THE IDE.
ST. FRANCIS ᴜғ ASSISI

BY

HILARIN FELDER, O.M.Cap.

TRANSLATED BY

BERCHMANS BITTLE, O.M.Cap.

PREFACE BY

JAMES J. WALSH, M.D., LL.D.

REVISED BY THE AUTHOR FOR THE
ENGLISH EDITION

NEW YORK, CINCINNATI, CHICAGO

BENZIGER BROTHERS

PRINTERS TO THE HOLY APOSTOLIC SEE

1925

APPROBATIO ORDINIS

Cum opus cui titulus *Die Ideale des hl. Franziskus* a R. P. Hilarino a Lucerna, Ordinis nostri in Provincia Helvetica Prædicatore et Lectore compositum et a duobus eiusdem Ordinis Theologis recognitum et probatum fuerit, praesentium virtute annuimus, ut præfatum opus typis demandari et publici iuris fieri possit, servatis tamen ceteris de iure servandis.

Datum Romæ, e Curia Nostra Generali,
die 20. Iulii 1923.

IOSEPHUS ANTONIUS
Minister Generalis

———————————

ST. FRANCIS OF ASSISI

PREFACE

NOTHING could be more appropriate than that this magnificent addition to the large body of literature on St. Francis in English, *The Ideals of St. Francis of Assisi* by Father Felder, should come from the press so opportunely just as we are entering upon the celebration of the seven-hundredth anniversary of the death of St. Francis. Ours, as everyone is willing to confess, is a material age and there probably never was a time when men needed to have emphasized for them the ideals of St. Francis so much as at the present moment. Our generation centers its interests mainly in this worldliness on happiness, comfort and success from a worldly standpoint. I need scarcely say that the one supremely characteristic element in St. Francis' interests and ideals was other-worldliness. Somehow or other this little man of Assisi who forgot about himself and thought only of others and was about as far as it is possible to conceive from the individualism of our time, won the hearts not only of his own generation but also of succeeding generations so that the world will not willingly forget him. There is probably no one not known because of his political or military glory who is so widely familiar to mankind as St. Francis of Assisi, though he loved to describe himself as the Little Poor Man of God.

Nothing is more surprising than the fact that there should be so much of interest in St. Francis in our time since his ideals represent such a contradiction to those that are popular now. It is hard indeed to understand how in this twentieth century, seven centuries after his death, St. Francis is written about more enthusiastically than perhaps any other man who has lived during the intervening period. There are more lives and sketches of him, above all more references to him in literature, than to anyone else who has lived these seven hundred years, and, most curious of all, that interest is increasing and not diminishing. Scarcely a year of the twentieth century has passed that has not seen the publication in some language or country of some important book embodying a complete tribute or at least a partial contribution to the life of the merchant's son of Assisi whose father was almost in despair because his boy was such an idealistic, such a hopelessly impractical, individual. Probably no one would be more surprised than St. Francis himself over the fact that educated men in every part of the world, many of them in parts of the world of which he knew nothing and scarcely even dreamed, should be interested in his life seven centuries after his death.

We have grown somewhat accustomed to multiple centenary celebrations during the twentieth century. Some five years ago we had the unprecedented spectacle of a world-wide celebration of the six-hundredth anniversary of the death of Dante. Probably never before did the educated world unite so cordially in the celebration of an anniversary, for we feel that Dante, in Ruskin's phrase, is "the central man of all the world," possessing in the highest degree the intellectual qualities of the race. During the preceding decade Oxford invited the scholars of the world to come to Oxford, not far from his birthplace, to celebrate the seven-hundredth anniversary of the birth of Roger Bacon. I think that it is perfectly clear that neither of these men had anything like the wide appeal to the sympathy of humanity as St. Francis. Dante himself was very proud to be a member of the Third Order of St. Francis and was probably buried as one of the lay sons of the Assisian. Roger Bacon was a member of the Franciscan Order and doubtless owed his education and his opportunities for study which have given him his name and fame in the modern world to his connection with the Franciscans. Both of these celebrations serve to reflect glory on St. Francis and add to the distinction with which he is regarded by the world because of the opportunity that he afforded to so many to make life a worthier thing than it could possibly have been if they were occupied mainly with worldliness. Neither of them, however, aroused anything like the popular appeal that the Centenary of St. Francis is manifestly to bring with it.

Very probably the most surprising feature of all in the preparations that are now being made for the appropriate celebration of the St. Francis Centenary, is the fact that our generation seems to be more interested in St. Francis than almost any preceding generation. His favorite idea in life was the love of poverty, so that the loftiest symbol of his career was his mystical marriage with Holy Poverty. That surely is the last thing in the world the people of our time have any inclination for. While governor of New York, Mr. Hughes once said, "The main occupation of men in our day seems to be the raising of a corruption fund for their children." We have learned to appreciate better than before how much of harm has been wrought to growing youth during the dozen years that have passed since that was said. The spirit which made St. Francis of Assisi choose the Lady Poverty for his bride and delighted to call himself *Il poverello di Dio,* "the little poor man of God," would seem to be entirely too impractical and utterly idealistic to have any particular appeal for our time. And yet literally more than a score of important lives of St. Francis have been written during the twentieth century, and our interest is growing, not waning. We are beginning to wake up to a realization of the fact that "things are in the saddle and ride mankind," and that things seem ever so much more important than thoughts, though it requires no special intelligence to understand what an utter contradiction of real values any such state of mind represents.

Not long before his death Mr. William James, professor of psychology at Harvard, often looked upon as the acutest of our thinkers in many problems of sociological psychology, said, "Among us English-speaking peoples especially do the praises of poverty need once more to be boldly sung. We have grown literally afraid to be poor. We despise anyone who elects to be poor in order to simplify and save his inner life. If he does not join the general scramble and pant with the money making street, we deem him spiritless and lacking in ambition. . . . It is time for thinking men to protest against so unmanly and irreligious a state of affairs. . . . The prevalent fear of poverty among the educated classes is the worst moral disease from which our civilization suffers."

There is no panacea for the many ills that have come from the dread of poverty and the love of riches that is so potent as the study of the life and the Ideals of St. Francis of Assisi. Hence the gladness with which I write the Preface to this latest contribution to the literature that has, in spite of our age's tendencies, gathered round the life of the Little Poor Man of God.

JAMES J. WALSH.

AUTHOR'S FOREWORD

THIS book can at least claim the distinction of not
being immature. It is in fact not the latest, but the
oldest work of the author. He began it when still
a young man, and he now stands at the threshold of old
age. More than thirty years ago he attempted to answer
for himself and for others the question: What was really
the Ideal of St. Francis, and what should our Ideal be?
Drawing on the material at his disposal and on his personal
knowledge—both very limited and meager—he produced
in his leisure hours a rather bulky manuscript, which
for the time being was used for the instruction of the
students under his charge. But in the course of time he
was forced to realize that the work was very unsatisfac-
tory because unseasoned, and that many problems remained
unsolved, partly on account of the prevalent state of Franciscan research, and partly on account of the limitations
of the writer. The several hundred pages of manuscript
were therefore locked away, and the writer resolved to
wait and prepare a better foundation for the work.

In the course of the following decades several Franciscan studies were published by the author, in particular
*Die Geschichte der wissenschaftlichen Studien im Fran-
ziskanerorden bis um die Mitte des 13 Jahrhunderts;* my
other publications, however, also stood psychologically in
close relation to the *Ideals of St. Francis,* above all my
recent work, *Jesus Christus.** It is only now when I
look back on the devious course of my literary and personal development, that I fully realize this. And as I

---

* *Christ and the Critics,* translated by John L. Stoddard, Benziger
Brothers, New York.

now, at the conclusion of this work, again take up the pages of that old manuscript, yellow with age, it becomes evident to me that the final product was embodied in the original manuscript as the fruit is embodied in the blossom—blossom and fruit, so distinct and yet essentially one, because both were born of the one purpose, that is, to develop as correctly and clearly as possible the Ideals of St. Francis.

The goal which I had to keep constantly in view was to discover the individual character of the person and the work of the Poverello, to trace this character clearly and correctly; in other words, to delineate the Franciscan Ideal. It would not do to graft modern ideas on the original with the view of favoring some pet idea or conception. It was even more necessary to avoid superimposing personal and subjective ideas on the image of the real Francis, as has been so frequently done within the past fifty years. My entire and sole endeavor was to portray quietly, respectfully and lovingly the Ideals of St. Francis in the light of all available sources, and to give these Ideals their proper place in the frame of his environment and time.

The main purpose, as well as the main difficulty, was not only to discover these Ideals in their inception, but to follow their growth and their development, their realization. "God indeed usually inspires the holy Founders with the general plan of the work which they are to accomplish, and this at times in a direct and miraculous manner; but the execution of this plan is frequently left to secondary causes, that is, the various happenings and experiences of their life, by which the gradual development of the original plan is brought about. This can be observed in the work of St. Francis no less than in the work of St. Dominic or of St. Ignatius. It is therefore a serious mistake to consider the first beginnings of the realization of a plan as the full expression of the Ideal, as its culmination, and to consider all further development

as a partial decadence or depreciation, and to stamp
the forces active in this development as harmful or destructive." *

This observation is of the greatest importance. Some
modern writers contend that the Ideals of Francis did
not survive the first phase of his enterprise, and declare
that all later modifications and developments were the
result of pressure brought to bear on him to abandon his
original purpose. That means to ignore important laws
of history and psychology, and to forget that it is a far
cry from the abstract ideal to its realization. For if this
ideal is to live not only in its originator, but is to become
incarnate in a world-embracing organization, then the
distance between ideal and realization is well-nigh immeasurable. It admits of no doubt that Francis was personally true to his Ideal to the very end; but its vaster
realization demanded a certain development. In some
respects this development was brought about only toward
the end of his life; in others, that is where exterior circumstances exerted more force, as, for instance, regarding
poverty, the apostolate, and science, many years passed
before the Ideal and its realization came to a perfect
balance. On this account we are able to restrict several
chapters of this book to the lifetime of the Saint, while
in other chapters we are forced to extend our scope to
the first generations of the Order.

It is peculiar that as yet no such work as the present
exists. We have several excellent biographies of the
Saint, also a number of works treating of various phases
of Franciscan history, and especially a copious literature
of critical studies on the Sources. Several very meritorious works have been published which in some respects
cover the same ground as this volume, such as: P. Ubald
d'Alençon, *L'âme françiscaine,*† Heinrich Tilemann, *Stu-*

---

* Franz Ehrle, S. J., *Die Spiritualen, ihr Verhältnis zum Franziskanerorden
und zu den Fraticellen,* in: *Archiv für Literatur-und Kirchengeschichte des
Mittelalters* III, 558 f.
† 2me éd., Paris, Librairie St. François, 1913.

dien zur Individualität des Franziskus von Assisi,† and
F. Imle, *Der Geist des hl. Franziskus und seiner Stiftung.*§
But they do not express fully the characteristic individuality of Francis, nor of his Ideal.

And yet this peculiar character is the most interesting and the most important element in the entire movement which centers in the Patriarch of Assisi. What interests us is not what he has in common with other heroes and saints of history, and particularly with other Founders of Religious Orders, but that which distinguished him from all others and which constitutes his individuality, his personality, his soul, his spirit, his genius, his Ideal.

This Ideal has created that wonderful period which we call the Franciscan Century. This Ideal would have been potent enough to save the following centuries from the crisis which led to the Western apostasy with all its dire results, and is still powerful enough to cure our present society of its almost fatal ills. This Ideal must be cherished especially by the sons of St. Francis, if they wish to bring about the salvation of the world and of themselves. This Ideal was incarnate in Francis and lived by him; and as it was lived by him, it was lived but once, so fully, so perfectly, so sublimely. But it must always remain the wish of his children to live it and to realize it to the fullest of their ability, albeit with due respect to the needs of the times, and to draw fresh inspiration from the one source, the Ideals of their Founder. For his Ideals were the ideals of the Gospel, and his own image was but the reflection of the Divine Image, our Lord and Saviour, Jesus Christ.

Hilarin Felder, O.M.Cap.

Freiburg, Switzerland
   June 24, 1923

---

† Leipzig-Berlin, Teubner, 1914.
§ Mergentheim, Ohlinger, 1921.

TRANSLATOR'S NOTE

AMONG recent contributions to Franciscan literature Father Felder's book occupies a pre-eminent place. His extensive learning, his deep piety, and his intimate knowledge of all things Franciscan acquired through many years of laborious research, qualify him as perhaps no other to undertake and successfully accomplish a task such as this work represents. The object of this work, in which is offered the fruit of lifelong labors, was, to use the words of the author, "to portray quietly, respectfully, and lovingly the Ideals of St. Francis in the light of all available sources, and to give these Ideals their place in the frame of his environment and of his times."

The enthusiastic reception accorded this work of the scholarly author in its original form as well as in its various translations not only proved its intrinsic merit, but at the same time prompted the desire to make it accessible to a wider circle of readers in the English-speaking countries. The great interest shown in late years in St. Francis, and the peculiar charm which this lovable Saint has ever exerted, seems to warrant the assumption that this inspiring book of Father Felder will likewise find a warm reception in its English dress.

The translator has deviated from the German original only in so far as to relegate the numerous and at times lengthy notes to the rear of the book, thus providing a continuous and unbroken text. For the student this will prove no further hardship, and those conversant with the Latin will no doubt find particular relish in the charming language of Celano and of the other biographers of the Saint. The bibliography has also been adapted to English readers, proper mention being made of the various works in the English language which are of recognized merit, in particular of the accepted translations of the various Franciscan sources.

In order to give proper credit where it is due, the translator wishes to state that he has utilized the scholarly English rendition of the writings of St. Francis made by the Rev. Paschal Robinson, O.F.M., wherever quotations are made of these writings in this book. He also desires to acknowledge his indebtedness to those of his confrères who have rendered such substantial help in preparing this translation.

BERCHMANS BITTLE, O.M.CAP.

MILWAUKEE, WISCONSIN
July 20, 1925

CONTENTS

xvi   CONTENTS

THE IDEALS OF ST. FRANCIS OF ASSISI

CHAPTER I

FRANCIS AND THE GOSPEL

THE disciples of St. Francis speak of a change in the life of their master which they call his conversion.[1] They understand under this term simply the passing of Francis from a worldly to an ascetical life, a term commonly used by the Western monks to designate the embracing of the religious life.[2] That a complete personal change took place in Francis in consequence of this transition, is recorded fully by Thomas of Celano and the Three Companions.[3] Francis himself does not hesitate to call the period preceding this conversion a life of sin, in contrast to the following life of penance.[4]

He did not, however, look back on a period of life which would have caused the average man severe remorse or called for a conversion, in the accepted sense of the term. His sins were an all too worldly frame of mind and course of conduct. His genial nature overflowed with the joy of life and a youthful yet healthy exuberance. Heart and fancy were filled with the songs of the troubadours, the provençal chansons de geste, fables and sirventes. His delight was to march through the streets of his native city at the head of the gay young bloods to the tune of a merry song, to be acclaimed the king of youth, to wear gorgeous garments, and to give sumptuous banquets to his comrades.[5] These were the faults of his earlier life, of which he later says: "When I was in sin . . . ."

---

[1] This and all subsequent figures refer to notes in Appendix.

I

Yet even among these shadows we find sunny traits which gave evidence of unusual natural endowments and presaged his calling to a life of perfection.

In the first place, his *unsullied moral purity.* His most intimate companions testify: "He was by nature and by principle a nobleman in word and deed. No one ever heard an insulting or offensive word uttered by him. Albeit he was such a jovial and reckless youth, he made it a rule never to answer scurrilous language. The towns-folk respected him in consequence, and many who knew him declared, that he would yet become a great man." [6] "Nowhere do we find signs that this period of his life was marred by a serious violation of his conscience." [7]

To this must be added his utter *disregard of wealth.* The son of the cloth merchant Peter Bernardone, Francis had been born and reared in wealth and luxury. As a young man he gave promise of becoming a successful merchant like his father. He had, however, as Thomas of Celano remarks, the one very unbusiness-like trait of being far too prodigal and extravagant. "He was the first in merrymaking, in sport and song, in soft and flow-ing robes, because he was very wealthy; not greedy, but prodigal; not miserly, but a waster of money; a prudent merchant, but withal a lavish spender." [8] He poured out money like water for himself and his boon companions, but also for the poor and needy. His parents rebuked him frequently for frittering away their substance as if he were not the son of a merchant, but of a great prince.[9]

Another feature was his *spirit of chivalry.* This trait is emphasized time and again by his biographers. His very prodigality was in truth nothing else but the out-growth of his chivalrous spirit. The leading rôle which his comrades accorded him at their feasts and revels, and in which he so much delighted, was in his eyes but the stepping-stone to the rank of knighthood, and its deeds and honors. A symptom in particular of this spirit was the irresistible attraction which he felt for soldierly adventures, calling for heroic efforts and the risk of life and blood. Hardly twenty years of age, Francis threw himself into the feud then raging between Assisi and Perugia; but as the reverses of war will have it, he was taken prisoner with many of his compatriots. In this predicament his inborn chivalry again asserted itself. The captivity had lasted a full year and his fellow-sufferers were about to succumb to despair; but Francis never for a moment lost his jovial mood, joking humorously about their vexing misfortune. His companions thought him mad for being so merry in a prison, but cheerily came his answer: "Would you know why I am so merry? I see the day when all the world will bow before me." It was due to this genial and chivalrous spirit that he succeeded in reviving the drooping spirits of the prisoners, in suppressing the unruly elements, and in composing the quarrels that arose.[10]

No doubt these three traits, moral purity, contempt for material wealth, and a chivalrous spirit, predisposed the youthful Francis for that higher spiritual life according to the Gospel, which demands chastity, the renunciation of all earthly things, and a soul at once chivalrous and heroic.

Before Francis could approach this higher calling, the way had to be cleared of two formidable obstacles: his fondness for worldly pleasures, and his ambition for the worldly glory of the knighthood. We shall presently see how Christ directed the earthly ideal of the knight to the higher conception of the spiritual knighthood.[11] But in order to sketch more fully the conversion of Francis, we must show how his fondness for the vain pleasures of the senses gradually died away under the powerful influence of divine grace.

A character such as Francis possessed, cast along noble and heroic lines, could not rest content with the pleasures which his mode of life afforded. The serious outlook on life which had acceded to his natural gaiety and levity while a captive at Perugia, asserted itself more and more.

He soon after fell a victim to a grave illness, which shook his soul to its very foundations. When finally—he was then about twenty-three years of age—he left the paternal house for the first time, convalescent but still in need of the support of a staff, the world had lost its former potent charm. The beauty of the fields, the bloom of the vineyards, and all that is fair to the eye, could in no wise gladden him. All things about him seemed to have changed, for the simple reason that a mighty change had taken place within himself.

Francis was amazed and vexed by this change, and hardly had he regained his strength, when he sought to escape the hand of God.[12] Goaded on by dreams of romantic adventures and restless for action, he set out for Apulia.[13] But the farther he rode, the more pensive he became.[14] A short way beyond Spoleto, the voice of God came to him, urging him to return to Assisi, where God's design in his behalf would be made known to him. So emphatic was the voice, that he forthwith turned about and returned to Assisi.[15]

Once more at home, he was again prevailed upon by his friends to arrange for a grand feast of youth. He yielded with reluctance. After the sumptuous meal, his companions, as they had done so often before, paraded, singing and shouting, through the streets of Assisi. Francis, the King of Youth, with a scepter in his hand, followed them for a short distance in silence and recollection. Suddenly the hand of the Lord touched him and deluged him with such sweetness of spirit that he could neither speak nor continue on his way.[16]

From this hour he became more thoughtful and absorbed. A deep loathing for himself and for all the things of which he had once been fond, settled upon him. He withdrew more and more from worldly affairs, yielding to the prompting of grace, which led him to a more intimate converse with God; for this reason he took refuge almost daily in a deserted spot outside the city, drawn by an irresistible force and filled with divine sweetness.[17] In spite of this, however, he suffered intensely with anxious doubts regarding his vocation, not knowing whither the voice of God was calling him. His soul was in a very turmoil of emotions, plan after plan forming in his mind only to dissolve again, and leaving him in a state of greater perplexity than before. He was on fire with an intense longing for an unknown ideal and with high resolves for the future, which was for him as yet completely dark; to these emotions there soon was added the most bitter remorse for the sins of his past life.[18] In a groping manner he felt that he was called to renounce the world and surrender himself to the service of God, but that was all.

Finally—he was now twenty-five years of age—[19] after he had trustfully invoked the Divine Mercy, the Lord put an end to his doubts by clearly manifesting His will to him. So great was the joy of Francis, that he could not contain himself. He began to speak of the good fortune which had befallen him, yet in terms so fanciful that his hearers thought that he had found a rich treasure, or that he was about to take a bride unto himself. He would then reply to their queries: "Indeed, I am about to espouse a bride, so noble and wealthy and charming as no other." [20] "In truth," remarks Thomas of Celano, "the Order which he embraced is the unspotted Bride of God, and the rich treasure which he sought so ardently is the heavenly kingdom. No wonder that the evangelical vocation was realized in him, who was to become a disciple of the Gospel in faith and in truth." [21]

The ground plan of his future vocation had now become clear to Francis. But as yet the full understanding of this plan remained a problem to him, and more so the details of its execution. Three years were yet to pass before this problem was fully solved.[22] Meanwhile Francis strove zealously to follow the path marked out for him, by detaching himself completely from all earthly things;

and each new light vouchsafed him, he followed faithfully, in order thus to come closer to his ideal.

The early biographers describe minutely the various steps in the development of this vocation.[23] Francis himself outlines them broadly in the first paragraphs of his Testament:

"The Lord granted to me, Brother Francis, thus *to begin* to do penance, for when I was in sin, it seemed to me too bitter a thing to see lepers, but the Lord Himself led me amongst them, and I showed mercy to them. And when I left them, that which had seemed bitter to me, was changed for me into sweetness of body and soul.

"And *afterward* I remained a little and I left the world. And the Lord gave me so much faith in churches that I would simply pray and say thus: 'We adore Thee, Lord Jesus Christ, here and in all Thy churches which are in the whole world, and we bless Thee because by Thy holy cross Thou hast redeemed the world.'

"*After that* the Lord gave me, and gives me, so much faith in priests who live according to the form of the holy Roman Church, that if they should persecute me, I would have recourse to them. . . .

"And after the Lord gave me some brothers, no one showed me what I ought to do, but the Most High Himself revealed to me that I *should live according to the form of the holy Gospel*. And I caused it to be written in few words and simply, and the Lord Pope confirmed it for me." [24]

In these plain and simple words is sketched the birth of the new man, the new Francis. Under the impulse of divine grace his innate tenderness now rises to the heroic heights of Christian charity. The heroism he displayed in nursing the lepers, spiritualized and deepened his entire religious life, manifesting itself by that simple-hearted, childlike reverence and service which he renders to churches, priests, and the Holy Eucharist. This deepening of his religious life was brought to a full conclusion when the Lord Himself directed Francis to set his life and his Order on the only foundation of all perfection, the Gospel of the Saviour.

2. It was on the 24th of February, 1209,[25] while attending Mass at the chapel of Portiuncula, that Francis heard the gospel wherein is related how the Lord sent forth His apostles to preach. After Mass he humbly requested the priest to explain more fully the words he had heard; and when he understood that a disciple of Christ should possess neither gold nor silver nor money, should carry neither scrip nor purse nor staff on his way, and wear neither shoes nor two coats, but preach the kingdom of God and penance, he rejoiced exceedingly and exclaimed: "That is what I wish to do, that is what I desire and seek with all my heart!" He immediately removed the shoes from his feet, cast away the staff he was carrying, girded his loins with a rope in place of the leather belt he wore, and fashioned for himself a garment of coarse material, with the figure of the cross, the emblem of penance, attached to it. "For," continues his biographer, "he was no listless hearer of the Gospel, but kept faithfully in mind all that he had heard, and was careful to fulfil all things literally." [26]

A few weeks later the first companions joined him, Brother Bernard of Quintavalle, and Brother Peter Catanii. In order to convince himself that these also, and likewise the future fraternity, should share the *life according to the Gospel,* Francis thrice at random opened a book of the Gospels, and each time he struck the passage describing the sending of the apostles. He saw in this the hand of God, and turned to his disciples with the words: "Brothers, this is our life and our rule, and that of all those who are to join our fraternity. Go, therefore, and do as you have heard." [27] It was the 16th of April, 1209, the birthday of the Franciscan Order. "From this day on," remark the Three Companions, "they lived together after the manner of the holy Gospel, as the Lord had manifested to them. And Francis declared later in his Testament: 'The Most High Himself revealed to me that I should live according to the form of the holy Gospel.' " [28]

As soon as the number of brothers had increased to twelve, they journeyed to Rome in order to obtain the sanction of the Church for their mode of life (1209 or 1210). It immediately became evident how clearly and firmly Francis had grasped the ideal set forth in the Gospel, and how tenaciously he clung to it. To all objections on the part of his protector, the pious and influential Cardinal John Colonna of St. Paul, he had but one answer, that he was called by divine inspiration to live according to the Gospel. The Cardinal finally approached Pope Innocent III and said: "I have found a saintly man who desires to live after the manner of the Gospel, and to observe evangelical perfection in all things; and I am convinced that God intends to restore the true Faith in the whole world through him." After the Pope himself had tested the invincible constancy of Francis, he consented, and approved the rule of the new fraternity by word of mouth.[29]

Unfortunately this primitive rule has not reached us. But we know that it consisted of a number of Gospel texts, to which Francis added several necessary ordinances. He declares expressly: "The most High Himself revealed to me that I should live according to the form of the holy Gospel. And I caused it to be written in few words and simply and the Lord Pope confirmed it for me." [30] Thomas of Celano amplifies this statement thus: "When the blessed Francis perceived that the Lord God increased the number of brothers from day to day, he wrote for those present and for those to come, simply and without many words, a form of life and rule for which he used mainly the words of the Gospel, after whose perfection he aspired most ardently. To this he added a few precepts which were necessary for the uniformity of a religious life." [31]   St. Bonaventure declares even more emphatically, that the observance of the Gospel was the inviolable foundation of the primitive Franciscan rule, while the inserted regulations had the sole purpose of guiding the brothers in their new mode of life.[32]   The exact nature of these regulations cannot be determined; but it is certain that the main body of the primitive rule comprised the texts relating to the sending of the apostles,[33] in which Christ demanded of them absolute poverty and renunciation of the world.[34]

These summary ordinances sufficed for the first years and the limited number of brothers. With the growth of the Order, further amplification and remolding of this rule became necessary. At the first Pentecostal chapter (1212), new additions were considered and adopted, "in order to observe more exactly the rule and the Gospel." [35] Further additions were likewise made at the various chapters held during the first decade of the Order.[36] Cardinal Jacques de Vitry states that the brothers assembled annually in one place, rejoicing together in the Lord, taking their repasts in common; and, with the help of good men, they adopted and promulgated holy precepts approved by the Pope.[37] Finally, at the chapter of 1221, Francis proposed a revised rule consisting of twenty-four chapters, greatly differing in length. [38] In this rule were incorporated all the ordinances of earlier years with several additions made necessary by the new conditions.

One thing, however, had to remain unchanged and unchangeable—the Gospel as the underlying basis of the rule. So strongly fixed was the determination of Francis in this regard, that he commissioned one of the brothers, Caesar of Speyer, who had gained fame as a Scripture scholar, to insert the various biblical texts in connection with the ordinances of his new rule.[39] The Prologue of the rule therefore contained the significant words: "This is the life according to the Gospel of Jesus Christ, for which Brother Francis has sought permission and approbation

from the Lord Pope Innocent, and which the Lord Pope
Innocent has permitted and approved for him and his
brothers present and future."[40] He designates the summary of precepts and admonitions which then follow,
simply as a formula for the observance of the evangelical
life.[41] Toward the end of the rule he admonishes again:
"Let us therefore hold fast to the words and the life and
the Gospel of Jesus Christ."[42]

But the rule had not yet reached its final form. The
experience gained by its practical application since 1221,
very soon demanded a modification of several regulations,
the addition of new ones, and the recasting of the whole
into a measure at least of uniformity. Francis accordingly journeyed with Brother Leo, his confessor and secretary, and Brother Bonizio, a learned jurist of Bologna,
to Fonte Colombo,[43] and having prepared himself with
forty days' fasting and prayer,[44] he caused the final rule
to be written as the Holy Ghost inspired him.[45] After the
drafting of each chapter, he again sought counsel with
the Lord in fervent prayer, to assure himself that all was
in harmony with the Gospel.[46] In order to emphasize the
evangelical character of the rule, and to impress the
brothers strongly that their calling demanded the full observance of the Gospel,[47] he placed the solemn declaration
at the beginning and at the end of the rule: "The rule
and the life of the Friars Minor is this, namely, to observe
the Gospel of our Lord Jesus Christ. . . . We have firmly
promised to observe the holy Gospel of our Lord Jesus
Christ."[48]

Several Ministers Provincial had raised objections to
various precepts of the rule, declaring them above human
strength.[49] Francis himself, moreover, was somewhat
troubled regarding the Papal approbation (given November 29th, 1223), and in consequence the following vision
was granted him.[50] It appeared to him that he was to
gather minute crumbs of bread from the ground and to
distribute them among the brothers. In doing this he was

seized with great fear lest the crumbs should fall from his hand. A voice then suddenly called to him, saying: "Francis, knead the particles into one host, and give of it to eat to those who will." This he did. Those who would not receive it reverently, or showed contempt, were forthwith stricken with leprosy. The following morning, Francis related the vision to his companions, full of sorrow for not being able to understand its meaning. Soon after, while at prayer, the voice again spoke to him: "Francis, the crumbs of bread are the words of the Gospel, the host is the rule, the leprosy is sin." [51]

As a result of this vision, Francis became still more inflamed with zeal for the rule, and until his last breath commended its observance untiringly. He was wont to say: "The rule is the book of life, the hope of salvation, the marrow of the Gospel, the way of perfection, the key to paradise, the eternal covenant. This rule all should possess and know, and it should be kept in mind reverently by all to combat weariness and to remind us of the vows which we have solemnly made. We should advert to it constantly as the norm for our conduct, and, what is more, die with it." [52]

The *Ideal* of Francis was therefore a life *"according to the Gospel," "after the manner of the Gospel," "according to the perfection of the Gospel."* What Francis meant by these words is evident from what has been said above, and is furthermore plainly expressed by the rule of the Order. Even the primitive Franciscan rule consisted mainly of the following sentences: [53] "This is the life of the Gospel of Jesus Christ, to live in obedience, in chastity, and without property, and to follow the teaching and example of Our Lord Jesus Christ, who said: 'If thou wilt be perfect, go sell what thou hast and give to the poor, and thou shalt have treasure in heaven: and come, follow Me.' [54] And: 'If any man will come after Me, let him deny himself and take up his cross and follow Me.' [55] Again: 'If any man come to Me, and hate not his father and mother and wife and children and brethren and sisters, yea, and his own life also, he cannot be My disciple.' [56] 'And everyone that hath left house or brethren or sisters or father or mother or wife or children or lands, for My name's sake, shall receive an hundredfold and shall possess life everlasting.'" [57]   The same is contained literally in the rule of 1221,[58] and in substance in the rule of 1223.[59]

The Friars were consequently to observe exactly all those things which the Saviour demanded of His apostles, and of all those who are called to evangelical perfection.[60] And since the Friars were called to this life of perfection, they evidently were bound to observe also the minor precepts of the Gospel.   Francis accordingly was fully justified in calling his disciples "apostolic men." [61]

Not satisfied with binding his own brothers to the evangelical manner of life, Francis in 1212 undertook the foundation of an Order for women, that of the Poor Ladies, or Poor Clares.[62]   These also, as far as it was practicable,[63] he bound to the observance of the Gospel, according to the example and under the direction of the Friars.   The primitive "little rule" (*formula vitæ*), which Francis wrote for them, contains only the one, but pregnant sentence: "Since, by divine inspiration, you have made yourselves daughters and handmaids of the Most High Sovereign King, the heavenly Father, and have espoused yourselves to the Holy Ghost, choosing to live according to the perfection of the holy Gospel, I will, and I promise to have always, by myself and by my brothers, a diligent care and special solicitude for you, as for them." [64]

But even this did not satisfy Francis.   As he himself and his disciples lived and preached the Gospel, or "penance," [65] so in like manner he founded a third branch of the Order (1221), for those living in the world and desirous of following the Franciscan Ideal.   The Three Companions and St. Bonaventure tell us that in a short time very many men and women practised the life of "penance" in their family circles under the direction of the Friars, and for this reason Francis called them Brothers of Penance (*Fratres de Pœnitentia*).[66]

Thus the entire Franciscan Movement assumed *its character and individuality from the Gospel.* Francis had no other aim than to lead back all classes of Christian society to the purity and the ideals of the Gospel by means of his three Orders.[67] The Friars were destined not only to be the leaders in this movement by their preaching of the Gospel, but more so by living it themselves in the fulness of its perfection. That was the aim of the Poverello, that was at all times his supreme Ideal.

3. Viewed in this light, and grasped with such depth, clearness, courage, and living force, *this Ideal was something entirely new;* it was, moreover, *peculiar to Francis alone.*

The novelty and peculiarity of this Ideal did not consist in regarding the Gospel as the rule and compass of Christian life and of moral perfection. How could any Christian, and, above all, the Founder of an Order, think otherwise! Every Christian is bound to the observance of the moral law of the Gospel. A Religious is furthermore bound by his vows to follow the evangelical counsels of perfection, of obedience, poverty and chastity. He is distinguished thereby from the ordinary Christian as the apostles were distinct from the other disciples. The Fathers of the Church do not hesitate, therefore, to designate the religious life as the only and truly evangelical and apostolical life.[68] Monastic life had indeed unfortunately lost much of its luster later on, due to the increasing worldliness and to the laxity of church discipline. In the period of the Crusades, however, it again revived with renewed splendor. Shortly before the appearance of Francis, Rupert of Deutz (died about 1130), and Bernard of Clairvaux (died 1153) wrote in glowing terms of the apostolic character of monastic life and rules.[69]

And yet not a single Religious Founder prior to Francis had based his rule on the Gospel and bound his followers expressly to its observance in its fullest sense. Neither Basil and Pachomius in the East, nor the Frankish and Irish monks in the West, placed this goal before their disciples. The two famous rules which were exclusively in use in the beginning of the thirteenth century, the Benedictine and the Augustinian,[70] in no manner made the Gospel as such the foundation of religious life. Nowhere do they intimate that the Order is based on the Gospel, nor that the individual Religious is bound by his profession to observe the Gospel and to imitate the apostolic mode of life; on the contrary, they expressly exclude very important features of this life. One need only mention, for instance, the *stabilitas loci* of the older Orders, and the obstacle it placed in the way of the apostolate of preaching.

For this reason Francis rejected most emphatically the suggestion to borrow from these rules. When this was suggested to him, he replied: "I do not wish that you propose to me any other rule, be it that of Benedict or Augustine or Bernard, nor in any other way a manner of life but that which the Lord has mercifully given and shown to me." [71] Neither would he listen to the proposal of St. Dominic to merge the newly founded Mendicant Orders of the Friars Minor and the Preachers into one.[72]

Francis was well aware that his institution was not merely a variation or a branch of another Order, but a new and distinct creation. And because he was firmly convinced of its divine origin,[73] he held fast to it with every fiber of his being. There was absolutely no consideration that could influence him to deviate from this course. Yes, even with his last breath he adhered to this conviction, breaking forth on his death-bed into praises for the evangelical mode of life, placing it before all other institutions.[74] His constant anxiety was the luster and purity of his heavenly Ideal. Humble and meek and submissive as he was, yet he was unrelentingly firm where the *soul*, the *substance*, the *individuality* of the Order was concerned, *its evangelical character*.

To have grasped this individual character fully and completely, to have preserved it untouched and to have made it a world-reality; that was and always will be the glorious distinction of St. Francis; that it is, which gives him his *historical significance*. The re-birth of the Gospel and of the primitive Church—that was the outstanding feature which drew the praises of his contemporaries upon the Poor Man of Assisi. Every biographer who depicts his life, every chronicler who has fixed his character, if only in a few lines, emphasizes his singular merit in leading the world back to the Gospel by means of his life and his work. Thomas of Celano declares briefly, but pregnantly: "He was the man with the evangelical vocation, in truth and in faith the servant of the Gospel. . . . His supreme desire, his ardent wish, and highest principle was, to observe the Gospel in all things and above all things." [75] In that lasting memorial which the Three Companions have erected to him in their *Legenda*, they state in the briefest terms that he was a perfect follower of the Gospel and of the apostles: "Emulating Christ most perfectly, the apostolic man Francis followed the life and the footsteps of the apostles." [76] "Many nobles and others," reports the Augustinian, Walter of Gisburn, "clerics and laymen followed this blessed Francis and walked in his footsteps. The holy Father taught them to observe the perfection of the Gospel, to bear the burden of poverty and to walk in the way of simplicity. He also wrote an evangelical rule for himself and for his brothers." [77]

Cardinal Jacques de Vitry, one of the most learned and pious men of his time, who was personally acquainted with Francis and his disciples, writes under the influence of this experience: "One consolation indeed I found in those regions [of Umbria]: many persons of both sexes, wealthy and prominent, gave up all for Christ and left

the world. They were called Friars Minor. . . . This
Order of Friars Minor is spreading so rapidly over the
whole world because its members imitate faithfully the
manner of life of the early Church. . . . To the three
Orders of the Hermits, the Monks, and the Clerics Regular, the Lord has added in these days the fourth religious
institution, the flower of monastic life and the essence of
monastic sanctity. Indeed, if we study more closely the
nature and form of the early Church, we find that he has
not so much discovered a new rule, as renewed the old;
namely, the evangelical manner of life. He has brought
to life the decadent and almost defunct religion, in order
to place in the field new warriors for the perilous times
of the anti-Christ, and to defend the Church by means of
this bulwark. This is truly the significance of the Order
of Poor Men of the Crucified, the Order of preachers
whom we call Friars Minor. They endeavor so zealously
to renew the fervor, poverty and simplicity of the primitive Church, to draw in the thirst and fire of their spirit
the pure waters from the fountain of the Gospel, that they
not only follow the precepts, but also the counsels of the
Gospel, and imitate most perfectly the manner of life of
the Gospel. . . . That is the holy Order of Friars Minor,
and the admirable society of those men whom the Lord
has raised up in these days." [78]

The Dominicans themselves regarded the Franciscan
Order as the only one which is entirely devoted and bound
to the fullest observance of the Gospel. Toward the
middle of the thirteenth century, the General of the Dominicans, Humbert de Romanis, makes the following
declaration: "The blessed Francis wished that the Friars
Minor observe the Gospel most perfectly. They are bound
to its observance not only in lighter matters, but also in
the most difficult, as for instance regarding the injunction: 'If anyone strike you on one cheek, offer him also
the other,' that they might be in truth perfect followers
of the Gospel." [79]

The return to the Gospel is, therefore, according to these authorities the one, great achievement of St. Francis. The Christian peoples indeed believed the message of the Lord; but to a great extent they failed to understand and to practise it. Thus the chasm between theoretical and practical faith became wider and wider among all classes and ranks of society. The foremost men of those times constantly complain of this. And most lamentable of all was the fact that the consciousness of this glaring disparity between faith and its practise had been lost. They no longer sensed the grandeur and sublimity of the Gospel, having become entirely engrossed in common and customary things. For Francis, however, to know the Gospel, meant to live it.

Its every word engraved itself upon his soul with startling freshness and keenness. Hardly had he read or heard it when he immediately set out to put it into practise. Whether this or that word of the Gospel were a precept or only a counsel, whether intended for all or only for certain persons, whether given for all times or only for the apostolic period, whether only a figure and parable or an actual occurrence—such exegetical questions were unknown to him. He heard the word of God, he understood it literally, and fulfilled it to the last iota, unless circumstances rendered its execution impossible.

He reads: "Give to everyone that asketh thee," [80] and he commands his disciples to give to those that beg alms their hood or half their garment if nothing else were at hand.[81] He reads again: "If a man will take away thy coat, let go thy cloak also unto him," [82] and he allows his habit to be taken from him without remonstrance.[83] And again: "Eat such things as are set before you," [84] and he permits his brothers to partake of all foods placed before them, contrary to the custom of other Religious Orders.[85] He reads that on entering a house the apostles are to say: "Peace be to this house," [86] and he commands his brothers never to enter a house without this greeting; [87] he begins his own sermons with it,[88] and in his Testament he again reminds his brothers: "This greeting the Lord revealed to me, that we should say: 'The Lord give thee peace.' " [89]

These and other words of the Saviour, with which he became acquainted through the daily reading or hearing of the Gospel,[90] formed the rule and compass of his life.[91] With touching simplicity and heroic firmness he lived the Gospel—that is the secret of his influence on the Franciscan Century.

That also, and that only, explains the newly awakened enthusiasm for St. Francis in our days. Since the thirteenth century there has never been so keen and widespread an interest for the Poor Man of Assisi as to-day. The last decades have brought forth a veritable flood of Franciscan literature. Men of various camps and of various convictions are enthused over the Poverello. This may be the result of a certain fashion or of modern decadent sentimentality, with some even an entirely false, anti-Catholic conception of the person and aims of the Saint. The main cause, however, of this phenomenon is undoubtedly that quality in the life and ideals of the Saint which is identical with that of the Gospel. The mainspring of this movement is a yearning for the simplicity and the purity of the ideals set forth in the Gospel; the Saint is esteemed so highly because since the days of the apostles no other has dared to live the Gospel in all its idealism as he did.

This alone gives to the Seraph of Assisi his historical significance and his place in the hall of fame; this alone explains the proverbial popularity of the Franciscan Order and its undiminished influence. If this Order is to be the salt of the earth, as its Founder wished it to be, it must always remain true in principle and in practise to the motto of St. Francis: "The rule and the life of the Friars Minor is this: to observe the holy Gospel of Our Lord Jesus Christ."

CHAPTER II

FRANCIS AND CHRIST

THE Gospel is embodied in the person of the Saviour. Jesus Christ is the heart and soul of the Gospel. To observe the Gospel means to make Jesus Christ the center of one's life. That St. Francis accomplished this, even a superficial study of his life will prove. But this does not express all. The peculiar character of the relation between Francis and the God-Man lies in this, that he was a *Knight of Christ,* that he devoted himself with truly chivalrous spirit and in a truly chivalrous manner to the *service,* the *imitation,* and the *love* of his Lord.

1. The life of a Christian has at all times been regarded as a military service of Christ. The Apostle of the Gentiles, who borrows many terms and figures from military life, demands of every Christian that he be "a good soldier of Christ." [1]

Those who embraced religious life especially, were always styled warriors of Christ. Jerome,[2] Augustine [3] and other Fathers use the term "soldiers of Christ" with preference when speaking of monks. The Father of Western monasticism thus addresses his disciples: "You have denied your own will, and have seized the strongest and best weapons of obedience, in order to battle for Christ, the Lord, the true King." [4]

Benedict and his predecessors regarded the monk as a soldier in the then prevalent sense of the term; i.e., as a Roman legionary, but in the period of the crusades the soldier becomes a knight, a noble liegeman of the Lord, a "champion of God." The term *miles* itself, which

19

previously connoted the common soldier, now signifies
the knight.[5]   The enthusiasm of the Crusaders for their
Saviour King waxed so strong in the Holy Land, that
even the secular knight sought his chief glory in being
"the cup-bearer and warrior" of Christ.[6]   His supreme
ambition was to be the "liegeman of the holy Christ, who
was martyred for us." [7]

Following out this ideal conception, the Christian
knights began to band together in Religious Orders.   It is
needless to say that thereby this conception of knightly
service rendered to Christ, was considerably strengthened
and deepened.   In the earliest rule of the Knights, that
of the Knights Templar,[8] the knight is made to appear
as the soldier of Christ, as His co-warrior and com-
rade.   He is constantly reminded that he once chose
knighthood from earthly motives, but now has become
a warrior for the sake of Christ, and in consequence will
receive his reward with Christ's soldiers.[9]

All this applied literally to the youthful Francis, to his
chivalrous ideas, and to his conversion to the knighthood
of Christ.   We have already made mention of his chivalrous character.   On the paternal side the son of a wealthy
merchant, on the maternal side the scion of a noble
(Provençal) family,[10] Francis knew no greater ambition
than to acquire the rank of knighthood.   This ambition
grew upon him from the day when he began his adventure with the knights of his native city.   Although a few
years later [11] he tired of earthly pleasures, his thirst for
knightly fame and knightly deeds remained unabated.[12]

The occasion to realize his ambition seemed to present
itself very soon.   An able leader of the noble family of
the Gentile of Assisi [13] made preparations for a military
expedition against Apulia.   Francis, though his inferior
in rank, but superior in nobility of soul and in courage,
joined the expedition as a common soldier.[14]   He was in
the certain hope of obtaining knighthood by this adven-

ture, and with knighthood also nobility of rank, wealth and fame.

At this point, when ready to set out on the expedition, he had a peculiar dream. He beheld a splendid palace, filled with arms, shields and various knightly trappings. Wonderingly Francis inquired to whom this palace and its splendors belonged, and he received the reply that he himself was the noble lord, and that he was awaited within the palace by his retainers and vassals. Joyously he exclaimed: "Now I know that I am to be a great prince!" [15]

But the following night he had another dream. It seemed to him that he was speaking with someone who inquired whither he was going. Francis replied that he was setting out for Apulia in the retinue of a noble compatriot in order to achieve wealth, fortune and knightly honors. "Who can bestow greater fortune, the lord or the servant?" Francis replied: "The lord." "Why, then, dost thou forsake the lord for the servant, and the ruler for the subject?" Francis then asked: "What wilt thou, Lord, that I do?" "Return to thy country, for thy vision shall find through Me a spiritual fulfilment." [16] In this moment "Saul became a Paul. Francis exchanged earthly weapons for spiritual, a worldly knighthood for the divine." [17]

The new Knight of Christ was forthwith put to the test. "The newly knighted warrior must exert himself to the fullest extent in the first tournament in order to win praise," is the injunction given in a contemporaneous instruction on knighthood.[18] In consequence of his conversion Francis soon became engaged in a truly heroic struggle. His own father persecuted him, his brother ridiculed him, all Assisi, which had recently acclaimed him as the King of Youth, now jeered at his apparent idiocy. "They saw that he had changed his former mode of life so completely, and regarded it as insanity. They reproached him severely, called him an idiot and fool, and threw stones and filth at him." [19]

At first he fled from the storm of abuse, and hid himself in a cave, waiting for the tumult to abate. "He was," remarks Thomas of Celano, "as yet only a novice among the champions of Christ." [20]   But his chivalrous nature soon again asserted itself; he felt a deep shame for his lack of courage, and he determined to meet the attacks of his enemies fearlessly. "Dauntless and determined, he quickly arose, girded himself with the sword of confidence in Christ, and, holding aloft the shield of faith, and burning with the fire of divine love, he went forth into the battle for his Lord. A true knight of Christ, he disdained all persecutions, and, unbroken and untouched by all insults, he thanked God for all." [21]   The prince of darkness likewise endeavored in vain to turn him from his purpose. "The most valiant knight of Christ," write the Three Companions, "laughed at his threats and prayed God to direct his way." [22]

From this hour Francis devoted the heroic spirit of chivalry, with which nature had endowed him, to the service of Christ: his bold resoluteness, his generosity, his fearlessness, his high-mindedness in thought and action. Heretofore his sole ambition had been to please the great men of the world and thus achieve nobility of rank and fortune, but henceforth his great desire was to know and fulfil his obligations as liegeman of Christ. He was convinced that he could never show himself sufficiently thankful for the grace and honor of divine Knighthood. Chanting spiritual minstrel songs,[23] he set to work with a bold and dauntless spirit. Whatever he knew to be the will of his sovereign Lord, he accomplished with zealous and unswerving loyalty.

At first he felt himself called to serve the poorest of the poor of Christ, the lepers. In these unfortunates the Middle Ages beheld none other than the suffering Saviour Himself. To serve them, therefore, appeared to Francis as the sweet task of a knight of the cross. The Lord Himself, as Francis declares, led him among these afflicted ones, who were ostracized by an unfeeling world.[24] Their horrible condition at first caused him deep disgust.[25] But mindful of his knightly calling, he reproached himself, saying: "Thou art not a knight of Christ, if unable to conquer thyself." [26] And with true soldierly daring he embraced the lepers and gave them the kiss of peace.[27]

A short time after, he heard the voice of the Lord speaking from the crucifix: "Francis, dost thou not see that My house is falling to ruins? Go, and repair it." Filled with awe and wonder he replies: "Gladly will I do so, Lord!" Thinking that the command referred to the material house of God, he set to work upon the church, begged mortar and stones, carried them upon his own shoulders, and toiled so strenuously at this unaccustomed labor, that he well-nigh exhausted the strength of his frail body. But he was joyous and happy withal, deeming it a high honor thus to serve his King and Lord.[28]

As soon, however, as the Lord revealed to him clearly [29] that He had called him to rebuild and renew His spiritual Church, Francis embraces and fulfils his apostolic vocation with the fiery zeal of a St. Paul. During his entire life it was a point of honor with him to follow the call of his Master like a loyal knight, not tarrying to explore the path to be taken, or to consider the hardships to be endured. Like a valiant soldier "he sought always to perform valorous deeds," declares his biographer.[30]

His one great and lasting desire was to perform the highest deed of heroism, to suffer martyrdom for Christ; and his greatest sorrow was that this coveted honor was not vouchsafed him.[31] And when, finally, broken down with toil and sickness, and unable to walk on account of the Stigmata, he could no longer be active in the apostolate, he let himself be led through villages and towns, inspiring the faithful by his example to carry the cross of Christ. To his brothers he said in the last days of his earthly life: "Brothers, let us begin to serve God, for as yet we have done so little." And he still thirsted to labor for the salvation of souls, and yearned to return to the service of the lepers. Without pity for his body broken with suffering and arduous labors, he still hoped to do great deeds of heroism for Christ, his King and Master.[32]

He had furthermore always endeavored to *educate his disciples* to the same spirit of chivalry with which he himself was animated. When receiving them into the Order, he was wont to instruct them in the duties of the new knighthood to which they consecrated themselves. To Brother Giles, who had asked to join the holy company, Francis replied: "Most beloved brother, God hath bestowed upon thee a great honor. If the Emperor came to Assisi and wished to choose one of the townsmen as his knight or chamberlain, many indeed would desire to be selected. How much happier oughtest thou be, seeing that the Lord hath chosen thee from among them all, and called thee to His own court." [33]   At another time, Francis met at Rieti a youthful knight of the noble family of Tancredi, proudly mounted on his charger and resplendent in brilliant armor. "Sir Knight," said Francis to him, "armor, sword and spurs are vain dross. How would it suit thee to wear a coarse rope instead of the girdle, to carry the cross of Christ in place of the sword, and the dust and dirt of the fields in place of spurs? Follow me, I shall make thee a knight of Christ." The young nobleman dismounted, and Francis received him into the knighthood of the cross. [34]   That was the conversion of Brother Angelo Tancredi; that was the spirit which had to animate every novice who wished to join the company of these knights of the cross.

Francis constantly conjured this ideal of spiritual knighthood before the mind of his disciples. He would remind the novice of the great heroes, Charlemagne and his Paladins, Roland and Olivier and their brave comrades battling for the faith and the cause of Christ.[35] In glowing terms he would speak of the twelve heroes of the Round Table, and then turning to his brothers, he would exclaim joyously: "These my brothers, they are my Knights of the Round Table!" [36] Francis himself wished to be a knight of Christ; those whom he received into his army, were likewise to be knights of Christ—men of zeal, of courage, of magnanimity, and of loyalty in the service of the Lord.

2. The main duty of a knight consisted in rendering *unflinching fealty* to his lord. Knightly honor was embodied in the *homo legalis,* the loyal soldier, ever ready and eager to follow his leader into battle, to stand by him in combat and in death. His loyalty must never fail, as God's fidelity never fails:

> "Be true—loyal without fail,
> As God Himself is ever true,
> And hateth the false knave,"

thus the knight is reminded.[37] To accuse the knight of disloyalty was to accuse him of the basest crime.[38] Felony, the violation of the oath of fealty, rendered him guilty of death, and led to the company of the "sulphur-burning hordes" of the devils in hell.[39]

The supreme duty of the spiritual knight was therefore to be a vassal of Christ, the Lord Most High. But the call of this sovereign Lord was not to bloody strife and battle. He, the "King of kings and Lord of lords," has come as "Prince of peace," has come to shatter the sword of steel, and to check the brutal force of war, which seeks to ruin and destroy. He challenges His knights to the spiritual combat against sin and Satan and the world, arming them with the spiritual sword of faith and truth and virtue. "Do not think that I came to send peace upon earth, but the sword," is His battle-cry. "He that followeth Me not," the Leader in the spiritual combat, "is not worthy of Me." [40]

Christ has become our Leader in the fight, our Exemplar in every perfection. He has gone before us, "leaving us an example that we should follow His steps." [41] This duty of spiritual vassalage He frequently recalls to our mind. "I am the Light of the world: he that followeth Me, walketh not in darkness, but shall have the Light of life." [42] "I have given you an example, that as I have done to you, so you do also." [43] There is no higher purpose on earth for the chosen knight of the cross. "For whom He foreknew, He also predestinated to be made conformable to the image of His Son; that He might be the first-born among many brethren." [44] The true knight of Christ must therefore follow his divine Leader step for step, and copy His life line for line, until he can exclaim: "I live now, not I, but Christ liveth in me." [45]

St. Francis was deeply convinced of the necessity of following Christ, and wholly carried away with the determination to proclaim and practise it. With the same earnestness with which he placed the observance of the Gospel before his brothers as their ideal in life, he also pointed out to them the Person and the example of Jesus Christ, in whom the Gospel had become a living reality.

There is no doubt that even the primitive rule contained the words: "The rule and the life of the brothers is this: namely, to live in obedience, in chastity and without property, and *to follow the steps of Our Lord Jesus Christ.*" [46]

In the rule of 1221, Francis again admonishes: "Let us therefore hold fast the words, the life and doctrine and Holy Gospel of Him who deigned for us to ask His Father to manifest to us His Name. . . . Let us therefore desire nothing else, wish for nothing else, and let nothing please and delight us, except our Creator, and Redeemer, and Saviour." [47]

He adjures the General Chapter: "Hear, my lords, my sons and my brothers, and with your ears receive my words. Incline the ear of your heart, and obey the voice of the Son of God. Keep His commandments with all

your heart, and fulfil His counsels with a perfect mind.
Praise Him, for He is good, and extol Him in your
works, for to this end He has sent you into all the world,
that by word and deed you may bear witness to His
voice." [48]

In his Admonitions to the Friars, Francis thus speaks
of the following of Christ: "Let us all, my brothers, consider the Good Shepherd, who, to save His sheep, bore the
suffering of the cross. The sheep of the Lord followed
Him in tribulation and persecution and shame, in hunger
and thirst, in infirmity and temptations, and in all other
ways; and for these things they have received everlasting
life from the Lord." [49]

From his death-bed Francis writes these few and simple
words as his last wish: "I, little Brother Francis, wish to
follow the life and poverty of Jesus Christ, our Most High
Lord, and of His Most Holy Mother, and to persevere
therein until the end. And I beseech you all, my ladies,
and counsel you, to live always in this most holy life
and poverty. And watch yourself well, that you in no
wise depart from it through the teaching or advice of
anyone." [50]

Thus Francis, the Knight of Christ, persevered until
his last breath in the loyal service of his Lord. Thomas
of Celano assures us: "His supreme endeavor, his most
ardent wish and foremost principle was to observe the
holy Gospel in all and above all things, and to follow perfectly, with all zeal, with the fullest ardor of his spirit,
with all the love of his heart, the doctrine of Our Lord
Jesus Christ, and to imitate His example. In constant
meditation he reflected on His words, and with deep
intentness he pondered on His works." [51]

The following of Christ in all conditions of life, in
thought and action, a practical, energetic, constant and
persevering following of Jesus Christ until death, is the
secret of St. Francis. In great things as well as small,
in the hidden life of the soul as well as in exterior con-

duct, he sought to become like to his Saviour. Görres says of him: "If the Saviour has found one since the times of the apostles, who has walked after Him in all His footsteps, followed His example in all His teachings, and clung to Him with all the strength of his soul, it was this fiery nature, who, sunning himself ceaselessly in His light, himself became a light-bearer, reflecting not only His splendor, but His very image." [52]

It is a partly naïve and extravagant, yet on the whole a faithful picture, which Bartholomew of Pisa draws of Francis in his work: *On the Conformity of Life of St. Francis with the Life of the Lord Jesus.* The main theme of this work is expressed in the first lines of the *Fioretti:* "Conformity of St. Francis with Christ. Let it be known in the first place, that our holy Father St. Francis was conformable to Christ in all things." The earliest biographer of Francis remarks: "In my judgment St. Francis was a most holy mirror of the sanctity of Our Lord, and the image of His perfection." [53] So close was this conformity that St. Bonaventure finds it but natural that the Saint finally became a perfect image of his Saviour by means of the Stigmata: "As the man of God had imitated Christ in the actions of his life, so, before he should depart from this world, he was to be conformed to Him likewise in the sufferings and pains of His passion. And although, by the great austerity of his past life and his continual bearing of the cross of Christ, he had become very feeble in body, yet he was not terrified, but prepared himself with good courage to endure the martyrdom set before him. For there had grown in him an invincible fire of the love of his good Jesus." [54]

3. This invincible *fire of love for Christ* was the fountain from which Francis drew his zeal in following Him as a faithful knight. Next to the duty of service, love and its devotion has always been an essential element of chivalrous knighthood. That applied also to the Assisian Knight of the Cross. By very nature he was a passionate lover.

To love great things, and to be great in love, had always been the need of his heart. Therefore his youthful enthusiasm for the glowing, yet withal wondrously chaste songs of romance, and for the valorous deeds of true knighthood. But from the moment when he was made a spiritual knight, he directed this love to Christ. The Three Companions write: "From the time of his conversion to his death, he loved Christ with his whole heart, bearing the memory of Him constantly in his mind, praising Him with his lips, and glorifying Him in good works. So ardently and tenderly did he love the divine Saviour, that, on hearing His sweet Name, he became enraptured and exclaimed: 'Heaven and earth should bow before the Name of the Lord.'" [55] In his letter to all the Friars, Francis writes: "When you hear His Name, adore ye with fear and reverence, prostrate on the ground; the Lord Jesus Christ, such is the Name of the Most High Son, blessed forever." [56]

In touching words "the brothers who had lived with him would delight in telling how he daily and constantly occupied himself with Jesus when conversing, how sweet and charming was his discourse, how mild and tender his talk of Jesus," declares Thomas of Celano; and he adds: "His tongue spoke out of the fulness of his heart, and the stream of enraptured love which filled his soul, overflowed outwardly. Always was he occupied with Jesus. Jesus he carried in his heart, Jesus in his mouth, Jesus in his ears, Jesus in his eyes, Jesus in his hands, Jesus in all his members. Oh, how often he forgot earthly food while at table, when hearing the Name of Jesus, or pronouncing it, or thinking of it; seeing, he then saw not; and hearing, he heard not. Often, too, when thinking of Jesus on his journeys or singing of Him, he lost sight of his way and invited all elements to the praise of Jesus." [57]

In his prayers also he besought the Saviour to grant him the grace of perfect love: "I beseech Thee, O Lord, that the fiery and sweet strength of Thy love may absorb my soul from all things that are under heaven, that I may die for love of Thy love, as Thou didst deign to die for love of my love." [58]

This flame of love he enkindled especially at the two beacon-lights of the earthly life of the God-Man—the mysteries of His *Incarnation* and His *Passion*. Thomas of Celano tells us: "The humility of the birth of Jesus and the love of His passion occupied the soul of the Saint in such measure that he could scarcely think of aught else." [59]

"The *feast of the Birth of the Infant Jesus* he observed with heartier rejoicing and sweeter devotion than the other great feasts. He called it the feast of feasts, because on that day the Most High Son of God became a poor little child. The images of the Babe he would kiss with avidity of the soul, and his affection for it, which was poured out in his heart, caused him to stammer words of sweet delight after the manner of babes." [60]

One year Christmas occurred on a Friday. Brother Morico remarked casually that this time no meat could be placed on the table. "Thou art in error, brother," replied Francis; "on Christmas there is no Friday. I wish that on this day even the walls should eat meat, and since they cannot do so, it should at least be rubbed on them." [61]

Many times he would say: "If I could speak with the Emperor, I should beg him humbly and heartily for an edict, commanding all people to strew corn and wheat on the roads for love of God, in order that the birds, and especially our sisters the larks, might revel in abundance on this high feast. All magistrates and lords should see to it that out of love and reverence for the Son of God, on the night in which the most Holy Virgin laid her sweet Babe in the manger between an ox and an ass, every master should provide more plentiful hay and better fodder for his ox and ass. The rich also should spread a bounteous table for the poor and hungry on Christmas

Day." [62] And at the same time he burst into tears, thinking of the extreme want of the Mother of God.[63] And since on this day our redemption was begun, he desired that every Christian rejoice in the Lord, and do good to all creatures for love of Him who gave Himself to us.[64]

The following episode shows how ingenious was his love for the Babe of Bethlehem. Three years before his death, he resolved to observe the feast of Christmas in a novel, hitherto unheard of manner. At Greccio he had a dear friend, Giovanni Vellita, who had given to Francis and his brothers a wooded cliff, lying opposite the city. A fortnight before Christmas, Francis called Giovanni to his retreat in Fonte Colombo and said to him: "Giovanni, if thou art willing to celebrate with us the holy feast, prepare diligently what I tell thee. I wish to present in lifelike and visible manner the birth of the Infant of Bethlehem. Therefore, prepare in yonder woods a manger filled with hay. An ox and an ass must also be there, just as at Bethlehem." Giovanni did as he was bidden. In the holy night his brothers and many of the simple countryfolk flocked together with torches, singing shepherd songs so that the rocks resounded. "The holy man of God stood before the Babe in the manger, shedding tears of love and overflowing with joy." [65] Then, vested as deacon, he read aloud the gospel of the birth of Jesus, and, thus writes Celano in his inimitable manner, "his voice, his strong voice, his sweet voice, his clear and sonorous voice announced in honey-sweet words the birth of the poor King of heaven. And often, when he was about to pronounce the Name of Jesus, the all too great fire of love overcame him, and he called Him only the Babe of Bethlehem. And the word 'Bethlehem' he said with the sound as that of a bleating lamb. But when he had said the word 'Jesus' or 'Bethlehem,' he let his tongue glide over his lips as if to taste the sweetness of this word with his palate and to relish it." [66]

His devotion to the *passion of Christ* was similarly

deeply tender and fervent. "The entire public and private life of the man of God," writes Celano, "centered about the cross of the Lord; and from the first moment in which he became a knight of the Crucified, various mysteries of the cross shone forth in him." [67]

The Saviour's cross had stood at the very crossroads of the Saint's life. After he had begun to withdraw from the world and to converse with God in peaceful solitude, one day "Jesus Christ appeared to him under the form of a crucifix, at which sight his whole soul seemed to melt away; and so deeply was the memory of Christ's passion impressed on his heart that it pierced even to the marrow of his bones. From that hour, whenever he thought upon the passion of Christ, he could scarcely restrain his tears and sighs." [68]

Two years later, he was kneeling before a crucifix within the crumbling walls of San Damiano. Suddenly a voice went forth from the image of the Crucified, and the overpowering grace of God poured into his heart, changing him completely. "From that hour," writes Celano, "he was pierced with compassion for the Crucified Saviour, so that for the rest of his life he bore in his heart the holy wounds, which later were also impressed upon his body. The sufferings of Christ were ever before his eyes, and filled them with ever flowing tears. Everywhere one heard his weeping; at the memory of Christ's wounds he was inconsolable." [69]

One time, shortly after his conversion, when he was walking alone in the road, not far from the church of St. Mary of the Portiuncula, he lifted up his voice in lamentation. A certain spiritual man meeting him, asked what had befallen him. "The suffering of the Saviour," replied Francis. "In this way I ought to go through the whole world, without shame lamenting the passion of my Lord." This he said with such an overwhelming sense of sorrow, that this man also began to lament with many tears.[70]

To become like to the Man of Sorrows and to experience in his own body the sufferings of the Crucified, was his most ardent desire. In this endeavor he knew no bounds. The soul, as well as the body, was subjected to constant mortification. Incredibly severe were the chastisements which he imposed upon himself without regard to the state of his health; he knew no respite in crucifying the flesh, so that at the moment of death he believed an apology due to Brother Body, for having treated him so severely. On rising from prayer his eyes were often suffused with blood, so intense was his weeping. He did not, however, confine his mortification to tears, but denied himself food and drink in memory of the sufferings of his Lord.

Even in his exterior he appeared as the Knight of the Crucified. His garb bore the form of the cross, thus to express his love and reverence toward the sacred symbol of salvation. His earliest biographer relates: "He wished to clothe himself with the cross, choosing a garment of penance which represented its image. Although he chose it because of its poverty, he also desired it to express the mystery of the cross. He wished his entire body to be clothed with the cross of Christ, even as his spirit had put on the Crucified; and since God had vanquished the powers of hell in this sign, so also the Franciscan army should serve its Liege Lord under this standard." [71] For this reason he employed no other seal but the Tau, or sign of the cross. With this sign he sealed his writings, and also the walls of the cells.[72] He likewise admonished his brothers to worship the holy cross with due devotion, wherever they should behold it.[73]

The Lord Himself considered Francis as a knight of the cross, and confirmed him as such. Brother Pacificus one day beheld the sign of Tau shining with dazzling splendor on the forehead of Francis.[74] Brother Monaldus one time saw Francis fixed to the cross, while St. Anthony of Padua was preaching on the mystery of Redemption.[75] Brother Sylvester at various times beheld a golden cross proceeding from the mouth of the Saint, its beam growing upward into the heavens, and its arms reaching unto the ends of the earth.[76] Brother Leo, however, beheld a wondrously beautiful cross moving before the face of Francis, and Christ hanging thereon. And when Francis stood still, the cross stood still; and when he moved, the cross moved; and whither he turned, the cross also turned. And it shone so brilliantly that not only the seraphic man of God, but all the surroundings, the air and the earth were bathed in a flood of light.[77]

Brother Hugolino therefore wrote some time later: "As St. Francis and his companions were called and elected by God to carry in heart, and to preach in word and in work, the cross of Christ; and as, both in appearance by reason of the habit which they wore, and in fact by reason of their austere life and their acts and conduct, they were crucified men, therefore they desired the more to undergo shame and contumely for the love of Christ, rather than to receive the honors of the world or the reverence and praises of men. They rejoiced in ill-treatment, they were sad in honors; and so they went through the world as strangers and pilgrims, taking nothing with them but Christ crucified." [78]

Whatever reminded Francis of the sufferings and loving patience of the Saviour was very dear to his heart. For this reason he so loved the lambs, because they put him in mind of the Lamb of God, who was so meek and suffered so patiently. One day, seeing a lamb grazing in the midst of goats and rams, he exclaimed with a voice choked with emotion: "Behold, thus Our Lord Jesus Christ walked amongst the Pharisees and high priests, mild, sweet and lowly." [79]

But if his eyes chanced to fall on a crucifix, he was overcome with love and compassion. He would then begin to sing, at first softly, then louder and louder, giving utterance in the French tongue to the passing sweet melody of the spirit within him, and the strain of the

divine whisper that his ear had caught would break
forth into a French song of joyous exulting. At times he
would pick up a stick from the ground, and setting it
upon his left shoulder, would draw across it another stick
after the manner of a bow with his right hand as across
a viol or other instrument, and, making befitting gestures,
would sing in French of Our Lord Jesus Christ.[80] But
all this show of joy would be ended in tears, and the
exultation would die out in pity of Christ's passion. And
in tears would he remain, drawing deep sighs, and with
redoubled lamentations he would hang in ecstasy, sus-
pended from heaven, forgetful of that which he held in
his hands the while.[81]

Early one morning—it was the feast of the Holy Cross,
1224—Francis again struggled with his crucified Love.
"O my Lord Jesus Christ," thus he prayed, "I pray Thee
to grant me two graces before I die; the first, that in
my lifetime I may feel in my soul and in my body, so far
as is possible, all the pain and grief which Thou, O sweet
Lord, didst feel in Thy most bitter passion; the second,
that I may feel in my heart, as far as is possible, that
excessive love by which Thou, the Son of God, wert
impelled willingly to sustain so great sufferings for
sinners." [82]

The longer Francis prayed for this twofold grace, and
the longer he contemplated the passion of Christ and His
infinite love, the stronger waxed the flame of love and
compassion within him, until he was wholly changed into
Jesus.

Suddenly he beheld the crucified Saviour descend
toward him in the figure of a seraph. The wondrous
apparition shone with a blazing light of glory and with
the searing flame of suffering. Blood-red were the marks
of the nails in hands and feet, and the gaping wound in
the side. And the Vision looked upon Francis with such
unspeakably tender and loving eyes that he fain would
have died for love and compassion. At the same time

he felt himself smitten with a fivefold agonizing pain. His hands and feet were pierced as if with fiery nails, his right side opened as if with a lance. The Stigmata of the Saviour glowed and burned in his flesh.[83]

From this day on, in consequence of an astounding and hitherto unheard of miracle, he was a living image of the Crucified,[84] "a crucified man."[85] But he was not content with the severe pains caused by the sacred wounds; he yearned for further suffering in order to endure in his entire body the torments of the Saviour. He would not have considered himself a worthy knight of Christ if he had borne only the marks of the passion, without its torture. The Lord soon granted his wish in fullest measure.

Shortly after the stigmatization, his body was visited with ills more severe than he had as yet experienced.[86] He was stricken with a very painful malady of the eyes, which never left him until death, necessitating inhumanly cruel operations, and ending with almost total blindness.[87]

Six months before his death, his body, already broken with constant austerities and superhuman labors, became afflicted with various maladies, so that hardly a single member remained sound. The stomach refused almost all nourishment, the liver became torpid; body, limbs and feet swelled to an alarming degree, frequent hemorrhages occurred. Reduced to a mere skeleton, he appeared a veritable figure of woe, and each day seemed to be his last.[88]

Once, being more grievously tormented than usual, a certain simple brother said to him: "Brother, pray to God that He will deal more gently with thee, for it seems to me that His hand is heavier upon thee than is meet." Francis rebuked him severely, saying: "But that I know the purity of thy simplicity, I should from henceforth abhor thy company, for that thou hast dared to find fault with the divine judgments which are executed upon me." And although sick to death, he cast himself upon the ground, all his weak bones being shattered by the fall.

And, kissing the ground, he said: "I thank Thee, O Lord, my God, for these my pains, and I beseech Thee, O Lord, to increase them a hundredfold, for this shall be most acceptable to me, that Thou spare not to afflict me with suffering, because the fulfilment of Thy holy will is to me an overflowing consolation." [89]

Another time, when asked by one of the brothers, which he would rather suffer, this slow and wearisome illness or a cruel martyrdom at the hand of an executioner, he replied: "My son, it has always been and always will be sweeter and more pleasing to me, whatever my Lord and God pleases to do in me and to me. My sole desire is to be found submissive and obedient to His will in all things. Still, in comparison to any form of martyrdom, it seems more grievous to me to bear this illness even for three days." [90] What others could hardly bear to see, that he bore willingly, smilingly and joyfully to the end.[91] Thus his confessor could justly say, "that from the apparition of the crucifix at San Damiano until his death, he had always been conformable to the image of Christ." [92]

Furthermore, as he had been an image of the living Saviour in life, of the dying Saviour in death, so after death his body was to bear the perfect semblance to the body of the Saviour.[93] Only now, when his soul had winged its way to eternal glory, and he lay on the bare ground, despoiled of all, his perfect conformity with Christ became manifest to all. Until now he had succeeded in hiding the Stigmata with truly ingenious humility, so that only the most intimate brothers knew them.[94] But now thousands beheld and reverently touched the sacred symbols of seraphic love, and it appeared to them as if Francis had just been taken down from the cross, so fresh and almost living seemed the seal and escutcheon of Christ, his Lord, which he bore in hands and feet and side.[95] In the service, in the following, and in the love of his Most High Liege Lord he had lived and died, in deed and in truth a *genuine Knight of the Holy Grail*.

CHAPTER III

FRANCIS AND THE EUCHARIST

WHEN Francis speaks of the Saviour, he has, above all, the Eucharist in mind. His knightly service, his imitation, and his love of Christ were so fervent, so real and living for the very reason that they did not refer to the Saviour distant in time or place, but to the immediate Person of Christ in the Holy Sacrament. Crib and cross, both he found here present. Here his divine Master lived and breathed. Here the knight of Christ stood guard day by day in the court and at the throne of his Most High King. The altar was for him the hearth of his faith, of his hope and his love, the goal of his thoughts and actions. In the Eucharist, and through the Eucharist, Christ became to him a living reality. *The Eucharist was the focus of his entire religious life.*

1. Francis fostered the *devotion to the Eucharist* as no saint before him. It was *the* devotion, not one of the devotions of the Seraphic Saint. Even unbelieving historians find it remarkable that the eucharistic cult "played such an important rôle in his religious ideals, and that this cult was to a certain extent the soul of his piety." [1]

Brother Leo, the confessor of the Saint, has already stressed in his charming and delicate way "this," as he expresses it, "exceeding great reverence and devotion of the blessed Francis to the body of the Lord." [2] Thomas of Celano declares: "Every fiber of the heart of Francis was aglow with love for the sacrament of the Body of Christ, and with exceeding great admiration he marveled

38

at the loving condescension and the condescending love of the Lord. He considered it an unpardonable negligence not to attend Mass each day whenever possible.[3] If illness prevented him from going to church, he would ask a priest to celebrate Mass for him in the sick-room.[4] If this also were not possible, he would have the gospel of the day read to him from the missal, and in this wise assist at Mass spiritually. For he said: 'If I cannot be present at Mass, I adore the body of Christ in meditation and with the eyes of the soul, in like manner as if I were present at Mass.' [5]

"He communicated often and with such devotion that he enkindled the hearts of others. Because he revered the Most Holy Sacrament with all his heart, he offered Him the sacrifice of all his members, and"—these are words of Celano—"whenever he received the sweet and spotless Lamb, he surrendered also to Him his spirit with that flaming ardor which ever glowed on the altar of his heart." [6] "He was, as it were, spiritually inebriated, and frequently rapt in ecstasy," adds St. Bonaventure.[7]

His predilection for French customs and the French language is explained not only by the fact that he descended from a French mother, and that the Provence was the home of true knighthood and of the troubadours; he loved France above all, because it was the "Friend of the Eucharist." [8] When he therefore resolved one day [9] to take up his abode in a distant province, he said to his brothers: "In the name of Our Lord Jesus Christ and of the glorious Virgin Mary, His Mother, I choose the province of France, where there is a Catholic people who more than other Catholics greatly reverence the body of Christ, which is to me a great joy, and therefore do I desire to converse with them." [10] He desired also to die in France out of reverence toward the Most Holy Sacrament.[11]

His reverence and love for the Eucharist was also the source from which sprang his ardent zeal for all those things which stood in remote or proximate relation to this sublime mystery.

As a young man of the world he frequently purchased precious ornaments and vessels which were used at the Holy Sacrifice, and sent them secretly to poor priests and churches.[12]

On the occasion of a pilgrimage to Rome, he took notice of the scanty offerings made by the people for the maintenance of St. Peter's. "What!" he exclaimed, "such small alms you give the church of the Prince of the Apostles?" Saying this, he drew a handful of coins from his purse and threw it upon the altar with such noise that all present were seized with admiration at his generosity.[13]

In later years he charged St. Clare and her daughters at San Damiano to make altar linens, vestments and other articles, to be used in those churches which were too poor to procure them. In spite of his extreme poverty, he desired to send a number of brothers in every direction with beautiful and neat vessels, and wherever they found the body of the Lord preserved in an unbecoming manner, they were to place it respectfully in the vessels which they had brought along. He was often seen washing the church linens, and baking the altar breads with artistically wrought irons; yes, he sent these irons into the various provinces, so that the Friars might be able to prepare beautiful and snow-white breads everywhere.[14] Wherever he found a neglected church on his journeys, he would seize a broom, sweep and garnish the house of God humbly and devoutly, and adorn the altars, so that his Lord might abide there with due honor and respect.[15]

From his early youth Francis felt himself impelled to repair poor and dilapidated churches. His first efforts were in behalf of the church of San Damiano, which later on became the mother church of the Poor Clares. Going from house to house, he gathered materials as well as helpers, and for many months he exerted himself so strenuously that his weak and delicate frame almost suc-

cumbed under the strain. When the work of restoration
was fairly completed, in 1207, he begged a sufficient quan-
tity of oil to have a lamp burn continuously before the
Most Holy Sacrament.[16]

His next undertaking was the restoration of the old
Benedictine church of San Pietro, which at present is
within the city, but at that time was beyond the walls.[17]
He then directed his attention to the little country church
Santa Maria of Josaphat, called later the Portiuncula, or
Our Blessed Lady of the Angels. This sanctuary—once
a famed place of pilgrimage, but at the beginning of the
thirteenth century deserted and in ruins—began to rise in
new beauty under the hands of Francis toward the end of
the year 1208, and in later years became the favorite
chapel of the Saint and the mother church of the Order.[18]
In 1213 Francis remodeled the church of the Holy Virgin
between San Gemini and Porcaria.[19] Three years later
he undertook the completion of the church Santa Maria
del Vescovado, in Assisi. This sanctuary was so destitute that nothing but a roof covered the altar of the
Sacrament. Moved by the poverty of his sacramental
God, Francis renovated the choir, and erected a beautiful
baldachin over the main altar.[20]

His devotion to the Eucharist inspired him furthermore
with an ineffable *reverence for the priesthood*. The de-
generacy of the clergy was at that time wofully great
and widespread. As usual, the masses held the entire
clerical state, yes, the very office of the priesthood itself
responsible for the sins of the individuals. The Cathari
and the Waldenses declared outright that priests who
were living in sin, had lost their priestly power itself.
Day after day these heresies drew larger circles, and thus
became a distinct menace to the Church. Francis combated this heresy with the sword of invincible faith in the
word of God and in the eucharistic God-Man, both of
which were entrusted to the priesthood.

The Dominican Stephen de Bourbon (died about 1261)

relates an incident which strikingly illustrates the love
and reverence of the Saint for the priesthood. Francis
was journeying at one time through Lombardy, and the
people of a certain village, clerical and lay, Catholics and
heretics, flocked to meet him. A member of the sect of
the Cathari elbowed his way through the throng, and,
pointing to the village pastor, said to Francis: "Tell us,
good man, how can this shepherd of souls demand faith
and reverence, since he is living in concubinage and notorious sin?" Walking over to the priest Francis knelt
down in the mire, kissed his hands and said: "I know
not whether these hands are unclean or not, but even if so,
the power of the sacraments administered by them is not
diminished thereby. These hands have touched my Lord.
Out of reverence for the Lord I honor His vicar; for
himself, he may be bad; for me, he is good." [21]

Francis constantly admonished his brothers to esteem
the priests above all others, out of reverence for the Holy
Sacrament. "Wherever they met a priest, whether rich
or poor, good or bad, they bowed humbly before him and
reverenced him." [22] Yea, the priests who administer the
sublime and most holy Sacrament, were to be honored
so highly, that not only were the Friars to bow before
them, to kneel down and kiss their hands, but even to kiss
the hoofs of the horse which had carried a priest, in order
thus to honor the priestly dignity.[23]

Repeatedly he would say: "Blessed is the servant of
God who exhibits confidence in clerics who live uprightly
according to the form of the holy Roman Church. And
woe to those who despise them: for even though they [the
clerics] may be sinners, nevertheless no one ought to
judge them, because the Lord Himself reserves to Himself alone the right of judging them. For as the administration with which they are charged, namely, of the most
holy body and blood of our Lord Jesus Christ, which
they receive and which they alone administer to others,

even so the sin of those who offend against them is greater than any against all the other men in this world." [24]

Even on his death-bed the Saint in the most touching words gave expression to his reverence toward the Holy Eucharist and to the priestly ministers of this sublime mystery. In that most solemn moment, when he felt himself impelled to entrust to his sons what was most dear to his heart and most holy on earth, he had Brother Leo write the words: "The Lord gave to me, Brother Francis, thus to begin to do penance; for when I was in sin it seemed to me very bitter to see lepers, and the Lord Himself led me amongst them, and I showed mercy to them. And when I left them, that which had seemed to me bitter was changed for me into sweetness of body and soul. And afterward I remained a little and I left the world. And the Lord gave me so much faith in churches, that I would simply pray and say thus: 'We adore Thee, Lord Jesus Christ, here and in all Thy churches which are in the whole world, and we bless Thee, because by Thy holy cross Thou hast redeemed the world.' After that the Lord gave me, and gives me, so much faith in priests who live according to the form of the holy Roman Church, on account of their order, that if they should persecute me, I would have recourse to them. And if I had as much wisdom as Solomon had, and if I should find poor priests of this world, I would not preach against their will in the parishes in which they live. And I desire to fear, love and honor them and all others as my masters; and I do not wish to consider sin in them, for in them I see the Son of God, and they are my masters. And I do this because in this world I see nothing corporally of the most high Son of God Himself except His most holy body and blood, which they alone consecrate and receive and they alone administer to others. And I will that these Most Holy Mysteries be honored and revered above all things and that they be placed in precious places. Wheresoever I find His most holy Names and written words in unseemly places, I wish to collect them, and I ask that they may be collected and put in a becoming place. And we ought to honor and venerate all theologians and those who minister to us the most holy divine words as those who minister to us spirit and life." [25]

It would indeed be difficult to find in all theological literature a treatise which sets forth so briefly and in words so profound and yet so simple the significance of the Eucharist and of the priesthood for religious life. "In this world I see nothing corporally of the most high Son of God, but His most holy body and blood, which they alone consecrate and receive and they alone administer to others." Words of living faith! The faith of Francis beholds behind the crystal of the monstrance, on the linen of the altar, and on the tongue of the communicant, the hands and feet, the eyes and mouth, the flowing blood and throbbing heart, the majestic personality and the saving grace of Him who once walked the fields of Galilee and Judea, and to whom he himself had sworn allegiance as a knight of the cross. And this unfathomable mystery and infinite treasure the priest calls back from the bygone days of Palestine into the presence of every tabernacle, from the height of heaven into the heart of the least of men. This thought is overwhelming, is staggering to the human mind. Francis was so overcome by it, that he constantly spent every effort in honoring and loving the eucharistic Saviour, the eucharistic sanctuaries, and the eucharistic priesthood.

2. He was, however, not content with this. The Eucharist occupied the first place not only in his private devotion, but also in his *apostolic activity*. Bartholomew of Pisa has already called attention to this fact. Among the doctrinal treatises of the Saint, he places the latter's utterances on the Eucharist above all others.[26] Even Böhmer, the Protestant editor of the *Analekten*, designates the Eucharist "the favorite theme of the Saint." [27] In fact, the Saint does not speak of the Eucharist in a casual

manner only; he treats of it at length in his writings. Of eight letters which are still extant, five treat exclusively, or at least extensively, of the Eucharist.[28] He felt himself impelled to impress this truth, which had penetrated every fiber of his heart, at all times and places upon the people, the princes, the clergy and his own sons: "In this world I see nothing corporally of the most high Son of God except His most holy body and His most holy blood. . . ."

At the head of his "Words of Holy Admonition" we find a catechetical instruction bearing the title: "Of the Lord's Body." In spite of its utter simplicity this instruction is an excellent dogmatic treatise and a practical exposition of the Saint's conception of the Eucharist. He writes: "The Lord Jesus said to His disciples:[29] 'I am the way, and the truth, and the life. No man cometh to the Father but by Me. If you had known Me you would, without doubt, have known My Father also, and from henceforth you shall know Him, and you have seen Him.' Philip saith to Him: 'Lord, show us the Father, and it is enough for us.' Jesus saith to him: 'Have I been so long a time with you and have you not known Me? Philip, he that seeth Me, seeth the Father also.' The Father 'inhabiteth light inaccessible,'[30] and 'God is a spirit,'[31] and 'no man hath seen God at any time.'[32] Because God is a spirit, therefore, it is only by the spirit He can be seen, for 'it is the spirit that quickeneth; the flesh profiteth nothing.'[33] For neither is the Son, inasmuch as He is equal to the Father, seen by anyone other than by the Father, other than by the Holy Ghost. Wherefore all those who saw the Lord Jesus Christ according to humanity and did not see and believe according to the Spirit and the Divinity, that He was the Son of God, were condemned.

"In like manner, all those who behold the sacrament of the body of Christ, which is sanctified by the word of the Lord upon the altar by the hands of the priest in

the form of bread and wine, and who do not see and
believe according to the Spirit and Divinity that it is really
the most holy body and blood of Our Lord Jesus Christ,
are condemned, He the Most High having declared it when
He said: [34] 'This is My body and blood of the New
Testament,' and: [35] 'He that eateth My flesh and drinketh
My blood hath everlasting life.' Wherefore, he who has
the Spirit of the Lord dwells in His faithful, he it is who
receives the most holy body and blood of the Lord; all
others who do not have this same Spirit and who presume
to receive Him, 'eat and drink judgment to themselves.' " [36]

"Wherefore, 'O ye sons of men, how long will you be
dull of heart?' [37] Why will you not know the truth and
'believe in the Son of God?' [38] Behold, daily He humbles
Himself as when from His 'royal throne' [39] He came
into the womb of the Virgin; daily He Himself comes to
us with like humility; daily He descends from the bosom
of His Father upon the altar, in the hands of the priest.
And as He appeared in true flesh to the holy apostles, so
now He shows Himself to us in the sacred bread; and
as they by means of their fleshly eyes saw only His flesh,
yet contemplating Him with their spiritual eyes, believed
Him to be God, so we, seeing bread and wine with bodily
eyes, see and firmly believe it to be His most holy body
and true and living blood. And in this way Our Lord is
ever with His faithful, as He Himself says: [40] 'Behold, I
am with you all days, even to the consummation of the
world.' " [41]

Who will fail to notice that in this instruction Francis
makes the Eucharist the center and heart of Christianity?
As the apostles beheld the divinity of Jesus through the
veil of His humanity, thus also we to-day behold and
believe the Son of God present under the eucharistic veil.
As Jesus Christ lived with His apostles as an historical
Person, thus truly and really does He live among us now
in the eucharistic Presence. As salvation and damnation
hinged on the belief in Him and the love to Him then, so

also will our soul's salvation hinge on our belief in and our love to the eucharistic God-Man. Whoever lives with and for and out of the Eucharist, he lives with and for and out of Jesus Christ even to-day as really and truly as at the time of the apostles. "Jesus Christ, yesterday, and to-day and the same forever."[42] Yesterday with the apostles in the fields of Galilee and Judea; to-day with us in all the tabernacles of the world; and forever with all the saints in the splendor and glory of heaven's bliss. That is the eucharistic message of St. Francis to the Christian people.

It was entirely natural, considering the chivalrous spirit of the Saint, that he should also carry this message to the *princes of the people*. Christ present in the Eucharist as the Prince of princes, as the Lord of hosts, to whose service every genuine knight is called, to be the vassal and liegeman of whom is an honor even for king and emperor! To Francis it was evident that the great men of the world especially should bear a special devotion to the Most Holy Sacrament, and that they should promote this devotion also among their subjects. So strongly was this conviction rooted in his mind, that he addressed a special letter "To the Rulers of Nations," in which he says: "To all potentates and consuls, judges and governors, in whatever part of the world, and to all others to whom this letter may come, Brother Francis, your little and contemptible servant, wishes health and peace to you. . . . I ask you with such reverence as I can, not to forget the Lord on account of the cares and solicitudes of this world, and not to turn aside from His commandments, for all those who forget Him and decline from His commandments are cursed,[43] and they shall be forgotten by Him.[44] Wherefore, I strongly advise you, my lords, to put aside all care and solicitude, and to receive readily the most holy body and blood of Our Lord Jesus Christ in holy commemoration of Him; and to cause so great honor to be rendered to the Lord by the people committed to you, that every evening it may be announced by a crier or by another sign, to the end that praises and thanks shall resound to the Lord God almighty from all the people. . . ." [45]

Again the plastic and living conception of the Eucharist as the center and focus of religious life: to believe in Christ the Lord, and to serve Christ the Lord, means to believe in the Eucharist and to honor the Eucharist. The eucharistic God-Man is to rule our whole life, public and private; princes and people are to gather around their eucharistic King in worshipful reverence. The eucharistic kingdom of God come to us all and rule over us all! To promote and to acknowledge this kingdom is the sublime and august duty of the great as well as of the small men of this world, but, above all, the duty of the *clergy*.

We have seen with what devotion and awe Francis revered the priesthood because of its power to consecrate and administer the Eucharist. The same devotion and reverence moved him to admonish the priests with holy frankness to live worthy of the sublime mystery entrusted to their care, to celebrate and receive it devoutly and to further its worship zealously among the faithful. Brother Leo, his constant companion, relates: "When he was at St. Mary of the Portiuncula and the number of the Friars was still small, blessed Francis went round the villages and churches in the lordship of Assisi preaching the Gospel and exhorting all men to penance; and he would carry with him a broom to sweep out the churches, for it caused him great pain when he saw any church not as clean as he thought it ought to be. Therefore, whenever he finished his preaching, he would invite the clergy into some place apart where he could not be overheard by the laity, and would speak to them on the salvation of their souls, and particularly exhort them to be solicitous in keeping the churches clean, as well as the altars and things belonging to the celebration of the Divine Mysteries." [46] Not content with this, he wrote a pastoral

THE STIGMATIZATION OF ST. FRANCIS

instruction on the Eucharist to all the clerics of the world. It reads thus: "Let us all consider, O clerics, the great sin and ignorance of which some are guilty regarding the most holy body and blood of Our Lord Jesus Christ and His most holy Name and the written words of consecration. For we know that the body cannot exist until after these words of consecration. For we have nothing and see nothing of the Most High Himself in this world except [His] body and blood, names and words by which we have been created and redeemed from death to life. But let all those who administer such most holy Mysteries, especially those who do so indifferently, consider among themselves how poor the chalices, corporals, and linens may be where the body and blood of Our Lord Jesus Christ is sacrificed. And by many it is left in wretched places and carried about disrespectfully, received unworthily and administered to others indiscriminately. Again, His Names and written words are sometimes trampled under foot, 'for the sensual man perceiveth not these things that are of the Spirit of God.' [47] Shall we not by all these things be moved with a sense of duty when the good Lord Himself places Himself in our hands and we handle Him and receive Him daily? Are we unmindful that we must needs fall into His hands?

"Let us, then, at once and resolutely correct these faults and others; and wheresoever the most holy body of Our Lord Jesus Christ may be improperly reserved and abandoned, let it be removed thence and let it be put and enclosed in a precious place. In like manner, wheresoever the Names and written words of the Lord may be found in unclean places, they ought to be collected and put away in a decent place. And we know that we are bound, above all, to observe all these things by the commandments of the Lord and the constitutions of Holy Mother Church. And let him who does not act thus, know that he shall have to render an account therefor before Our Lord Jesus Christ on the day of judgment. And let him who may cause copies of this writing to be made to the end that it may be the better observed, know that he is blessed by the Lord." [48]

However zealously Francis sought to inspire the people and the clerics with reverence toward the Eucharist, he endeavored still more to promote it among his *brothers*. They were to be shining examples unto all men in their glowing love for the eucharistic Saviour. The Three Companions assert that "he admonished them constantly to hear Mass devoutly and to adore the body of the Lord with utmost reverence." [49] "Having confessed contritely," thus he charged them in the rule of 1221: "Let them receive the body and blood of Our Lord Jesus Christ with great humility and veneration, calling to mind what the Lord Himself says: [50] 'He that eateth My flesh and drinketh My blood hath everlasting life,' and: [51] 'Do this for a commemoration of Me.'" [52]

At the General Chapters of the Order he repeatedly counseled the brothers in like manner.[53]   Toward the end of his life, when he was unable to attend the Chapter, he addressed to the assembled Friars one of those wonderful missives in which he writes as it were with his own heart's blood:

"I conjure you all, brothers, kissing your feet and with the charity of which I am capable, to show all reverence and all honor possible to the most holy body and blood of Our Lord Jesus Christ, in whom the things that are in heaven and the things that are on earth are pacified and reconciled to almighty God.[54]

"I also beseech in the Lord all my brothers who are and shall be and desire to be priests of the Most High, that when they wish to celebrate Mass, being pure, they offer the true Sacrifice of the body and blood of Our Lord Jesus Christ purely, with reverence, with a holy and clean intention, not for any earthly thing or fear or for the love of any man, as it were pleasing men.[55] But let every will, insofar as the grace of the Almighty helps, be directed to Him, desiring thence to please the high Lord Himself alone, because He Himself alone works there [in the Holy Sacrifice] as it may please Him, for He says: [56] 'Do this for a commemoration of Me'; if anyone does otherwise, he becomes the traitor Judas and is 'made guilty of the body and blood of the Lord.' [57] Call to mind, priests, my brothers, what is written in the law of Moses: how those transgressing even materially, died by the decree of the Lord without any mercy.[58] How much more and worse punishments he deserves to suffer 'who hath trodden under foot the Son of God and hath esteemed the blood of the testament unclean by which he was sanctified, and hath offered an affront to the spirit of grace.' [59] For, man despises, soils, and treads under foot the Lamb of God when, as the Apostle says,[60] not discerning and distinguishing the holy bread of Christ from other nourishment or works, he either eats unworthily, or, if he be worthy, he eats in vain and unbecomingly, since the Lord has said by the Prophet: [61] 'Cursed be the man who doth the work of the Lord deceitfully.' And He condemns the priests who will not take this to heart, saying,[62] 'I will curse your blessings.'

"Hear ye, my brothers: If the Blessed Virgin Mary is so honored, as is meet, because she bore Him in her most holy womb; if the blessed Baptist trembled and did not dare to touch the holy forehead of God; if the sepulcher, in which He lay for some time, is venerated, how holy, just, and worthy ought he be who touches with his hands, who receives with his heart and his mouth, and proffers to be received by others Him who is now no more to die, but to triumph in a glorified eternity: on whom the angels desire to look.[63]

"Consider your dignity, brothers, priests, and be holy because He Himself is holy.[64] And as the Lord God has honored you above all through this mystery, even so do you also love and reverence and honor Him above all. It is a great shame and a deplorable weakness when

you have Him thus present, to care for anything else
in the whole world.   Let the entire man be seized with
fear; let the whole world tremble; let heaven exult when
Christ, the Son of the living God, is on the altar in the
hands of the priest.   O admirable sublimity and stupendous condescension!   O sublime humility! that the Lord
of the universe, God and the Son of God, so humbles
Himself that for our salvation He hides Himself under
a morsel of bread.   Consider, brothers, the humility of
God, and 'pour out your hearts before Him,' [65] and be
ye humbled that ye may be exalted by Him.[66]   Do not
therefore keep back anything for yourselves, that He may
receive you entirely, who gives Himself up entirely to
you." [67]

The soul of a St. John speaks in these words.   He
alone, who has rested on the bosom of the eucharistic
Saviour as did the Beloved Disciple, he alone, who has
drunk from the Source of infinite love, can speak in such
glowing terms of the Mystery of Love.

Francis, however, could not rest content with enjoining
the most tender reverence toward the Eucharist on his
sons.   Not only personally were they to foster this devotion above all else; they were to *promote* it to the utmost
of their endeavor also among others, among the clergy and
the faithful.   He stresses this again in another wonderful
letter directed to the Custodes, and through them to all the
Friars of the Order:

"I entreat you more than if it were a question of myself,
that, when it is becoming and it may seem to be expedient,
you humbly beseech the clerics to venerate above all the
most holy body and blood of Our Lord Jesus Christ and
His Holy Name and written words which sanctify the
body.   They ought to hold as precious the chalices, corporals, ornaments of the altar, and all that pertain to the
Sacrifice.   And if the most holy body of the Lord be
lodged very poorly in any place, let it according to the
command of the Church be placed by them and left in a

becoming place, and let it be carried with great veneration and administered to others with discretion. The Names also and written words of the Lord, wheresoever they may be found in unclean places, let them be collected; and they ought to be put in a proper place.

"And in all the preaching you do, admonish the people concerning penance and that no one can be saved except he that receives the most sacred body and blood of the Lord. And while it is being offered up by the priest in the sacrifice of the altar or it is being carried to any place, let all the people on bended knees render praise, honor and glory to the Lord God, living and true.

"And you shall so announce and preach His praise to all peoples, that at every hour and when the bells are rung, praise and thanks shall always be given to the almighty God by all the people through the whole earth.

"And to whomsoever of my brothers, custodes, this writing shall come, let them copy it and keep it with them and cause it to be copied for the brothers who have the office of preaching and the care of the brothers, and let them unto the end preach all those things that are contained in this writing: let them know they have the blessing of the Lord God and mine. And let these be for them through true and holy obedience. Amen." [68]

Francis would have embodied these directions in a separate chapter of the rule, if he had not been restrained from doing so by the misgivings of several of the Ministers Provincial. "For Blessed Francis," thus relates Brother Leo in the *Speculum perfectionis,* "had the highest reverence and devotion for the body of Christ, and wished to have it inserted in the rule, that the Friars in every province where they dwelt, should show great care and solicitude in this matter, exhorting all clerics and priests that they should reserve the body of Christ in good and decent places, and if they neglected this, the Friars were to do so for them. He also desired to insert in the rule, that when the Friars found the Name of the Lord, and those words that made the body of the Lord, not well and safely taken care of, the Friars should collect them and see to it that they be kept in a decent place, paying honor to the Lord in His words. And although these things were not written in the rule, the Ministers not thinking it suitable that the Friars should be commanded to do this, in his Testament and other writings he left to the Friars his will in this regard." [69]

In view of these documents it may be regarded as established beyond doubt: Francis desired that his sons be the bearers of *a world-wide eucharistic mission.* At that time this was something unheard of. At a time when the churches were to a great extent in a deplorable condition, when the Sacrament was treated with shameful indifference and neglect on the part of the clergy and laity,[70] the Seraphic Knight sounded the clarion-call to his "Brothers of the Round Table" to undertake an eucharistic crusade. They were to form the honor guard of the body of the Lord, to serve the Saviour, really, truly, and substantially present in the Holy Sacrament, as genuine knights of the Holy Grail, and to promote His glory with every ounce of their strength.

This was the Ideal before the mind of Francis, this his disciples understood and sought to accomplish.

Clare of Assisi, the noble daughter of the Saint, is symbolized with the vessel bearing the Holy Eucharist. "How great," thus writes Thomas of Celano, "was the devotion St. Clare felt toward the Sacrament of the Altar is shown by the fact that during the severe illness which had confined her to bed, she had herself raised to a sitting position and supported by props, and thus she spun the finest linens. From these she made more than fifty sets of corporals, and, enclosing them in silken and purple burses, sent them to different churches in the plains and mountains about Assisi. When about to receive the body of the Lord, Clare shed burning tears and approached with awe, for she feared Him not less hidden in the Sacrament than ruling heaven and earth." [71]

John Parenti, the successor of St. Francis as Minister General, ordained at the Chapter of 1230 that "the Most Holy Sacrament be preserved in all places in ivory or silver ciboria and that these be placed in well-locked tabernacles, because neither in heaven nor on earth can anything be found which deserves similar veneration." [72]

Anthony of Padua was the wonder-worker,[73] Berthold of Ratisbon the preacher of the Eucharist.[74] Alexander of Hales, Bonaventure and Duns Scotus, the luminaries of Franciscan science, became the theologians of the Eucharist.[75] Paschal Baylon is the patron of the eucharistic works and societies.[76] Joseph Plantanida of Ferno was the author of the Forty Hours' Adoration,[77] the entire Franciscan Order, the defender and promoter of the feast of Corpus Christi and of the eucharistic devotions.

That is the true Franciscan heritage, the true Franciscan spirit. As surely as Francis and his sons are called to the knighthood of Christ, so surely are they called to the cult and the apostolate of the Eucharist.

CHAPTER IV

FRANCIS AND THE CHURCH

AS CHRIST lives among us in the Eucharist in a sacramental manner, thus also He lives in the holy Church in a mystical manner. Yes, even more. As the Eucharist is the true, real and substantial body of Christ, so the Church of God is the mystical Christ: He is our Head, we His members, and the divinely established authorities of the Church are as so many links that bind us to Him and communicate to us His life, His grace, His salvation. That is the conception of the Church as expressed by the Gospel, by the Pauline epistles, by primitive Christianity, by Catholic teaching.

Francis grasped this truth with all the depth of his faith, and all the warmth of his heart. Hence his touching reverence for the clergy, the bishops, the Apostolic See, the ecclesiastical institutions and decrees; hence also the fruitful results of this relation between him and the Church.

1. We have shown how deeply Francis revered the *priesthood* on account of its direct relation to the Holy Eucharist. But, aside from this, his esteem for the priesthood and for the clergy in general was so marked for the simple reason that he beheld in them the bearers of divine authority, and the dispensers of the divine Mysteries. Even before his conversion he had frequently given proof of his love and esteem for priests;[1] from the very first moment of his conversion, however, he endeavored to be always in closest contact with them, to serve them,[2] and at all times showed them the devotion and honor due to

56

their state. "For," thus remarks Thomas of Celano, "since he himself was about to embrace the apostolic life and mission, and was entirely imbued with the Catholic faith, he was filled from the very beginning with reverence toward the servants and the service of God." [3]

In the course of his life this reverence developed to an astonishing degree of love and submission toward the various orders of the hierarchy.[4]

In his sermons he constantly and fervently admonished the faithful to be loyal and devoted to the priests, the theologians, and all the ministers of the Church.[5] It is obvious that he also instilled this spirit of devotion into his brothers. He never tired of inculcating the duty of reverence, of love, of loyalty and of submission to the clergy.[6] This duty he left to his brothers as a legacy, so to speak, in his Testament, and one of the final admonitions which he gave on his death-bed was this: "Be ever devoted and submissive to the prelates and the clergy." [7]

He had docile pupils. Following the example and the injunction of their Father, they constantly rendered deepest homage and devotion to the clergy.[8] "Wherever they met a priest, whether rich or poor, good or bad, they bowed humbly before him and reverenced him. And whenever they were forced to seek shelter, they would turn rather to the priests than to the laymen." [9] They placed their confidence in the priests unreservedly, without regard to their degree of learning or their mode of life. They confessed their sins to them, not considering whether the confessor were a just or a sinful man.[10] Yes, in their deep humility and respectful love, they found it difficult to believe that their fellow-man, and above all a priest, could sin.[11]

One day Brother Giles returned from a dense wood with a bundle of twigs, and, passing a church, he threw down his burden, and knelt and adored his Saviour. A priest who happened to see him, called him a hypocrite, which grieved him so sorely that he could scarcely refrain from tears. Asked by another Friar the cause of his weeping, Giles said: "Because I am a hypocrite, as a certain priest told me." "Believest thou this," asked the other, "because he said so?" Giles answered: "I believe, because it is a priest that said it; for I do not believe that priests lie." Whereupon the other said: "Father, the opinions of men, who are liable to err, are often at variance with those of God." On hearing this, Giles was consoled, and his usual happy frame of mind returned to him.[12]

Francis inculcated reverence to the clergy not only on account of their dignity, but also because of the apostolic mission entrusted to himself and to his brothers. Hence he would say: "We are sent to aid the clergy for the salvation of souls, and to supply in ourselves what is wanting in them. Each one receives his reward, not according to his authority, but according to his work. Know, brothers, that the gaining of souls to salvation is most acceptable to God, and this we can do better by living in peace and not in discord with the clergy. If these should place an obstacle in the way of the people's salvation, God will be their judge, and will repay them, but be ye subject to the prelates and see that it be not your fault if any jealousy arise. If you are the children of peace, you will gain over both the clergy and the people, and this will be more acceptable to God than if the people only were gained and the clergy scandalized. Conceal their faults and supply their defects, and when you have done all this, be all the more humble yourselves." [13]

2. Still more did Francis honor and respect the *bishops*. Shortly after his conversion, his father, Bernardone, invoked the aid of the magistrate of Assisi, to force him to restore the goods he had taken from the warehouse. When the court-servant approached Francis with the order to appear and answer the charge, the latter refused politely but firmly, saying that he was no longer answerable to the civil authorities, having devoted himself to the

service of the Most High.   The Bishop only, he replied, was the competent authority, according to the existing law. But as soon as he had received the summons of the Bishop, he exclaimed joyfully: "To the Bishop I will go, for he is the father and lord of souls."   And when the latter admonished him to return the goods to his father, he forthwith threw his purse and his clothing at the feet of his avaricious sire, and stood before the prelate of the Church naked and poor.   Filled with admiration of such heroic determination, Bishop Guido covered him with his own mantle, kissed and embraced him.   And from that hour he became the friend and guide of Francis, and loved him most dearly.[14]   He pleaded for him at the Papal Court,[15] visited him frequently at Portiuncula, conversed with him as with a most dear friend,[16] sheltered him, nursed him in his illness in his own palace,[17] and mourned his death as that of a dear father.[18]

Francis strove constantly to establish a similar relation of respectful love toward all bishops.   As soon as he entered a city, he would first visit the Bishop, or in the latter's absence, the priests.[19]   He made it a rule for himself and for his brothers never to preach in any place without the episcopal consent and approbation.[20]   In most cases the bishops welcomed the unassuming preachers with open arms.   If they failed to do so, Francis succeeded in winning them over by his childlike confidence and simplicity. One day he arrived at Imola in the Romagna, went to the Bishop, and requested his permission to preach.   The Bishop replied: "Trouble not thyself, brother, I shall preach to my people myself."   Bowing his head humbly, the Saint turned and left.   After a while he returned. The Bishop, not a little surprised, said to him: "Brother, what hast thou come for now?"   Francis smilingly gave answer: "Lord, if the father send his son out of one door, he must needs return by another."   Completely disarmed by these humble words, the Bishop embraced Francis and exclaimed joyously: "Henceforth thou and thy brothers may preach in my diocese without hindrance; such saintly humility deserves nothing else." [21]

In no wise would Francis allow any measures to be employed to force the bishops' permission to preach. Several of the Friars one day complained to the Saint: "Father, dost thou not see that at times the bishops will not permit us to preach, and that we must wait whole days before we can announce the word of God? It were better and more helpful to the welfare of souls, if thou wert to obtain this privilege from the Lord Pope." Francis rebuked them saying: "You Friars Minor do not know the will of God, and you do not allow me to convert the whole world as God wishes, since I desire, in the first place, to convert the bishops; who, seeing our life and holy and humble reverence, will themselves call you to preach and convert the people; which will avail more than your privilege, that will only lead you to pride." [22]

That was final. The Friars no doubt succeeded in gaining the approval of the majority of the prelates.[23] Since the year 1219 they nevertheless carried with them Papal credentials, declaring them to be wandering preachers, approved by the Church and recommended as such.[24] It was left to the bishops, however, to grant permission to preach or to refuse it. Indeed, Francis expressly forbade his brothers in his Testament to "ask letters from the Roman Court under pretext of preaching." [25] He would rather see the apostolate suffer than the harmonious relation with the ecclesiastical superiors.

Francis applied the same prohibition to letters granting the right to establish new houses for the brothers.[26] They were never to force permission for a new establishment by asking Papal privileges; on the contrary he gave the following specific injunction: "If the Friars come to a city where they have no place, and there are those who wish to give them ground where they can build and have a garden and have all things needful . . . they must go to the Bishop of the city and say to him: 'My lord, such a man wishes to give us some land, for the love of God, and the good of his soul, that we may build thereon. We come to you first, because you are the father and master of all the flock committed to you, and of all the Friars who will live in this place; will you allow us, with God's blessing and yours, to build?' " [27]

And to give his words more weight, he reminded his brothers of the principle they were ever to bear in mind: "The Lord has called us for the help of his faithful people, of the clergy and prelates of the holy Roman Church. Hence, by all means in our power we should always love, honor and reverence them. For this we are called Friars Minor, that both by our name and actions we should ever set an example of humility to all men. At the beginning of my conversion the Lord placed His word in the mouth of the Bishop of Assisi, that he might advise and confirm me in the service of Christ; for this and many other excellent things I honor and respect not only bishops but also poor priests, desiring to love and reverence them, and look upon them as my masters." [28]

3. From the foregoing we may surmise how closely Francis wished to be united to the *Holy See*. There is no doubt that he placed at the head of the primitive rule, which he composed for himself and his first companions, the vow to render obedience and respect to the Roman Pontiff.[29] His filial love and reverence toward the Church is evinced by the words which he addressed to his companions at the beginning of the Order: "Brothers, I see that God in His mercy wishes to increase our number. Let us therefore go to our Mother, the holy Roman Church, and make known to the Pope what God has deigned to begin through us, so that we may continue what has been begun, with the approval and the command of the Apostolic See." [30]

A few days later he stood with his family of Friars before the great Innocent and the College of Cardinals. How humbly and prudently he knew how to win the Pope,

is well known.[31] Overwhelmed by the impression which
the Poor Man of Assisi made on him, and moved at the
same time by a heavenly apparition, Innocent exclaimed:
"This is of truth the pious and holy man through whom
the Church of God is again to be raised up and supported."
He then embraced Francis, approved the rule submitted
to him, and granted to Francis and his companions permission to preach penance wherever they wished. Francis
threw himself on his knees, and humbly vowed obedience
and reverence to the Vicar of Christ, as he had written in
the rule.[32] From that hour Francis had found a warm
friend and patron in Innocent III.

The same holds true of the Papal Court in general.
When the band of apostolic men arrived in Rome, they
were presented by the Bishop of Assisi, then present in
the city, to Cardinal John of St. Paul, the most prominent
and influential adviser of the Pope. They soon endeared
themselves so deeply to him, that he not only overcame all
obstacles to their undertaking, which, humanly speaking,
seemed reckless beyond measure, but wished to be regarded in future as a Friar Minor himself.[33] Through
his influence the other cardinals were gradually won over
to their cause; yes, they became so enthused over it, that
each wished to have at least one of the brothers at his
court.[34]

After the death of Cardinal John of St. Paul, God
raised up another equally devoted friend of the Order
in Cardinal Ugolino, Bishop of Ostia. Not a friend
only, for Ugolino loved and protected them as if he
were the father of all.[35] He met Francis for the first
time at Florence in 1217.[36] The Cardinal received the
Poverello with joy and said to him: "I place myself entirely at thy disposal and that of thy brothers, and am
willing to assist you in word and deed, if only you are
mindful of me in your prayers." Francis gratefully replied: "Lord Cardinal, very willingly do I accept thee
as the father and protector of the Order, and I com-

mand that the brothers remember thee in their prayers."
And he requested the Cardinal to attend the Chapters of
the Order in future, in order thus to become acquainted
with its affairs.[37]

In view of the many difficulties which threatened the
Order from within as well as from without, Francis very
soon determined to obtain the Papal approval for the
protectorate of the Cardinal. In this proposal he was
strengthened by a vision. He beheld a small, black hen
surrounded by a brood of chicks, so numerous that they
could not find shelter under her wings. "The hen," he
said to himself, "am I, small of stature and dark of appearance. The chicks are the brothers, increasing in numbers and in the grace of God. The strength of Francis no
longer suffices to protect them from the enmity of evil
tongues. I will therefore go and recommend them to
the Roman Church, by whose powerful scepter the evil-
doers are put to naught, the children of God, however,
enjoy full liberty to open more and more the treasure of
eternal salvation. From this the brothers may know the
sweet blessings of their Mother, and follow her direction
with greater piety." [38]

An unforeseen event soon led to the realization of this
plan. During the sojourn of Francis in the Orient in
1219, a crisis broke out in the Order.[39] According to his
usual procedure, Francis hastened to the Papal Court, to
obtain counsel and direction. Ugolino obtained an audience for him with Honorius III. But, fearful lest he
appear troublesome, the humble Friar waited at the door
of the Papal apartments until the Holy Father should
appear. As soon as the latter emerged from his room,
Francis bowed deeply before him and said: "Lord Pope,
may God grant thee peace!" Honorius replied: "God
bless thee, my son!" "Lord, since thou art a mighty ruler,
and art often detained by grave affairs, the poor cannot
always find access to thee when in need of thy help. Thou
hast given me many popes. Appoint one of them with

whom I may speak, whenever it is necessary, and who may give heed and settle the affairs of the Order in thy place." "Whom, then, dost thou desire?" replied Honorius. "The Lord of Ostia," said Francis. The Pope consented, and from this hour Francis regarded Cardinal Ugolino of Ostia as his "Pope." [40]

In fact, from that time there was hardly a weighty affair of the Order, aside from the organization of the fraternity and the final editing of the rule, in which Ugolino did not have a hand. Francis and Ugolino henceforth seemed as but one heart and one soul, so that Thomas of Celano could declare: "St. Francis clung to him [Ugolino] as a son to his father, and as an only child to its mother; he slept and reposed carefree on the bosom of his kindness. Ugolino truly fulfilled the office of a shepherd in regard to Francis; but the name of shepherd he left entirely to Francis himself. The blessed Father ordained whatever was necessary; but that praiseworthy lord executed the enactments. Oh, how many lay in wait to destroy the seed of the new Order, particularly at its birth! Oh, how many endeavored to choke the chosen vine which the hand of the Lord had planted so mercifully in the world! How many strove to steal and consume the first and purest fruits of this vine! All these were routed and put to naught by the sword of this venerable Father and Lord Cardinal. For he was a stream of eloquence, a bulwark of the Church, a champion of truth, a friend of the lowly. Blessed therefore and memorable the day on which the Saint entrusted himself to so exalted a lord!" [41]

At the time when Celano penned these words (1228-1229), Ugolino had just ascended the Papal throne as Gregory IX (1227). Among the first and most important acts of his pontificate was the canonization of his friend,[42] and the exposition of the rule of the Order in the spirit of its blessed Founder.[43] A large number of documents give proof of the constant and touching loyalty of Gregory IX to the heritage of St. Francis.[44] The following incident strikingly illustrates the familiarity with which the brothers at all times turned to their illustrious protector and friend. In 1238 Jordan of Giano, who relates the incident himself, journeyed to Rome in order to appeal against the arbitrary conduct of the General, Elias of Cortona. Gregory, who was sick abed, welcomed Brother Jordan heartily, but, owing to his indisposition, soon dismissed him. The latter, however, was by no means anxious to leave the room, but running to the bed of the sick Pontiff, he drew one foot of the Pope from under the covers, kissed it, and said jokingly to his Friar companion: "Brother, such relics we have not in Saxony." The Pope again bade them to leave the room, but Jordan hastened to say: "Not so, Lord, we have nothing to ask for the present. By your grace we are well provided and happy. For you are the Father, Protector and Corrector of the Order. We came for one thing only, to see you." At these words the Pontiff's mood changed; he became very affable, and, rising up in his bed, he began to speak of the affair which had brought Jordan to him, and promised relief.[45]

As Jordan correctly points out, Francis and his Order beheld in the Cardinal Protector not only a friend who would foster and protect the Order, but also the guardian and disciplinarian, who would at times remind them of their duties toward the Apostolic See and the holy Catholic Church. When the Saint, together with Ugolino, definitely fixed the institution of the Cardinal Protectorate, he commanded: "I command the Ministers by obedience that they petition our Lord the Pope for one of the Cardinals of the Holy Roman Church, who shall be the governor, protector, and corrector of the fraternity; so that, being always subject and submissive at the feet of the same holy Roman Church, and steadfast in the Catholic Faith, we may observe poverty and humility and the Holy Gospel of Our Lord Jesus Christ, as we have faithfully promised." [46]

4. That was, in fact, the motto of Francis: *to be ever subject and submissive to the holy Roman Church.*

In his *sermons and instructions* he admonished the faithful, the clergy and his own brothers to adhere most closely to the Church. Celano graphically describes the preaching of Francis in these words: "So great was the faith of men and women, so deep their reverence toward the Saint of God, that whosoever touched but the hem of his habit, deemed himself indeed blessed. Whenever he entered a city, the clergy rejoiced and rang the bells, men and women became jubilant, the children gleefully clapped their hands, broke branches from the trees, and met him with songs of joy. The damnable heresies were routed, the faith of the Church strengthened, and while the faithful rejoiced, the heretics were put to flight. . . . He declared most strongly that in all things and above all things, the Faith of the holy Roman Church should be maintained, revered and observed; that in this Faith alone was salvation, and by this Faith alone all could be saved. At the same time he respected the priests, and esteemed every clerical dignity very highly." [47]   The clergy, on the other hand, were admonished that in their life and their doctrine they should follow the "commandments of God, and the precepts of our holy Mother, the Church." [48]   He exhorted his brothers even more strongly "that they observe faithfully the Holy Gospel and the rule, which they had embraced, and that they be in a special manner reverent and devout in regard to the Divine Office and the decrees of the Church." [49]

The various *precepts of his rule* breathe the same spirit. Aside from the vow of obedience which he renders to the Holy See, as mentioned above, the following precepts are contained in the first rule: [50]   "It shall not be lawful" for any brother "to pass to another Order, nor to wander about beyond obedience, according to the commandment of the Lord Pope." [51]   Furthermore: "No one shall be received contrary to the form and institution of the Holy Church." [52] Then he prescribes that the brothers should follow the regulations of the Church in regard to the Divine Office: the clerics should recite it as other clerics; [53] the lay-brothers, by praying a certain number of "Our Fathers" for each canonical hour, as the Church had already provided for the rule of the Knights Templar at the Council of Troyes (1128).[54] In the chapter on the preachers he commands: "Let none of the brothers preach contrary to the form and the institution of the holy Roman Church." [55] The nineteenth chapter bears the explicit inscription, "that all the brothers must live in a Catholic way." Then follow these trenchant words: "Let all brothers be Catholic and live and speak in a Catholic manner. But if anyone should err from the Catholic Faith and life in word or deed, and will not amend, let him be altogether expelled from our fraternity. And let us hold all clerics and Religious as our masters in those things which regard the salvation of souls, if they do not deviate from our religion, and let us reverence their office and order and administration in the Lord." [56] In the twentieth chapter he speaks of the confidence which the brothers should show the "Catholic priests" in confessing their sins.[57] Toward the end of the rule he entreats not only the brothers, but all the faithful, to remain loyal to Catholic doctrine and Catholic life: "And all we Friars Minor, useless servants, humbly entreat and beseech all those within the holy Catholic and Apostolic Church, wishing to serve God, and all ecclesiastical orders, priests, deacons, subdeacons, acolytes, exorcists, lectors, doorkeepers, and all clerics; all religious men and women, all boys and children, poor and needy, kings and princes, laborers and husbandmen, servants and masters, all continent virgins and married people, laics, men and women, all infants, youths, young men and old, healthy and sick, all small and great, and all peoples, clans, tribes and tongues, all nations and all men in all the world, who are and shall be, that we may persevere in the true Faith and in doing penance, for otherwise no one can be saved." [58]

The same spirit of reverence toward the Church permeates the final rule. In this rule, however, these exhortations are more condensed and precise, corresponding to the shorter and more definite form of this rule. The entire tenor of the second rule is therefore logically carried forward to the final harmonious accord: "so that, being always subject and submissive at the feet of the same holy Roman Church, and steadfast in the Catholic Faith, we may observe poverty and humility and the Holy Gospel of Our Lord Jesus Christ, as we have faithfully promised." [59]

The same is true of the *Testament* of St. Francis. In the beginning of this inspiring document the dying Patriarch declares: "The Lord gave me, and still gives me, such faith in priests who live after the manner of the holy Roman Church, on account of their orders, that, if they persecuted me, I would still have recourse to them." And in the course of his last will he gives the following injunction, which can be understood only in view of his most loyal adherence to the Church: "If any Friar be found who is not really Catholic, in such case all the Friars wherever they are, shall be bound by obedience to bring him before the Custos of the nearest place where he is found. And the Custos is strictly obliged under obedience to keep him as a prisoner day and night, so that the Friar cannot be taken out of his hands, until he can personally put him into the hands of the Minister. And the Minister is strictly bound by obedience to send the Friar with others, who shall guard him as a prisoner day and night, until they present him before the Lord Cardinal of Ostia, who is the Lord and Protector and Corrector of this fraternity." Finally Francis declares emphatically, that he has made his Testament for the purpose only "that we may in a more Catholic manner observe the rule we have vowed to the Lord." [60]

Thus we find Francis to be personified loyalty to the
Church.   To believe with the Church, to pray, to live,
to work, to think, to feel with the Church—*sentire cum
Ecclesia*—is for him an axiom as self-evident as the axiom
to follow in all things the Holy Gospel.   There is not one
moment and not one episode in the life of the Saint, nor
a single passage in the authentic biographies of him,
which could disturb in any manner this delightful harmony between the Poverello and the Church.[61]   In no
other Founder of a Religious Institute before him—and
they were all loyal to the traditions of the Church—do
we find the truly Catholic sense so fully developed and
so charmingly, yet so strongly and frequently expressed,
as in the Patriarch of Assisi.   The Premonstratensian
Prior, Burchard of Ursperg (died 1230), who was well
acquainted with the work of Francis and of his first disciples, lays great stress upon this characteristic: "The
Friars Minor are submissive to the Apostolic See in all
things." [62]   The Church herself, in the liturgical Office of
the Saint, has accorded him the singular title: "Francis,
the Catholic":

> "Franciscus, vir catholicus
>   Et totus apostolicus,
>   Ecclesiæ teneri
> Fidem romanæ docuit,
>   Presbyterosque monuit
>   Præ cunctis revereri." [63]

5.   The *far-reaching and fruitful results* of this deeply
Catholic sense were as pronounced for the Church herself
as for the Order.

Although the Popes of that period joined an ardent
zeal for reform to their worldly position of splendor and
power, the condition of the Church was nevertheless all
but hopeless.   Bishops and priests struggled in vain to
check the flood of licentiousness which was spreading
among all classes of society, due in part to the fact that

they themselves had become infected with the spirit of worldliness, and in consequence gave an example far from edifying; with the result that the respect due their exalted office had almost reached the zero point.

This condition of affairs produced a fertile soil for the propaganda of certain heretics generically known as the Cathari, or the Pure. They rejected the Old Testament, claiming that its God was no other than Satan; condemned marriage; denied the dogma of the resurrection of the body; and declared the eating of flesh-meat and the killing of animals as sinful and forbidden. The oath was placed in the same class as murder and adultery. The images of the saints, the cross, the sacraments, the entire ceremonial of the Church—all these were regarded by them as an abomination. The Church itself, the Papacy, bishops and priests, they designated as the society of the anti-Christ. They attacked the civil authorities with equal vehemence, and thus undermined the power of the State as well. At the same time they indulged in the most shameful practises of lust under the guise of extreme continence, and infected all society with their poisonous doctrines. Southern France especially, and northern Italy became the hotbed of their activities, but gradually all countries of western Europe were infested by these nefarious sects.[64] Some time before, about 1150, St. Hildegarde had already urged kings and princes and all the faithful "to expel from the Church these heretics, who contaminated the whole earth, despised the divine law which bade men to increase and multiply, who grew lean with fasting and at the same time gave themselves to most shameful lust, who contemned all laws given by God through Moses and the Prophets, and finally through His own Son." She declared that they should be punished with confiscation of their goods, but not with death, since they also were created to the image of God.[65] Toward the end of the century, according to the testimony of Cæsar of Heisterbach, the Cathari had devastated nearly one thousand cities, and threatened the ruin of all Europe.[66]

On several occasions men indeed arose within the pale of the Church, who sincerely strove to accomplish needed reforms. We need but mention Waldus and the Poor Men of Lyons and of Lombardy. These movements, however, shortly after their inception—about 1170— began to conflict with Catholic doctrine and with the hierarchy of the Church. The remedy invariably proved more harmful than the evil itself. The Church was finally forced to view with distrust every new movement toward reform.

This was the state of affairs when Francis appeared before Innocent III. It is obvious that the great Innocent at first showed great reluctance. It was the unconditional surrender of the Poverello to the cause and the teachings of the Gospel, joined to his unreserved submission to the ecclesiastical authorities, which convinced Innocent that the Poor Man of Assisi was indeed called to save the Church from utter ruin. By his sincere and earnest endeavor to carry out the work of reform in complete submission to the spiritual authorities, Francis became, with St. Dominic, the savior of Christendom in times of extreme peril, became "a reformer of most far-reaching importance, whose saving influence reaches out through the centuries, comparable to the pure, unsullied fountain of the Gospel, springing forth from eternal wisdom and love." [67]

For his Order also Francis established the most secure foundation, anchoring it to the twofold pole: return to the Gospel, and complete submission to the Church. Without the wise and benevolent guidance of the Church, Francis, more idealist than realist, could never have built up his institution to a strong, living organization. And much less could he have saved it from the rocks of heresy. The history of the Waldenses and of the Humiliati let us surmise what may have become of the Franciscan Order

had it not followed strictly and faithfully the guiding
hand of the Church in carrying out the ideal of the
Gospel. Men of great promise had arisen and preached
against the crying evils and vices of the times, had chosen
poverty, penance, humility, charity and brotherly love as
their standard, and sought to enlist others under their
colors. As barefooted mendicants they traversed city
and country, embracing in their ranks clerics and lay,
nobles and artisans, lettered and unlettered. What had
become of them? Obstinate heretics, adventurous dream-
ers, buddhistic ascetics, fanatic seducers.

That Francis was preserved not only from these pit-
falls, but also from any false step in carrying out his
ideals, he owes to the influence of the Church, and to
his loyal submission to her wise guidance. Under her
protection and motherly care he was able to develop
fully his own splendid personality, and his world-embracing undertaking. She was to him indeed a true
Mother and guide, who not only understood how not to
smother his fiery idealism, but to guide, bless and bring
it to fruition.

The Saint was fully conscious of this. That he constantly emphasized and practised devotion and loyalty to
the Church, was the result of his deep conviction and
manifold experience that the Church, the divine institute
of salvation upon earth, was his greatest benefactress and
safest guide. His beloved disciple Giles expressed this
in his wonted wise and simple manner: "O Holy Mother
Roman Church! We ignorant and miserable ones do
not know thee or thy kindness. Thou teachest us the
way of salvation; thou preparest and showest us the
path, by which if anyone walketh, his feet shall not stray,
but attain to glory." [68]

In fact, it has been shown repeatedly that the institute
of the Patriarch of Assisi proceeded safely and unerringly
on its march through the ages only when its compass
pointed unfailingly toward the Church. As soon as the

needle of this compass wavered in any manner, or deflected from this course, the Order experienced periods of decadence and internal dissension. We need but point to the Spirituals, who, while endeavoring to realize the Ideal of St. Francis in its utmost purity and rigor, yet perished so miserably because they strove to accomplish this without obedience to the Church. The return to the Gospel under the guidance of the Church—that must ever remain the motto of the Franciscan Order if it is to preserve untarnished the Ideal of its Holy Founder, and thus be the means of sanctification unto itself and unto the world.

CHAPTER V

FRANCIS AND HIS LOVE OF POVERTY

HE poverty of St. Francis! It might seem indeed
at first sight as if this chapter interrupted the course
of thought hitherto developed, which was merely
an elucidation of the Ideal of Francis: the return to the
full and exact observance of the Gospel. It will be seen,
however, that poverty according to the conception of
the Poverello of Assisi, is simply the basis of evangelical
perfection; that to Francis the life after the manner of
the Gospel is identical with a life of poverty. For this
reason this subject must be treated more fully than any
other, if we are to understand properly the spirit of the
Seraphic Saint. Of immediate interest to us in this regard
is his *love of poverty,* a love so singular and significant
both as regards *the fact* as well as the *motive.*

1. In Francis the love of poverty was a gift of nature
and of grace as well. God had endowed him with a
generous and sympathetic love toward the poor and needy.
This happy disposition grew in him from childhood, and
gradually developed in his character a trait of such
benevolence, that, even then a docile pupil of the Gospel,
as St. Bonaventure remarks, he resolved never to refuse
a beggar, above all when appealed to for the love of God.[1]

In this regard not only his chivalrous nature, but also
his youthful prodigality was a contributing factor. At
one time, when he had regaled his comrades with a sumptuous feast, he entered into himself and said: "If thou
art so liberal and courtly toward men from whom thou
canst receive naught but empty and transitory favor, it is

74

but just, that thou shouldst also be liberal and courtly toward the poor for the love of God, who is most generous in rewarding." From that moment he began to love the poor more dearly, and to give alms with a lavish hand. And, as the Three Companions remark, though he was a merchant by profession, he had the most unbusinesslike trait of giving away money most freely.[2]

On one occasion, however, when he happened to be very busy at the cloth-counter, he repulsed a beggar who had asked an alms for the love of God. But hardly had he realized how thoughtlessly he had acted, when he was seized with deep remorse and he said to himself: "If that poor man had asked thee for something for the sake of a great count or baron, thou wouldst surely have given it; how much more shouldst thou have been generous for the sake of the King of kings and the Lord of all?"[3] Deeply imbued with the spirit of faith, Francis had already begun to behold in the poor man the ambassador of the Most High, and his chivalrous spirit regarded it a most discourteous act not to place this ambassador above petty nobility, and to receive him with truly royal honors. Roused to sudden action by this thought, Francis hurried from the shop, rushed after the beggar and, having found him, gave him a generous sum of money; and he resolved never in future to refuse a request made in the name of God, a resolve which he kept unbroken until death, and which obtained for him God's choicest blessings in the course of his life.[4]

The most signal grace was no doubt this, that henceforth he made the cause of the poor his own, and began to strive after poverty as a most desirable treasure. One day, as often before, he had gathered his boon companions about him for a festive banquet. The feasting being over, they marched as usual through the streets of Assisi, singing and rollicking, with Francis at their head in the rôle of King of Youth. Suddenly he was touched by the hand of God. He stopped as if transfixed, his soul flooded with such sweetness that he neither saw nor heard. His friends roused him from his seeming reverie, and teasingly asked him: "Whereof wast thou dreaming, Francis, and why dost thou not follow us? Art thou thinking of taking to thyself a bride?" Francis replied joyously: "Ah yes, truly! I was thinking of taking a Bride, one more noble and wealthy and beautiful than you have ever seen." This answer, of course, gave his comrades more cause for raillery; but, thus remark the Three Companions, he said this not of himself, but by divine inspiration, for the Bride, more noble and wealthy and charming than all others, was the holy Lady Poverty, whom he was to espouse.[5]

From this hour "he began to withdraw more and more from the vanities of the world, and to hide the treasure which he strove to acquire at the cost of all earthly things, from the eyes of fools. . . . He had been heretofore a benefactor of the poor, but now they became his most dear friends. As often as he met a beggar on the street, he would give him money; if by chance he had no money to give, he would part with his head-covering or his shoes, so as not to let the beggar go away empty-handed. If he had not even this to give, he would hasten stealthily to some obscure spot, divest himself of his shirt, and send the beggar thither with the behest to take it for the love of God. He purchased various things for churches and sent them secretly to poor priests. One time, in the absence of his father, he was to take his repast alone with his mother, yet he ordered the entire table to be set. When his mother asked him wonderingly why he had so many portions of bread prepared, he replied that he intended to distribute them to the poor, since he had promised never to refuse anyone who asked alms for the love of God. . . .

"His sole desire was to visit the poor and listen to their pleadings, so as to give them alms. Moved by divine grace, he desired, though still in the world, to be in some city where he was unknown, and thus able to exchange his clothing with the rags of some beggar, and to beg alms like them for the love of God.

"Some time later, on the occasion of a pilgrimage to Rome, he found a number of beggars on the steps of the church, and, borrowing the clothing of one, unnoticed, he exchanged them for his own sumptuous garments, and began to beg alms in French with the other poor people. He then returned the beggar's clothes, put on his own garments, and returned to Assisi, beseeching God to reveal to him the way of poverty. But he made known his secret to none except to the Bishop of Assisi. For at that time no one professed true poverty, which he desired above all things of this world, and in which he resolved to live and die." [6]

Nevertheless, he could not refrain from repeating that he was indeed courting the noblest, richest, and most beautiful Bride, whenever his friends asked him about his marriage plans.[7] Completely fired by this thought, he now set out to woo his chosen Bride.

Taking with him several bales of cloth, he mounted a horse, and set out for Foligno. There he disposed of the cloth, and also of the horse, and, with the proceeds of the sale, returned to Assisi. His only thought was now, what to do with the money he had thus obtained, for his conversion to the cause of poverty had now reached the stage, that even the money he carried with him had become a burden and a cause of anxiety. Approaching his native town, he met a poor priest at the sadly neglected church of San Damiano. He reverently kissed the hands of the priest, gave him the entire sum of money, and explained to him the plan which had ripened in his mind. But the latter, no doubt fearing the wrath of Peter Bernardone, refused to accept the money; whereupon Francis threw it upon the ledge of a window, regarding it as so much dust. "For, he desired to possess the wisdom that is more precious than gold, and the prudence that is more precious than silver." [8]

This chivalrous wooing of Lady Poverty was not to be accomplished without the cost of heroic sacrifice. His father, Peter Bernardone, much wroth both over the loss of the money and over the seeming folly of Francis, had him put in chains, cast into prison, and finally brought before the episcopal court, with the avowed purpose of either bringing him to his senses, or at least of regaining the money so carelessly thrown away. On the advice of the Bishop, Don Guido Secundi, Francis sent for the money, which was still lying undisturbed at San Damiano, and returned it to his father. He likewise divested himself of his clothing, with the exception of his hair-shirt, and cast them at the feet of his father, exclaiming: "Hear ye all, and understand: until now I have called Peter Bernardone my father; but because I propose to serve the Lord, I return to him his money, and all the clothes I had of him: for now I wish to say no longer: father Peter Bernardone, but, Our Father, who art in heaven." [9]

Such was the betrothal of St. Francis with Lady Poverty, as sung by the poet of the *Divina Commedia* in the immortal lines:

"A dame, to whom none openeth pleasure's gate,
  More than to death, was, 'gainst his father's will,
  His stripling choice: and he did make her his,
  Before the spiritual court, by nuptial bonds,
  And in his father's right: from day to day,
  Then loved her more devoutly." [10]

Supremely happy in the love of his newly found bride, Francis walked with her in the way of perfection, which the Lord was to show him more and more plainly. He wore no clothing, save the hair-shirt and an old cloak which he had received from a servant of the Bishop. This he marked with a cross, the escutcheon of the knighthood of Christ. One day he fell in with robbers, and was

stripped of even this poor garb; he then obtained from
a friend at Gubbio a dress similar to that worn by hermits
and pilgrims: a short tunic with a leather girdle, shoes and
a staff. In this apparel he toiled for two years in building and repairing churches, living the while on the charity
of kind people, and surpassingly happy in the love of his
bride, Lady Poverty.

Then it happened that one day—it was the 24th of
February, 1209 (1208)—he heard at Portiuncula the
gospel of the Mass describing the sending of the apostles:
"And going, preach, saying: The kingdom of heaven is
at hand. Heal the sick, raise the dead, cleanse the lepers,
cast out devils: freely have you received, freely give. Do
not possess gold, nor silver, nor money in your purses:
nor scrip for your journey, nor two coats, nor shoes,
nor a staff.[11] . . ." These words sounded in his ears like
a new revelation. "That is what I seek, what I desire
with all my heart!" he exclaimed joyfully, cast away staff
and shoes, exchanged the leather girdle for a rope, and
fashioned a garment for himself out of coarse material.[12]

Now Francis was poor in the fullest sense of the
Gospel. He soon realized that he was to be the founder
of a fraternity of men as poor as himself. Inspired by
his example, a nobleman of Assisi, Bernard of Quintavalle, came to Francis and said: "Brother, I wish to distribute all my earthly possessions according to thy word,
out of love to God, who has given them to me." Francis,
loath to give an immediate decision, answered: "To-morrow morning we shall go to the church, and see from the
Book of the Gospels, what the Lord has taught His
disciples."

Early the next day—it was the 16th of April—Francis
and Bernard went themselves to the church of St. Nicholas at Assisi, with a third companion, Peter Catanii, a
lawyer.[13] After fervent prayer, Francis requested the
priest to open the Gospel three times at random. The first
time they read: "If thou wilt be perfect, go, sell all thou

hast, and give to the poor, and thou shalt have treasure in heaven, and come, follow Me." The second time: "And he commanded them that they should take nothing for the way, no scrip, no bread, nor money in their purse . . . and that they should not put on two coats." And the third time: "Who will come after Me, let him deny himself, and take up his cross, and follow Me."

With a heart overflowing with joy, Francis thanked the Lord, who had deigned to point out the way of poverty for himself and his companions. Then he exclaimed: "Brothers, that is our life and our rule, and that of all those who are to join our fraternity. Go, therefore, and fulfil what you have heard." They went accordingly, gave all they had to the poor, garbed themselves as Francis had done, and "lived with him after the form of the Gospel, as the Lord had revealed." [14]

And they rejoiced exceedingly, as if they had found a priceless treasure in the possession of Lady Poverty, for love of whom they despised all earthly things as so much filth. And whithersoever they went, they exulted in the Lord, and Francis more than the others, and he sang the praises of the Lord after the manner of the French minstrel singers with a loud and clear voice, glorifying the mercy of the Most High, who had given them the long-lost treasure of Lady Poverty. [15]

Having passed the springtime, so to speak, of their new life in rapturous joy, and tested their endurance in observing absolute poverty, they journeyed to Rome to obtain the Papal approval for their mode of life. "Let us go to our Mother, the holy Roman Church, and make known to the Pope what God has begun to do through us, that we may continue what we have begun, according to His will and decree," said Francis. [16] And he caused the new rule to be written with few and simple words. [17] This rule consisted, with the exception of a few regulations, almost entirely of the passages from the Gospel relating to poverty, as he heard on the day of

the birth of the Order.[18] This rule he defended before
Innocent III with such persuasive eloquence, that the
Holy Father finally approved it, although harboring grave
misgivings as to the possibility of its observance.[19] In
writing the later, as well as the final rule, Francis was
guided likewise by his ardent love for poverty; for though
he was later on forced by the change of conditions to
modify the original rule, "he still commended poverty
above all else in all his rules." [20]

The same ardent love for poverty inspired his entire
life; it burned in his heart with an undying flame, and
found utterance in all his words. Ofttimes he spoke to
his disciples on poverty, reminding them of the words of
the Gospel: "The foxes have holes, and the birds of the
air nests, but the Son of Man hath not whereon to lay
his head." [21] He would often repeat the warning: "In
the same measure as the brothers recede from poverty,
the world will recede from them; they will seek and shall
not find. But if they hold fast to my Mistress, Holy
Poverty, the world will provide for them, for they are
given to the world for its salvation." Bound as he was
to Lady Poverty with indissoluble ties, he awaited not
her present, but her future dowry. The psalms dealing
with poverty, such as: "The hope of the poor shall not be
lost forever," and: "The poor behold and rejoice," he
would sing with greater love and jubilation than others.[22]
Frequently he greeted the love of his heart with the
words: "O my Lady, Holy Poverty, may God preserve
thee!" [23] On every occasion he extolled her beauty and
charm, yes, even in his dreams he beheld her revered
image.[24] "There never has been a troubadour who sang
to his lady love a song so bold, and words of such burning
love, as Francis sings to the queen of his heart in his
ideally chivalrous love of poverty." [25]

This truly chivalrous love of Francis for Lady Poverty
finds its echo after many years in the words of his biographer: "The blessed Father, as long as he tarried in this

vale of tears, despised all treasures of men as dross. He aspired after the highest degree of perfection, and embraced poverty with most ardent love. The Son of God Himself had been poor, and so he wished to espouse her whom everyone shunned, with undying love. And having become the lover of her image, he not only left father and mother, but renounced all things, so as to cling more faithfully to his spouse, and to be two in one spirit with her. He therefore embraced her in chaste love, and suffered himself never to live otherwise than as her spouse. He declared that this Lady Poverty was for his sons the way of perfection, the pledge and earnest of eternal treasure. No one can desire wealth as ardently as he desired poverty; no one guards a treasure as diligently as he guarded this pearl of the Gospel. Nothing saddened his eye more than when he beheld within or without the house anything that was contrary to poverty. And, truly, his sole riches consisted, from the beginning of his life in the fraternity to his death, in a habit, a cord, and the breeches; more he had not. His poor garb showed where he had laid up his treasure. For this reason he was joyful, carefree, and happy; for he rejoiced that he had exchanged all perishable treasure for a hundredfold." [26]

When the Saint felt his end approaching, he roused himself once more to sing in his Testament that touching swan-song to his beloved Poverty.[27] Then he gave vent to the rapturous joy of his heart, for, having kept his troth with Lady Poverty inviolate,[28] he admonished his sons to ever love and revere her with a chivalrous spirit,[29] and passed away in the embrace of his all-beloved spouse.[30]

"Then the season came that He,
Who to such good had destined him, was pleased
To advance him to the meed, which he had earn'd
By his self-humbling; to his brotherhood,
As their just heritage, he gave in charge
His dearest Lady: and he enjoin'd their love

And faith to her; and, from her bosom, will'd
His goodly spirit should move forth, returning
To its appointed kingdom; nor would have
His body laid upon another bier." [31]

Truly a wondrous love for poverty! So wondrous,
that it appears indeed as one of those charmingly romantic plays of the Middle Ages. Many have attempted
to solve its meaning. Mystic asceticism, beginning with
the charming allegory, *Mystical Nuptials of Blessed
Francis with Lady Poverty;* [32] legendary literature, since
the appearance of the ever-fragrant *Little Flowers of St.
Francis of Assisi;* the love of the masses, as expressed
in the incomparable term "Il Poverello," "the Poor Little
Man of Assisi"; poetry, since the day of Dante Alighieri
and Jacopone da Todi; painting, since Giotto and Sas-
setta; historical research of seven centuries up to our
own day—all have endeavored to depict and extol the
love of our Saint for holy poverty. The secret of this
love will, however, remain unfathomed, if we fail to discover its cause, its real, true motive.

2. The reason why Francis dedicated himself and his
Order to poverty, seems to be none other than that God
Himself so enjoined it. In his endeavor to discover the
will of God, the Saint requested to have the Gospel opened
three times at random, as we have seen, and each time
he read the law of evangelical poverty. He never doubted
for a moment that this remarkable coincidence was a
direct revelation coming from God. Throughout his life,
and even on his death-bed, he appeals to this fact: "After
the Lord had given me brothers, none showed me what
I should do, but the Most High Himself revealed it
to me." [33]

However, this would demonstrate only that Francis
regarded the strict observance of poverty as a duty, and
that he fulfilled this duty with fullest resignation to God's
will. But if we ask why he embraced poverty with such

unprecedented, such bridal love, the answer is: because
he beheld in poverty the basis of *evangelical perfection,* of
the *evangelical apostolate,* and of the *knighthood of Christ.*

That poverty was an essential element of the *Gospel
perfection,* no one could ignore who was at all conversant
with the Gospel.   For this reason there never existed a
Religious Order which did not prescribe it and consider it
a necessary factor in the life of perfection.   In the age
of the Crusades the esteem for poverty was revived in a
few chosen souls, together with the newly awakened enthusiasm for the Holy Places.   The foundation of "The
Poor Knights of the Temple," [34] and of the Knights of
St. John,[35] the writings of St. Bernard of Clairvaux,[36] and
of the Benedictine Abbot Rupert of Deutz,[37] as well as
the entire movement toward poverty of the twelfth century, prove sufficiently that prior to Francis wide circles
of thinking men were convinced of the necessity of poverty as a factor in a life of perfection.

Francis belonged to this group of men long before his
direct calling to a life of poverty was revealed to him by
the threefold opening of the Gospel.   On this occasion,
however, the words of the Master became burdened with
a new meaning for himself and his disciples.   "If thou
wilt be perfect, go, sell all thou hast, and give to the poor,
and thou shalt have treasure in heaven, and come, follow
Me." [38]   He now became firmly convinced, that poverty
was not only *one,* but *the* basic condition of evangelical
perfection.

It is significant that, although Francis enjoined the
observance of the Gospel in general, yet the original rule
consisted almost exclusively of the scriptural texts relating
to poverty.   The Three Companions declare expressly that
these texts embody that perfection after which Francis
aspired with his whole soul.[39]   Of his first disciple Francis
remarks: "The first Friar given me by the Lord was
Brother Bernard, who was the first to accept most completely the perfection of the Holy Gospel, giving away all

his substance to the poor." [40]   Cardinal John of St. Paul
presented Francis to Pope Innocent III, referring at the
same time to the former's ambition in regard to the observance of poverty: "I have found a most perfect man,
who desires to live after the manner of the Gospel, and
to observe evangelical perfection in all things." [41]   Because of her great love for poverty, St. Clare of Assisi is
called "the foremost emulator of St. Francis in preserving
evangelical perfection." [42]   Francis himself declares that
Clare and her daughters have chosen by means of poverty "a life according to the perfection of the Holy Gospel." [43]   Before his death, he again admonished his daughters to strive after the perfection of the Gospel, when he
wrote to them these words: "I, little Brother Francis,
wish to follow the life and poverty of Jesus Christ, our
Most High Lord, and of His Most Holy Mother, and to
persevere therein to the end.   And I beseech you all, my
ladies, and counsel you, to live always in this most holy
life and poverty.   And watch yourselves well that you in
no wise depart from it through the teaching or advice of
anyone." [44]

Since Francis beheld in poverty a life of perfection,
he calls it simply the evangelical manner of life, a life
according to the form of the Holy Gospel.   "He desires
to live after the form of the Holy Gospel," Cardinal John
of St. Paul declares of him.   "They lived after the manner of the Holy Gospel, which the Lord had revealed to
them," [45] the Three Companions say of Francis and his
first disciples.   The Saint asserts the same in his Testament: "And after the Lord gave me some brothers, no
one showed me what I ought to do, but the Most High
Himself revealed to me that I should live after the form
of the Holy Gospel. . . . And those who came to take
this life upon themselves, gave to the poor all that they
might have, and they were content with one tunic, patched
within and without, by those who wished, with a cord and
breeches, and we wished for no more." [46]

It is evident, then, that under the Gospel, which he had chosen as a norm of life, Francis understood poverty before all else. In consequence of their poverty Francis styled himself and his sons simply, "the evangelical men." [47] Even in death he admonished his brothers to the faithful observance of poverty, "placing the Holy Gospel before all other rules." [48] There can be no doubt, therefore, that he recognized and cherished poverty as the basic element of evangelical perfection.

As the basic, but not as the exclusive element. Besides his Lady Poverty, Francis praised the entire crown of virtues which adorn the soul in company with poverty and give to it the fulness of harmonious beauty.[49] But of one thing Francis was firmly convinced: that poverty was the *basis,* as well as the *fruitful soil* of all other virtues.

One day the brothers asked him by what virtue we become dearest to Christ, and he answered: "Poverty, my brothers! Know, that poverty is the special way to salvation, for it is the food of humility, and the root of perfection, the fruit of which is manifold, though hidden. Poverty is the treasure, of which we read in the Gospel, which was hidden in the field; to buy which you must sell all, and in comparison with which, all that can be given for its purchase, is to be accounted as nothing." [50] This pre-eminent importance of poverty Francis beheld one day in a vision. There appeared to him a wondrously beautiful lady, who was adorned with precious jewelry, but covered with a poor mantle. The soul of Francis was evidently represented by the beautiful figure, his virtues by the precious jewelry, and his poverty, which protected and preserved these virtues, by the poor mantle.[51] Jacopone da Todi therefore makes Poverty declare, in the dialogue between Francis and herself, that she never appears without the company of the seven virtues inseparably united to her—charity, obedience, humility, continence, chastity, patience, and finally hope, who is the "maid-servant" of the others:

> "Ch'io haggio qui sette sorelle,
> Tutte pretiose e belle.
> Me aver non puoi senza elle;
> Che tra se se l'han giurato.
>
> Queste son la Charitade,
> Ubidienzia e Umiltade,
> Continentia e Castitade,
> Patientia en sommo stato.
>
> Cameriera è la Speranza,
> Che ci dona consolanza,
> Onde avemo gran baldanza,
> Che lo ben sia meritato." [52]

Francis furthermore esteemed and practised poverty as the *soul of the three evangelical counsels and religious vows.* One day a marvelous thing befell him. On the way from Rieti to Siena he suddenly met three poor women, so completely alike in stature, age and countenance that they could not be distinguished one from another. As the Saint drew near, they bowed respectfully before him and greeted him with the words: "Welcome to Lady Poverty!" Francis was filled with inexpressible joy, because they had greeted in his person his most dear Lady Poverty. The apparition then vanished.[53] St. Bonaventure remarks hereon: "By these women was signified the beauty of evangelical perfection, namely, of chastity, obedience, and poverty, all which shone forth in the holy man in equal beauty and glory, although he had chosen to glory in the privilege of poverty above all others." [54]

The *calling to the apostolate* was for Francis a further incentive to poverty. The Saviour had sent His apostles in poverty to convert the world: "Going, preach, saying: The kingdom of God is at hand. Heal the sick, raise the

dead, cleanse the lepers, cast out devils: freely have you
received, freely give. Do not possess gold, nor silver, nor
money in your purses, nor scrip for your journey, nor two
coats, nor shoes, nor a staff; for the workman is worthy
of his meat." [55] That these words of Christ were to be
the norm of conduct for the Franciscan apostolate, became clear to Francis by divine revelation, and soon after
also to his disciples.[56] We know that Francis was always
firmly convinced of the divine origin of this revelation.
That was sufficient to determine him to choose his Lady
Poverty as the constant and inseparable companion of his
apostolic activity.

He was confirmed in this determination by the need
and the spirit of the times. Money and wealth was the
watchword of the century. The Crusades indeed roused
in some hearts the love for the poverty of the Saviour;
but on the other hand they brought to the West a knowledge of the luxury and the treasures of the Levant, and
thus became the occasion of a hitherto unknown greed for
wealth and pleasure. The clergy also soon became infected with this cancerous disease. In place of devoting
themselves to the care of souls, a large part of the clergy
indulged in frivolous amusements and idle luxury, or
became absorbed in the pursuit of filthy lucre.[57] Innocent III, in the year 1200, stigmatized the clergy of the
entire province of Narbonne in the following words:
"All, from the highest to the lowest, allow themselves to
be led by avarice, seek donations, and are open to bribery,
so that they absolve the impious, and deprive the just of
their rights for the sake of remuneration." [58] The prelates lived a luxurious life, wore lavish garments, kept
a splendid court, and appeared at their visitations with
such numerous retinue that the pastors were often forced
to sell the church vestments in order to defray the costs
caused by this extravagance.

Since the ordinary revenue did not suffice to satisfy
the greed for luxury and money of the clergy, recourse

was had to the dreadful evil of simony. Although this evil was combated by the Papacy since Gregory VII (1073), it continued, practically unabated, to infest the body of the Church. The bishops devised various ways and means to extort money from the priests, and these in turn indemnified themselves by seeking benefices, by legacy-hunting, and by demanding scandalously exorbitant fees for their priestly functions.[59] The Church employed alternately mild and severe measures,[60] but without signal success. Innocent III still complained that in spite of all exertions of his predecessors, this simonistic pest could neither be cured by remedial measures, nor cauterized by fire.[61] Thus the secular as well as the religious clergy lost every vestige of influence over the masses, who on the other hand clamored for apostles of poverty, and turned eagerly to those who declared war on the avaricious clergy.

This the heretical Poor Men of France, Italy, and Germany had done in the last decades of the twelfth century. The Waldenses and their followers endeavored to lead back the clergy as well as the laity to the Gospel by imitating the poor life of the apostles. But instead of following out this ideal in submission to the ecclesiastical authorities, they openly declared war on them, maligned and reviled them,[62] and thus were the cause of great spiritual havoc among the masses. They finally perished miserably in consequence of their unchurchly apostolate of rebellion and insubordination.

St. Francis, on the contrary, combated this heretical movement by preaching and practising poverty, but allowing himself to be guided and directed by the Church.[63] Thus, poverty became the most powerful factor in the exercise of his apostolate, and the source of boundless blessings for Christendom as well as of the never failing popularity of his Order. For this reason he cherished his noble Lady Poverty with undying love and the most loyal constancy.

The love of Francis for poverty was furthermore

the natural result of his ideal conception of *Christian knighthood*. Only by keeping this in mind can we solve the secret of that mystical relation of the Saint to his spouse, Holy Poverty. As Christ was the sovereign Liege Lord of the Saint, thus poverty was the beloved Lady of his heart.

That was the natural result of his romantic and chivalrous character. A knight cannot be conceived without the services of chivalry rendered to his lady love. The Christian knight, however, abhorred the licentious philandering of a pagan and decadent knighthood, and devoted his life to deeds of heroism, achieving victory or death for his king and country. Chaste worship of womanhood and the virtuous love of his lady have always been the outstanding characteristic of the true Christian knight.[64] At the tourney and the various contests the knight paid homage to his lady love, and received the prize from her hands. In combat and in battle he drew courage and inspiration from the memory of his beloved. He worshiped his wife and bride with an affection at once strong and tender, for in the last instance his worship of womanhood was rooted in the worship of the glorified womanhood of the purest of maidens, the Mother of the Saviour. It is a well-known fact, that the Meistersingers Walter von der Vogelweide, Werinher von Tegernsee, Konrad von Wuerzburg, Gottfried von Strassburg, Brother Philip the Carthusian, Jacopone da Todi, and others, sought to promote the true honor and worship of woman by singing their choicest lays in honor of our blessed Lady with the divine Child.

This noble conception of love we find fully developed in Francis, the true Christian knight. His love, however, as his knighthood, was of a purely spiritual nature. He loved with an inspired love, and his beloved was the Bride of his Saviour, the most noble Lady Poverty.

How touching is the loyalty with which the Saviour loved His beloved Spouse, Holy Poverty! From the highest throne of heaven the Lord of angels came to earth to seek the Queen, shunned and despised by men. And lo! she awaited Him impatiently in the stable at Bethlehem, in the company of His Virgin Mother. She accompanied Him as His loyal Spouse through life, and was praised and cherished by Him above all things of this earth. And when the hour of disgrace and suffering had struck for Him, and He was abandoned by all, Poverty left Him for not a moment. She remained with Him when He was outraged and blasphemed. She remained with Him when He was spit upon, scourged and crowned with thorns. She did not abandon Him when He was nailed to the cross, naked and despoiled of all. And as He hung on the tree of shame, between heaven and earth, cast off by the earth and abandoned by heaven, she clung to Him and consoled Him. And though even His own Mother could not mount the cross with Him, sweet Poverty held Him in her loving embrace until death.[65]

And after her divine Spouse had passed from this earth, no one was found who loved her as the Saviour had loved her, until Francis chose her for his bride.

> "She, bereav'd
> Of her first husband, slighted and obscure,
> Thousand and hundred years and more, remain'd
> Without a single suitor, till he came.
> Nor aught avail'd, that, with Amyclas, she
> Was found unmoved at rumor of his voice,
> Who shook the world: nor aught her constant boldness
> Whereby with Christ she mounted on the cross,
> When Mary stay'd beneath. But not to deal
> Thus closely with thee longer, take at large
> The lovers' titles—Poverty and Francis." [66]

In these words the prince of poets has designated the true source from which sprang the love of the Poverello for poverty: the knight of the cross loved his Lady Poverty, because she, now reviled and shunned, had once been the Spouse of Christ; he loved her for the sake of Christ, in order to love and imitate the sovereign and divine Lover of Holy Poverty.

Thomas of Celano asserts expressly: "Francis strove constantly to espouse Poverty with perpetual love, because she had been the companion of the Son of God, but now was an outcast in the eyes of the whole world. He therefore became her faithful suitor, so that for the sake of this Spouse he left not only father and mother, but all things of this world." [67]

The Saint has formulated his life's program, so to say, in these simple words: "I, little Brother Francis, wish to follow the life and poverty of Jesus Christ, our Most High Lord, and of His Most Holy Mother, and to persevere therein until the end." [68] That explains why he was so deeply touched, if anyone asked alms for the love of God,[69] or if he chanced to meet a beggar: "In the poor he beheld the Son of our poor Lady." [70] He would often burst into tears when meditating on the poverty of Jesus Christ and His blessed Mother.[71]

He found it impossible even to think of the poverty of the Virgin Mother and her divine Child without shedding tears. "One day, while he was sitting at table, a brother chanced to speak of the poverty of the Most Blessed Virgin, and how the divine Child was so completely despoiled of all things. Immediately the Saint arose from the table with mournful sighs, and ate his bread with tears, kneeling on the bare floor. For this reason, he said, this virtue is the royal virtue, because it shone so gloriously in the divine King and Queen." [72] And he added: "I will not lay aside this royal dignity which Our Lord Jesus Christ assumed when He became poor that He might enrich us by His poverty, and so make the poor in spirit to be kings and heirs of the kingdom of heaven. I will not lay it aside, I say, for the gift of all the false riches, which, for a short time, are granted." [73]

That is the touchstone and token of the true knighthood

of the Seraphic Saint: tender, yet strong love for the noble
Lady Poverty, for love of the God-Man and His blessed
Mother. His brothers were to prove themselves likewise
true Knights of the Round Table by this sublime conception of Holy Poverty.

He inspired his first disciples to despoil themselves of
all earthly possessions, because thereby they would return
all things to their Saviour.[74] He admonished them in the
first rule: "Let all brothers strive to follow the humility
and poverty of Our Lord Jesus Christ. . . . And let
them not be ashamed thereof, but rather remember that
Our Lord Jesus Christ, the Son of the living and omnipotent God, was poor, and a stranger, and lived on alms,
He Himself, and the Blessed Virgin, and His disciples." [75]
This love of poverty for the sake of Christ, Francis established as the perpetual and fundamental law of his Order
in the final rule: "The brothers shall appropriate nothing
to themselves, neither a house, nor a place, nor anything.
And as pilgrims and strangers in this world, serving the
Lord in poverty and humility, let them go confidently in
quest of alms; nor ought they to be ashamed, because the
Lord made Himself poor for us in this world." [76]

CHAPTER VI

THE FRANCISCAN IDEAL OF POVERTY

THE love of Francis for poverty is the proper criterion by which we may also rightly estimate his Ideal of poverty. This Ideal is as singular and as sublime as his love for it. The Ideal of Francis may be expressed in two words: *total renunciation* of earthly things, and the greatest possible *moderation in the use of* these things.

1. The *renunciation of property* without restriction, was unknown in the history of Religious Orders before Francis and Dominic. Even the latter was influenced by the example of the Poverello.[1] The older religious institutions indeed observed the vow of poverty, but it meant only the personal renunciation of property on the part of the individuals, while the monastery and the Order as such always possessed property in common. "The most excellent and wise men of religious life before Francis and Dominic, renounced their possessions in this wise, that they held them in common," remarks St. Bonaventure very correctly.[2] The old monasteries could not have existed, nor have achieved their purpose in promoting divine worship and civilization, without property. But, unfortunately, the possession of landed properties by abbeys and other monastic institutions reached such vast proportions, and caused such luxury among the monks, that often barely a trace of the true ideal of poverty remained.

Since the tenth century several Reform Congregations endeavored to return to the state of poverty and simplicity which true religion demanded, but without decisive

or lasting results. The most powerful reform movement
in this direction was begun in the twelfth century by the
Cistercians, and through the influence of St. Bernard
spread to the various Orders of Knights.[3] But even the
Cistercians never thought of renouncing their property.
The reform consisted solely, with the exception of the
elimination of all extravagance in the household, in man-
aging and cultivating their lands personally, contrary to
the prevailing system of renting them to tenants.[4] But
this system of personal management, which meant cheap
labor and consequently high profits, again led to the rapid
enrichment of the abbeys.

As a result of this state of affairs, the complaints against
the enormous wealth of monasteries and of the feudal
clergy became louder and more vehement in the course
of the twelfth century. The reaction against this abnormal
condition, started by Peter Waldes (since 1173), who
advocated the total renunciation of property,[5] degenerated,
after the lapse of a decade, into heresy.[6]

When, therefore, Francis espoused the same cause, and
attempted to realize the ideal of absolute poverty, the
most zealous and intelligent among the princes of the
Church doubted the advisability of this plan. Bishop
Guido, of Assisi, to whom the Saint had made known
his project, though filled with admiration for Francis and
his brothers, could not forbear to remark: "Your mode of
life, to possess nothing in this world, appears to me severe
and difficult." Francis replied: "Lord, if we were to
have possessions, we should need weapons to defend our
property. This would lead to lamentable law-suits and
litigations, whereby the love of God and of the neighbor
is so frequently violated. We therefore prefer to possess
no temporal goods in this world." [7] He replied in like
manner to Cardinal John of St. Paul, who endeavored to
induce Francis to join an Order possessing property, and
professing either the Benedictine or the Augustinian rule.[8]

Pope Innocent III also pointed out the almost insuperable difficulties in which an Order such as Francis proposed, would find itself involved: "My dear sons," thus he addressed Francis and his disciples, "your life appears to Us too hard and bitter. Although We believe that you in your fervor may be able to bear it, still We must consider those who are to follow after you, and to whom such manner of life may seem too arduous." It was only after the Pope had tested the invincible enthusiasm of Francis for the evangelical ideal of poverty, and at the same time had recognized in him the man supporting the walls of the Lateran church, as had been shown to him in a vision, that he approved their manner of living in absolute poverty, and he exclaimed: "Truly, that is the man by whom the Church of God will be supported and raised up again!" [9]

It is not difficult to understand, on the one hand, the prudent reserve of the Church in regard to the reform advocated by Francis; nor, on the other, the firmness of the latter in advocating it. Celano makes it clear that Francis declined the suggestions made by the ecclesiastical superiors humbly, but firmly, not because he deemed them unworthy of consideration, but because he valued his Ideal more.[10] His guide and norm in this matter, as in all others, was the Gospel.

The poverty which the Saviour had embraced, and which He commended to His disciples, plainly excluded all possession. Christ declared of Himself: "The foxes have holes, and the birds of the air nests; but the Son of Man hath not where to lay His head." [11] To the rich young man He said: "If thou wilt be perfect, go, sell all thou hast, and give to the poor, . . . and come, follow Me." [12] For those who wished to become His disciples, He laid down the one condition: "Every one of you that doth not renounce all that he possesseth, cannot be My disciple." [13] And to His disciples, when sending them out to preach the Gospel, He said: "Freely have you received, freely give. Do not possess gold, nor silver,

nor money in your purses, nor scrip for your journey,
nor two coats, nor shoes, nor a staff; for the workman
is worthy of his meat." [14] And on all His disciples He enjoined: "Sell what you possess, and give alms. Make
to yourselves bags, which grow not old, a treasure in
heaven which faileth not." [15]

One thing was evident to Francis: in word and by
example Jesus demanded of His disciples complete renunciation of all earthly possessions. They were to call
nothing their own, neither in person, nor in common; yes,
even the terms "personal" and "common" were unknown
to the Saint, as they were unknown to the Gospel. The
ideal of poverty, as set forth in the Gospel, meant literally: complete dispossession in favor of the poor.

Francis understood and practised poverty in this literal
sense of the Gospel.[16] Whatever he called his own before
his conversion, he gave to the poor; and whatever he
owed his father, Peter Bernardone, he returned to him,
even the garments which he wore at the time.[17] He then
clothed himself in a hermit's garb, which was given him
by a servant of the Bishop; this he exchanged later for
the "evangelical" clothing, after hearing the words of
the Saviour forbidding His disciples to wear two coats
or shoes.[18] "His entire riches consisted, from his entrance into religious life until his death, in a single tunic,
a cord, and breeches; more he possessed not." [19]

Two years later, Bernard of Quintavalle also resolved
"to give all he had to the poor, and to follow Francis in
his manner of life and clothing." He sent for Francis
and said to him: "If one does not wish to keep the little
or much which he has received from the Lord and possessed for many years, what shall he do with it?" Francis
replied that he ought to return it to the Lord, from whom
he had received it. Bernard gave answer: "Brother, I will
give away all my earthly substance, as it seems best to
thee, for love of my Lord, who has given it to me." They
thereupon requested the priest to open the Book of the

Gospels thrice at random, and having thrice read the words of the Saviour demanding full renunciation of all earthly possessions, Bernard sold all he had, gave the proceeds to the poor, and clothed himself as Francis had done. Peter Catanii, the third one to join the holy company, did likewise.[20]

This course was followed whenever a new disciple asked to be received into the fraternity. Francis declares expressly in his Testament: "Those who came to take this life upon themselves, gave to the poor all that they might have, and they were content with one tunic, patched within and without, by those who wished, with a cord and breeches, and we wished for no more." [21]   And he later admonished his brothers constantly, "that, as he had learned by revelation, the beginning of religion must be the fulfilment of the words of the Gospel: 'Go, sell all thou hast, and give to the poor, and thou shalt have treasure in heaven; and come, follow Me.'   Therefore, he would admit none to the Order except such as would strip themselves of all things, retaining nothing for themselves, as well in obedience to the words of the Holy Gospel, as to avoid the dangers and scandal which the reserving of earthly goods might occasion to the soul." [22]

In this dispossession, or renunciation of the world (*renunciatio sæculi*), it was demanded that the novice distribute his substance to the poor, and not among his relatives, in accordance with the word of the Gospel. When a certain man, in the March of Ancona, asked to be received into the Order, Francis replied: "If thou wilt become one of the poor of Christ, give thy goods to the poor." The man went his way, and, being led astray by carnal affection, he left his property to his kinsfolk, and not to the poor. When the holy man heard of this, he rebuked him severely, saying: "Go thy way, Brother Fly, for thou hast in no wise gone forth from thy kindred and from thy father's house. Thou hast given thy goods to thy family, and hast defrauded the poor; thou art not worthy to be a follower of holy poverty. Thou hast begun with the flesh, and hast sought to raise a spiritual building upon a ruinous foundation." The man returned home, and reclaiming his goods, which he was unwilling to give to the poor, he quickly forsook his holy purpose.[23]   Celano, who relates this incident, remarks hereon: "Many are deceived in these days by such a deplorable distribution of their substance, seeking to attain to eternal life by worldly barter.   For no one gives himself to God by enriching his own kindred, but only by atoning for his sins at the price of generosity, and by gaining eternal life at the price of good works." [24]

Francis only then permitted relatives to profit from this renunciation if they themselves were poor.   One day a peasant who was plowing the field with a yoke of oxen, asked to be received into the fraternity.   Francis as usual directed him to give all he had to the poor, according to the words of the Gospel.   The young man in his simplicity then unharnessed one of the oxen, and leading the beast to Francis, said: "Brother, I have served my father and all my house for many years, and as for this there is a debt owing to me, I will take this ox as my portion and give it to the poor, as seems best to you."   As soon as the parents and the family of the young man heard of this, they began to lament bitterly, partly because he was to leave them, partly because of the loss of the ox, for it was a large and helpless family.   The Saint thereupon bade them make ready a meal, and when they had eaten with much gladness, he said to them: "This your son wishes to serve God, and instead of opposing him, you should be glad thereat.   For not only in the sight of God, but in that of the world, it is counted a great honor and advantage, both for soul and body, when one of your flesh and blood devotes himself to the Lord; and all our Friars will be your sons and brothers.   And since he is a creature of God, and desires to serve his Creator, to serve whom is to reign, I cannot restore him to you; but to comfort you, I do not wish him to despoil you of the ox, but that he should give it to you as to the poor, though according to the Holy Gospel it should be given to the other poor." At these words all were consoled and they rejoiced, most of all because they were to keep the ox, which they had thought lost.[25]

For the same reason Francis would not permit his brothers to accept anything from the postulants, except in case of momentary need: "Let the brothers and the ministers of the brothers . . . not receive any money, either themselves or through any person acting as intermediary; if, however, they should be in want, the brothers may accept other necessaries for the body, money excepted, by reason of their necessity, like the other poor." [26] But even in these cases of necessity, Francis was very loath to permit the Order to receive anything from postulants. For the sake of example, and in order to avoid the appearance of taking undue advantage of the good will of the postulants, he preferred to have recourse to other benefactors.[27]

Under no circumstances would he permit the brothers to accept temporal goods for the purpose of retaining them for future use. Brother Peter Catanii (died 1221), at that time Vicar of the Order, complained one day that the poverty at St. Mary of the Angels was so great that the guests could not be properly received, and begged permission to reserve a part of the goods of the novices, so as to be able to supply the wants of the brothers in time of need. Francis, however, replied: "God forbid, beloved brother, that for any man whomsoever we should thus sin against the rule. I would rather have thee strip the altar of the glorious Virgin, should necessity so require, than infringe in the slightest degree the vow of poverty, and the due observance of the Gospel precept. For rather would the Blessed Virgin see her altar unadorned, and the counsel of the Holy Gospel perfectly observed, than that her altar should be ornamented, and the counsel of her Son set at naught." [28]

The views of the Seraphic Saint regarding this point are reflected in the second chapter of the final rule, which reads: "If any wish to embrace this life, and come to our brothers, let them send them to their provincial ministers, to whom alone and not to others is accorded the power of receiving brothers.   But let the ministers . . . tell them the word of the Gospel, that they go and sell all their goods, and strive to distribute them to the poor.   If they should not be able to do this, their good will will suffice.   And the brothers and their ministers must take care not to be solicitous about their temporal affairs, that they may freely do with their affairs whatsoever the Lord may inspire them.   If, however, counsel should be required, the ministers shall have power of sending them to some God-fearing men, by whose advice their goods may be distributed to the poor.   Afterward let them give them clothes of probation; namely, two tunics without a hood, and a cord, and breeches, and chaperon reaching to the cord,[29] unless at some time the same ministers may decide otherwise according to God." [30]

Thus the renunciation of property was as complete and as true to the Gospel as possible.   Before entering, each postulant had to strip himself of his possessions, if possible, in favor of the poor; after his admission, the novice as well as the professed brother possessed nothing but the clothing designated by the words of the Mission. Outward conditions, as we shall see, soon made necessary the use of various articles for personal or common service. These, however, could never become the property of the individual or of the Order.   On this point Francis remained inexorable until the end of his life.

Before 1223, the rule contained the words: "Let the brothers take care, that wherever they may be, whether in hermitages or in other places, they never appropriate any place to themselves, or maintain it against another.   And

whoever may come to them, either a friend or a foe, a
thief or a robber, let them receive him kindly." [31]   The
rule of 1223 contained substantially the same: "The
brothers shall appropriate nothing to themselves, neither
a house, nor a place, nor anything.   And as pilgrims
and strangers in this world let them serve the Lord in
poverty and humility. . . . This is the height of the most
sublime poverty, which has made you, my dearest brothers,
heirs and kings of the kingdom of heaven: poor in goods,
but exalted in virtue.   Let that be your portion, for it
leads to the land of the living; cleaving to it unreservedly,
my best beloved brothers, for the Name of Our Lord
Jesus Christ never desire to possess anything else under
heaven." [32]   At the moment of death the Saint is urged to
admonish once more: "Let the brothers take care not to
receive on any account churches, poor dwelling places and
all other things that are constructed for them, unless they
are as is becoming the holy poverty which we have promised in the rule, always dwelling there as pilgrims and
strangers." [33]

Shortly after the demise of the blessed Father, some
laxists nevertheless thought that at least the movable
goods which they had in use, were the common property
of the Order.   The more zealous brothers became greatly
saddened because of these suggestions, and feared for their
own conscience as well as for the ideals of the Order.
This caused Gregory IX to declare, as early as 1230,
that, as an intimate friend of Francis, and his collaborator
in compiling the rule, he knew perfectly the mind of the
Holy Founder,[34] and he continued: "We declare, that the
brothers may not possess property either in common or
personally, but they should have implements and books
and other movable goods for use only, and the brothers
should use them according to the direction of the General
and Provincial Ministers in such wise that the title of
those to whom the places and houses belonged, be not
violated." [35]

What strikes us most forcibly is, that Francis grasped the ascetical importance of this rigid poverty almost intuitively. To renounce all earthly possession meant to him to be stripped of everything earthly, and to belong entirely to God. "Holy poverty," he was wont to say, "confounds cupidity and avarice, and the cares of the world." [36] "Poverty is that heavenly virtue by which all earthly and perishable things are trodden under foot, by which all obstacles are removed in order that the spirit of man may freely unite itself to the eternal Lord and God. It enables the soul still dwelling on earth, to converse with the angels in heaven" [37] and in the moment of death "to go to Christ stripped of all things." [38]

This conception of poverty is so ideal, that it includes not only the renunciation of all material things, but also of the inordinate affection for spiritual things. "He who would attain to this height of perfection," Francis declared, "must lay aside not only earthly prudence, but even all knowledge of letters, that, thus stripped of all things, he may come to see what is the power of the Lord,[39] and cast himself naked into the arms of the Crucified. Neither does he perfectly renounce the world, who keeps a place for the treasure of his own will in the secret of his heart." [40]

2. The Franciscan ideal of poverty demands, besides the renunciation of earthly property, also the *limited use* of earthly things. Francis did not originally recognize the distinction between property (*proprietas, dominium*), and use (*usus*). Aside from the coarse food which he procured either by the labor of his hands, or by begging, the Poverello had nothing, and needed nothing, but his poor habit. But whether he possessed this habit, or merely had the use of it, was of no concern to him in those early days. It was in perfect accord with the Gospel, and it had been revealed to him by the Gospel. That sufficed.

As Francis thought and lived, so the entire fraternity

at first thought and lived: "We were content with one tunic, patched within and without, by those who wished, with a cord and breeches. And we wished for no more." [41] Thomas of Celano describes the poverty of the first years in these words: "Because the disciples of most holy poverty possessed nothing and desired nothing, neither did they fear to lose anything. They were content with one tunic, which was frequently patched within and without. There was nothing fanciful about it, but all contempt and poverty, so that they might appear wholly crucified to the world. Girded with a cord, they wore cheap breeches, and they were firmly resolved to remain faithful to this, and to accept nothing more." [42]

That the brothers should have been able to live without the use at least of other articles, can be understood only if we consider briefly the mode of life in the first decades of the Order. Those years were the period of itinerary preaching, in exact accordance with the Gospel. After the manner of Jesus and His disciples, Francis and his companions went forth into the world two by two, preaching penance. From time to time they returned to a designated place, to rest from their labors and to refresh their spirits. A fixed dwelling-place they had not; food and shelter they obtained from day to day *per amore di Dio*— for love of God.

Francis chose Portiuncula as the first point whence their activities were directed. It was situated a little below Assisi. There the Benedictines of Monte Subasio possessed a small deserted church, called "Mary of the Angels," [43] and it was here that Francis and his disciples first assembled. In order to protect themselves against the inclemency of the weather, they constructed a poor hut made of clay and willows next to the chapel, in which they lived together for a while.[44]

But only for a while. As soon as the disciples had rested from their apostolic labors in the surrounding country, Francis again sent them out into all quarters of the compass to preach. A frugal meal was always assured them in hospitable Umbria. Shelter for the night they had to seek frequently in the porches of churches and of other buildings, in ovens,[45] in grottoes, caves,[46] or under the open sky; for in many instances they were regarded as thieves and vagabonds, and in consequence they found the doors closed against them.[47] At the appointed time they would assemble again at the chapel of Portiuncula. The Three Companions remark: "They had claim in no wise to property, but used the books and other things in common, according to the rule handed down by the apostles." [48]

After a brief sojourn at Portiuncula, the apostolic band—they now numbered twelve—journeyed to Rome, in order to beg the approval of the Holy Father for their mode of life. On their return from Rome, they interrupted their missionary labors, making a stay of a fortnight in a deserted place near the town of Orte. Thomas of Celano describes their sojourn in this place, giving at the same time valuable information regarding the question of poverty: "Some of them went to the city and procured the necessary food, and the little which they had begged from door to door, they brought to the other brothers, and they ate it in common with hearty gratitude and rejoicing. But if by chance something remained over, and they could not give it to anyone, they preserved it for the next day in a cave, which at one time served for the burial of the dead. The place was solitary and deserted, and was sought out by few or no people. The brothers rejoiced exceedingly, because they neither saw nor possessed anything which could have given them vain or carnal pleasure. Thus they began to have sweet converse with Holy Poverty,[49] firmly resolved to remain faithful to her, here as elsewhere. Free from all earthly cares, and open to divine consolation only, they were irrevocably determined to be neither depressed by tribulations, nor shaken by temptations, nor separated from the embrace of Lady Poverty by anything. Although the charm of the place, which so easily may harm the strength of the spirit, in no wise diminished their zeal, they nevertheless resolved to journey elsewhere, lest the attachment to a place give the impression, even outwardly, that they possessed property." [50]

They therefore continued their apostolic journey until they arrived at Rivo Torto, about one mile from Portiuncula, where they found an empty hut. This hut was in every way according to the heart of Francis, "For," he remarked, "one goes more quickly into heaven from a hut than from a palace." [51] The place was, however, so small that the brothers could scarcely sit or lie one next to another. In order to prevent any disturbance, when one wished to rest and another to pray, Francis gave to each one a place by writing his name on the rafters. Here they lived in great poverty, devoid of all things. Bread was frequently so difficult to obtain that they were forced to satisfy their hunger with turnips, which they had begged from the peasants in the country about Assisi. There was neither a church nor a chapel in the vicinity, and so the brothers assembled for their devotions before a large wooden cross which they had erected in front of the hut. Thus the days passed, until one day a mule-driver appeared with his beast and began to disturb the silence of the place with coarse and abusive language. Francis thereupon said to the others: "Brothers, I know that we are not called to give shelter to this beast, and to be disturbed by men, but to promote the salvation of souls by our preaching, our good counsel, our prayers and gratitude." [52] And they forthwith returned to the chapel and hut at Portiuncula.

Here they remained during the following years, the brothers steadily increasing in numbers, and gradually extending their journeys beyond the boundaries of Umbria into the various provinces of Italy,[53] even occasionally as far as Syria and Morocco.[54] Once or twice a year they assembled at Portiuncula for Chapter, living under the open sky or in tents.[55]   In the intervals between Chapters they would occasionally find shelter for a few days or weeks in some deserted place, preferably in an improvised hermitage.   The remainder of the time was spent in apostolic labors, wandering from place to place, and preaching penance.   Naturally there was no question of a permanent abode and of the things necessary thereto, in this mode of life.   The Three Companions remark, not without indicating the gradual change and development of conditions: "The brothers went through the world as pilgrims and strangers, and carried nothing with them on the way, except the books from which they prayed their hours. . . . And when evening began to fall, they took refuge with the priests, rather than with the people of the world.   But if they found no shelter with priests, they stayed rather with spiritual and God-fearing people, until God inspired pious persons to prepare a hospice in the cities and villages, which the brothers wished to visit, as long as no places (loca) had been erected for them in the cities and towns." [56]

Jacques de Vitry (died 1240), who became closely acquainted with Francis and the Friars in Italy in 1216, and again in the Orient in 1219, found conditions in the Order substantially the same as we have described them. The following is the testimony of the famous Cardinal and historian: "That is truly the religion of the poor men of the Crucified, the Order of preachers, who are called Friars Minor.   They are in truth Friars Minor, and by reason of their clothing and poverty and contempt of the world and humility they surpass all Religious of their time. . . . They endeavor so zealously to renew the faith, poverty and humility of the primitive Church, and to draw the pure waters of the evangelical fountain in the thirst and fire of the spirit, that they, following not only the precepts, but also the counsels of the Gospel, strive most faithfully to imitate the apostolic life, renouncing all their

possessions, denying themselves, and, destitute of all, following the poor Saviour. . . . They are sent out two by two into the world to preach, as if going before the face of the Lord, and to prepare His coming. And these poor of Christ carry on the way neither purse nor scrip, nor bread, nor any money in their girdles, nor have they at all gold or silver or shoes. For no brother of this Order is permitted to possess anything whatsoever. They have no monasteries, nor churches, nor lands, nor vineyards, nor beasts, nor houses, or any property, nor as much as where to lay their heads. They wear neither furs, nor linen, but only tunics with a hood, not to mention surplices and cloaks and cowls, and such like garments. If anyone invites them to table, they eat and drink what is placed before them. If anyone gives them alms, they do not keep it for future use. Once or twice a year they assemble at a given time and place to conduct the General Chapter, with the exception of those who would.have to make too long a journey by land or by sea. After the Chapter they are sent out again by the superiors, two by two, or more in number, into various regions and provinces and cities. Not only by their preaching, but more by the example of their holy life and their perfect conduct, they incite many people of the lower estate as well as of distinguished and noble rank, to despise the world, so that they leave their cities, their castles, and their lands, bartering away all their earthly substance for the blessed exchange of the clothing of the Friars Minor; namely, a tunic of little value with which they are clothed, and a cord with which they gird themselves. . . . .
. . . . . . For the brothers give to those who enter, a cord only with the tunic; all else they leave to Divine Providence." [57]

As admirable as this carefree life of missionary activity may have been with its well-nigh heroic practise of poverty, the need of organization soon became apparent. Think of a fraternity without a novitiate, without train-

ing of its members, with perfect liberty to enter to-day
and leave to-morrow; without legislation, with only a rule
still in the formative period; without provincial and local
superiors—welded together and guided solely by the personal prestige of the Founder! In consequence of this,
the difficulties increased from day to day, the more numerous the brothers, and the more extensive their sphere of
activity became. When, therefore, Francis undertook the
realization of his wider and greater purpose, the missionizing of the whole world, he was confronted with the alter-
native of either forcing his fraternity into the bonds of a
firm organization, or of leading it to the brink of an
inevitable catastrophe.

Ominous signs of this impending catastrophe had already begun to multiply. We read in the life of Blessed
Giles that many brothers succumbed to the temptation of
leaving the Order and returning to the world when occasion offered itself.[58] The contemporaneous rhetorician
Buoncompagno, of Bologna, likewise laments the incon-
stancy of many Friars, some of whom were mere youths
and striplings, who roamed about the world without check
or restraint, and who made themselves guilty of various
indiscretions, because they were left to themselves without
the proper ascetical schooling and discipline.[59] Jacques
de Vitry also states in one of his letters, dated 1220, that
the Order, sublime though it be, still was beset by great
dangers, for the reason that not only men of mature age
and tried virtue, but also unfledged youths, who were still
in need of monastic training, wandered about the world.[60]

After the Chapter of 1219 Francis had sent out brothers
not only into the various Italian provinces, but also to
France, Germany, Austria, Hungary and Spain, while he
himself set out for Syria.[61] Hardly had he left for his
destination, when dark clouds gave portent of the impending storm. Rumors from the Orient began to reach Italy
that the holy Founder had died; that sufficed to start a
dissolution, as it were, of the Order in Europe, attempts

being made to reform the organization.[62]   Francis immediately recognized the tragedy of these events, returned
with haste to Italy, and, having sought counsel with Pope
Honorius, he set to work with Cardinal Hugolino to give
the Order a definite and lasting Constitution.[63]   In this
manner the first rule of 1221 was written, and two years
later the final rule of 1223.   In this rule the Order is
divided into provinces and custodies, a complete hierarchy
of superiors is established, from the Ministers General
down to the guardians; a novitiate is prescribed, terminat-
ing with the perpetual vows, and every brother is placed
under the obedience of his immediate superior.[64]

This was of the greatest moment in the development of
the practise of poverty.   In the first place, the ever changing lodgings gave way to fixed *"places"* (*loca*), consisting
of a *"house"* for the brothers, and a *church* or *chapel* for
conducting divine services.   The chronicles of Thomas of
Eccleston and of Jordan of Giano establish the fact that the
brothers everywhere settled in friaries even during the lifetime of the Saint.   The rules of the Order, and the Testament of St. Francis place this fact beyond the pale of
doubt.

But in every way these Friaries had to correspond with
the ideal of poverty.   Whenever there was a question of
building or accepting a house, Francis would remind his
brothers of the word of the Saviour: "The foxes have
their holes, and the birds of the air nests, but the Son of
Man hath not where to lay His head." [65]   And he added:
"When therefore the brothers go into a city where they
have as yet no house, and someone is found who wishes
to give them ground to build thereon a 'place,' with a
garden and the other necessary things, let them take care
above all, how much space suffices for them, considering
poverty and the good example which we are bound to give
in all things." [66]   On this ground the brothers were then
to build poor dwellings, preferably of wood and clay.[67]
Francis, however, would not fix any definite rule regard-

ing the material to be used, since he well knew that in some localities buildings of wood entailed greater cost than those of stone.[68]   Another reason soon presented itself. It is stated thus by St. Bonaventure: "Wherever we are able, we build houses of stone; they are not destroyed so quickly by fire or age." [69]

But whether the house was built of wood or stone or other poorer material, Francis wished them to be small and to have space only for a limited number of Friars, as it was difficult to observe poverty amongst a large number.[70]

Not even at Portiuncula, where at the time of the General Chapters hundreds, yes, thousands of Friars assembled, would Francis allow large buildings to be erected. The only building which existed there, was the hut which he had built of clay and willows and covered with straw.[71] The many hundreds of capitulars who had flocked thither from all quarters of the land, were forced to live under the open sky, or in tents.[72]   The Council of Assisi was anxious to remedy this condition, and, during the absence of the Saint, the good townspeople had erected a large building of stone.   When Francis arrived for the Chapter and saw this mighty structure, he became sad, for he feared that the Friars would erect similar buildings in other places if such were allowed at Portiuncula, the cradle and model of the Order.   He quickly climbed upon the roof, and began to tear off the tiles and laths, exhorting the brothers to give aid in destroying the building.   But hardly had he begun the work of destruction, when the town-guard, whose captain happened to be the brother of Francis,[73] arrived and commanded him to halt, saying that the building had been erected by the Council of Assisi, and therefore was the property of the city.   "If that be the case," replied Francis, "I will not touch your property." And he permitted his brothers to live therein as guests.[74]

He insisted also that the churches of the Order be small, even if they could not accommodate the masses on occasions of preaching or other solemnities; "for," thus Francis reasoned, "humility is greater and the example more potent if the brothers betake themselves to other churches to preach. And if perchance prelates, clerics, Religious and lay people come to the place of the Friars, the poor houses, the cells and the small churches·will preach, and they will be edified thereby more than by words." [75]

During the first years of the Order, when the brothers wandered about preaching, such small houses sufficed for their wants. A few years, however, of living in established Friaries brought the conviction that it was in the interest of health and monastic discipline to build more spacious dwellings, however, poor and simple they might be. The words of Bernard of Bessa in this regard are noteworthy: "Francis was pleased with poor dwellings, and with wooden ones more than with those of stone. He would often sojourn with a few brothers in hermitages, where hedges of thorns served as enclosure, and small huts as dwellings. In the cities, however, neither the sinfulness of men, nor the number of Friars would allow such poverty." [76] St. Bonaventure amplifies this statement thus: "People of the world, who frequently travel, are in no need at home of a change of air; Religious, however, who are enclosed in narrow cells, soon become ill and indisposed and unfit for mental labors if they have not fresh, healthful air in their houses.[77] We prefer large houses to the small; for in these discipline can be more easily upheld . . . ; devotion is deeper, order more exact, Divine Office more beautiful, and the training of novices better." [78]

In one point, however, Francis would countenance no relaxation: the brothers were to accept all buildings *for use only,* and to avoid everything that savored of proprietorship. At one time he sojourned in the vicinity of Bologna, and when he chanced to hear that the brothers had a house of their own in the city, he would not stay with them. He ordered, on the contrary, that the house be vacated at once, not excepting a brother who was lying

THE MYSTICAL MARRIAGE OF ST. FRANCIS WITH LADY POVERTY

ill at the time. It was only after Cardinal Hugolino had
assured him that the house was his own, that Francis allowed the brothers to return.[79] Another time a Friar
spoke of a cell as being the cell of Francis, and the latter
forthwith replied: "Because thou hast given this cell the
name of Francis, and thus appropriated it to me, thou
mayest seek another dweller for it: I will never again enter
it." [80] He would not allow the Friars to occupy even the
smallest place, unless someone claimed it as his own. For
it was his wish that the brothers "follow the custom of
pilgrims, who seek shelter under strange roofs, journey
onward in peace, and long for their own country." [81] We
have already seen that Francis embodied this wish in the
rules of 1221 and 1223, and likewise in his Testament.[82]

For the very reason, that the brothers "should, after the
manner of the poor, build for themselves poor little huts,
and should not look upon even these as their own, but
dwell in them as pilgrims in the houses of others," [83] these
dwellings were not called monasteries (*monasteria, claustra*), but "places" (*loca*), or at most only houses
·(*domus*). The older monasteries were units in themselves, situated outside of towns and villages, after the
manner of lordly castles or estates. They were econom-
ically independent, and the inmates, Benedictines, Cistercians, Carthusians, even the canons-regular, promised the
stabilitas loci,[84] that is, their vows were made for a definite
monastery, and they remained bound to it for their lifetime. The Friars, however, dedicated themselves to the
service of God without limiting themselves to a certain
place or house, because they wished to labor everywhere [85]
and claimed no lasting home in this world. They "pil-
grimed for the sake of Christ," according to the words of
the Psalmist: "Thy justifications were the subject of my
song, in the place of my pilgrimage." [86] This term could
be applied at first both figuratively and literally, as long as
the brothers had no fixed residences, but lived perhaps in
a cave, a deserted hermitage, a hut made of willows, or

some other "place." But after their wandering mode of life had been restricted, the dwellings erected to shelter the brothers were called "houses." They were never termed monasteries in the earliest Franciscan literature. When in 1225 the citizens of Erfurt asked Brother Jordan of Giano whether they should build a house for the Friars after the manner of a monastery, the latter, never having seen a monastery in the Order, replied: "I know not what a monastery is; build us a house near the river, that we may go down to the water to wash our feet." [87]

The establishment of houses for the brothers brought about another development; namely, the necessity and the licitness of the use of *movable goods*. The various implements necessary for manual labor had to be available,[88] as well as the books which were indispensable to carry on the missionary work of the Order. Provisions had to be made to give the sick brothers the proper care and attention. In short, all those things which are needful for the maintenance of the household, however poor, had to be on hand. That was self-evident, and Francis allowed the use of these things either expressly, or tacitly; "for the contrary," remarks St. Bonaventure, "would be unreasonable." [89]

But, on the other hand, every vestige of luxury or extravagance in these articles was forbidden. It is significant that he forbade the keeping of beasts and riding on horseback.[90] The former was prohibited because it savored of proprietorship, the latter because it was proper only to the rich.[91]

Francis furthermore "forbade in every way that the brothers exceed the measure of poverty in the houses or churches or gardens or in all other things which they had in use." [92] Regarding books, as Celano states, they were to seek the testimony of God, not costliness, edification or beauty.[93] The author of the *Speculum* further remarks that as regards the beds and their covering, such abundant poverty reigned among the Friars, that they imagined themselves sleeping on soft mattresses if their straw was covered with a tattered sheet.[94]

Many and valuable utensils were an abomination to Francis. He abhorred everything, as Celano states, in the furnishing of the table, which reminded one of the world, and he desired that all things which the Friars had, bespeak their state of pilgrimage and exile.[95] Superfluous things he would not tolerate; even the smallest article had to be removed from the house if it were not absolutely necessary. He was wont to say that it was very difficult to satisfy the needs, without yielding to self-indulgence.[96]

One time, it was the feast of Easter, the brothers had prepared the table in the hermitage at Greccio with greater care, using linens and glassware. Francis came down from his cell and saw the table decked out so lavishly, but the festive board did not put him in a happy frame of mind. He withdrew quietly and stealthily, and, placing the hat of a beggar on his head and taking a staff in his hand, he waited before the door until the brothers had begun to eat; for they usually did not wait for him if he did not appear on the signal. While they were sitting at table, he called out from the door: "For the love of God the Lord, grant an alms to a poor and weak pilgrim." The brothers replied: "Enter, friend, for the love of Him, whom thou hast called upon." Francis then entered and made himself known to them. Great was the consternation of the brothers when they recognized the pilgrim, and still greater when he asked for a small dish, sat down upon the floor, and set the dish in the ashes at his side. "Now," he said, "I am sitting at table like a Friar Minor." And, turning to the brothers, he continued: "To us example of the Son of God must be more binding than to other Religious. I beheld the table prepared and adorned, and did not recognize it as the table of the poor, who beg alms from door to door." [97]

The expansion of the Order throughout the world brought about a third development, or rather relaxation, in

the practise of poverty; namely, in the *clothing* of the
Friars. Francis had followed literally the command of
the Saviour, not to possess gold, nor silver, nor money,
nor scrip, nor two coats, nor shoes, nor a staff.[98] He
therefore allowed his disciples to wear nothing but the
tunic with a cord, and, of course, breeches. At the most
he allowed them, for the sake of humility as well as for
greater warmth, to sew coarse patches on the tunic "if
they wished, within and without." [99]   To allow more,
seemed to him contrary to the Gospel.

The Saviour had indeed spoken thus on the occasion of
their first mission. Later on, however, when He sent them
into more distant regions, He allowed them sandals and
a staff.[100] When finally the time of His sacred passion
and of persecution had come, He permitted them, contrary to His first command, to take with them also a
purse, a scrip and a cloak.[101] Francis seems to have overlooked these passages, and for this reason would not allow
any relaxation in the clothing of the brothers. But circumstances forced him, as they had forced the Saviour,
to mitigate his earlier austerity.   Such circumstances
were physical illness and the severity of the weather, even
while the fraternity was restricted to the sunny clime of
Italy. After it had spread to the northern countries, the
spare clothing in use at the beginning of the Order was
soon found to be wholly inadequate.   In fact, the first
brothers who had been sent to Germany, Austria and
Hungary by Francis in 1219, wore an upper and under
garment and breeches.[102] Some time later this clothing
was made official for the entire Order. According to the
rule of 1221 the professed brothers received a tunic with
a hood, and if necessary, another without a hood, with a
cord and breeches.[103] Since the tunic and hood formed
the figure of the cross,[104] it naturally became the privileged
dress of those who had taken the cross of Christ upon
themselves. The novices received for the same reason

two tunics without a hood, and in place of the latter the so-called chaperon,[105] with breeches and the cord.

The prohibition of two coats was accordingly omitted from the text of the mission, and limited to the following: "The brothers should carry nothing by the way, neither bag, nor purse, nor bread, nor money, nor a staff." [106] Two years later, the Ministers prevailed upon Francis [107] to omit even these words from the rule,[108] and a second tunic was allowed unconditionally to all brothers. The wearing of shoes, which had been forbidden altogether in the first years,[109] and which was not yet mentioned in the rule of 1221, was made permissible in case of necessity.[110]

To this was added the admonition: "Let all the brothers be clothed with mean garments, and they may mend them with sackcloth and other pieces, with the blessing of God." [111] Thomas of Celano remarks hereto: "Francis wished that under no circumstances the brothers should wear two tunics, although he permitted them to patch them with pieces of cloth. He commands them to avoid precious material, and he reprimanded most severely in the presence of others, those who acted contrariwise. The brothers, however, who were forced by illness or other necessity, he allowed to wear a soft under-garment on their body, yet so that in outward appearance poverty and severity was observed." [112]

Whatever the weakness of human nature, and conditions "of places and times and cold climates" [113] made necessary, Francis freely permitted. Yet he constantly feared that his Order might also be contaminated by the oft-lamented luxury in clothing which was prevalent at that time among the seculars and the Religious.[114] However, he would not have the brothers sit in judgment over others who wore luxurious clothes: "I admonish and exhort them not to despise or judge men whom they see clothed in fine and showy garments, using dainty meats and drinks, but rather let each one judge and despise himself." [115] He further admonished and warned them:

"Let all the brothers be clothed with mean garments. . . ;
for the Lord says in the Gospel: 'They that are in costly
apparel, and live delicately, and they that are clothed in
soft garments, are in the houses of kings.' And although
they should be called hypocrites, let them not cease to do
good; let them not desire rich clothes in this world, that
they may possess a garment in the kingdom of heaven." [116]
In spite of this warning, Francis foresaw the influence of
worldly fashions on the Order, and he declared with great
sadness of heart: "Austerity will in time decrease in such
measure and such laxity will prevail that the sons of the
poor Father will not fear to wear even scarlet clothing,
changing only the color." [117]   Thomas of Celano was
forced to state, only a short time later,[118] that "it was
plainer than day, and becoming plainer each day," how
correctly Francis had spoken.

To prevent as much as possible by his own example such
violations of poverty, the Poverello was content during
his lifetime with one tunic, a cord, and the breeches.[119]
On this tunic he sewed a coarse sack, and he commanded
that his burial habit be also covered with an ugly sack.[120]

In his last hour he had himself laid upon the ground,
and his sacklike habit taken off. His guardian divined the
wish of the dying man, and hastened to tender him another habit, with a loin cloth, and a hood made of sackcloth, of which he was in need on account of a recent
operation performed on his eyes. Then he said to the
dying Saint: "Know that this tunic, with the hood and
breeches, is loaned to thee in the name of holy obedience.
But that thou mayest know that thou hast no right of
possession, I deprive thee of the power to give it to another." At these words the Saint became jubilant, and his
heart overflowed with holy joy, because he saw, that he
had kept his troth with Lady Poverty unbroken unto the
end. . . . [121]

That is the true ideal of poverty of St. Francis: complete renunciation of earthly things, extreme moderation in

their use. The renunciation of property he demanded absolutely and unconditionally; to possess anything in person or in common, was incompatible with his ideal. The moderation in the use of things is obviously to be governed by the conditions under which the individual Franciscan as well as the Order perform their proper functions; in consequence of the manifold, inevitable needs that arose, a development in this regard could not be avoided even during the lifetime of the Saint, and more so in later years.

For the very reason that many brothers lost sight of these two guiding stars in the practise of Franciscan poverty, they provoked that unhappy dispute of the thirteenth and the fourteenth century,[122] which inflicted serious wounds on the Church and society, and particularly on the Order itself. The laxists among the Friars finally arrived at the point of allowing the possession of lands, thus depressing the Franciscan Ideal to the level of the other Orders. The rigorists, on the other hand, became so extreme as to condemn not only the moderate use of things as sanctioned by the Church, but also every reasonable use, attempting to model the practise of poverty on the basically different conditions of the first years of the Order, thereby rendering the apostolic and literary activity of the Friars impossible, destroying that sweet, mild, and cheerful spirit which made Francis and his Order so popular, and finally allowing themselves to be driven to stubborn resistance to the authorities of the Church. The history of the Franciscan Order proves that only under the guidance of the Church, the Franciscan Ideal of poverty can be correctly understood and followed out, for the immeasurable good of human society.

CHAPTER VII

FRANCISCAN LIVELIHOOD

WE HAVE not yet fully developed the Franciscan Ideal of poverty. The Poverello had solved the problem with the utmost simplicity: to possess nothing, and to use only what was necessary to live. A further problem, however, presented itself: in what manner were the Friars to gain their livelihood, considering their rigid poverty? Francis answered: by their own labor, and if this did not suffice, by begging alms, with the restriction however, that money was not to be accepted, either as wages, or as alms.

That is the briefest formula to which the Franciscan mode of living can be reduced. To form a more correct estimate of this formula, and to understand how exactly it agreed with the Gospel Ideal of Francis, it will be necessary to give our attention to the three factors of this formula: *money, labor,* and *alms,* and their place in the Franciscan household.

1. *Money* and its commercial use had in the days of Francis achieved an importance heretofore undreamt of. It had always been the medium of exchange to a limited extent; but with the growth of cities and their markets in the Middle Ages, the sale of agricultural products for money had become quite common. Toward the end of the twelfth century, money as a medium of exchange had, to all practical purposes, replaced the old system of trade and barter. Side by side with the productivity of land and of labor, the productivity of money now became a dominant factor; the capitalist had become a power to be

reckoned with as well as the landowner and the laborer. The latter also strove to become capitalists: the landowner by liquidizing his products in the market; the laborer by capitalizing his wages, which no longer took the form of land tenure, but mostly of money. And forthwith began the struggle of class against class. Enormous wealth on the one side; poverty of the masses on the other; and on the part of both, the insatiable greed for mammon—that soon became the dread symptom of the time. Poets and preachers of the thirteenth century, in particular the Franciscan Berthold of Regensburg, depict in somber colors these evil results of the new system of economics.[1]

Francis had been a witness from earliest youth of the spread of this new system; he himself had experienced the passionate greed of his own father. The result was an irresistible repugnance to everything which meant money or its equivalent. We still remember how restless he remained at the time of his conversion, until he had rid himself of the money which he carried in his purse.[2] The repudiation of money finally became the supreme law of his new life, after he had heard the words of the Saviour: "Do not possess gold, nor silver, nor money in your purses."[3] His contempt for all earthly things directed itself in particular against money. He instinctively sensed the demoniacal power which lies in this artificial wealth, and he consequently commanded his followers to flee money as the devil himself. The motto which he placed before them was: "Give to money the same value as to dung."[4]

A practical exemplification of this motto presented itself very strikingly at the admission of the first disciples into the Order. Bernard of Quintavalle, who had been very wealthy, was distributing the proceeds from the sale of his property quietly to the poor.[5] Francis stood aside, an edified witness of this procedure, praising and glorifying God in his heart.[6] Suddenly a secular priest, Sylvester by name, made his way through the throng of beggars; it was

the same priest from whom Francis had purchased stones
to repair the Church of San Damiano.   Seeing Bernard
handing out the coins so lavishly, the priest was seized
with greed, and he exclaimed ill-humoredly: "Francis,
thou hast not paid me sufficiently for the stones which
thou hast bought from me."   On hearing this unjust
charge, the lover of poverty and despiser of money reached
down into the pockets of Bernard, drew out a handful of
coins, and gave them to the priest. A second handful was
also dropped into the outstretched palms, and then he
asked: "Hast thou been paid enough now, sir priest?"
The latter declared that he was satisfied, and went home
delighted. His delight, however, soon changed into remorse; he became ashamed of his greediness and filled
with admiration over the contempt of money which
Francis had shown, and soon afterward became the third
disciple of the Poverello.[7]

In similar manner many seculars were soon won over
to the Order, inspired by the absolute contempt of earthly
treasure displayed by Francis and his companions. At the
time of their first apostolic journey, Brother Bernard and
his companion were forced to seek shelter one night at
Florence, and finally obtained permission from a kind-
hearted peasant woman to pass the night in the bakery.
When her husband came home and heard of what she had
done, he became very angry; she appeased his ire, however, by remarking that at most they could possibly steal
some wood. After the brothers had passed the night,
which was rather cold, without any covering, and clothed
only "with the garment of Lady Poverty," [8] they went to
the nearest church to pray. Soon after, their kind-hearted
hostess also entered the church, and finding the brothers
absorbed in deep prayer, she said to herself: "If these men
were vagabonds and thieves, as my husband thinks, they
would not pray so long and devoutly." In the meantime
a certain charitable man named Guido was distributing
alms in the church to the poor; but when the brothers'

turn had come, they refused to accept the money offered them. At the surprising question, why they refused alms although they appeared so poor and destitute, Bernard replied: "Poor we are indeed; however, poverty is not a burden to us as it is to the other poor, for by the grace of God, whose counsel we follow, we have become poor of our own choice." Guido was greatly astonished at hearing such words, and more so when he heard that these men had once possessed great wealth. And from that hour he became a staunch friend and benefactor of the brothers.[9]

This episode illustrates the natural and deep impression which the Franciscan scorn of money made upon their money-hungry contemporaries. Cardinal Jacques de Vitry, and the chronicler Burchard of Ursperg likewise shared this deep impression.[10] The Three Companions on their part remark: "When the people saw that the Friars were full of joy in their tribulations, and devoted to constant and zealous prayer, neither accepting money nor carrying such with them, and showing each other great charity, their persecutors were deeply touched, and begged their forgiveness for the injuries inflicted upon them." [11] The Friars, on their part, took occasion from this "to love poverty still more, and in particular to tread money under foot like so much dust; yes, counting it of equal value as the dung of asses, as they had been told by Francis himself." [12]

One of the Friars, however, failed to show sufficient contempt for money, as it seemed to Francis. A stranger one day had entered the church of Portiuncula and placed a number of coins at the foot of the crucifix. The Friar in question unthinkingly took the money into his hand, and threw it on the ledge of a window. The Saint heard of this and ordered the brother to appear before him. The latter came in haste and threw himself upon his knees, asking pardon, and ready to accept the chastisement which he thought he had deserved. Francis rebuked him severely for having touched the money, and bade him take it down with his own mouth and deposit it on a dung-heap beyond the hedge of the enclosure. The other Friars were filled with great awe at this, and they henceforth despised still more that which was placed on the same level with dung; and they were encouraged in this sentiment by almost daily examples of this kind.[18]

Thomas of Celano relates a very striking incident which greatly helped to confirm the brothers in their contempt for money. The man of God was one day passing by the city of Bari, in Apulia, accompanied by another Friar. On the way they found a heavy purse, all swollen as if full of money. His companion earnestly besought Francis to let him take it from the ground and distribute the money among the poor. He appealed to his charity and generosity, begging him to let the poor share in the fortune. But the Saint refused, and declared that there was some diabolical delusion hidden in the purse, saying: "We may not take away strange goods, my son; to give away the property of another brings not Heaven's reward, but punishment." They left the purse lying in the road, and hastened on their way. But the Friar, deluded by a vain show of pity, could not be appeased. Then Francis, in his meekness, agreed to return to the place, not to fulfil the will of the brother, but to reveal to him the fraud of the devil. He called a boy, who happened to be sitting near a well at the side of the road, in order to have a third witness, and having first prayed to God, he commanded the Friar to take up the purse. The Friar did so tremblingly, being struck with sudden terror as if at the presence of the devil; but in obedience to the command of Francis he stretched out his hand to take the purse, when lo! a large serpent slipped hissing from the bag, thus revealing the diabolical deception to the Friar. The Saint, however, said to him: "Money, my brother, is to the servants of God but the devil and a venomous serpent." [14]

In accordance with this view, Francis embodied the strictest prohibition of money also in his rules. The exact wording in which this prohibition was originally couched, is unknown. The Three Companions state simply that Francis proscribed the acceptance of money in all his rules.[15] But it appears evident from the severe regulations of the rules of 1221 and 1223, that actual conditions made the enforcement of the original prohibition more and more impossible, at least in its full rigor. One feels how strongly ideal and reality conflicted on this point, and how sorely the mind of the Saint was troubled in this regard.

In the rule of 1221, the brothers are enjoined "in no wise to accept money" from the novices, "neither themselves, nor through an intermediate person." [16] They are allowed, however, to "receive for their labor all necessary things, money excepted." [17] Then follows a lengthy chapter with the inscription: "That the Brothers must not receive money." The wording of this chapter is as follows: "The Lord commands in the Gospel: 'Take heed, beware of all malice and avarice, and guard yourselves from the solicitudes of this world, and the cares of this life.' Therefore let none of the brothers, wherever he may be or whithersoever he may go, carry or receive money or coin in any manner, or cause it to be received, either for clothing or for books, or as the price of any labor, or indeed for any reason, except on account of the manifest necessity of the sick brothers. For we ought not to have more use and esteem for money and coin than for stones. And the devil seeks to blind those who desire or value it more than stones. Let us therefore take care, lest, after having left all things, we lose the kingdom of heaven for such a trifle. And if we should chance to find money in any place, let us no more regard it than the dust we tread under foot, for it is 'vanity of vanities, and all is vanity.' And if perchance, which God forbid, it should happen that any brother should collect or have money or coin, except only because of the aforesaid necessity of the sick, let all the brothers hold him for a false brother, a thief, a rob-

ber, and one having a purse, unless he should become truly
penitent. And let the brothers in no wise receive money
for alms or cause it to be received, or money for other
houses or places; nor let them go with any person seeking
money or coin for such places. But the brothers may perform all other services which are not contrary to our life,
with the blessing of God. The brothers may, however,
for the manifest necessity of the lepers ask alms for them.
But let them be very wary of money. But let all the
brothers likewise take heed not to search the world for any
filthy lucre." [18]

From the above, it is obvious that Francis wished to
uphold the prohibition not to accept money in its full
force, "except in case of necessity for the sick brothers."
In this case the brothers are permitted to accept money
personally; and the same permission is granted in favor
of the lepers, with the warning, however, that the brothers
may not collect money for themselves.

Two years later, Francis repeats the regulation forbidding money, in the final rule, in which he says: "I strictly
enjoin on all the brothers that in no wise they receive
money or coins, either themselves or through an intermediate person. Nevertheless, for the necessities of the
sick and for clothing the other brothers, let the ministers
and custodes alone take watchful care through spiritual
friends, according to places and times and cold climates,
as they shall see expedient in the necessity, saving always
that, as has been said, they shall not receive coins or
money." [19]

It will be noticed that in this rule the acceptance and
the use of money is forbidden even in the case for which
an exception was made in the first rule; that is, for the
needs of the sick brothers. But the necessity of caring
for the sick and of providing proper clothing for the Friars
grew more urgent from day to day; and since the needful
articles could be procured only by means of money, the

Ministers are directed in the rule of 1223 to meet these needs by having recourse to the spiritual friends.

This provision of the rule was, however, not sufficiently explicit. The more zealous of the Friars, therefore, requested Pope Gregory IX, the friend of Francis and the co-editor of the rule, to state the exact sense of this regulation. The answer was: The Friars may deposit monetary alms with the spiritual friends, and seek relief in times of need through them; they may even have recourse to these spiritual friends in all cases of necessity, especially if the latter proved careless or ignorant of the needs of the Friars. The spiritual friends, the Pope stated, are not to be regarded as intermediaries of the *Friars* in this case, but of the *benefactors.*[20]

If we compare these regulations of 1221 with those of 1223, it becomes obvious how Francis strove to harmonize the principle of the absolute prohibition of money with the actual conditions of life. These conditions had forced him in 1221 to allow the acceptance of money at least for the proper care of the sick. Nevertheless, the principle involved had thereby suffered a serious infraction; moreover, this exception did not solve the problem, since a great many other needs arose, in particular for the clothing of the Friars, necessitating the use of money. Thus Francis, no doubt with the help of Cardinal Hugolino, who later became Pope Gregory IX, endeavored to solve the problem by permitting the acceptance of money through the spiritual friends. In this manner he was able to uphold the principle at stake, and still make provision for all needs of the Friars.

This solution quieted the Saint, but it did not completely satisfy him. In the first place, it was all too complicated for his simple mind. Then again, he had earnestly desired that the Friars should subsist without the use of money, even if it were procured and disbursed by others. Finally, and this was the weightiest consideration, the question presented itself to him: would it suffice at all times and in all cases, that the spiritual friends accept money "for the needs of the sick and for the clothing of the brothers?" Would not such needs arise that might make it imperative for the Friars to receive and disburse money themselves and for themselves?

Francis rejected this thought resolutely, because he believed himself bound fully to the Gospel. Christ had forbidden the apostles to carry money with them; the only one of their number who did not follow this precept, became a traitor. Francis was deeply convinced that the precept of the Gospel applied to himself and to his Order; and the fate of the traitor was a source of constant terror to him, as we learn from the rule of 1221. But however great our reverence for the Seraphic Saint, we must concede the fact, that in this matter he went beyond the Gospel. The Saviour had indeed forbidden the apostles to carry money with them at the time that He sent them to preach in the neighboring country. But when later He sent them into distant and inhospitable regions where they would be in need of money, He allowed, yes, commanded them to carry a purse and coins.[21]   When He Himself was asked for the coin of tribute at Capharnaum, He procured the necessary money in a miraculous manner, and directed Peter to give it to the authorities.[22]   Judas had indeed become a traitor, but through his own personal greed; he was, however, the lawful treasurer of the apostolic band,[23] appointed to receive and disburse money in favor of the sick, the poor, and for Christ Himself and the apostles, whenever occasion demanded.[24]

Francis himself had experienced that the use of money could at times not be wholly avoided. When about to return to Italy after his first journey to Syria in 1212 or 1213, he begged the crew of a ship to take him on board as a passenger. But the captain of the ship refused to listen to his request, since he lacked the necessary money. Francis and his companion thereupon secreted themselves on the ship, trusting in Divine Providence, and they suc-

ceeded in crossing to Italy as stowaways.[25]   It is obvious
that this procedure cannot be approved by any means, although it can be excused by the good faith of the Friars.
It was but a proof, if such were necessary, that the Friars
could not altogether avoid the use of money under certain
circumstances.

Still more significant is an occurrence which took place
a few months before the death of the Saint.   The missionary Friars, whom he had sent to Morocco, in that
country received no other alms but money, and this they
were forced to accept in order to buy food and clothing.
They applied to the Pope for a solution of this problem
and the latter approved their conduct, saying: "We dispense you from the prohibition of money for the above-
mentioned regions, as long as the necessity exists, on the
condition that you do not allow yourselves to be seduced
by cupidity to misrepresent the actual conditions." [26]

This wise and prudent attitude, assumed during the
lifetime of the Saint by Honorius III, who had approved
the Franciscan rule, is the same attitude taken to-day by
the Church and the Order in this matter.   The dispensation granted by the Church allowing the use of money,
became more frequent, however, in the course of centuries, in consequence of the constantly increasing commercial use of money.   To-day this commercial use has
become so common and so general that the Order simply
could not exist nor carry on its work properly without
such dispensation.   No one deplores this more than the
sons of the Poverello.   Every true Franciscan regards it
as a bitter tribute to the demands of the modern economic
system, as often as he is forced to accept money for his
livelihood, be it in the form of alms, or as a stipend for
his labor.

2. *Labor* is the first source of Franciscan livelihood.
Christ and the apostles had dignified labor by word and
example, and recommended it to their followers.   The
monks and hermits of the first centuries had lived by the

labor of their hands.[27]   Later, when the monasteries already possessed property, St. Augustine testifies that in every well-ordered monastery the day was divided between manual labor, reading, and prayer.[28]   The Patriarch of Western monasticism accordingly later on also prescribed manual labor for certain hours of the day, besides the *opus Dei* (Divine Office) and spiritual reading.[29]   The monk who showed himself careless in his spiritual reading and meditation, or was unfit for it, was directed to occupy himself with manual labor exclusively.[30]

From the eighth to the tenth century, the Benedictine Order became very active in the field of education.   The consequence was that the monks were divided into two groups, the educated *(litterati)*, who devoted themselves to studies, and the uneducated *(illitterati, idiotæ)*, who were occupied with manual labors, in addition, of course, to the religious exercises.   Then followed a period during which the proverbial Benedictine spirit of industry began to decline, both in the field of literature as well as in agriculture; and with this decline the genuine Benedictine spirit also began to wane.   In the twelfth century the Cistercians again resumed activities in both fields of labor, in consequence of a very energetic reform movement. They esteemed it an honor when the monks of Cluny ridiculed them, saying: "What new fashion of monkhood is this, where fields are plowed, forests are cleared, and dung is carried around?"[31]   Their principle was expressed in the answer: "We devote ourselves to agriculture, which God has created and ordained, and labor together, we [the monks] and our brothers [*conversi*] and the day-laborers, each according to his strength."[32]

In the course of time, however, the Cistercians again returned to the division of labor in such wise that the lettered monks devoted themselves to the pursuit of knowledge, while the others shared the labors in field and house with the servants and lay-laborers.[33]

This brief historical review of the evangelical, the apostolical, and the monastic conception of labor is important to understand properly the attitude of the Poverello regarding labor. The example of Christ and of the apostles induced him to encourage manual labor. This all the more, since the ancient monks, the great majority of whom were lay-brothers like the first Franciscans, had always held labor in high esteem. And since manual labor had always been held an obligation for the uneducated monks, Francis also emphasizes the fact that he and the first Friars were simple (unlettered) and subject to others, and for this reason performed manual labor: "We were simple *(idiotæ)* and subject to all. And I worked with my hands, and I wish to work, and I wish firmly that all the other brothers should work at some labor which is compatible with honesty." [34]

Labor, however, among the Friars occupied a position differing from that in the Benedictine Order. The latter worked for the sake of income, and on their own land; the Franciscans, however, not possessing property, worked in order to gain their livelihood, and were therefore forced to seek occupation abroad. In other words Franciscan poverty made labor a necessity. According to medieval ideas, poverty and labor were synonymous. The laborer was necessarily poor, because he received nothing but his bare sustenance for his toil; the poor man was necessarily a laborer, because he could in no other way gain his livelihood. [35] Thus Francis and his first companions, according to all contemporaneous records, appear as poor laborers working for their daily bread.

From the first day of his conversion, Francis devoted himself to the service of the lepers, a service which everyone shunned, and for which even the Saint at first felt a deep repugnance; but by the grace of God it soon became his favorite occupation. [36] Later on, we find him acting as servant in a monastery. Wearing a coarse work-blouse, he performed the hard and humiliating work of a kitchen-boy, receiving as wages only a small portion of soup; this position he was forced to leave because the monks would not even replace the poor garment which robbers had taken from him.[37]

His next occupation was repairing churches, the first one being the Church of San Damiano. The Three Companions relate how he labored and toiled as a mason, almost exhausting the strength of his frail body in this unaccustomed work. But they state also that he tasted fully the nobility and the joy of manual labor, singing French romances at his work, and inviting the passing citizens of Assisi to lend a helping hand.[38]

This love for lowly, but honest labor Francis preserved until the very end, Thomas of Celano declares: "He himself, the model of all perfection, worked and toiled with his hands, and would not allow a particle of the precious gift of time to pass without advantage." [39] Whenever he sojourned in a solitary place, where no occasion for labor offered itself, he would nevertheless endeavor to occupy himself in some way. Thus Celano remarks casually that during the season of Lent Francis carved a small wooden dish, in order to put his free moments to some use.[40] Even a short time before his death, he resolved to do great things with the grace of God, and to place his exhausted body once more in the strenuous service of the lepers, as he had done in the beginning of his conversion.[41]

The first companions of the Poverello were animated by the same spirit. Whenever they assembled at the poor Friary of Portiuncula they immediately put into practise the motto: "Pray and work," in order to ward off idleness, that insidious enemy of the soul.[42] If there was work to be found in the neighboring country, they zealously made use of the opportunity, assisting the poor peasants in their toil, and accepting as reward a piece of bread.[43] During their sojourn at Rivo Torto they likewise busied themselves with various occupations.[44] Though the hut in which they dwelt was hardly fit for habitation, Francis nevertheless chose it because of its very poverty and its nearness to the lepers' hospital, where the Friars could offer their services in ministering to the wants of these unfortunates.[45]

The greater part of the time, however, the brothers journeyed from place to place, as we have seen, finding shelter for the night as Providence directed them, and preaching or otherwise occupying themselves during the day as occasion demanded. Cardinal Jacques de Vitry writes of them in 1216: "By day they come into the cities and villages to win others by their preaching, and rendering other services; at night they return to a hermitage or some solitary spot to meditate." [46] Thomas of Celano likewise says: "They are not concerned in the least for their nightly shelter. Frequently they had none, and passed the nights in ovens, or grottoes, or caves. By day, those who were able, labored in the lepers' hospitals or other places, serving everyone humbly and devoutly. They would never accept work which might cause scandal, but always performed holy and just, honest and useful labors, thereby giving an example of humility and patience." [47]

Among the early Franciscan documents, the life of Blessed Giles is most explicit regarding the life of the first Friars. Wherever Giles happened to stay with his companions, he sought an opportunity for work. He hired himself as a day-laborer, yet so that several hours of the day were reserved for his devotions, and in particular for the Divine Office.[48] At work he always showed great cheerfulness and alacrity.[49]

Any occupation, however lowly, was welcome to him, as long as it was honest.[50] At Fabriano, in the March of Ancona, whither he had been sent by Francis in 1214, Giles made containers for drinking vessels, rush baskets and similar articles, carrying them to the city to be sold, and accepting in return anything they needed in the form of food or clothing. So diligently did he labor that he

received enough in return to clothe another Friar, poorer
than himself.[51]   A year later he made a pilgrimage to
Palestine.   While waiting for the ship at Brindisi, he
procured a water-jug, and began to peddle water about
the town, accepting in payment whatever he and his companion were in need of for their livelihood.   On the return
journey, while detained for some days at St. Jean d'Acre,
in Syria, he procured the necessary food by making rush
baskets, and by carrying the dead to the cemetery.   When
such means failed him, he had recourse "to the table of the
Lord," begging alms from door to door.[52]

During a subsequent sojourn at Rome, Giles lived as
usual by the labor of his hands.   After attending Mass
early in the morning, he would go to a wood about eight
miles from the city, and having gathered a bundle of
fuel, would carry it back and exchange it for bread
and other things useful for the life of the body.   One
day he thus met a woman who wished to buy some
wood.   Having come to an agreement, she tried to pay
him more than the bargain called for, having recognized
in him a Religious.   But Giles answered: "I do not wish
to be overcome by avarice," and he not only refused to
accept her offering, but returned half of the stipulated
price.

When the time of vintage arrived, Giles helped to
gather grapes for the peasants, and trod them in the
winepress.   At one time he met a man on the road who
wished to engage someone to beat down nuts from a
walnut tree.   But he could find no one willing to do
so, because the tree was so tall and hard to climb, and
far from Rome.   Giles himself offered to help, agreeing to
accept a share of the nuts in return for his labor.   Having arrived at the place, he signed himself with the cross,
bravely climbed the tree, and struck down the nuts.   The
share of these, however, which fell to his lot was so
great that his pocket would not hold them, so taking off
his habit, and tying the hood and arms, he made a sack

of it to hold the nuts. On his way back to the Friary he distributed them to the poor.

When the corn was being cut, Giles went with the other poor into the field to glean the ears. If anyone offered him a sheaf, he refused to take it, saying: "I have no granary in which I could store it." The ears which he had gathered himself, he gave to the poor.

While staying with the monks at the monastery of Santi Quattro, near the Lateran, the baker sought someone to clean the flour. Giles heard of this, and offered his services, agreeing to take seven loaves of bread for each three measures of meal which he cleaned. He also drew water for the monks from the fountain of San Sisto, helped in baking, and received in return several loaves of bread.[53] Some time later, he was the guest of Cardinal Nicholas of Tusculum at Rieti. At the instant urging of the Cardinal, he agreed to dine with him, but made the stipulation that he be allowed to earn his own bread. He went to work daily, helped in gathering olives, and turned his hand to whatever work he happened to find. When he sat down to dine, he brought the bread which he had earned in the sweat of his brow. Once he was kept indoors because of stormy weather, so he spent his time sweeping the house and polishing rusty or soiled knives, accepting a few loaves of bread as payment. At the approach of Lent he took leave of his host, in order to pass the holy season in solitude with his companions. Seized with admiration as well as sympathy, the Cardinal exclaimed: "Whither are you going? You wander as the birds, who have no nest." [54]

In view of the foregoing we understand clearly the chapter of the rule of 1221: "Of the manner of serving and working." This chapter reads: "Let the brothers in whatever place they may be among others to serve or to work, not be chamberlains, nor cellarers, nor overseers in the houses of those whom they serve, and let them not accept any employment which might cause scandal or be injurious to the soul, but let them be inferior and subject to all who are in the house. And let the brothers who know how to work, labor and exercise themselves in that art they may understand, if it be not contrary to the salvation of their soul, and they can exercise it becomingly. For the prophet says: 'For thou shalt eat the labor of thy hands; blessed art thou and it shall be well with thee'; [55] and the Apostle: 'If any man will not work, neither let him eat.' And let every man 'abide in the art or employment wherein he was called.' [56] And for their labor they may receive all necessary things, except money. And if they be in want, let them seek for alms like other brothers. And they may have the tools and implements necessary for their work. Let all brothers apply themselves with diligence to good works, for it is written: 'Be always busy in some good work, that the devil may find thee occupied'; [57] and again: 'Idleness is the enemy of the soul.' [58] Therefore, the servants of God ought always to continue in prayer or in some other good work." [59]

Francis here speaks, in the first place, of the brothers who are employed as servants or day-laborers: they may hire themselves for work, on condition that they accept no position as master, nor any work which might cause scandal or might be injurious to the soul. In the next place, he speaks of skilled laborers, or artisans: they should remain true to their trade, even after entering the fraternity; for that reason they may have the necessary tools and implements; they may accept all things needful for their livelihood, money excepted; if these be withheld, they should go in quest of alms like the other brothers. The Saint finally admonishes the "other" brothers, who work neither as laborers nor as artisans, to apply themselves in some useful occupation, even if it be for the sole purpose of not remaining idle.

This regulation reflects accurately the attitude and the practise of the first Franciscans. We have made it sufficiently clear that the first Friars earned their livelihood when not occupied in preaching, by being employed among the lay-people as servants, day-laborers or artisans; whenever they withdrew to a hermitage or some other place for a brief time, they sought to be actively and usefully engaged in some other work. Consequently, it is evident that the chapter on the manner of working was embodied in the rule before 1221; indeed, far from being an addition to the rule of 1221, it in fact no longer corresponded with the conditions prevailing at that time. Two years later, these new conditions necessitated the incorporation of the following chapter in the final rule, in place of the one contained in the rule of 1221:

"Let those brothers to whom the Lord has given the grace of working, labor faithfully and devoutly so that in banishing idleness, the enemy of the soul, they do not extinguish the spirit of holy prayer and devotion, to which all temporal things must be subservient. They may, however, receive as the reward of their labor, the things needful for the body for themselves and for their brothers, with the exception of coins or money, and that humbly, as befits the servants of God and the followers of most holy poverty." [60]   Entirely in accord with this chapter is the admonition of the Saint in his Testament: "I wish firmly that all the brothers should work at some labor which is compatible with honesty. Let those who know not [how to work] learn, not through desire to receive the price of labor, but for the sake of example, and to repel idleness. And when the price of labor is not given us, let us have recourse to the table of the Lord, begging alms from door to door." [61]

Since 1223, therefore, the regulations regarding the work among lay-people are omitted: there is no mention whatever made of serving, of day-labor, or of trades; there is simply a regulation regarding labor in general, and in such manner that not only manual labor, but also the pursuit of studies is included in the scope of the rule.[62]

A radical change has evidently taken place. How can it be accounted for?

The transition from the former wandering mode of life to the settled living in Friaries, which took place since 1219, was accompanied also by a change in the conditions of labor. Henceforth the brothers restricted their work almost entirely to the houses of the Order. This was the natural result of the decree of Honorius III, prescribing a year of probation for the aspirants of the Order, and forbidding the professed brothers to wander about freely.[63] The consequence was a crisis in the labor question. The great majority of the Friars at that time were unlettered (*illitterati, nescientes litteras, idiotæ, laici*).[64] These were limited exclusively to manual labor; they were forbidden, according to the will of the Founder, to study or even to learn the Psalter.[65] Most of them were not fitted to devote themselves to a life of constant prayer. The work which the Friars might be called upon to do for people in the world, was no doubt not very plentiful; in fact, this kind of work no longer was of any consequence.[66] The domestic tasks within the small and poor dwellings likewise did not suffice to keep all the Friars busy. Indeed, before 1240 there did not even exist a vegetable garden which the Friars could have cultivated! [67]

Thus a very real danger existed that the lay-brothers fall a prey to idleness. It is not without reason that in his rules and in his Testament Francis warned so emphatically against idleness.[68] In this regard he showed the utmost severity, declaring that the Friars who were remiss in their duty to occupy themselves with diligence, would soon be spit out of the mouth of God. He could not bear to see anyone idle without rebuking him severely. He would then say: "I wish that all my brothers should work and exercise themselves, and that those who know not how to work, should learn a trade, lest we become a burden to men, and heart and tongue be seduced through idleness to sinful things." [69]

Thomas of Celano, who has preserved for us this exhortation of the Saint, nevertheless was forced to exclaim some twenty years later: "Permit me, holy Father, to cry out to thee in heaven over those who should be thine. Many to whom the exercise of virtue is repugnant, wish to rest before ever working, and thus prove themselves sons of Lucifer and not of Francis. We have an abundance of weaklings instead of valiant fighters, although they, born to labor, ought to regard their life as a warfare. It suits them not to lead an active life, and for the contemplative they are not fit. Having perplexed others with their vagaries, they work more with their throats than with their hands; they become hostile to those who punish them as superiors, and do not let themselves be touched with the point of a finger. According to the word of Francis, I marvel more at their impudence, since at home they would be obliged to live by the sweat of their brow, and now they live without work, and thrive on the sweat of the poor. Strange prudence! for though they do nothing, yet they always seem occupied. They never miss the time to eat, and if hunger seizes them, they accuse the sun of having slept. Should I, esteemed Father, regard these monsters as worthy of thy glory? No, not even of thy habit! Thou hast ever taught during this short and fleeting life, to acquire a treasure of merits, so that we be not forced to go begging in the world to come. They, however, have now no share in the heavenly fatherland, and afterward they shall be sent into exile. This great evil exists among the subjects, because the superiors act as if they should not later share in the punishment of those whose laziness they tolerate." [70]

In these words the earliest biographer of Francis describes the sad condition resulting from the preponderance of lay-brothers, who lacked the opportunity, and frequently the good will, to work. Fortunately the only effective remedy soon appeared: increase of the clerics and priests in proportion to the number of lay-brothers. Not many years after the death of the Saint this change in the personnel had developed to such an extent that the Minister General, Elias of Cortona, was able to obtain a majority of votes only by employing high-handed methods against the clerics.[71] A little later, St. Bonaventure declared: "To manual labor are bound the healthy and strong brothers, who in the world gained their livelihood by such work, and of these the number was much larger in the beginning of the Order; now, however, their number is much smaller in comparison to the others." [72] This smaller number had at that time, and to-day also, the worthy and meritorious vocation to perform the various tasks in the house and garden, to nurse the sick, to go in quest of alms; in a word, to make it possible for the clerics or educated Friars *(Fratres litterati)* to devote themselves without hindrance to their studies.[73]

It was taken for granted that the educated Friars were not bound to perform manual labor.[74] As the Seraphic Doctor expounds at length, mental labor demands the intensive employment of all human faculties.[75] Such labor is furthermore more precious and profitable than any form of manual labor.[76] For this very reason, it may lay claim with greater justice to a decent livelihood.[77] Indeed, mental labor is in general the most perfect manner of gaining a livelihood, since mechanical labor can be properly compensated, while spiritual labors cannot be measured by the standard of ordinary values.[78]

This held force all the more since the labor of the educated Friars in all its forms served the true and foremost purpose of the Order—the apostolate. The younger clerics devoted themselves to their studies with the express purpose of fitting themselves for their later activity as preachers.[79] As soon as they had proved their fitness, they were employed, for the most part, in apostolic labors, and continued to do so until the end. A smaller number devoted their efforts to the office of teaching and writing.

The office of teaching, also, was an apostolate in the fullest sense of the term, since its object was the training of future apostles; it stood in unbroken and intimate contact with the office of preaching; it was, in fact, an uninterrupted preaching of the word of God.[80] The same was true, according to the ideal conception of the Middle Ages, of the office of writing. "As many books as we write," remarks a contemporaneous author, "so many heralds of truth we send forth, and we hope to be rewarded by the Lord for all those who are cured of error by means of them, or are strengthened in the Catholic Faith, and no less for all who repent of their sins and vices, and are inflamed with a desire for the Heavenly Fatherland." [81]   Thus, all the spiritual labors of the educated Friars find their fullest and highest expression in the apostolate.

For this reason these labors gave not only a valid, but also an evangelical title to a livelihood. At the mission of the apostles the Saviour had said: "The workman is worthy of his meat." [82]   Those who received the word of God from their mouth, should also in return give them their sustenance.[83]   That was the motto and norm followed by the Saviour Himself and the apostles.[84]   St. Paul likewise appeals to this law: "Have we not power to eat and to drink? . . . Who serveth as soldier at any time at his own charges? Who planteth a vineyard, and eateth not of the fruit thereof? Who feedeth the flock, and eateth not of the milk thereof? . . . If we have sown unto you spiritual things, is it a great matter if we reap your carnal things? . . . So also the Lord ordained that they who preach the Gospel, should live by the Gospel." [85]

Francis was so clearly conscious of this divine ordinance, that when Innocent III expressed his fears for the proper livelihood of the Friars, he exclaimed: "If God gives temporal things to sinners for love of their children who must be nourished, how much more will He grant them to evangelical men, to whom they are justly due." [86]   In accordance with this view, the Saint wished that the clerics of the Order, whose lifework was the apostolate, should devote themselves exclusively to their studies and that they should not be hampered in this work by any other occupation.[87]

One occupation was indeed to hold rank over all others—prayer. "The brothers," thus Francis directs in his final rule, "to whom the Lord has given the grace to work, should labor faithfully and devoutly, so that in banishing idleness, the enemy of the soul, they do not extinguish the spirit of holy prayer and devotion, to which all temporal things must be subservient." [88]   In fact, prayer is the highest form of mental and corporal labor, since it places not only reason, will and heart in the service of God, but also the bodily senses and faculties.   For this reason it is the most important work of charity rendered by the Friar to humanity, and therefore gives him a valid and full claim upon a livelihood.

3. However plain it may have been that the Friars were to gain their livelihood by their labors, yet on the other hand—an apparent contradiction—they were to depend solely upon *alms*.   It is obvious that the Friars living in the monastery were dependent on alms whether they performed mental or manual labor, since they received no return for their labor from the world, and since the monastery had no income whatever from property. But even the Friars who were active in the apostolate outside the monastery, were totally dependent on alms.   For though the servants of the altar and of the Gospel should live by the altar and the Gospel, according to St. Paul, nevertheless their support was always regarded in the Church as a work of Christian charity.   In fact, even the Friars who were employed as servants and laborers, were not to demand a return for their labor as a matter of justice, but accept it as alms, if offered freely to them; if refused, they were to "beg from door to door" for their daily food.[89]

In the Middle Ages this mode of life, dependent on alms, was designated as the state of *mendicatio*, or *mendicitas*, and the Religious living on alms were called "mendicants." This term, however, was not used in the stricter sense, nor did it have the unpleasant savor which is associated with the common term "begging" in our days; it denoted simply the state of life depending on charity, whether this were offered voluntarily, or were asked for the love of God. St. Bonaventure defines *paupertas quoad mendicitatem*, or *mendicare pro Christo* thus: *Voco mendicare eleemosynam quærere seu de quotidianis eleemosynis vivere.*" [90] In these words the Seraphic Doctor points out the essential and yet very unessential difference which exists between the secular clerics and monks on the one hand, and the mendicants on the other. Both live on alms he explains, since the possessions of churches and of abbeys are also alms of the poor.[91] Secular clerics and monks, however, live on ample and large alms, offered and invested in the form of endowments;[92] while the mendicants content themselves with the daily and poor offerings of charity.[93]

That this mode of life alone was in perfect harmony with the ideal poverty of the Gospel, was self-evident to Francis. It was based on the words of Christ: "Do not possess gold, nor silver, nor money in your purses, nor scrip on the way, nor two coats, nor shoes, nor a staff: for the workman is worthy of his meat." [94] According to this basic principle of Gospel poverty, the apostles were to go forth to preach the word of God, despoiled of all, and depending solely on the generosity of those to whom they announced the glad tidings. Christ Himself had preceded them with His sublime example, living on alms Himself during His public life.[95] No doubt, therefore, if Francis wished to observe poverty in all its perfection after the example of Christ and His apostles, he would live like them on alms offered by charity.[96]

In fact, Francis did not hesitate a moment to make

this mode of life his own. Indeed, he preferred alms
that had been begged, to those that had been offered
voluntarily.[97] Only this could satisfy his desire to mortify
himself for love of his Lady Poverty. He realized that
self-denial could reach no higher point than when he
begged his daily bread from door to door for the sake of
his Beloved.[98] One glance at his prime favorites, the
poor, proved that in this manner alone he could be really
and truly poor. The most needy among them, the beggars,
lived on alms. Having vowed rigid poverty for the love
of Christ, he also must needs beg alms for the love of
Christ, and thus become poor not only in spirit, but also
in fact and deed.[99] He was to be, and wished to be,
poor as a beggar, asking alms like them *"per amore di
Dio."* [100]

Francis made the first attempt while yet in the world,
as soon as he had come to know by divine inspiration
that he was to choose Lady Poverty as his bride. His
earnest wish was then to be in some strange city, unknown to all, and to exchange his garments for the rags
of a beggar and to beg alms for the love of God. He had
occasion to do this shortly after, while on a pilgrimage
to Rome.[101]

After he had betrothed himself to Lady Poverty forever, his first step was to devote his strength and energy
to the repairing of the Church of San Damiano. He
begged the materials in Assisi, going from street to street
and calling out: "Who giveth one stone, shall receive a
single reward; who giveth two stones, a twofold; who
giveth three stones, a threefold." The priest at San
Damiano provided his daily food, but when Francis became aware that the good priest was anxious to set healthy
and savory food before him, he began to ponder and said
to himself: "Wilt thou always find a priest who will show
thee such charity? That is not the life of the poor which
thou hast chosen; but go rather as a beggar from door
to door, with a dish in thy hand, and gather therein the

remains of food. Joyfully and willingly shalt thou live thus for love of Him who was born poor, lived as the poorest of the poor in this world, hung naked and poor on the cross, and was buried in the grave of a stranger." And taking a dish, he went into the city, begging alms from door to door. But when he was about to eat the remains of food all mixed in the dish, he was seized with an almost unconquerable disgust, for he was not accustomed even to look upon such a mixture, much less to eat it. After a brief struggle, however, he overcame his disgust, and while eating the food, it seemed to him that he had never before tasted such dainty morsels. At the same time he rejoiced exceedingly in the Lord, so that his body also, although feeble and exhausted, was strengthened to bear all painful and bitter things for the Lord. He therefore thanked the Lord, who had changed the bitter into sweetness, and had thus wonderfully refreshed him. And he requested the good priest of San Damiano to prepare food for him no longer, nor to have others prepare it for him.[102]

When his father, Peter Bernardone, beheld him in this state of extreme poverty, he was seized with chagrin and rage, and cursed him. Francis, however, paid no attention to these outbursts, but chose a poor old man to be his father, and said to him: "Come with me, and I shall share with thee the alms which are given me. As often as thou hearest my father curse me, thou shalt sign me with the cross and bless me in his stead." [103]

At one time, while begging in the streets of Assisi, he chanced to pass a house where a company of men were engaged in a game of chance. Fearing that perhaps some of his former comrades might be among the number, he was ashamed to appear before them as a beggar, and passed on. But he had hardly gone a few steps, when he began to rue his cowardice. He returned hastily to the house, and confessed humbly before the whole company that he had been ashamed to beg in their presence.

Then, using the French tongue, he began to ask alms for the love of God.[104]

Whenever he was invited by wealthy people to a sumptuous table, he went about it in such manner that he should not offend his Lady Poverty. He would go and beg a few crusts of bread in other houses, and with these return to the table, rich in all his poverty.[105] One day he was the guest of Cardinal Hugolino, the later Pope Gregory IX. When the hour to sup approached, the Saint hurried away, and on his return he placed several pieces of bread, which he had begged in the meantime, on the table of the Cardinal. When the latter became aware of this, he was greatly embarrassed on account of the guests whom he had invited. Francis, however, beaming with joy, began to distribute the morsels of bread among the dignitaries and nobles, all of whom accepted them with great reverence; some ate them, others took them as keepsakes. After the repast Hugolino arose, called the man of God to himself, embraced him, and said: "My brother, why hast thou dishonored me and my house, which belongs to thee and the Friars, by going about asking for alms?" The Saint replied: "My lord, I have thus greatly honored thee, inasmuch as I have honored a Lord greater than thou. For the Lord delighteth in poverty, and more than all in that beggary which is embraced for love of Christ. Nor will I lay aside that regal dignity which Our Lord Jesus Christ assumed when He became poor that He might enrich us by His poverty." And he added: "I feel more consoled, both in body and soul, when I sit with the poor at their table and see before me the poor alms which they have gathered for the love of God, than when I am seated at tables that are spread with rich viands in abundance and manifold variety." At these words the Cardinal was greatly edified, and he said to Francis: "My son, do whatever seems best in thy eyes, for truly God is with thee, and thou with Him." [106]

It was his constant practise, when opportunity offered, to go begging on the principal feasts, saying that in holy poverty the prophetic words are fulfilled: "Man shall eat the Bread of Angels." "Bread of Angels," remarks the Seraphic Doctor, "Francis justly calls that which is asked for the love of God, and, by the suggestion of the angels, is given by the charity of those at whose doors it is begged by Holy Poverty." [107]

In the beginning the Saint was wont to go alone in quest of alms, out of loving regard for the timidity of the first disciples.[108] He was, however, unable to perform this arduous task for a long time, his health being of a delicate nature and broken with incessant toil and penance. The other Friars furthermore were likewise called to a life of poverty, although they did not seem to realize this, since no one offered himself to assist in this laborious task.[109]

Francis therefore endeavored to encourage them prudently and kindly to take this burden upon themselves. "He called the shame which made them recoil from begging, the enemy of salvation, but the feeling of shame while actually begging, he regarded as holy fear. He would praise the Friar when the blush of shame rose on his brow while begging, but rebuked him when he allowed himself to be overcome by it." [110]

"The brothers," thus the Saint admonishes, "shall not be ashamed to go for alms, but rather remember that Our Lord Jesus Christ, the Son of the living and omnipotent God, set His face [in disgrace] as a hard rock.[111] He was poor and a stranger, and lived on alms, He Himself and the Blessed Virgin and His disciples. And when men treat the brothers with contempt and refuse to give them alms, let them give thanks for this to God, because for these shames they shall receive great honor before the tribunal of Our Lord Jesus Christ. And let them know that the injuries shall not be imputed to those who suffer them, but to those who offer them. And alms is an in-

heritance and a right which is due to the poor, which Our
Lord Jesus Christ purchased for us. And the brothers
who labor in seeking it, will have a great recompense, and
they will procure and acquire a reward for those who
give; for all that men leave in this world shall perish, but
for the charity and almsdeeds they have done, they will
receive a reward from God." [112]

Often he would encourage the Friars to go in quest of
alms by such words as these: "Go forth, for the Friars
Minor have been given in these last days to the world
that the elect by their means may obtain the praise of the
great Judge and hear those most sweet words: 'Inasmuch
as you have done it to the least of these My brethren,
you have done it unto Me.' Mark well: the least of these
My brethren, *Fratribus Minoribus*. Thus the Divine
Prophet has expressly announced and privileged our
Order. It is a joyful thing to beg under the name of a
Friar Minor, seeing that it is the very name uttered by
the mouth of the Master of evangelical truth when He
spoke of the reward of the just." [113]

When some of the Friars who were of noble rank
failed to recognize their calling and their duty to beg
alms, Francis added the following admonition with truly
fatherly love: "My dearest brothers, the Son of God, who
made Himself poor in this world for our sake, was of
nobler rank than we. For love of Him we have chosen
poverty; let us not then be ashamed to go for alms.
It is not meet that the heirs of the kingdom of heaven
blush for the pledge of their heavenly inheritance. I
say to you that many noble and wise men will join our
fraternity and will deem it an honor to beg alms. You,
however, who are the first of them, be glad and rejoice,
and refuse not to do that, which you are to transmit to
them for imitation." [114]

This admonition was all the more necessary because
of the unfriendly reception which they met at first. In
Assisi they knocked almost everywhere in vain. In place

of alms they received coarse insults; they were told that they had surrendered their own property only to live on that of others. Their own relatives persecuted them relentlessly. The people regarded them as idiots or insane. It was simply something unheard of in those days, that anyone should strip himself of all things for love of God, and beg alms from door to door.[115]

The Friars fared no better when they appeared elsewhere for the first time. When several of them were on their way to Germany, they stopped near Salzburg, and went forth in pairs to beg something to eat, for their hunger was extreme. But at every door they were greeted with the words: "God forbid!" Finally one of the Friars remarked good-humoredly: "This 'God forbid' will yet kill us to-day." Being somewhat of a wit, when they were greeted at the next house with 'God forbid!' he acted as if he did not understand German, sat down upon a bench, and cheerfully got ready for a meal. The peasant and his wife laughingly looked at each other, and finally gave the impertinent beggar bread, eggs and milk. When the Friar noticed that by this innocent stratagem he should be able to relieve the needs of the other Friars, he repeated it at the next twelve houses, until he had received sufficient supplies for the others.[116]

Francis no doubt enjoyed this innocent prank as much as the others when he heard of it, for that was exactly the spirit which he wished his brothers to possess. He himself was never so full of joy than when he saw them go in search of alms in a cheerful mood, and return as cheerfully. One day—it was in the beginning of the Order—several Friars returned from their begging near Assisi. Each one presented his prize to Francis, happy when the Saint expressed his satisfaction. They then teased each other gaily, one saying to the other: "I have captured more alms than thou." Francis rejoiced greatly at this, and from that day everyone gladly asked leave to go and beg for alms.[117]

Another time Francis was staying at St. Mary of Portiuncula, when one of the Friars returned from Assisi, carrying his beggar's sack, and singing loudly and gaily. When Francis saw him, he hastened to him full of joy, and kissed him on the shoulder where the sack was lying. He then relieved him of his burden, and carried it into the Friars' dwelling, exclaiming: "Blessed be my brother, who goes forth willingly, begs humbly, and returns joyfully!" [118]

Francis recognized herein the token of the genuine spirit of the Order. For this reason he declared that a Friar Minor should not tarry long before going in search of alms. "The nobler my son is," he added, "the more willingly should he undertake this task, for by so doing he adds merit upon merit." [119]   When the Friars were at Rivo Torto, thus relates Thomas of Celano, there was among their number one who counted as naught when begging alms, but for several when eating. As soon as the Saint heard of his conduct, and saw that this Friar was living on the labor of others, but would not work himself, he said to him: "Brother Fly, go thy way, since thou consumest the labor of others and art slothful in the work of the Lord. Thou art like the barren and idle drone, who earns nothing and does not work, but consumes the honey of the working bee." At these words the carnal-minded man returned to the world, which he had not sincerely left. He left the Order; "for he who counted as naught in begging alms, was no longer a Friar," remarks Celano.[120]

But in spite of his deep esteem for alms and mendicancy, Francis wished in no wise to plead the cause of lazy and covetous beggary.

That *covetous* beggary should have no place in the Franciscan household, was obvious from the admonition of the Saviour: "Be not solicitous for to-morrow, for the morrow will be solicitous for itself." [121]   Francis considered this Gospel axiom as an essential element of true poverty. He time and again called the attention of the brothers to it.[122] So deeply imbued was he with the importance of this axiom that he forbade the brother cook to steep in warm water the day before,[123] the vegetables which were to be served the following day. Cardinal Jacques de Vitry (1223-1226) and the Benedictine Prior Roger of Wendover (1219-1235) state expressly that the Friars did not keep food of any kind until the following day, in order that poverty, which they observed in spirit, should also be manifest in deed and example.[124] Brother Leo adds that in many places the Friars never accepted more than was necessary for the day, especially in cities, where the needful alms could always be procured.[125]

This, of course, could not be observed at all times and in all places. Jordan of Giano relates that the Chapter of the Mats had to be prolonged for two days because a large amount of bread and wine was still on hand for the capitulars, who numbered three thousand.[126] St. Bonaventure does not hesitate to say: "If we consider the Gospel closely, it is clear that it forbids us to be *solicitous,* but not *provident* for the morrow. Solicitude denotes anxious care, as well as the illicit procuring and greedy storing up of superfluous things. For just as we should put our ·hope in the Lord in matters of salvation,[127] so we should also leave the care for our bodily sustenance to Him, but so that we provide the needful things, inasfar as it can be done without injury to our spiritual welfare, and not tempt God to procure our daily food in a miraculous manner. Although, therefore, the first Friars out of zeal for higher perfection were wont to gather less alms than is done now, it was nevertheless not forbidden then, nor is now, to think of the future and to provide the necessary things for a certain time, in particular those things which we cannot beg when we are in need of them." [128]

But in no case would Francis allow the Friars to accept more alms than was necessary. He repeatedly said to the Friars: "Let us not act like thieves in asking for or accepting alms beyond what is necessary. I have always taken less than I needed, that the other poor might not be defrauded of their portion; to do otherwise would be dishonest." [129] Even while accepting necessary alms, he looked more to the spiritual welfare of the donors than to the needs of his own body. For whether accepting alms or giving them, he always edified others by his example.[130]

Francis debarred not only by covetous beggary, but no less *lazy* beggary. This is evident if we consider his attitude toward the question of labor. The Friars were to obtain their livelihood by diligent and prayerful labor, if possible. They were to have recourse to begging only, if they received no return for their labor, or if no occasion to work offered itself.

The life of Blessed Giles illustrates this principle most strikingly. He made it a point never to go for alms unless unable to earn his daily bread. He considered himself bound to this course by the express command of St. Francis.[131] The latter allowed begging only in case of necessity, according to the earlier rule: "When it may be necessary, let them go for alms." [132]

That this necessity arose often enough, is obvious if we consider the rigid poverty of the Friars and the fact that they directed their efforts more to preaching than to manual labor.[133] As soon as the Order was established in fixed houses, we find that the Friars no longer worked for wages among the people, and that the occasion for work within the houses themselves was anything but abundant. For this reason Francis commends begging in more general terms in the rule of 1223: "Let the brothers go confidently in quest of alms, nor ought they be ashamed, because Lord made Himself poor for us in this world. This, my dearest brothers, is the height of the most sublime poverty, which has made you heirs and kings of the kingdom of heaven." [134]

Toward the end of the Saint's life, wage-earning on the

part of the Friars had practically ceased to be a factor. To some Friars it therefore seemed that labor as such had lost its importance, and thus the danger was imminent that the Friars might lapse into a life of lazy beggary. Francis warns strongly against such a life in his Testament: "I worked with my hands and I wish to work, and I wish firmly that all the other brothers should work at some labor which is compatible with honesty. Let those who know not [how to work] learn, not through desire to receive the price of labor, but for the sake of example and to repel idleness. And when the price of labor is not given us, let us have recourse to the table of the Lord, begging alms from door to door." [135] The further development of conditions brought it to pass that the Friars, however diligently they occupied themselves with manual or spiritual labor, were soon forced to depend upon alms as the only source of livelihood.

In this connection a comparison between the Franciscan Order and the other mendicants who lived prior to the time of Francis, will not be out of place. From the fourth century on, we meet frequently with monks who made begging a business, both from greed and from laziness. St. Paulinus of Nola scourges them in the sarcastic verses:

> "Qualia vagari per mare et terras solent
>   Avara mendicabula,
> Qui deierando monachos se vel naufragos,
>   Nomen casumque venditant." [136]

St. Augustine describes in scathing terms the idleness and greed of these monks more explicitly in the work *De opere monachorum,* in which we read: "By virtue of his extreme deceitfulness the enemy has scattered many hypocrites under the garb of monks, hypocrites who wander about the provinces, sent nowhere, settled nowhere, quiet nowhere. Some have relics of martyrs for sale, if they be such; others boast of their lappets and tassels after the manner of the Pharisees; others state deceitfully that they have heard of their parents and other relatives living in this or that country, and that they wish to visit them, and all of them seek, all beg either the luxury of greedy poverty, or the price of a hypocritical piety." [137]   It is obvious that Francis and his disciples were the very contrary of these notorious beggar monks.

At the beginning of the thirteenth century the "Catholic Poor Men" resolved, following the example of the Waldenses, to live solely on the charity of the faithful, so as not to be hampered in their apostolic labors by the necessity of earning their livelihood. [138]   Several years later (1216), the Canon-Regular Dominic also chose this mode of life.   But he, as well as his Order, was actuated likewise in choosing mendicity by the desire to enjoy full freedom in the pursuit of study and in preaching.   They became mendicant Friars not from love of poverty, but for the sake of the apostolate. [139]

Francis had also been actuated by the same motive in embracing a life of absolute poverty.   We have adduced sufficient proof for this, and in 1219 Honorius III declared it expressly: "Francis and his companions have renounced all vain things of this world in order to scatter everywhere the seed of the word of God after the manner of the apostles." [140]   The apostolate, however, was neither the sole, nor the principal purpose which determined the Poverello to choose a life based on begging.   His determination sprang, in the first place, from his love of poverty, and from the desire to follow the Saviour in the most perfect manner.   This is obvious from what has been said on this subject in the foregoing pages, and is emphasized again by Honorius III: "The Friars Minor imitate Christ in leaving all things, becoming poor for love of Him, and living in perpetual poverty." [141]   St. Bonaventure [142] treats at length of this twofold purpose of Franciscan mendication.   The Friars, he explains, live on alms to preach Christ as well as to imitate Christ. "To preach Christ, *pro Christo evangelizando*": they place their word, their service, their strength, their entire selves in the service of the Gospel, and are justified thereby in expecting material alms of those to whom they give spiritual alms. "To imitate Christ, *pro Christo imitando*": whoever becomes a beggar for love of Christ, imitates the Saviour by self-contempt, humbling himself most deeply; by charity toward his neighbor, whom he edifies and moves to compassion; by loyalty to God, whom he serves with unshackled devotion, unburdened by earthly cares.[143] By giving the world this threefold good example, the Friars obtain a right to alms in greater measure.[144] St. Francis therefore said repeatedly: "There exists an agreement between the world and the Friars: these owe the world a good example; the world owes them a livelihood. If the Friars turn away from poverty, the world will turn away from them; they shall seek and not find. If they, however, remain true to my Lady Poverty, the world will sustain them, for they are given for the salvation of the world." [145]

The mainspring, however, of the Poverello's assurance for the livelihood of the Friars was his supreme and unshakable *trust in Divine Providence*. This trust at the same time is the solution of the problem of Franciscan economics. The living faith of the Poverello in Divine Providence—that, and that only, is the solution of the problem.

The Saviour Himself had placed His whole life in the providence of His heavenly Father, and in all earthly things He beheld forever new revelations of divine bounty. It was this way of childlike trust which He pointed out to His disciples, and time and again He preached to them the Gospel of Providence in the most impressive manner: "Are not five sparrows sold for two farthings, and not one of them is forgotten before God? Fear not, therefore: you are of more value than many sparrows. Yea,

156 THE IDEALS OF ST. FRANCIS

the very hairs of your head are numbered. . . . [146] Therefore I say to you: be not solicitous for your life, what
you shall eat; nor for your body what you shall put on.
The life is more than the meat, and the body is more than
the raiment. Consider the ravens, for they sow not,
neither do they reap, neither have they storehouse or
barn, and God feedeth them. How much are you more
valuable than they? Consider the lilies how they grow:
they labor not, neither do they spin. But I say to you, not
even Solomon in all his glory was clothed like one of
these. Now, if God clothe in this manner the grass that
is to-day in the field, and to-morrow is cast in the oven,
how much more you, O ye of little faith?" [147]

Francis accepted and understood this Gospel of trust
in God with the same childlike and literal faith as the
Gospel of poverty. His absolute poverty, the poverty of
a beggar, was in the last instance but the echo of his living
faith in Divine Providence. To him God was in reality
the Father of all, who embraces all His creatures in loving
care, and provides for all their needs. And the more
completely the creature strips itself of all earthly things
for love of God, the more lovingly God provides for it.
God is therefore the Father and Provider of the evangelical poor. This certainly came to Francis at the moment when he renounced the world; he was completely
conquered by it when he returned all, even his clothes,
to his father, Peter Bernardone, and exclaimed: "Henceforth I shall say: Our Father who are in heaven!" [148]
This carefree trust in the fatherly love of God accompanied the Saint from this moment to the end of his
life. It was the only treasure which he entrusted to his
disciples on their way through life.

Thomas of Celano relates how Francis equipped his
first disciples for their missionary journeys. After in-
structing them on the kingdom of God, the contempt of
the world, the denial of self-will, and the subjugation
of the body, he said to them: "Go, most beloved brothers,

two by two into all quarters of the globe, and preach to all men peace and penance unto the remission of sins. Be patient in tribulations and firmly convinced that God will keep His promise." He then embraced them, and spoke meekly and humbly to each: "Cast thy care upon the Lord and He will nourish thee." [149] While they went forth in all directions, he himself with Brother Masseo set out for France. The *Fioretti* tells us of his deep faith in Divine Providence, in one of those chapters redolent with that delightful sweetness and charm which characterize the "Little Flowers," and stamp them with the seal of truth:

Coming one day to a certain town and being very hungry, they went, according to the rule, to beg bread for the love of God; St. Francis going down one street and Brother Masseo down another. But, because Francis was a man of mean appearance and small of stature and accounted a vile beggar by those who knew him not, he received nothing but a few mouthfuls and crumbs of dry bread; whilst Brother Masseo, being tall and comely in person, had good pieces and large and plentiful given to him, and entire loaves. When they had begged enough, they went together to a place outside the town, where there was a beautiful fountain that they might eat; and beside which was also a broad and convenient stone, on which each placed all the alms which he had begged. And St. Francis, seeing that the pieces of bread which Brother Masseo had, were larger and better than his own, had great joy and spoke thus: "O Brother Masseo, we are not worthy of such great treasure." And as he repeated these words several times, Brother Masseo answered him: "Father, how can this be called treasure, when we are in such poverty, and lack the things of which we have need; we, who have neither cloth, nor knives, nor plates, nor platter, nor house, nor table, nor manservant nor maid-servant?" Then said St. Francis: "And this is what I call a great treasure, that there is nothing here provided by human industry, but everything is provided by Divine Providence, as we may see manifestly in this bread which we have begged, in this stone which serves so beautifully for our table, and in this so clear fountain; and therefore I desire that we should pray to God that He would cause holy poverty, which is a thing so noble that God Himself was made subject to it, to be loved by us with our whole heart." And when he had said these words and they had made their prayer and partaken for bodily refreshment of the pieces of bread and drunk of the water, they arose and went on their way to France.[150]

This episode affords us a deep insight into the secret of the Poverello's faith and trust in Divine Providence, and gives us also the key to his solution of the problem of Franciscan livelihood. God is in a direct and infallible manner his Father and Steward. The creatures, who consciously or unconsciously are his benefactors, are to the Saint merely the channels which receive and in turn dispense their bounty from the divine source of goodness. They accordingly can never fail, even as the divine source can never fail. The more directly they are in touch with this source, and the more untouched they are by mortal hands, by human calculation and artificial providence, the more forcibly the Providence of the Creator reveals itself in them. Thus every creature becomes to St. Francis Brother and Sister and Benefactor in God; the whole universe becomes the instrument of Divine Providence unto him. And the less he possesses himself, the more securely he finds himself sheltered in God and in His world. Most high poverty is, therefore, his precious treasure, which he desires to love and keep with every fiber of his heart.

With these sentiments firmly rooted in his heart, Francis appears before Innocent III with his eleven companions, to seek the approbation of his rule, which had been written in the meantime. The Pope, one of the greatest executives who ever lived, became hesitant and anxious when he realized that Francis was determined to base his undertaking entirely and solely on Divine Providence. He bade the Saint to pray for further inspiration from above. In obedience to the Pope's command, Francis prayed long and fervently, and the Lord revealed to him the following allegory: "In a desert place there lived a poor but beautiful lady. A king, seized with admiration for her beauty, desired her for his wife, that she might bear him beautiful children. After the marriage had been entered upon, many sons were born therefrom. When these had grown up, the mother said to them: 'My sons, be not ashamed, for you are children of the king. Go, therefore, to his court; he will provide you with all needful things.' When they stood before the king, he marveled at their beauty, and seeing that they resembled him greatly, he asked whose sons they were. They answered, the sons of a poor lady in the desert. The king thereupon embraced them with great joy and exclaimed; 'Fear not, you are my children. If strangers eat at my table, how much more you, to whom the inheritance is justly due!' He then commanded the poor lady to send all her children to the court, there to be reared by the king." [151]

After completing his prayer, Francis again appeared before the "dear Lord Pope," related the allegory which God had revealed to him, and added: "Lord Pope, I am the poor lady whom God has chosen and enriched with many children. The King of kings has assured me that He Himself wishes nourish all children which are begotten through me. For if He nourishes strangers, surely he must also nourish His own children. Since God gives temporal things to sinners that they may nourish their children, He must all the more provide evangelical men with those things which are justly their due." Innocent hesitated no longer, and not only approved their rule and manner of life, but gave his fatherly blessing to them and their undertaking.[152]

Was it foolhardiness? Human shortsightedness may

call it thus, but history does not. Cardinal Jacques de
Vitry, a contemporary, is puzzled which to admire more:
the trusting faith of the first Friars, or the bounty of
Divine Providence in their behalf. "As many as seek to
join the Order," he writes, "the Friars receive them all
without hesitation. They do so with all the more confidence since they surrender themselves completely to the
generosity and providence of God, and are firmly convinced that God will preserve them. They give to those
who come to them only a habit and a cord, and leave all
else to heavenly Providence. In fact, the Lord gives to
these His servants a hundredfold even in this world; and
wherever they go, His eyes are constantly upon them, so
that the word of Scripture is fulfilled in them: 'God
loveth the stranger and giveth him food and raiment.' [153]
Those count themselves blessed, whose hospitality and
alms the servants of God do not refuse." [154]   The Three
Companions, likewise eye-witnesses, assert the same:
"The Lord at all times prepared shelter for them, and
had all needful things offered them." [155]   In view of the
countless proofs of divine bounty manifested during the
life of the Poverello, Thomas of Celano does not hesitate
to declare: "Not only all creation served this man of God
at every nod; the providence of the Creator was at his
disposal according to his own pleasure. The fatherly
love of God anticipated his wishes and fulfilled them
before they were uttered. Need and supply, desire and
fulfilment were always one." [156]

Whenever Providence failed to supply their wants by
the ordinary means, it failed not to do so in an extraordinary, yes, marvelous manner.

At the time when the Saint and his band returned from
Rome, they arrived one day in a deserted region where
no food could be obtained. Suddenly a man stood before
them, gave them a loaf of bread, and disappeared. The
"Poor of God" beheld in this food the confirmation and
reward for their trust in Providence, and they encouraged

each other to expect all things from the bounteous mercy of God.[157]

Several years later (1212-1213), Francis embarked for Syria, but was cast upon the Slavonian coast, and after a long, hazardous voyage he landed again at Ancona. The sailors had refused to take Francis on board, seeing his poor and destitute condition. But God provided not only for the sustenance of the Saint, but through him also for the entire crew on their stormy voyage. Thus it happened, says Celano, that those who were unwilling to give passage to the man of God, were saved by him, and moved to praise and bless the providence of Him who never forsakes his own.[158]

Shortly after (circa 1213-1215), Francis set out for Morocco with the desire to obtain the palm of martyrdom, but fell seriously ill in Spain. As he dragged himself along, weary and exhausted, in company with Brother Bernard, he expressed a desire for some meat. And lo! a rider came along and offered the sick man a savory dish prepared of fowl, saying to him: "Servant of God, eat with relish what Divine Providence herewith sends thee." [159]

Again at a later time he was lying ill in the Bishop's palace at Rieti. Since the habit which he wore had become thin and threadbare, he asked his Guardian to procure him some cloth for a new habit. While the latter was pondering how he should be able to fulfil the wish of his Father, a knock was heard at the door, and a man stood there with a roll of cloth, saying: "Brother, accept this cloth for six habits for love of God; keep one for thyself, and distribute the others at thy pleasure." [160]

Another time, thus relates St. Bonaventure, when the man of God wished to go to a certain desert place, that he might give himself the more freely to contemplation, being very weak, he rode upon an ass belonging to a poor man. It being a hot summer's day, the poor man, as he followed the servant of Christ, became weary with the long way and the steep ascent, and, beginning to faint with fatigue and burning with thirst, he called after the Saint: "Behold," he said, "I shall die of thirst, unless I can find a little water at once to refresh me." Then without delay the man of God got off the ass, and, kneeling down with his hands stretched out to heaven, he ceased not to pray until he knew that he was heard. Having finished his prayer, he said to the man: "Hasten to yonder rock, and there shalt thou find living water, which Christ the Merciful hath even now brought forth therefrom that thou mayest drink." O marvelous goodness of God, who thus easily inclines to the prayer of His servants! The thirsty man drank of the water drawn from the hard rock by the power of prayer. Never was flowing water in that place before; neither, however diligently sought for, could it ever be found there afterward.[161]

Toward the end of his life, when the Saint was suffering with a serious malady of the eyes, a certain physician was accustomed to visit him frequently in the hermitage and to attend him. One day Francis invited this physician to dine with the Friars, wishing to show his gratitude in this manner, and to give him pleasure. But the Father Guardian remonstrated: "Father, we are ashamed to invite the physician; at present we are so very poor." The Saint replied: "O ye of little faith, must I repeat it again?" The physician himself wished to appease them, saying: "Dearest brothers, I shall reckon it the greatest honor to share your poverty with you." The Friars then hurried to collect whatever they could find in kitchen and cellar; namely, some bread and wine and vegetables. But the table of the Lord was more bountiful than the table of the poor; a lady appeared at the door of the Friary and handed the brothers a basket filled with fine bread, fishes and a crab patty, and covering all was some honey and grapes. The joy of the Friars was great, but still greater was the admiration of the physician for the sanctity of Francis and the bounty of Divine Providence.[162]

"At the time when the Saint was sojourning at Nocera," thus relates Thomas of Celano, "and the people of Assisi heard that he was near death, they sent messengers from the city to bring him back, fearing that they might be deprived of the possession of his sacred body. While bringing him back on a horse, they came to a poor little town named Sarziano. Being the hour of dinner, they were all hungry and went to buy some food, but finding nothing, they returned empty-handed. The messengers then said to Francis: 'Thou must give us of thy alms; for here there is nothing to buy.' 'Then,' said the holy man, 'you have found nothing because you trust more in your flies than in the Lord [by flies he was wont to signify money] ; return, therefore, to the houses which you have already visited, and humbly ask for alms, offering the love of God instead of money. Be not ashamed, for, after sin committed, God, the great Almsgiver, grants to all, worthy and unworthy, all things needful as alms with a lavish hand.' Then laying aside their false shame, they went and asked for alms, and this time they purchased more for the love of God than for money. The people vied with one another in giving food, and thus it befell that the hunger which by money could not be relieved, was relieved by the bounty of Lady Poverty." [163]

St. Bonaventure derives the following admonition from this marvelous providence of God in behalf of Francis and his Friars: "Therefore, let the poor man of Christ lay aside all distrust. For if the poverty of Francis was so abundantly sufficient to supply by its wonderful power the wants of all those who in any way assisted him, so that they lacked neither food nor drink nor house when all supply of money and all natural power and faculties failed them, much more shall they deserve to receive those things which the order of Divine Providence is accustomed to grant indifferently to all men. If, I say, the dry rock at the voice of the poor gave forth abundant water for the need of that poor thirsty man, never will Our Lord deny anything to those who have left all things for the Author of all things." [164]

"In no place and at no time do we read," the Seraphic Doctor writes elsewhere, "that one who strove to serve God in poverty, starved from lack of food. . . . For since all earthly things are the property of God, he who belongs to God shall lack nothing, if he but fail not God, nor become disloyal to Him. . . . It is therefore no hazardous venture, but a safe refuge, to leave all things in order to devote oneself entirely to God." [165]

Since these words were written, nearly seven centuries of Franciscan history have passed, and hundreds of thousands of Friars have lived from the "Table of the Lord," and all attest that faith and trust in Providence has never failed. All attest that "the fatherly eye of God never overlooks His own, but feeds them with all the greater love and care, the poorer and more destitute they are; yes, that the table of the poor of God is spread more lavishly than the table of princes, just so much more lavishly as the generosity of God surpasses that of men." [166]

The poor of Christ content themselves with simple food and raiment, still they are infinitely more happy than the rich man in purple and linens at his sumptuous banquet. The *Fioretti* episode of Francis and Brother Masseo repeats itself time and again. Franciscan poverty is still, according to the words of the poet, exceedingly rich in its neediness, because all things needful are provided by God Himself:

> "Son colei, che tu dimande
>   Con le povere vivande.
> Ogni cosa mi par grande,
>   Che per Dio mi sia donato." [167]

That is the blessedness of Franciscan poverty. These two terms are synonymous: to renounce all earthly things for love of God, and to be provided with all needful things by God; to despise every shred of earthly substance which manacles the heart of man to this earth, and to eat at the table of God, to live on His bounty; to seek nothing from the world, and to hope all things from God. That is the source of Franciscan joviality, the ever smiling Franciscan cheerfulness of the ever happy family of the Poverello of Assisi.[168]

CHAPTER VIII

FRANCISCAN HUMILITY

THE broad and deep conception of poverty, and its courageous realization as Francis achieved it, did not include merely the renunciation of material things. To be *truly poor* according to the example of the Saviour, the Poverello wished also to embrace *humility* as the companion of poverty, the poverty in spirit, the love of being small. It is obvious that this love of littleness is included in true and genuine poverty. It is both the soul and foundation as well as the necessary fruit of true poverty. To be poor and to be little are well-nigh synonymous. It has therefore been rightly said: *"Humilitas—that is perfect poverty."* [1]

In speaking of poverty, Francis time and again mentions humility in the same breath. He greets both as sisters: "O Lady Holy Poverty," he exclaims, "the Lord preserve thee with thy sister, holy humility! . . . Holy poverty puts to shame avarice, greed and the cares of the world. Holy humility puts to shame pride and all men of this world, and all things which are of this world." [2] He considers the union of both as the foundation of his Order.[3] He commends both most ardently to his brothers: "Let all the brothers follow the humility and poverty of Our Lord Jesus Christ. . . . Let all the brothers serve the Lord in poverty and humility as pilgrims and strangers in this world. . . . Let them observe the poverty and humility and the Holy Gospel of Our Lord Jesus Christ." [4] In his instructions he constantly reverted to the virtues of poverty and humility, and charged his brothers to hold fast to them without fail.[5]

Several fragments of his *instructions on humility* have come down to us. We cannot resist the temptation to repeat them here. In substance as well as in form they remind us strongly of the inspired wisdom of the *Imitation of Christ*.

In order to warn his brothers against vain self-complacency, he shows that no man has reason to glory in anything: "Consider, O man, how great is the excellence in which the Lord has placed you, because He has created and formed you to the image of His beloved Son according to the body, and to His own likeness according to the spirit. And all the creatures that are under heaven serve and know and obey their Creator in their own way better than you. And even the demons did not crucify Him, but you together with them crucified Him and still crucify Him by taking delight in vices and sins. Wherefore then can you glory? For if you were so clever and wise that you possessed all knowledge, and if you knew how to interpret every form of language and to investigate heavenly things minutely, you could not glory in all this, because one demon has known more of heavenly things and still knows more of heavenly things than all men, although there may be some man who has received from the Lord a special knowledge of sovereign wisdom. In like manner, if you were handsomer and richer than all others, and even if you could work wonders and put the demons to flight, all these things are hurtful to you and in no wise belong to you, and in them you cannot glory; that, however, in which we may glory is in our infirmities, and in the bearing daily the holy cross of Our Lord Jesus Christ." [6]

The brothers were to glory least of all in their virtues and graces. Repeatedly he would say: "Because of all things which a sinner may do, no one has reason to flatter himself with vain praise. The sinner can fast, pray, weep, chastise his own flesh; but one thing he cannot do: remain true to his Lord. Let us therefore glory in this, that we give God the honor, if we, loyal in His service, ascribe to Him all things which He grants us. The greatest enemy of man is his flesh. It knows not how to recall anything by which it may be moved to sorrow; it knows not how to foresee anything in order to walk in fear. It knows but one thing: to abuse the present moment. But far worse is this, that it arrogates to itself the gifts which have been granted to the soul, and uses them for its own praise. It demands praise for virtue and grace, applause for watching and praying. It leaves nothing to the soul; indeed, it demands its tribute even from tears." [7]

If, therefore, the brothers possess virtues or graces, they should manifest them in deeds, and not in words: "Blessed is that servant who does not speak through hope of reward and who does not manifest everything and is not hasty to speak, but who wisely foresees what he ought to say and answer. Woe to that Religious who, not concealing in his heart the good things which the Lord has disclosed to him, and who, not manifesting them to others by his work, seeks rather through hope of reward to make them known to men by words: for now he receives his recompense, and his hearers bear away little fruit." [8]

Francis accordingly admonishes all Friars in touching words to love humility: "I beseech in the charity, which is God, all my brothers, preachers, prayers, or laborers, both clerics and laics, that they study to humble themselves in all things and that they glory not, nor rejoice, nor inwardly exalt themselves on account of good words and works, nor indeed for any good which God may sometimes say or do and operate in them or by them, according to what the Lord says: 'But yet rejoice not in this, that the spirits are subject unto you.' [9] And let us know for certain that nothing belongs to us but vices and sins. And we ought rather to rejoice when we fall into divers temptations, and when we bear some afflictions or sorrows of soul or body in this world for the sake of eternal life. Let us then all, brothers, avoid all pride and vain-glory. . . . And let us refer all good to the Lord God most high and supreme; let us acknowledge that all good belongs to Him, and let us give thanks for all to Him from whom all good proceeds. And may He, the Most High and Supreme, only true God, have, and may there be rendered to Him and may He receive, all honors and reverences, all praises and benedictions, all thanks and all glory, to whom all good belongs, who alone is good." [10]

He reminds especially those Friars who, because of their calling, are exposed more than others to the danger of vain-glory, of their duty to be humble: the preachers, the theologians, and the superiors.

The *preachers* were constantly admonished by him to give glory to God alone in their success, and to remain indifferent to the praise and favor of men: "Thus," he would say, "may the servant of God know if he has the spirit of God: if when the Lord works some good through him, his body—since it is ever at variance with all that is good—is not therefore puffed up; but if he rather becomes viler in his own sight and if he esteems himself less than other men. . . . Blessed is that servant who is not more puffed up because of the good the Lord says and works through him than because of that which He says and works through others. A man sins who wishes to receive more from his neighbor than he is himself willing to give to the Lord God." [11]

As highly as Francis esteemed the office of preaching, so severely did he rebuke those preachers who sold their merit for the silver of earthly glory. In reprimanding those who had become puffed up because of their success as preachers, he would say: "Why do you glory because of those who have been converted, since they have been in

fact converted by the prayers of my simple brothers?"
The prophetic word of the barren one who bears many
children, while the fruiftul one does not,[12] he explained
in this wise: "The barren one is my poor little brother,
who is not called to bring forth sons in the Church. He
will bear many on the day of judgment, because the Judge
will reckon to his account the souls which he now con-
verts by his secret prayers. The woman who has many
sons, will be found barren; that is, the preacher, who
rejoices over many converted, as if he had begotten them
of his own power, will then know that he has had no
part in their conversion." Those also were hateful to the
Saint, who sought to shine more as orators than as preachers, since they indulged more in verbosity, instead of
speaking from heartfelt emotion.[18]

He admonished the *learned Friars* to renounce in like
manner for the love of God the fame of erudition. "If
a great scholar enters the Order," he remarked, "he must,
as it were, renounce learning itself in order to throw
himself naked into the arms of the Crucified, stripped
even of this spiritual possession. For, learning renders
many learned men indocile and stubborn in the humble
practises of religious life. Therefore I desire that such
a learned man should say first of all: 'Behold, brother, I
have lived a long time in the world and have not truly
known my God. I beg thee therefore for a cell removed
from the clamor of the world, where I can meditate on my
past life, shut out all distractions and order the affairs of
my soul.' What think you," Francis added, "will become
of a learned man who thus begins his religious life? Certainly he will then become like a lion freed of his chains,
and able to do all things. . . . If he be appointed to teach,
his mouth will overflow with the fulness of his spirit." [14]

According to the mind of the Saint, even the greatest
erudition was to be paired with a humble disposition.[15]
He considered just this as the direct object of learning and
its bed-rock foundation: to know oneself, and thus in-

crease in humility.[16]   That alone gave him security that
the efforts of the Friars in acquiring knowledge would
be born of, and permeated by, the spirit of God, which is
a spirit of humility and holy simplicity.[17]   Whoever rears
the structure of science on this foundation, will thus
prosper immeasurably in the science of God itself.[18]

Still more frequently and ardently he admonished the
superiors to humility. He was wont to say: "It is good
and pleasing in the eyes of God to have care of others,
but only those should have the care of souls, who seek
not themselves in anything, but are mindful in all things
of God's will alone. Only those should hold the office
of superiors who prefer nothing to the salvation of their
souls, and do not seek the favor of their subjects but their
welfare; who desire not the praise of men, but honor
before God; who fear, more than seek, the office of
superior; who, when they are chosen as superiors, are
humbled instead of puffed up, and who, when they are
deposed, do not feel themselves humbled, but exalted."
He reminded the Frairs repeatedly that in this time of
increasing wickedness and sin, it was a dangerous thing
to rule, but a profitable thing to be ruled.[19]

"Let those," remarks the Saint, "who are set above
others, glory in this superiority only as much as if they
had been deputed to wash the feet of the brothers; and if
they are more perturbed by the loss of their superiorship
than they would be by losing the office of washing feet,
so much the more do they lay up treasures to the peril of
their own soul. . . . Woe to that Religious who is elevated in dignity by others, and who of his own will is
not ready to descend. And blessed is that servant who is
raised in dignity not by his own will, and who always desires to be beneath the feet of others. . . . Blessed is
that superior who shall be found as humble among his
subjects as if he were among his masters!"[20]

In accordance with this idea of humility, Francis laid
down the following norm for the superiors in ruling their

brothers: "Let the ministers [servants] receive their brothers charitably and kindly and show so great familiarity toward them that they may speak and act with them as masters with their servants, for thus it ought to be, since the ministers are the servants of all the brothers." [21]

This leads us to the *true source* whence Franciscan humility derives its *sublimity* and *peculiarity*: the Gospel. In designating the superiors as ministers or servants, Francis appeals directly to the words of the Saviour,[22] who says of Himself: "The Son of Man is not come to be ministered unto, but to minister," and who commands His apostles: "Whosoever will be the greater among you, let him be your minister. . . . He that is the greater among you, let him become as the younger, and he that is the leader as he that serveth." [23] Following this injunction of the Saviour, Francis soon after the foundation of the Order [24] called his brothers *"Minores, Fratres Minores* —the least, the smallest, Friars Minor." He would not allow any other name to come into use.[25] For again he read in the Gospel: "Amen, I say to you, as long as you did it to one of these my least brethren, you did it to Me. . . . Amen, I say to you, as long as you did it not to one of these least, neither did you do it to Me." [26] The very name by which they were designated was to be a reminder to the Friars "that they had come to the school of the humble Saviour Jesus Christ in order to learn humility." [27]

Francis wished that his brothers be not only in name, but also in deed and in truth the *least and smallest of all, Friars Minor*. He emphasized the fact that God commanded him to call his sons "Friars Minor" because they were to be a poor and humble people.[28] Again and again he admonished them: "By our fault we are all wretched and corrupt, foul and worms, as the Lord says by the Prophet: 'I am a worm and no man, the reproach of men and the outcast of the people.' We should never desire to be above others, but ought rather to be servants and subject 'to every human creature for God's sake.' " [29]

He had hardly gathered the first Friars Minor about himself, when he charged them to go and serve the lepers. Because they were destined to be the servants of these poorest of all men, they were to become completely humble, and to remain conscious at all times what it meant to be called a Friar Minor, and to be one.[30] Whenever they served in the houses of lay people, they were to be bound by the precept forbidding them the position of masters, and commanding them to be "inferior and subject to all in the same house." [31]

This precept indeed could not be enforced literally later on because of the complete change in the mode of living of the Friars. However, as great and varied as the activity of the Friars might be, it was always repugnant to the Saint to see his brothers occupying a position of honor. He frankly and emphatically defended his attitude in this regard even before Cardinal Hugolino. The latter desired to promote the Friars to the office of bishops and prelates, declaring that in the primitive Church such men were promoted to this dignity who excelled in poverty and charity. Francis replied to the Cardinal: "Lord, my brothers have been called 'Minors' for this reason, that they should not presume to become the greater. Our calling teaches us to remain standing in the lowland, and to follow the humble steps of Christ, whereby the Friars will one day be exalted above others in the order of saints. If you desire that they bear fruit in the Church of God, leave them and preserve them in their primitive vocation, and lead them back to the lowland, whether they will or not. Lest therefore you make the poor proud, who exalt themselves above others, I beseech you, Father, never to allow them to be raised to places of honor." [32] Those Friars who even showed ambition to occupy places of honor, he no longer considered as Friars Minor.[33] And justly so! For "man is," according to the Seraphic Doctor, "humble by reason

of his love to be less and smaller; to be humble means to
be the least of all; . . . to be humble means to be a Friar
Minor." [34]

From all that has been said above, it becomes evident
that Francis wished to establish an Order conspicuous for
humility, and that this Order and the Friars should moreover be more humble, that is, more submissive, more unassuming, more lowly than the other Orders and other
Religious.

2. But, above all, Francis endeavored constantly to
humble himself, to be the *least and lowliest of all* himself.

That was directly contrary to the spirit of the time. It
was a time marked by social unrest, by ambitious craving
for aggrandizement, by a mad scramble for honors and
fame. The princes despised the lower nobility, the nobility despised the bourgeoisie, these despised the peasants,
and these again the serfs as lesser and meaner. On the
other hand, the lower classes were vigilant striving
by honorable or dishonorable means to rise above their
state, the serfs struggling to become free peasants, the
peasants aspiring to the citizen class, these to the nobility,
and the smaller nobles to untrammeled supremacy. Francis also, by birth half bourgeois, half noble, was fired by
the ambition to parade as King of Youth in his native
town, and to climb as rapidly as possible to the state of
knighthood and nobility.

And now, what a change! From the first day of his
conversion, he rejoices in the mockery and the gibes of
his townsfolk, he glories in being the laughing-stock of
all, and in casting his lot with the poor and despised. "He
showed himself submissive to all," remarks the Anonymus
Perugian.[85] He himself is able to say of himself and his
first disciples: "We were simple and subject to all." [86]

Although he belonged to the clerical state, yet he desired
to occupy with his brothers the last and lowest place.
"Let us hold all clerics and Religious as our masters in
those things which regard the salvation of souls," [87] was

his axiom. And he remained faithful to it until death, so
that he declares in his Testament: "I desire to fear, love,
and honor them [the poorest priests of this world] and
all others as my masters." [38]

In his endeavor to preserve this submissiveness to clergy
and laity, he adds: "I strictly enjoin by obedience on all
the brothers, that wherever they may be, they should not
dare, either themselves or by means of some intermediary, to ask any letter in the Roman Curia either for a
church or for any other place, nor under pretext of preaching, nor on account of their bodily persecution; but,
wherever they are not received, let them flee to another
land to do penance, with the blessing of God." [39]

This attitude he maintained during his whole life. At
one time the Friars counseled him to apply for a Papal
privilege empowering them to preach everywhere without
conferring with the clergy. He refused to do so, saying:
"You Friars Minor do not know the will of God, and you
do not allow me to convert the whole world as God wishes,
since I desire, in the first place, to convert the bishops,
who, seeing our life and holy and humble reverence, will
themselves call you to preach and convert the people; this
will avail more than your privilege, that would only lead
you to pride." [40] When Brother Philip nevertheless obtained a privilege in favor of the Poor Clares, he rebuked
him, "preferring to overcome all difficulties by humility
rather than by decrees of the court." [41]

In his ingenious humility, Francis succeeded even in
obtaining the last place among the brothers. In speaking
of the first regulations which the Saint made for the
young fraternity, the Three Companions add: "Although
Francis was above all the Friars, he nevertheless appointed
one of the brothers who dwelt with him as his guardian
and lord, whom he obeyed humbly and submissively, in
order thus to avoid all occasion of pride. Among all the
brothers he bowed his head to the earth, in order to make
himself worthy to be exalted by God among the saints and

elect." [42] He regarded it as self-evident that in an Order
whose characteristic was littleness, he should be the least
of all, who was the father and exemplar of all. At times
he would say to his companions: "I should not deem myself a Friar Minor, if I possessed not the spirit which I
shall describe to you."   And he said: "Behold, as the
superior of the Friars I go to the Chapter.   I preach to
the Friars and admonish them, and at the end of my discourse it would be said: 'Such an ignorant and contemptible man is not fit to be over us; we shall suffer
thee no longer to rule, for thou knowest not how to speak
and art simple and ignorant.'   Finally, I am set before the
door with rough words, despised by all.   I say to you, if
I do not endure these words with even countenance, with
an even gladness of heart and an even purpose of sanctity,
I am by no means a Friar Minor."   And he added: "In
prelacies lurks the fall, in praise the abyss, but in the
humility of the subject lies gain for the soul.   Why then
do we seek perils more than merit, since we have chosen
the occasion to gain merit?" [43]

How sacredly serious these words were meant, he
proved by actual fact. As soon as the condition of the
Order permitted, he resigned the office of Minister General (1219). All prayers and tears of the brothers were
unable to shake his determination. "He desired," says
Celano, "to preserve the virtue of humility; he therefore
remained a subject until death, proving himself more
humble than any Friar." [44]

For a time he agreed to be accompanied by one of the
Friars, being unable to find his way about on account of
a grave malady of the eyes. But he soon dismissed this
Friar, saying to the Vicar General, Peter Catanii: "I do
not wish to enjoy any privilege by having a special companion according to my pleasure, but let the Friars give me
a companion from place to place as God shall inspire
them." And he added: "I once saw a blind man who

The Feast of the Christmas Crib

had but a dog to lead him, and I would not be better off than he." [45]

In order to avoid even the appearance of grandeur, he would not tarry in the palaces of great men, even if they were prelates of the Church. Cardinal Leo of Santa Croce, thus relates St. Bonaventure, having once prayed him to remain with him awhile at Rome, Francis humbly consented to his desire, for the reverence and love which he bore so great a man. On the first night, as he desired to take some rest after his prayers, the demons arose in great fury against the soldier of Christ, and having severely beaten him, they left him as it were half dead. When they had gone, Francis called his companion, who came to him at once, and to him the holy man related what had happened, adding: "I believe, brother, that the demons, who can do nothing but by the disposition of Divine Providence, have beaten me now so cruelly because it is not well that I should abide in the courts of princes. My brethren, who dwell in poor places, will perhaps think when they see me living with cardinals, that I am meddling in worldly matters, or seeking after honors, or enjoying delicacies. Therefore I judge it far better that he who is to give an example to others should fly from courts, and dwell humbly among the humble in humble places, that he may be able to strengthen those who suffer poverty and are ill at ease, seeing that he endures the same things himself." The next morning therefore he offered his humble excuses to the Cardinal, and took his leave.[46]

The greatest charm of this passionate love for littleness —at the same time the genuine touchstone of humility— was the *deep reverence and respect with which Francis regarded others.* "Because he was the humblest of all," remarks Celano, "he was considerate to all men; he accommodated himself to the ways of all. Among the saints he was the greatest saint, among sinners he was as one of them." [47] "He met the prelates and priests," thus the Three Companions testify, "with greatest reverence, the aged with deep respect, the nobles and wealthy with esteem, the poor with heartiest love and compassion, all men with perfect submission." [48]

Examples of this charming reverence and humble submission toward all classes and all men abound in the life of the Saint. Let us mention but one. On his return from the Orient, the Saint was one day accompanied by Brother Leonard of Assisi. Being greatly fatigued from the journey, Francis rode part of the way on an ass. His companion, who followed on foot and who was no less fatigued, was seized with resentment and thought to himself: "His parents and mine were of the same rank, and now he rides, while I go on foot and lead his beast!" Hardly had this thought passed through his mind, when the Saint dismounted and said: "Nay, brother, it behooveth not that I ride and thou goest on foot; for thou wert once greater and nobler than I in the world." And he compelled Brother Leonard to mount the beast, while he himself became the driver. [49]

It was not difficult for Francis, indeed, it was natural, to be submissive to all men, because he regarded himself as the *greatest sinner and the most unworthy of all men.* The *Fioretti* has preserved for us a confession of the Saint which bears the genuine stamp of truth, and discloses his charming humility.

Once, thus the *Fioretti* relates, St. Francis was lodged with Brother Leo in a place where there were no books with which to say the Divine Office. And when the hour came for matins, St. Francis said to Brother Leo: "My beloved, we have no Breviary with which to say matins, but in order that we may spend the time in praising God, I will speak and thou shalt answer as I shall instruct thee, and take heed that thou say not a word other than as I tell thee. I will say thus: 'O Brother Francis, thou hast done so many evils and so many sins in thy time, that thou hast merited hell'; and thou, Brother Leo, shalt answer: 'Truly, and thou dost merit the deepest hell.'"

And Brother Leo, with the simplicity of a little dove, replied: "Willingly, Father; begin in the name of God." Then St. Francis began to say: "O Brother Francis, thou hast done so many evils and so many sins in thy time, that thou hast merited hell." And Brother Leo replied: "God will work so much good through thee, that thou shalt go to paradise." Then said St. Francis: "Say not thus, Brother Leo, but when I shall say: 'Brother Francis, thou hast committed so many iniquities against God, that thou art worthy to be accursed by God,' do thou answer thus: 'Verily thou art worthy to be placed among the accursed.' " And Brother Leo replied: "Willingly, Father."

Again St. Francis, with many tears and sighs, beating his breast, said with a loud voice: "O my Lord, Lord of heaven and earth, I have committed against Thee so many iniquities, and so many grievous sins that I am worthy to be accursed of Thee for them all"; and Brother Leo replied: "O Brother Francis, God will make thee such that amongst the blessed thou shalt be singularly blessed." And St. Francis, marveling that Brother Leo answered contrariwise to what he had imposed on him, reproved him, saying: "Wherefore dost thou not answer as I have instructed thee? I command thee by holy obedience to answer as I will tell thee. I will speak thus: 'O Brother Francis, thou wicked little one, dost thou think that God will have mercy on thee, knowing that thou hast committed so many sins against the God of mercy and God of all consolation, that thou art not worthy to find mercy?' And thou, Brother Leo, little sheep, shalt answer: 'By no means art thou worthy to find mercy.' " But when St. Francis said: "O Brother Francis, thou wicked one," and the rest, Brother Leo answered him: "God the Father, whose mercy is infinitely more than thy sins, will show thee great mercy, and, more than this, will add to thee many graces." At which reply, St. Francis, gently angry and patiently wroth, said to Brother Leo: "And wherefore hast thou presumed to act contrary to obedience, and

180 THE IDEALS OF ST. FRANCIS

so many times answered the contrary to what I imposed
on thee?" Brother Leo replied humbly and reverently:
"God knows, my Father, that each time I had it in my
heart to answer as thou hadst commanded me, but God
makes me speak as it pleases Him, and not as it pleases
me." At which St. Francis marveled, and said to Brother
Leo: "I pray thee from my heart that this time thou wilt
answer me as I have told thee." And Brother Leo answered: "I speak in the name of God, for this time I will
answer as thou desirest." And St. Francis said, weeping:
"O Brother Francis, thou little wicked one, dost thou think
God will have mercy on thee?" Brother Leo replied:
"Yea, rather, thou shalt receive great grace from God,
and He will exalt thee, and glorify thee to all eternity,
because he that humbleth himself shall be exalted, and I
cannot say otherwise for God speaks by my mouth." And
in this humble contention, with many tears and much
spiritual consolation, they continued until the break of
day.[50]

That God had decreed to exalt Francis according to the
measure of his self-humiliation, was revealed to Brother
Pacificus in a marvelous vision. While this saintly man
was absorbed in prayer one day, he was lifted up and rapt
into heaven; and he saw in heaven very many seats, and
one amongst them was raised above the others, glorious to
behold, adorned with splendor and many precious stones,
so that he marveled at its great beauty, and wondered
whose seat this could be. And he heard a voice that said:
"This was the seat of Lucifer, and in his place will be
seated the humble Francis." When he had returned to his
senses, he asked St. Francis what he thought of himself.
To which Francis answered: "It seems to me I am a
greater sinner than anyone else in the world." And when
the brother replied that this was not in accordance with
the truth, Francis said: "If Christ had shown such great
mercy to a criminal, however wicked he may be, he would
be tenfold more perfect than I." [51]

These words open the door to the innermost secret of the Saint's humility. He deemed himself so inexpressibly low and unworthy, because he was conscious that *all that was good and great* in him *came from God* and *belonged to God.*

He did not, however, by any means fail to recognize the good which the Lord wrought in him and through him. To overlook this or to deny this would have been insincerity or shortsightedness, and at any rate false humility. On the contrary, Francis found so much of divine grace and goodness in his life that his wonder never ceased. He was at all times mindful of the signal proofs of divine beneficence which had been vouchsafed him and his brothers.[52] He declared unreservedly that it was due to this divine munificence only, if he and his sons possessed or achieved anything good.[53]

It was for this reason that he sought to hide from the world all favors and achievements from which worldly fame might ensue. He was convinced that fame and notoriety became a distinct liability as far as the real soul merit was concerned, and he would often declare that it were less dangerous not to possess virtue, than to misuse virtue for self-glorification.[54] He went so far as to forbid the reading of the legend of the Moroccan martyrs, because it contained flattering mention of himself.[55] In like manner he studiously endeavored to conceal the Stigmata during his lifetime.[56] And the admonition he gave to the Friars he observed literally himself: "Blessed is the servant who treasures up in heaven the good things which the Lord shows him and who does not wish to manifest them to men through the hope of reward, for the Most High will Himself manifest His works to whomsoever He may please. Blessed is the servant who keeps the secrets of the Lord in his heart." [57]

Whenever the fame of his virtue nevertheless was noised abroad, he would point to the excess of grace to which all credit was due. He would then repeat his favorite comparison: "Francis, if the Most High had deigned to grant so many graces to a robber, he would show himself more grateful than thou." [58]   While others marveled at his sanctity, he would remind them: "I may yet commit grave carnal sins. Do not praise me as if I were secure. He is not worthy to be praised whose end is uncertain." [59]

In his own heart he was firmly convinced that God had favored him so singularly because he was the most unworthy of all men and thus all honor would redound to God alone. "Why after thee? why after thee? why after thee?" Brother Masseo one day exclaimed to Francis, wishing to test his humility. Francis replied: "What is it thou wouldst say?" And Brother Masseo made answer: "Tell me, why is it that all the world runs after thee, and everybody desires to see thee, and to hear thee, and to obey thee? Thou art not a man either comely of person, or of noble birth, or of great knowledge; whence, then, comes it that all the world runs after thee?" Hearing this, Francis, filled with joy in his spirit, raised his face toward heaven, and remained for a great while with his mind lifted up to God; then, returning to himself, he knelt down and gave praise and thanks to God; and then, with great fervor of spirit, turning to Brother Masseo, he said: "Wouldst thou know why after me? wouldst thou know why after me? why all the world runs after me? This comes to me, because the eyes of the most high God, which behold in all places both the evil and the good, even those most holy eyes have not seen amongst sinners one more vile, nor more insufficient, nor a greater sinner than I, and therefore to do that wonderful work which He intends to do He has not found on earth a viler creature than I; and for this cause has He elected me to confound the nobility and the grandeur and the strength and the beauty and wisdom of the world; that all men may know that all virtue and all goodness are of Him and not of the creature, and that none should glory in His presence, but that he who glories should glory in the Lord, to whom is all honor and all glory in eternity." [60]

The more, therefore, he was praised and honored, the more contemptible he appeared to himself, and the more he abased himself. He suffered grievously in mind whenever others praised him and extolled his virtue. In the midst of popular acclamation he would be heard sighing and groaning for utter sadness. While all others were loud in their praise of his deeds and virtues, his sole endeavor was to kill in the germ the faintest feeling of self-complacency, in order not to offend the eye of God and to cause it to turn from him.[61] While the impassioned enthusiasm of the crowds rose and surged about him, he would turn to someone and beg him to shower insults and reproaches upon him. Or he would call a Friar and say to him: "I command thee by obedience, that thou revile me and speak the truth to me contrary to the lies of these people." If then the Friar, although unwilling, would call him a vile and useless man, he would smile joyously and applaud heartily, saying: "May the Lord bless thee, for thou speakest the truth; such things the son of Peter Bernardone deserves to hear." [62]

The praise of men was only then a source of joy to him when it redounded to the glory of God alone. One day he was preaching with great success at Terni. At the conclusion of the sermon the Bishop said to the people: "In these latter days God has favored His Church through this poor and despised, simple and ignorant man; therefore it behooves us to thank God, because we know that He does not grant these blessings to every country." When Francis heard the Bishop giving praise to God, but representing him, Francis, as a contemptible person, he threw himself at his feet and exclaimed with holy joy: "Lord Bishop, thou hast honored me greatly; others rob me of what is mine, thou alone hast left it untouched. Thou hast separated what is precious from the vile, and as a discerning man hast given to God praise and honor, to me, however, contempt." [63]

Francis accordingly wished to be but a shadow before the Light Eternal, or rather, even this shadow was to be swallowed up in the Light. He compared the true servant of God with a painting which represented and glorified the Saviour or His blessed Mother Mary. The painting laid no claim to the honor which belonged to the Saviour; its object was to promote the honor of God. Thus man is naught but a picture representing the blessings of the Most High; yes, man is less than a pitcure, less even than the wood on which it is painted; he is a pure nothing before God. And for this reason he must surrender all honor to God. [64]

That is the secret of the humility of Francis: he thought and acted and lived as if none else existed on earth but himself and God alone. He was so overpowered by the glory of God that the entire world sank into nothingness before it. From this sentiment was born that word full of wisdom, so justly admired by the author of the *Imitation of Christ:* "How much soever each one is in the eyes of God, so much he is and no more." [65] A truly golden, truly honest and unselfish, thoroughly chivalrous zeal for the honor of his divine Liege Lord! Had not Christian knighthood inscribed this humble confession on its banner? [66] Had not Francis vowed to live and fight for his Lord alone as a spiritual knight? Had he not promised to follow Christ the Lord as His loyal liegeman? And was it not evident that the Son of God had descended from the bosom of His Father to our lowliness chiefly for this, that He might become the teacher of humility by word and example? [67]

Francis therefore forswore all honor which did not redound to the glory of Christ. [68] As the true herald of Christ, he walked before all men on the path of humility. [69] "On this foundation, which Christ had pointed out to him, he placed himself and his Order. Humble in his conduct, more humble in his heart, most humble in judging himself, this prince by the grace of God excelled all others in this jewel only: that among the Friars Minor he was the least of all." [70]

It need not surprise us, then, that Francis founded through his disciples *a real school of humility.* Thomas of Celano was the first to give expression to this thought [71] and he declares: "They were in truth Friars Minor, submitting themselves to all men, and endeavoring constantly to occupy the last place, filling such places only which were regarded as the lowest, in order thus to rear without difficulty the spiritual edifice of all virtues on the firm foundation of true humility. . . . Serving all men humbly and with devotion, they drew all men to humility and patience." [72]   The Three Companions likewise note this characteristic of the first Franciscans: "They were so firmly founded and rooted in humility and charity that each one honored the other as his father and master; and those who excelled among them by virtue of their office or any other superiority, appeared as the lower and meaner." [73] Bernard of Bessa attests, that the nobles in particular who had joined the fraternity became possibly even more humble and meek and simple than all others, being conscious of the fact that nothing can be nobler and greater than to be a true knight of Christ.[74]   The Benedictine Prior, Roger of Wendover, also stresses the fact that the outstanding feature of the Order of Friars was, next to poverty, their gracious and charming humility.[75] Cardinal Jacques de Vitry, however, considers, aside from poverty, this love of littleness, of lowliness and humility as the distinctive mark which sets the Friars aside from all other Religious: "That is in truth the Order of the poor preachers of the Crucified, whom we call Friars Minor," he writes.   "They are in truth Friars Minor because in their clothing, in their complete renunciation of all earthy things they are humbler than all other Religious of this time." [76]

CHAPTER IX

OBEDIENCE AND SIMPLICITY OF ST. FRANCIS

MOST intimately united, yes, almost synonymous with humility is the *obedience* and *simplicity* of Francis. These two virtues were rooted in his humility, and were stamped by it with a peculiar, singular character.

1. *Obedience,* as evangelical counsel, is indeed vowed by all Religious Orders. It is placed, accordingly, at the head of the Minorite rule, but with the distinct emphasis that the Gospel is its norm and basis: "The rule and the life of the Friars Minor is this; namely, to observe the Holy Gospel of Our Lord Jesus Christ, by living in obedience, without property and in chastity." [1] Francis indeed, in this "evangelical life in obedience, without property and in chastity," placed the greatest weight on the vow of poverty. His conception of poverty was, however, so sublime that it could not be realized without obedience; or rather, that, in conjunction with humility, obedience was the final word in the question of poverty. Francis was wont to say very ingeniously, that whoever retained the purse of self-will, had not yet left all things for God.[2] In reality, Franciscan poverty, as we have seen, reached its zenith in the humble denial of self, in the love of littleness, lowliness, submissiveness. This *spirit of deepest humility,* is, however, evidently at the same time the *spirit of obedience.* Should not monastic obedience under the divinely appointed superiors be self-evident to him who renders himself small, lowly and submissive to all men?

186

It is therefore not to be marveled at that Francis was *as obedient as he was humble*. At the head of the regulations intended for his brotherhood, he placed the declaration that he himself desired to be obedient to the Lord Pope. The first step in the new undertaking was to journey to Rome with his companions in order to make the vow of obedience personally in the hands of Innocent III. How reverent and childlike his devotion and submission to the Apostolic See was at all times, we have shown elsewhere.[3]

This, however, did not satisfy the Saint. In his ingenious love for obedience, he devised a means to be dependent on the will of an inferior even as Minister General. "Although Francis was placed above all the Friars, he nevertheless appointed one of them who dwelt with him, as his guardian and lord, to whom he was devoutly and humbly obedient," the Three Companions record.[4]

But even this solution of the problem did not satisfy him. However studiously he sought to be constantly under the orders of another—the *Fioretti* relates many touching incidents of this kind [5]—according to law he was the head of the Friars and had no other superior but the Pope. He found peace and contentment from that day only, when he gave over the direction of the Order into the hands of Brother Peter Catanii. He knelt down humbly before him and promised constant and inviolable obedience. But in order to feel the reins of obedience without respite even in the absence of Brother Peter, he requested the latter to appoint a Friar as his guardian, to whom he could be subject in all things.

From this hour he obeyed the brother who was placed over him, with childlike simplicity. "I know the fruit of obedience," he said. "Not a moment is he without merit who bends his neck under the yoke of another." [6] It was of no concern to him what was commanded, or from whom the command came. He confessed candidly: "Among other graces which Divine Mercy granted to

me was this, that I should render obedience to a novice
who had just entered an hour ago, if he were appointed
my guardian, as diligently as to the oldest and most experienced brother.   The inferior," he added, "should not
behold in the superior the man, but God, for love of
whom he is subject to others. The more contemptible the
superior is, the more pleasing to God is the humility of
the obedient Friar." [7]

His entire conduct was inspired by this lofty sentiment.
In his Testament he declares: "I wish to obey the Minister
General of this brotherhood strictly and the guardian
whom it may please him to give me. And I wish to be
captive in his hands so that I cannot go or act beyond
his obedience and his will, because he is my master." [8]
His greatest consolation in the hour of death was that
he was allowed to render the last act of obedience toward
his guardian.[9]

Every member of the primitive Franciscan family
was animated by the same *spirit of obedience*. The Three
Companions attest of Francis and his first disciples: "All
placed themselves completely in the service of obedience.
As soon as the command of the superior was given, they
fulfilled it quickly, without considering whether the command were just or unjust. In every command they recognized the will of God, and because of this, obedience
was sweet and easy." [10]   Thomas of Celano likewise says:
"These most obedient knights would not have ventured
to prefer anything to the commands of holy obedience.
The superior had not yet uttered the command when they
set about to fulfil it. Without passing judgment on the
command, much less objecting to it, they fairly upset
themselves in executing it. . . . As disciples of their
saintly master the brothers endeavored to fulfil zealously
not only whatever the Blessed Father said in brotherly
counsel or commanded with fatherly authority, but also
whatever he thought or wished, if they became aware of
it by any sign. For the Blessed Father said himself that

holy obedience does not only fulfil the word, but also the thought; not only the command, but also the wish of the superior. Not only then when the brother hears the voice of the superior, but as soon as he knows his will in any manner, he should render obedience without delay and put the wish into deed." [11]

The earliest chroniclers have quite casually and artlessly preserved several interesting snapshots, as it were, of such perfect obedience.

When the Vicar of the Order, Brother Elias, was recruiting brothers at the command of Francis for the mission to Germany, there was among many others present at the Chapter also Jordan of Giano. Elias left him the choice of either going to Germany or remaining in Italy. But this freedom of choice greatly disturbed Brother Jordan. On the one hand, it seemed to him that the Vicar was inclined to send him on the mission; but on the other, he feared for the salvation of his soul, since he thought that the Germans would immediately put him and the Friars to death, and he felt that his courage was not equal to this ordeal. At the same time he was distressed that he could not comply with the wish of his superior to make the choice himself. He finally begged Brother Elias humbly to command him to enlist for Germany and martyrdom, or command him to remain. Elias then made known his wish, and Jordan joyously joined the ranks of the brave band. [12]

In the following year, 1222, the brothers, who had then settled at Salzburg, received a letter from Cæsar of Speier, the first German Provincial, advising them that he left the decision in a weighty matter to their own judgment. The letter placed them in quandary. Had they not placed themselves completely in his hands, and surrendered their own judgment by the vow of obedience? How, then, could he leave them the freedom of choice in spite of their vow? It was only after the Provincial had expressed in plain terms what he desired in the matter, that these disciples of obedience could rest content.[13]

Somewhat later, Brother Nicholas, "the humble," formerly a distinguished lawyer, came to Germany, and at Gotha he met Brother Jordan of Giano without recognizing him as his new superior. Both greeted each other heartily and conversed with each other in the most cordial manner. Suddenly the third companion, Peter of Eisenbach, asked roguishly: "But, Brother Nicholas, dost thou not recognize our king and master?" Nicholas quickly folded his hands and replied humbly: "Certainly, I recognize my lord and am willing to serve him." "Behold then," answered Peter, "this is our Custos." Nicholas thereupon threw himself upon his knees before his superior, begged his pardon for having received him so disrespectfully, and from that moment showed such childlike obedience that Brother Jordan felt the greatest reluctance in giving commands to such a learned and obedient man.[14]

In 1224 the Friars came to England. The French Provincial, who had been charged with the mission, turned to a young cleric with the question whether he also wished to go to England. The latter, however, named William of Esseby, replied instantly that he did not know whether he wished to go or not. Seeing the surprised look on the face of the Provincial, William explained that he did not in fact know whether he wished to go, since his will was not his own, but that of his minister. Later on, the superior allowed him to choose the house where he wished to be, and William again replied obediently that the place which suited him best was the one designated by his superior.[15]

The same spirit of childlike obedience was characteristic of Brother Giles, one of the "Knights of the Round Table," as Francis called him because of his courageous obedience and his instant readiness to undertake any task assigned to him.[16] One day he asked the Saint what he should do and whither he should go. Francis replied: "Whatever thou wilt and whithersoever thou wilt." Giles thereupon wandered about for four days as the mood led him. Soon, however, this freedom of action disquieted him to such an extent that he returned to Francis and said: "Father, send me whither *thou* wilt, for in such free obedience my soul cannot find rest." [17]

Some time later he was recalled from Agello, near the Lake of Trasimene, to Assisi. The order reached him when he happened to be outside the Friary. He instantly set out for his new destination, and nothing could induce him to return for a while to the Friary. "I have been told to go to Assisi, and not that I set my foot once more in my former dwelling," was the answer of the obedient knight.[18]

From the above it may be seen that the disciples were animated by the same spirit of obedience as their master, who had declared: "I wish to obey the Minister General of this brotherhood strictly and the guardian whom it may please him to give me. And I wish to be captive in his hands so that I cannot go or act beyond his obedience and his will, because he is my master."

It was this *complete submission to the will of the superior* which Francis placed before his disciples as the only true obedience. He declared that obedience was only then perfect when the self-will of the subject played absolutely no part. Thus, one might be called "obedient" if the superior were asked to grant a favor and he then gave his consent. But entire and complete obedience implied that the superior give commands of his own accord. The former was permission, the latter obedience in the true sense of the word. The former suffices for salvation, the latter alone, however, leads to sanctity.[19] After these remarks Francis sighed: "There is hardly one Religious in the whole world who is perfectly obedient to his superior." When the Friars urged him to describe more fully the perfect and most sublime obedience, he compared the obedient man with a corpse, saying: "Take a dead body and place it anywhere you please. You will see it offers no resistance against being moved, it complains not against its position, it will not cry out if you let it go. If you seat it on a throne it will not look up or down, and to clothe it in purple but makes it more pale. Thus is the truly obedient man. He reasons not why he is sent; he minds not where he is placed, nor insists upon being sent elsewhere. If he be promoted to office, he still remains humble; the more he is honored, the more he counts himself unworthy." [20]

This perfect submission to the will of the superior must be rendered by the Friar *in all things, under all circumstances,* and *at all times.*

In all things. Francis prescribes in each of his rules that the brothers are to obey in all things "which are not against their souls and our rule." [21]   In his Words of Admonition he explains this more fully: "The Lord says in the Gospel: 'He that doth not renounce all that he possesseth, cannot be My disciple.' [22]   That man leaves all he possesses and loses his body and his soul who abandons himself wholly to obedience in the hands of his superior, and whatever he does or says—provided he himself knows that what he does is good and not contrary to the superior's will—is true obedience. And if at times a subject sees things which would be better or more useful to his soul than those which the superior commands him, let him sacrifice his will to God, let him strive to fulfil the work enjoined by the superior. This is true and charitable obedience, which is pleasing to God and to one's neighbor. If, however, a superior command to a subject anything that is against his soul, it is permissible for him to disobey; but he must not leave the superior, and if in consequence he suffer persecution from some, he should love them the more for God's sake. For he who would rather suffer persecution than wish to be separated from his brethren, truly abides in perfect obedience, because he lays down his life for his brothers.[23] For there are many Religious who, under pretext of seeing better things than those which their superiors command, look back [24] and return to the folly of their own will.[25] These are homicides, and by their bad example they cause the loss of many souls." [26]

The brothers should obey *under all circumstances.* Francis would allow no excuses or subterfuges, however justified they might seem, when there was a question of obedience. On one occasion one of the Friars had a great longing to see the Blessed Father. The guardian would not grant permission to go, and the brother undertook the journey on his own responsibility, trusting in the kindness of Francis. The latter, however, rebuked him severely, and then commanded him to remove his cowl. He then took it and cast it into the fire. And lo! though lying in the midst of the raging flames, it was not consumed by the fire. "A sign," remarks Celano humorously, "that Francis had spoken rightly, and perhaps, too, that the erring brother had not sinned so grievously." [27]

Some of the brothers were of the opinion that at least prayer and meditation were preferable to obedience. Thus a Friar one day came to Brother Giles and said with a touch of indignation: "Father, I was just now in my cell at prayer, and my guardian bids me go begging; now it seems to me that it is better to pray than to beg." Giles, who had inherited the true spirit of Francis, made answer: "Brother, believe me, thou knowest not yet what prayer is, for the most true and perfect thing is to do the will of thy superior." Another time he said: "He who places his head beneath the yoke of obedience, and afterward, that he may follow the path of perfection, withdraws his head from beneath the yoke of obedience—this is a sign of great hidden pride. A truly obedient Religious is like a soldier, well-armed, seated upon a good horse, who passes safely among the enemy and no one can harm him. But the Religious who obeys murmuringly is like an unarmed soldier seated upon a poor and stubborn horse, who, passing among the enemy, falls and is at once taken by the foe, chained, wounded, imprisoned, and then put to death. It seems to me, that if one were in such great grace that he might speak with the angels, if he were called by a man to whom he had promised obedience, he ought to leave off his colloquy with the angels and obey the man, because while he is subject in this world, he is bound to obey the man to whom he is subject for love of the Creator." [28]

The brothers were to obey *at all times*. That is perhaps the most notable feature of obedience as conceived by Francis. As he himself was disquieted whenever he was beyond the immediate direction of a superior, he also admonished the brothers never to be outside the pale of obedience, since obedience alone called down God's blessing, just as disobedience brought His curse.[29]   Brother Giles expressed the same sentiment when he said: "The more a Religious is held beneath the yoke of obedience for the love of God, so much the greater fruit will he reap. So long as the ox holds his head beneath the yoke it fills the granaries with grain; on the contrary, the ox not holding his head beneath the yoke, and which wanders about, seems to itself to be a great lord, but the granaries are not filled with grain. The great and the wise humbly put their heads beneath the yoke of obedience, and the foolish withdraw their heads from beneath the yoke and will not obey." [30]

Francis went even further. If the superior chanced to be absent, he desired that the Friar should obey any other brother who happened to be present. He was, of course, well aware that this was not the strict obedience due only to the lawfully appointed superior, but rather the zealous fostering of the spirit of obedience, or, as he expressed it, the voluntary obedience of love.   "The brothers," he said, "should willingly serve and obey each other in the spirit of charity; and this is the true and holy obedience of Our Lord Jesus Christ." [31]

Still more. In order to practise the virtue of obedience constantly and perfectly, they were to be submissive to all men; yea, to all creatures. Francis declares expressly of himself and his first disciples in his Testament: "We were simple and submissive to all men." [32] In his Praise of Obedience he says: "Holy obedience confounds all bodily and fleshly desires and keeps the body mortified to the obedience of the spirit and to the obedience of one's brother, and makes a man subject to all the men of this world, and not to men alone, but also to all beasts and wild animals, so that they may do with him whatsoever they will, insofar as it may be granted to them from above by the Lord." [33]

With this well-nigh heroic conception of obedience, Francis merely makes the final deduction from his conception of humility, according to which he and his disciples are to be the smallest, the least, the most submissive of all men, and thus be in truth *Minores,* Friars Minor, after the words of the Gospel. [34]

This unrestricted condition of service and submission on the part of the subjects would indeed have led to slavery and tyranny if Francis had not on the other hand likewise placed the *relation of the superiors toward their subjects* entirely on the Gospel. The Gospel makes the superiors the ministers and servants of their subjects and designates every form of domineering as pagan abuse of power. Francis accordingly says: "The ministers and servants [*minstri et servi*]"—that is the official title, the purely evangelical title of superiors—"should remember what the Lord says: 'I have not come to be ministered unto, but to minister.' . . . Let there not be power and authority among the brothers, for as the Lord says in the Gospel: 'The princes of the Gentiles lord it over them: and they that are the greater exercise power over them.' It shall not be thus among the brothers, but 'whosoever will be the greater among them, let him be their minister and servant, and he that is the greater among them, let him be as the younger.' " [35]

That is the main feature and the most important element in the constitution of the Franciscan Order, that the superiors are regarded as *"ministers and servants."* Francis stressed this point frequently and emphatically. These terms occur so frequently [36] that no one can fail to realize how great a weight Francis laid on this conception. He expressly declines the titles customary in other Orders, such as the name Prior, "the first." [37] Thus, the custom of addressing the superior of the entire Order as "Minister General," of a Province as "Minister Provincial," was sanctioned even during the lifetime of the Saint. The superior of a smaller number of houses was called "Custos," the superior of a house "Guardian": both terms are a degree lower than that of Minister, having the sense of a watchman, overseer, menial, body-servant. [38]

Francis repeatedly impressed the superiors with their duty to conduct themselves in truth as the ministers and servants of their brothers, in accordance with their designation. He describes the true *Minister General* as one who is at the service of all brothers, accessible to all, and helpful to all in word and deed; who receives and serves without distinction the little and simple ones as well as the great and learned ones; who, the more learned he himself is, shows himself all the more condescending and accessible. [39]

The same qualities must also adorn the *Ministers Provincial*. They are to be friendly in their converse with even the least of the brothers, and filled with such kindness and benevolence that even the sinners do not fear to open their hearts to them. They should be moderate in commanding, lenient toward offenses, more willing to suffer wrong than to avenge it, foes to wrong-doing, physicians to the sinners. [40]

He counsels *all superiors*: "Command seldom in obedience! Do not quickly have recourse to severe measures! Do not easily take the sword in hand!" [41]   And he admonishes them: "Let him to whom obedience has been entrusted and who is considered greater, become as the lesser and the servant of the other brothers, and let him show and have the mercy toward each of his brothers that he should wish to be shown to himself if he were in the like situation.   And let him not be angry with a brother on account of his offense, but let him advise him kindly and encourage him with all patience and humility." [42]   He commands all the superiors of the Order: "Those brothers that are ministers and servants of the other brothers . . . shall humbly and charitably correct them. . . . And let them receive the brothers charitably and kindly and show so great familiarity toward them that they may speak and act with them as masters with their servants, for thus it ought to be, since the ministers are the servants of all the brothers." [43]

The superiors, however, who are thus in truth the minor brothers of their brothers, Francis wishes to be revered and honored and loved for Christ's sake, because they bear in the name of God the cares and burdens of all, and are worthy of the supreme reward before God.[44] He calls them "blessed": "Blessed is that superior who shall be found as humble among his subjects as if he were among his masters!" [45]

Francis himself had been such a superior, calling himself in his Testament "the little one and servant" of the brothers.[46]   Superiors of this kind are repeatedly met with among the disciples of Francis.   One instance is worthy of mention, being typical of the Franciscan Ideal. In 1225 a Custos was to be appointed for Saxony.   Blessed Albert of Pisa, at that time Provincial of Germany, had selected for this office Brother Nicholas of Reno, with whom we have already become acquainted.   Foreseeing that the latter would refuse the office because of his profound humility, he did not send the appointment by letter,

but went in person to persuade him to accept the office.
Brother Nicholas demurred, saying that he lacked admin-
istrative ability, and could not act the part of prelate and
lord. The Provincial took him at his word and said with
seeming indignation: "Ah, brother, thou canst not act
the part of a lord! Are we, then, lords who hold office
in the Order? Confess thy fault instantly, brother, because thou hast called the offices in the Order which are
in reality burdens and services, lordships and prelacies."
And as penance Nicholas was then commanded to assume
the office of Custos. He filled it with his accustomed
humility, being always the first when there was a menial
task to be performed, such as cleansing the dishes or
washing the feet of the brothers. Whenever he was
forced to impose on a brother the penance of sitting on
the floor or of taking the discipline, he performed the
penance with him in true humility. Yet he punished
severely every show of stubbornness, in order to prove
by word and example how great an evil disobedience is
and how the brothers should obey in all simplicity.[47]

That is the Ideal of Franciscan obedience: superiors
and subjects in humble contention for the last place, and
united in this rivalry—as we shall see—by the bond of
true brotherly love.

2. The *simplicity* of Francis, like his obedience, is the
product of his humility. Both humility and simplicity
are so closely related that only the keenest eye can detect
the difference. He is humble who desires to be accounted
no more than he is; simple who desires to appear no other
than he is.[48] To be accounted more than one is, detracts
from simplicity; to appear other than one is, detracts from
humility. For this reason Francis so frequently mentions
simplicity and humility in one breath, and speaks of the
former with such rapturous enthusiasm that a child of
the world is justly astounded.

For the world has at best only a deprecating smile for
simplicity, often even contempt and mockery. The very

word itself has become an expression of contempt. The majority of men will rather suffer to be called clever, shrewd, cunning, crafty, false, tricky and double-tongued, than to be called simple. This noble virtue has been so thoroughly proscribed, that it requires almost heroic courage to break a lance in its defense, and more so to practise it in all conditions of life. Pretense and boastfulness, hypocrisy and deceit, duplicity and double-dealing rule not only commerce, politics and worldly culture, but also the mutual conventions of society; yea, even the most intimate relations of family life are infected by this virus. We have even forgotten to be honest, upright and simple with ourselves and with God. Duplicity is in fact the true spirit of the world and of our time.

But the *spirit of Christianity is simplicity*. What is more charming than the simplicity of the Saviour, that simplicity which attracted the children to Him strongly and which scandalized none but perverse Phariseeism! And what is more appealing than the Gospel of simplicity of the Saviour: "Amen I say to you, unless you become as little children, you shall not enter the kingdom of heaven!" [49] Unless you become as little children— frank, open, candid, upright, natural, unaffected, true and straightforward, in a word: simple!

This simplicity is the distinguishing mark of the saints, and of every genuine Christian. If duplicity or hypocrisy could be charged against them, all virtues would not counterbalance this one defect. The character of simplicity was impressed especially on the Christian culture and mysticism of the Middle Ages. *And its most charming blossom was St. Francis of Assisi.*

Thomas of Celano declares: "Holy simplicity, this daughter of grace, sister of wisdom, mother of justice, was fostered by the Saint with exceeding great zeal in himself and cherished by him in others. Yet not every kind of simplicity did he call good, but that alone which, content with its God, counted all other things as little." [50]

A profound conception of simplicity! Duplicity and deception aim to appear different, better in the eyes of the world than one really is in the eyes of God. Simplicity, however, aims to appear as one is in the judgment of the all-knowing and all-just Judge, without regard to the judgment of creatures. This was the simplicity which animated Francis. His constant endeavor was *never to appear before men better* than he was and thought and acted *in the eyes of God.*

One day, being ill and weak, he rode on a beast and chanced to pass a peasant's dwelling. The peasant hastened to him and inquired whether he were Brother Francis. When Francis nodded humbly, the peasant admonished him: "Take heed that thou be as good as thou art said and praised to be; for many have faith in thee. Therefore I admonish thee never to appear other than people believe." Hearing these words Francis quickly dismounted, cast himself on his knees before the peasant and kissed his feet, thanking him heartily for having thus admonished him.[51]

This principle of conduct conveyed by the naïve words of the peasant had in fact been always observed by Francis with scrupulous anxiety. Thomas of Celano describes at length how the Saint was animated from the very beginning by the sole endeavor to become perfect before God, without the least thought of the judgment of the world. He then adds: "He was constantly solicitous for holy simplicity."[52] How truly this is said, is evident to everyone who has acquainted himself with Francis and his life. He not only avoided every shadow of hypocrisy; he was, on the contrary, simply not capable of such. And this is the very element which renders his deep, rich and extraordinary personality so easily understood, so close and intimate, and so natural, because he appeared never other than he was, always candid, clear, plain and simple as a child.

As soon as he became aware that what he did in secret

did not harmonize with the favorable impression which his public actions made, he would call the attention of the people to it. At one time he lay ill in the hermitage at Pogglio during the Advent fast, and was in need of more nourishing food. Preaching to the people around Christmas time, he began his sermon with the words: "You consider me a holy man and have therefore piously journeyed hither. But I confess to you that during this entire season of fast I have taken food prepared with bacon." [53]

Another time, convalescing from illness, he partook of some chicken meat. As soon as he was able to leave the house, he hastened to Assisi in order to preach in the market place. Having arrived at the gate of the city, he commanded his companion to place a rope around his neck, to lead him as a bandit through the streets and to call out like a town-crier: "Behold the glutton who fattened himself on the meat of fowls, which he ate without your knowledge." In this manner he frequently exposed himself to the people.[54]

During the winter his guardian had at one time procured him a piece of fox fur and said to him: "Father, thou art suffering grievously, I beg thee for the love of God to allow me to sew this piece of fur beneath thy habit, at least so as to cover the stomach." The Saint replied: "If thou wilt that I wear it underneath the habit, then place also a like piece on the outside, in order to let the people know that there is a fur hidden within." All remonstrances were to no avail, so that the guardian was finally forced to sew a piece within and without, and the sick man thus appeared outwardly as he was in secret.[55] The biographer remarks hereto: "O thou, the same in word and deed, the same within and without, the same as subject and as superior! Thou hast never loved the praise of men, nor the praise of self, who hast ever gloried in the Lord alone!" [56]

If at times even a thought arose in him which seemed

to him an imperfection, he did not hesitate to confess it openly. He wished to be at all times as clear as crystal, and thus entirely transparent to all. While walking through the streets of Assisi one day, he met an old woman who asked an alms of his charity. Having nothing with him but his mantle, he joyously gave this to her. Soon after, however, a temptation to vain-glory arose in his heart. He immediately confessed before all present that he had felt a sense of pride because of his act of charity.[57]

On one occasion he felt a desire to speak with Brother Bernard. The latter, however, was so rapt in God that he did not heed the voice of Francis. This annoyed the Saint somewhat and he secretly fretted because of this disobedience of the brother. But as soon as he became aware of his fault, he confessed it openly, cast himself on the ground, and said to Brother Bernard: "I command thee under holy obedience, that in order to punish my presumption and the rashness of my heart, when I shall cast myself down upon the ground, thou shalt put one foot on my throat and the other on my mouth, and then pass over me three times from one side to the other, speaking to me reproachfully and contemptuously, and especially saying to me: 'Lie there, miserable little son of Peter Bernardone; whence comes to thee so much pride, seeing thou art a most vile creature?'" [58]

In his simplicity Francis frequently subjected himself to similar humiliations because of such imperfections in thought. Thomas of Celano writes in general terms: "He did many things of this kind, in order to render himself altogether contemptible and to encourage others to strive after imperishable glory. To himself he appeared as an unworthy vessel; . . . he exposed himself without mercy to every dishonor, lest self-love lead him to desire earthly things." [59] Truly, "a man with the simplicity of a dove," remarks a contemporaneous chronicler.[60]

Francis impressed the same character on his disciples.

Among the virtues which he enjoined on them from the first day, simplicity always occupied a prominent place. "The blessed Father taught them to fulfil evangelical perfection, to observe poverty, and to walk in the way of holy simplicity," writes a contemporary.[61] In order to test the simplicity of his brothers he at times resorted to measures that appear to us almost childish, as when he commanded Brother Masseo to turn in a circle until he became dizzy and fell to the ground, or when he sent Brother Rufino to Assisi to preach without a habit.[62] He punished faults against simplicity severely, as in the case of the young Friar who out of charity or humility would not confess to the Saint that he had been harshly treated by his older companion.[63]

He thus educated his brothers to an almost incredible degree of simplicity. They revealed to him the most secret thoughts and emotions of their heart.[64] Simplicity had become as it were a second nature to them, so that every form of insincerity or duplicity was unknown to them, and their entire life was one of marvelous purity and innocence.[65]

The primitive days of Franciscan history present many splendid examples of saintly simplicity. Besides the above-mentioned Brothers Masseo and Rufino, may be pointed out: the first Friars in England, who joined with a great zeal for learning a truly childlike simplicity in speech and action;[66] Brother Giles, whose entire life was a picture of simple wisdom and wise simplicity; Brother Juniper, whose dovelike simplicity caused the Saint to exclaim: "My brothers, my brothers, would that I had a whole forest of such junipers!";[67] Brother James, "the Simple," who went to such extremes in nursing the lepers with whose service he was charged by Francis, that the Saint was forced to rebuke him mildly;[68] Brother John, likewise called "the Simple," whom Francis wished to have about himself constantly because of his simplicity. Brother John had but one wish—to become like his master in all things. If he beheld Francis at prayer, he imitated the least of his gestures. If Francis spit out, John did likewise; if Francis coughed, John coughed also; if Francis wept and groaned, John wept and groaned; if Francis raised his arms to heaven, John did likewise. When questioned by the Saint why he did thus, he replied: "I have promised at my entrance into the Order to live exactly as thou; it were perilous to act otherwise in the least." Francis laughed joyously at his naïve simplicity and explained to the brother that it was not meant just so. It would suffice if he were to follow the rule of the Order with the same simplicity and sincerity of mind. A short time afterward the Brother died, simple as he had always been. Francis often pointed to him later as a model of simplicity, and never called him Brother John, but always the Blessed John.[69] And rightly so. For according to the words of the Saviour [70] this childlike character, this guileless, unassuming, unselfish simplicity is the quintessence of all perfection and sanctity.

For this reason *Francis wished that his Order preserve this spirit of simplicity and sincerity under all circumstances and for all times.* Whenever he was urged to adapt himself and the Order more to the life of the Benedictines, Cistercians or Augustinians, he declined quickly and firmly, saying: "My brothers, my brothers, the Lord has called me to the way of simplicity and humility, and this way He has revealed to me in truth for myself and for all who wish to follow me." [71] In his dying moments he admonished his brothers to understand the rule and to live according to it in the spirit of simplicity: "As the Lord has given to me to speak and to write the rule and these words [the Testament] simply and purely, so shall you understand them simply and purely and with holy operation observe them until the end." [72]

In his solicitude for holy simplicity *he constantly warned the present and future brothers against the spirit and the wisdom of the world,* which seeks more the appearance than the truth, more affectation than sincerity, more exterior ostentation than inner perfection.[73] "Brothers," he said, "let us keep ourselves from the wisdom of this world, and the prudence of the flesh; for the spirit of the world wishes and cares much for words, but little for work; and it seeks not religion and interior sanctity of spirit, but wishes and desires a religion and sanctity appearing from without to men. And these are they of whom the Lord says: 'Amen, I say unto you, they have received their reward.'[74] But the spirit of the Lord wishes the flesh to be mortified and despised, and to be considered vile, abject, and contemptible; and it studies humility and patience, pure simplicity and true peace of mind, and always desires above all things divine fear and divine wisdom, and the divine love of the Father and the Son and the Holy Ghost."[75] And again: "Let us not be wise and prudent according to the flesh, but let us rather be simple, humble and pure."[76]

Francis nevertheless recognized that *wisdom directed toward God and united with God,* was no enemy of simplicity. Indeed, he praised both as two sisters: "Hail Queen, Holy Wisdom! May the Lord save thee with thy sister holy pure Simplicity!"[77] He constantly admonished the Friars who were occupied with studies to exercise themselves equally in science and simplicity: "I would have my brothers to be disciples of the Gospel and so to increase in knowledge of the truth that they may grow at the same time in purity and simplicity, so that they may not separate from the wisdom of the serpent the simplicity of the dove, which our Divine Master joined together with His blessed mouth."[78]

He went even further. His axiom was: the more simple and humble the learned brother was, the more progress will he make in the science of God,[79] and the greater his learning, the simpler he should strive to be in his thoughts and actions.[80]

At the same time the Saint did not fail to see that the *unlettered lay-brothers* would be of marked influence in preserving the character of simplicity in the Order. Their very station and condition demanded simplicity, and Francis accordingly called them his "simple brothers," and he esteemed them highly as an essential element of the Order. Whenever he had his tonsure cut as cleric, he would say to the Friar performing this task: "Do not make the crown too large, so that my simple brothers may also find place on my head." [81]

For the sake of simplicity he therefore wished the Order to embrace unlettered lay-brothers as well as educated clerics. "Before God," he said, "there is no respect of persons, and the Minister General of the Order, the Holy Ghost, rests on the poor and simple ones as well as on the rich and learned." He had even wished to insert these words in the rule, but could not do so because it had already been approved by the Pope.[82] Both classes of brothers were to vie with each other for the palm of simplicity.[83] Both, united by the bond of simplicity, were to become a spectacle unto heaven and earth. "Our Order," he said, "is like an immense gathering, in a measure a general council, which convenes from all parts of the world under one mode of life. Therein the wise draw profit from that which is of the simple, because they see how the unlearned seek the heavenly things with fiery zeal and how the simple brothers become wise in spiritual things through the Holy Spirit. Therein the simple likewise draw profit from that which is of the wise, seeing how most learned men condescend to them, although they might lead a life of fame in the world. In this," he concluded, "shines forth the beauty of this blessed family, whose manifold charm delights the heavenly Father." [84]

CHAPTER X

CHASTITY AND PENANCE OF ST. FRANCIS

AS OBEDIENCE and simplicity are the two main branches on the tree of humility, thus *chastity* is its fragrant blossom. Just as it is impossible to be chaste without humility—theology and experience both bear witness to this—so also it is easy for the humble man to remain chaste, and to him it is self-evident that he must esteem and cherish chastity above all else. We need not marvel, therefore, if it is said of Francis: "Next to humility, which is the foundation of all virtues, the Saint loved and esteemed in his brothers especially the virtue of chastity in all its purity and beauty." [1]

Both nature and grace seemed to have predestined Francis to a rare excellence in this virtue. He had been born and reared by a mother who stands forth as a perfect model of moral greatness and purity.[2] From her motherly pride sprang the one ambition to behold her son grow up with the same moral greatness and purity, so that she was wont to say: "What do you think will become of my son? With the aid of grace he will surely become a man of God." [3]

Even in the midst of the reckless frivolity of his youth, Francis preserved his innocence unsullied. The Three Companions are able to testify: "He was, as it were, by nature and by generous resolve, of a noble character in conduct and speech. Never did he utter an unseemly word. Yea, although a youth of great joviality, he made it a rule never to answer ribald language. For this he was greatly esteemed in the entire vicinity, and many who knew him declared that he would yet become a great man." [4]

After he had said a final farewell to worldly pleasures, and had espoused Lady Poverty, he guarded the purity of his heart and life with redoubled zeal.[5] Whenever he experienced an improper emotion or sensation, he resorted to measures which make us shudder. In the middle of the most severe winter he plunged himself into icy water, remaining therein until the carnal desire had completely vanished.[6] This extreme severity surprises us all the more, since there was evidently no question of temptation to impurity, but merely to sensuality. He declared, however, that it were incomparably more bearable to a spiritual man to suffer great cold in the body than to feel even in slight measure the fire of sensuality in the spirit.[7]

He thus preserved mind and body from every blemish until death. Although he declared himself to be the greatest of sinners, yet he never confessed himself guilty of any failing against chastity.[8] Brother Leo, his confessor, never detected in him even a shadow in this regard. One day the unstained innocence of the Saint was revealed to Brother Leo in a vision. He beheld a lofty mountain, on the peak of which Francis walked alone. At his surprised query what this vision signified, a voice answered: "The mountain is virginity, on whose height Francis, truly the most chaste servant of God, constantly abides." [9] His unstained purity was impressed even on his countenance. Whoever approached him, instinctively felt the childlike innocence of the Saint, of whom his first biographer writes: "Oh, how beautiful, how glorious he appeared in the innocence of his life, in the purity of his heart, in his angelic countenance!" [10]

In order to forestall every danger, Francis observed the

greatest caution and reserve in his dealings with the opposite sex. He designated familiarity with women as sugared poison, which causes the weakling to fall, and often exposes the strong to severe temptations. He said, "To deal with women and still to escape their harmful influence, is, except for a man well-tried in virtue, as easy (as it is written) as to walk through fire and not burn the soles of his feet." [11]

He therefore commanded his brothers to shun the society of women as much as possible. He explained this injunction by saying that a Friar should speak with them only in case of confession, or for the sake of brief admonition and instruction. He remarked: "What has a Friar Minor to say to a woman, except in confession or for the sake of encouragement to a more spiritual life?" [12]

He himself was guided by this principle during his whole life. It was only with the greatest reluctance that he conversed with women. As soon as their tedious gossiping conflicted with his brief and humble speech, he broke off and resorted to silence with downcast eyes. He would often then raise his eyes to heaven, as if he wished to draw thence the words with which to reply to their vapid talk. Those, however, who came to him with the earnest desire to be instructed in matters of spiritual life and who utilized their conversation with him for true progress in virtue, he instructed with wondrously wise, but few words. When speaking with a woman, he would raise his voice in such manner that all could hear him.[13]

At the same time he observed scrupulously great modesty of the eyes. In this he went so far that he was able to confess to his companion on one occasion: "I assure thee, most beloved brother, I should not recognize any woman by countenance, if I were to look at her, except two. These two I know, but none other." [14] Thomas of Celano, who records these words of the Saint, adds the following incident. Francis was one day on the way to Bevagna, when he collapsed at the roadside, exhausted by a long and severe fast. He sent his companion to a pious woman to ask for some bread and wine. The woman came in haste with her daughter, who had consecrated herself to God, to render aid to the Saint. After Francis had recovered somewhat and strengthened himself, he in turn strengthened mother and daughter with the word of God. While he spoke, he did not once raise his eyes to their faces. When they had left, the companion remarked: "Brother, why hast thou not looked at this saintly virgin, since she came to thee with so great reverence?" Francis replied: "Who should not fear to gaze upon the spouse of Christ? If one is to preach with eyes and mien, she should look at me and not I at her." [15]

His chaste reserve in regard to the female sex was prompted by his spirit of chivalry. As a true knight of Christ he was filled with a profound reverence for womankind, and especially for those consecrated to Christ. He recommended this spirit of chivalry to his disciples in the form of the following allegory. A pious and powerful King sent to the Queen two messengers in succession. When the first messenger returned, he spoke only of the things connected with his embassy and said nothing about the Queen. He had wisely kept his eyes to himself, and had not once lifted them to look at the Queen. The other returned and after a few words began with great animation to speak of the beauty of the Queen. "Truly, my Lord, I have seen the most beautiful of women; happy he to whom she belongs!" Then said the King: "Thou wicked servant, who hast dared to lift thine impudent eyes to my spouse! It is clear that, by cunning, thou didst desire to obtain her thou didst gaze upon." He then sent for the first one and asked him: "What is thy opinion of the Queen?" "The best of opinions, since she so willingly and patiently listened to me," thus answered this wise man. Then said the King: "Thinkest thou she is beautiful?" He replied: "My Lord, her beauty is for thy gaze; I had but to repeat the words of thy message." Then the King passed this sentence: "Thou, because thine eyes are chaste, shalt be in my chamber, chaste of body and a partaker of my delights; but this impudent one must be turned out of the house, that he may not pollute my chamber." Francis added hereto the remark: "If one feels too secure, he guards himself less well against the enemy. Give the devil a hair, and he will soon make it grow into a beam. And if he succeeds not in conquering the tempted one for many years, he complains not, if only he yields in the end. That is truly his handicraft, at which he busies himself day and night." [16]

It was this chaste and wise sentiment which prompted Francis to write the twelfth chapter of his first rule: "Let all the brothers, wherever they are or may go, carefully avoid unbecoming looks and company of women, and let no one converse with them alone. Let the priests speak with them honestly, giving them penance or some spiritual counsel. And let no woman whatsoever be received to obedience by any brother, but spiritual counsel being given to her, let her do her penance where she wills. Let us all carefully watch over ourselves, and hold all our members in subjection, for the Lord says: [17] 'Whosoever shall look on a woman to lust after her, hath already committed adultery with her in his heart.'" [18] In the final rule the Saint gives the following injunction, under the direction, no doubt, of Cardinal Hugolino, who was well versed in the prevalent ecclesiastical law: "I strictly command all the brothers not to have suspicious intimacy or conferences with women, and let none enter the monasteries of nuns except those to whom special permission has been granted by the Apostolic See. And let them not be godfathers of men or women, that scandal may not arise on this account among the brothers or concerning the brothers." [19]

Even regarding the "Poor Ladies of San Damiano"

Francis commanded his brothers to observe the greatest reserve; yea, they were to be all the more cautious in their dealings with the Poor Clares, since they stood in closer relationship to the Friars as members of the same Order. The Saint charged only such Friars with the direction of the nuns, who had proved themselves fit for this office by a virtuous life, and who were reluctant to assume this burden.[20] He punished without mercy those who made unnecessary visits to them,[21] and he himself appeared very seldom and only for very weighty reasons in San Damiano.[22]

These severe measures, however, sprang in no wise from an exaggerated hatred of womankind or from a similar vagary, but were dictated solely by the Saint's solicitude for his own virtue and that of others. The tender as well as holy friendships of Francis with Clare of Assisi and with Giacoma de Settesoli furnish abundant proof of this.

Toward Clare his whole life was one of fatherly friendship in the full sense of the word. In this he was guided by the thought that the one and same spirit had led himself and his brothers on the one hand, and Clare and her daughters on the other from the world, and the same spirit should also underlie their mutual bond of love.[23] When the Friars, therefore, showed surprise that he so seldom gave the handmaids of Christ the pleasure of his bodily presence, he replied: "Think not that I do not love them perfectly. If it were not allowed to love them in Christ, it were still more wrong to espouse them to Christ. Had I not called them to the religious life, I should have done them no wrong; but to leave them after I have called them, would be great cruelty. If I nevertheless rarely go to see them, I do it for the sake of example, that you may do as I have done." [24]

In consequence of his visits to San Damiano becoming more and more rare, St. Clare was seized with anxiety lest her spiritual father should abandon her completely,

and Francis thereupon wrote her the following lines:
"Since, by divine inspiration, you have made yourselves
daughters and handmaids of the most high Sovereign
King, the heavenly Father, and have espoused yourselves
to the Holy Ghost, choosing to live according to the perfection of the Holy Gospel, I will, and I promise to have
always, by myself and my brothers, a diligent care and
special solicitude for you, as for them." [25]   He kept this
promise faithfully until the end, and enjoined it most
earnestly on the conscience of the Friars in the hour of
death.[26]

The same strong and loyal friendship bound him to
Giacoma de Settesoli. This noble and saintly Roman
lady had merited the affectionate love of the Saint in
consequence of her remarkable virtue and her bountiful
charity toward the Order.[27]   On her part she was devoted
to the Saint with her whole heart until his death.[28] Francis therefore did not wish to pass from this life without
having bidden her farewell. A few days before the end he
had a letter sent to her, requesting her to come in all haste,
and to take with her various articles for his last hours
and for his burial. At the very moment when the messenger was about to depart for Rome, a commotion was
heard before the house, and when the door was opened,
Giacoma with her sons and a large retinue stood before
the entrance. On hearing these tidings, Francis was
overcome with joy, and he exclaimed: "Blessed be God,
who has sent to us Lady Giacoma, our brother. Open
the doors and lead her within, for the law forbidding
women to enter the convent does not bind Brother Giacoma." The meeting of the two friends was exceedingly
touching. Giacoma had brought with her the very articles
which Francis had requested in his letter: candles, an
ash-colored cloth to be used as a shroud, linen for his
face, and a pillow for the bier. In her thoughtful love
she had not even forgotten to take along with her the
favorite dish of the Saint which she was wont to place

before him on his visits to Rome. Francis was strengthened in such measure by this visit, that he seemed to take
a new lease of life. Nevertheless he foretold to his benefactress the day of his death, and requested of her the
final act of charity of remaining until after his burial.[29]

Truly, an exemplary regulation of the relation toward
the other sex as becomes a Friar Minor! Exemplary
the modest reserve, as well as the chivalrous reverence
toward womanhood. Exemplary also the conscientious
solicitude for the welfare of the souls entrusted to his
care, as well as the grateful appreciation for the charity
shown to him. And exemplary, above all, the unrelenting
severity with which Francis charged his brothers to flee
all improper or scandalous dealings with women, in order
to anchor their innocence and purity firmly in God.

2. To the avoidance of danger Francis joined *the practise of penance*.

The New Testament designates the entire Christian
conception of life in general as penance, a life of penance.[30] Since the purpose of the Poverello was to lead
back the entire world to a life based on Christian principles and Christian ideals, the Franciscan form of preaching and the Franciscan movement as such, was called, in
brief, "the preaching of penance" and "the movement to
penance." [31] The Friars Minor themselves, who were
the pioneers of this movement, styled themselves originally "Brothers of Penance of Assisi." [32] And in his
Testament, in which the Saint reviews the first days of
his new life, he remarks: "The Lord gave me, Brother
Francis, thus to begin to do penance." [33] In conjunction
herewith the entire life of poverty, humility, simplicity,
chastity, which the brothers promised and practised, had
all the elements of a life of penance. In fact, this life
demands in a high degree the spirit of penance, and represents its uninterrupted practise.

Francis raised both to a degree truly heroic. From
the first day on which he began to withdraw from the

world, he imposed such severe penances upon himself that he was derided as a fool.[34]   When soon afterward he appeared before the Bishop of Assisi and divested himself of his sumptuous garments, returning them to his father, Peter Bernardone, he wore on his body nothing but a hair-shirt.[35]   Later on, he fashioned for himself an exceedingly rough and poor garment, in order to crucify his flesh night and day.[36]   When on one occasion a soft garment was given him, he fastened some rough cords within; for, he said, according to the word of the Eternal Wisdom, one should not seek soft garments in the huts of the poor, but in the palaces of princes.[37]   Being asked how he could endure the severity of the winter's cold in that poor clothing, he made answer in the fervor of his spirit: "If we burn within with a fervent desire for our heavenly country, easy it is to endure this exterior cold." [38] He spoke in this manner in order not to confess that he frequently almost perished with cold, finding so little protection in his poor clothing.   One day he was walking along the road during winter time in the face of a very cold wind.   A sense of discouragement began to weigh him down, but as soon as he became conscious of this, he roused himself and went up into a mountain, and taking off his habit, he exposed himself thus to the cutting wind.   He then said to himself: "How well would it be now to be clothed even in one tunic!" [39]

Even at night he retained his rough clothing.   This, with a chain girdle, was his only protection against the cold night air.   Never would he use a covering.   His bed was the naked floor.   His sleep was brief, and taken mostly in a sitting posture.   His pillow was a stone or a block of wood, or at most a rolled-up sack.[40]

Not only in his clothing, but also in his food he exercised the utmost rigor, denying himself all that was not absolutely necessary to sustain life.[41]   His axiom in this regard was that it is hardly possible to satisfy the needs of the body without indulging the sensual appetite.[42]   He spent the greater part of the year in rigorous fasting. At one time he fasted forty days, partaking of no food whatever, in order thus to imitate the example of the Saviour. But toward the end of this fast he ate a half loaf of bread, lest he should boast of having fasted continuously as his divine Master had done.[43]

Even outside the ordinary seasons of fast he was most abstemious both in regard to the amount and the quality of food. He would seldom eat cooked food, and, when doing so, he rendered it unpalatable by mixing into it water or ashes. Lest the brothers should ascribe this to a spirit of penance, he explained that Brother Water and Sister Ashes were chaste. He resorted to the most ingenious methods of this kind even when invited to dine with persons of note. But in order not to offend his host, and to follow the injunction of the Gospel to eat of all things placed before him,[44] he would eat sparingly of the meat and other delicacies, but hide the rest in the folds of his habit, continuing, however, to put his hand to his mouth, so that no one suspected what he was doing. He partook rarely and sparingly of wine; indeed, he would not even drink enough water to quench his burning thirst.[45]

To these mortifications he added others no less severe. He treated his poor body like a beast of burden, which must be continuously held in check. Brother Giles no doubt spoke the mind of the Saint when he said: "The body of the brother of penance is as a beast of burden. Although it may bear heavy burdens, and although he may feed it well withal, it will not go along the road aright if it feels not the rod of correction."[46] Francis accordingly chastised his body with incredible severity, whether in good or ill health.[47] He never spared it and treated it by word and deed as if it were his worst enemy.[48] Whenever it dared to show signs of rebellion, whether from itself or by the instigation of Satan, it was made to suffer doubly. Thomas of Celano relates the following incident, which he had heard from the mouth of a reliable eye-witness.

Francis had exhausted his frail body one night in the hermitage at Sarziano by incessant prayer and penance. Suddenly the tempter cried out: "Francis, Francis, Francis!" The latter replied: "What wishest thou?" And the Evil One gave answer: "There is no sinner in the whole world whom the Lord will not pardon if he but repent; but whoever destroys his life by severe penance, will not find mercy in eternity." The Saint immediately detected the ruse of the enemy, who wished to seduce him to tepidity. Undaunted by the temporary failure, the tempter began to point out to him that he, Francis, was deceiving himself in depriving himself of the happiness of a home and family, and at the same time he painted the pleasures of married life in the most glowing colors. Francis, recognizing the hand of the tempter, took off his habit and began to scourge himself cruelly with the cord, saying: "Ah, Brother Ass, it behooves thee thus to feel the scourge. The habit belongs to the Order, this may not be stolen. But if thou desirest to run away, then run." But although his whole body had been bruised by the scourge and bled freely, the temptation did not yield. Then, opening the door of his cell, Francis went out into the garden and plunged himself into a pile of snow. And gathering up the snow with his hands, he formed seven mounds or pillars of snow, and placing himself before them, he addressed his body thus: "Behold, this large pillar is thy wife; the next four are thy two sons and daughters; the other two are thy servant and maid, whom thou needest for thy service. Hasten now to clothe them all; for they are dying with cold. But even if thou art burdened with manifold care in their behalf, yet must thou serve thy only Lord zealously." Then the illusion vanished.[49]

This constant and merciless chastisement gradually brought his body to complete subjection under the soul.

The latter ruled over it as over a most willing servant. The soul henceforth was free to rise to the utmost heights —the body never again resisted; yea, it appeared to outstrip even the soul. The fire of his spirit had so lightened the body that it vied with the soul in thirsting for God, as the Scripture says: "For Thee my soul hath thirsted; for Thee how mightily my flesh!" [50]   The daily and uninterrupted habit of following the rule of the soul and of clinging to it most closely, became a necessity for the body, indeed, a second nature.[51]

In the two last years of his life, when the Lord Himself put him through the school of suffering, the heroism of the Saint reached the loftiest heights. Nailed to the cross with Christ by the sacred Stigmata, exhausted by incredibly painful maladies,[52] he preserved not only his accustomed cheerfulness of soul, but he refused steadfastly to grant his body the least alleviation. In their love and anxiety, the brothers urged him to desist from his harsh treatment of his body, yet he could not be brought to yield to their entreaties.[53]   Finally, one of the brothers prevailed upon him in this manner: "Tell me, Father," he said, "has thy body, as long as it could, rendered zealous obedience to thy commands?" Francis replied: "Certainly, my son; this testimony I must give to it, that it was obedient in all things, never spared itself, but on the contrary hastened head over heels as it were, to fulfil all commands. It shirked no labor, avoided no hardships, so long as it could follow my wishes. In this we have both been perfectly at one, to serve Christ without the least discord." The brother then said: "Where then, Father, is thy benevolent heart, where thy sympathy, where thy most tender compassion? Is that the reward worthy of a true friend, to accept blessings and then in the time of need to refuse to repay the benefactor according to merit? What couldst thou have accomplished in the service of thy Lord Jesus Christ without the assistance of thy body? Has it not, as thou hast said, exposed itself to every danger?" "I confess, my son, this is very true," replied Francis. The brother continued: "Is it, then, just that thou shouldst not succor such a true friend in this need, who has sacrificed himself and his own to death for thy sake? May that be far from thee, Father, thou joy and staff of the sorrowful, far from thee be such a sin before the Lord." These words struck a responsive chord in the heart of the Saint. He looked with pity on his emaciated body, broken with pains and suffering and near death, and he said: "Rejoice, Brother Body, and forgive me; in future I shall willingly comply with thy wishes and lovingly listen to thy complaints." [54] His compassion with the loyal friend whom he had treated all his life as an enemy, was as genuine and sincere as his former severity. On the very day of his death he believed himself bound to an apology and confessed candidly that he had sinned greatly against Brother Body.[55]

Francis likewise *trained his disciples in the school of penance and mortification.* He warned them not to seek the cause of their faults and imperfections outside themselves, but to attribute them to their own flesh, which constantly militates against the spirit. "There are many," he said, "who if they commit sin or suffer wrong, often blame their enemy or their neighbor. But this is not right, for each one has his enemy in his power—namely, the body by which he sins. Wherefore, blessed is that servant who always holds captive the enemy thus given into his power, and wisely guards himself from it; for so long as he acts thus, no other enemy, visible or invisible, can do him harm." [56]

The Saint accordingly urged his brothers constantly to watch over and guard both the interior and exterior senses.[57] A single example will suffice to illustrate the severity of the Saint in this regard. Toward the end of the year 1204, Emperor Otto IV, who had just·received the imperial crown at Rome, passed through Assisi.[58] The cavalcade was journeying on the road which led close by the hut at Rivo Torto, where Francis was then staying with his brothers. The crowds flocked together from all sides to view the German Emperor in all his magnificence, with his numerous and gorgeous retinue. Francis, however, would not so much as set foot before the hut, nor would he allow any of the Friars to witness the glorious spectacle. One Friar, however, was sent by him to accompany the cavalcade and to remind the Emperor continuously of the vanity of earthly fame.[59]

The disciples of Francis, moreover, hardly stood in need of encouragement to the practise of penance: The example of their father alone sufficed to incite them to similar severity.[60]   The entire Franciscan school of those first days was animated by a spirit of penance so fervent that every Friar regarded it as highly improper to indulge in any bodily comfort whatsoever.[61]   Their entire mode of life was so severe, that the rhetorician Buoncompagno of Bologna, a contemporary of those days, writes: "The Friars Minor can in truth be numbered among the disciples of the Lord, because they spurn all earthly lusts, torture their flesh, and follow Christ with unshod feet and a garb of penance." [62]   Other eye-witnesses were seized with awe at the sight of this austere life of penance, and declared that only saints or fools could thus crucify themselves.[63]   The Friars on their part were affected neither by the one nor the other opinion of the world, and persevered steadfastly on the narrow and steep path of evangelical penance.[64]

Their clothing was so poor and coarse that it appeared to serve more for the torment than the protection of the body. In food and drink they restricted themselves to what was absolutely necessary to life, and whenever they perchance exceeded this measure because of great hunger or thirst, they abstained for several days from all food in punishment for their indulgence. After laboring arduously the whole day, they spent a great part of the night in prayer and meditation. If sleep nevertheless demanded its rights mercilessly, they resorted to various ingenious methods to keep themselves awake; they would often bind themselves to a hanging rope, lest they fall over from sheer exhaustion and thus disturb the others in their devotions. They spoke rarely and only what was strictly necessary. They would hardly hear or see even those things which could possibly not be avoided. All their senses and their entire exterior conduct were regulated in like manner by complete self-control. If they were mocked and jeered at, despoiled, scourged, shackled, imprisoned, persecuted in every way, they not only did not seek any defense, but praised and blessed God for the injury inflicted on them. To this they added other chastisements, such as plunging themselves into icy water, or rolling themselves among sharp thorns until covered with blood. Many wore iron rings on their body, or carried girdles studded with wooden prongs, or resorted to similar instruments of torture in order to crucify Brother Body.[65] Some of the Friars would have rendered themselves ill by means of this excessive severity, or at least unfit for labor and prayer, if Francis had not prudently and firmly intervened.[66]

For *the Saint forbade resolutely all such lack of moderation.* "In this point alone," remarks his biographer, "his example did not harmonize with his teaching." [67] He himself treated his body with inhuman cruelty, because he thought that, on the one hand, he was a greater sinner than the others; and that, on the other, he was bound to do more in this regard than others.[68] But for his brothers and for the Order itself, his conduct was not to be directive. At public Chapter he therefore reprimanded those who exceeded the bounds of prudence in their vigils, in fasting and other practises of penance. He forbade this strictly, and commanded them to treat Brother Body mildly and sensibly.[69]

In his private instructions he likewise admonished the brothers frequently to season their severity with prudence and forbearance. "One must treat Brother Body with kindness," he said, "lest a storm of rebellion break out on his part. One must not give him any reason to murmur, that he may not tire of watching and praying devoutly. Otherwise he could complain: 'I perish for hunger; I cannot bear the burden of thy good works.' But if he has received sufficient nourishment and still shows signs of rebellion, then may he know that the lazy beast of burden deserves the spur and the idle ass the prod." [70]

Fortunately we are able to learn through Thomas of Eccleston and Thomas of Celano how lovingly Francis put these principles into practise. The former relates the following incident told him by Blessed Albert of Pisa himself. Brother Albert, later on Minister General (1239-1240), was at one time staying with the Saint at a hospital. To the arduous labor of caring for the sick, Albert joined a rigorous fast. Francis became aware of this and commanded him forthwith to eat henceforth a double amount of what he had hitherto taken. Brother Albert learned from this to care for his subjects in later years with the same kindness and discretion. He looked after the wants of the sick and delicate brothers with the love of a mother, and at one time sharply rebuked a guardian and his procurator, because they had not provided more abundant food on a festival day after the brothers had labored strenuously in the care of souls.[71]

Thomas of Celano relates an even more touching incident. Francis at one time had retired for the night with the brothers. In the middle of the night, while the others were sleeping, one of the Friars suddenly cried out: "I am dying, brothers, I am dying for hunger." The good shepherd arose immediately and hastened to succor the poor hungry sheep. He had a table prepared with various homely delicacies, water taking the place of wine, which was often lacking. Francis was the first to begin eating, and urged the others to do likewise, lest the hungry brother be ashamed to eat. When the love feast was finished, Francis spoke at length on the virtue of moderation in fasting as well as eating, in the care of the body as well as in its mortification. Every sacrifice, he said, which is offered to God, must be seasoned with the salt of prudence. Everyone must consider his own strength in the service of God. He even declared that it was just as sinful to exceed moderation in depriving the body of the necessary nourishment, as to surfeit it with superfluous food for the sake of indulging the appetite.[72] The brothers were to follow prudence in all things as the guide of all virtues; not that prudence, however, which is prompted by the flesh, but which Christ has taught, whose most holy life is the shining example of all perfection.[73]

That was the *supreme norm of all his Ideals* and especially of *penance: Jesus Christ, His life, His Gospel*. This explains how judiciously Franciscan penance was tempered and softened by its *characteristic mildness*. We know that the Friars Minor had taken on themselves all the austerities of the evangelical life, and for this express reason were called "Brothers of Penance." Yet it would be an easy matter to furnish the proof that the Franciscan Order nevertheless emphasized the spirit of mildness, which permeates the Gospel, more than the older monastic institutions. As points of comparison may be mentioned, in order not to digress too far, only two: corporal punishments and the precepts regarding food.

None of the older monastic rules discard corporal chastisement; that is, daily punishment of offenses by stripes, scourging, etc., on the part of the superior. The most severe chastisements were ordained by St. Columba (545-615). The more serious as well as trivial offenses were punished according to his rule with cudgeling. Whoever forgets to make the cross over the spoon before eating; omits the Amen after prayer; talks too loudly; speaks of himself; excuses himself after a reprimand; coughs unnecessarily; whoever makes himself guilty of a dozen such misdemeanors, is subject to chastisement. Everywhere blows are threatened, distributed and counted exactly, six, twelve, fifty, a hundred, so that the monk was hardly able with the best of intentions to finish a day with a whole hide.[74]   It was because of this almost barbaric severity of the Columban rule, besides others, that from the seventh century the rule of St. Benedict (480-543) was introduced into most monasteries of the West.   The cultured and refined Roman, Benedict, rescinded the merciless system of chastisement, but without relinquishing corporal punishment altogether.   In the first place he ordains that the younger and unlettered inmates of the monastery, who lacked the proper understanding for other penances, should be punished for more serious offenses "either by extraordinary fasting or with sharp stripes." [75]   The other monks are to be punished with stripes or scourging if previously punished without amending themselves.[76]   The statutes of the Cluniac reform (composed after 1123) still prescribe corporal chastisement of a very severe nature, at which the offending monk "according to ancient custom" was stripped and beaten with a sharp scourge.[77] Even the Dominicans retained the old custom of having the Religious who was guilty of more serious faults, beaten at public Chapter at the feet of each conventual.[78]

Such regulations are simply unthinkable in the Franciscan rule, so thoroughly is it permeated by the spirit of evangelical mildness.   The entire penitential discipline of the Minorite rule is contained in the words: "If among the brothers, wherever they may be, there should be some brother who desires to live according to the flesh and not according to the spirit, let the brothers with whom he is, admonish, instruct and correct him humbly and diligently. And if after the third admonition he will not amend, let them as soon as possible send him, or make the matter known to his minister and servant, and let the minister and servant do with him what may seem to him most expedient before God.   And let all the brothers, the ministers and servants as well as the others, take care not to

St. Francis in the Embrace of the Crucified Jesus

be troubled or angered because of the fault or bad example of another, for the devil desires to corrupt many through the sin of one; but let them spiritually help him who has sinned, as best they can; for he that is whole needs not a physician, but he that is sick." [79]   Corporal chastisement is not even provided for those grave offenses which necessitate the ejection of the Friar from the Order.   In these cases the sinning brother is simply directed to leave the Order and do penance in the world.[80]

Not only in regard to the discipline of penance, but also in regard to the *regulations concerning food,* Francis deviated essentially from the older Orders.   He indeed prescribed, like other Founders, fasting for a great part of the year.[81]   Fasting was then understood to mean that the Friars ate but once a day, toward evening, and then only Lenten food.[82]

But while all other Orders forbade the use of meat even on days not of fast,[83] Francis permitted it unreservedly on these days, within and without the monastery.[84]   In this he adhered simply to the injunction of Christ to the apostles: "Eat what is set before you." [85]   He ordains expressly in the third chapter of both rules: "According to the Holy Gospel, it is lawful to eat of all foods set before them." [86]

This innovation, unheard of in the history of monastic institutions, caused no little sensation.   Even some of the Friars were of the opinion that the Saint had exceeded all bounds in his clemency.   While Francis was absent on his mission to the Orient, in 1219, the two Vicars to whom the direction of the Order was entrusted meanwhile, assembled a number of Friars of like sentiment at a Chapter, and ordained that the Friars should henceforth no longer procure meat for themselves, but partake of it only when given by benefactors.[87]   Francis received notice of this unauthorized encroachment on the constitution of the Order while he chanced to be sitting at table with Brother Peter Catanii before a dish of meat.   "Well now, Sir

Peter," he said, "what is to be done?" The latter replied: "Ah, Sir Francis, whatever pleases thee, for thou hast the power." In their mutual polite respect they always addressed each other as lords. Francis did not hesitate long, but remarked gaily: "Let us, then, eat, according to the Gospel, what is set before us." [88]

CHAPTER XI

FRANCISCAN JOY

NOT a virtue in the proper sense of the word, but the fragrant aroma of all the virtues hitherto considered, the everlasting spring-charm of Franciscan life, the bright golden atmosphere of the entire Franciscan movement—that is, the joy of the Poverello and of his disciples. It is for this very reason the characteristic mark of the Franciscan Ideal, and forms the colorful setting on which this Ideal is mounted.

1. *Francis himself was by very nature gay and joyous,* as the Three Companions attest.[1] He was in this a true son of his mother. Donna Pica, a child of the gay Provence, rich in song and music, had endowed him with a heart so joyous that it could not be clouded even by the somber, calculating and mercenary spirit of his father, Peter Bernardone. Even the partnership in the paternal business failed to dampen his youthful gaiety. Though prudent and shrewd in commercial affairs, he retained his sunny disposition, "a youth full of the joy of life, merry, and devoted to mirth and song," as the biographers declare.[2]

The *gaya scienza,* the "gay science" of the troubadours served even more to weave a sweet charm about his joyous conception of life. All great and small courts, all towns and cities of Italy, resounded at that time with the minstrel-songs and ballads of the troubadours and jongleurs, those knightly poets and bards. Francis himself provided his native town with a "court" of such joyous fellows. Clothed in the colored garb of a minstrel,[3] and

with a scepter in his hand, he passed as King of Youth
from feast to feast in company with his friends,[4] at all
places "the first in frolic, in mirth and song." [5]

But through all his joviality there ran a strain of seri-
ousness. His ambition was to become a knight, or perchance a prince; and knighthood was not to be thought
of without the gay doings of the troubadours. Wherever
we read of knightly courts and tournaments, we meet also
the knightly and courtly minstrels. The knights themselves deemed it an honor to be as expert with the lyre
as with the sword. Gaiety, in fact, seems to hold the first
place among the qualities which become the knight.[6] "The
newly invested knight must be gay," is the injunction
given in an instruction on knighthood; "for this is the
handicraft of arms: great clamor in the field, and great
joyfulness at home." [7] Francis was so imbued with the
truth of this axiom that he would not allow himself to be
deprived of his gaiety even while a prisoner in bonds.
During the entire time that he languished in captivity at
Perugia with the knights of his native town, while all
the others succumbed to discouragement and depression,
he alone preserved his usual imperturbable cheerfulness.[8]

This characteristic mood was not destroyed by his conversion to the knighthood of Christ, but was *translated
into the spiritual and supernatural realm* and thus greatly
ennobled and enhanced. At every step which he took in
the realization of his new vocation, his biographers note
an ever increasing joy of mind and heart. They relate
the vision which presaged his spiritual knighthood for the
first time, and add: "From that hour he was filled with
such joy that he could no longer contain himself, but was
forced to manifest his interior jubilation in the company
of men." [9] They relate how he began to show his chivalrous love for God by rendering heroic charity toward the
lepers; and they emphasize the fact that in this, humanly
speaking, loathsome and disgusting occupation he experienced an excessive sense of joy.[10] They tell us how

his divine Liege Lord soon after made the nature of his spiritual knighthood clear to him, and remark that in consequence of this revelation an overpowering sense of heavenly bliss took possession of him.[11] They describe, finally, how he appeared as a finished knight of Christ, singing spiritual ballads in the French tongue. At one time he was stopped by robbers, and when they asked who he was, he replied joyously: "I am the minstrel of the great King; what is it to you?" The miscreants thereupon seized him, abused him roughly, and finally threw him into a ditch filled with snow, saying mockingly: "Lie there, thou boorish minstrel of God!" Francis, however, shook himself free of the snow, climbed out of the ditch, and wandering through field and forest he began with greatest joy to sing the praise of God.[12]

His entire life was henceforth attuned to this basic note of joy. Thomas of Celano assures us: "The Saint constantly endeavored to persevere in this gladness of heart, to keep ever fresh the unction of the spirit and the oil of joy. With utmost solicitude he avoided the greatest evil of ill-humor; . . . With imperturbable calmness and cheerfulness of mind he sang to himself and to God songs of joy in his heart." [13] His ceaseless endeavor was to keep himself interiorly and exteriorly in a joyous mood.[14] In the intimate circle of his brothers he likewise knew how to sound the pure key-note of joyfulness and to make it swell to such full harmony that they felt themselves raised to an almost heavenly atmosphere. The same joyful note pervaded the converse of the Saint with his fellow-men. Even his sermons, in spite of their burden of penance, became hymns of gladness,[15] and his mere appearance was an occasion of festive joy for all classes of people.[16]

Joy transfigured even his constant weeping for the sufferings of the God-Man and for his, as he thought, countless and grievous sins. Bonaventure points out this feature in the character of the Saint in the words: "He never ceased to clarify his soul in the rain of tears, aspiring after the purity of supernatural light and counting as little the loss of his bodily eyes. Yet though he shed streams of tears, he was filled with a certain heavenly joy, which gladdened his spirit and his countenance. In the stainlessness of his holy conscience he overflowed so with the oil of joy, that his spirit was constantly dissolved in God and he unceasingly rejoiced over the works of the Lord." [17] Thomas of Celano relates how the interior melody and the sweet whisperings of the Holy Ghost in the soul of Francis would break forth in rapturous songs rendered in the French tongue,[18] and he adds: "He would often take a piece of wood from the ground, as we have seen with our own eyes, lay it on his left arm, and holding with his right another piece bent by means of a cord, would draw it across the wood as across a violin, making gestures at the same time (after the manner of the troubadours) and singing ballads in the French tongue to the Lord. At times this ecstasy of joy would turn into weeping, and the jubilation ended in piteous sighs for the passion of the Lord." [19]

Joy assuaged and sanctified even his own *sufferings and maladies*. The Three Companions remark: "His heart rejoiced so much in the Lord, that his weakened and mortified body became strong enough to endure all hard and bitter things most joyously for God the Lord." [20] Even when his sufferings grew to a veritable martyrdom he preserved his wonted smiling cheerfulness.[21]

Only once, at the approach of death, his usual cheerfulness threatened to leave him. Tortured by unspeakable pains, he struggled one night in prayer for knightly fortitude until the end. Suddenly he heard in spirit a consoling voice: "Rejoice, brother, and exult in thy weakness and tribulation, and trust so confidently as if thou wert already in My kingdom." The following morning his soul rose to the sublimest heights and composed that hymn of joy, the Canticle of the Sun,[22] which "lets all natural joy and all joys of nature and all supernatural joy of the believing and God-loving soul flow together and sends it as a crystal-clear, rapturous fountain toward heaven, into the ocean of divine glory and eternal bliss." [23]   This Canticle of the Sun Francis requested the brothers to sing to himself again and again in those last days and nights.[24] When Brother Elias remarked to him quietly that such a preparation for death might offend others, Francis answered smilingly: "Permit me, brother, to rejoice in the Lord and in His praise and my own infirmities, since by the grace of the Holy Ghost I am so united and joined to the Lord that by His mercy I well may rejoice greatly in Him." [25]   A few hours before his death he summoned all his remaining strength and intoned the One Hundred and Forty-second Psalm.[26]   When he had finished, evening had fallen, the day of his life had drawn to a close. Singing, he passed into eternity.

The famous master Zurbaran (1598-1662) portrays the Saint meditating on a skull.   Since then, Francis is seen so frequently in pictures and paintings with a skull, that the impression is given as if this representation were typically characteristic.   And yet it is a travesty of the Saint, a simply impossible attitude, warranted neither by his life nor his death.   His life was one hymn of joy, and to "Brother Death" he sang the last, most touching strophe of his Canticle of the Sun.   He was a virtuoso of joyfulness, than whom history knows none more expert. Had history not called him the "Poor Man of Assisi," he would have to be known as the "joyous" Francis.

Francis impressed the same character of joy on his Order.   The primitive Franciscan days were as a single melody full of spiritual joy.   One becomes entranced in roaming through this paradise at the hand of the *Fioretti*, whose charming poetry is in this regard more historical than history itself could ever be.   But also the oldest biographies and chronicles of the Order give proof that the Franciscan family lived constantly in a well-nigh heavenly atmosphere of joy. This is so evident and so well known, that more need not be said.

To one as familiar with the needs of spiritual life as Francis, it was clear that *cheerfulness is indispensable to the Religious.* He regarded it outright as the infallible remedy against the countless snares of the enemy.[27] He was wont to say: "The devil rejoices most when he can rob the servant of God of the joy of the spirit. Satan's game is won when the heart is opened ever so little to allow him to inject a speck of dust with which to tarnish the candor of the mind and the purity of life. But as long as the heart is filled with spiritual joy, the serpent endeavors in vain to instil his deadly poison. The devils cannot harm the servant of Christ so long as they behold him filled with holy joy. But when the soul is in ill-humor, if discouraged and desolate, it easily becomes a prey to complete unhappiness or turns to vain pleasures." [28]

The interior joy of the soul did not, however, suffice for the Saint. *His brothers were to be joyous in their exterior appearance and conduct as well.* One day he noticed that a companion showed a mournful and sad countenance. Francis rebuked him severely: "It behooves not a servant of God to show himself sad and ill-humored before men; he should, on the contrary, always be of good cheer. If thou hast sinned, go, and examine thyself in thy cell and weep over thy sin before God. But when thou returnest to thy brothers, put aside thy sadness and be cheerful as the others." [29] Turning to his brothers, he then added: "The enemies of man's salvation envy me exceedingly, and since they cannot rob me of my cheerfulness, they endeavor constantly to disturb my brothers." [30]

From the very beginning of the Order, Francis had therefore embodied cheerfulness in his program. Mindful of the admonition of the Gospel: "Be not, as the hypocrites, sad," [31] he inserted these words in his first rule: "Let them take care not to appear exteriorly sad

and gloomy like hypocrites, but let them show themselves
to be joyful and contented in the Lord, merry and becomingly courteous." [32]   He considered this command so important that he had it placarded at one of the General
Chapters, so that it might give the entire assembly the
character of joy.[33]

The Chapters of the Order were in fact feasts of joy
and brotherliness, according to the eye-witness Jordan
of Giano; [34] yes, Cardinal Jacques de Vitry declares that
the fostering of universal joyfulness was one of the main
objects of the annual meetings of the Order.[35]

Not content with being joyful in the Lord themselves,
the brothers were to be *messengers and harbingers of joy
for the whole world*.   The object of their apostolic activity was to promote and encourage true joy among the
masses by word and song and example.   Preaching and
singing they were to pass through the world.   With the
Gospel of the "glad tidings" they were to sound the
praises of the Lord as knightly troubadours.[36]   "For,"
thus he declared on his death-bed, "what else are the
Friars but joyous minstrels of the Lord, who move and
excite the hearts of men to spiritual joy?" [37]

2. We have considered the Franciscan spirit of joy as
a *fact*. Let us now try to discover from the Saint also
the *secret* of his joy. For, the problem still remains to
trace the singular *character* and the deep-welled *source* of
Franciscan joyfulness.

In the first place, it is evident from the foregoing that
there is no question of the talmi-gold of riotous or sensual
pleasures.   The Saint constantly recommended *spiritual
joy*, the *joy of the soul*, and his zeal in fostering this joy
was as ardent as his zeal in avoiding all unbecoming
hilarity.[38]   As unbecoming he regarded not only that a
Religious should find pleasure in earthly amusements and
vanities,[39] but also in vain and idle laughter and gossip.
He, the lover of decorum and gravity, would not consider
such as true joy of the spirit, but as vanity and folly.[40]

He strongly admonished his disciples: "Blessed is that Religious who feels no pleasure or joy save in most holy conversation and the works of the Lord, and who by these means leads men to the love of God in joy and gladness. And woe to that Religious who takes delight in idle and vain words and by this means provokes men to laughter." [41]

Francis was, of course, not oblivious of the fact that man is composed of body and soul, and that the soul cannot rise freely and joyously to God if hindered by the body. We have already shown how discreetly and mildly the Saint judged of these things in spite of his rigorous penance, and how he often admonished the brothers to treat Brother Body kindly and show him mercy in all his needs, that he might thus willingly serve the soul.[42] It was truly Franciscan when the saintly Provincial, Peter of Teukesbury, remarked: "Three things are necessary to keep one in bodily health—food, sleep, and a joke," and when he enjoined as a penance upon a brother of a melancholy disposition that he drink a tankard full of the best wine, saying to him: "My dear brother, if such a penance were given to you frequently, you would surely have a better conscience." [43]

Francis himself would often resort to music and song in order to render soul and body cheerful. Thus, one day when the affliction of his eyes weighed heavily on him, he called to himself a companion, who had been a lute player in the world, and said: "Brother, I wish that thou go and borrow a lute in secret, and compose a song, and thus bring comfort to my Brother Body, who is full of pain." The companion replied: "I fear much, Father, that the people might attribute this to levity on my part." The Saint then answered: "Well, then, brother, be it so. It is good to omit many things, lest we give scandal." But while the man of God was praying the following night and was rapt in God, suddenly there sounded in his ears the marvelously sweet melody of a lute. He saw no one, yet he heard, now from this side, now from that, the music of a lute player as if he were walking to and fro. His spirit was filled with such heavenly joy because of this angelic music, that he thought himself already in the other world.[44]

Music and song played, indeed, an important part in those primitive days of the Order.[45] Religious song was fostered by Francis and his sons in all places and in all its forms: as choral, as hymn and prose, as unison and polyphonic cantilena, as rhyme poetry in the Latin as well as in the vernacular tongue. That is one of the chief reasons why the Order appealed so strongly to that exceptionally musical and poetic period: that explains why many a gifted troubadour joined the choir of the poor minstrels of God, and dedicated his muse, which had hitherto sung the praises of knightly adventure and love of fair lady, to the praise of Eternal Love and the sweet Virgin Mother.

But this must be stressed constantly: Francis wished to cultivate the *spiritual song* for the sake of *spiritual joy*. He styled himself time and again the joyous minstrel of the Lord, and deplored deeply that musical instruments served any other purpose but to sound the praises of God.[46] "Joyous minstrels of the Lord," he styled his disciples, for this reason: that they had tuned the harp of the troubadour to the praise and the love of God.[47] Thus, we read of Brother Juniper: "Brother Juniper was an excellent minstrel of the Lord, singing of the Lord frequently in burning words." [48] Thus, too, of Brother Giles: "This holy man was always cheerful and joyous. And when he spoke with someone of the words of the Lord, he was filled with wondrous joy; in his ineffable ecstasy he could then kiss straw and stones and do many such things from pure devotion. But when he found himself in such marvelous grace, it seemed bitter to him to turn away from God and to eating; he then wished to be able to live from the leaves of trees, lest he lose even for an hour the grace of conversing with God. When he finally returned to the brothers, he walked joyous and jubilant and praising God, saying: 'No tongue can express, no writing describe, and no heart of man perceive, what the good God has prepared for those who love Him.' " [49]

In a similar manner the joy of prayer, and prayer itself, became for Francis an overflowing fountain of joyfulness. As soon as he noticed that a mere breath of sadness threatened to becloud the joyous candor of his soul, he turned quickly to prayer in order to regain his wonted cheerfulness.[50] He also admonished his brothers to turn to God without delay whenever sadness began to weigh them down, saying: "If a servant of God, as it may easily happen, is sad for any reason, he must turn to prayer immediately and tarry before the face of the most high Father until He restores His salutary joyfulness. For, if he remain longer in this sadness, this Babylonian [all disturbing evil] will increase, and, unless finally destroyed by tears [of prayer] it will leave in the soul a lasting harm." [51]

We thus understand the essence of Franciscan joy and the source from which it springs. Francis and his brothers rejoiced in the greatness and the goodness of God, which is revealed in all His creatures and which becomes a soul-satisfying and living experience especially through the personal contact with God, by living under His eyes, and in constant converse with Him. Franciscan joy is the *joy in God, of God,* and *from God.*

Its second characteristic feature is *joy of poverty.* According to the universal testimony of history, the Franciscans were from the very beginning so unspeakably content and happy not only in spite of their poverty, but directly because of their poverty. The contemporaneous witnesses cannot speak of the poverty of Francis and his disciples without emphasizing constantly that in the retinue of Lady Poverty cheerfulness occupied a prominent place.

They relate how Francis dwelt near the poor little church of Portiuncula with the first three Friars in a wretched hut, and add: "These four dwelt together with unceasing jubilation and ineffable joy of the Holy Ghost." [52]   They tell of the first missionary efforts of the Saint and his companions, and remark: "While they journeyed to the March of Ancona, they rejoiced exceedingly in the Lord; Blessed Francis, however, sang with a loud and clear voice songs of praise in the French tongue, blessing and glorifying the mercy of the Most High. They were filled with such joy as if they had found a great treasure in the possession of evangelical poverty, for love of which they despised as dung with a generous and joyous heart all earthly things." [53]   They stress the fact that the brothers were happy in the lack of all things save a poor habit with the cord and the breeches, and add the psychologically fine observation: "Since the disciples of most holy poverty possessed nothing and loved nothing, neither did they fear to lose anything." [54]   They show furthermore how constantly new friends were attracted by the joyousness of the disciples of poverty,[55] and how the latter also found the treasure of joyfulness in their utter despoilment: "They became exceedingly joyful because of their poverty, since they desired no riches, but despised all perishable things. They rejoiced unceasingly in the Lord, because they had nothing, neither inwardly nor outwardly, by which they could have been grieved in any way." [56] They then afford us an insight into the intimate companionship of the brothers with Lady Poverty, and confess: "The brothers rejoiced inexpressibly, since they neither saw nor possessed anything which could have given them vain or carnal pleasure. They began thus to cultivate bridal converse with Holy Poverty, and, filled with consolation because of the lack of all earthly things, they vowed to remain faithful to her in all places and for all times. And since they were comforted by divine consolation only, free of all earthly care, they resolved not to allow themselves to be weighed down by any tribulation, nor shaken by any temptation, nor torn away from the embraces of Lady Poverty by anything." [57]

Promise and expectation found their fulfilment. "The espousals of the Order with poverty became in fact an unending marriage-feast amidst song and rejoicing." [58] Not only in Umbria and the surrounding provinces, the carefree home of the Order; in fact, in every place poverty and joy accompanied the Friars. We behold them in a short while passing through southern Tyrol across the Brenner into Austria, Germany and Hungary. Their constant companion is carefree and unburdened Joyousness. Even when forced to content themselves with a morsel of bread and a few turnips to save themselves from starvation, their hearty cheerfulness does not leave them.[59] Similarly in England. It frequently happened that the first Friars sent thither by St. Francis had to satisfy both hunger and thirst with a soup made from the dregs of beer. Each would dip a cup into the pot and drink in turn, speaking some word of edification when his turn came, thus seasoning the mess with overflowing cheerfulness and hearty joy.[60] At all times these Friars were so joyful and merry amongst themselves that even when they were silent their countenances seemed to laugh.[61]

This was exactly according to the heart of Francis. In spite of all poverty to sing joyously as the larks; joyously to labor for their daily bread; joyously to go in quest of alms; joyously to return from begging;[62] joyously to share the alms of Providence [63]—this he constantly recommended to his brothers. And, to express all in one word, he coined the motto: *"Paupertas cum lætitia*—poverty with joyfulness." [64] Whoever understands poverty as Francis did, as the voluntary renunciation of all earthly substance for love of God, with complete trust in Divine Providence, and in imitation of the poor Saviour, he gains through poverty an inexhaustible treasure of spiritual freedom, hearty contentment and supernatural happiness.

A third feature of Franciscan joy is *happiness in suffer-ing*. That Francis was cheerful even in suffering and in spite of suffering, we have already seen.[65] But that does not express all. He was joyous *because* of suffering; suffering itself became for him a source of joy. The sweetness of the cross of Christ was verified in his entire life of poverty, humility and penance. The Three Com-panions assert of him after his conversion: "His heart became so joyous in the Lord that his body, although weak and delicate, received strength to endure all hard and bitter things joyously for the Lord."[66] The same is true of his first disciples: "In persecutions, hunger, thirst, cold and nakedness, they endured immeasurable trials and tribulations. All this they suffered bravely and patiently, as they had been admonished by Blessed Francis. They never became sad or ill-natured, nor did they revile those who did them evil; but, as perfect and evangelical men, they rejoiced in it loudly in the Lord and regarded it as great joy when they could suffer these and similar things."[67]

The life of Francis and of his disciples in the following years differed in no wise from the first. To suffer for Christ and for love of God was their joy most pure and mighty. The Saint himself has expressed it in wondrously charming manner in his conversation with Brother Leo "on perfect joy," as related in the *Fioretti*.

Once as St. Francis, with Brother Leo, went from Perugia to Saint Mary of the Angels in the winter, they suffered greatly from the severity of the cold, and St. Francis called to Brother Leo, who was walking a little in advance: "O Brother Leo, although the Friars Minor in these parts give a great example of sanctity and good edification, write it down and note it well that this is not perfect joy." And having gone on a little farther, he called to him a second time: "O Brother Leo, even though

the Friars Minor should give sight to the blind, and loose
the limbs of the paralyzed, and though they should cast
out devils, and give hearing to the deaf, speech to the
dumb, and the power of walking to the lame, and although
—which is a greater thing than these—they should raise
to life those who had been dead four days, write that in all
this there is not perfect joy." And going on a little while
he cried aloud: "O Brother Leo, if the Friars Minor knew
all languages and all the sciences and all the Scriptures,
and if they could prophesy and reveal not only things in
the future, but the secrets of consciences and of men's
souls, write that in all this there is not perfect joy."
Going still a little farther, St. Francis called aloud again:
"O Brother Leo, thou little sheep of God, even though
the Friars Minor spoke with the tongues of angels, and
knew the courses of the stars, and the virtue of herbs,
and though to them were revealed all the treasures of the
earth, and they knew the virtues of birds and of fishes and
of all animals and of men, of trees also and of stones and
roots and waters, write that not in this is perfect joy."
And going yet a little while on the way, St. Francis called
aloud: "O Brother Leo, even though the Friars Minor
should preach so well that they should convert all the infidels to the Faith of Christ, write that herein is not perfect joy."

And as he spoke in this manner during two good miles,
Brother Leo in great astonishment asked of him and said:
"Father, I pray thee, for God's sake, tell me wherein is
perfect joy." And St. Francis replied to him: "When
we shall have come to Saint Mary of the Angels, soaked
as we are with the rain and frozen with the cold, en-
crusted with mud and afflicted with hunger, and shall
knock at the door, if the porter should come and ask
angrily, 'Who are you?' and we replying: 'We are two of
your brethren,' he should say: 'You speak falsely; you
are two good-for-nothings, who go about the world steal-
ing alms from the poor; go your way'; and if he would

not open the door to us, but left us without, exposed till
the night to the snow and the wind and the torrents of
rain, in cold and hunger; then, if we should bear so much
abuse and cruelty and such a dismissal patiently, without
disturbance and without murmuring at him, and should
think humbly and charitably that this porter knew us
truly, and that God would have him speak against us, O
Brother Leo, write that this would be perfect joy.   And
if we should continue to knock, and he should come out in
a rage and should drive us away as importunate villains,
with rudeness and buffetings, saying: 'Depart from this
house, vile thieves; go to the poorhouse, for you shall
neither eat nor be lodged here'; if we should sustain this
with patience, and with joy, and with love, O Brother
Leo, write that this would be perfect joy.   And if con-
strained by hunger, and the cold, and the night, we should
knock again, and beg him with many tears, for the love
of God, that he would open to us and let us in, and he
should say still more angrily: 'These are importunate
rascals, I will pay them well for this as they deserve,'
and should come out furiously with a knotted stick and
seize hold of us by our hoods and throw us to the earth,
and roll us in the snow, and beat us all over our bodies;
if we should bear all these things patiently and with joy,
thinking of the pains of the blessed Christ, as that which
we ought to bear for His love, O Brother Leo, write that
it is in this that there is perfect joy.   For, above all the
graces and gifts of the Holy Spirit, which Christ has
given to His friends, is that of conquering oneself, and
suffering willingly for the love of Christ all pain and ill-
usage." [68]

If we now again seek the key to the secret of Franciscan
joy, the answer is very simple. As the minstrels and troubadours were the sunshine of knighthood, thus joyousness
lent a sweet charm to the spiritual knighthood of St.
Francis. As genuine Knight of Christ, Francis was inex-

pressibly happy to serve his Liege, to follow Him in poverty and to be like unto Him in suffering; and this blissful happiness in the service, the imitation, and the suffering of Christ he announced as knightly Minstrel and Troubadour of God to the whole world.

CHAPTER XII

FRANCISCAN BROTHERLINESS

THE joyfulness of Francis, his blissful happiness so firmly anchored in God, was in fact but a fruit and result of his extraordinary love of God. This love of God was by very necessity reflected as extraordinary love of men. The peculiar character of this extraordinary love for men consisted in his observing perfectly the injunction of Christ: "All you are brethren." [1] *Franciscan brotherliness*—this term perhaps expresses properly what is meant by his great love for his fellow-men.

The members of older monastic institutions were called monks; it was only among themselves and in contrast to their superiors that they called themselves brothers. [2] Francis does not know the term monk, monastic Order or rule, but replaces them with the name *brother, brotherhood, Order of friars, rule of the friars*. [3] Any other title is prohibited. The office of the superior is suggested by the term "servant" (*minister*) or "guardian" (*custos*); but all, superiors as well as subjects, are to be called simply "brothers." [4] We are told expressly in the first rule, that the Saint had the text quoted above, in mind when writing on brotherly love. [5] The latter was, then, evidently to be characteristic of his brothers.

He constantly held this *Ideal of brotherly love* before their eyes. Thomas of Celano assures us repeatedly: "The Blessed Francis admonished all to charity, kindness and brotherly affection. He said: 'I desire that my brothers show themselves as sons of *one* mother, and if the one ask the other for a habit, a cord or anything else, it should be given him generously. Books and all things which one may wish, they should share with one another, or rather one should urge the other to accept it.' . . . The constant desire and unceasing endeavor of the Saint was to preserve intact the bond of unity among the brothers, in order that those whom the same spirit had called, and the same father had begotten, should be nurtured peaceably in the bosom of the same mother. The superiors were to be one with the subjects; by brotherly affection the learned should be united to the simple; the present were to be joined to the absent by the bond of love." [6] With Poverty he greeted Love as the mistress of the Order, and the conviction was rooted firmly in his mind, that love not only beautifies the companionship of the brothers, but also affords a most powerful protection for the spiritual welfare of each.[7]

In accordance with this, he established the fostering of brotherly love in various parts of his rule as law. "Let the brothers willingly serve and obey each other in the spirit of charity. . . . And let them love one another, as the Lord says: [8] 'This is My commandment, that you love one another, as I have loved you.' And let them show their love by the works they do for each other, according as the Apostle says: [9] 'Let us not love in word or in tongue, but in deed and in truth.' . . . And wherever the brothers are and in whatsoever place they may find themselves, let them spiritually and diligently show reverence and honor toward one another without murmuring. . . . And wheresoever the brothers are and may find themselves, let them mutually show among themselves that they are of one household. And let one make known his needs with confidence to the other; for, if a mother nourishes and loves her carnal son, how much more earnestly ought one to love and nourish his spiritual brother!" [10]

Francis consequently regarded his disciples as united by the bond of such tender and cordial love, that the entire Order was thereby fused into one family. In thoughts, words and actions, inwardly and outwardly, whether near and known intimately or absent and unknown, all were to show one another genuine brotherly love. Yea, more than brotherly love: a mother's love, not indeed of the carnal order, but a much higher and sublimer, a spiritual motherly and filial love. The superiors, above all, were to take the place of father and mother in regard to their subjects, as the Saint repeatedly declares.[11]

Francis, in consequence, reproved in the most severe terms every violation of brotherly love: "Let not any brother do evil or speak evil to another . . . And let all the brothers take care not to calumniate anyone, nor to contend in words; let them indeed study to maintain silence as far as God gives them grace. Let them also not dispute among themselves or with others, but let them be ready to answer with humility, saying: 'We are unprofitable servants.'[12] And let them not be angry, for 'whosoever is angry with his brother shall be in danger of the judgment. And whosoever shall say to his brother 'Raca,' shall be in danger of the council. And whosoever shall say 'Thou fool,' shall be in danger of hell fire.'[13] . . . Let them not judge and not condemn, and, as the Lord says,[14] let them not pay attention to the least sins of others, but rather let them recount their own in the bitterness of their soul."[15] He also warned them against the vice so destructive of charity, against jealousy of the superior gifts and greater success of others: "Whosoever envies his brother on account of the good which the Lord says or does in him, commits a sin akin to blasphemy, because he envies the Most High Himself, who says and does all that is good."[16]

The Saint had a pronounced loathing for those who touched the honor and good name of a brother. He declared that they had poison on their tongues, and with it infected others.[17] Thomas of Celano assures us as eyewitness, that Francis avoided whisperers and detractors, "these vicious fleas," wherever he could, and that he

turned away from them as soon as they began to speak.[18]
At one time he heard of a brother having slandered another, and turning to his Vicar, Peter Catanii, he uttered
the terrible words: "The Order is threatened by a crisis
if the detractors are not checked. Very soon the good
name of many brothers will be sullied if the mouth of
these slanderers is not stuffed. Rise, rise, examine carefully, and if thou find an accused brother as innocent, then
inflict on the accuser a hard and public punishment. Give
him into the hands of the Florentine pugilist"—thus he
called Brother John of Florence, a man of gigantic
stature and immense strength—"if thou canst not punish
him thyself. Thou shalt see to it most diligently, thou
and all the ministers, that this pest spread no farther." [19]

On several occasions Francis commanded the one who
had defamed the good name of his brother to be robbed of
his hood, and declared him to be unworthy to raise even
his eyes to God until he repaired the injury done. In
consequence of this, the brothers at that time declared a
relentless war on detraction and slander, and endeavored
to avoid strenuously all that might injure the good name
of another, or whatever might detract from his reputa-
tion.[20] Francis confirmed them in this endeavor by stig-
matizing the slanderers in these severe words: "The
slanderer says to himself: 'Perfection of life I have none;
neither does my ability suffice for science or special grace,
and thus I have honor neither with God nor with men. I
know what I will do: I will repute dishonor to the elect,
and thus curry favor with the superior. I know that my
superior is also human and acts at times as I do, and if
we thus succeed in felling the cedars, then they will see
in the woods only us, the underbrush.' Yes, thou miserable one, fatten thyself on human flesh, and since thou
canst not live otherwise, gnaw the bowels of thy brothers!
Such men strive to appear good, not to become good;
they reprove vices, but do not put them aside themselves.
They praise only those by whose power they hope to be

favored; where praise does not promise to reflect on the flatterer, they are silent. Even their pale fasting mien they parade for the sake of pernicious praise, in order to be considered as spiritual men; they judge all things, but will not be judged by others. They desire to be saints in opinion only, not in fact; angels in name only, not in deed." [21]

From the above we may conclude that the Ideal of brotherliness such as Francis conceived, was not always realized. Where there are human beings, there are human frailties. Yet, though exceptions were found at all times, *the Franciscan family as such was always distinguished for its most cordial and happy brotherliness.* Although the members of this immense fraternity were gathered from all parts of the globe, yet they were raised up to *one* temple of the Holy Ghost by the cementing bond of love. Indescribable was their mutual love and cordiality. When dwelling together, they vied with one another in loving friendship and friendliness, each one seeking only how he might gladden the heart of the other. No privation was then able to disturb their joyousness; the thought of future separation alone burdened their heart. When the moment of leave-taking arrived, they became inconsolable, and their only solace was to accompany the departing Friars for a long way, saying farewell with many tears. If they chanced to meet one another on their journeys, whether known to one another or not, that day was for them always a feast day. They greeted each other with the word of peace and the kiss of brotherhood, conversed with each other merrily, and shared with each other whatever they chanced to have. If obedience again led them back to the monastery, the occasion became a happy reunion between brothers, a joyous return of sons to their parents. They loved and served and cherished one another as tenderly as only a mother can love and serve her only beloved child.[22] All lived for one and each one for all in such wise that no particular love was allowed to arise to destroy the mutual harmony of the family, and that each one was willing to sacrifice himself for his brother. "So greatly did charity glow in them," attest the Three Companions, "that it seemed an easy matter for them to endure death not only for love of Christ, but also for the bodily or spiritual welfare of their brothers." [23] On one occasion two Friars were journeying together. Suddenly they encountered a demented young man who in his rage began to cast stones at one of the Friars. Without hesitation one sprang forward in order to let himself be stoned in place of his brother.[24]

So great was the solicitude of the Friars to preserve mutual charity, that for every violation of brotherly love they punished themselves severely. It happened that a certain Friar, Brother Barbarus, made use of injurious words to another Friar. When he perceived that this Friar was troubled thereby, the offender was seized with a strong desire to punish himself, and picking up the dung of an ass, he put it into his mouth, saying: "Let the tongue that turned the poison of its anger on my brother eat dung!" [25] If but a word of anger or impatience escaped them, they remained unhappy until they had confessed their fault and performed penance for it. The offending Friar would cast himself quickly on the ground, confess his fault and beg the other to place his foot on the offending mouth. Remonstrance availed nothing. If the offender was a subject, he requested the superior to command his punishment; if a superior himself, he commanded the offended one to execute the sentence.[26]

The superiors were, in fact, the most zealous promoters of brotherliness, as Francis had wished and commanded. Franciscan history tells of many touching incidents of this kind. Mention may be made of only a few. Brother John de Pian di Carpine, Minister Provincial of Germany, Bohemia, Hungary, Poland and Norway, "cherished and guided all his brothers so peaceably, tenderly and devotedly as a mother her sons and as a hen cherishes and guides her brood." [27]   Brother Stephen, the first guardian of Salisbury, "was a man of great sweetness and cheerfulness and of exceeding charity and compassion, so that he could not behold anyone sad." [28]   One day two Friars stopped at an English convent, hot and thirsty from their long journey.   Nothing to drink could be found in the house but water, and the poverty was so great that they lacked even the means of purchasing anything.   Finally, the compassionate superior succeeded in obtaining a pot of beer.   This was passed first to the guests, and then to the other Friars, but the latter placed only their lips to the pot without drinking, in order that the travelers might have plenty and yet not be ashamed to drink alone." [29]

With similar tenderness St. Clare was concerned for the bodily as well as for the spiritual welfare of her daughters.   During cold winter nights she would often make the rounds in the dormitory in order to look after the comfort of the Sisters and to arrange their covering with her own hands.   As great as her zeal was for the common observance of the rule and of discipline, no less great was her loving solicitude for those whose infirmities demanded exemptions from the severity of the rule. Whenever she beheld a Sister burdened with temptations or sorrow, she would call her to herself and comfort her with tears of compassion.   At times she would cast herself at the feet of the afflicted Sister and soothe her sorrow with motherly caresses.[30]   The result of her example was such perfect unity and harmony among the Poor Ladies, that all seemed to have but one soul and one will, although at times forty or fifty of them lived together.[31]

The most splendid example of brotherly love *was given, however, by Francis himself.*   The various expressions and precepts of the Saint on the fostering of brotherly love as quoted above, afford abundant proof of this; they are but the echo of his own personal and practical charity. He was, in fact, as an elder brother to all, or rather as father and mother to them in God. With what cordiality he received each brother, guided him and cared for him! [32] How keenly he suffered when he had to send them out on a mission; how tenderly he embraced them and recommended the departing Friars to Divine Providence! [33] How he longed for the day of their return; how joyfully he praised the Most High when all returned safely, and what a joyous feast to him were the moments of their renewed companionship! [34] How friendly and yet how courteous were his speech and manner! How prudently he knew how to adapt himself to the learning, the customs and the state of each! How openly sincere his look, how tender his words, how joyous his mien, how lovable his entire conduct! [35]

He never failed to give expression to his affection for all by rendering every possible aid and by serving the brothers whenever occasion offered itself. We remember how he had the table set for the hungry brother in the middle of the night and shared the meal with him, lest the poor Friar be ashamed to eat. [36] Every wish of his brothers was for him a command which he sought to fulfil without delay. One day two Friars arrived from France, whose most ardent desire had always been to behold the Saint with their own eyes. Their joy was all the greater when Francis embraced them with fatherly affection and spoke most kindly to them. Finally, one of the guests ventured to ask the Saint for his habit. Francis forthwith took it off and gave it to the bold petitioner, taking in exchange the much poorer one of the latter. Thomas of Celano remarks hereto: "Not only these and similar things, but everything which was asked of him he gave most joyfully; indeed, he was ever willing to give himself for love." [37]

Not content with devoting his strength, his time, his

heart, yea, himself to his brothers, he devoted to them also his ceaseless prayers. Thomas of Celano expressed this in his inimitably beautiful manner: "Who could ever describe the solicitude of Francis for his brothers? Constantly he held his hands raised to heaven for the true children of Israel, and often he forgot himself to think first of the welfare of his children. Prostrate at the feet of the Divine Majesty in adoration, he offered the sacrifice of his spirit for his sons, in order thus to draw down God's blessings upon them. His perfect love for the little flock which he had drawn after himself never left him without fear that they might lose heaven, after having renounced the world. He feared that he should not attain to glory himself if he should not lead those to glory who were entrusted to him, those whom his spirit had brought forth with greater travail than the maternal womb." [38]

When finally God was calling him to eternal glory, one thing only saddened his heart: the farewell from his brothers. He called all present to himself, encouraged them to steadfastness and perseverance in their vocation, and blessed them, placing his hand on each. It caused him great anguish that he could not see all the brothers for the last time, and so he blessed also the absent ones, those who then belonged to the Order as well as those who were to follow in his footsteps in the ages to come.[39] He then remembered that the Saviour had celebrated a love-feast with His disciples before His death. In this Francis also wished to become like to Him. He asked bread to be brought, blessed it, broke it, and gave to each weeping brother a piece. It was the symbol and the pledge of his tender and lasting love as their father and brother.[40] Thus the word of the Gospel also became true of him: "Having loved His own who were in the world, He loved them unto the end." [41]

We might properly conclude here, having seen how exemplary was the love which Francis bore all his sons. But

it remains to point out that Francis showed a peculiar predilection for the *sick,* the *sorrowful,* and the *erring*
brothers.

For the *sick brothers* he always evinced a tender compassion and loving solicitude.[42] It is touching to see how
attentively, unselfishly and lovingly he cared for them.
Although suffering at times greater afflictions than others,
his last thought was always for himself. If kind friends
offered him more delicate and substantial food, he distributed it among the sick, though he himself was in
greater need of it than they. Even in days of better
health he would break his fast so that the sick would not
hesitate to eat with him. Indeed, he was not ashamed
to beg openly in the streets, even during a season of fast,
and to the great wonderment of the people, that the sick
might have more strengthening food.[43] He had the lovable faculty of reading the wishes of others from their
eyes, and he strove to fulfil these wishes without revealing
that it was a hardship for himself. One day he noticed
that a sick brother had a great desire for grapes, but did
not venture to express his wish; for the Friars at that
time were very rigorous toward themselves whether in
good or ill health. Francis led the Friar to a neighboring
vineyard and sat down with him by a vine richly laden
with luscious grapes. He then began to eat the grapes, in
order that this Friar should not be ashamed to eat alone.
And all the days of his life this Friar would tell, with
tears in his eyes, of the loving pity and compassion of the
Blessed Father, and relate what happened on this occasion.[44] If Francis found himself unable to relieve the
needs of a sick brother, he manifested his sincere and
deep compassion; in fact, he felt the sufferings of the
afflicted brothers as keenly as if they were his own.[45]

So anxious was the Saint to provide for the care of the
sick brethren, that he enjoined the greatest solicitude for
them in his rules. In the first years it was very difficult,

on account of the migratory life of the Friars, to find a proper home for the sick and to give them the necessary care. The Saint therefore prescribed in his first rule: "If any of the brothers fall into sickness, wherever he may be, let the others not leave him, unless one of the brothers, or more if it be necessary, be appointed to serve him as they would wish to be served themselves; but in urgent necessity they may commit him to some person who will take care of him in his infirmity." [46] In the meantime, conditions had undergone a change. The Friars had settled in houses, and in each house the best cell was reserved for the sick. For this reason Francis had but to repeat in his final rule: "If any one of them should fall into illness, the other brothers must serve him as they would wish to be served themselves." [47] Similar precepts were given to the Second Order. In consideration of their great severity, he admonished the Poor Ladies to partake joyfully and gratefully of the alms tendered them, in order to protect themselves against illness.[48] Whenever the condition of the Sisters demanded it, any kind of food was to be given them—although they otherwise never ate meat—even if it could be obtained only with great difficulty.[49]

Notwithstanding his loving solicitude for the bodily welfare of his sons and daughters, Francis nevertheless admonished them to be ever mindful of their calling to the Knighthood of the Cross and to the service of the Crucified Saviour. He reminded the Poor Clares, the sick as well as those who were charged with their care, to give at all times an example of patience.[50] The same admonition is given to his brothers in the final rule.[51] In the more explicit rule of 1221 we read: "I ask the sick brother that he give thanks to the Creator for all things, and that he desire to be as God wills him to be, whether sick or well; for all whom the Lord has predestined to eternal life [52] are disciplined by the rod of afflictions and infirmities, and the spirit of compunction; as the Lord says: [53] 'Such as I love, I rebuke and chastise.' If, however, he be disquieted and angry, either against God or against the brothers, or perhaps eagerly ask for remedies, desiring too much to deliver his body which is soon to die, which is an enemy to the soul, this comes to him from evil and he is carnal, and seems not to be of the brothers, because he loves his body more than his soul." [54]

Francis himself gave in his many sufferings the most splendid example of patience and resignation, of unselfishness and gratitude. Obedience alone could prevail upon him to accept the attentions and the care which his illness demanded.[55] He bore the most excruciating pains with sublime calmness and joyousness of mind.[56] So great was his anxiety that he was becoming a burden to his brothers, that he felt himself bound to ask their pardon whenever they rendered him a service. He feared that they might become discouraged for devoting so much of their time and labors in his behalf, instead of using their time for their own prayers and labors, and he consoled them in these words: "My best beloved brothers and little children, do not get wearied of your labors because of my infirmities, since the Lord for love of me, His little servant, will restore to you all the fruit of your works, at this time and in the future, which you cannot now do because of my illness—indeed, you shall have a greater reward than you could gain for yourselves, since He who helps me aids all the Order and life of the Friars, and you can say of this, 'Whereas we spend ourselves upon you and for you, the Lord will hold Himself our debtor.' " [57]

Still greater sympathy was manifested by the Saint toward the brothers *afflicted in mind*. Although the Friars breathed the atmosphere of almost constant joy, they were not spared trials and storms, either sent by God, or temptations caused by the evil spirit, or tribulations arising from their own nature. Francis well knew the torture of such sufferings,[58] and could fully sympathize with those afflicted in like manner. On the other hand, he well knew the importance, yea, the necessity of temptations and trials for the furtherance of spiritual life; and of this he constantly sought to convince his brothers. On one occasion he replied to a Friar who was sorely tried by a grievous temptation and who had recommended himself to the prayers of the Saint: "Believe me, my son, that I only now regard thee as a servant of God, because thou art tempted; and the more grievous the temptation becomes, the more be thou assured of my love," And he explained this further, saying: "Truly, I say to thee, no one can consider himself a servant of God, unless he has endured temptations and trials. A temptation conquered is, as it were, a ring by means of which the Lord espouses to Himself the soul of His servant. Many are joyful because they have gathered merits for many years and have never suffered temptations. Let them know that God has had compassion for their weakness, well knowing that they would succumb before the battle for sheer fright. Him only does the Lord place in the struggle, in whom He finds well-tried virtue." [59]

Whenever he uttered such words of encouragement, he spoke with so tender a voice and so compassionate a heart, that it usually sufficed to instil new courage into the heart of the afflicted one. He, in truth, became sad with the sorrowful and afflicted with the suffering, and in consequence he consoled the Friars with such touching words that the temptation and sadness immediately vanished.[60]

No wonder, then, that the Friars placed unbounded confidence in him and never despaired of finding solace and help when turning to their Father. In times of severe temptations they cast themselves at his feet, revealed to him their most secret needs, and, having received his blessing, departed again with peace in their hearts.[61]

The mere thought that they stood in the good graces of
their Father, sufficed to pour soothing balm on their
troubled hearts; while, on the other hand, the fear to have
incurred his displeasure, caused them acute anguish.
Brother Rizzerio, "noble by birth, but nobler by virtue,"
as Celano says, was firmly convinced that he stood in the
good or ill favor of God accordingly as he stood in the
good or ill favor of the Saint. And since he deemed himself unworthy of the former, he became tormented by
grave fears. Francis, to whom the sore plight of the
Friar was made known by God, called him to himself and
said with motherly affection: "Let not this temptation
trouble thee, my son, nor this doubt embitter thee; for
thou art very dear to me and canst be assured that among
all my beloved ones thou art worthy of my particular
esteem and friendship. Come to me whenever thou wilt,
and avail thyself without fear of this friendship." Rizzerio was speechless with joy, and from that moment was
filled with a confidence in God as strong as his confidence
in his fatherly friend.[62]

Francis, however, was not content with manifesting his
solicitude in mere words. Night and day he was at the
service of every afflicted brother and ready to fulfil their
slightest wish. At one time Brother Leo, tormented in
spirit by a grievous temptation, requested the Saint to
write down a few devout words, that he might regain at
all times his wonted cheerfulness of mind. The Saint
told him to fetch paper and ink without delay, wrote
a few lines to the praise of God and also a short formula
of blessing, and gave this precious relic to Brother Leo,
who preserved it as a priceless treasure all the days of
his life, constantly finding therein joy and consolation.[63]
Another Friar, living at Lago Fucino, exclaimed at one
time with childlike simplicity while laboring under a sore
trial: "If I had with me only a piece of the fingernails
of the blessed Father, I believe this storm of temptation

would vanish and with the help of the Lord peace would return to me!" He hastened to Rieti, where Francis was lying ill at the time, and made known his naïve request to another Friar. The latter, however, replied: "I fear I shall not be able to give thee a piece of his nails, for he commands us to throw away the parings, and will not allow us to save them." He had hardly spoken these words when the Saint called him to his bedside and asked him to cut his nails, and then gave the parings to the tempted Friar, who immediately regained his peace of mind.[64]

What we admire in Francis in this as in all other things is: his loving attentiveness to all forms of suffering, and his constant readiness to help the afflicted ones wherever and whenever he could. In this he remained true to himself to his very end. We have already seen how tenderly he strove to console all the Friars in his last days. One of them especially was seized with almost uncontrollable sadness, Brother Leo, who had been closest to him as his confessor and constant companion. In his desire to console him, Francis bequeathed to him his habit, the only article of which he could dispose. "I give thee this habit," he said; "accept it, it shall henceforth be thine. As long as I live, I shall wear it; after my death it shall belong to thee." [65] His next thought was for his bereaved daughters at San Damiano. Unable to speak words of encouragement to them personally, he dictated to them words of solace and edification, and added to this some words set to a melody, with the wish that the Sisters sing it for their own consolation and for the praise of God.[66]

Most deeply, however, did Francis sympathize with the misfortune of the *erring brothers*. Great as was the joy he experienced because of his loyal and perfect disciples,[67] so keen was his compassion for those who succumbed in time of temptation, or even became untrue to their vocation. He was indeed most vigilant in regard to the faults

of his subjects. He reproved every violation of the rule
or discipline, punished the stubborn and rebellious Friars
with due severity,[68] and uttered his woe over those
brothers especially who by their evil example caused
scandal to others.[69] Yet he at all times joined inexhaustible patience and kindness to his words of warning and
reproof.[70]

It is remarkable how frequently and earnestly he stresses
kindness and charity. In the older rule he gives the following directions regarding the correction of erring
brothers: "If among the brothers, wherever they may be,
there should be some brother who desires to live according to the flesh, and not according to the spirit, let the
brothers with whom he is, admonish, instruct, and correct
him humbly and diligently. And if after the third admonition he will not amend, let them as soon as possible
send him, or make the matter known to his minister and
servant, and let the minister and servant do with him what
may seem to him most expedient before God." [71] In the
final rule he says: "If any of the brothers, at the instigation of the enemy, sin mortally by those sins for which it
has been ordained among the brothers that recourse.
should be had to the provincial ministers alone, the aforesaid brothers are bound to have recourse to them as soon
as possible, without delay. But let the ministers themselves, if they are priests, impose penance on them with
mercy; if, however, they are not priests, let them have it
imposed by other priests of the Order, as it may seem to
them most expedient, according to God. And they must
beware lest they be angry or troubled on account of the
sins of the others, because anger and trouble impede
charity in themselves and in others." [72]

Shortly before writing the final rule, he addressed the
following words to a minister: "By this I wish to know
if thou lovest God and me His servant and thine; namely,
that there be no brother in the world who has sinned, how

great soever his sin may be, who after he has seen thy
face shall ever go away without thy mercy, if he seek
mercy, and, if he seek not mercy, ask thou him if he
desires mercy. And if he afterward appears before thy
face a thousand times, love him more than me, to the end
that thou mayest draw him to the Lord, and on such ones
always have mercy. And this thou shouldst declare to
the guardians, when thou canst, that thou art determined
to do thus of thyself." [73]

In his description of a good superior he says: "He
must be a man who comforts the sorrowful, who is the last
refuge for the tempted, lest the sick, when all means of a
cure fail, become a prey to despair. In order to win over
the rebellious ones, he should cast himself at their feet,
and at times forego his right, in order to win the soul
of the erring one for Christ. Even to those who have
left the Order, he should not close his pitying heart as to
lost sheep, knowing that the temptations must be indeed
severe which lead to such a fall." [74] And when he resigned from the direction of the Order, he prayed to God:
"Lord, I recommend to Thee the family which Thou hast
entrusted to me until now. Since I can no longer care
for them because of the infirmities of which Thou knowest, I entrust them to the ministers. Let them render
account to Thee on the day of judgment, if by their
negligence or evil example or their too severe correction
any brother is lost." [75]

Thus the Ideal of brotherliness runs like a golden thread
through the entire conception and organization of the
Franciscan institute. From beginning to end the relation
of Friar to Friar, of superior to subject and vice versa is
governed by the Gospel axiom: "You are all brothers."

Still more: the Franciscan sun of love shed its glowing
rays over the entire world. *Francis regarded all men as
brothers and sisters.* For all he had a tender and loving
heart, all were dear to him, for all he was solicitous.[76]

Wherever he commends the fostering of brotherly love to his own disciples, are interwoven at the same time admonitions to love with a brotherly love all fellow-men, whether friendly to the Franciscan Ideal, or worldlings in the full sense of the word.[77] He forbade strictly that the Friars pass judgment on anyone, or look askance at those who lived riotously and were clothed in soft and splendid garments. "God," he said, "is their Lord and ours, mighty enough to call them to Himself, and to sanctify those who are called." He commanded the brothers to regard even these worldlings as their brothers and masters: as their brothers, because created by the one Creator; as their masters, because they made possible a life of penance to the good, providing for them their necessary livelihood.[78]

Furthermore, his disciples were enjoined to extend their love even to *their enemies*. That indeed is but the fulfilment of the Gospel precept, binding on all those who profess Christian ideals. But it is noteworthy how vividly and determinedly Francis conceives this precept, how universally he appplies it, and how frequently he urges its practise. Let us mention a few relevant instructions and precepts.

When sending out the first Friars on a mission, the Saint addressed them as follows: "Go, most beloved, two and two into the various quarters of the heavens, preach to men peace and penance unto remission of sins, suffer patiently persecutions, and be nothing solicitous, for the Lord will fulfil His design and His promise. If you are asked, answer humbly; if they persecute you, bless them; if they do injustice and spread calumnies against you. thank them, because for this the eternal kingdom is prepared for us." [79]

In his rules the Saint is just as emphatic in commanding his brothers to love their enemies as Christ Himself has taught and practised: "Let them not resist evil,[80] but if anyone should strike them on the cheek, let them turn to him the other; and if anyone take away their garment, let them not forbid him the tunic also. Let them give to everyone that asketh them, and if anyone take away their goods, let them not ask them again.[81] And let all the brothers, wherever they may be, remember that they have given themselves, and have relinquished their bodies to Our Lord Jesus Christ; and for love of Him they ought to expose themselves to enemies both visible and invisible, for the Lord says: 'Whosoever shall lose his life for My sake, shall save it'[82] in eternal life. 'Blessed are they that suffer persecution for justice' sake, for theirs is the kingdom of heaven.'[83] 'If they have persecuted Me, they will also persecute you.'[84] If, however, they should persecute you in one city, flee to another.'[85] 'Blessed are ye when they shall revile you, and persecute you, and speak all that is evil against you, untruly, for My sake; be glad in that day and rejoice, for your reward is great in heaven.'[86] . . . Let us all, brothers, give heed to what the Lord says: 'Love your enemies, and do good to them that hate you,' For Our Lord Jesus, whose footsteps we ought to follow, called His betrayer 'friend,' and offered Himself willingly to His crucifiers. Therefore, all those who unjustly inflict upon us tribulations and anguish, shames and injuries, sorrows and torments, martyrdom and death, are our friends whom we ought to love much, because we gain eternal life by that which they make us suffer."[87]

Francis went to such extremes in his brotherliness as to treat even *robbers,* those outcasts of humanity, as his brothers. He commanded expressly: "Whoever may come to them, either a friend or a foe, a thief or a robber, let them receive him kindly."[88] How sincere he was in this regard, is charmingly illustrated by a chapter of the *Speculum perfectionis.*

To a certain hermitage of the Friars near Borgo San Sepolcro, begging for bread came some robbers, who lay

in wait in the woods for passing travelers, to despoil them.
Some of the Friars maintained that it was not fitting to
give them alms, while others out of pity relieved them,
hoping thus to move them to repentance.   Meanwhile
Blessed Francis came to that place, and the Friars asked
him if it were right to give them alms, and Blessed
Francis answered. "If you will do as I tell you, confiding
in God, you shall gain their souls. Go, therefore, and
take with you good bread and good wine to the woods
where they dwell, and calling to them, say, 'Brother robbers, come to us who are your brothers, and who bring
you good bread and good wine,' When they come, spread
a white cloth on the ground and place thereon the bread
and wine, and serve them humbly and cheerfully while
they eat. When they have eaten, speak to them the Word
of God, and, at the end, beg them for the love of God, as
your first petition, that they will promise you not to kill
or wound anyone. If you ask too much of them at first,
they will not listen to you; but this much for the sake of
your humility and charity they will promise you.   Then
another day, because of their good promise, take with the
bread and wine eggs and cheese, and serve them as before
while they eat. And when they have eaten say to them,
'Why do you stay here to die of hunger and suffer so
many hardships in order to do evil in will and deed, for.
which you will lose your souls unless you are converted
to the Lord? Better is it to serve the Lord, who in this
world will give you all you need for your bodies and.
finally save your souls.'   Then, inspired by the Lord,
they will be converted because of the humility and
patience you have shown them." The Friars did all that
Blessed Francis had told them, and these robbers, by the
grace and mercy of God, listened to them, and observed
literally and in every point all things the Friars had
humbly begged of them. And further, because of the
humility and kindness of the Friars, they humbly served

them, carrying wood for them to the hermitage, and some amongst them entered the Order. Others, confessing their sins with true repentance, made a promise to the Friars to live henceforth by the labor of their hands and never more commit the like offenses.[89]

CHAPTER XIII

FRANCISCAN CHARITY

THE foregoing pages will no doubt have rendered it evident that Francis exemplified in his own person that Ideal of brotherliness of which St. John says: "My little children, let us not love in word or in tongue, but in deed and in truth." [1] Active, practical charity was at all times the Ideal of the Seraphic Saint. Its soul is his knighthood of Christ, its sphere principally the *care of the sick,* and the *relief of the poor.*

1. The movement for the *care of the sick* received a strong impetus during the period of the Crusades. The same enthusiasm that moved countless warriors to leave house and home and stake their lives and limbs for the redemption of the Holy Places from the tyranny of the infidels, spurred on numberless souls to devote themselves to the ministry of the sick, those helpless ones whom the Saviour Himself in by-gone days had consoled and healed with such tender mercy. A vast number of hospitals arose, richly endowed with alms and property, as likewise a great number of Orders and fraternities which were dedicated to the service of suffering humanity.

This service assumed a truly heroic character when dedicated to the *lepers*. The Arabian leprosy, carried into Europe even before the Crusades,[2] became in a short time the most dreaded plague in all countries. The greater part of the population would have succumbed to its ravages, had the lepers not been isolated from the society of their fellow-men. They were forced to live apart, in huts or colonies removed from towns and villages and from the public highways.

The privilege of entering the Community was granted them only at Easter and Christmas, and even then they were bound to the regulations imposed on them at their isolation; i.e. to make known their approach by means of a clapper, to indicate with their staff what they wished to purchase, to wear their distinctive garb, etc. The inn-keepers were prohibited under heavy penalty from harboring them, and even the churches were closed to them.[3] The law obliged them to give warning whenever someone approached their dwelling-place, so that all contact with them could be avoided. The alms which Christian charity always had ready for them was placed in a dish set at the roadside.[4] Condemned to a slow death, and already looked upon as dead, they received their only solace and assistance from the Church and Christian charity.

The Church regarded them as consecrated to God, accompanied them into their exile, with touching cere-monies, and attended to their wants with motherly love and devotion. Christian charity was ever mindful that the Saviour always had shown special tokens of love toward the lepers;[5] moreover, that it was written of Him: "He hath borne our infirmities and carried our sorrows; and we have thought Him as it were a leper and as one struck by God and afflicted."[6] The Christian world accordingly perceived in the lepers Jesus Christ Himself, who like them was ostracized by the world as an outcast, and reputed as the Man of Sorrows.

This deeply religious view led in a short time to the foundation of leper hospitals in countless places. Every city, yes, every village almost, had its lazaretto situated in an isolated spot. During the lifetime of St. Francis there existed two thousand of these in France.[7] The chronicler Matthew of Paris some years later records the number of these hospitals as close to nineteen thousand.[8] The Knights of St. Lazarus as well as fraternities and individuals of both sexes devoted themselves to the care of the lepers, prompted by the example and the love of Christ.

This was the most severe penance which one could take upon oneself. Cardinal Jacques de Vitry writes in his History (1223-1226) : "Suffering violence for the sake of Christ, they patiently bear almost unthinkable hardships amid the filth and stench of the afflicted, so that no other penance can be compared with this holy and heroic martyrdom before God." [9] The Dominican General, Humbert de Romanis, is in full accord with this statement when he declares that among many thousands hardly a few had enough courage to minister to the sufferers, so terrible was the disease and so intolerable the impatience and ingratitude of the lepers.[10] St. Francis confirms this statement by his own experience.

As a young man of the world, he had an invincible repugnance toward the lepers. The mere thought of them filled him with disgust. Their presence was so insufferable to him, that, as he confessed later on, he turned away and held his nose whenever he saw a leper colony even from a distance of two miles. The most horrid monstrosities in the world did not appear so terrifying to him as the lepers. Not that he was indifferent to their sufferings, but his antipathy was stronger than his sympathy, and when he perchance met a leper, he tendered his alms through the hands of another person, while he himself hastened away.[11]

This repugnance remained with him until the day on which Our Lord revealed to him that he was called to the knightly service of the cross. "From that day on," remarks St. Bonaventure, "it seemed to be made known to him that the spiritual combat must begin with the contempt of the world, and that the soldier of Christ must begin by victory over himself." [12] Yet, however strong this conviction may have become, it was powerless to overcome the disgust and repugnance toward those unfor-

tunate ones, until God spoke to him: "Francis, barter
away that which thou hast heretofore loved with vain
and carnal pleasure, for the spiritual; conquer thyself
and choose the bitter instead of the sweet, if thou wishest
to know Me; in reward the bitter will then be sweet to
thee." [13]

Francis was soon to experience this. While riding one
day over the plain of Assisi he met a leper, whose sudden
appearance filled him with fear and horror. But he
quickly recalled to mind the resolution he had made to
follow after perfection, and remembered that if he would
be a soldier of Christ he must first overcome himself. So
dismounting from his horse, he went to meet the leper,
and when the poor man stretched out his hand to receive
the alms, Francis kissed it and filled it with money. Having again mounted his horse, he looked around him over
the wide and open plain, but nowhere could he see the
leper. Being filled with wonder and joy, he gave thanks
to God, and resolved within himself to proceed to do still
greater things than these.[14] He then galloped homeward,
and taking with him a large amount of money, he rode
to the hospital of the lepers, and gathering about him the
sufferers, he kissed their hands and distributed the money
among them. And when he had left the place, that which
had appeared to him bitter was in fact turned into sweetness.[15] In his Testament he testifies to this himself:
"When I was in sin, it seemed to me very bitter to see
lepers, and the Lord Himself led me amongst them and I
showed mercy to them. And when I left them, that which
had seemed to me bitter was changed for me into sweetness of body and soul." [16]

From that time on, he frequently sought out the leper
hospitals, supplied the wants of the inmates with a generous hand, and kissed their hands and mouth with heartfelt
sympathy, for he beheld in each one the Saviour Himself.[17] Especially after he had renounced the world he
became the friend and companion of the lepers, devoting

himself entirely to their service and showing them every
manner of kindness for the love of Christ. He washed
their feet, bound their sores, cleansed them, bathed their
limbs, in fact, in his heroic devotion he caressed their
festering wounds.[18]

His first companions vied with him in this heroism of
love. In the beginning they lived, for the most part, in
or near the leper hospitals, and rendered to the sick the
most lowly service with true humility and sincere devotion.[19] It was the express wish of the Saint that his sons
devote themselves to this work at least for a time. Even
the proud nobles and pampered worldlings who applied
for admission into the Order were told that their dwelling
would be the leper hospital and their duty to minister to
the lepers.[20] In his first rule he likewise ordained that
the Friars were to solicit alms for the lepers in case of
necessity.[21]

No matter how disgusting, impatient and ungrateful a
leper might appear, Francis commanded that he be served
with all the greater devotion and attention. And when
at times the Friars became disheartened in the face of
this superhuman task, the example and encouraging words
of the Saint spurred them on anew.[22] On one occasion,
however, Francis thought himself guilty of harsh treatment toward a leper. Brother James the Simple had
brought with him a leper who had been entrusted to his
care by Francis, from the hospital at Rivo Torto to
Portiuncula. When Francis became aware of this, he
said somewhat reproachfully to Brother James: "Thou
shouldst not take these Christians abroad, since it is fitting
neither for thee nor for them." For although he had
desired him to serve them, he did not wish that they
should be taken beyond the hospital, since they were
greatly afflicted and men held them in abhorrence, and
this Brother James, out of sheer simplicity, would let the
lepers accompany him from the hospital to St. Mary of
the Angels as if they were his fellow-Friars. St. Francis

himself always called the lepers "Brother Christians."
As soon as he had spoken these words, Francis reproached
himself, thinking that the leper would be offended and
shamed because of what he had said to Brother James.
In his desire to make reparation to God and the leper,
he confessed his fault to Brother Peter Catanii, saying:
"Wilt thou confirm the penance I desire to perform for
this fault, and not oppose it?" The latter replied:
"Brother, do as it pleases thee." Francis then said:
"This is my penance, that I eat out of the same bowl with
my Brother Christian." When they were seated at table,
Francis with the leper and all the other Friars, one bowl
was placed for Francis and the leper, who was covered
with running sores, especially the hand which he dipped
into the bowl to take out the pieces of meat. Seeing
this, Brother Peter and the other Friars were greatly
troubled, but dared not remonstrate because of the fear
and the reverence they had for the holy Father.[23] Even
now the narrative of the chronicler, who was an eye-
witness, seems to quiver with agitation in relating this
incident.

In the course of time the Friars found it impossible
to devote practically all their time to the service of the
sick, being occupied to a larger extent with apostolic
labors and living in established communities.[24] Yet they
never failed to give some attention to this phase of Christian charity. In 1218 Razzardo di Rocco Pazza, a feudal
lord of Umbria, donated to a priest by the name of Bono
an extensive piece of land for the purpose of erecting
thereon a hospital for the lepers and a church. The
care of this hospital was entrusted to the Friars, because
of their great influence on the sick as well as on those
in charge of them.[25] No doubt the Friars retained their
connection with leper hospitals in many other places. The
chronicler, for instance, of Brother Jordan of Giano mentions the fact that he was guardian in the leper hospital
at Speyer in 1223 and that the Minister Provincial, Albert

of Pisa, presided over a Chapter convened in the same place.[26] In the following year Brother Jordan was sent with several Friars to establish a new monastery at Erfurt, in Thuringia; and while their house was in the course of construction, they lived in the quarters of the chaplain of the leper hospital.[27] In the same year the first Franciscans set foot on English soil, and a number of them likewise found shelter in the hospitals at Canterbury and Northampton.[28] No doubt the Friars in many instances made their temporary home in various hospitals during the last years of the Saint. Francis himself, shortly before his death, being no longer able to preach because of his illness, desired to return to his beloved lepers and to perform the most lowly services for them.[29]

In response to the earnest wish of their Father, the Friars ever afterward proved themselves true friends of the sick. The number of spiritual and corporal works of mercy which they practised in hospitals and private homes during seven centuries, defies computation. Thousands of Franciscan Friars and nuns died in the service of the lepers and the plague-stricken. The Third Order especially, which was not hampered by the duties of the apostolate and the restriction of the cloister, developed a widespread social activity in behalf of suffering humanity. Already the oldest Tertian rule, which in the main dates back of St. Francis, contains regulations for the care of the sick.[30] The two great luminaries of the Order, King Louis IX of France and the royal princess, Elizabeth of Hungary, set a glorious example for all others.

Not only did Louis IX build many hospitals with his own means;[31] he ministered to the lepers in person, bathing and cleansing their sores and kissing them reverently. His tender compassion for them even led him to share his meals with them and to eat the victuals which they had touched with their loathsome hands and cast aside, out of reverence for the Saviour.[32]

The good and lovable St. Elizabeth sequestered herself in the hospital at Marburg, which she had established, in order to devote the evening of her life entirely to the sick. Day and night she spent in their service, cleansing and dressing their sores, administering the remedies, consoling them and leading them to God. Even the most repugnant tasks could not make her recoil. The lepers were her darlings, and to them she consecrated herself with incomparable heroism and unspeakable joy. With heroic love she took to her bosom a poor girl afflicted with the leprosy, whom the dreaded disease had so badly deformed that no one in the hospital had the courage to approach her, or even to look upon her. Elizabeth brought her to her own room, gave the sufferer her own bed, cleansed her sores, and kneeling down before her, she removed the girl's shoes, cut her nails, and spent many hours with her, playing games with her and speaking to her with motherly affection and tenderness. "O how fortunate we are," she exclaimed to her companions, "how fortunate we are to be permitted to wash and clothe Our Lord and Saviour in the person of the lepers!" One day she declared to the Minister Provincial, Brother Gerard: "O my Father, the most ardent desire of my heart is to be considered and treated like a leper. I wish that they would construct for me as for the poor people a little hut of hay and straw, and hang in front of it a piece of linen to warn the passers-by, together with a poor-box, wherein alms might be placed." [33]

These illustrious examples were followed by nearly all the numerous congregations which professed the Tertian Rule, as likewise by the millions of pious souls that observe the same rule in the midst of the turmoil of the world.

2. *The relief of the poor* was as dear to the heart of Francis as the care of the sick. Indeed, while he became the friend of the lepers only after his "conversion," he showed and fostered from earliest youth a special love for the needy of every description. With every step which

he took in the realization of his evangelical vocation, this love for the poor deepened and grew until the day when he chose the portion of the poor and of the outcasts.[34] From this time on, he became the Knight of Lady Poverty and of Christ, the King of Poverty. How else could he have truly become the Knight of Christ, if he had not made the lot of the poor his own? If the worldly knight at his investiture vowed to be the lifelong protector of the needy,[35] how much more this Knight of the Cross, who beheld in the poor and the sick his own divine Master?

His biographers hardly find words enough to express adequately his surpassing *love for the poor*. "He loved the poor most tenderly, was most compassionate toward them, and was the humble servant of all," is the testimony of the Three Companions.[36] Thomas of Celano, however, writes: "What tongue can express how compassionate this man was to the poor? He was, in truth, by very nature most compassionate, and this compassion was increased by the love which was granted to him from above. For this reason the heart of Francis went out to the poor; and for those whom he could not assist bodily, he showed most tender sympathy. The needs and misery of his fellow-men he referred in spirit to the person of Christ. Thus, he beheld the Son of the Poor Lady in all the poor by carrying Him poor and naked in his heart, whom she carried poor and naked in her arms. And although Francis had banished every thought of envy from his heart, yet he could not repress the envy of poverty. Whenever he met one poorer than himself, he immediately envied him, and forthwith began the contest for poverty, full of anxiety lest he be vanquished by the poorer one."[37]

One day, as the man of God was going about preaching, he chanced to meet a poor man on the street. When Francis beheld the destitute condition of the beggar, he exclaimed with great emotion to his companion: "This

The Death of St. Francis

man's poverty puts us to shame and contains a grievous complaint against our poverty." "In what manner, Brother?" asked the other. The Saint replied with a voice choked with sobs: "For my only treasure, yea, for my Queen I have chosen Poverty, and behold her more resplendent in him than in me. Or art thou not aware that the cry has resounded throughout the earth, that we are the poorest of the poor for the sake of Christ? But this poor man convinces us of the fact that it is not truly so." [38]

His compassion for the poor and the envy of their poverty was the source of that *profound esteem* and that *sincere friendliness* which he manifested toward them at all times. Though he instructed his followers to greet and to treat both the honored and the lowly with all courtesy and brotherliness,[39] yet he wished them to prefer the little ones of this world to all others. In very decisive terms he gives the following precept in his first rule: "They ought to rejoice when they converse with mean and despised persons, with the poor and the weak, with the infirm and the lepers, and with those who beg in the streets." [40]

All this was self-evident to him. The poor who were unable to alter their lot, and the Friars who voluntarily shared this lot with them, obviously were of the same company. Whether the poverty of the former was self-caused or not; whether it was in reality as great as it appeared; whether it was the lot of one worthy or unworthy: such distinctions were of no consequence to Francis. Whenever he beheld poverty standing before him, he beheld Christ in spirit, and forthwith the Knight of Poverty was filled with profound sympathy and compassion.

For this reason he could not bear to hear others speak or judge harshly of the poor.[41] It happened on one occasion that a Friar uttered the harsh words to a beggar who had begged alms of him: "Take heed that thou dost not feign poverty, whilst thou art in fact rich!" Francis was deeply grieved when hearing these words spoken. He reproved the Friar severely, and commanded him to take off his habit in the presence of the beggar, to kiss his feet and to implore his forgiveness. He then added: "Whoever insults a poor man, does injury to Christ Himself, whose noble image he bears; for He has become poor in this world for our sake." [42] Another time Francis met a man who was not only poor, but ill. This double misfortune sorely grieved the Saint. While pursuing his way, he began to converse with his companion on poverty, until his heart glowed with compassion and love for the sufferer. His companion listened attentively, but doubted in his heart whether the poor man was content with his lot. Finally he remarked: "It is true, brother, the man is poor; but perhaps there is no one in this whole region who covets riches more than he." The Saint became aroused at this remark, and when the Friar had confessed his fault, Francis commanded him: "Go quickly, take off thy habit and prostrate thyself at the feet of the poor man, and confess to him thy fault. But do not only ask his pardon, beseech him also for his prayers." The Friar obeyed, did as he was told, and returned. Francis then counseled him most gravely: "Whenever thou seest a poor man, O brother, thou seest an image of Our Lord and His poor Mother. In like manner also, when thou seest a sick man, remember the infirmities which He has borne for us." [43] Thomas of Celano adds hereto: "Thus it was in truth: Francis constantly gazed upon the countenance of his Christ; everywhere he beheld the Man of Sorrows, Him who was acquainted with infirmity." [44]

In the same measure, however, as Francis encouraged his disciples to esteem and love the poor for love of God, he also *encouraged the poor themselves to regard their poverty, and to bear it, in the light of the same Ideal.* One day he met near Colle, in the domain of Perugia, a beggar whom he had previously known in the world as a man of moderate wealth. Full of pity, Francis approached him and asked: "My brother, how farest thou?" The latter began to rail vehemently against the master to whom he had been subject and who had deprived him of all his possessions. "By the fault of my master," he said, "whom the almighty God may damn, I am in this sorry plight." At these words Francis was seized with even greater pity for the unfortunate man, more on account of his immortal soul than for his body, by reason of the deadly hate which he bore his master, and he said to him: "Brother, for the love of God, forgive thy master, and thus unburden thy conscience; it may then come to pass that he will return to thee thy stolen property. If not, thou hast lost thy property, and thy soul as well." The other retorted angrily: "I cannot forgive him unless he returns what he has taken from me." Seeing that words availed nothing, Francis took off the mantle which he wore on his shoulders and said: "Behold, I give thee this mantle, and beseech thee to forgive thy master for the love of God, thy Lord." This act of generosity softened the heart of the other; he accepted the gift, and willingly forgave the injustice done him.[45]

Thus, Francis was not content with reconciling the poor to his fate, showing him loving kindness and condescending to his poverty, and placing before him the divine Ideal: *he endeavored to relieve poverty by practical charity.* It is, however, his own secret how he accomplished this, since he personally could call nothing in this world his own.

In the first place, he shared the scanty food which Divine Providence prepared for him, with the poor. It was self-evident to him that the hungry poor were entitled to be received by the Friars as guests. In giving alms his manner was so charmingly kind and affectionate that it seemed as if he were receiving a favor instead of the poor. The result was that whenever he had occasion to relieve the needs of others, he at the same time conferred a lasting benefit on their souls.[46]

He was inconsolable when there was nothing in the house to give to the needy. On such occasions he would give away even the most necessary articles. One day, when he was living at St. Mary of the Angels, a poor old woman, who had two sons in the Order, came and begged alms of Francis. He immediately turned to Brother Peter Catanii, who at that time was Minister General, and said: "Have you anything we could give to our mother?" For he spoke of the mothers of the Friars as if they were the mothers of himself and all other Friars. Brother Peter answered: "In all the house there is nothing we can give her; that is, nothing that would satisfy her bodily needs. In the church we have only one New Testament from which to read the lessons at Matins." Then Francis said to him: "Give our mother the Testament that she may sell it for her needs, for I firmly believe this will be more pleasing to God and the Blessed Virgin than that we should read out of it." It was given to her, and thus the first Testament which the Order possessed, was disposed of by an act of charity.[47]

In cases of extreme necessity Francis did not hesitate to give away even the clothing which he wore. Thomas of Celano remarks that he delighted to perform this work of mercy from earliest youth. How often did he not strip himself of his costly attire to give it to the first beggar whom he met![48] Now, however, he was poor himself, and could not part with his only habit. For this reason he at times allowed himself to be persuaded to accept a mantle, so as to be able to give it to the next beggar whom he chanced to meet.

Once during a severe winter he was staying in the vicinity of Celano. To protect himself from the cold, he covered himself with a piece of cloth, which a friend of the Friars at Tivoli had given him. Meeting an old beggar woman who asked an alms of him, he immediately took off the covering from his shoulders and gave it to her, saying: "There, make thyself a warm dress, for thou art surely in need of it." The woman with a laugh seized the goods from the hands of the Saint, and filled with both joy and fear hastened home and cut it up, so as not to give the donor time to ask its return. When, however, she discovered that the cloth did not suffice for a dress, she returned to Francis and informed him of her plight. Francis looked at his companion, who wore a similar covering, and said to him: "Hearest thou, brother, what the poor woman is saying? For the love of God let us endure the cold and give the cloth to this woman who is in want, that she may have sufficient to make a full garment." He had given his mantle, the brother gave his own, and both remained uncovered, but the old woman had sufficient cloth to make herself a dress.[49]

Similar scenes were enacted frequently. If the Saint, so exceedingly rich in poverty, had nothing wherewith to clothe the poor, he would go to some rich friends and ask them for a loan of a garment or a mantle of fur. When they had joyfully complied with his request, he would say gratefully: "I accept this loan on one condition only, that in no wise you expect its return." On the very next occasion he would then joyfully dispose of the garments obtained in this manner.[50]

The Friars in consequence were often in great fear for the well-being of their Father, who, though almost constantly ailing, always disposed of the winter garments which kind friends had donated. So they procured a mantle themselves, thinking that he would not give it away without their consent. Francis, however, had recourse to an ingenious stratagem. He was staying at Cella, near Cortona. A poor man came to him who had recently buried his wife, and had a large family of small children to provide for. The Saint's sole resource was his mantle, which the Friars had procured and of which he was not free to dispose. It recurred to him that the mantle

could be used as a pawn. He therefore said to the poor
man: "For the love of God I will surrender this mantle
to thee, but do not part with it unless well paid for." The
Friars saw what was going on and hastened to take away
the mantle, but the poor man beheld the encouraging looks
of the Saint, and so he fought for the garment with might
and main as if it were his own. The Friars were finally
forced to abandon the struggle, and agreed to redeem the
mantle themselves.[51]

When such means did not achieve the desired result,
the Saint appealed to the supreme Ideal of poverty, which
entitled him to be poorer than the poorest beggar. Meeting a beggar one day while returning from Siena, he said
to his companion: "Brother, let us restore this cloak to this
poor little one to whom it properly belongs. We have
accepted it for our use until we should meet some one
more needy than ourselves." The Friar remonstrated with
the Saint, and endeavored to convince him that the cloak
was more necessary for himself, and that it were wrong
to despoil himself of it. Francis, however, replied: "I do
not wish to be a thief; for it would, in truth, be accounted
a theft unto us if we failed to give it to him who is in
greater need of it than ourselves." The Friar then was
silent, and Francis gave away the cloak.[52]

At times, however, the generosity of the Saint met with
serious obstacles, because the superiors, whom he obeyed
like a child, were more concerned about him than about
the poor. He would then plead so touchingly and earnestly, until he had scored a victory. At the time that
he was staying in the Bishop's palace at Rieti, he was in
the care of a physician, a serious illness of the eyes threatening him with blindness. While at the physician's house,
he met a poor woman who suffered from a like evil. Turning to his superior, he said in the most friendly manner:
"Brother guardian, we must now again return our strange
goods." The guardian replied: "If anything is found that
does not belong to us, let us return it without delay."

"This mantle," said the Saint, "which was loaned to us by
that poor woman, must now be returned to her, for she
has nothing in her purse wherewith to pay the physician." "Brother," answered the guardian, "this mantle
is mine, and no one has loaned it to us; use it as long
as it pleases thee, but if thou no longer desirest it, return
it to me." For the guardian had shortly before purchased
the mantle for the use of the Saint. The latter, however,
would not be quieted, but continued pleading: "Brother
guardian, thou hast always been so gracious to me; grant
me now, I beseech thee, also this favor." The guardian
then replied: "Well, then, Father, do as it pleases thee
and as the spirit prompts thee." Francis thereupon summoned a pious friend and said to him: "Take this mantle,
together with twelve loaves of bread, and go to that poor
woman and say: 'A beggar to whom thou hast loaned
this mantle, renders thee sincere thanks for its use, and
begs thee to accept again what is thine.'" The friend
went and did as he was told. The woman, however,
thought that he was making sport of her and exclaimed
full of anger: "Leave me in peace with thy mantle; I
know not what thou art prating about." The man, however, insisted, and finally gave her the mantle as well as
the bread. When she saw that he was in earnest, and,
fearing that she might be again deprived of the things she
had acquired so easily, she hurriedly departed, forgetful
of both physician and her affliction, and returned home
with the mantle.[53]

When he had nothing else at his disposal, Francis would
often exchange his poor habit for the much poorer garment of a beggar whom he chanced to meet.[54] At other
times he would tear off the lower part of his habit and
give it to a beggar. Yes, time and again he took off
even his breeches and gave them away.[55] If he had
nothing of his own to share with the poor, he would lend
them the help of his hands. Whenever he met poor
people carrying bundles of wood and other burdens, he

hastened to relieve them and took the load on his own weak shoulders.[56]

Thus, he loved the poor with every fiber of his compassionate heart, and imitated most faithfully his divine Master, the Friend of the poor.[57]

No wonder, then, that *the love of the poor was bequeathed to his disciples and to his entire Order as a precious heirloom!* We have already shown how conscientiously the first Friars adhered to the instruction of Francis to distribute their substance to the poor whenever possible on their entrance into the Order.[58] Not content with this, they freely and joyously shared with the poor the alms they received as true followers of the Poverello. If no food was at hand to dispose of, they would often give away part of their clothing. Repeatedly they cut off the hood or a sleeve from their habit, that the beggar might not depart empty-handed, and to fulfil the injunction of the Gospel: "Give to everyone that asketh thee." [59] It would be interesting and edifying to illustrate in particular how solicitous the disciples of Francis were for the poor; let us record a few instances.

Blessed Brother Giles, the third companion of the Saint, had but shortly joined his company. While on the way to Assisi in quest of some cloth for a habit, he met a beggar woman. Immediately the novice took off his upper garment and gave it to the beggar.[60] Further on, he encountered another beggar, but having nothing except the habit which Francis had given him, Giles tore off the hood and gave this to the beggar. For twenty days he then traveled about without a hood.[61] He not only provided his own livelihood by the labor of his hands, but frequently supported other poor in like manner.[62] Indeed, he considered it the duty of every Friar to feed the poor, to clothe them, and to relieve their needs generously and plentifully.[63]

Blessed Luchesio, who was converted by the preaching of Francis, sold his vast estates and divided the proceeds among the poor. He retained for himself and his wife but one small piece of ground, to insure his own livelihood and that of his subjects. At regular intervals he made the rounds of the neighboring hamlets, villages and towns, seeking out the needy, the sick and the aged, and sheltering them in his own home. It was of frequent occurrence that he carried one cripple on his shoulders, and led two others on each side. If his resources failed to satisfy their wants, he took a basket, went from door to door in quest of alms, and returned heavily laden with foods of all kinds. And with such tender and glowing words did he speak of the love of poverty, that the unfortunates not only were content with their lot, but soon learned to bear it with rejoicing.[64]

St. Elizabeth of Thuringia was accustomed to search out all the huts far and near, and personally distributed among the poor, meat, bread, flour, and other necessities of life. She looked over their clothes and beds, and examined closely into their needs, in order to succor them all the more effectively. Her own precious jewels, silk garments, and other treasures were sold and divided among the poor; even her own princely dowry found its way one day into the hands of twelve thousand poor. If perchance on her errands of mercy she met beggars who were reduced to the last extremity and despised by all, she sheltered them in her own house, shared her food with them, and served them as a maid. Her confessor, Father Conrad, endeavored to separate her from these poor outcasts, but she implored him: "No, my dearest master, do not take them from me; be mindful of my former worldly life with its pomp and vanity; henceforth I must live with the poor and the lowly. Their company obtains for me countless graces. Permit me to rejoice in their presence." [65]

St. Louis daily fed one hundred and twenty of the poor in his palace; during Lent and Advent the number reached two hundred. Very often he made the rounds personally with plates, pitchers of wine, and bread, cut their bread for them, and distributed money among them. On days of fast or on vigils he never took his place at table before he had personally attended to all the wants of the poor. His special favor was enjoyed by the very poor, toward whom he was more bountiful than to others. Three of these were selected each day, taking turns in eating with him at noon and in the evening. They were served with each course before the others, and on their departure each received a generous sum of money. Besides this, he supported countless poor families, established poor-houses, endowed poor convents, and aided indigent students. When his courtiers began to murmur against this unheard-of lavishness, he remarked curtly: "In one way or another a king is bound to be extravagant; I prefer to be extravagant in almsgiving for the love of God, rather than to be extravagant in worldly and transitory things. In this manner the immoderate expenditures which must often be made for the sake of worldly undertakings, are overlooked and balanced by excess in spiritual things." [66]

Space does not permit us to enumerate further examples of Franciscan lovers of the poor. Their number is endless. Millions of Tertiaries have devoted their substance during the course of centuries for the relief of bodily suffering in all its forms. Countless also is the number of Friars who have renounced all earthly possessions to enrich the poor; who lived from the labor of their hands and their mind, and from frugal alms in order to ennoble, yea, sanctify poverty; who made every effort and used every influence to alleviate the sufferings of the poor. Thus, history has at all times justified the title which contemporaries accorded the Poverello: *"Pater pauperum pauper Franciscus*—the poor little Francis, the father of the poor." [67]

CHAPTER XIV

THE FRANCISCAN PEACE MOVEMENT

FRANCISCAN charity did not, however, confine itself to the care of the sick and the relief of the poor: the Poverello became the benefactor of all ranks of society by his peace movement.

1. A true child of "sweet Assisi"—*la dolce Assisi*—and of balmy Umbria, Francis was predestined by nature for a mission of peace. All that was gentle and mild attracted him, while on the other hand he had an instinctive abhorrence for all that was severe, rough or unbrotherly. He showed marked preference for Brother Little Lamb of God, for Brother John the Simple, Brother Juniper, Brother Masseo, Brother Giles, and other equally lovable characters; likewise for the lambkins, doves and nightingales; while for the cruel swine he had but threats,[1] and for Brother Wolf the command to change his mode of life.[2]

Even as a youthful prisoner of war at Perugia his patience conquered the haughty and embittered character of an imprisoned knight, and prevailed upon his fellow-prisoners to receive the latter again in their midst.[3] His work for the promotion of universal peace, however, took definite shape when he was called by God to embrace the life as outlined by the Gospel. On that occasion he heard the gospel on the Mission of the apostles, together with the injunction given them: "And when you come into the house, salute it, saying: Peace be to this house."[4] He regarded these words, as well as his vocation, as a direct revelation to himself. As long as he lived, he clung to the reality of this revelation, and even when at death's door, he declared: "The Lord revealed to me this salutation, that we should say: The Lord give you peace." [5]

In accordance with this conviction, he embodied this salutation in the rule of his Order, and he commanded his brothers to wish peace to all men, wherever they be, and to say on entering a house: "Peace be to this house!" [6] At first this greeting caused no little surprise. When one of the Friars was going about the country and greeted men and women while at their work with these words, some laughed, others became indignant, and asked: "What means this strange greeting?" Intimidated by such experiences, the brother asked Francis that he might employ some other greeting. "Heed them not," the Saint replied, "for they know not what is of God. Be not ashamed of it, for the time will come when even the rich and the princes of this world shall revere thee and thy brothers because of this greeting." [7]

Francis himself was the first to extend this greeting to all whom he met. He did so with such warmth and genuine sincerity, that thereby many who had lived in enmity and hatred, found peace with themselves and with their fellow-men. The burden of his sermons particularly was a constant appeal for peace. Every sermon began with the words: "May the Lord give you His peace!" [8] Whenever he heard that strife and discord reigned in any place, his entire discourse was directed toward the restoration of peace. [9]

The brothers were enjoined to follow this example when setting out to preach. The first mission on which he sent them was one of peace. He took leave of them with the words: "Go, dearest brothers, two by two into all the country, and preach to men peace and penance unto the remission of their sins." [10] And the last mission on which he sent them was again one of peace. We feel obliged to deal with it more in detail, because it shows with what originality and confidence Francis and his disciples undertook the work of promoting peace, and how indefatigably they carried it on.

The Saint had arrived at Assisi sick unto death, when he heard that a great discord had arisen between the Bishop and the Governor of the city. The Bishop had excommunicated the Governor, and the latter ordered that no one should sell to the Bishop, nor buy from him, nor make any contract with him. Francis was moved with great pity, especially as no one tried to make peace between them, and he said to his companions: "It is a great reproach for the servants of God that the Bishop and the Governor hate each other, and that no one tries to make peace between them." And then he added another verse to the Canticle of the Sun on this subject as follows:

"Praised be my Lord for those who for Thy love forgive
And weakness bear and tribulation.
Blessed those who shall in peace endure,
For by Thee, Most High, shall they be crowned."

Then he called one of his companions and said to him: "Go to the Governor and beg him for me that, with the chief men of the city and such others as will join them, he go to the Bishop's palace." When this Friar had departed, he said to his other two companions: "Go before the Bishop and the Governor and those who are with them, and sing the Canticle of Brother Sun, and have confidence in God that He will humble their hearts, and cause them to return to their former love and friendship." When all were assembled in the cloister of the Bishop's palace, the two Friars arose, and one of them said: "Blessed Francis during his illness has made The Praises of the Lord by All His Creatures, in honor of the Lord, and for the edification of others; and now he beseeches you to listen to it with great devotion." And they began to recite and sing it. The Governor also rose and, with joined hands and arms, as if at the Gospel of the Lord, with much devotion and many tears, listened intently, for he had great faith in, and devotion for, Blessed Francis. When the Friars had ended singing the Praises, the Governor said before all those present: "Verily I say to you, that not only the Lord Bishop, whom I desire and am bound to hold as my Lord, but, had anyone slain my kinsman, or my son, him also would I forgive." With this he fell at the Bishop's feet, saying: "Behold, I am ready to make you any satisfaction that it may please you to demand, for the love of Our Lord Jesus Christ and His servant, Blessed Francis." Then the Bishop took him by the hand and raised him up, saying: "By the virtue of my office it is fitting I should he humble, but as by nature I am prone to anger, I pray you to pardon me." Then with much kindness and love they embraced and kissed each other. All the people however, praised God, who had restored peace and harmony through the efforts of Blessed Francis.[11]

In order to promote their mission of peace, Francis and his brothers avoided all that might disturb harmony among themselves, or entangle them in any dispute with others.[12] Their constant endeavor was to render their association with all men of the most peaceable nature.[13] Francis counseled his disciples repeatedly: "As you preach peace by word, so you should also possess peace, and superabundant peace in your hearts. Anger no one, nor vex any man; but by your meekness urge others to be peaceful, meek and merciful. For we are called to heal the wounded, to succor the injured, and to bring back the erring to the ways of righteousness."[14]

It is not due to mere chance that as early as 1258 a Franciscan, Gilbert of Tournay, a professor at the University of Paris, wrote a treatise for the Friars "On Peace and Tranquillity of Soul." His main objective is to convince his readers that they must possess peace within their own soul if they wish to impart it to others. He then remarks very ingeniously that peace of heart is the fruit of the knightly service of Christ. "Now, therefore," he exclaims, "brandish the sword with the left hand as with the right, and be brave, that the word may apply to thee: 'Peace be to thee, most valiant of men!' If the knights of this world fight undauntedly in order to stir up the wind of popular favor, how much more zealously must the knights of Christ battle for the eternal crown. And as, according to martial law, the land which is given to the knights as spoils, is used partly for their sustenance, and partly is reserved for future times, lest they become impoverished because of mal-administration, in like manner thou shalt also, according to the measure of thy fealty to the Lord, be given true peace of heart in this world, and God's eternal peace will be reserved for thee in the next." [15]

2. To be an apostle of peace in that era presupposed this nobility and idealism of heart and mind. For there was a crying need of restoring harmony not only between individuals and families, but only too frequently between whole cities and provinces, rent asunder by petty strife. The cause of this deplorable condition must be sought mainly in the *social evils inherent in the feudal system.*

The feudal system implied that by an extensive gradation the lower classes were ruled by the higher. The ruler of a country held sway over his immediate vassals, to whom he gave part of his kingdom in fief. These vassals of the crown in turn lorded it over their feudatories, and so on down to the last class, who were mere retainers. This socio-political institution was of a most salutary nature as long as the lower strata of society were in need of the protection of the higher, and as long as the primitive relations of feudatory dependence prevailed. But when this relation underwent an essential change, due to the new monetary and economical system, the lower classes began to aspire after fuller liberty and independence. The *Minores,* that is, the artisans and smaller merchants, began to struggle for equal rights and a share in the government with the *Maiores*, that is, the ruling class of wealthy merchants, the nobles and knights.[16] This long-drawn-out struggle frequently led to bloody civil strife.

In Assisi the strife between the two factions reached its climax at the beginning of the thirteenth century. As early as 1198 the populace rebelled, and drove out the much-hated feudal lords. These allied themselves with Perugia, the ancient enemy of Assisi, and prepared to make war. In the hope of more easily warding off the attack of the powerful enemy, the remaining Maiores of Assisi agreed to compromise with the Minores and conceded certain rights to them. The war of 1204 nevertheless ended with a rather humiliating defeat for the Assisians. Many of them, among whom we find Francis, were led captive to Perugia and imprisoned for one year.[17]

When peace had been restored, the Minores of Assisi pressed the Maiores to grant them still greater civil rights. The decisive solution was reached on November 9, 1210, when the representatives of both factions signed an agreement, which may be styled the Magna Charta of the democracy of Assisi. It begins thus: "In the name of God, Amen. The grace of the Holy Spirit be with you. To the honor of Our Lord Jesus Christ, of the Blessed Virgin Mary, of the Emperor Otto, and Duke Leopold. This is the ordinance and covenant made between the Maiores and Minores of Assisi for all future times. Without mutual consent they may not enter into an alliance, neither with the Pope, nor with his nuncios or legates, nor with the Emperor or the King and their legates and nuncios, nor with any city or fortress, nor with any powerful lord; but in all things they should agree as to what is more necessary for the honor, welfare and prosperity of the city of Assisi." Then follow a number of acts, according to which the feudal lords acknowledge full equal rights to their subjects.[18]

It is beyond all doubt that the lion's share in this peaceable triumph of democracy belongs to St. Francis. Since 1198 his sympathy had indeed been with the Minores.[19] From that time he followed with keen interest the steadily growing democratic movement. He openly manifested his preference for the lower classes by selecting for himself and his disciples the title of *Minores,* Friars Minor.[20] But his one desire was to secure a peaceable settlement of the mighty conflict. Day after day he and his followers exhorted great and small to make peace. Time and again his appeal for peace resounded in the cathedral of his native city.[21] In consequence, the desire for a lasting peace prevailed and led to the peace pact of 1210.[22]

In other places the Saint likewise acted as mediator in the conflict between the struggling classes. One day he arrived at Arezzo and found the entire city in revolt. High and low were engaged in a bloody combat; the city seemed doomed to certain destruction. Francis sent his companion, Brother Sylvester, ahead and commanded him: "Hasten to the gate of the city, and in the name of the Most High bid all the devils of discord leave the city at once." The brother followed the instruction of the Saint in all simplicity, and the Saint then stepped before the excited mob with the customary greeting, and in a short while peace was restored. The man of peace became the savior of the city.[23]

The lower classes, indeed, often resorted to unlawful means in their struggle to wrest their rights from the lords, but in this they were but apt pupils of the lords themselves. Only too frequently did the latter abandon the Christian ideal of knighthood, and engage in *petty wars and plunder.* Their insatiable greed for power and wealth induced them not only to exploit their subjects, but also to carry on feuds with one another. The words

which Pope Urban II spoke to the knights in his appeal
for the Crusade at the synod of Clermont in 1095 are
significant: "The arms which you have stained with
blood in your murderous feuds, now wield against the
enemies of the Christian faith and name. Cleanse yourselves from theft, plunder and arson by a work pleasing
to God. Ye who have oppressed orphans, robbed the
widows, murdered your Christian brethren, plundered
Church property, and committed every manner of crime,
desist now from these abominations, and fight for your
brethren against the hostile nations." [24] By following this
call, the unbridled warlike spirit of the knights was
checked and directed toward the accomplishment of a holy
and noble cause, and knighthood itself was thereby
ennobled. Nevertheless, many representatives of the
feudal nobility availed themselves as heretofore of the
law of might, and all the efforts of the Church and of the
State to abolish these abuses remained futile. We meet
with instances of this sort also in the life of Francis.

The lords of Perugia were noted far and wide for
their ruthless tyranny. No neighboring city was safe from
their attacks, and Assisi especially was frequently made
the objective of their animosity. Francis nevertheless
hoped to bring about their reform. He journeyed to
Perugia and began to preach. The people gathered about
him in large numbers; the knights, however, had resolved
to disturb the apostle of peace. They held a grand tournament and caused so great a clamor that the preacher could
not be understood. Francis then turned to the disturbers
and exclaimed with indignation: "O the folly of unfortunate men! You consider not, nor do you fear the
judgments of God! Hear ye, then, what the Lord tells
you through me, the poor little one. The Lord has exalted you above all that dwell in these confines; you should
therefore also excel in charity and gratitude toward God.
But instead you are ingrates, you attack your neighbors
with the force of arms, murder them, and plunder their

possessions. I say unto you that this will not pass un-
avenged, but for your greater chastisement God will
plunge you into civil strife, so that you will strike one
another in common revolt. For whoever does not heed
God's will, will suffer His anger." A few days later the
conflict actually broke out in their midst. The populace
demanded their rights with the force of arms, their rage
being directed especially against the lords. The result
was a slaughter so appalling that the neighboring cities,
who had but shortly before been attacked by Perugia, had
pity on the unfortunate city.[25]

In Bologna, however, the efforts of the Saint to restore
peace were crowned with greater success. The nobility of
that city had for a long time been engaged in a deadly
feud. Their mutual hatred had often resulted in cruel
bloodshed, and it appeared as if the warring factions could
never be reconciled again. Francis preached to the people
on the feast of the Assumption, 1222. Nearly all the
inhabitants of the city were assembled in the public square.
Francis announced his theme: "The angels, men, the
devils." In fact, however, his entire sermon dealt with
the laying aside of enmities and the resuming of covenants
of peace. He spoke with such unction and conviction
that not only the common people were carried away by
their enthusiasm, but also the warring families, who then
and there became reconciled to each other.[26]

In like manner Francis succeeded frequently in breaking up the feuds which existed between the lords themselves and between the people subject to them.

The apostolic peacemaker of Assisi, however, aimed to
exterminate the evil at its root. This lay in the fact that
the vassal was compelled to swear allegiance to the lord
in whose domain he dwelt. Consequently, he was bound
to render feudal service to his lord, especially to bear
arms at the demand of his liege. This promoted and
facilitated petty wars and raids on the part of the lesser
lords, and aggressive wars on the part of the greater,

including kings and emperors. Francis paralyzed this abuse of the feudal system by inserting into the rule of the Brothers of Penance, or Tertiaries,[27] the following precepts:

"The brothers may not receive arms to be wielded against any person, nor bear them on their person. Let all refrain from taking solemn oaths, except in those instances decreed by the Pope; namely where peace, the Faith, or a juridical oath is at stake. . . . If the Brothers and Sisters are troubled contrary to their right and privilege, or by the rulers of the places where they abide, let their own prefects together with the council of the Lord Bishop resort to measures which may appear to them proper." [28]

From the standpoint of law no objection could be raised against this regulation. For though the Tertiaries lived in the world, they were Religious in the full sense of the term, and hence subject only to ecclesiastical authority. The socio-political and religious importance of this measure adopted by Francis was simply incalculable. By prohibiting the Tertiaries to bear arms and to take the military oath, feudalism was stricken to the heart; for the latter consisted essentially in the oath-bound obligation of the vassal to draw arms and to follow his liege lord in strife, and war. We understand, then, why the feudal lords, from the lowest class even to the crown, declared war on the Tertiaries. We understand this all the more clearly when we consider the feud which existed at that time between the Guelphs and the Ghibellines. The imperial faction of the Ghibellines found its main support among the feudal lords, while the Papal faction of the Guelphs found theirs among the citizenry. The latter severed the ties which bound them to the feudal party by entering the Third Order, and thus the cause of the Ghibellines and with it the entire anti-Papal power of the unfortunate Frederic II was given the death-blow.

The reaction against the imperial power set in at Faenza

only a few months after the foundation of the Third Order. The citizens of that city had always favored the Guelphs, and in consequence were made to suffer grievously at the hands of their Ghibelline masters. As early as 1221 large numbers of these citizens entered the Third Order, prompted undoubtedly by the desire of freeing themselves from the yoke of fealty and from the obligation of bearing arms for their feudal lords. When these sought to employ compulsory measures, the Tertiaries appealed to the Bishop of Rimini, who in turn referred the matter to Pope Honorius III. On December 16, 1221, the Pope declared that the Tertiaries were to be exempt from the oath of fealty, and that it was the Bishop's duty, in virtue of the apostolic power conferred upon him, to protect the Tertiaries against the lords who attacked their rights.[29]

Upon this the faithful in large numbers clamored for admission into the Third Order. In a few decades half of Italy, not to mention other lands, were gathered about the religious and democratic standard of St. Francis of Assisi. A contemporary, writing of a secular cleric, inspired by envy against the Mendicants and their Tertiaries, complains: "Not only do the Franciscans and Dominicans reap what they have not sown, and intrude into ecclesiastical dignities; not only do they presume unto themselves the conferring of the sacraments of Baptism and Penance, of Extreme Unction, and the burial of the dead in their own cemeteries: in order to destroy our rights completely, and to turn away the faithful from their allegiance to us, they have now founded two new brotherhoods, and have received men and women into its ranks in such masses, that there is hardly a person whose name is not inscribed in the one or the other." [30] In all probability "we may assume that the great majority of religious organizations also belonged to the Third Order [of St. Francis]." [31] By far the greater number of Tertiaries were citizens, peasants and artisans; but many members of all ranks of nobility, some even of royal blood, likewise sought to become disciples of the "Poor Little Man" by joining the Third Order. King Louis IX of France, and the royal princess, Elizabeth of Hungary, are but the most noted and celebrated among them. Following their example, as Humbert de Romanis, an eye-witness testifies, "many men and women of distinguished birth, especially in the provinces of Italy, embraced this mode of life." [32]

For a time many of the feudal lords had still endeavored to check this movement by striving to impose their yoke upon them. But the Tertiaries were protected by the strong arm of the Church. Upon the death of Honorius III, Gregory IX ascended the Papal throne. As Cardinal Hugolino, he had assisted his friend and protégé Francis in organizing the Third Order.[33] Two months after his election, on May 26, 1227,[34] he addressed an encyclical letter to all the Bishops of Italy, and ordained that the "Penitents" be protected against those in power, and the fraternity be encouraged by all possible means. He complains that the lords everywhere strive to coerce the Tertiaries to swear allegiance to them, to bear arms, and to assume public offices. He decrees that they are, however, to be free from all these obligations, and bound only to pay the customary taxes and tributes as other citizens.[35] In another letter, dated March 30, 1228, he inveighs against those lords and magistrates who molest the Tertiaries with their oaths and a thousand other petty annoyances in order thus to avenge themselves for the refusal to take the oath of fealty.[36] In the years 1230, 1231 and 1234 the Bishops are merely enjoined to uphold the rights and privileges of the Tertiaries in regard to the feudal powers.[37] Thereafter similar instructions cease. It appears that henceforth the feudal lords had yielded to the existing conditions and acknowledged the rights of the Tertiaries.

Considering the above mentioned facts, we must admit

that St. Francis achieved the stupendous task of introducing a social reform far-reaching in its scope, without in any way disturbing the peace; or rather that the peace movement begun by him paved the way for a social reform of the widest influence, and that this social reform was truly a work in the interest of peace of first magnitude.

That St. Francis was a social reformer, whose equal the world has not seen since the time of Christ, is generally admitted by the authorities of various camps and convictions.[38] He was not, however, a socialist, much less a revolutionary. There is no doubt that he enthusiastically espoused the cause of the oppressed and enslaved people. Aside from the fact that in particular instances he guided the efforts of the Minores to a happy issue, the Franciscan conception of poverty and humility, of universal brotherhood, was in itself a powerful factor in promoting the cause of the people;[39] indeed, it has been said very appropriately, that the Franciscan rule was the consecration, and in a manner the cradle of democracy, especially in Italy.[40]

But St. Francis was far from agitating the people against the wealthy and governing classes, or from preaching the overthrow of the existing social order. We know that on the contrary, in spite of his preference for the poor and the little ones, he esteemed the rich and honored those of superior rank.[41] It was not wealth which he impugned, but the overvaluation of wealth, as well as the prevalent contempt of the poor and of poverty. It was not power and authority which he condemned, but its abuse; the oppression of the people, the exploiting of the subjects, the misuse of the feudal system for petty warfare and for the law of might. In a word, it was the social and the socio-political evils which the apostle of peace impugned; and the means he employed to abolish them was the mutual adjustment of wealth and poverty, of power and submission, and the equalization of master

296 THE IDEALS OF ST. FRANCIS

and servant, of lord and vassal, by the law of Christian brotherhood and charity.

Even the regulation forbidding the oath of allegiance and the bearing of arms, so incisive in its effect, served this noble purpose. Francis entertained no scheme of revolt against the lords, nor did he desire to obstruct the lawful defense of home and country. The former is out of the question, because he commanded the Tertiaries to pay taxes and tribute to the lords, and frequently acted the rôle of peacemaker between the lords and their liege-men.[42] The latter likewise, because prior to, as well as after, his conversion he was an ardent patriot of his native city,[43] a staunch lover of his fatherland as no other *"il più italiano dei santi e il più santo degli italiani."* He issued the prohibition forbidding the bearing of arms merely in reference to *wars of aggression.* By this means he endeavored, as far as he was able, to prevent the abuse of might, and in the last instance to prevent all war in general.

Indeed, an incomparably far-sighted and far-reaching plan! It surpassed in many ways the hitherto customary "Peace of God" (*Treuga Dei*), which forbade acts of violence or the bearing of arms on certain days of the week and at particular seasons of the year.[44] The *Treuga Dei* which St. Francis contemplated, admitted no exceptions and no interruption; its meaning and purpose were akin to that eternal peace of God, which the Saviour praised so highly in the Gospel: "Blessed are the peacemakers, for they shall be called the children of. God." [45]

This *peace program* should be fostered and realized by the members of the Third Order to the fullest of their ability, and this *Ideal of peace* the members of the First Order should keep constantly before the eyes of the world by means of their daily apostolate: the greatest peace movement ever launched, and the most sublime peace Ideal ever proclaimed!

CHAPTER XV

THE FRANCISCAN APOSTOLATE

THE peace movement is only a part of the extensive program of the Franciscan apostolate. The latter occupied such a prominent place in the life of Francis that he is honored with the title: "The apostolic man Francis." Thus his first disciples styled him;[1] the Church herself from the very beginning glorified him thus,[2] and as such he lives forever in the grateful memory of all ages. We of the twentieth century perhaps no longer find anything extraordinary in this distinction. For the contemporaries of Francis, however, it was something unprecedented that the Founder of an Order should dedicate himself and his followers to the apostolate.

We emphasize: the apostolate in its proper sense. It was not simply a question of the ordinary pastoral care of souls, or rather, there was no question whatever of this. Far from binding himself to a definite place and a definite spiritual charge, Francis wished, in imitation of the apostles, that the Order founded by him should regard the whole world as its field of activity, and in this field devote all its faculties to *the upbuilding of the Faith at home* as well as to the *conversion of the infidels*. This he understood as apostolic activity, and this was essentially the nature of the apostolic life which he had in mind.

1. The *ancient monks* no doubt also regarded their vocation as an apostolic one. They, however, wished to express thereby that the monk, as follower of the apostles, was bound not only to the observance of the commandments, but also of the evangelical counsels.[3] That he was

bound like the apostles to labor at large and to exercise the apostolate in the proper sense of the term, never occurred to them. *St. Columba* alone included missionary activity in his program.[4] In his rule, however, there is no mention made of preaching.[5] If he and his disciples nevertheless gained for themselves lasting merits by the preaching of the Gospel, it must be ascribed mainly to the Irish tradition, according to which the monasteries were to be centers of pastoral activity. The same holds good in regard to the Anglo-Saxon Benedictine abbeys, from which Boniface and his disciples came forth.

The *Benedictine rule,* as such, shut off the monk completely from the world, and thereby rendered missionary activity on his part impracticable. Besides this, the large majority of the inmates of the abbeys were lay-brothers. Clerics, not to mention priests, were rare exceptions, and were received reluctantly, and just as reluctantly admitted to Holy Orders. A monk who was at the same time a priest, was not permitted to preach even in the monastery, much less to seculars. The sole functions allowed him were various blessings and the celebration of Mass.[6] For the rest, he was obliged to divide his time as the other monks between choir duty and labor.

In later centuries priest-monks became more numerous, and began to exercise the office of preaching in their own churches. When the Clerics Regular, who dated from the eleventh century, complained of this, the Abbot Rupert of Deutz (died about 1130) wrote an apology of monasticism under the title: "On the Truly Apostolic Life." He explains therein that a priest-monk receives with ordination the right to preach and baptize; but although the exercise of these rights makes him more conformable to the apostles, yet the essence of apostolic life consists simply in his following Christ by the observance of the three vows. In consequence, every true monk, though he observe but the latter, is a true apostle, just as the apostles were, on the other hand, true monks.[7] The apostolate as applied to preaching was therefore foreign to the rule of St. Benedict. The teaching office was exercised, in consequence, by the monks only exceptionally, and then only within the walls of the monastery,[8] with the exception of a few instances, when on extraordinary occasions, as in the case of St. Bernard, the monks directed their powerful appeals to the masses, to the astonishment of the whole world.[9]

More than this. Canon law of former centuries flatly deprived the monks of the right to preach,[10] according to the ancient axiom: *"Monachus non doctoris habet, sed Plangentis officium."* [11] A few decades before the appearance of Francis, Alexander II (1061-1073) decreed: "In conformity with the regulation of St. Benedict, we command that the monks remain within their monastery; we forbid them to journey through villages, hamlets and towns, and demand that they in no wise preach to the people." [12] As late as the middle of the thirteenth century, Berthold of Regensburg declares that the Cistercians and other monks support the Church with their prayers only, but the Minorites and Dominicans also with their preaching.[13] Not even the *Canons Regular* or Augustinian Clerics devoted themselves to the office of preaching. They indeed asserted that among all Religious they alone possessed the right to preach. They were, in fact, incumbents of parishes and benefices.[14] They argued that the care of souls, and with it, the office of preaching, was therefore not only a right but also a duty. But they were restricted in every way to these charges. There could be no question of exercising missionary activity after the manner of the apostles. When therefore St. Dominic, who had been an Augustinian Cleric, took up the work of preaching, it was said of him that he had changed from a cleric to an apostolic man.[15] Humbert de Romanis also remarks that the Dominicans had injected an essentially new element into the Augustinian rule by assuming the office of preaching.[16] In the same sense St. Thomas says of the Benedictines and Augustinians: "Both Orders, that of the monks as well as that of the Clerics Regular, are destined for the work of the contemplative life," [17] not for apostolic activity.

In contrast hereto, Francis—the same may be said of St. Dominic—turned to the labor of the apostolate with the same zealous ardor and singleness of purpose with which he devoted himself to the apostolic or evangelical life.[18] In this sphere he had forerunners insofar as during the twelfth century several itinerant preachers had arisen, some in full accord with the authority of the Church, others in opposition to her. Among the former may be mentioned St. Norbert of Xanten and Robert of Arbrissel; [19] among the latter Waldus and the Poor Men of Lyons.[20] As late as 1201 the Lombardic Humiliati,[21] and in 1207 the so-called Catholic Poor Men,[22] had obtained permission to preach from Innocent III.

Shortly after, Francis likewise resolved to devote himself to the apostolate. The assumption that he was influenced in this by his forerunners appears well founded. And yet it was not so. We are acquainted with the sentiments of St. Francis at the beginning of his conversion well enough to declare that he was led to choose the apostolic life and apostolic labor neither by the example of others, nor by personal choice, nor by the need of the times. The determining factor was solely the call from above.

When he set out on the new life following his conversion, he was ruled by the one, great idea of spiritual knighthood. He would be a knight of Christ; he would serve the Most High Lord of heaven valiantly and with every fiber of his being.[23] But he was as yet completely in the dark as to the form and manner of this service. Of one thing he was, however, certain: that he was called to an active, not merely contemplative, life. For every true knight was reminded: "Heroism will not rest idly at home, but go abroad and labor and seek everywhere deeds of arms, and adventure."[24] In accordance herewith, Francis devoted himself for the time being to the service of the lepers, a service well worthy of a true knight of Christ.[25] Yet not even then could he rest content. An irresistible impulse stormed within him to announce to the whole world the greatness and the loving kindness of his Lord. He wandered through fields and woods, singing the praises of the Most High after the manner and in the tongue of the troubadours. When he was seized one day by robbers and was asked for his name, he straightway gave answer: "I am the herald of the Great King, what is it to you?"[26] Kings and emperors had their heralds, whose duty it was to announce the tournaments and contests of the knights and other weighty decrees.[27] The herald of the Lord Most High was to announce the greatness and the works of his Lord; wherefore preachers were commonly styled "heralds of God."[28] One sees how Francis begins to feel the call to an apostolic life dawn within him in those hours of profound devotion and high enthusiasm. Yet he was far from recognizing this calling as coming from God. Not daring to make the decision himself, he prayed ardently for enlightenment from above.[29]

While still in the throes of doubt and uncertainty, he one day passed the little church of San Damiano, which had almost fallen to ruins. Following the interior call of grace, he entered and cast himself on his knees before the image of the Crucified, imploring the Saviour with all the ardor of his soul to make known His divine will. Suddenly he heard from the cross the words sweet and distinct: "Francis, dost thou not see My house falling to ruins? Go, and restore it." Bewildered and trembling he stammered: "Most willingly, O Lord!" And he forthwith set himself to rebuild the ruins of the church.[30] That Christ had in mind the spiritual House of God, for whom He had shed His blood, was as yet hidden to Francis. It appeared incomprehensible to him that he was chosen to rebuild the Church of Christ throughout the world by means of his apostolate.[31]

A long lapse of time intervened before Divine Providence finally lifted the veil, behind which the vast field of his apostolate stretched forth. We have previously made mention of the events which were the decisive factor in his calling to the evangelic-apostolic *life*.[32] We are forced to touch upon them again in reference to his calling to apostolic *activity*.

It was in the church of the Portiuncula on February 24, 1209 (1208). Francis had listened with rapt attention to the gospel of the Mass, which contained the mission of Christ to the apostles. Deeply moved, he begged the priest after the Mass to explain the gospel which he had just heard. When he was told that the true follower of the apostles should possess neither gold nor silver nor money, should take with him neither purse nor scrip nor staff, nor wear shoes nor two coats, but, stripped of all things, should *preach the Kingdom of God and penance,* he rejoiced exceedingly and exclaimed: "This is what I desire, this is what I seek, this is what my whole heart craves!" [33]

Thus, by a bright ray from Heaven his entire course of life was lighted up before him. He was to be, as Brother Jordan of Giano remarks, "a follower of evangelical poverty and at the same time a zealous preacher of the Gospel"; [34] his task was the renunciation of the world together with the apostolic labor in the world and for the world. And both conjointly, apostolic poverty and preaching, apostolic renunciation and activity, apostolic life and labor, were to be equally essential elements in the calling of Francis, just as they were essential elements in the calling of the apostles, and inseparably bound up in the Gospel of the mission.

Francis hastened to comply with the Gospel without delay, cast from him staff and purse and shoes, put on a poor, rough garment [35] and "began to preach penance to all with ardor and rejoicing of spirit, edifying his hearers by his simple speech and generous manner. His word was as a flaming fire, penetrating the inmost heart and filling the minds of all with wonder." [36]

The impression made by this new apostle was so over-powering that the people were not only converted in masses,[37] but several men of noble and generous mind resolved to cast their lot with the poor preacher and to make his life and purpose their own. Francis led them to the nearest church and had the Gospel book opened before them, in order to assure themselves that they were also chosen to the life and labor of the apostles. Thrice the holy book was opened at random, and thrice their wondering eyes beheld the words relating the mission of the apostles. The leader then turned to his disciples and said: "Brothers, this is our life and rule, and the life and rule of all those who would join our company; go, then, and do as you have heard." [38] They went, sold all their possessions, and gave the money to the poor; they then set out on their first missionary journey, under the leadership of Francis.

The new brotherhood counted at first but four members. According to the injunction given to the apostles, they went forth two and two. Francis with Brother Giles took the road to the March of Ancona, Brother Sylvester of Assisi with Bernard of Quintavalle turned in another direction. The manner in which they exercised the apostolate was indeed singular. Francis journeyed on, singing with a loud and clear voice, as was his wont, lyrics in the French tongue, sounding the praises of the Most High and His boundless mercy. Whomever he met on the highways and byways, in villages and towns, he urged to love and fear God, and to do penance for his sins. Brother Giles, however, admonished the hearers to heed Francis and to believe him, for he counseled them well.[39]

When the brothers met again after a short space of time, four others joined their company.[40] Without delay

Francis reminded them of their apostolic vocation in the words: "Let us consider well our vocation, most beloved brothers, and bear in mind that God in His mercy has called us unto the salvation not only of our souls but of many, that we go through the world exhorting all nations by word and example to do penance for their sins and to observe the commandments of God. Fear not if ye are regarded as mean and contemptible and ignorant, but preach penance with courage and simplicity; trusting that the Lord, who has overcome the world, will speak in you and through you by His Spirit to move all to be converted to Him and to observe His commandments. You will find some believing, kind and meek, who receive you and your words with joy; and you will find still more unbelieving, proud and godless men, who will mock you and resist your words. Resolve therefore in your hearts to accept all things patiently and humbly." [41]

Having tried them for a while in their new vocation, he sent them out with the words: "Go, most beloved, two by two into the world and preach to men peace and penance unto the remission of sins. Be patient in sufferings, convinced that the Lord will fulfill His promise and His design. If ye are asked, answer humbly. Bless those who persecute and abuse you, and thank those who calumniate you, since for all this the kingdom of heaven is prepared unto us." [42]

The brothers accepted with joy the commands of obedience; they cast themselves at the feet of the Saint, eager to labor for the conversion of the world, and to go whithersoever he might wish to send them. Francis embraced each one and said: "Cast thy care upon the Lord, He will preserve thee." The plan of the mission was quickly outlined: Francis drew on the ground the figure of the cross, with its arms pointing to the four quarters of the globe, and sent out the brothers in these directions. Brother Bernard and Brother Giles chose Compostella in Spain as their goal; the rest selected other places.[43] Whenever the

Friars came to a church or a cross, they knelt down and greeted their Lord and Saviour with the words they had learned from the lips of their Father: "We adore Thee, O Most Holy Lord Jesus, and praise Thee here and in all the churches which are in the whole world, for by Thy holy cross Thou hast redeemed the world.[44] When entering a city, a village, a hamlet or a house, they gave the greeting of peace, and summoned all to fear and love the Creator of heaven and earth, and to keep His commandments. Toward friend and foe alike they were meek and kind, edifying all and winning all for God by word and deed. After a time they returned to their meeting place at Portiuncula, seeking recollection in prayer and meditation, relating their experiences and successes, and strengthening each other thus to renewed labor in the vineyard of the Lord.[45]

These first apostolic attempts appear in all respects similar to those of the apostles. The complete renunciation of all earthly things, their mission into all quarters of the world, the command to preach penance, the return of the disciples to their Master [46]—everything is in full accord, with the exception of the power of miracles, which Christ imparted to His apostles. The plan of Francis obviously tended to imitate the activity of the apostles in every respect.

In the meantime the number of the disciples of the Poverello had increased to twelve. Francis now realized the necessity of obtaining the approval of the Church for their mode of life, and the formal *Mission* of the Church for his apostolate. "Brothers," he said, "I see that God deigns to increase our brotherhood. Let us then go to our Mother, the holy Roman Church, and relate to the Pope what the Lord has begun to do through us, that we may continue what we have begun, according to his will and command." [47] Their pilgrimage to Rome became another missionary journey, similar to those preceding. In the

Eternal City they unexpectedly found in Cardinal John Colonna of St. Paul a powerful advocate. The latter beheld in the despised poor man of Assisi the future champion of God's cause, and introduced him to the Papal Court with the words: "I have found a most perfect man, who desires to live after the manner of the Gospel and to observe evangelical perfection; through him God intends, as I believe, to renew the Church in the whole world." [48]

Innocent III himself had beheld in a vision a man who supported the Church of the Lateran with his shoulders, and when Francis appeared before him he exclaimed: "Truly, this is the man who will support the Church of Christ by deed and word." [49] Having tested the constancy of the twelve Friars, he approved their rule and their apostolate with the words: "Go, then, brothers, with the blessing of God, and preach penance to all as God will deign to inspire you. And as soon as the Almighty has blessed you in numbers and grace, report to Us, and We shall concede to you even greater things and commit even greater tasks to you with fuller confidence." [50] The Pope added expressly that all the disciples of Francis should be entitled to exercise the apostolate in the entire world, if only they received the permission to preach from their Founder.[51] He then admitted the twelve to the tonsure, receiving them into the ranks of the clergy,[52] who alone were entitled to exercise the office of preaching.[53]

Herein lay the decisive and far-reaching *importance* of the Papal Mission. Until then the men of Assisi had spoken to the people only brief, impressive admonitions to do penance and to amend their lives, as the Three Companions expressly declare.[54] It had been a purely lay apostolate, which could be exercised even without formal authorization of the Church. "From now on, however," the same biographers continue, "Blessed Francis exercised the *office of preaching* in the fuller and wider sense; for he was now a preacher strengthened by apostolic authority." [55] With this agrees also the characterization which

the Three Companions give to his apostolic activity. [56]
Thomas of Celano is likewise in full accord when he
pens the following inimitable description:

"The most brave knight of Christ, Francis, traversed
the cities and hamlets announcing the kingdom of God, not
in the persuasive words of human wisdom, but in the word
and power of the Holy Ghost, preaching peace, teaching
salvation and penance unto the remission of sins. Sus-
tained by the apostolic authority granted him, he bore himself in all things with perfect trust, without flattery and
vain eloquence. He understood not how to palliate the
faults of certain of his hearers, but attacked them fearlessly; far from defending the life of sinners, he impugned
it with keen reproof. Since he had proved by his own
actions what he required of others, and therefore feared
no rebuke, he preached the truth with such courage that
even the most learned men, however great their fame
and dignity, admired his words and were seized with
wholesome fear at his appearance. The men pressed
about him, the women flocked to him, the clerics hastened
to him, even the Religious sought eagerly to see and hear
the man of God, who appeared to them as a man from
another world. Every age and sex hastened to behold
the wonders which God worked through His servant in
the world. Everyone, whether he met Francis in person,
or knew him only from report, everyone was convinced
that a new light from heaven had been sent to the earth,
to dispel the night of darkness which had sunk upon
almost the entire world, so that no one found a remedy.
For such an abysmal godlessness and such a deadening
indifference had overcome almost all men, that they could
scarcely be awakened from the death of their old and
deeply rooted vices. Then Francis shone forth like a
glittering star in darkest night, and spread as a radiant
dawn over the darkness. Thus it came to pass that soon
the face of the earth was renewed and showed a joyous
mien, without even a trace of the former ugliness. Gone

was the long drought, and on the swaying field the grain ripened unto the harvest. The hitherto unpruned vine put forth its sprouts full of heavenly odor, unfolded of its own strength sweet-smelling blossoms, and matured into the fruit of honesty and virtue. Everywhere prayer and praise resounded, so that many, because of the life and teaching of the most blessed Father Francis, renounced the care of earthly things, came to know themselves and aspired only after the love and reverence of the Creator. Many of the people, nobles and citizens, clerics and laics, moved by divine inspiration, began to join the holy Francis and desired to serve as knights under his direction and leadership. All these the Holy Spirit, as a stream overflowing with heavenly grace, bedewed with His extraordinary gifts and adorned the soil of their hearts with the flowers of virtue; for he was the chosen workmaster, by whose example, rule and doctrine, and under whose standard, which he carried aloft, the Church is renewed, and the threefold body of knights leads the triumphal march of the elect. But to all others likewise he marked the course of life and pointed out to men and women of every station the way of salvation." [57]

At first only Umbria and central Italy experienced the blessings of the Franciscan apostolate. It was only exceptionally and temporarily that the Franciscan preachers penetrated into more distant regions. The primary and immediate need was to prove and train the few laborers at the disposal of Francis in this restricted field. Yet Francis never for a moment forgot that the whole world was the field of action for himself and his Friars. Both are equally astounding: the immense power of the propaganda by means of which the Franciscan Ideal gained numerous workers in such a short time,[58] and the incomparable daring with which these were constantly placed in the service of the world-wide apostolate.

The Three Companions testify that at the very first Chapters of the Order the chief efforts of St. Francis were directed not only toward the interior upbuilding of the Order by inculcating the faithful observance of the rule, but also toward the extension of its activity by dispatching preaching Friars into all provinces.[59] In 1216 Bishop Jacques de Vitry writes that the new apostles had conquered the whole of Italy, from Lombardy to Apulia and Sicily, and that everywhere the blessings of this apostolate were being felt.[60]

Already at the Pentecost Chapter of 1217, was begun the intensified march into the northern countries. Francis placed himself at the head of the missionaries destined for France. However, his journey was unexpectedly ended at Florence, where Cardinal Hugolino persuaded him not to leave Italy for the time in the interests of the Order.[61] In his place Brother Pacificus, the "King of Verses," was commissioned to travel beyond the Alps with several companions.[62] This expedition unfortunately failed of its purpose at the time, because both bishops and people suspected the Friars of being members of the Albigensian sect.[63] In 1219 a second band of Friars set out for France. This time they carried a Papal letter of recommendation directed to all archbishops, abbots, priors and prelates of the entire kingdom. In this document the Friars are recommended to the kind favor of all friends, because "Brother Francis and his companions of the Order of Minors have renounced the world and all worldly things, live after the manner approved by the Roman Church, and journey from place to place after the example of the apostles in order to preach the word of God." [64]

At the same Chapter of 1219 Francis dispatched missionaries into all the other provinces of the European continent.[65] The German-speaking countries alone resisted this invasion. The Friars, numbering nearly sixty, who had made their way into these countries under the leadership of John of Penna, were regarded as Lombardic heretics, and were forced to return to Italy under unspeakable

hardships.[66]   However, after a few years, in 1221, Francis
made a second attempt.   At his request ninety Friars,
"filled with zeal for the cause of God and the salvation
of souls, and animated by the desire for martyrdom," [67]
volunteered to journey with the Provincial, Caesar of
Speyer, to the country of the dreaded Teutons.[68]   Jordan
of Giano, who accompanied the band, was soon able to
report a tremendous activity on the part of the German
Province.[69]   The British insular kingdom still remained.
In 1224 the invasion of the Isle was attempted, and in a
short while the English Province excelled as the model
of all provinces.[70]

Thus the Friars had become active apostles throughout
Christian Europe during the lifetime of the Saint.   The
prophecy of Cardinal John of St. Paul, that Francis was
to renew the Church of God in the whole world,[71] was
gloriously fulfilled.   Thomas of Celano reviews the
apostolate exercised by Francis himself or by his sons in
his usual graphic manner: "At a time when the evangelical doctrine was everywhere neglected, Francis was
sent by God to give testimony unto the truth in the whole
world after the example of the apostles.   Thus it came
to pass that by his word he branded all wisdom of the
world as obvious folly, and by the simplicity of his preaching led all men to the true wisdom of God under the
leadership of Christ.   For, the new evangelist of these
latter days has watered as a stream of paradise the whole
earth with the waters of the Gospel, and has preached
the way of the Son of God and the true doctrine by word
and deed.   In him and through him the earth received
the unexpected glad tidings and the new message of
salvation; the dying shoot of the old religion was quick-
ened by him unto new, vigorous life.   A refreshing spirit
streamed into the hearts of the elect, and the unction of
salvation was poured out into their midst, when the
Servant and Saint of Christ blazed forth as a star in the

heavens. . . . While still living amongst us sinners, he wandered and preached throughout the whole world." [72]

2. Not content with the world-wide apostolate among the faithful, Francis had included also the *conversion of the infidels* in his program from the very beginning. To live and die for the spread of the Faith, had always been his most ardent desire.[73] This we understand without difficulty if we bear in mind the chivalrous spirit of the Saint on the one hand, and on the other the flaming enthusiasm of Christian knighthood for the Faith.

To battle for the Faith and for the Church against the infidels, and in particular against Mohammedanism, the ancient arch-enemy of the Christian name, was the sublime goal of the knight in the days of the Crusades. The Crusades were in fact a gigantic conflict, in which the religious enthusiasm of Christian knighthood entered the lists with the religious fanaticism of the Saracens. Marked with the cross, the symbol of their common endeavor, and with the cry "God wills it!", the Crusaders left home and country, bore with heroic fortitude the most dreadful privations, and marched into the bloody battle as if it were a nuptial feast. All this in order to deliver the Holy Places from the grasp of the infidel and to either convert or destroy a godless paganism. The spread of Christianity, the conquest of the whole world for Christ and the Church, was the motto and the battle-cry of every true knight.[74] Happy the one who was fortunate to give his life in this holy struggle! His was in fact the crown of martyrdom. It is significant of the character of Christian knighthood, when Konrad sings of the Paladins of Charlemagne in the *Rolandslied*:

> Their knightly heart was chaste and pure,
> E'en death they gladly would endure,
> That God show mercy to their soul.
> This e'er their most desired goal
> As martyrs all for God to die,
> For heaven's glory thus to vie.[75]

And again:

> Nor fire feared they nor the sword.
> In truth 'twas granted by the Lord
> What they desired with ardent glow,
> The while they lived on earth below:
> Achieved the martyr's bright renown
> And everlasting heaven's crown.[76]

We have seen how vividly the *Rolandssage* ever dwelt in the mind of Francis [77] and how perfectly he embodied the ideal of Christian knighthood. No wonder then that he was fired with the ambition to sacrifice life and blood for the conversion of the infidels, and of the Saracens in particular.

The Assisian Knight, however, understood the apostolate among the infidels in an essentially different manner than the Crusaders. Their sole effort, their heroic struggle and death, was devoted to the *apostolate of the sword*, forced upon them by the fanatical hate of the infidels, and yet freely chosen. Just as the sword had often, indeed, too often, in the early Middle Ages been the means of missionizing, so now the Crusades were launched to conquer Mohammedanism by military, material and political means, and to make it amenable to Christianity. Francis on the contrary spiritualized the idea of the Crusades. With his eyes fixed on the example of Christ and the apostles, he went forth as a preacher of the Gospel of peace, of penance, of grace and of truth.

Hardly three years after the foundation of the Order (1212-1213), that is, at a time when the Friars had not yet gone far beyond the boundaries of Umbria, he launched his mission among the infidels. Thomas of Celano lays stress on this: "Glowing with divine love and burning with the desire for martyrdom, the blessed Father Francis set out in the direction of Syria, in order to preach the Faith and penance to the Saracens and other infidels." [78] A severe storm, however, threw him with his companion upon the coast of Slavonia, and he was forced to return to Italy by way of Ancona.[79]

His hope of reaching the stronghold of oriental Islam having been shattered, he shortly afterward (1213-1215) fared forth on foot for the Moroccan kingdom of the Saracens in Spain, passing through Lombardy and southern France. His biographer again stresses the purely evangelical character of his crusade: "The servant of God, Francis, now leaves the sea, traverses the land, works it with the plow of his word, sows the seed of life and brings forth manifold fruit. His goal was martyrdom; a great yearning for it burned in his heart. The road led to Morocco, in order to preach the Gospel to the Sultan Miramolin and his followers. He was driven forward by such desire, that he at times left his companion, and, as one carried away by the spirit, ran before him, in order the sooner to accomplish his purpose. But it pleased God to show mercy to me and to many. For when Francis had already reached Spain, the Lord stood in his way, sending him an illness, so that he could go no farther, and thus recalled him from the journey he had undertaken." [80]

But even then Francis was not to be discouraged. After he had dispatched Friars to the distant countries of Europe at the Pentecost Chapter of 1219, he set out with Brother Peter Catanii for Damiette, in Egypt, where the army of the Crusaders battled with the hosts of Sultan Malek-al-Khamil. "It should not appear," remarks Jordan of Giano, "as if the Blessed Father sought rest, while he sent out the brothers to suffer and to labor for the sake of Christ; on the contrary, he wished to go before all on the way of Christ in the generosity of his soul. When he therefore sent out his sons to the preaching of the Gospel, which was beset with so many perils, he himself braved the dangers of the sea, reached the infidels, and hastened to the Sultan." [81] Truly a hazardous undertaking, since the Sultan had placed a prize on the head of every Christian.[82] Francis, however, bore himself with such meekness and humility, and at the same time with such courage and holy daring, that the tyrant not only did not suffer any harm to come to him, but listened willingly to his words, and allowed him to preach the Christian Faith. But as soon as he became aware that Francis attacked the faith of Islam, he had him escorted back to the camp of the Christians with military honors. Again Francis had failed to realize his burning desire to suffer martyrdom for the Faith.[83]

After his return to Italy, he began to put the final touches to the earlier rule. It contains two chapters on the work of the apostolate, the one (chap. 17) dealing with preaching to the faithful, the other (chap. 16) with preaching "to the Saracens and other infidels." [84] Two years later, he wrote the final rule, in which we find these chapters in briefer form, but with the same content.[85] Regarding the apostolate among the infidels, Francis decrees for all times: "Let all the brothers who by divine inspiration desire to go amongst the Saracens and other infidels, ask leave therefor from their provincial ministers. But the ministers must give permission to go to none except those whom they see are fitted to be sent." [86] Hereby mission work among the infidels is proclaimed as an essential element of the Franciscan Ideal and of Franciscan activity.

Still more, Francis regarded missionary activity among the heathens as the noblest and highest task of the Order. When speaking of the various obediences, that is, of the tasks undertaken by the Friars under obedience, he said: "The most sublime obedience, in which flesh and blood have no part, consists in this, that one go among the infidels by divine inspiration, be it for the salvation of our neighbor, or from desire for martyrdom. To request this obedience from the superiors, is above all pleasing to God." [87]

In the beginning Francis directed his attention principally to the missions among the Saracens, because Islam was at that time the most formidable enemy of Christendom and threatened Europe from the East, the South, and the West. Not only did Francis himself set out to preach the Christian Faith to the Saracens, he time and again appointed new Friars to this mission. Brother Giles was sent at a very early date to Tunis.[88] In 1218 he sent a band of missionaries under the leadership of Brother Elias of Bombarone to Syria.[89] At the time that Francis was with the Crusaders at Damiette (1219), a considerable number of Friars were active in the various cities of the Syrian sultanate.[90]

Contemporary with this oriental mission, a second was attempted among the Moors in Spain and Morocco. The five missionaries: Bernard, Peter, Otto, Adjutus and Accursius preached in the then Saracen city of Seville, and after suffering the most cruel tortures in that city, they were finally beheaded in Morocco on January 16, 1220, by Sultan Miramolin himself.[91] The joy of Francis over their martyrdom was as great as if he himself had obtained this honor and happiness. Now he knew that he had had five true Friars Minor, he exclaimed when he received the message. And turning in the direction of Portugal, he greeted and blessed the monastery of Alenquer, whence the martyrs had set forth.[92] Fired by the example of these Moroccan martyrs and by the miracles that accompanied the return of their bodies, the noble Portuguese youth, Don Fernando, later on Anthony of Padua, resolved in 1220 to enter the Order, and to volunteer for the African missions.[93] One year later (1221), the Friars: Daniel, Samuel, Domnus, Leo, Hugolinus, Nicolaus and Angelus set out for the Moroccan sultanate and shed their blood on the peninsula of Ceuta for the love of Christ.[94]

The success of these and other heroic sacrifices was, however, small. Bishop Jacques de Vitry, who witnessed the labors of the Friars among the Mohammedans, writes: "The Saracens admire the humility and perfection of the

Friars Minor, receive them kindly and furnish their livelihood, wherever they appear as fearless preachers. . . .
They even listen willingly to their preaching on the
Christian Faith, until they begin to attack the deceitful
and perfidious doctrines of Mohammed. From that
moment they cruelly beat the missionaries and drive them
from their cities." [95] The same hopeless experience, which
has been repeated for the last seven centuries, already
marked the pretentious beginnings of the Franciscan
missions among the Saracens: the Moslems are converted
only in the most rare cases.

The Franciscan missionaries therefore turned their attention more and more to the conversion of other infidels.
Only a few years after the death of St. Francis, they
developed an exceedingly fruitful activity in various
oriental mission fields, among the schismatics as well as
among the heathens; [96] even before the middle of the
thirteenth century they penetrated into the very heart
of the Mongolian empires in India and China.[97] In the
course of this century we find Franciscan missionaries in
almost all countries of the then known globe.[98] Dominic
de Gubernatis prefaces his history of the Franciscan missions with the words: "I set out upon a vast ocean, the
description of the glorious as well as numerous labors,
sufferings and martyrdoms which the Friars Minor have
endured for the defense and the spread of the Catholic
Faith throughout the world." [99]

This magnificent spirit of sacrifice and the restless
energy displayed by the sons of St. Francis throughout
the centuries and in all fields of missionary endeavor,
need not surprise us. For the Order is by its very nature
a missionary Order. Francis, among all the Founders
of Religious Institutes, was the first to include foreign
missions in his apostolic program. He is the father of
the modern missionary movement, which he originated
and which has developed so wonderfully up to the
present time. Indeed, it may be said without exaggera-

tion, that since the days of the apostles he was the first herald of faith to emblazon on his banner the conversion of the whole world in literal observance of the words of Christ: "Go ye into the whole world and preach the Gospel to every creature." [100]

We marvel at this and ask how the Poverello of Assisi could venture to include the world-wide activity in the home as well as the foreign missions in the program of his unworldly Institute. But for Francis this was altogether patent. Had he not vowed to observe the Gospel after the manner of the apostles? Had he not learned from this Gospel, that his Master sent him into the missionary field, as He had once sent His twelve disciples? And furthermore, did he not read in the same Holy Book the last Will and Testament of Jesus to the apostles to exercise their apostolate without restriction of space or time? The will of Christ was therefore clear to him, and this will was for the Knight of Christ sovereign law. Another reason was added to this: the example of the Saviour, who lived and died for the salvation of souls. *Zeal for souls after the example of Christ, became the pole-star of the Franciscan apostolate.*

Thomas of Celano adds weight to this when he writes: "Francis again and again declared that nothing was to be preferred to this labor for the salvation of souls, because Christ had deigned to hang on the cross for them. For this the constant wrestling of the Saint in prayer, his zeal in preaching, the excess of his good example. He would not have deemed himself a friend of Christ had he not loved the souls which Christ has loved. This also was the impelling cause of his exceeding reverence for the teachers of the word of God: he beheld in them the associates of Christ, since they exercised with Christ the office of saving souls." [101]

It would be erroneous to think that Francis overlooked the immense difficulty of combining harmoniously the contemplative life of the Order with an active apostolate.

On the contrary, this problem engrossed his attention and that of his disciples from the first. Shortly after having received the permission to preach from Innocent III, they deliberated in all earnestness, whether it were not better to withdraw into solitude than to live among men and to labor for them. Arguments for and against were placed in the balance and considered gravely and prayerfully. The solution was reached solely by realizing their calling to the knightly service of Christ. Christ had lived and died for the salvation of souls. The new knight of Christ should, then, also live not only unto himself, but unto those for whom Christ had died.[102]

This zeal for souls, called forth by the example of Christ, later on compelled him time and again to persevere in his apostolic calling, despite the attraction to a purely contemplative life so frequently and so strongly felt. Returning one time from his hermitage, he could not rid himself for several days of the doubt whether he should not relinquish the office of preaching. He finally laid the question before his companions, that they might decide. "What is your counsel, brothers?" he asked. "What do you advise? Shall I devote myself to prayer, or wander about as preacher? For I, simple, plain man, incapable of speech, have received the grace of prayer in higher measure than the grace of preaching. In prayer is profit and fulness of grace, in preaching is the distribution of the blessings imparted from above. In prayer is the cleansing of the inner emotions, union with the one, true, and highest Good, growth in virtue; in preaching there is soiling of the feet, manifold distraction, relaxation of discipline. In prayer we speak with God and hear Him, praying we converse with the angels and in a manner lead an angelic life; in preaching we must condescend exceedingly to men, live in their midst as men, think and speak and hear as men. One thing, however, is against the choice of the purely contemplative life of prayer, and appears to outweigh before God all reasons which speak for it: the only-begotten Son of God, the most high Wisdom, has come down from the bosom of His Father for the salvation of men. He wished to be an example for the world and to preach to men the word of salvation, to redeem them by His precious blood on the cross, to renew them in the fountain of regeneration, to nourish them with the Eucharist; He kept back nothing which He could give generously for our salvation. Since we are to follow His example in all things, it appears to me that it is most pleasing to God if I interrupt my quietude and go forth to labor."

Though he pondered this thought for many days, he could nevertheless reach no conclusion. He therefore sent a messenger to Brother Sylvester, who was engaged in incessant prayer on a mountain beyond Assisi, that he might obtain God's answer to this question and impart it to him. He also requested St. Clare and her daughters to pray for enlightenment in this weighty matter. When Brother Masseo, whom he had dispatched as messenger, returned, Francis knelt down before him, crossed his arms, and asked humbly: "What is the command of my Lord Jesus Christ that I should do?" Masseo declared: "It is His good pleasure that thou shouldst go forth to preach, since God has called thee not only for thy sake, but also for the salvation of thy fellow-men." When the Saint heard this answer, he rose immediately and fared forth. "He went forth," says St. Bonaventure, "with such fervor to do the will of God, and ran with such haste as if the hand of God upon him had endued him with new strength from on high." [103]

This indefatigable and insatiable zeal henceforth dominated his whole future life. Thomas of Celano reviews and recapitulates it in the pithy sentences: "For eighteen years his body had little or no rest, for he traversed various and far distant regions, in order that the ever willing spirit which dwelt in him, the devout spirit, the fervent spirit, might scatter everywhere the seed of the word of God. He filled the whole world with the Gospel of Christ in such wise that in one day he visited four to five villages or even cities, preaching everywhere the kingdom of God, and rendering his whole body a tongue, in order to edify his hearers by his example as well as by his words." [104]

During the last two years of his life, when the holy Stigmata prevented him from walking, he had himself carried on a poor little beast through cities and towns in order to animate the faithful to bear cheerfully the cross of Christ,[105] so insatiable was his zeal for souls. A knight unto the last hour of his life and unto the last fiber of his being, "he resolved to perform even greater deeds for Christ, his Leader, and though the members of his body were weary and feeble, yet his spirit was strong and fervent, so that he hoped to wage a fresh warfare against the enemy, and to attain a glorious triumph. For there is no place for languor and sloth where the stimulus of love is ever urging to greater things." [106]

This glowing zeal for souls was passed on by Francis to his sons as a precious inheritance. "Francis desired that his sons be perfectly like unto him in that zeal for souls with which he was completely filled, " writes the oldest biographer.[107] In fact, this fervent zeal became the prized inheritance of the first Friars [108] as well as of those great Franciscan apostles of all centuries, of an Anthony of Padua, Berthold of Regensburg, Bernardine of Siena, John of Ducla, Peter of Alcantara, Francis Panigarola, Cornelius Musso of Piacenza, Lawrence of Brindisi, Mark of Aviano, Joseph of Leonissa, Procopius of Templin, Martin of Cochem, Leonard of Porto Maurice, Didacus of Cadiz, and others. Zeal for souls must ever remain the guiding star of the Franciscan apostolate and the perennial fountain from which it draws ever fresh strength and inspiration.

THE APPARITION AT PORTIUNCULA

CHAPTER XVI

THE FRANCISCAN APOSTOLATE
(Continued)

THE essential *pursuits of the Franciscan apostolate* were preaching and hearing confessions. In the first years the Friars did not, of course, administer the *sacrament of Penance*. Francis and the majority of his first disciples were not even priests,[1] and those who were invested with the priestly office did not possess the jurisdiction necessary for hearing confessions.

Innocent III granted the Friars (1209-1210) merely the authority to preach.[2] He did, however, promise greater concessions.[3] That he did not at the time have in mind to grant permission to hear confessions, is quite evident from the decree *"Omnis utriusque sexus,"* which he published a few years later (1215) at the Fourth Lateran Council, and which reads: "All the faithful of both sexes are bound to sincerely confess all their sins at least once a year to their own priest. . . . If, however, one wishes to confess to another priest for a just cause, he must first request and obtain permission from his own priest, since otherwise the former cannot absolve him."[4] Thus the administration of the sacrament of Penance was reserved to the parish clergy, with the exclusion of Religious, who were forbidden by the prevalent Church law to hear the confessions of the seculars.[5]

For this reason Francis makes no mention of this element of the apostolate, neither in the later rules, nor in his other utterances. He decrees merely that the priests of the Order may absolve their own brothers from sins, and that the Friars, whenever possible, should have recourse to the confessors within the Order.[6]   However numerous the priests had become in the Order in the first years following its establishment,[7] we find nowhere, until shortly before the death of Francis, that the priests of the Order heard the confessions of seculars.

Yet their magnificent activity could not be restricted very long to preaching.   Many of the faithful, with increasing insistence, demanded to be allowed to confess to the mendicant priests for the relief of their conscience, partly because these were strangers and were regarded as more perfect; partly because the secular clergy were to a great extent unworthy, or incapable, or too limited in numbers.[8]   The Friars therefore assumed the burdensome, as well as important, office of confessors in many places, with the permission or at the request of the pastors.

If we mistake not, the first record of this kind dates from 1224.   Brother Haymo of Faversham, the later Minister General, in that year was visiting a parish church in Paris, where a large number of the faithful were assembled.   In his anxiety lest many might approach the Lord's Table in an unworthy state, he delivered a sermon on the reception of the Eucharist.   His discourse was so impressive that many postponed the reception of the Sacrament until they had confessed to him.   For three full days he sat in the church and heard confessions, to the great consolation of the parish.[9]   During Lent of 1231 St. Anthony of Padua preached daily and heard the confessions of his almost countless hearers from morning to evening.[10]   Without doubt the Saint had been active not only as preacher, but also as confessor, from the beginning of his apostolate (1222).   Frequently as many as thirty thousand people flocked together to hear him,[11] and the crowd of penitents was so great that the large number of Friars and secular priests who followed the saintly preacher, were unable to hear all who were desirous of confessing.[12]

It is merely by accident that we receive these reports of

Haymo, of Anthony, and of the confessors accompanying the latter. It is highly probable that many Friars heard confessions at this date, perhaps even earlier. Thomas of Eccleston declares expressly that in England numerous Friars, who were not even preachers or lectors, were promoted to the office of confessors by the extraordinary favor of prelates;[13] as for instance Brother Solomon, Maurice of Derham, Vincent of Wygorn, Galfrid of Saresbury, Eustace of Merc, and others.[14] Other bishops outside England no doubt acted in like manner.

Very many, even of the higher and lower clergy, however, far from allowing the Friars to hear confessions in their dioceses, even demanded of the Mendicants that they confess to the pastors themselves, receive holy communion from them, render tribute to them; in short, be subject to them in every manner. Gregory IX, in 1231, put an end to these encroachments by several Bulls, forbidding them under the most severe penalties to violate or restrict in any manner the privileges granted to the Friars by the Popes.[15]

The great friend and mentor of St. Francis on the chair of Peter was, however, not content with this. He wished that the Friars should exercise without hindrance the office of confessors not only in their own churches, but also in the whole world in the same manner as they exercised the office of preaching. The respective decree is dated April 6, 1237.[16] Prior to this time Gregory had merely insisted, as Innocent III had done before him, that the Friars should everywhere preach freely and without restraint.[17] He had likewise demanded that they be permitted to erect their own oratories within the parishes, and to preach in them.[18] As regards the missionary districts, which had neither bishops nor parish clergy, he had furthermore granted the Friars unlimited authority to administer the sacrament of Penance as well as the other sacraments.[19] Now, however, he commands the entire secular clergy of all Christian countries not only to assist the Friars zealously in the exercise of the office of preach-

ing, but also to allow the faithful to confess to them freely
and without hindrance.[20]

From this moment the sons of St. Francis—the same
can be said of the Dominicans—were active in the confessional with the same zeal as in the pulpit. Preaching
and hearing confessions were regarded by them as sowing
and reaping, respectively, in the harvest field of the
Church.[21] By means of the latter as well as of the former,
they achieved an immeasurable amount of good, and gained
the universal confidence of the faithful.

This, however, again roused the jealousy of many of
the secular clergy, who believed their rights and revenues
endangered by the Friars. They raised such vehement
and constant protests before Emperor and Pope [22] that
Innocent IV, who had shortly before defended the privileges of the Mendicants to the fullest extent,[23] now (1254)
restricted the faculties granted by his predecessors, and
in particular forbade Religious to hear confessions without
the express permission of the respective pastor.[24]

Alexander IV, however, rescinded this decree after but
one month[25] and soon afterward commanded all bishops
and secular priests to assist the Mendicants in the defense
and the exercise of all privileges granted them by the
Popes.[26] The enemies of the two Orders indeed protested
all the more vehemently, in particular the Parisian professor, William of St. Amour, who at this period (1255)
published his notorious work: *On the Perils of the Latter
Days*. These foes of the Mendicants were, however, refuted decisively by the two intellectual giants Thomas of
Aquinas and Bonaventure of Bagnorea,[27] and condemned
by the Church.[28]

The apology which St. Bonaventure wrote in defense of
the activity of the Friars as preachers and confessors,[29]
bears throughout the imprint of his sublime mentality as
well as of true Franciscan charity and reverence toward
the secular clergy. Its dominating thought is: far from

striving to rival the secular clergy, the Friars desire to lead all humanity to God in co-operation with them.[30] The Friars are aware that they preach and hear confessions solely by a special Papal privilege,[31] while the pastors possess the right and the duty of the ordinary care of souls. The Friars accordingly are merely the fishermen in the second boat, who are called by those in the first when the catch becomes too great.[32] They divide the labor and exertion of the secular clergy, without encroaching on their office or their revenue.[33] In their sermons they constantly remind the faithful of their duties toward the clergy [34] and are far from discouraging the people to attend their instructions.[35] In the confessional they give their service to those only who come of their own choice, and send every penitent to the pastor if he has not confessed to the latter within the lapse of a year.[36] In all these things the Friars follow the authorization and the command of the Apostolic See, which has empowered them to instruct and direct as preachers and confessors not only the faithful of the whole world, but the clergy and Religious as well.[37]

More exact records of the manner and the method according to which the Friars administered the sacrament of Penance are not extant, because this element of their apostolate is naturally beyond the pale of closer research.

2. Of the individuality of the *Franciscan sermon,* however, which was the oldest and most important element of the apostolate,[38] we are able to glean definite information. The nature, the content, the method of the sermon as regards composition and delivery; finally, the relation of sermon to actual life, appear clearly marked and defined.

In order to understand correctly the *nature of the Franciscan sermon* we must examine more closely the difference, as previously pointed out, between the *simple exhortation* and the *formal discourse.*[39]

In the beginning, Francis and his companions restricted

themselves altogether to the former. After the example of
the apostles, they spoke to the people in the houses where
they labored or chanced to enter, on the streets, in public
places, in the open field and wherever occasion offered
itself, few and simple words of exhortation, and naturally
these aphoristic addresses in no wise bore the character of
a formal discourse.

Wherever Francis found a group of people, he greeted
them with the words of the Gospel: "The Lord give you
His peace!" To this he joined in the fervor of his spirit
and with holy joy his exhortation, which by its very simplicity and sublimity withal edified his hearers greatly.[40]
Yet, however deep the impression made by his words, and
however astounding the results produced by them, it is
expressly noted that there was no question of a sermon
in the strict sense, but merely an exhortation to penance,
to peace, to virtue; and when the master had finished, his
companion Brother Giles would then add: "Believe him
and heed his words, because he is a man who speaks
well." [41]

When Brother Giles himself appeared as preacher, he
followed the same method. The "Aurea dicta of blessed
Giles," [42] which were collected by his hearers, are not of
direct bearing on this matter, since they were addressed
almost exclusively to his brothers in the Order; yet they
show that Giles had the very happy faculty of uttering
brief, striking and wise words of admonition even in converse with his brothers. His life, on the other hand, represents him as exercising this faculty in the most original
manner. We find him now in a hermitage, now on a
journey to Rome, to Compostella, to Syria and Palestine;
he earns his livelihood by gathering bundles of fagots
and carrying them to the city, by harvesting and pressing
grapes or gathering nuts and baking bread; at one time he
peddles water in the city, another time he makes rush
baskets or carries the dead for burial.[43] In all these occu-

pations he speaks to men and women words of instruction and encouragement to love God and to do penance, wherever occasion offered.[44]

The other disciples of Francis did likewise. "Whenever they entered a city, a hamlet, a village or a house, they announced peace and exhorted all to love and fear the Creator of heaven and earth, and to observe His commandments," we read in the Legend of the Three Companions.[45] They adhered to this form of exhortation long after they had been empowered to preach formal sermons. Cardinal Jacques de Vitry testifies to this in his description of their activities, written in 1216. Day after day the Friars leave their houses and repair to the surrounding villages to earn their livelihood; yet their one desire and ambition in laboring thus was to elevate their fellow-men to virtue and piety by their example and their words.[46]

The exhortatory form of preaching was to remain in practise even later, independent of the formal sermon. Francis emphasizes this expressly in the rule of 1221, and adds a sketch of a sermon of exhortation, which is worthy of attention. Under the title: "Of the Praise and Exhortation Which All the Brothers May Make," we read: "This or the like exhortation and praise, all my brothers may announce with the blessing of God, whenever it may please them, among whatever men they may be: Fear and honor, praise and bless God, give thanks and adore the Lord God almighty in trinity and unity, Father, Son, and Holy Ghost, the Creator of all. 'Do penance, bring forth fruits worthy of penance';[47] for know that soon we must die. 'Give, and it shall be given to you. Forgive, and you shall be forgiven.'[48] And if you do not forgive men their sins, the Lord will not forgive you your sins.[49] Confess all your sins. Blessed are they who shall die in penitence, for they shall be in the kingdom of heaven. Woe to those who do not die in penitence, for they shall be the children of the devil, whose works they do, and they shall go into eternal fire. Beware and abstain from all evil, and persevere in good until the end." [50] With such simple exhortations all the brothers, clerics and lay brothers, could take part in the apostolate.

Apart from these, however, the *formal sermon* also had its place, but was not permitted to all indiscriminately. These formal discourses were not, as we shall presently see, Scripture or homiletic sermons, but merely moral, or sermons on "penance." The latter did not differ essentially from the above-mentioned exhortatory sermon. The preaching of the formal sermon, however, was done in the name and by the authority of the Church; it bore therefore an official character, and was permitted not only outside the churches, but also within them and at the liturgical functions.[51] For this very reason the formal sermon could be permitted to those Friars only who possessed the proper fitness for this office. That Innocent III did not only have in mind the simple exhortation, but the preaching of sermons in the above-mentioned sense when he gave his approbation of the Franciscan apostolate, can hardly be doubted. For, the simple exhortation, which is open to every Christian, did not require the official authorization of the Church. Furthermore, in order to make use of the simple admonition, Francis and his companions would not have stood in need of the tonsure, but they necessarily had to be clerics in order to preach sermons in the strict sense. Finally, if there had been merely a question of the simple exhortatory form of preaching, the Pope would not have decreed that among the future Friars only those should be permitted to preach who would obtain leave from Francis; [52] for, this form of preaching, as we know, was free to all the Friars without exception.

That Francis did, in fact, understand the Papal approbation in this sense, can be definitely proved. Immediately after his return from Rome he made use not only of the simple exhortation, but, according to our previous statement,[53] he appeared as preacher in the stricter sense. He preached in the churches and at the Sunday services even at the time that the Friars were living in the hut at Rivo Torto. It was his custom at the time to go to Assisi on Saturdays, passing the night in prayer in a small garden-house belonging to the cathedral chapter, and to preach on Sunday at the early Mass in the cathedral church.[54]

In like manner, by virtue of the authority granted by Innocent III, he permitted a chosen group of specially fitted Friars to exercise the office of preaching. Each year, on the occasion of the General Chapter, these Friars were selected and sent into the various provinces, that they might preach to the people.[55] In this matter Francis did not consider whether the Friars were clerics or lay brothers, but granted leave to preach to all those who possessed the spirit of God and the required eloquence.[56] It may be assumed that he had the tonsure conferred on the lay brothers who were selected for this office, to receive them thus into the ranks of the clergy, just as he and his eleven companions had received the tonsure for the same reason.

In the course of the next years the Saint became more rigorous in the requirements for the office of preaching. For a time indeed he left the selection of the preachers to the provincial ministers. The great expansion of the Order and the constantly increasing number of Friars, advised this innovation. But in making it, strict regulations were imposed at the same time on the ministers as well as on the preachers. The rule of 1221 ordains expressly: "Let none of the brothers preach contrary to the form and the institution of the holy Roman Church, and unless this has been conceded to him by his minister. But let the minister take care that he does not grant this leave indiscreetly to anyone. . . . And let no preacher appropriate to himself the office of preaching, but let him give up this office without any contradiction, at whatever hour it may be enjoined him." [57]

Experience, however, did not seem to commend this manner of procedure. At least the approbation for the office of preaching was restricted to the General of the Order in the final rule of 1223, and made dependent on an examination to be made before him: "Let no one of the brothers dare to preach in any way to the people, unless he has been examined and approved by the Minister General of this brotherhood, and the office of preaching is conceded to him by the latter." [58]

We are also informed how this regulation was enforced during the lifetime of the Saint and shortly after. All candidates for the office of preaching, without exception were obliged to travel in person from all parts of the globe and submit to an examination by the General of the Order. This entailed so many difficulties, that already in 1230 the question was submitted to Gregory IX, whether the General should not be permitted to appoint special examiners, by whom the Friars could be examined in their own provinces. The answer was negative. The future preachers were to appear before the General of the Order as heretofore on the occasion of the General Chapter, and be examined by him in the presence of their provincial minister. Exemption was granted in favor of those Friars only who, because of their theological training, their eloquence and other obvious qualifications, were not in need of an examination.[59]

However, after ten years the same Gregory IX realized the necessity of abrogating this decree, for the simple reason that the large number of Friars and the great distances to be traveled by them rendered its observance impossible. He accordingly conceded that the candidates who had received their theological training, should submit to an examination before their ministers and definitors at the Provincial Chapter, and then receive their patent.[60]

All this leads to the evident conclusion that from the very beginning the authorization to preach was made dependent on certain conditions, and that furthermore these conditions became more and more stringent even during the lifetime of the Saint. Innocent III had entrusted (1209-10) the permission to preach to the judgment of the Founder. The latter granted it during the first decade of the Order even to the unlettered Friars if they possessed the proper qualities. During the second decade of the Order, however, these requirements no longer sufficed. An examination became indispensable to prove the candidates sufficiently trained in theology; and in consequence only the educated Friars were selected for the office of preaching. The requirements demanded of the preachers are therefore an index to the *content of the Franciscan sermon.*

The latter was designated from the first as preaching *to penance.* When Francis received the evangelical message at the time of his calling, making it clear that the apostles were sent by Christ "to preach the kingdom of God and penance," he exclaimed: "This is what I desire, this is what I seek, this is what I wish to do with all my heart." [61] He immediately set about "to preach penance to all with great fervor of spirit and joy of heart." [62] His first disciples received the same charge: "Most beloved, go forth two and two into all countries of the world, preaching to men peace and penance unto the remission of their sins." [63] As soon as their number had risen to twelve, they journeyed to Rome to request the approbation of the Church. Innocent III "granted to Blessed Francis and his brothers leave to preach penance everywhere," and added that he would make larger concessions as soon as the young band had increased and proven itself.[64]

From this it becomes evident with utmost clearness that Francis and his Institute were restricted at first to the preaching of penance. What is the exact import of this term?

It must be observed in the first place that the Friars designated their life as one of "penance" just as definitely as they styled their preaching "the preaching of penance." The dying Francis looks back on his original life in the Order and views the present and future life of his brothers, and joins both in the term "to do penance." [65] The earliest disciples of the Saint are "moved to do penance by the example of the Saint." [66]   To the questioning of the curious populace regarding their origin, the Order to which they belong and the life which they lead, the first companions make answer simply: "We are penitents, natives of the city of Assisi." [67]   Humbert de Romanis condenses the entire Franciscan perfection in the one term: "Penance." [68]

Since Franciscan life was called and is a life of penance, one might assume that the preaching of penance was essentially a means of propaganda for the spread of the Order: that the Friars aimed at the one thing in their preaching, to urge their hearers to follow the same calling, to become members of their fraternity. In fact, this was partly the object of Franciscan preaching.

Cardinal Jacques de Vitry finds the immediate object and the incisive effect of these preachers herein: they exert themselves to the utmost to wrest the souls of their fellow-men from earthly vanities and to gain them for themselves, a task in which they succeeded admirably.[69] Thomas of Celano and the Three Companions are still more definite. In large groups the hearers follow the preachers to their hermitages.[70]   The women, who could not of course join the Friars, imitated their life of "penance" in their own convents under the guidance of St. Clare; others, hindered by the ties of position and family, remained in the world, "doing penance." [71]   Thus the three Orders of St. Francis were regarded originally as Orders of penance. "To preach penance," therefore, signified in its most restricted sense: to bring the world into affiliation with one of the three Orders of St. Francis and thereby to a life after the Gospel, along the lines laid down by him in his rules.[72]

And yet this could not have been the exclusive meaning of this term if we consider the nature of the reform which was inaugurated by the Franciscan preachers and which permeated all classes of the people. That the whole world should observe the Gospel to that degree of perfection which Francis had in mind for his institute, was not to be thought of. The Saint aimed, as Bernard of Bessa remarks, at mapping out the path of perfection or "penance" for the entire human race as it was suitable and possible for all,[73] as it was made obligatory for all men by the law of the Gospel. To preach penance, therefore, in its wider sense, meant to urge all classes of humanity to observe the laws and precepts of the Gospel, to rouse them to conversion and the correction of their lives, to lead them back to practical Christianity.

This conclusion is brought home to us by all the reports of the biographers regarding the preaching of Francis and his disciples. The Three Companions relate that the Saint on his first missionary journeys "went about through cities and villages, urging all men to fear and love God and to do penance for their sins."[74] His disciples did likewise,[75] following the instructions imparted by the master. "For," thus spoke the latter, "the Friars Minor have in these latter days been sent by God to this, that they show the path of light to those who are enveloped in the night of sin. Let us consider well, most beloved brothers, the calling to which God has called us, not only unto our salvation, but unto the salvation of many, that we go through the world and urge others more by our example than by word, to do penance and to heed the commandments of God."[76] Thomas of Celano likewise emphasizes that the preaching of Francis aimed at the thorough conversion and correction of his hearers,[77] that it rebuked all sins and vices, roused the sinners and effected a complete change of heart and life among all classes of the people.[78]

With this agree fully the sketches of sermons made by Francis and still extant, also his "Admonitions" to all Christians,[79] as well as the records of his discourses delivered on the occasion of the wolf plague at Greccio,[80] at the so-called Chapter of the Mats at Portiuncula (1221),[81] and during the feud of the noble families of Bologna (1222),[82] and likewise the elementary themes which he places in the mouth of a simple and of a learned Friar respectively at the imaginary Chapter of all the Religious of the world.[83]   Even more significant is the address embodied in the rule of 1221, and which we have previously reproduced.[84]   The latter shows that he understands by the "sermon on penance" what we are accustomed to designate as "moral sermons."   Francis accordingly defines the usual content of the Franciscan sermon thus in the rule of 1223: "I warn and exhort the same brothers that in the preaching they do, their words be fire-tried and pure for the utility and edification of the people, announcing to them *vices* and *virtues, punishment* and *glory,* with brevity of speech, because the Lord made His word short upon earth." [85]

The preaching therefore, as granted by Innocent III and practised by Francis and the first generation of his brothers, was evidently the simple *moral sermon,* in contradistinction to the *Scriptural sermon,* which aimed at expounding the moral as well as the dogmatic content of Revelation by means of the inspired text, and which for this reason was termed *doctrinal sermon.*

That the Friars were entrusted with the preaching of moral sermons in distinction to the Scriptural or doctrinal sermon, becomes still more evident if we consider the law of custom which prevailed at that time in regard to popular preachers. Whenever the permission to preach was granted to laymen, or unlettered clerics, the Scriptural sermon was always excluded. This was restricted to the educated clerics. The popular preacher Peter Waldes and his followers came in conflict with the Archbishop of Lyons, because they dared to undertake the exposition of the Scriptures and the preaching of doctrinal sermons.[86] Innocent III granted the Lombardic Humiliati the permission to preach moral sermons (1201) with the explicit exclusion of sermons on the articles of faith and the sacraments,[87] i. e. on dogma.[88]

The Catholic Poor Men were the first (1208) to successfully solicit the permission to preach doctrinal sermons, on the ground that the members of their society were for the greater part clerics and trained in theology.[89] Two years later the re-united Lombards obtained this concession on the same grounds.[90]

In the meantime the Poverello with his eleven companions, who were almost all unlettered,[91] had appeared before Innocent III (1209-10). They requested and received permission to preach penance.[92] Beyond doubt this meant the authorization to preach moral sermons, in direct contrast to doctrinal sermons.

The Pope, however, gave them hopes of preaching the latter in the near future, when he added that he would "concede still greater things and entrust more to them with more secure confidence, as soon as they had increased and proven themselves [as preachers of penance]." There is no record to show when the Church regarded this condition as fulfilled. The first attempts at preaching doctrinal sermons occurred, however, but a few years after the establishment of the Order.

Of great significance in this direction is the inauguration of the missions among the infidels dating from 1212-13. Francis himself went forth at that time "to preach the Christian Faith and penance to the Saracens and other infidels." [93] From that time the heathen missions were fostered by him and his sons with increasing zeal, so that they were in need of more definite organization as early as 1221. In the apposite chapter of the rule the Holy Founder designates the twofold manner in which the missionary Friars were to exercise the apostolate among the Saracens and other infidels. The first consisted in simply furnishing the example of a truly Christian life and professing their faith steadfastly; the second, in preaching the truths of the Faith, above all the mysteries of the Trinity, the Incarnation and Redemption.[94]

Contemporary with the missions among the infidels, the Friars began to preach doctrinal sermons also to the Christian people. In this regard the Franciscans, in common with the Dominicans, found a wide gap to be filled. Religious instruction left much to be desired in the beginning of the thirteenth century. Time and again various synods admonished the parish clergy to teach the faithful at least the Apostles' Creed [95] with the Ten Commandments of God [96] the Lord's Prayer [97] and the Angelical Salutation.[98] In larger parishes the occurring gospel or epistle were to be expounded on Sundays and holydays.[99]

Yet even this minimum of religious instruction was hard to realize. This was due to the lack of zeal on the one hand, and on the other more frequently to the lack of knowledge on the part of the secular clergy. Many pastors were so ignorant that they were directed to hear other preachers and be instructed by them before they attempted to instruct their own parishioners.[100] Occasionally the archdeacons were enjoined to instruct the clergy under them in the elementary truths of the faith and in simple terms, in order that the latter might be able to impart the most necessary knowledge to the faithful.[101] Bishops, even, were found lacking the knowledge requisite to the preaching of doctrinal sermons.[102]

In the face of this unfortunate state of affairs, the

Fourth Lateran Council decreed in 1215, that the bishops were bound under the most severe penalties to appoint in all places suitable preachers, who were to go from parish to parish and announce the word of God and administer the sacrament of Penance.[103] The two Mendicant Orders, which had been founded expressly for the purpose of itinerant preaching, were to assume the major part of this task. The Dominicans, being an Order of clerics, were engaged from the beginning in the preaching of doctrinal sermons. The Franciscans followed as soon as they were able to place sufficiently trained men in the field.

In fact, as early as 1219 Honorius III speaks not only of the sermon on Penance in his first letter of recommendation of the Franciscan preachers addressed to the bishops, but declares simply that the Friars Minor "sow the seed of the divine word after the example of the apostles." [104] Shortly after, it is recorded that St. Anthony of Padua (since 1222) preached as a new evangelist in many places not only to the faithful, but also refuted the heretics in public discourses and converted them from their errors in large numbers.[105] He dealt the enemies of the Faith such severe blows that his contemporaries accorded him the name "Hammer of Heretics." [106]

It is worthy of note that Anthony developed his glorious activity as preacher of faith and morals at the very time when Francis, under the mentorship of Hugolino, the later Pope Gregory IX, was writing the rule in which he mentions explicitly only the moral sermon; that is, the preaching on "the vices and virtues, punishment and glory." [107] The rule of 1223 did not therefore exclude doctrinal sermons outright, as little as the non-Franciscan instructions on preaching of the thirteenth century excluded it, although these also mention only the moral sermon.[108]

Numerous other Franciscans were also engaged like St. Anthony in preaching sermons on the Faith. As early as 1237 Gregory IX declares: "Because impiety has grown beyond bounds, and the love of very many has grown cold, the Lord has raised up the Order of the beloved sons, the Friars Minor, who have devoted themselves to the preaching of the word of God, to extirpate heresies as well as other deadly evils." [109]   Soon after, Alexander IV bestows the following encomium on the two Mendicant Orders: "These are the men who battle against the enemies of souls with the shield of faith, the armor of justice, the sword of the spirit, the helmet of salvation, the spear of perseverance, and thus seek to effect the increase of faith, hope and charity in all Catholics, that the path of truth be opened to all unbelievers and the error of heretical perversity vanish." [110]

We are now in a position to form a fairly accurate idea of the contents of the Friars' sermons. In the beginning they restricted themselves to the subject of penance; i. e., in their exhortations as well as in their formal sermons they simply admonished their hearers to change their morals and to lead a better life. Later on, the Friars who were able to do so, were permitted to preach Scriptural sermons, that is, to explain on Scriptural grounds the entire matter of revelation, from the moral as well as from the dogmatic standpoint. Whenever they addressed Catholic, and not infidel or heretic audiences, they laid chief stress as heretofore on moral and practical truths; in other words, they preached moral sermons grounded on dogma; and even when they treated topics of faith they never lost sight of the fact that by their calling they were preachers of penance, called to edify, to uplift, to rouse, to convert the masses.

The manuscript sermons of the thirteenth century which we possess,[111] all bear this character, especially those of the greatest preacher of them all, Father Berthold of Regensburg.

The majority of Berthold's sermons,[112] whether intended for Sundays, for festivals of the Lord and of the Saints, for special occasions, or hearers, must be designated as moral sermons solidly grounded on dogma. A remarkable thing about these sermons is how often the Friar takes up the cudgels against the heresies of his time.[113] In consideration of the havoc wrought by false teachers, and of the needs of his hearers, he was accustomed, whenever possible, to weave catechetical instructions into his discourses, particularly into those intended for the early Masses.[114] Besides these, there are extant purely dogmatic sermons, especially on the sacraments. Nevertheless, even these, not to mention his strictly moral sermons, are never purely doctrinal; always and everywhere we note a tendency to reach the masses in the problems of their daily life, to expose and to heal the wounds which festered in the body social of his day. Hence Roger Bacon holds him up as the unsurpassed model of the popular style of Franciscan oratory.[115]

Bacon bases his opinion not only on the practical contents, but more so on the eminently *popular method* of Berthold's sermons, in contrast to the cumbersome method in vogue with so many preachers of his time.

Up to the eleventh century all preachers were accustomed to explain Holy Writ and to make applications according to the homilies of the early Fathers. With the advent of Scholasticism, however, this form of preaching began to wane. Holy Scripture, of course, remained the chief source of inspiration both for pulpit eloquence and scientific theology. Anselm of Canterbury, (died 1109), the "Father of Scholasticism," expressly declares: "We preach and teach nothing accruing to the welfare of men, unless our instruction comes forth from the Scriptures, fructified by the Spirit of God, or can be reduced to the same source." [116] In spite of the trend of progressive speculation, this conviction remained deeply rooted in all the schools during the twelfth and thirteenth centuries.[117]

But just as the Scholastic method supplanted the continuous citation of Scripture texts with the "Sentences" and with the systematic exposition of the inspired books, so the preachers began to favor the selection of a single Bible text as the subject of their discourse, and to elaborate this "theme" according to the Scholastic method. In this way the simple homily was superseded by the rhetorically correct *sermo*. Clear division of topics, carefully ordered dispositions, logical construction and expansion of the entire discourse were the advantages of the new method of preaching. Only too often, however, these qualities were upheld at the cost of the graphic, practical, and stirring popular style. Yes, they became the very ruin of pulpit eloquence as soon as the Scholastic sermon method degenerated into dialectic hair-splitting and word play. Unfortunately this was frequently the case when, from the middle of the thirteenth century, the Aristotelic-Porphyrian method of dialectics assumed prominence in theological schools. The majority of preachers at this time seemed to forget that the sole object of their discourse was to instruct and confirm their hearers in the Faith and to guide them to a godly way of living. Instead, they spent their efforts in endless splitting of texts and opinions, divisions and distinctions, and the empty turning of harmonious phrases. It seemed as if their whole aim was to weave fragile webs of bombast in which the hearts and minds of their auditors became hopelessly enmeshed. One sought in vain among their scholarly orations for traces of the wisdom and strength of the old, genuine popular sermon.[118]

For St. Francis and his immediate followers there existed no danger of being infected by this improper method of preaching. They were the products of everyday life, not the exotics of the halls of learning. Their preaching was therefore free from oppressive erudition, mimicry, and stereotyped methods. It was the sporadic outflow of their divinely inspired zeal for souls, which knew no other objective than the conversion and the uplift of mankind through "penance." Unfortunately, his hearers have handed down to us no complete sermon of the great preacher of penance of Assisi. Nevertheless, it suffices to know that his words found a loud echo in the hearts of all, drawing into their magic circle all grades of society, the lowest as well as the highest,[119] in order to establish the fact with unfailing certainty that he was one of the greatest popular preachers that ever lived. Even his exhortations, instructions and letters that have come down to us, insignificant as they may be when compared with his living word, betray a preacher after the heart of God in their straightforwardness and simplicity, their heartiness, their unction, warmth and vigor. As an example we cite his touching admonition on the veneration of the Holy Eucharist,[120] and the dramatic effect he lends to the description of the death of the impenitent sinner.[121] These afford us an insight into the charming originality of the oldest Franciscan sermon.

We dare not pass over the deep reverence which these preachers evinced for the Holy Scriptures. It would be an error to conclude that these unlettered Friars, in contrast to the schooled oratory of their contemporaries, made no use of the Bible. It is true, in the beginning the purely Scriptural sermon, that is, the homiletic interpretation of the Scriptural pericope, was forbidden them for the very reason that they were not trained in theology. That their discourses on penance, however, were grounded on Scripture, is evident from what has been said above. No one understood this art of preaching in the spirit of the Gospel better than Francis of Assisi, he who had taken the Gospel in its fulness as the norm of his life. How copiously he used the words of the divine volumes we leave the reader to judge. Those of his writings which we still possess, reveal a manifold choice of Scripture citation from nearly every book of the New Testament. It seems that he as a

rule spoke freely on any particular truth, illustrating and
supporting his ideas wherever possible by passages from
the inspired text. Sometimes, however, and this is worthy
of note, he took a single Scripture text and expounded it
thematically after the custom of the schooled preachers of
his day.

Jordan of Giano, an eye-witness, tells us that Francis
preached in this way at the Chapter of the Order in 1221,
taking as his text the Psalm verse: "Blessed be the Lord,
my God, who teacheth my hands to fight," [122] with the
avowed object of enthusing the thousands of Friars there
assembled to give the world an example of virtue.[123]
Again in his allegory of the General Chapter of all the
Religious of the world, he depicts a simple brother holding
a thematic sermon on the Psalm text, whereas a learned
one admonishes his hearers in simple fashion: "Great are
the things we have promised: still greater are those that
were promised to us! Let us observe the former and
strive to attain to the latter! Pleasure is short; punishment everlasting; the suffering slight, the glory infinite.
Many are called, few are chosen; retribution awaits all." [124]
At Bologna, on the feast of the Assumption in 1222,
Francis announced the following division of his sermon
matter: "The angels, men, the devils." He treated this
subject with the intention of extinguishing existing feuds
and reconciling the citizens estranged by enmity.[125]   In
all this, however, he avoided all artificial and affected
oratory.[126]

The more this Franciscan method of preaching penance
extended into the region of dogmatic and moral theology,
the closer it copied the method of preaching prevalent in
those days. In spite of this it succeeded in preserving the
character of simplicity, naturalness, and popularity, even
when the analytic method of preaching had become quite
common. Roger Bacon scourges the "Porphyrian" orators
of that time in a way [127] which proves that both he and

others of his Order had a deep understanding of and a deeper enthusiasm for, the genuine popular style of preaching.

Even those Franciscans who were caught in the toils of the Scholastic-analytic form, adopted a much simpler tone and exerted in proportion a more telling influence on their hearers than the Dominicans and other preachers.[128] Friar Berthold of Regensburg especially had a pronounced talent for utilizing the advantages of Scholastic learning without prejudice to true rhetorical art, and of bringing sacred oratory to the height of perfection, and thus, as Bacon testifies, of achieving more than all other Franciscans and Dominicans combined.[129]

Popular as Francis was in the treatment of his sermon matter, he was equally popular, in the best sense of the word, in *his delivery*. It is well known to us that he began his apostolate as a "ministrel of God," singing with a loud and clear voice ballads on the goodness of the Most High.[130] Love of God and enthusiasm for God were the spiritual atmosphere in which he constantly lived and out of which he spoke. The uninterrupted walking in the presence of God and the continuous meditation on the things of God enabled him to preach without much thought the most soul-stirring sermons. Close preparation seemed rather to hinder than to help him. A few times when he had carefully prepared a sermon, it happened that he forgot all he had learned, and was unable to continue. In such a predicament he would humbly acknowledge to his hearers that he had thought long and deeply over what he had wished to preach, and that he now knew not what to say. Finding himself at a loss for words, he would then dismiss the people with his blessing, and this blessing, coupled with his humility, did more to move their hearts than the most effective sermon. Usually, however, after he had humbly acknowledged his unfitness, the Spirit of God would move him. Without further anxiety about his prepared sermon, he would speak impromptu and with such eloquence that the assembled hearers were carried away with admiration.[131]

He could, above all, never bring himself to follow the custom of so many preachers of his time of memorizing and delivering the sermons of others.[132] Only once, when he had to preach at Rome in the presence of Honorius III and the Papal Court, he attempted to memorize a sermon prepared by Cardinal Hugolino according to all the canons of rhetoric. When, however, the man of God stood up in this strange armor, his memory failed him entirely. Quickly recovering himself, he opened his breviary, came across the Psalm text, "All the day long my shame is before me; and the confusion of my face hath covered me," [133] and applying this text to the assembled prelates, he showed them how they were the face of the Church, and therefore should not cause it shame, but honor; he pictured how dreadful is the scandal and how terrible the responsibility of bad prelates, and admonished them to illumine the faithful with the light of their virtues. He spoke with such profound knowledge, experience and ease that his august hearers were not only astonished, but deeply moved.[134]

It was because Francis was so intimately united with God and absorbed in God's interests, that he could appear before the choicest and largest audiences with an ease and confidence as though he were conversing with a trusted friend. He held large assemblies of hearers as easily in control by his eloquence as he would one person, and he preached with the same care and enthusiasm to one as to many thousands.[135]

As soon as he began to speak, the inner fire that glowed within his soul broke forth in his countenance and flashed from his whole person. Thomas of Celano describes his delivery in a few bold strokes: "He was a man of unusual eloquence; his countenance beamed with joy; the expression of his face was replete with kindness, his speech meek, fiery and moderate, his voice strong, sweet, clear and sonorous . . . Christ, the true Strength and Wisdom, imparted to his word power and force." [136] According to the testimony of the Three Companions and of the Seraphic Doctor, his word was like a flaming torch, which sent its rays into the deepest recesses of the heart and inflamed his hearers with its ardor. One felt instinctively that he spoke not with human artificiality, but at the movement and inspiration of God.[137]

The appealing force of his sermons was enhanced by his unusual, characteristic gesticulation. The Bolognese student, who heard him preach on the feast of the Assumption in 1222, was so astounded that he remarked: "Francis spoke not after the manner of ordinary preachers, but as a man of the people to the people." [138] Everything about him was life, movement, attraction, so much so, that the masses went not only to hear him, but also to see him.[139] "His whole body," says Thomas of Celano, "became to him a tongue." [140] The whole man spoke, and his entire speech became a spectacle in the best and noblest sense of the word.

This can be explained on the one hand by the fact that in Francis the orator and the poet were united in one; on the other, by the fact that his sermons, as we have had occasion to remark before, were the outpouring of a heart deeply sunk in God; in a word, of an apostle fired with enthusiasm for the cause of God. Both factors considered together, furnish the full explanation; that is, that the Poverello was in fact a "spiritual troubadour, a minstrel of God." It has been rightly remarked that Francis at all times felt an irresistib'e tendency to expression. "A child's tendency to play—I know no other but this profane term—clung to him till his death; he 'plays' beggar; he 'plays' pilgrim; he 'plays' Christmas; he 'plays' the Last Supper. Indeed his entire life fashions itself into a 'playing' in the highest meaning of the word: for with him the following of Christ became a literal imitating of Christ, a living with the Redeemer and according to the life of the Redeemer, even to the agony of Golgotha." [141] No wonder, then, that he "played" preacher also, that he "performed" the truths of Christianity, exactly as the profane Jongleurs and minstrels played and performed their *Chansons de geste*.

He never laid aside this highly popular style of preaching whether he addressed simple folk or the learned and the mighty. Even in the face of the Papal Court he retained it. He spoke before this august audience of Pope and cardinals with such fiery ardor and enthusiasm that he was carried out of himself and at almost every word that dropped from his lips he moved his feet in such a manner as if he were about to leap. This was not mere theatrical display, but the unconscious exhibition of the raptures of divine love controlling him, so that the spectators were not moved to ridicule, but on the contrary to sorrow and compunction. Hugolino himself, who was present, had been very anxious before and had prayed that the simplicity of the man of God might not be ridiculed, now rejoiced with the entire assembly at this wonderful sermon of the minstrel of God.[142]

Up to the very end of his life the Saint showed how dear to him was this method of preaching. He had just composed the Canticle of the Sun. Thereupon he sent for Brother Pacificus, the "King of Verses" and a gifted singer. To him Francis confided the mission of journeying through the world, accompanied by a number of Friars, preaching, and singing the Canticle of the Sun. The most eloquent among them was to preach to the people, then the Canticle was to be sung by all in chorus, as true minstrels of God. When the last note of the song had died out, the preacher, after the manner of the profane troubadours, was to ask payment in these words:

"We are minstrels of God and wish to be repaid by you for our sermon and song by your perseverance in penance." And the Saint added: "What else are we servants of God but in a measure His minstrels, who should uplift the hearts of men and move them to spiritual joy?" [143]

But just as the Friars were called to represent the Gospel after the manner of the minstrels, they were admonished by the Saint to *realize the Gospel* also in their own life as true knights of Christ. His oldest biographers assert that Francis preached with such overwhelming persuasion because he always observed personally what he demanded of others; [144] deeply conscious that men needed the force of good example to move them, he first reduced the truths of Christianity to daily practise in his own life, following the example of the apostles, in order to be able to preach them afterward in words, and thus effect the conversion of the world both by word and by deed. [145] Contemporary chroniclers also record that the example of the apostolic life led by the early Friars endowed their preaching with that irresistible power which brought about the conversion of the masses sunken in vices; indeed, even led many into the Order itself. [146]

Francis himself insisted strongly on the harmony that should exist between living and preaching, between word and deed, between teaching and example. However great his zeal in announcing the truths of the Gospel, his efforts to live this Gospel perfectly himself were even greater. [147] He declared that the Friars Minor were called by God to shed the bright ray of their good example unto all that sit in the darkness of sin; [148] their motto should be, "to go through the world admonishing everyone more by example than by word to do penance and to keep God's commandments." [149] He was, in fact, of the opinion that the Order had no title to existence and support unless it benefited the world by good example. [150]

From all this, the one inevitable conclusion can be

drawn; namely, that no Friar Minor can exempt himself from the obligation of preaching to the world by good example. Not everyone is fit to preach by word, yet Francis says distinctly: "Let all the brothers preach by good works." [151] A professor of theology once asked him the meaning of the passage in Ezechiel: "If thou declare it not to the wicked nor speak to him that he may be converted from his wicked way and live: I will require his blood at thy hand." [152] Francis answered: "A servant of God should be so inflamed with inner holiness of life, that he correct everyone by the light of his example and the speech of his life. Thus the light of his life and the odor of his fame will proclaim to the godless their iniquity." [153]

At every Chapter of the Order and on every other occasion, he therefore never failed to warn the brothers against giving scandal.[154] At the very thought that some of the brothers might in future bring shame on the Order through bad behavior or scandal, he lifted his hands heavenward and, with tears streaming down his cheeks, he uttered these words of prayer, or rather of imprecation: "Lord Jesus Christ, who hast chosen twelve apostles, among whom one fell, the others however, animated by one and the same Spirit, preached the Holy Gospel, Thou, O Lord, being mindful of Thy mercy, hast in our time planted the Order of Friars Minor that they might be a support to Thy Faith, and that through them the mystery of the Gospel might be realized. Who will be able to render Thee satisfaction for them if they do not show the light of a good example, as they are called to do, but instead do the works of darkness? May they be cursed by Thee, Most Holy Lord, by Thy heavenly court, and by me, Thy least servant, who by their bad example undermine and destroy what Thou hast once built up through the holy brothers of this Order, and which Thou never ceasest to build up." [155]

On the other hand, he declared that he was filled with

the sweetest odor and refreshed with precious ointment when he heard great things of the brothers scattered throughout the world. He rejoiced in spirit that these brothers were leading back the sinners to the love of Christ by word or deed, and he showered upon them his most choice blessings.[156] Almost carried away with rapture over such brothers, he lifted up his voice in praise to the Almighty and sang out of the depths of his soul: "I thank Thee, O Lord, who sanctifiest and guidest the poor, that Thou hast deigned to let me hear such gladsome tidings of the brothers. I beseech Thee, bless with Thy richest blessings those brothers, and sanctify all who render their religious state illustrious by their good example, with the special gifts of Thy grace." [157]

CHAPTER XVII

FRANCISCAN SCIENCE

*A*POSTOLIC *activity* and *apostolic life* are also the two standpoints from which Francis viewed the question of science in the Order. The work of the apostolate imparted the impulse to Franciscan science; apostolic life became its norm.[1]

1. Francis and his disciples knew only one ideal sphere of activity: *apostolic labor.* For this reason science interested them only in so far as it had direct or indirect bearing on the office of preaching and the administration of the sacrament of Penance. A science which was its own goal, never existed in the Order. St. Bonaventure stresses this fact even at a time when studies had reached their zenith in the Order.[2] With much more force does this hold good for the first decades of the Order, and especially for the lifetime of the Founder.

Francis himself was neither learned nor educated. It may be mentioned as a mere curiosity of history that Roger Wendover (died 1236), and his successor, Matthew of Paris, assert that Francis "applied himself from tender years to the study of sciences and theology, and mastered them completely."[3] His biographers stress, on the contrary, that he was uneducated and grew up without instruction.[4] Francis personally designates himself *idiota.*[5]

Yet one should not take this too literally. In the Middle Ages it was customary to designate as *idiotæ* not only those who were unlettered, but the laity in general, in distinction to the clergy, because these almost exclusively were the representatives of higher learning. In Order parlance especially, the lay brothers were called simply *idiotæ* to distinguish them from the priests.[6]   In this sense only can this term be applied to Francis and to his first companions,[7] though many of them were not uneducated, as education was then understood.[8]   In fact, Francis had learned to read and write as a boy,[9] was acquainted with French [10] and Latin,[11] and was familiar with the poetry and the art of singing of the Duecento. In a word, he possessed the education proper to the sons of the wealthy merchants of the time.[12]

This limited knowledge he strove to augment during his religious life not only by prayer, but also by study.[13] Whenever he felt low-spirited, when sufferings and sickness menaced the buoyancy of his spirit, he sought solace in the reading of the Scriptures, including the Old Testament, and found in their perusal the enlightenment, rest, peace and joy he sought.[14]   At other times he also loved to read the Scriptures, and whatever he had once grasped with his mind, remained indelibly stamped on his heart. Thus his memory served him as a ready reference book, since he constantly meditated on whatever he had heard or read.   This method of learning, in contrast to the injudicious and excessive reading of many things, he considered the best way of cultivating his mind.   In order to increase whatever knowledge he acquired in this manner, he would discuss disputed questions with the Friars, and although the scientific terminology failed him, the acumen and penetration of his intellect became all the more prominent.[15]   "Where many another, in spite of scholarly attainments and mental application, in spite of methodical processes, could achieve nothing, he strikes the right solution; he was gifted with clearness of vision and that intuition of genius which without effort and, as it were spontaneously, grasps things which even greater talents fail to grasp after great efforts.[16]

But far more important than these natural sources of

knowledge were the supernatural, extraordinary illumi-
nations which he received from God.

The authorities agree that in theological matters Francis
possessed a knowledge all his own. He spoke on the
deepest mysteries of faith, on the most difficult religious
problems, on the most abstruse passages of Scripture
with an astounding clearness, precision and thorough-
ness. Even learned priests, doctors and prelates sought
out the *idiota* for enlightenment where science failed
them.[17] A doctor of theology of the Dominican Order
confessed after such a conference with Francis: "My
brothers, the theology of this man soars aloft to heaven
on the wings of truth and contemplation like an eagle,
while our science laboriously creeps on the earth." [18]

This knowledge he owed, if not to the direct interven-
tion of God, at least to the liveliness of his faith and the
fervor of his love, by means of which even the simplest
men at times clearly and thoroughly grasp the most difficult things, whereas great and learned men see only
darkness. Cardinal Hugolino ascribed this knowledge of
his holy friend to supernatural inspiration.[19] Thomas of
Celano also assures us that not human study, but divine
light furnished him with the understanding of the mysteries of faith, and that the intensity of his love penetrated
where the cold learning of the professors dared not intrude.[20] This love-inspired contemplation of God on the
one hand, and the continuous enlightenment from God on
the other, filled him with a wisdom more sublime than
that of the greatest scholars of his time.[21]

Because of this knowledge, drawn from supernatural
sources, the Patriarch is given in the art creations of the
Renaissance a place of honor among the Doctors of the
Church,[22] and the Prince of poets represents him in company with Thomas and Bonaventure in the sunburst of
Paradise.[23] Everything in the life of the Saint which
reveals deep, scientific knowledge must have sprung from
this supernatural source. Even if one were to designate

Francis and Dominic, according to the opinion of two of their greatest disciples, as cherubim resplendent with knowledge,[24] yet the science of the former flows from the seraphic fountain of his glowing love of God, while the latter must be accorded the palm of cherubic wisdom:

> ". . . . . One, seraphic all
> In fervency; for wisdom upon earth;
> The other, splendor of cherubic light." [25]

From this the preaching of St. Francis especially derived the greatest benefit. As highly as his contemporaries esteem his inborn talent for oratory, they nevertheless emphasize particularly: "The most brave knight of Christ, Francis, preached the kingdom of God not with the persuasive words of human wisdom, but in the teaching and the strength of the Holy Ghost." [26] "He drew out of the fulness of his heart what the Holy Ghost prompted." [27] In regard to Francis the question therefore remains, whether and in how far he trained himself for the office of preaching by scientific study.

The same holds good regarding his first disciples. These were, as we know, for the most part lay brothers, therefore *idiotæ,* without scientific training. No doubt they feared to accept the office of preaching; Francis nevertheless sent them out with the consoling admonition: "Fear not because you appear little and mean and ignorant, but preach penance courageously, trusting that the Lord, who conquered the world, will speak through you and in you by the power of His spirit." [28] After the number of Friars had increased, Francis allowed only those to preach who showed special fitness for it, whether clerics or lay brothers; higher education, however, was not the determining factor in this choice, but the fact that the chosen ones were animated by the spirit of God and possessed the proper oratorical ability.[29]

This might have sufficed as long as the Friars restricted

themselves to preaching penance, or to moral sermons in a strict sense. This privilege had been granted, as we know,[30] to various lay institutes even before Francis, and the latter had obtained for himself and his disciples the privilege of preaching without reference to the duty of study. Consequently it appears that theological training was not regarded as a necessary requirement for preaching toward the end of the twelfth and the beginning of the thirteenth century.

It was an entirely different matter in regard to the office of preaching in the strict sense of the word. Whoever wished to preach the "Scriptures," that is, to expound the entire matter of revelation both in its dogmatic and its moral content, was obliged to study "Scripture," or as we should say, theology. All the homiletes of those times emphasize this fact. Thus Alanus of Lillie (died 1202): "For preachers learning is necessary; they must be acquainted with both Testaments, and skilled in the application of their passages."[31] The synodal statutes of Odo de Sully, Bishop of Paris (ca. 1197), forbid itinerant preachers under pain of excommunication to preach within or outside of churches, and prohibit others to listen to them under the same penalty.[32] The provincial synod of Trier (1227) inhibits preaching to all "uninstructed priests, lest they become exponents of error," and ordains that "the Word of God be frequently propounded by capable men."[33] The Fourth Council of the Lateran (1215) enjoins on all bishops to appoint as preachers of the Word of God well-trained men only, and demands the same even of prelates.[34]

Fully in accord with this was the attitude of the Church toward those religious associations which sought the privilege of preaching. When the Waldenses, claiming fitness for this task, attempted to preach "Scripture," they were refused by the Archbishop of Lyons.[35] And when they insisted by appealing to the Third Council of the Lateran (1179), Walter Mapes replied that they were practically unlettered and consequently should not be listened to.[36] The Poor Men of Lombardy were likewise refused the privilege by Innocent III in 1201, because they were not trained in theology; shortly afterward, however (1208), permission was given to the Catholic Poor Men by the same Pope in consideration of their theological training.[37] Some years later (1215), St. Dominic founded the Order of Preachers. But just as preaching was emphasized as the object of the Order, just so essential was study regarded as the indispensable means to this end.[38]

As early as 1212-13 the Franciscans advanced from the preaching of penance to missions among the infidels, and assumed the office of preaching in its fullest sense both as regards Catholics and heretics, and including also doctrinal sermons; this was a few years after the Dominicans.[39] Then followed the administration of the sacrament of Penance.[40] The beginning of theological studies must consequently be assigned also to this time.

We say "the beginning of theological studies." That theology alone was concerned, or, more exactly, the study of Scripture, is beyond doubt, and will be explained later.[41] It is likewise beyond doubt that the study of Scripture was very limited. For, as severely as the Church demanded education from her preachers in the beginning of the thirteenth century, the amount of knowledge with which she had to be contented was at best only small.[42] Even the Dominicans in 1228 exacted of the *prædicatores generales,* who were active among the heretics, only three years of study, while ordinary preachers were admitted to the pulpit after one year.[43] In the beginning the requirements must have been still less. Among the Franciscans the achievements were no doubt even poorer. Most likely they restricted themselves to the reading (*studium*) of the Scriptures.

The latter, however, Francis also demanded from those brothers who were entrusted with the office of preaching.

Bonaventure writes against William of St. Amour, the enemy of Franciscan studies: "In order that you may know how highly Francis esteemed the study of the Scripture, hear the following. A brother who is still alive, related to me that at his time there was only one Testament at hand, and consequently the Scriptures were not available to all the Friars of the house. Francis therefore cut up the book and distributed the loose leaves among the brothers, in order that they might all study and not disturb one another." [44] This obviously has reference to the first ten years of the Order. Later, when Francis could no longer read because of the ailment of his eyes, he recalled his former zeal in reading the holy Book, and recommended it strongly to the brothers as a means of broadening their knowledge of theology.[45] He wished, according to the testimony of Thomas of Celano, that the preachers of the divine Word apply themselves to sacred studies to the exclusion of all other occupations; this was demanded by their office, according to which they were set aside by Divine Providence to announce to the people the decrees which they had heard from the lips of their Great King.[46]

In full accord with this are the precepts which he embodied in the *final rule* a few years after he had begun the preaching of the Scriptures. Express regulations on study, it is true, are not to be found in it, and cannot be expected. None of the older Orders legislated on the nature of studies.[47] Not even St. Dominic did this, although he always laid great stress on study.[48] Francis likewise at first only in a general way determines the occupations of the Friars, be they clerics or lay brothers: "Let those brothers to whom God has given the grace to work, labor faithfully and devoutly, so that they shun idleness, which is the enemy of the soul, and not destroy the spirit of prayer and devotion, to which all other things must be subservient." [49] In another place it has been shown that he thereby wished to oblige the clerics to apply themselves to mental pursuits as zealously as the lay brothers to manual labor.[50]

This is evident also from the precept of the rule which reads: "Let not those who are ignorant of letters care to learn letters."[51] In other words, the lay brothers should not study. This was always a principle with Francis. From the very beginning he gave them an Office which could be said even by the illiterate; he even went so far as to forbid them the reading of the Psalter;[52] and he never allowed a lay brother to apply himself to studies. All, lay brothers as well as clerics, were to remain true to their respective calling and its proper pursuits.[53]

Herewith it is expressed plainly that clerics are obliged to the studies of their state. On this score Francis had already passed a decision. The question once having been put to him, whether the educated men who had entered the Order should pursue the study of Holy Scripture, he answered unhesitatingly in the affirmative.[54] St. Bonaventure comments on this as follows: "I say, therefore, that the rule does not forbid study to the educated and the clerics, but only to lay brothers. It wishes, according to the word of the Apostle,[55] that everyone should be true to the calling in which he is called; that no one may change from the brotherhood to the priesthood, that on the other hand the clerics may become lay brothers by neglecting their studies; otherwise one would be forced to consider Francis himself as an infringer of his rule. For he, who enjoyed only a modest education, as a Religious made progress in learning, not only by means of prayer, but also by diligent study."[56]

In the chapter of the rule "On the Preachers," the obligation to study is imposed still more distinctly on the clerics. We read therein: "Let no one of the Friars dare to preach in any way to the people, unless he has been examined and approved by the Minister General of this brotherhood, and the office of preaching conceded to him by the latter."[57] Now it is evident that an examination for the office of preaching presupposes commensurate study. Gregory IX, a co-editor of the rule, as is known, furthermore states what degree of learning was required of the candidates. Scarcely four years after the death of Francis, this Pontiff states that the required test must establish that the future preacher "has been instructed in sacred theology and oratory." [58] In substance he says the same in another Bull, wherein is ordained that only such Friars be promoted to the office of preaching who "are versed in the Holy Scriptures." [59] Since it was a question of approbation for the preaching of the Scriptures, it is clear that the study of the same and knowledge of Scriptural theology is thereby demanded.

The final words of this chapter of the rule are to be understood in accordance with the above: "I warn and admonish the same brothers that in the preaching they do, their words be fire-tried and pure, for the utility and edification of the people, announcing to them vices and virtues, punishment and glory, with brevity of speech, because the Lord made His word short upon earth." [60] Roger Bacon in his droll way, and not without a thrust at the "porphyrian" method of preaching then in vogue, comments on this in the following manner: [61] "Many things necessary for the salvation of men are easy, such as the understanding of virtues and vices, the heavenly glory, and the punishments of purgatory and hell. About these not only the Religious, as theologians, but also all clerics and laics and old women know much. For there is enclosed in every heart a great book on the vices which each one has committed himself from youth and which he has seen others commit. Thus even peasants and old women know how to discourse convincingly on virtue and vice, on reward and punishment, not only among Christians, but also to the Saracens and other infidels. Besides, every Christian from his customary religious instruction has an extensive knowledge of what is necessary to eternal happiness. For this reason it is not difficult for the studying Orders (the Mendicants) to speak to the people of virtue and vice, of punishment and glory; and that, all the more since in Holy Writ there are many things self-evident to the ordinary man who can read and who studies the works of the Fathers." [62]

Nevertheless, the text of the rule in question should not be restricted, after the above considerations, to the mere moral content of the sermon, although in a literal sense it mentions only this. It refers also to the practical Scripture sermon [63] and accordingly demands also a corresponding knowledge of the Scriptures and of theology. At the close of the twelfth and the beginning of the thirteenth century, theology in general as well as preaching laid the greatest stress on the practical side of the revealed truth. Thus, for instance, the renowned teacher and orator Peter Cantor (died 1198) in his *Verbum abbreviatum* writes only *"ad vitiorum singulorum redargutionem et ad virtutum et morum commendationem et operum nostrorum directionem."* [64] The *Verbum abbreviatum* was to be considered an epitome of the theological-homiletic course of the author. In a similar sense there must have been demanded of the Minorite preachers since 1223 a summary knowledge of theology or of the Holy Scriptures, with their practical application to everyday life.

In fact, Thomas of Eccleston testifies of the Friars studying under Robert Grosseteste at Oxford since the year 1225 as follows: *"Sub quo inestimabiliter infra breve tempus tam in quæstionibus quam prædictioni congruis subtilibus moralitatibus profecerunt."* [65] The expression "subtile moralities" and much less that of "questions," should not be rendered by the general term "moral doctrine." We know for certain that the Franciscan doctor, Grosseteste, used not only the entire Bible as a basis for his lectures, but philosophy and the natural sciences also were copiously drawn upon in the interest of a solid and practical exegesis. [66] Furthermore, at this time we hear of the Famous Dominican, John de St. Aegidio,

professor at the University of Paris, being called *"suavis-*
simus moralizator,[67] and also of his confrère Master
Richard Fitzacre being greatly lauded for his "splendid
moralizings." [68]   In both cases the sense is: these men
knew how to combine in a striking manner theological
depth in the study of Scripture with a happy application
to everyday life.   When we therefore read that in England between the years 1224-1236 the Minorites were promoted to the office of preaching because of the "subtile
moralizings" which they had acquired from the schools,
this can mean but one thing: they studied the Scriptures
with constant stress on its theological content as well as
on its practical value and its adaptation to preaching.
Thomas of Eccleston interprets his own words when in
his Collation on "The Promotion of Preachers" he says:
"Although the [first English] Friars endeavored earnestly
to preserve in all things the greatest simplicity and the
purity of conscience, still they were so zealous in hearing
the divine law and in their scholastic exercises, that they
were not deterred from going daily barefoot, in bitter
cold or through deep mire, to the schools of theology, no
matter how distant these might be." [69]

In those days progress in the sciences did not perhaps
keep equal pace in all provinces of the Order; yet by the
singularly rapid advance which studies made in the Mendicant Orders of the twelfth century, the intellectual *niveau*
of the Friars set aside for preaching was constantly on the
ascent.[70]

It may be readily concluded from the above that the
development of the *schools* of the Order kept abreast of
the progress of the sciences taught in them.   Up to the
time of the final codification of the rule, the brothers were
thrown upon their private resources for study.   Soon
after, however, they attended lectures on theology either
outside their houses or at home.   The first teacher of the
Order appointed by Francis himself was St. Anthony of
Padua.[71]   Most likely the Founder imposed the office of

teaching upon him the same year in which the rule was approved by Papal Bull.[72] To manifest his reverence for the teacher of theology, he addressed Anthony with the title: "To Brother Anthony, my Bishop."[73] We meet with this extraordinary reverence for the teachers of theology often in the life and writings of the Saint. Regarding his journey to the Orient in 1219 the Chronicle of Jordan of Giano recounts the following: "Because Brother Peter [Catanei] was a learned man and of noble mind, Francis in his politeness always addressed him 'Lord' [not Brother], in order thus to honor him. And this mutual reverence they observed not only beyond the sea, but also in Italy."[74] The oldest biographer adds that from the time that learned men began to enter the Order, Francis always treated them as lords and respected learning in them.[75] Whenever he gives expression to his reverence for teachers, he always emphasizes the fact that the teachers of theology deserved greater marks of veneration.[76] Even in his Testament he admonishes the brothers to honor the teachers of sacred theology and to esteem them highly as men dispensing spirit and life.[77] Francis was therefore devoted to the teaching of theology from innermost conviction.

To this was added the external circumstance that *the number of clerics in the Order was on the increase from day to day.* Francis had scarcely entered the field of preaching, before the Order experienced a remarkable increase in the number of its clerics.[78] When the Founder soon afterward (1212-13) undertook his apostolic journey to Syria and afterward to Spain, a large group of clerics joined him at Ancona,[79] and likewise on his return to St. Mary of the Angels.[80] A sermon which he delivered at Alcoli had the same result.[81] Soon this increase of clerics became a daily occurrence.[82] Already, before 1216, a multitude of clerics and educated men had joined the Friars, if we are to place any credence in the testimony of the Chronicler Matthew of Paris.[83] In 1219 Cardinal

Jacques de Vitry himself was an eye-witness of the influence which the sermons of St. Francis and his Friars wielded over the educated knights of the army before Damietta. A large number of the Cardinal's circle of clerical friends instantly joined the Order, while others could be persuaded only by great effort to remain in the army and in the diocese.[84] Even during the lifetime of the Saint, great numbers of scholars joined the Franciscans at Paris, Oxford and at other places.[85] It is only logical to conclude that these young men, who evidently were to continue their studies, had to be instructed in theology.

But even aside from this it was *the wish of the Church* that the Mendicants should occupy themselves with teaching as well as with preaching, for the benefit of the secular and regular clergy. For no matter how active intellectual life had become at the universities in the beginning of the thirteenth century, and no matter how meritorious the few other special studies may have been for the training of the clergy, they were able to influence only narrow circles of the priesthood. The majority of the priests, especially in rural districts, were ignorant; they mastered scarcely enough Latin to read the Breviary. Synods and Popes constantly raised protest against this sad state of affairs, and demanded the founding of schools. But to no avail; even the regulation of the Fourth Council of the Lateran demanding the appointment of a teacher of grammar in every episcopal see, and a doctor of theology at every metropolitan church, was left unheeded. The reform of studies remained a burning question which neither the secular clergy nor the older Orders could or would solve.[86]

In this strait the Church turned to the two so-called "teaching Orders." [87] The Papacy, attacking the task of the reform of studies with all vigor, found that it could marshal the flying squadrons of St. Dominic and St. Francis fully and freely. At that time the Mendicant

Orders were engaged with their final organization, and this task they accomplished while remaining in closest touch with the Roman Curia. Hence it was but natural that this desire of the Curia to reform the studies, should also become dear to them. The Dominicans, immediately after the approval of their rule (1216), set out with sails spread for the goal of intellectual activity assigned to them. That the Franciscans would soon follow in their wake, was to be expected all the more since the three great personalities who were directing this reform with such admirable zeal, had mapped out the entire course for the Order: Innocent III (died 1216), Honorius III (1227), and Gregory IX (died 1241). Especially, since Honorius III was represented among the Franciscans by two of the most prominent promoters of science, Cardinal Hugolino, afterward Gregory IX, and Brother Elias of Cortona,[88] the Order felt itself obliged to aid in the reform of studies. The fact, on the other hand, that Francis himself chose Hugolino as Cardinal Protector of the Order (since 1221), and with whom he remained in closest friendship until death,[89] proved anew how deeply the Holy Founder was concerned about the study of sciences in his young Order.

We find in fact that even during the lifetime of the Saint the Friars began to attend the three most famous seats of learning, the universities of Bologna, Paris and Oxford.[90] At these intellectual citadels, whither scholars congregated by the thousands, where the student fraternities formed cities of their own within the cities, where the most illustrious doctors appeared as preachers of the Word of God, where therefore preachers and students were educated together, a successful training could be accomplished only on the basis of a thorough theological schooling. It became consequently a necessity that provision be made for capable preachers, and accordingly for the alumni of the Order, in such wise that the Order could command respect from the standpoint of science as well. The entrance of many scholars and teachers into the Order increased this demand still more and gave it a practical expression in so far as individual teachers who had assumed the poor habit of St. Francis with their hearers, began to continue their lectures henceforth in the monastery; and thus the colleges of the Minorites gradually developed into the most frequented of the university schools.

And just as Bologna, Oxford and Paris became the standard-bearers of the entire development of the medieval universities, thus, as can be readily proved, the early Franciscan schools took their rise at these three centers of higher learning, and gradually ramified into a vast network of schools throughout the entire Order. We know that already at the beginning of the thirteenth century the secular clergy at the University of Paris fomented a bitter strife against the Dominican and Franciscan schools, prompted by pure jealousy. On this occasion St. Thomas Aquinas proved that up to that date the secular clergy had not succeeded in carrying out the injunction of the Fourth Lateran Council with regard to the establishment of the most essential schools of learning, whereas the Mendicants had achieved far more than the Church had ever dared demand.[91] The hostile professors themselves complain in 1254 that the Mendicants held all the chairs of theology in all the cities and in the larger towns, so that secular professors hardly found an audience.[92] Roger Bacon's statement agrees with this complaint. He writes in 1271: "Never was there seen such a budding forth of knowledge, nor so great a zeal for study in so many schools and in so many places, as in the last forty years. Everywhere we now find teachers; especially in theology there are doctors to be found in every city, in every town and important village. This is the case only since the last forty years, and it is due mostly to the activity of the two teaching Orders." [93]

Thus within a few decades the Mendicants had solved

the problem of the Church in regard to studies, not only for themselves, but also for the secular clergy. For, as can be gleaned from the assertions of St. Thomas, the Paris professors and Roger Bacon quoted above, it is clear that the secular clergy to a great extent studied with the Mendicants [94] and that these were the chief support of the entire system of ecclesiastical culture, or pedagogy, science and literature. The dependence of the clergy on the Mendicants was so marked that Roger Bacon declares: "In the last forty years the secular clergy have not written a single book of theology, and they are convinced that they know nothing unless they have spent ten or more years in study with the members of the two Orders. They do not risk reading the Sentences, nor to advance in theology, nor to hold a lection, a disputation, or a sermon, unless it be taken from the books of the beggar monks. All this is evident to everyone, at the University of Paris as well as elsewhere." [95]

We are now in a position to understand how fully this Franciscan activity in the schools found an outlet in the Franciscan apostolate. The same Holy Scripture was expounded on the chair as on the pulpit, there in a more scientific, here in a popular form; what the sermon was for the simple faithful, that the lecture was for the learned theologian. The lecture was simply the sermon for the clerics. Moreover, in the school the clerics were trained and fitted out for the office of preaching; the school was thus the breeding cell of the apostolate of the world. Even this is saying too little; the school was only the beginning, so to say, of the office of preaching, just as preaching was the fulfilment and the end of all scholastic study; both together formed the two integral parts of the one religious system of teaching.[96]

Francis no doubt did not grasp the full significance of science for the apostolate of his disciples, and still less did he originate or even imagine the mighty development which science experienced in his Order. This development, however, lay hidden as in a germ in the idea of the apostolate which he enjoined on his brothers; it was simply the direct continuation of the development which the Order had begun even in his time; it was, in the last instance, but the echo of the admonition of the dying Saint: "Let us honor and esteem all the theologians and those who preach to us the word of God [Holy Scripture], because they impart to us spirit and life."

2. For Francis, however, the problem remained of harmonizing science with the *Apostolic life*. He could approve only such a science as did not interfere with his apostolic Ideal. The points where a collision threatened were *poverty, humility* or *simplicity,* and *piety.* It is evident that learning might in many instances conflict with this triple constellation of seraphic virtues, and so it needed no gift of prophecy but just human prudence and knowledge of the world on the part of Francis to cause him to look forward with anxiety to this intellectual activity in the Order.

The most difficult part of the problem, as later years showed, was to pair the rigid *poverty* of the Order with science; more directly, to join the complete renunciation of all earthly things with the possession of necessary books. Let us seek to discover from the tangle of confused reports what Francis in reality thought of this matter.

For a better understanding of this question let it be remarked that besides the primitive sources, also the *Speculum perfectionis,* the writings of the leaders of the Spirituals, Angelus of Clarino and Ubertinus of Casale, are critically of value to us. The *Speculum* treats our subject chiefly in the second chapter, in the very part which can be traced with the greatest evidence and certainty to Brother Leo, the secretary of St. Francis.[97] Angelus of Clarino supports his assertions on the relevant statements of Brother Leo;[98] Ubertinus repeatedly asserts that for his communications he has drawn on a manuscript of Brother Leo, as well as on the *"Rotuli fratris Leonis,"* and that, besides, he had his views confirmed by personal friends of St. Francis.[99]   When we consider that these testimonies were written in the heat of the conflict over the ideals of poverty, and could never be refuted by the Community, one is not inclined to dispute their evidence.   Besides, it happens that they are in full accord with the oldest biographies.   All this entitles us to ascribe the statements traced by the *Speculum,* by Angelus and Ubertinus to Brother Leo; in fact, to this secretary and companion of the Holy Founder.   This is so far of prime importance, since these accounts contain very weighty confirmation and supplements to the other sources of information on the question of poverty.

First of all, it is established that *Francis did not intend to forbid books to his brothers and monasteries.* He allowed indeed only the use of those things which were necessary to their livelihood and becoming to their vocation.   Under this category, however, he reckoned no doubt the indispensable books.   Even in the oldest houses we find books for the common use of the brothers, as the Three Companions relate.[100]   According to Thomas of Celano, Francis warned only against luxury in books: the brothers should seek in books only the word of God, and not costly bindings; edification, and not the beauty of furnishings.   He desired, however, that some books be always at hand, which might be supplied to the brothers as they might need them.[101]   St. Bonaventure explains that Francis neither would nor could forbid books to the brothers.   The Friars, writes the Seraphic Doctor, are obliged by the command of their Founder to preach.   If they are not to preach fables, but the Word of God, and if they cannot know this without reading it, which is impossible without books, it follows, obviously, that to possess books belongs just as strictly to the perfection of Franciscan life, as to preach.   And as little as it compromises the poverty of the Order to keep Missals for reading Mass, or Breviaries for reciting the canonical hours of the Church, just so little does it injure poverty to have and to retain the Holy Scriptures and other books necessary to the proper exercise of the office of preaching. Thus books are by no means forbidden to the Friars.[102] Ubertinus also declares that he agrees with this view, and that Brother Leo once related as witness that Francis wished a common library in every house, supplied with sufficient, though plain and not superfluous and precious, volumes.[103]

In the lifetime of the Saint a common library with a few volumes was considered sufficient. Not only Francis, but the Order in general, as we shall presently see, demanded that studies be limited to theology; and this study consisted in a comparative exegesis of Holy Scripture, to which were added commentaries from the words of the Fathers: *"in dictis sanctorum et textu bibliæ comparativæ."* [104]   One could thus content himself with the Scriptures and some writings of the Fathers, with a textual concordance of the latter, respectively. With the mighty development which studies underwent, both in depth and in extent, these monastic libraries had to be accordingly expanded. The question was therefore to take into account the new inevitable conditions and yet exclude all ownership of books and movable property. The only possible settlement of this problem was that the Church assume the ownership of these things and then entrust them to the Friars for their use. In 1230 Gregory IX gave his sanction to this solution, of the question of books and libraries, and declared that this was in accord with the well-known intentions of his friend, Francis.[105] The same view forms the basis of the decree of Nicholas III, *Exit qui seminat* of the year 1279.[106] Ubertinus, in the name of the Spiritual zealots, accepts this view in the sense that smaller or larger libraries should exist according to the needs and importance of individual houses, and that books might be given to the individual Religious as their

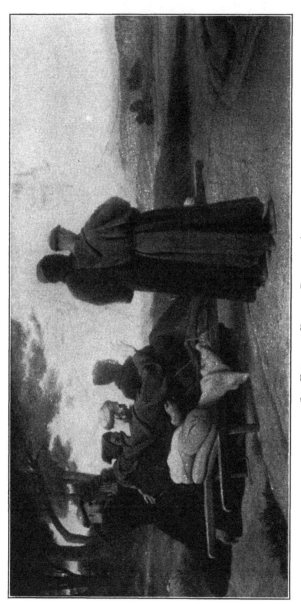

St. Francis, Dying, Blesses Assisi

calling and office demanded: after they had been used, however, or after their term had expired, these books were to be restored to the common library, so that other Friars might use them also.[107]   .

As certain as it is that Francis permitted books in common, so certain it is that *he allowed no brother to have a private collection of books.* Thomas of Celano [108] and the Three Companions [109] insist most emphatically on this point. They stress the fact that the Holy Founder allowed libraries common to the entire Community only. Thomas of Celano moreover relates that a certain Provincial approached Francis for permission to retain for himself some ornamented and costly books. Francis answered laconically: "I will not lose the Gospels, which I have promised to observe, on account of thy books. Do as thou pleasest, but thou shalt never do it with my consent." [110] This anecdote and others of a similar nature are recorded by Brother Leo.[111] For in this matter more than in any other it is to be emphasized that the authors of these accounts stubbornly cite the manuscript relics of Brother Leo and of other first disciples of Francis without fear of being charged with falsehood.[112]

The declaration made to Brother Riger by Francis is significant. To the question whether it could be justified to possess an amount of books for personal use under the pretext that these belonged to the Order and not to the person, the Saint replied: "My first and last will was and is, that the Friars possess nothing but habit, cord and breeches." [113] Francis repeatedly gave the same answer to similar casuistic questions, always with reference to the question of poverty.[114]

From the instances mentioned above, it is clear that there was no question of allowing or refusing proprietary rights over books to any individual Friar. That such ownership was not even to be considered, was self-evident. The question was of an entirely different nature. A Friar Minor is not affiliated with a particular house; he travels much and often. May he carry with him from place to place the books he thinks of personal service? Francis denied this, as Ubertinus of Casale expressly adds.

It is true, he says, that Francis desired books to be at hand in every house. "Nevertheless it was by no means the intention of our Blessed Father Francis that individual Friars might collect a bag of books and own them, carrying them with themselves whenever their residence was changed." [115] On the contrary, no Friar whatsoever was permitted to dispose of a single book according to caprice, or to carry it with him from place to place, not even when this was given him as a present by friends, or as a memento by relatives.[116] Everyone should draw on the common library for the books required by his need and office and talent, and replace the same when finished.[117] If he be removed to-day or to-morrow, he should take with him only the garment he wore at the time [118] and his Breviary, in order to pray the canonical hours.[119]

There was indeed no lack of Friars who objected to the view of the Saint on this point.[120] Several of these demanded permission to keep certain books and to carry them with them in exceptional cases.[121] Although the Saint at times tolerated this in silence,[122] he personally nevertheless clung to his original principle.[123] Even at the end of his life he demanded of his successor that he be no collector of books, but should content himself with one small book, together with writing materials and the seal for the affairs of the Order.[124]

Yet the constantly increasing demands became stronger than the primitive Ideal. The complaints of the *Speculum* and Ubertinus, which were traced to Brother Leo, show that the Friars often took with them from place to place the books which they thought indispensable. The Chronicler Matthew of Paris also notes about the year 1225 that the Friars carried with them on their journeys a small collection of books in a bag.[125] Five years later

St. Bonaventure regulated this matter in the oldest constitutions of the Order at the General Chapter held at Narbonne in 1260. It was conceded that individual Friars might have a certain number of books for private use and take them along from house to house, indeed, even from province to province; yet it was ordained that they must have permission for this from their provincial, and that after the death of the brother in question, the books should be returned to his home province.[126]

"To be poor" meant for Francis [127] not only to renounce all temporal possessions, but also spiritual ownership; and with the renunciation of "mine" and "thine" to regulate the no less egotistic "I," and to sanctify it by *humility* and *simplicity*. We have already seen how these two virtues were to shine forth in Franciscan savants and to give the entire Franciscan system of science its peculiar trait.[128] It also becomes evident how nobly and comprehensively Francis conceived the harmony which should exist between learning and humility; how far he was from stressing humility at the expense of science, or science at the expense of humility; and how firmly he was convinced that genuine science tends toward humility, simplicity and modesty.

But the renunciation of self and of the world through humility and poverty did not suffice. Francis demanded that student Friars strive for union with God through *piety*. What he prescribes to the lay brothers in regard to manual labor, applies clearly and in a special manner to those engaged with intellectual pursuits: "Let those brothers to whom the Lord has given the grace of working, labor faithfully and devoutly, so that in banishing idleness, which is the enemy of the soul, they do not extinguish the spirit of holy prayer and devotion, to which all temporal things must be subservient." [129] In this strain Francis likewise expressed his views on the relation between study and prayer when he wrote to St. Anthony.[130]

The chief stress was to be laid on prayer; learning should guide prayer, and prayer enlighten learning.[131]

It pained him deeply to behold some of the Friars neglecting the inner life in order to apply themselves to study. At such times he was wont to say: "Those brothers who allow themselves to be misguided by a vain curiosity for learning will find themselves empty-handed on the day of reckoning. I would much rather they were strong in virtue, in order that when the time of tribulation overtakes them, they might have the Lord with them in their need. For tribulation will come on them when books will avail them naught, but will be cast into crevices and corners." [132]   Thomas of Celano remarks hereto: "Francis spoke thus, not that he wished to discourage the study of the Holy Scriptures, but because he wished to restrain all the Friars from immoderate curiosity in learning, and would rather that they were proficient in the perfection of charity, than filled with vain knowledge. He foresaw, moreover, the not far distant time when learning would be an occasion of ruin, but the spirit remains always to religious men a support." [133]   He even then already pointed out that "many bent all their energies by day and by night to the acquisition of learning alone, and in this way became disloyal to their vocation, to holy and devout prayer." [134]

As far as this vocation was regarded, Francis believed not only that prayer was to be preferred to every kind of learning, but he recognized and recommended only theological studies.

If we compare the various utterances of the Saint on the subject of studies in his Order, we find only such expressions as "spiritual study," "study of wisdom," "study of Holy Scriptures," "science of holy theology." We know that all these terms denote one and the same thing: theology. Nowhere do we find mention of the secular sciences, or of philosophy.[135]   The question whether these were permissible in the Order or not, seems never to have been put to him. Had he been asked, he no doubt would have answered in the negative.

In those days this was understood without further ado. Before the thirteenth century, philosophy was not taught in the schools of Europe.[136] Whoever wished to enter the professions of theology, law or medicine, needed only the knowledge of grammar, that is, a working knowledge of Latin, the tongue of the cultured, and perhaps a smattering of logic, which was merely an introduction to the forms of speech in vogue in the schools. The Aristotelian dialectics first became general among the Western scholars in the twelfth century; in the beginning of the thirteenth century, the Aristotelian physics, metaphysics and works on the natural sciences began to become known through translation.[137] Thus suddenly the unsuspected treasures of Greek culture were opened to the literary world.

Their exploitation however seemed unworthy of Christian science, more especially of theology. They were furthermore accompanied with dangers to the Faith. With all his geniality the Stagirite was replete with the spirit of paganism. Added to this was the fact that the translations of his works were made by the Arabic philosophers and were imported together with the commentaries of Avicenna and Averroes from the Moorish peninsula of Spain. There was therefore in fact a question of Arabic philosophy, which, built upon a much falsified Aristotelism, lent support to Hedonism and Deism, and would have become more dangerous to Christian Europe than the arms of Islam. The Church looked forward to this threatening evil with anxiety. Since 1210 she repeatedly forbade the Parisian faculty to hold lectures on Aristotelian physics and metaphysics until the errors contained therein were expunged, and admonished the theologians to expound the Word of God according to the commentaries of the Fathers, instead of having recourse to godless pagan philosophers.[138]

The Religious Orders sounded the warning clarion even more loudly. Not to mention the monks who were not occupied with science, we read in the oldest constitutions of the Dominican Order: "The brothers should study no pagan philosophers, except they merely scan their works cursorily. They should not take up any secular science, unless the Master General or the General Chapter wish to make an exception for the one or other Religious. All others, young as well as old, may read only theological works." [139] We have seen that Francis and the first Franciscans were opposed just as firmly to the study of philosophy, and we now fully understand their attitude.

Soon, however, a change of opinion in favor of Aristotle set in all along the line. Efforts were made to eradicate the errors from his works and from the commentaries of his exponents, and to render their colossal intellectual products fertile for Christian science. This was significantly sooner the case at the Franciscan schools of Oxford and Paris than anywhere else. Since 1225, the learned Franciscan Robert Grosseteste of Oxford had drawn not only the natural sciences and philology, but also the study of philosophy into the service of theology. His disciple, Adam of Marsh, continued this work until the time of Roger Bacon. Bacon, who was a product of their school, does not hesitate to place both teachers at the side of Aristotle and Avicenna, and to acknowledge that he himself follows "those wonderful trails" which they had blazed for him.[140]

The school of the Parisian Minorites underwent a similar transformation about the year 1231, under the leadership of the great master, Alexander of Hales. As the pioneer among the Summistae he introduced the complete works of the Stagirite into theological literature; applied in numberless passages the speculations of the Philosopher and of his exponents Avicenna and Averroes to Christian dogma; corrected false views, and exposed the sophisms of the Arabic philosophers. He rendered the entire forces of Aristotelian dialectics subservient to theological research, with the firm conviction that Scholasticism would receive a truly gigantic impetus through Aristotle. Thus he paved the way on which the future intellectual heroes Albertus, Thomas, Bonaventure and Duns Scotus were to press on to immortal fame.[141] His disciple and successor, John de Rupella (died 1245), went in fact so far as to not only disapprove, in a public sermon, of the heated opposition to Aristotle and his philosophy, but even branded such antagonism as called forth by Satan. Commenting on a passage of Scripture he says: "Now there was no smith to be found in all the land of Israel; for the Philistines had taken the precaution, lest the Hebrews should make them swords or spears.[142] The smiths are the teachers of philosophy. Behold how they forge their unbending, invincible objections which pierce the mind like a sword; behold how their arguments penetrate like gleaming lances. For this reason Satan sets everything in motion to make the study of philosophy impossible; for he does not wish that the faithful possess a keen intellect." [143]

After the example of the two general study houses of Oxford and Paris, philosophy was introduced into other colleges of the Order during the generalate of Crescentius of Jesi (1244-1247). Angelus of Clarino says expressly that under Crescentius "the Egyptian plagues of the black arts of Aristotle descended on the Order," [144] and that, besides other excesses contrary to the rule, "an insatiable craving for learning" had become prevalent, which at all costs "aimed at introducing worldly sciences and erecting a multitude of schools for these branches." Especially in Italy, he continues, there were many Friars who "preferred the vain and barren learning of Aristotle, neglecting their prayers, and who eagerly desired to hear the doctrine of the natural sciences and dialectics, and increased the study of the same with burning ardor." [145] It was at this juncture that the opposition of the Spirituals to profane studies set in with full might [146] and became more and more bitter, until it in the end aided as a powerful factor in the final separation of these zealots from the Order.

The Spirituals of former times had complained only of the immoderate study of philosophy and science in general, at the cost of piety and the spirit of prayer. Thus, the Minister General John of Parma (1247-1257) very emphatically asserts that the structure of the Order rests on two buttresses, virtue and learning; he deplores however (with reference to the dialectic treatment of theological truths), that they had built the buttress of learning "higher than the heavens," but that of virtue far too low.[147]   Peter John Olivi (died 1297) also deplores the excessive emphasis placed on profane learning; although he concedes that such study can well be reconciled with the Franciscan Ideal, if it be made subservient to theology and does not extinguish the spirit of prayer.[148]

The later, extreme Spirituals, however, especially Angelus of Clarino and Ubertinus of Casale, condemned all philosophic studies on the ground that they did not exist at the time of Francis.[149]   They forgot completely that in the meantime conditions had undergone a change; Greek philosophy had become permeated with the Christian Faith; by the aid of Aristotelian philosophy religious science had made wonderful progress; the most enlightened and saintly of men had devoted themselves to Scholasticism, which is not thinkable without Aristotle; the Church guarded Scholastic learning as the apple of her eye; and Francis himself, the most obedient son of the Church, in consideration of the changed conditions, would have declared himself in harmony with the movement. Only the Spirituals took in this, as in other questions, an extremely rigorous stand, allowed the study of theology and the apostolate to languish more and more, rebelled against the Order, the Pope and the Church, and were shipwrecked on the reefs of fanaticism (1317-1318).

The *only proper position which science could assume in the Order* under the changed conditions since the death of Francis, had long ago been defined by St. Bonaventure, the "second Founder of the Franciscan Order," equally great as theologian and as saint. Against the attacks of outsiders and the excesses of the laxists as well as the rigorists within the Order, he drew up the following regulations for the scholastic activity of his brothers.

A. The *study of theology* or of the *Holy Scriptures* is an essential obligation of the Friars because of their calling to the apostolate. He writes: "Since the Order is bound, by virtue of the profession of the rule, to the office of preaching and of hearing confessions, and these offices presuppose the knowledge of Holy Scripture, it is necessary that we have study houses and teachers of Holy Scripture." [150] And again: "These poor Friars are engaged with the care of the souls of their neighbors; this they cannot do without the help of the Holy Scriptures, and the Scriptures they cannot understand thoroughly except through the study of theology, which consists in the reading, meditation, prayer, hearing, discussion and preaching of the Scripture texts. Hence, they are bound to this spiritual activity, which because of its difficulty taxes the entire man and surpasses all bodily labor in sublimity." [151] Even when the Friars apply themselves to other branches of learning "they should never wander too far from the home of Holy Scripture," [152] and when they adapt these sciences to theology they must do so with moderation. "One must not mix too much water of philosophy in the wine of Holy Scripture, lest the wine become watery. This would be a sad miracle! Christ changed water into wine, not wine into water." [153]

B. Nevertheless, the *study of philosophy,* and of the *profane sciences* respectively, is justified and necessary when they are employed in the interests of theology.

Bonaventure censures those Friars who waste time on vain and unprofitable studies, or cultivate profane sciences for their own sake.[154]   Philosophical studies are only in so far permissible as they are auxiliary to theology, prepare for it, acknowledge it as their goal, and in this way become sanctified.[155]   Thus understood, Bonaventure ascribes to them great importance.   His treatise *"De reductione artium ad theologiam"* is a hymn on the harmony of all natural science with supernatural knowledge and faith.   "All science," he writes, "has its value for the understanding of Holy Scripture; in this they find their goal; by this they are perfected, through it they are directed to the Eternal Light. . . . It is consequently evident that the manifold wisdom of God, so brightly communicated in the Holy Scriptures, lies hidden in every science, and that every science is serviceable to theology. And the chief fruit of all learning consists in furnishing material for the strengthening of the Faith." [156]   Yes, he adds, philosophy is not only useful, but simply indispensable.   Without philosophy the understanding and the defense of dogmatic truths is often impossible; many passages of Holy Writ are beyond comprehension without the aid of the profane sciences.[157]   Philosophy constructs from its investigations of the things of nature, a mirror in which theology can behold the divine truths.   Both sciences together form a Jacob's ladder, whose foot rests on the earth of philosophy, and whose top pierces the heaven of theology, and all this through Christ Jesus, the Lord of the natural as well as the supernatural world and truth.[158]

C. On this ladder the brothers should constantly mount to heaven by the study of philosophy and theology in the *spirit of piety.*   Herein, according to Bonaventure, lies the peculiar character of Franciscan science.   Dominicans and Franciscans distinguish themselves from all other Religious by scientific speculation, he explains.   He then adds the distinctive mark of Dominican and Franciscan science:

"The Dominicans are occupied mostly with speculative science, then with piety; the Franciscans mostly with piety, then with speculation. O that this piety and this unction may never be given the second place!" [159]

The embodiment of this Franciscan science we find in St. Bonaventure himself. His intimate friend and secretary, Bernard of Bessa, testifies of him: "In the same measure as one beheld Bonaventure advance with wonderful ability in the light of the sciences, and especially in Holy Scripture, he also made constant progress in grace and devotion. He transformed every truth which he grasped with his mind into prayer and praise of God, and contemplated them in unceasing elevations of his heart." [160]   This constant converse with God imparted to his works that marvelous unction and mystical tone which won for him undying fame as the *Doctor devotus* and *Doctor seraphicus,* the devout and seraphic Doctor.

CHAPTER XVIII

THE PIETY OF ST. FRANCIS

"IN FRANCIS medieval piety reaches its clearest and strongest expresssion," writes Adolf Harnack.[1] And Henry Tilemann agrees: "The piety of Francis reveals the type of the religious spirit of the Middle Ages in its perfection."[2] Since non-Catholics think thus, piety must evidently be the sum, center and substance of the Ideals of St. Francis. How is it, then, one might ask, that this subject is treated only now and in a special chapter? I should like to answer this objection with the counter question: how is it that we are to speak of the piety of Francis in particular, since the whole book treats of it?

Piety is the directing of the entire man to God; *Christian* piety is the following, the imitation and copying of the God-Man, Jesus Christ; piety as understood by all the *Founders of Orders* prior to Francis, was merely a higher form of this following, imitation and copying of Jesus Christ, insofar as the Religious observed the counsels of the Gospel in addition to the commandments of God. The *piety of the Saint of Assisi* differed from this in that he strove to fulfil perfectly the entire Gospel in spirit and letter, to become like to the Saviour in every way, not only in His hidden and contemplative, but also in His public and active life. That was the peculiar trait of his Ideal of piety. Up to his time either active *or* contemplative life was the motto; Francis declared for contemplative *and* active life joined in one, removing the antithesis by the higher unity of an all-sided following of Christ. To serve one's neighbor by works of charity and by the apostolate for love of Christ, constituted the zenith of his piety. Thus, life itself with its manifold aspects becomes for Francis religious piety. When we consider the Ideals of this man of God, it is as if we were wandering through the halls of a vast cathedral. There remains for us yet to penetrate into the innermost sanctuary of the temple in order to consider the *piety of the Poverello* in its stricter acceptation:—his *life of prayer,* his *practises of prayer,* his *spirit of prayer.*

1. The term *life of prayer* is no exaggeration when applied to St. Francis. The cordial communion with God assumed, in fact, so prominent a place and so wide an extent in his life, that his entire existence became as it were one continuous prayer. His entire life was "a holy leisure," in which his heart occupied itself with the Eternal Wisdom, as one of his biographers remarks.[3] Prayer made up his happiness on earth, the cloudless sunlight of his years, the safe harbor in which his heart lay anchored. He did not restrict his devotion to moments of time, but extended it as long as possible; it seemed he could no longer separate himself from God, before whom he lay prostrate in humble, unceasing and childlike prayer; wherever he went or tarried, in his cell and without, at work or at rest, while eating and drinking, always and everywhere he prayed, so much so that the impression was forced upon one that he devoted not only his heart, soul and body, but also all his actions and all his time to prayer.[4]

Everything that might disturb this prayerful mood was scrupulously avoided. With untiring zeal he strove to keep himself free from all worldly interests, in order that the heavenly joy of his soul might not become clouded even for an hour with the dust of the earth. He became, so to say, insensible to all distractions from without; he guarded his external senses so carefully and governed every movement of his soul so constantly, that he could find no other attraction but in God. With preference he dwelt "in the clefts of the rock, and in the hollow places of the wall he made his abode." [5]   He loved to tarry in secluded nooks which were especially suited to prayer, and when he grew tired and exhausted, he rested all the longer and all the more lovingly in the wounds of the Saviour.[6]

Whenever he was forced to interrupt his prayer to devote himself to any business or to receive visitors, he withdrew again into the interior of his soul as quickly as he could; he was so accustomed to heavenly sweetness and to divine joys, that everything human and earthly became unsavory and almost unbearable.[7]   If he was not able to rid himself of importunate visitors, he was wont to recite the Psalm verse: "Thy words I have hidden in my heart, O Lord, that I may not sin against Thee." [8]   As soon as he uttered these words, the Friars knew that it was time to lead the visitors away politely and to dismiss them.[9]

At one time the Bishop of Assisi called at a moment when the Saint was wrapt in deepest prayer in his cell at Portiuncula. Out of curiosity, and over-reliant on the intimacy of friendship, he knocked rapidly and opened the door without waiting for a summons; but he had scarcely protruded his head within the narrow door when he began to tremble from head to foot, and became speechless with terror. In an instant he was forcibly driven out by an irresistible power, that he might not witness the mysteries of the Saint in prayer.[10]   Francis was loath to have even the Friars know that he held continuous converse with God. Early in the morning he would rise noiselessly from his pallet, and steal away, that no one might notice how early he began his orisons. In the evening, however, when he retired, he was wont to cause a stir, almost a noise, that all might become aware that he was about to retire.[11] This was his customary conduct *at home* and *in his cell*.

But also *when traveling* Francis understood how to cultivate uninterrupted and hidden prayer. When the presence of God began to overwhelm him, he would send his companions in advance, and, slacking his own pace, he would surrender himself to the delights of the heavenly visitation. If he was unable to withdraw himself completely from company, he would use his mantle as an improvised cell to preserve his recollection and to conceal his interior agitation. Had he no mantle, he would conceal his face with the sleeves of his habit, in order that the heavenly Manna might not be profaned by impertinent eyes. If even this ruse failed, he became adept in diverting the attention of onlookers to various objects, that they might not notice the presence of his Beloved. If all else failed, he would make his bosom a hidden sanctuary, and remained wrapt in God, instead of giving free rein to the agitation of his soul in exclamations, deep sighs, groans and motions.[12]

Occasionally he became so carried away by contemplation, even in the street among crowds of people, that he fell into ecstasy and, absorbed in divine sweetness, became unconscious of what was transpiring about him. Thus, one day he was riding toward Borgo San Sepolcro, whence he intended to reach a leper hospital which he had chosen as shelter for the night. When the country folk heard that he was passing by, they streamed out to meet him and to touch his hands and feet with their customary reverence. They took hold of him, tugged at his habit and cut off pieces from it to preserve them as relics. Francis, however, neither felt anything nor knew what was happening to him or around him. Finally the little party neared the end of their journey and had already left the town of Borgo far behind them. Suddenly the Saint came out of his ecstasy and inquired anxiously how far it was still to Borgo. These experiences were of frequent occurrence, as his companions have recorded from their own observation.[13]

Not even the *work of the apostolate* was able to distract him from prayer. At first blush this seems incredible, considering the prominent place the apostolate occupied in his life and in his Order. This was, however, his secret of true piety, that his work in the world be based on prayer and tend to prayer as well as the various occupations at home. Whatever he undertook for the welfare of his fellow-men, he first recommended to God in fervent prayer.[14] He often declared that it was a poor division if any priest devote all his strength and time to preaching and have little or nothing left for devotion. Only that preacher was worthy of praise who thought of his own soul first and attended to its needs.[15] His motto was: "The preacher must first draw from hidden prayer what he wishes to communicate afterward in holy discourse; he must first become inwardly warm himself, or he will afterward speak only cold words." [16]

As the brothers turned from prayer to preaching, they were also to return from preaching and from contact with the world to prayer as quickly as possible. Jacques de Vitry asserts that in the beginning the Friars followed this advice: "The Friars Minor," he says, "concern themselves in no way with temporal things, but apply themselves day and night with burning zeal to win back from the vanities of the world the souls that have gone astray. . . . By day one sees them going from town to town to save their fellow-men by means of the active life; at night, however, they retire to their solitary dwellings, in order to devote themselves to contemplation and prayer." [17] Francis himself was accustomed to spend the greater part of the night in prayer after the labors of the day. Brother Bernard observed how he spent whole nights, with but a brief interval, in the praise of God and of His holy Mother.[18] Indeed, Thomas of Celano relates that he often began his prayer in the evening and persevered in it till morning.[19]

Not content with this, he often interrupted his apostolic

labors for a longer or shorter period, in order to betake himself to some secluded *hermitage* and there devote himself entirely to contemplation. "He had," as Bonaventure says, "learned to dispose of the time given to him to gain merits so prudently, that he applied one half of it in meritorious work for his fellow-men, and the other in silent meditation. After he had labored for the salvation of souls, as place and circumstances demanded, he would leave the multitudes and seek a solitary place, in order to give himself more freely to God and to wipe away the dust that might have settled on his soul." [20] He was irresistibly attracted to Greccio near Rieti, to Celle near Cortona, to the Carceri on Mount Subasio, to Sarziano, La Verna, and other hallowed spots, which like oases of seraphic peace and sweetest surrender to God, still live in the history of the Saint and of his disciples. He had his cell built under a projecting rock or in the woods where he could be near his brothers and yet give himself entirely to heavenly devotion.[21]

In the morning he withdrew to his hermitage, spent the whole day in prayer and returned only at night to sup with his brothers. Yet he had no fixed time for his return, because his spirit wished to enjoy contemplation to the full before the body dared demand its rights.[22] What passed between him and God at such times, he never revealed to anyone.[23] When he came from prayer he was very careful to act as the others, in order not to betray the inner fire which had almost transformed him into another man.[24] He often said to his confidants: "When a servant of God is visited by Him in prayer, he should lift up his eyes to heaven at the end of prayer and speak thus with folded hands: 'This consolation Thou, O Lord, hast sent to me, a sinner and ingrate, from heaven, and I confide this grace to Thy protection, that Thou mayest preserve it for me; for I feel that I am a robber of Thy treasure.' Or: 'Lord, take Thy gift from me in this world and preserve it for me for the future world.'

When he returns from prayer he should conduct himself as a most poor sinner, as though he had received no special grace. For," he continued, "one can barter a priceless grace for a small price and cause the Giver not to be so generous with His gifts a second time." [25]

In spite of this, his companions discovered many things about his prayerful solitude. At times they stole after him that they might observe him and hear him secretly. They then saw and heard how he filled the woods or the hermitage with sighs, how he bedewed the earth with tears, how he struck his breast and held communion with the Lord as with an intimate friend. In the solitude he answered his Judge, he implored his Father, he conversed with his Friend. With burning tears he interceded with the Divine Mercy in behalf of sinners, and lamented loudly over the sufferings of his Saviour, as though these were visible to his eyes. They observed how he was lifted above the earth, his hands outstretched in the form of a cross, and how a cloud, as proof of the marvelous illumination of his soul, gleamed about him. Frequently, too, he spoke only inwardly, his lips remaining immovable, and while he withdrew within himself, he lifted his soul upward to God. He directed all his mind and will and love to God alone, so much so, that when he prayed, he did not seem to pray, but his very being became a living prayer: *"Totus non tam orans, quam oratio factus."* Thus Thomas of Celano.[26]

This preference of Francis for solitary places of prayer and union with God communicated itself also *to his brothers.* Many of these lived in hermitages for a time, others constantly. The Saint saw himself obliged to draw up a particular *"modus vivendi"* for such, which reads: "Let those brothers who wish to live religiously in hermitages, be three brothers or four at most. Let two of them be mothers, and have two sons, or at least one. Let the former lead the life of Martha, and the other two the life of Mary Magdalen. Let those who lead the life of

Mary have one cloister and each his own place, so that they may not live or sleep together. And let them always say Compline of the day toward sunset, and let them be careful to keep silence and to say their Hours and to rise for Matins, and let them seek first 'the kingdom of God and His justice.' And let them say Prime and Terce at the proper time, and, after the Hour of Terce, they may break silence and may speak and, when it is pleasing to them, they may go to their mothers and ask alms from them for the love of the Lord God, like little poor ones. And after that let them say Sext and None and Vespers at the appointed time. And they must not allow any person to enter into the cloister where they live, or let them eat there. Let these brothers who are mothers endeavor to keep apart from every person and, by the obedience of their custos, let them guard their sons from every person, so that no one may speak with them. And let these sons not speak with any person except with their mothers and with their custos, when it shall please him to visit them with the blessing of God. But the sons must sometimes in turn assume the office of mothers, for a time, according as it may seem to them to dispose. Let them strive to observe all the above diligently and earnestly." [27] The greatest joy overcame Francis when he heard of any brothers who faithfully led this life of uninterrupted recollection and constant prayer.[28]

As a rule, however, Francis and his sons could not forsake the world very long because of the demands of the apostolate. They endeavored therefore to combine the active and the contemplative nature of their vocation by settling in the vicinity of cities and villages, yet outside of them. As early as 1224 Honorius III granted them the privilege "to celebrate Mass and the other divine mysteries on a portable altar in their places and oratories, because they wish to avoid the noise of the masses so contrary to their calling and to live by preference in hidden seclusion, in order the better to cultivate the spirit of prayer in

holy solitude." [29]   Ubertinus de Casale certainly grasped
this Ideal of the Saint fully when he wrote: "Francis
never neglected to withdraw from time to time into solitude, although he remained recollected and sunk in prayer
day and night, as well as he could, even when among men.
This was the manner of living and preaching which he
always prescribed to his brothers. For this reason he
desired that the houses of the brothers be in the neighborhood of human dwellings, that they might be ready to
assist their fellow-men zealously. However, in order to
guard against a too intimate intercourse with the world
and to preserve the spirit of silent meditation and prayer,
he wished to be a neighbor to men in such wise that he
still remained a stranger; he desired to erect the houses
near the people, yet so that they might be situated outside
of the settlements, in places of quiet solitude." [30]

Although he emphasized the apostolate so much, the
chief care of the Saint was therefore the *cultivation of
the spirit of prayer*. The grace of prayer, he insisted,
must be desired above all things by a Religious; and since
he was convinced that without it no one can progress in
the service of God, he animated his brothers in every
possible way to be zealous at prayer.[31] He personally instructed them how to pray; [32] he bound them strictly to
avoid everything that could lessen the aptitude of the
soul for prayer, even though it were only a vain talking
outside the time of prayer; [33] he incited them mostly by
his example to work without ceasing for the grace of
prayer. In this manner he reared those choice families
of devout supplicants, about whom all the chronicles of
early Franciscan history are so eloquent.[34]

2. Let us now turn our attention to the various *practises
of prayer* observed by St. Francis. In the first place, we
must put aside the thought that the piety of the Saint consisted in many and complicated devotions. *His one* devotion was the childlike, humble and joyous adoring and
glorifying of the *Triune God*. "Always adoring and con-

templating the Lord, the living and true God," this was
the sum total of his life of prayer.[35] One need but read
the first rule of the Order to understand how thoroughly
he practised devotion to the Most Holy Trinity and how
zealously he recommended it to his brothers.

In the seventeenth chapter of this rule, he desires that
they should seek "above all things divine fear and divine
wisdom, and the divine love of the Father, and the Son
and the Holy Ghost." Then he admonishes them as follows: "Let us refer all good to the Lord God most high
and supreme; let us acknowledge that all good things
belong to Him, and let us give thanks for all to Him from
whom all good proceeds. And may He, the most high and
supreme, only true God, have, and may there be rendered
to Him, and may He receive, all honors and reverences, all
praises and benedictions, all thanks and all glory, to whom
all good belongs, who alone is good. And when we see
or hear evil said or God blasphemed, let us bless and thank
and praise the Lord who is blessed forever. Amen." [36]

In the twenty-first chapter there is an admonition which
all the brothers, clerics and laics, should deliver to the
people. This begins with the words of praise; "Fear and
honor, praise and bless God, give thanks and adore the
Lord God almighty in Trinity and Unity, Father and Son
and Holy Ghost." [37]

In the twenty-second chapter Francis admonishes the
brothers still more forcibly: "Let us all, brothers, watch
much, lest under pretext of some reward or labor or aid
we lose or separate our heart or mind from the Lord.
But I beseech all the brothers, both ministers and others,
in the charity which God is, that, overcoming all obstacles
and putting aside all care and solicitude, they strive in the
best manner they are able, to serve, love and honor the
Lord God with a clean heart and a pure mind, which He
seeks above all. And let us always make in us a tabernacle and dwelling-place for Him, who is the Lord God
omnipotent, Father, Son and Holy Ghost." [38]

The entire rule concludes with the wonderful chapter entitled: "Prayer, Praise, and Thanksgiving" and which reads as follows: "Almighty, most holy, most high and supreme God, holy and just Father, Lord King of heaven and earth, for Thyself we give thanks to Thee because by Thy holy will, and by Thine only Son Thou hast created all things both spiritual and corporal in the Holy Ghost, and didst place us, made to Thy image and likeness, in paradise,[39] whence we fell by our own fault. And we give Thee thanks because, as by Thy Son Thou didst create us, so by the true and holy love with which Thou hast loved us, Thou didst cause Him true God and true Man, to be born of the glorious and ever Virgin, most blessed and holy Mary, and didst will that He should redeem us captives by His cross and blood and death. And we give thanks to Thee because thy Son Himself is to come again in the glory of His majesty to put the wicked who have not done penance for their sins, and have not known Thee, in eternal fire, and to say to all that have known Thee and adored Thee and served Thee in penance: 'Come, ye blessed of My Father, possess the kingdom prepared for you from the beginning of the world.' [40]

"And since all we wretches and sinners are not worthy to name Thee, we humbly beseech Thee, that Our Lord Jesus Christ, Thy beloved Son, in whom Thou art well pleased,[41] together with the Holy Ghost, the Paraclete, may give thanks to Thee as it is pleasing to Thee and Them, for all; He suffices Thee always for all through whom Thou hast done so much for us. Alleluia!

"And we earnestly beg the glorious Mother, the most blessed Mary ever Virgin, blessed Michael, Gabriel, Raphael, and all the choirs of the blessed Spirits, Seraphim, Cherubim and Thrones, Dominations, Principalities and Powers, Virtues, Angels and Archangels, blessed John the Baptist, John the Evangelist, Peter, Paul, the blessed Patriarchs and Prophets, Innocents, Apostles, Evangelists, Disciples, Martyrs, Confessors, Virgins, blessed Elias and Enoch, and all the saints who have been and are and shall be, for Thy love, that they may, as it is pleasing to Thee, give thanks for these things to the most high, true God, Our Lord Jesus Christ and the Holy Ghost, the Paraclete, forever and ever. Amen. Alleluia!

"And all we, Brothers Minor, useless servants, humbly entreat and humbly beseech all those within the holy Catholic and Apostolic Church wishing to serve God, and all ecclesiastical Orders, priests, deacons, and sub-deacons, acolytes, exorcists, lectors, door-keepers and all clerics, all religious men and women, all boys and children, poor and needy, kings, and princes, laborers, husbandmen, servants and masters, all virgins, continent, and all married people, laics, men and women, all infants, youths, young men and old, healthy and sick, all small and great, and all peoples, clans, tribes and tongues, all nations and all men in all the earth, who are and shall be, that we may per-severe in the true Faith and in doing penance, for other-wise no one can be saved. Let us all love with all our heart, with all our soul, with all our mind, with all our strength and fortitude, with all our understanding and with all our powers, with our whole might and with all our affection, with our innermost parts, our whole desires and wills, the Lord God, who has given and gives to us all, the whole body, the whole soul and our life; who has created and redeemed us, and by His mercy alone will save us; who has done and does all good to us, miserable and wretched, vile, unclean, ungrateful and evil.

"Let us therefore desire nothing else, wish for nothing else, and let nothing please and delight us except our Creator and Redeemer and Saviour, the only true God, who is full of good, all good, entire good, the true and supreme Good, who alone is good, merciful and kind, gentle and sweet, who alone is holy, just, true and upright, who alone is benign, pure and clean, from whom and through whom and in whom is all mercy, all grace, all glory of all penitents and of all the just, and of all the blessed rejoicing in heaven. Let nothing therefore hinder us, let nothing separate us, let nothing come between us. Let us all, everywhere, in every place, at every hour and at all times, daily and continually believe truly and humbly and let us hold in our hearts, and love, honor, adore, serve, praise and bless, glorify and exalt, magnify and give thanks to the most high and supreme, Eternal God, in Trinity and Unity, to the Father and Son and Holy Ghost, to the Creator of all, to the Saviour of all who believe and hope in Him and love Him, who, without beginning or end, is immutable, invisible, unerring, ineffable, incomprehensible, unfathomable, blessed, praiseworthy, glorious, exalted, sublime, most high, sweet, amiable, lovable, and always wholly desirable above all for ever and ever. Glory be to the Father and to the Son and to the Holy Ghost, as it was in the beginning, is now, and ever shall be, world without end." [42]

Truly a canticle to the Most Holy Trinity whose equal we can find nowhere in depth, piety and childlike simplicity! Francis, who himself was wholly "Prayer, Praise, and Thanksgiving," calls upon heaven and earth, and especially upon his brothers, to adore, praise, and love the Triune God.[43] This is *the* devotion of the Man of Prayer of Assisi.

This devotion, however, turns with preference to the Second Person of the Divinity, to the *God-Man, Jesus Christ*. It is self-evident that Christ always occupied a prominent place in Christian piety. However, since the era of the Crusades, since the time when the Christian world became inflamed with the desire of conquering the Holy Places hallowed by the feet of the Redeemer, it was as though the early days had returned when the faithful were simply known as "Invokers of the name of Jesus," and "Adorers of the Lord Jesus." [44] The beginning was made by the great preacher of the Crusades, Bernard of Clairvaux; but what began with him and his times as a bud, "broke forth in the holy Beggar of Assisi into full bloom, filling the world with its fragrance." [45] Christ was the center not only of the piety of the Poverello, but of his entire life, as we have already shown in the opening chapters of this book. What has been said there, may be condensed in the pithy sentence of Thomas of Celano: "With his whole soul he thirsted after Christ alone; to Him he consecrated not only his heart, but also his whole body." [46] His devotion to Christ found its expression in the "Office of the Passion," [47] composed by him. This Office is made up of Psalms taken mostly from Holy Scripture, but partly also composed by him and written in the most touchingly childlike and devout spirit. Its object was to awaken in him and in others "veneration and remembrance and the praise of the Passion of Our Lord." [48] Strictly speaking, however, it is not only an Office of the Passion, but of Christ Himself, for in it the chief mysteries of the life of the God-Man are praised, yet so that the Cross and Crucified are made the focus of devotion. Even the Psalm for the Vespers of Christmas, which gives expression to joy at the birth of the divine Child, concludes with the recollection of the Passion of Christ:

> Rejoice to God our helper; shout unto God, living and true, with the voice of triumph.
> For the Lord is high, terrible, a great King over all the earth.
> For the most holy Father of heaven, our King, before ages sent His beloved Son from on high, and He was born of the Blessed Virgin, Holy Mary.
> He shall cry to Me: Thou art My Father; and I will make Him My first-born, high above the kings of the earth.
> In the daytime the Lord hath commanded His mercy: and a canticle to Him in the night.
> This is the day which the Lord hath made: let us rejoice and be glad in it.
> For the beloved and most holy Child has been

given to us and born for us by the wayside, and laid
in a manger because He had no room in the inn.

Glory to God in the highest, and on earth peace
to men of good will.

Let the heavens rejoice and the earth be glad, and
let the sea be moved and the fulness thereof.

The fields shall rejoice and all that is in them.

Sing to the Lord a new canticle, sing to the Lord,
all the earth.

For the Lord is great and exceedingly worthy to
be praised. He is to be feared above all the gods.

Bring to the Lord, O ye kindreds of the Gentiles,
bring to the Lord glory and honor.

Bring to the Lord glory unto His name. Bring
your own bodies and bear His holy cross and follow
His most holy precepts unto the end.[49]

This devotion of St. Francis to Christ spread to his
entire Order, yea, even to the whole period which we
call the Franciscan Era. It is a known fact that his sons
guarded this devotion as a precious heirloom. This is
evident from the coat of arms which the Order selected
and which distinguishes it, and from the custody of the
Cross which it has kept through thirteen hundred years
up to the present day in the Holy Land, and from the
devotion to the Stations of the Cross, which it has popu-
larized and spread throughout the world. The Franciscan nuns, from the day of St. Clare to the present
time, propagated the devotion to Christ and the Cross
with the same zeal as the First Order. Thomas of Celano
tells us that Clare daily suffered a mystical death with
the Crucified Saviour; that she recited the Office of the
Passion, composed by Francis, with the same fervor as
he himself; that she constantly prayed to the Wounds
of the Saviour; in a word, that she bore the most tender
and ardent devotion to the Crucified and never wearied
of recommending it to her daughters.[50] Her letters to
the Blessed Agnes of Prague reveal a most touching love
for the divine Redeemer.[51] When she was on her death-

bed, the gospel of the Passion and the last words of Christ had to be read to her for the last time; then she had Brother Juniper summoned to her side and begged him with a joyous smile to say something new to the praise of God, for she knew that this "excellent troubadour of God understood how to say wonderful things about the Lord." [52]

Simultaneously the Franciscan mystics took up the pen to carry the devotion to the divine Redeemer into the widest circles. As early as the middle of the thirteenth century, Brother David of Augsburg composed, besides other Latin and German works, meditations and prayers on "the dearly beloved Lord Jesus Christ," so tender in tone and depth, so charming in their appeal, that their equal can scarcely be found.[53] It seems as if he sang a refrain to these when he adds the verses:

"O Jesus, Thou art my sweet delight,
Art to my spirit sun and light,
Which in my inner shines:
When with longing for Thy love it pines,
What heavenly blissfulness it wins,
When for Thy honey-sweet Divinity it burns!" [54]

A still more powerful impetus to the devotion to Christ was given by St. Bonaventure, the Prince of Mystics. In almost countless passages of his works he commends the devotion to the Crucified as the shortest and surest way that leads beyond all degrees of prayer directly to mystic union with God. The soul, desirous of penetrating into the mysteries of the spiritual life, must purify itself in the blood of the Crucified, must allow itself to be carried on by a burning love to the Crucified, must adore, contemplate and glorify the Crucified without ceasing.[55]

The influence of this Franciscan devotion to Christ on the later Middle Ages is reflected in the almost divine book of Thomas à Kempis (1379-1471). The attempt to trace the *Following of Christ* to St. Bonaventure was indeed abortive. However, it is undeniable that Thomas à Kempis was conversant with, and utilized, the works of the Seraphic Doctor,[56] and that everywhere he reveals the particular piety proceeding from St. Francis.[57] Before the Franciscan Era no one would have dared to write a book with the title, "The Following of Christ." Every chapter of the *Imitation* is Franciscan in thought and prayer; the intimate union of the soul with the Cross and the Tabernacle is especially Franciscan; Franciscan, above all, the sovereign principle which controls all others: "Let it be our chief study to meditate on the life of Jesus Christ. . . . When thou hast Christ, thou art rich, and He is sufficient for thee." [58] The self-same thought was the lodestar of St. Francis: "I know Christ, the poor Crucified. More I need not." [59]

With Christ and because of Christ, he was devoted to the *Blessed Virgin Mary*.[60] From earliest youth he was filled with "an ardent devotion to the Mother all-loving" and "Mistress of the world." [61] He was attached to her with such ineffable love because she "gave us the Lord of majesty as our Brother." [62] He could rejoice like a child over every mark of love and esteem shown her. "The Blessed Virgin Mary," he remarked, "is justly honored so greatly, because she bore the Lord in her most holy womb." [63]

His love for Mary, however, was based not only on her divine Motherhood, but also on this, that Mary shared the poverty of her divine Son, and thus had become the model for the Friars Minor.

Again and again he returned to this idea. He praised poverty as "the queen of virtues, because it sparkled with such brightness in the King of kings and in His queenly Mother." [64] Alms-begging was esteemed so highly by him "because Our Lord Jesus Christ was poor and a stranger and lived on alms, He and the Blessed Virgin." [65] Every beggar that he met he considered "a reflection of the Lord and of His poor Mother." [66] It was only with many tears that he could recall the great privations to which the Blessed Virgin and her Divine Child were exposed.[67] Once at dinner a Friar mentioned how poor the Blessed Virgin had been on Christmas Day when she gave birth to the Saviour. This was enough to affect Francis most strongly. He rose instantly from the table, seated himself on the bare floor, and thus finished his frugal meal amid bitter tears.[68] The example of Christ and of His blessed Mother alone was sufficient to urge him and his Brothers and Sisters to a life of poverty. For this reason he once wrote to Clare and her Sisters at San Damiano: "I, your least brother, Francis, will follow the life and poverty of Our Lord Jesus Christ and of His blessed Mother and persevere therein till the end. And I beg and beseech you all to persevere always in this most holy manner of life and poverty." [69]

For this reason also he consecrated himself and his Order to Mary, the Mother of God, and Mother of the Poor. The small sanctuary of Mary of the Angels, or Portiuncula, was, and remained, the cradle and home of his Order. In this chapel "he poured forth," as St. Bonaventure says, "constant prayers to her who had conceived the Word full of grace and truth, that she might vouchsafe to be his advocate. And now, by the merits of the Mother of Mercy, he conceived and brought forth the spirit of evangelical truth." [70] To this chapel he always led the brothers who joined the brotherhood, "that the Order of Friars Minor, which had been born there by the merits of the Mother of God, might there also by her aid receive its increase." [71] This chapel of the Virgin Mother of God "became the source and center of the new Order, the soul of his foundation. Here sprang up the fountain, which flowed in many thousand glittering rills of silver, humble and unassuming, through the divine garden of the Church, and changed so much sterile and desert land into green and blossoming fields. Hither

Francis always returned after his distant journeys into the Orient and Occident; after he had strengthened and consoled his brothers on his journeys by his presence, founded monasteries, clothed princes and lords, poor and lowly, men and women with the garb of poverty, consoled the sorrowful, reconciled enemies, distributed spiritual and temporal alms—hither he felt always drawn, to the home-like little church, the cradle of the Order." [72] He loved this little sanctuary more than any other place on earth, and on his death-bed commended it to the care of his brothers.[73] In its shadow he also wished to die,[74] after he had chosen the Blessed Virgin as Patroness and Advocate of his Order and of his brothers for all times.[75]

From this we may conclude how often and how zealously he prayed to Mary. He was not satisfied with the prayers which are found in the liturgy, nor with the Office of the Blessed Virgin which he added to these.[76] Thomas of Celano assures us: "He dedicated to the Mother of Jesus special hymns of praise, addressed special prayers to her, and breathed so many and such intimate aspirations of love to her, that no tongue is capable of describing it." [77] After Christ, he placed all his confidence in her; [78] to her confessed all his faults, and through her he daily hoped to obtain pardon of his imagined sins.[79] He spent entire nights in the praise of God and of the glorious Virgin.[80] Every Hour of his Office of the Passion began and ended with the antiphon: "Holy Virgin Mary, there is none like unto thee born in the world among women, daughter and handmaid of the most high King, the heavenly Father! Mother of our most holy Lord Jesus Christ, Spouse of the Holy Ghost, pray for us with St. Michael Archangel, and all the virtues of heaven, and all the saints, to thy most holy Son, our Lord and Master." [81] Still more charming is the "Salutation of the Blessed Virgin," composed and often recited by him:

Ave Domina sancta, regina sanctissima, Dei genitrix Maria!

Quæ es Virgo perpetua, electa a sanctissimo Patre de cælo!

Quam consecravit cum sanctissimo dilecto Filio et Spiritu Paracleto!

In qua fuit et est omnis plenitudo gratiæ et omne bonum.

Ave palatium eius!
Ave tabernaculum eius!
Ave domus eius!
Ave vestimentum eius!
Ave ancilla eius!
Ave Mater eius!

Et vos omnes sanctæ virtutes, quæ per gratiam et illuminationem Sancti Spiritus infundimini in corda fidelium, ut de infidelibus fideles Deo faciatis!" [82]

Hail, holy Lady, most holy Queen, Mother of God, Mary!

Who art ever Virgin, chosen from heaven by the mostly holy Father!

Whom He has consecrated with the most beloved Son and the Spirit, the Paraclete!

In whom was and is all the fulness of grace and all good.

Hail thou His palace!
Hail thou His tabernacle!
Hail thou His house!
Hail thou His garment!
Hail thou His handmaid!
Hail thou His Mother!

Hail, all ye virtues which by the grace and illumination of the Holy Ghost thou infusest in the hearts of the faithful, that from infidels ye may make them faithful to God!

Besides his devotion to the Queen of heaven, he had also a tender veneration toward the *angels and saints*. In genuinely knightly fashion he reckoned the angels as our champions in the battle against the powers of darkness. Everywhere, he was wont to say, we are surrounded by these heavenly Paladins; closest, however, to us are our Guardian Angels.[83] He could not bear that they should detect in him anything that might sadden their eye, or that one should dare to do anything in their presence that he feared to do before men. In the knowledge that the angels unceasingly sang hymns of praise before the Most Holy Sacrament, he desired that whenever possible

the brothers should come to the choir and there chant
their Office in union with the heavenly spirits.[84]

In a special manner Francis loved the archangel Michael.
As the knightly conqueror of the dragon he was the
patron of warriors.[85]   Under his standard they marched
to the conflict, and far and wide echoed the battle-cry:

> O invincible, valiant hero, Prince Michael,
> O guard us through life,
> O help us in strife,
> Prince Michael, Prince Michael![86]

The spiritual Knight of Assisi placed himself under the
leadership of this Prince of heaven, all the more since
the latter burns with zeal for souls, and has been assigned
the office of leading them to heaven.[87]   Francis fasted
forty days in his honor, beginning with the feast of the
Assumption, and during this time applied himself to most
zealous prayer.[88]   He did not hold the brothers to this
fast, but remarked: "Let each offer to God a special
praise or other tribute in honor of so exalted a Prince." [89]

Of the saints he honored with deepest devotion the
Princes of the Apostles, Peter and Paul, because they
excelled in glowing love for Christ, and were to him
splendid examples in the exercise of the apostolate.   He
prepared himself yearly for their feast by a fast of forty
days.   The other saints were also dear to his heart.   Their
memory constantly spurred him on to ever increasing love
of God.[90]   Whatever pertained to their cult was especially
dear to him, in particular their relics.[91]   Their imitation
was, however, of prime importance to him.   He was wont
to remind the brothers not only to praise the servants of
God, but like them to be loyal to God in sorrow, persecution and contempt, in sickness and temptation and similar
trials.[92]   On such occasions he would declare in his
romantic way: "Emperor Charles, Roland and Olivier, and
all brave knights and warriors, fought in battle against
the infidels in heat and hunger, won great victories and

died as holy martyrs for their faith in Jesus Christ. Now, however, there are many carpet knights, who desire to be honored and praised only because they know how to speak of such exploits and of such heroism. Thus, there are many, even among us, who place their entire glory in speaking and preaching about the great deeds of the saints." [93]

Francis preferred the *Divine Office* to all private devotions. As was to be expected, the liturgical functions could not be conducted in the poor and small churches of the Friars with that solemnity and splendor which accompanied them in the great abbeys and cathedrals. But the zeal with which the Friars practised liturgical prayer could not be surpassed by monks or canons. In the rule of 1221 the Saint prescribes: "Let all the brothers, whether clerics or laics, say the Divine Office, the praises and prayers which they ought to say. The clerics shall say the Office, and say it for the living and the dead, according to the custom of clerics." [94] Even in his Testament Francis bears witness that at first he and his followers prayed the Office as did the other clerics.[95] In the final rule he exchanged, with the exception of the Psalm version, the form of Office then commonly in use, for the one used by the Roman Church, that is, in the Papal chapel. He now ordains: "The brothers shall recite the Divine Office according to the order of the Holy Roman Church, with the exception of the Psalter." [96] The faithful retention and the conscientious recitation of this Office was always a matter dear to his heart. When he was nearing his end, and was no longer able to read because of his poor health and almost total blindness, he had a cleric read the Office to him daily. He inflicted the severest penalties on those brothers who were negligent in this matter.[97]

As we have seen elsewhere,[98] the Office was to be recited if possible in common, in spiritual union with the angels. It was not only recited, but, whenever possible,

sung after the manner of the Roman choir.[99]   Francis
implores the brothers to practise this chant with all possible dignity and devotion: "The clerics should recite the
Divine Office with devotion before God, so that they pay
not so much attention to the melody of the voice as to
the harmony of their spirits, so that the voice is united
with the spirit, the spirit, however, with God, so that
they may please God through purity of conscience and
not flatter the ears of men by the quality of their
voices." [100]   He also admonished the brothers to recite
the Hours with the same reverence and devotion whenever they could not be present in the choir.

In this as in all other things Francis gave the most
splendid example.   He chanted the Psalms with such
interior recollection as if he beheld God present.[101]   Although he suffered from illness of his eyes, his stomach,
his kidneys and his liver, he would not lean on anything
while reciting the Office, but prayed in an upright position,
with his hood thrown back, never allowing his eyes to
wander, or interrupting it in any way.   If he happened
to be on a journey, he would make a stop; if in the saddle,
he would dismount.   Even when the rain poured down
upon him he would not depart from this custom.   "If
the body," he said, "which is the prey of worms, is
allowed to enjoy its food in quiet, with how much tranquillity and peace must the soul take its food, which is
God Himself!"   He considered it a great fault if his
soul occupied itself a single instant with vain fancies
during prayer, and he hastened to atone for the sin by
immediate confession.   In this manner he succeeded in
remaining recollected to such an extent that he was
scarcely ever pestered by the "gnats of distraction."   Once
during Lent he had made a small earthen vessel, in order
not to waste a single moment of time.   While he was
reciting Terce, his work fastened itself upon his mind
and distracted him for an instant.   This caused him such
sorrow that after the completion of Terce he said to his

brothers: "Fie upon this idle work which has such a hold on me that it draws my spirit away! I will sacrifice it to God, whose sacrifice it has hindered." With these words he seized the vessel and flung it into the fire.[102]

In the first years of the Order the brothers did not yet understand how to recite the Office. For this reason Francis ordained that they should replace it with the *Our Father*.[103] Thus at every canonical Hour, and in fact at every interval at their disposal, they prayed and sang the Lord's Prayer with the greatest zeal.[104]

As soon, however, as the number of clerics increased, he prescribed, as we have seen, the ecclesiastical Office for them, while he obliged the lay brothers to recite a certain number of Our Fathers.[105] This ordinance of 1221 was embodied almost without change in the rule of 1223: "Let the clerics perform the Divine Office according to the order of the holy Roman Church, with the exception of the Psalter; wherefore they may have Breviaries. But let the laics say twenty-four Pater Nosters for Matins, five for Lauds; for Prime, Terce, Sext and Nones—for each of these Hours, seven; for Vespers, however, twelve; for Compline seven; and let them pray for the dead." [106]

A similar lay Breviary was already in use among the Knights Templar,[107] and among the lay brothers of the Cistercians.[108] This may not have been unknown to Francis. Yet evidently he was not induced by this, but by his love for the Gospel, to recommend heartily the devotion to the Lord's Prayer to his sons, lay as well as cleric. In the beginning [109] and later on [110] he constantly urged them to say the Our Father, repeating the words of the Saviour: "When ye wish to pray, say: Our Father, who art in heaven." [111] In order to lead *his* brothers, lay and cleric, to a deep understanding of the Our Father, he composed a striking paraphrase on it and recited it before every Hour of the Breviary, and before the Office of the Blessed Virgin Mary.[112] We dare not

withhold this pearl of prayer from our readers in its
own precious setting:

Our Father, most holy, our Creator, Redeemer, and
Comforter.

Who art in heaven, in the angels and in the saints,
illuminating them unto knowledge, for Thou, O Lord,
art light; inflaming them unto love, for Thou, O
Lord, art love; dwelling in them and filling them
with blessedness, for Thou, O Lord, art the highest
Good, the eternal Good, from whom is all good and
without whom is no good.

Hallowed be Thy name: may Thy knowledge shine
in us that we may know the breadth of Thy benefits,
the length of Thy promises, the height of Thy
majesty, and the depth of Thy judgments.

Thy kingdom come, that Thou mayest reign in us
by grace and mayest make us come to Thy kingdom,
where there is the clear vision of Thee, the perfect
love of Thee, the blessed company of Thee, the
eternal enjoyment of Thee.

Thy will be done on earth as it is in heaven: that
we may love Thee with the whole heart by thinking
of Thee; with the whole soul by always desiring
Thee, with the whole mind by directing our intentions to Thee and seeking Thy honor in all things
with all our strength, by spending all powers of body
and soul in the service of Thy love and not in anything else; and that we may love our neighbors even
as ourselves, drawing to the best of our power all to
Thy love; rejoicing in the good of others as in our
own, and compassionating with them in troubles and
giving offense to no one.

Give us this day, through memory and understanding and reverence for the love which He had for us
and for those things which He said, did and suffered
for us—*our daily bread,* Thy beloved Son, Our Lord
Jesus Christ.

And forgive us our trespasses, by Thy ineffable
mercy in virtue of the passion of Thy beloved Son,
Our Lord Jesus Christ, and through the merits and

intercession of the most blessed Virgin Mary and of all Thy elect.

As we forgive those who trespass against us, and what we do not fully forgive, do Thou, O Lord, make us fully forgive, that for Thy sake we may truly love our enemies and devoutly intercede for them with Thee, that we may render no evil for evil, but in Thee may strive to do good to all.

And lead us not into temptation, hidden or visible, sudden or continuous.

But deliver us from evil, past, present, and to come. *Amen.*[113]

3. The practises of piety as thus far recounted, by no means exhaust the Saint's life of prayer; they merely exhibit various phases of it. Brother David of Augsburg writes: "Prayer is threefold. First, when we say prayers composed by the Holy Ghost through the mouths of others, as the Psalms, hymns, the Our Father and similar prayers. Second, when we converse intimately with God and the saints from out of our hearts, according as the Holy Ghost moves us, reveal what distresses us, and beg for what we desire, and render thanks for what we have received—for ourselves and for others. The third is in the heart, does not make use of words, consists in pure desire, is hidden in the longings of the heart, and cannot be uttered in words by the tongue. The first is good, the second better, the third best." [114] From what has been said above, it is evident that Francis was a master of all three kinds of prayer. It now remains but to examine the *spirit* that animated him at prayer.

Briefly expressed, it is the spirit of *contemplation.* The Saint himself designated it as his Ideal. "Always to adore and contemplate the Lord, the living and true God." [115] His immediate disciples esteemed in him above all else "the contemplation and wisdom of the eternal truths." [116] And Bonaventure declares: "Filled with the Spirit of God, Blessed Francis was inflamed with the

desire to cling to God through the enjoyment of uninterrupted contemplation." [117]

The term contemplation in this connection connotes not
only piety in general, but *affective* piety, the prayer of
the heart. It is true, the mind had its share in Francis'
life of prayer, as it has necessarily in every prayer. But
in him the source and the focus of prayer was nevertheless his heart, his emotions, his God-tending will, his
absorption in and union with God. The prayers composed by him are proof of this. He occupies himself
prayerfully with the deepest speculative mysteries of the
Holy Trinity; but despite the deepest speculation, his
prayer unwittingly becomes an unbroken chain of inner
aspirations.[118] He meditates on the mysteries of the
human-divine life and of the passion of Jesus Christ,[119]
yet so that his prayer to Christ, as Thomas of Celano
remarks, always ended with the desire to be dissolved and
to be with Christ.[120] He bore an inexpressibly tender
devotion to Mary, and always and everywhere it becomes
a childlike, loving and intimate lisping to the Mother in
heaven.[121] He prays the Divine Office, and every Hour
becomes to him a living, throbbing experience, and every
Psalm a touching cry to God.[122] He prays and para-
phrases the Lord's Prayer, and petition after petition
becomes on his lips like a sunlit prism, in which the rays
of his enthusiastic love of God are refracted.[123] What,
then, must have been those hours, yea, days and nights
of almost ceaseless intimate prayer, during which his soul
remained irrevocably wrapt in the Most High! [124]

As prayer with him was more the outpouring of his
heart than the cold product of his mind, it did not spring
from labored reasoning, but gushed forth *spontaneously*
from his absorption in God. In this lies the essential
mark of higher mystic contemplation. Everyone engaged
in prayer, both beginners and the advanced, should regard
discursive mental activity *(meditatio)* only as a means
to the end of arousing the affections and of entering into

close union with God; it is, however, a prerogative of
the advanced and perfect only, or the result of an extraordinary grace, to attain to this union without the use of
this medium. Francis possessed this mystic quality of
the soul in a high degree. A single glance at a church
or a cross,[125] a single word casually dropped about the
Saviour or the Mother of God,[126] transported him into
the state of deepest contemplation. Indeed, a purely acci-
dental reference to a divine truth sufficed to place this
truth before his soul in its full light and life, to penetrate
and enthuse his heart, to inflame his will, to engulf the
entire man in holy wonderment, sweetness and bliss.
Thus, without effort he could hold converse with God
unceasingly, whether eating or drinking, whether moving
about or standing, whether at home or on a journey.[127]

Often, however, neither an exterior cause nor interior
meditation was needed, but the presence of God would
overpower him unconsciously or rather miraculously with
such force that he became lost in Him, either retaining
the normal control of his senses or transported into
ecstasy.[128] A pilgrim on earth in the flesh, his soul
soared among the angels in heaven, in such manner that
only a thin wall seemed to separate him from the vision
of God.[129] It appeared as if he were already at home
in the eternal mansions,[130] and as if the harmonies of
eternity were echoing in his prayerful soul.

The dominant notes to which his spirit of prayer was
attuned, were *love* and *praise*.

That the piety of Francis was born of his *love of God,*
need but be intimated here. We have already shown in
the first chapters of our book,[131] that he was a knight of
the love of God, and that his entire life was one long
prayer of love. All that has been said of his piety may be
here recapitulated in the *one* word—love: love is the secret
of the Saint's life of prayer; love is the strain that ever
quivers through all his practises of prayer; and if we are
to designate his spirit of prayer as affective and direct

contemplation, it is again thereby expressed that the
dominant note of his piety is above all things a burning
and overwhelming love of God.   This is universally
pointed out as the characteristic trait of the Saint.   "In-
toxicated with divine love," the Three Companions declare.[132]   "Glowing with divine love," he is described by
Thomas of Celano.[133]   "If he but heard the word of the
love of God mentioned, he immediately became moved,
warmed, inflamed, as though one had struck the hidden
chords of his heart and set them in vibration." [134]   "Who
can describe the fervor of the love with which Francis,
the friend of the Bridegroom, burned!" exclaims St.
Bonaventure.   "Like a glowing coal he appeared to be
wholly consumed by the flame of divine love." [135]   "He
was wholly seraphic in the fire of his love," sings the Poet
of the "Divine Comedy." [136] The whole world therefore
accords him the title "the Seraphic Francis."

Because of his love of God, his life and his prayer were
a continuous *praise of God*.

As the profane jongleurs proclaimed the glory of their
heroes, so this spiritual troubadour of Assisi wished to
announce God's glory and God's greatness to all the world.
Scarcely had he heard the first call to the knighthood of
Christ, than he appeared as a minstrel of Christ and began
to sing through field and forest the praise of his Creator
in the tongue of the Provençal troubadours.[137]   Shortly
afterward he felt called upon to promote the honor of his
Lord by restoring poor and ruined churches.   For this
purpose he traversed the streets of his native town, singing and praising God as though carried out of his senses.
When he had finished his song, he would beg from door
to door, and begin anew the praises of the Lord.[138] After
the first brothers had joined his company, he sent them out
to preach, two by two.   He himself, together with Brother
Giles, bent his steps toward the Marches, singing in a loud
and clear voice the praise of God and the goodness of the
Most High.[139]   Thus he continued during his whole life.

Often words failed him to express his love and enthusiasm for God. At such times he imitated some musical instrument, singing and playing to the glory of God, as the knightly minstrels were wont to do.[140]

Whenever he was wrapt in ecstasy, as it happened at times, the brothers were instructed to praise God in the meantime and to pray to the Lord for him.[141] Without end he urged them to praise the Most High. Their whole life was to be such that it served as a hymn of praise and moved others to glorify God.[142] Once he stopped amid a downpour of rain in an open field and wrote to the brothers, urging them to sing joyously to the Holy Trinity: "Let us bless the Father and the Son and the Holy Ghost." [143] Another time he sent them the written message: "You shall so announce and preach His praise to all people that at every hour and when the bells are rung, praise and thanks shall always be given to the almighty God by all the people through the whole earth." [144] And another time he addressed a "Letter to All the Faithful" with the request: "Let us love God and adore Him and offer Him praises by day and by night. . . . O how glorious and holy and great to have a Father in heaven! O how holy, fair and lovable to have a Spouse in heaven! O how holy and how beloved, well pleasing and humble, peaceful and sweet and desirable above all to have such a Brother who has laid down His life for His sheep. . . . And since He has suffered so many things for us and has done and will do so much for us, let every creature which is in heaven and on earth and in the sea and in the abysses, render praise to God and glory and honor and benediction; for He is our strength and power who alone is good, alone most high, alone almighty and admirable, glorious and alone holy, praiseworthy and blessed without end forever and ever. Amen." [145]

Thus he molded his life and that of his brothers into one great prayer of praise. This applies all the more to his special devotions. They are, as has been explained, focused as much on the praise as on the love of God.[146] Yet, not content with this, he wished to frame, as it were, all religious exercises with specially composed prayers, which in the full sense of the word are canticles of praise (*Laudes Dei*), and were thus called by him.

Before every Hour of the three Offices said by him daily ; that is, the canonical Office, the Office of the Blessed Virgin, and the Office of the Passion, he recited the *Laudes Dei*,[147] which are as follows :

Holy, holy, holy Lord, God almighty, who is and who was and who is to come. Let us praise and exalt Him above all forever !

Worthy art Thou, O Lord, our God, to receive praise, glory and honor and benediction. Let us praise and exalt Him above all forever !

The Lamb that was slain is worthy to receive power and divinity and wisdom and strength and honor and benediction. Let us praise and exalt Him above all forever !

Let us bless the Father and the Son and the Holy Ghost. Let us praise and exalt Him above all forever !

All ye works of the Lord, bless ye the Lord. Let us praise and exalt Him above all forever !

Give praise to God, all ye His servants and you that fear Him, little and great. Let us praise and exalt Him above all forever !

Let the heavens and the earth praise Him, the Glorious, and every creature which is in heaven and on the earth and under the earth, and in the seas and all that are in them. Let us praise and exalt Him above all forever !

Glory be to the Father and to the Son and to the Holy Ghost. Let us praise and exalt Him above all forever !

As it was in the beginning, is now, and ever shall be, world without end. Amen. Let us praise and exalt Him above all forever ! [148]

To this he added the oration: "Almighty, most holy, most high and supreme God, highest good, all good, wholly good, who alone art good. To Thee we render all praise, all glory, all thanks, all honor, all blessing, and we shall always refer all good to Thee. Amen." [149] At the conclusion of the Office he added: "Let us praise the Lord, the living and true God. Let us always render to Him praise and glory and honor and benediction and all good! Amen. Amen. Fiat! Fiat!" [150]

Two years before his death, when he had just been blessed with the Stigmata of the Crucified, he wrote, out of the endless gratitude of his heart, a "Praise of God," "a Te Deum, than which a more glowing was never sung:" [151]

Tu es sanctus Dominus Deus solus, qui facis mirabilia.

Tu es fortis. Tu es magnus. Tu es altissimus.

Tu es Rex omnipotens, tu Pater sancte, Rex cœli et terræ.

Tu es trinus et unus Dominus Deus, omne bonum.

Tu es bonum omne bonum, summum bonum, Dominus Deus, vivus et verus.

Tu es caritas amor.
Tu es sapientia.
Tu es humilitas.
Tu es patientia.
Tu es securitas.
Tu es quietas.
Tu es gaudium et lætitia.

Thou art holy, Lord God, who alone workest wonders.

Thou art strong. Thou art great. Thou art most high.

Thou art the almighty King, Thou, holy Father, King of heaven and earth.

Thou art the Lord God, Triune and One, all good.

Thou art good, all good, highest good, Lord God, living and true.

Thou art charity, love.
Thou art wisdom.
Thou art humility.
Thou art patience.
Thou art security.
Thou art quietude.
Thou art joy and gladness.

Tu es iustitia et temperantia.

Thou art j u s t i c e and temperance.

Tu es omnia divitia ad sufficientiam.

Thou art all riches to sufficiency.

Tu es pulchritudo.

Thou art beauty.

Tu es mansuetudo.

Thou art meekness.

Tu es protector.

Thou art protector.

Tu es custos et defensor.

Thou art guardian and defender.

Tu es fortitudo.

Thou art strength.

Tu es refrigerium.

Thou art refreshment.

Tu es spes nostra.

Thou art our hope.

Tu es fides nostra.

Thou art our faith.

Tu es magna dulcedo nostra.

Thou art our great sweetness.

Tu es vita æterna nostra, m a g n u s et admirabilis Dominus Deus omnipotens, misericors Salvator.

Thou art our eternal life, great and admirable Lord God almighty, merciful Saviour." [152]

Francis never ceased to sing these canticles of praise to God even when his bodily infirmities had become almost unbearable. On the contrary, his spirit became more resigned to God, more united to God, more joyous in God. In his last days he continuously sang the praises of God and taught his disciples to praise and bless Christ the Lord. All other creatures he also called upon to praise God, and urged them to love God; and he requested to have the Canticle of the Sun, which he had composed in the midst of his suffering,[153] sung again and again, that sublime song of praise which he himself entitled "The New Canticle of Praise of the Creatures of the Lord." [154]

CHAPTER XIX

FRANCIS AND NATURE

THAT Francis possessed a *love of nature* of rare tenderness and vividness, is beyond the need of proof. The oft-repeated assertion that the early Middle Ages had no eye for the beauties of nature, is a gross exaggeration,[1] and it is utterly false to ascribe the awakening of the sense of the natural to the Renaissance.[2] The first impetus was already given by the Poverello of Assisi.[3] Long before Dante, Boccaccio and Petrarch penned their immortal verses, Francis had walked through nature, carried away with ecstatic joy and with wonderment at the charming scene of hill and dale, at the beauty of flower and animal, at the majesty of the inanimate elements. In him were united all the qualities of the thoughtful observer and sensitive friend of nature: the innocent eye of a child, the lively fancy and the heightened sensibility of a poet,[4] and the joyful, loving, godly heart of a saint. Important as the two first qualities are, nevertheless the third is the very root of his joy in the things of nature and of his love of nature. *His entire relation to nature is essentially religious.* It begins and ends with nature's God. It may be condensed in the two words: *from Creator to creature,* and *from creature to Creator.*

1. From *Creator to creature.* Not the manifold attraction and beauties of nature itself, nor yet the personal temperament of the Saint, but his *all-embracing love of God* must be assigned as the source of his love of nature. The *Speculum perfectionis* expresses this in the words: "Entirely absorbed in the love of God, the Blessed Francis

saw the goodness of God reflected in every creature in a perfect manner, and because of this he was devoted to created things with a special and heartfelt love." [5]

Thoroughly imbued himself with the consciousness of being a child of God, he considered all his fellow-creatures as his kin, as members of the *one, great family of God*. In all of them he marveled at the wisdom, power and goodness of the Creator.[6] A mere glance at the sun or the moon and stars, at creatures great or small, filled him with inexpressible joy.[7]

And because all came from God, all entered into the closest kinship with him. To him all were *Brothers* and *Sisters*. No matter how small, lowly and insignificant they were, his eye penetrated into the deepest meaning of all things earthly, into the very essence of every creature, reaching the last and Supreme Cause of all things; and in consequence there rose from his heart naturally and spontaneously the name: "Brother, Sister in God, the Creator and Father of all things." [8] Nor was this name an empty sound; it was the expression of the deepest conviction, or rather, of the plain reality as he saw it. He felt the closest kinship to all created things. Not only human beings, but also irrational animals, everything that crept and moved upon the earth, even lifeless things he loved and cherished with every fiber of his heart.[9] As if by instinct he felt urged to protect all, to help all. He could not suffer to see even the least of them hurt or mis-treated, were it only by an offensive word.[10]

Thus he flung around the world a *bond of blessed harmony* similar to that which existed between man and nature at the dawn of Creation. His love-call resounded throughout the entire sense-world and was echoed back to him in the loving esteem and obedience of all nature. His association with the *animals* especially was vested with all the magic charm of this sweet harmony. A few instances will suffice for illustration.

Once the Saint came to the little town of Alviano to

preach the word of God. He mounted an elevated place in order that all might see him; he then signaled for quiet. The people held their peace and stood about reverently; but a multitude of swallows twittered noisily nearby, building their nests. When the noise became so loud that Francis could not be heard by the people, he turned to the birds and said: "My Sisters Swallows, it is time now for me to speak, you have spoken enough. Listen to the word of God and be still and peaceful until the sermon is over." And lo! the birds ceased their twittering, and did not even move from their places until the sermon was ended, to the utter amazement of the people.[11]

A nobleman from the vicinity of Siena once sent a pheasant to the man of God while he was ill. The latter accepted it joyfully, not because he had any thought of eating it, but because he always found delight in such beautiful animals. He then said to the pheasant: "Praised be our Creator, Brother Pheasant!" Then turning to the brothers he said: "Now we shall see whether Brother Pheasant prefers to remain with us or to fly back to his haunts, because they please him more." A brother was charged by Francis to set the fowl down in the vineyard; but the bird flew back straightway to the hut of the Saint. Then Francis ordered it to be carried still farther away, yet the bird again returned to the door of the hut, slipping between the habits of the brothers, who were blocking the doorway, in order to reach Francis.[12]

On another occasion, while Francis was staying at Greccio, a man brought him a hare which had been caught alive in a snare. Francis gazed at it kindly, and said compassionately: "Brother Hare, come to me. Why didst thou allow thyself to be so outwitted?" The brother, who was holding the hare, set it free, and it immediately sprang into the arms of the Saint, hiding itself in his loving embrace. After it had rested there awhile, Francis fondled it as a mother would fondle her child, and then set it down that it might escape to its home in the woods.

Yet, as often as he set it down on the ground, it sprang back into his arms, until Francis finally commanded the brothers to carry it back to the woods. A similar incident is related in regard to a wild rabbit, while the Saint was staying on an island in the lake of Perugia.[13]

Francis showed the same loving kindness toward the fishes. Those which had been caught alive he would toss back into the water, with the warning not to let themselves be caught again. One day he was sitting in a boat on the lake of Rieti, and a fisherman brought to the Saint, as a token of his esteem, a large fish which he had caught. Francis accepted the fish joyfully and kindly, called it his Brother Fish, and began to sing aloud the praises of God. He then placed the fish in the water alongside of the boat, and as long as the Saint remained in prayer, the fish hovered near the boat, playing in the water, until the Saint granted it leave to swim away.[14]

Another time, he entered a boat to ferry across the same lake to his beloved hermitage of Greccio. The ferryman offered him a water-fowl, which he had just captured. Francis took it into his hands, stroked it gently for a while, and then opened his hands to let it fly away. The fowl would not leave him, however, but nestled down into his palms; Francis, lifting up his eyes, was lost in prayer. After a long time he returned to himself as from a distance, and in sweet tones he assured the bird not to fear, but to return to its haunts. It lingered until he had blessed it, then with evident signs of joy it soared aloft and flew away.[15]

To these and similar historical incidents, legendary tradition has added others which are not authenticated, or at least not sufficiently so as to be accepted as genuine. We mention only the well-known anecdote of the Wolf of Gubbio, as related in the Fioretti. It is no easy task to separate fact from fiction in this tale. It is certain that Francis fearlessly encountered the wolf in the vicinity of Gubbio,[16] and that on another occasion he freed the

ST. FRANCIS AND THE WOLF OF GUBBIO

neighborhood of Greccio from the wolf scourge.[17]   And
since at that time this scourge was regarded as a serious
calamity, than which a more dreaded could hardly befall
the countryside, the love of Francis for animals and his
power over them, springing from this love, was perhaps
typically expressed in the charmingly poetic and popular
legend "Of the Most Fierce Wolf Who Was Converted by
Francis to the Greatest Tameness." [18]

Even the *lifeless elements* were drawn into the magic
circle of the Saint's love. When in great need, the miracle
of the multiplication of the loaves was repeated at his
word,[19] water was changed into wine,[20] springs gushed
forth from the barren rock,[21] and fire lost its fierce power.
When suffering with a grievous illness of his eyes at
Fonte Colombo near Rieti, the Saint had to submit to the
cruel operation of cauterization with a glowing iron. Before undergoing the ordeal, he consoled his body, shrink-
ing with fear, and thus spoke to the fire : "Brother Fire, the
Most High has made thee most strong, beautiful and
useful beyond all other elements. Be merciful, then, to
me in this hour, be kind, because I have always loved thee
in God. I implore the great God who created thee, that
He may moderate thy ardor, so that thou mayest burn
mildly and I may be able to bear thy heat." With this he
made the sign of the cross over the fire and was ready for
the operation. The physician took the iron glowing to a
white heat and applied it to the Saint. Sizzling it sank
into the tender flesh and burned away a strip from the ear
to the eye. Francis bore it without a tremor. When the
brothers, who had fled in terror at the sight, returned, he
addressed them smilingly : "O ye fearsome cowardlings,
why did you flee? I assure you that I felt neither the
torture of the fire nor any other pain," and turning to the
physician : "If it is not well, apply the iron again."
Utterly amazed, the latter exclaimed : "I have witnessed a
miracle today !" The biographer remarks : "I believe that

he had returned to the primitive condition of innocence, to whose will heartless nature showed itself merciful." [22]

In fact, the relation of the Saint toward animate as well as inanimate nature appears to us as a scene from *Paradise Regained*. Something akin to the condition of man before the Fall lends its potent charm to the world of Francis and his Friars. Toward this man with the heart of gold, with the heart pulsating with brotherly love toward all creatures because of his love toward the Maker of all, animals know no fear or dread. They serve and obey him, and even the elements are subject to his bidding. "It is marvelous," remarks his first biographer, "that even irrational creatures recognized the fondness of Francis for them and felt the power of his most sweet love." [23] "They endeavored to repay the Saint for his love and to prove themselves duly grateful. If he caressed them, they seemed to smile; if he requested anything of them, they acquiesced; if he commanded them, they obeyed." [24]

At times this docility of creatures appeared as the natural echo of the Saint's love for them, and again it seemed the supernatural and directly miraculous reward of his love of nature. The basis and the cause of this mutual relation is the Saint's love of God. All the biographers of Francis are one on this point. "It is not to be wondered at that all creatures honored him who so loved their Creator," says Thomas of Celano.[25] And elsewhere: "The glorious Father Francis trod the way of obedience so faithfully and bore the yoke of subjection to God so perfectly that the obedience of creatures became the signal mark of favor on the part of God." [26]   Bonaventure likewise: "Since the man of God had attained to such a degree of purity that his flesh was subject to his spirit, and his spirit to God in a wonderful harmony and agreement, it came to pass by divine disposition that all creatures were thus in marvelous subjection to his will and command, who was himself the faithful servant of the Creator." [27]   The singer Julian of Speyer, shortly after the death of the Saint, expressed the same thought in the beautiful lines:

> "Hic creaturis imperat,
> Qui nutui subiecerat
> Se totum Creatoris;
> Quicquid in rebus repperit
> Delectamenti regerit
> In gloriam Factoris." [28]

2. From *creation to the Creator*.   In the same measure as the love of God led the Saint to nature, *nature in return led him to God*.   The word of the Psalmist became to him an actual experience: "O Lord our Lord, how admirable is thy name in the whole earth!" [29]   At every turn he beheld the truth of the word of St. Paul that God's eternal power and majesty, although invisible, yet manifests itself in the realms of creation, whose very existence and perfection proclaims the eternal perfections of the Creator.[30] Every being became to him a guide on the way to the fatherland; in every masterpiece of creation he praised the Eternal Artist; the entire universe was as a mirror reflecting the love of God.[31]   He rejoiced in all things made by the hand of God, and in the things so joyously beheld, he recognized the life-giving Infinite Mind and Cause.   In all things beautiful he saw the Source of all beauty; from all things good he heard the voice calling to him: "He who has created us is the Sovereign Good." In the footprints impressed on all creatures he followed everywhere his Beloved; out of created things he fashioned a ladder that led upward to the throne of God.[32]

Those objects that served as *symbols of the Son of God* he prized with special affection.[33]   They spurred him on anew to knightly service of Christ, who to him was the Sovereign Lord.[34]

Christ called Himself "the Light of the world," [35] and said: "I came to cast fire on the earth, and what will I but that it burn." [36]   Even in themselves fire and light are

so beautiful and so useful that they reflect most clearly the
divine beauty and generosity. For this reason Francis
loved fire and light above all created things, and would
never hinder their activity.[37] He would never extinguish
a burning light, lamp or candle, because his hand should
not smother the gleam which was a symbol of the Eternal
Light.[38] Once when he sat near the hearth, his habit
caught fire. A brother hastened to extinguish the blaze,
but Francis begged: "Dearest Brother, do not injure
Brother Fire." He would never permit a torch or partly
burned piece of wood to be thrown away. They had to
be laid carefully on the ground out of reverence for Him
whose creatures they were.[39]

Christ called Himself "the Living Water, the Fountain
which flows unto eternal life"; He made water the symbol
of spiritual purification, and with it instituted the sacrament of Baptism. The Saint accordingly prized this element second only to fire.[40] Whenever he washed his
hands, he did so in a place where the waste water could
not be trodden under foot.[41]

In the Sacred Scriptures Christ is called the Rock.[42]
Francis was ever mindful of this when he walked over
stones. He stepped on them as lightly as possible out of
reverence for his Lord. When he came across the Psalm
verse: "Thou liftest me up onto a rock," [43] he read instead with great devotion: "Thou hast exalted me under
my feet," for he did not wish to raise himself above the
rocks which were to him symbols of the Saviour.[44]

Christ died on the wood of the cross, and again Holy
Writ says: "A tree hath hope; if it be cut, it groweth
green again, and the boughs thereof sprout." [45] For this
reason Francis prevented the brothers, when cutting trees,
from destroying them completely, in order that they still
might have a chance of growing again.[46]

Of Christ it is written: "I am the Flower of the field
and the Lily of the valley." [47] Flowers are, as it were,
relics of the carpet of paradise on which the Eternal trod

when He walked the earth. It is indescribable with what exquisite joy Francis beheld their beauty, considered their fair features, and enjoyed their delightful odors. At once his eyes were lifted to that glorious Blossom which sprouted forth from the rod of Jesse in the springtime, [48] whose fragrance has restored to new life thousands and thousands of the dead.[49] He accordingly ordered the gardener not to plant vegetables everywhere, but to leave free spaces round about the garden where greening herbs and pretty flowers might speak of the dear Father who is in heaven. He always had one bed set aside in every garden for fragrant and flowering plants that they might remind the beholders of the everlasting bliss of heaven.[50]

The Saviour exclaims in the words of the Psalmist: "I am a worm and no man." [51] Reason enough for Francis to love the worms with tender affection. He would lift them carefully from the ground and lay them in a safe place, that they might not be crushed by those passing by.[52]

His wonder and admiration knew no bounds when he saw bees at work. They were to him the reflection of the Infinite Wisdom. Their remarkable sagacity and artistic structures carried him away to loud praise of the Lord, at times spending a whole day in their praise. During the winter he had honey and the best wine placed in their hives, that they might not suffer from the cold.[53]

Most tenderly, however, he loved the lambs, because Christ is the Lamb of God which takes away the sins of the world,[54] and because they typify the meekness and humility of the Saviour.[55] At one time the Saint was staying at the monastery of St. Verecundus near Gubbio. In the same night a sheep gave birth to a lamb, which was soon afterward devoured by a wild sow. Francis, on hearing of this unfortunate incident, was moved to great pity, and, thinking of the Spotless Lamb of God, bewailed the death of the lambkin and said: "O my Brother Lamb, innocent little creature, who remindest men of Christ!

Cursed be the wild beast that devoured thee; neither man
nor beast shall eat of its flesh!" Wonderful to say, the
sow sickened forthwith and died after three days, the car-
cass being thrown into the ditch near the monastery.
There it lay a long time, dried out completely, and no animal touched it.[56]

Passing one day through the March of Ancona he
espied in the fields a shepherd holding watch over a flock
of goats and rams. Among these was a little lamb which
meekly ran alongside the flock and nibbled quietly.
When Francis saw this, he slackened his pace and said to
Brother Paul who was accompanying him: "Seest thou
that little lamb which grazes so peacefully among the
goats and rams? Thus Our Lord Jesus Christ walked
mild and meek among the Pharisees. I charge thee, therefore, my son, out of love toward Him to have pity on
this poor little lamb even as I, to buy it and lead it out
of that company of goats and rams." Brother Paul
marveled at the sympathy of his Father and was likewise
overcome with pity. But having nothing except their
poor habits, they knew not where to obtain the purchase
price. Luckily a traveling merchant just then happened
along and gave them the money needed for the purchase
of the lamb. Accompanied by Brother Lamb they continued their way toward the city of Osimo. There Francis
preached on the parable of the lamb and Christ, the Lamb
of God.[57]

On another occasion he was traveling through the same
country when he met a man on the way to the market with
two lambs hanging trussed from his shoulders. The
servant of God heard the little creatures bleating, and was
profoundly moved. He approached the man, stroked the
lambs, and showed as tender sympathy as a mother toward her weeping child. He then said to the man:
"Brother, why dost thou plague my little lambs so, trussing
and hanging them up?" The latter answered: "I am
carrying them to the market in order to sell them. I am

in sore need of money." The Saint replied. "And what
will become of them?" The man rejoined: "The buyers
will slaughter them and eat them." "That shall not be,"
answered the Saint. "Here, take this mantle which I have,
and give me the lambs." The man agreed and the deal
was closed. Francis now had the lambs, but he was at a
loss what to do with them. Finally he returned them to
the man, but insisted that he was not to sell them again,
nor to harm them in any way, but to keep them and care
for them.[58] In this manner Francis frequently redeemed
lambs that were being led to the shambles, out of love to
that meek Lamb who allowed himself to be led to the
slaughter for the redemption of sinners.[59]

Theology recognizes in the devout reflection on the
works of God, no less than in the study of the supernatural truths of religion, a means to, and a gauge of
contemplative life.[60] Francis was a past master of this
genuine mysticism of nature. The consideration of the
universe with everything in it which lives and moves and
breathes, that glitters and glows and gleams, stirred him
to deepest devotion. At every step he heard the thousand-
fold Sursum Corda echoing from the works of creation,
filling him with the knowledge, the praise, and the love
of God.

But he, too, sang his ceaseless Sursum Corda into the
heart of creation. As nature led him to God, so he in
return *led it to God*. With the simplicity of a dove he
urged every creature to love its Maker.[61] As the Three
Young Men in the fiery furnace called upon the elements
of the universe to honor and praise the Father of all
things, so too this friend of God never tired of praising,
loving and blessing the Author and Preserver in all the
elements and in every living thing.[62] With unheard-of
intimacy he pressed these his Brothers and Sisters to his
heart and conversed with them of God.[63] When he came
upon a meadow sown with flowers, he preached to them
and invited them to praise the Lord as though they pos-

sessed reason. The swaying grain fields, and vineyards, rocks and woods, smiling pastures and babbling brooks, earth, fire, air and wind—all, everything he admonished in the crystal purity of his heart to love and praise and serve God with joy.[64]

The animals, above all, that were naturally nearer to him than the other creatures, and which had been endowed more highly by the Creator, he admonished to be the more grateful to God and the more ready to serve Him.

At Portiuncula a lamb was one time presented to him. He exhorted it to pay heed to the praise of God and not to disturb the brothers in their prayers. The little creature carefully followed this instruction. For when it heard the Friars chanting in the choir, it also went into the church, bent its knees, and remained in this position, as if to repair the irreverence of the ungodly, and to spur on the devout to honor the Holy Sacrament.[65]

While living in his hermitage he became a close friend of a falcon which was building its eyrie nearby. Each night the bird would sing its carol before the Saint rose for Matins. Francis rejoiced at this exceedingly, for it prevented him from missing the time appointed for prayer. Once when he was very ill, the falcon spared him and did not announce the hour as early and as loudly as usual. Only at the first streak of dawn, and as if instructed from on high, it began to sound the clarion call to prayer.[66]

Near the cell of the Saint at Portiuncula a cricket sat on a fig-tree, chirping in its familiar, homely way. At times Francis would stretch out his hand toward it and say: "My Sister Cricket, come here to me!" And the little creature would climb into his hand. He then said to it: "Sing, Sister Cricket, and praise the Lord, thy Creator, with thy joyful tones." It obeyed immediately and began to chirp, not ceasing until the Saint, who had joined it in a song of praise, bade it return to its accustomed perch. There it remained, as if glued to the spot,

for eight days. Whenever the Saint came down from his
cell, he would caress it with his hand and bid it to sing
the praises of its Creator, and forthwith the cricket would
do his bidding. Finally the Saint said to his companions:
"Let us now grant a furlough to our Sister Cricket; for
she has enlivened us long enough with her praises of God."
The cricket, now granted leave, went away, and never
again appeared.[67]

One day Francis was passing through the valley of
Spoleto. Drawing near to Bevagna he came to a place
where a large flock of birds, pigeons, crows and jackdaws
were assembled. He went up to them and greeted them
as his Sisters, as was his custom. He was not a little
astonished that the birds did not take alarm and prepare
for flight as usual, and filled with joy he bade them hear
the word of God. Among other things he said to them:
"My feathered Sisters, you especially ought to praise your
Creator, since He has given you down for your raiment
and wings for flight. Among all His creatures God has
created you most wonderfully, and has allotted the pure
air for your element: you neither sow nor reap, and in
spite of this He protects and guides you without the least
care on your part." At these words the birds began to
show their joy after their fashion, stretching their necks,
spreading their wings, and looking at him with gaping
beaks. Francis then passed up and down among them
and stroked them with the hem of his habit on their heads
and backs. Finally he blessed them with the sign of the
cross and bade them fly away. He then departed with
his brothers from the place, praising and thanking God,
whom all creatures honor in their way. In his simplicity
of heart he began to chide himself for not having preached
to the birds long before. And from that time on he was
accustomed to invite all the birds, the quadrupeds, the
reptiles and all inanimate creatures to love and praise
their Creator.[68]

"Laudans laudare monuit,
Laus illi semper affuit,
Laus, inquam, Salvatoris.
Invitat aves, bestias,
Et creaturas alias
Ad laudem Conditoris." [69]

When at last his bodily eyes were closed to the beauties of the external world, his inspired and blissful love of nature became all the more interior, clarified and fervent. He became all the more mindful of the countless benefits and comforts which he had received from creatures all his life. His soul was overwhelmed with gratitude and joy. He struck the full chords of his poetic heart and sang "The Praises of the Creatures," in order that all the world might be moved to the praise of God, and that all men might honor God in His creation.[70]

Just as his pious love of nature ever found its source in God and reverted to God, so now, in this Canticle, he sinks before God into the very dust and confesses His infinite majesty and his own nothingness. He then lifts up the eye of his soul to the lordly sun, because it is more beautiful and beneficial than all other creatures, and because it is the image and the symbol of the Lord, whose countenance shines like the sun,[71] and who calls Himself the Sun of Justice.[72] With Brother Sun, the Sisters Stars and Moon announce the goodness and greatness of the Eternal. And wind and tempest, clouds and air, how beneficent they show themselves to their fellow-creatures in the vault of heaven and on earth below, how loudly they call into the fathomless spaces their praise of God! And Sister Water, so useful and humble and sweet and pure, and Brother Fire, so beautiful and joyful and strong and mighty, and Mother Earth, so loving in her care for man and beast and herb and flower: water and fire and earth and all that it bears and nourishes, should praise the Lord! Those favorites of God also, the meek, the suffering and the lovers of peace should praise Him!

And Brother Death, who leads the world-weary children
of God back into the arms of the Creator, should praise
Him! All should praise and love and glorify the Lord!

"Most high, omnipotent, good Lord,
Praise, glory and honor and benediction all, are Thine.
To Thee alone do they belong, Most High,
And there is no man fit to mention Thee.
Praise be to Thee, my Lord, with all Thy creatures,
Especially to my worshipful Brother Sun,
The which lights up the day, and through him dost
    Thou brightness give;
And beautiful is he and radiant with splendor great;
Of Thee, Most High, signification gives.
Praised be my Lord, for Sister Moon and for the
    Stars,
In heaven Thou hast formed them clear and precious
    and fair.
Praised be my Lord for Brother Wind
And for the air and clouds and fair and every kind
    of weather,
By the which Thou givest to Thy creatures nourish-
    ment.
Praised be my Lord for Sister Water,
The which is greatly helpful and humble and precious
    and pure.
Praised be my Lord for Brother Fire,
By the which Thou lightest up the dark.
And fair is he and gay and mighty and strong.
Praised be my Lord for our Sister, Mother Earth,
The which sustains and keeps us
And brings forth diverse fruits with grass and flowers
    bright.
Praised be my Lord for those who for Thy love
    forgive
And weakness bear and tribulation.
Blessed those who shall in peace endure,
For by Thee, Most High, shall they be crowned.
Praised be my Lord for our Sister, the bodily Death,
From the which no living man can flee.
Woe to them who die in mortal sin;

Blessed those who shall find themselves in Thy most
  holy will,
For the second death shall do them no ill.
Praise ye and bless ye my Lord, and give Him
  thanks,
And be subject unto Him with great humility.
  Amen." [73]

"The Canticle of the Sun" this sunny song was called
by the Saint.[74] Like the sun it mounts to the very heavens
and lays the tribute of love and of praise of every creature
before the throne of God: "Praised be Thou, my Lord,
with all Thy creatures, praised, praised, praised. . . ."
Like the sun it should travel throughout the wide world;
wherever the Friars Minor, the Minstrels and Jongleurs
of God appeared, there should also this Canticle be en-
toned, to enthuse men thereby to the service of God and
to the true joy in God.[75] Like the sun this Canticle moved
Francis himself to utter joy and to closest union with
God in the midst of suffering; by day and by night he
had it sung unto himself during the martyrdom of his
last weeks and months.[76] And when the hour of departure struck, he added the stanza on Brother Death,[77]
and on the wings of this his swan-song he passed from
this world to the Father of all.

The Canticle of the Sun is, however, more than the
swan-song of the Saint; it is the *symbol and the genius
of his life and his Ideals.* For was he not called to be
the Knightly Herald of God? Was not every beat of his
heart a hymn of divine love? Did he not pass through
the world as a Troubadour of the Lord, singing the
chansons de geste of his Master? In a word, did he not
even in his last hour urge his brothers and disciples of
all times: "We are the Minstrels of God, who should
lift up the hearts of men, and move them to divine
joy"?[78] "Thus he molded out of humility and love his
life into a poem—he, the greatest poet that lived at the
time." [79] This life was a single, uninterrupted Canticle

of the Sun, a song of such enchanting power, of such sweet melody, that the godless and joyless world, even of to-day, after seven hundred years, is charmed by it, and can be saved by it. With this Canticle, which we with the holy Minstrel of Assisi call the Canticle of the Sun, ends the harmonious finale and the last chord of his life, so full of melody and sunshine.

BIBLIOGRAPHY

The following works will help to acquaint the student with the sources bearing on the life of St. Francis and early Franciscan history: H. Böhmer, *Analekten zur Geschichte des hl. Franziskus von Assisi* (large edition) Tübingen, Mohr 1904, LXIII-LXXII; Walter Götz, *Die Quellen zur Geschichte des hl. Franz von Assisi,* Gotha, Perthes 1904; Paul Sabatier, *Examen des quelques travaux récents sur les opuscules de St. François (opuscules de critique historique,* fascic. X), Paris, Fischbacher 1904; Léon de Kerval, *Les sources de histoirie de Saint François d'Assise,* Perouse, Unione tipographica cooperativa, 1905; G. Schnürer, *Neuere Quellenforschungen über den hl. Franz von Assisi,* in: *Historisches Jahrbuch* 1907, 10 ss. P. Gratian, O. M. Cap., *Les sources de la vie de S. François,* in: *Études franciscaines* t. XVIII (1907) 359-383; J. Jörgensen, *Der hl. Franz von Assisi,* Kempten und München, Kösel, 1908; H. Tilemann, *Studien zur Individualität des Franziskus von Assisi,* Leipzig, Teubner 1914, 6-46; P. Fidentius van den Borne, O. F. M., *Die Franziskus-Forschung in ihrer Entwicklung dargestellt,* München, Leutner 1917; Fr. Cuthbert, O. M. Cap., *Life of St. Francis,* new edition, London, Longmans, 1921, 492-527; Le Monnier, *Histoirie de S. François,* nouvelle éd., Paris, Librairie S. François, 1923, Introduction.

A critical estimate of these research works would exceed the scope of this book and bring to light very little that is new. We restrict ourselves therefore to the bare mention—with the exception of a few explanatory comments—of those sources from which we have principally or at least frequently drawn. They can be classified into the following groups: I. the writings of St. Francis; II. Biographies of Francis compiled in the 13th century; III. Compilations made by the Spirituals in the beginning of the 14th century; IV. Biographies of early companions of St. Francis; V. The earliest Franciscan chronicles; VI. Records not of Franciscan origin.

I. THE WRITINGS OF ST. FRANCIS

Edited by H. Böhmer, also by P. Leon. Lemmens, O. F. M., *Opuscula S. Patris Francisci Assisiensis,* Ad Claras Aquas

431

(Quaracchi), Collegium S. Bonaventuræ, 1904. It is noteworthy that both editions, although appearing simultaneously, contain the same text, with the exception of a few minor discrepancies. Since perhaps only one of these editions is available to the reader, we quote both, thus: *Opusc.* ed. Böhmer . . . Lemmens. . . . A German version of the *Opuscula* has been made by Fr. Maternus Rederstorff, O. F. M., Regensburg, Pustet 1910; a French version by Fr. Ubald d'Alençon, O. M. Cap., *Les Opuscules de Saint François d'Assise,* Paris, Poussielgue 1905; and an English one by Fr. Paschal Robinson, O. F. M., *The Writings of St. Francis,* Philadelphia, Dolphin Press, 1906, followed shortly after by that of Countess de la Warr, *The Writings of St. Francis,* London, Burns and Oates 1907. An Italian translation has been made by Fr. Vittorino Facchinetti, O. F. M., *San Francesco d'Assisi,* Milano 1921. These writings of St. Francis, though not extensive, are nevertheless of greatest importance in writing his story and especially for the proper estimation of his Ideals.

II. BIOGRAPHIES OF ST. FRANCIS OF THE XIIITH CENTURY

1. FR. THOMAS DE CELANO, *St. Francisci Assisiensis vita et miracula,* ed. Fr. Eduardus Alenconiensis, O. M. Cap., Romæ, Desclée, Lefèbre et Soc., 1906. For other editions cf. *Bibliotheca hagiographica latina* n. 3096 sq. 3106 sq. The *Legenda Prima* (1228/1229), the *Legenda Secunda* (1245/1247) and the *Tractatus de miraculis* (1253) by Thomas de Celano are marked by running numbers in the excellent edition of Fr. Ed. d'Alençon, so that they can be quoted very simply thus: Thom. Cel. I, n. 5=Thomæ de Celano, *Legenda Prima,* n. 5; Thom. Cel. II, n. 7=*Legenda Secunda,* n. 7; *Tract. de mir.,* n. 9=Thomæ de Celano, *Tractatus de miraculis,* n. 9. The English translation of the Celanese Legends by Dr. Rosedale, London, Dent, 1904, is of very little scientific value. The reader will find it advantageous to compare the Latin original with my quotations in the course of this book. The *Legenda Prima* was written by Celano partly in his character as witness, partly on the oral communications of other witnesses; for the *Legenda Secunda* he made use chiefly of the written records compiled by various companions of Francis, in particular of those by Brothers Leo, Angelus and Rufinus, written by order of the General Chapter of 1224.

2. LEGENDA TRIUM SOCIORUM, ed. Faloci-Pulignani, in: *Miscellanea francescana,* vol. VII, p. 81 sqq., and as a separate publication, Foligno 1898. We quote simply: *Tres Soc.* with the running number of the aforementioned edition. Regarding earlier editions

cf. *Bibliotheca hagr. lat.* n. 3114-3117. The Legend of the Three Companions originated no doubt between the years 1244 and 1246, but is not the work of the Brothers Leo, Angelus and Rufinus, as it represents at best only a fragment of the writings compiled by them. The attempt to reconstruct the entire Legend of the Three Companions made by Marcellino da Civezza and Teofilo Domenichelli, O. F. M., is a failure. *(La Legenda di San Francesco, scritta da tre suoi compagni, pubblicata per la prima volta nella sua vera integrità,* Roma, 1899). An English translation was made by Miss E. Gurney Salter, *Legend of the Three Companions,* London, Dent 1902.

3. Fr. IULIANUS A SPIRA, *Vita S. Francisci,* ed. Van Ortroy, S. J., in: *Analecta Bollandiana* t. XXI, 160-202, also *Officium S. Francisci,* ed. Fr. Hilarin Felder, O. M. Cap., *(Die liturgischen Reimoffizien auf die heiligen Franziskus und Antonius gedichtet und komponiert von Fr. Julian von Speier,* Freiburg in d. Schw. 1901). The author of this *Vita,* who died in 1250, bases his work almost exclusively on the *Legenda Prima* of Celano.

4. S. BONAVENTURA, *Legenda* (maior) *S. Francisci* ed. a PP. Collegii S. Bonaventuræ, Ad Claras Aquas, 1898. This edition is a special publication taken from t. VIII of the best known Bonaventure edition of Quaracchi, with the omission of the variants. We quote thus: S. Bonav., with chapter and number.— The General Chapter of 1260 commissioned Bonaventure with the elaboration of this comprehensive Legend; the General Chapter of 1263 approved it; the General Chapter of 1266 finally ordered the suppression of all earlier Legends for the sake of uniformity and harmony. An abridgment of this biography of S. Francis was made by Bonaventure for choir use and designated as *Legenda Minor.* The *Legenda* was done into English by Miss Lockhart, London, Washbourne, 4th ed. 1898; also by E. Gurney Salter, London, Dent, 1904.

5. Fr. BERNARDUS A BESSA, *Liber de Laudibus Beati Francisci; accedit eiusdem auctoris: Catalogus Generalium Ministrorum* ed. Fr. Hilarinus a Lucerna, O. M. Cap., Romæ, Typographia editrice industriale, 1897. Another edition appeared almost simultaneously in the *Analecta Franciscana,* t. III, 666-692.—The General Chapter of 1277 ordered the Brothers of all Provinces to collect and transmit all as yet unknown records regarding Francis and his companions. The meager returns of this inquiry were then utilized by Fr. Bernard of Bessa, a former secretary of St. Bonaventure, to compile his *Liber de Laudibus.* More important than the *Liber* itself is the appended catalogue of the first Ministers General of the Order.

6. ANONYMOUS PERUSINUS, *Legenda S. Francisci* ed. Van

Ortroy, S.J., in: *Miscellanea franciscana,* Vol. IX, Foligno 1902, p. 33 ss. This Legend was also the result of the above mentioned decree of the Chapter of 1277. Its author introduces himself in n. 2 as a "disciple of the first disciples of Francis." With the exception of a few original passages, it represents an abridged copy of the Legend of the Three Companions. According to Van Ortroy both are based on a common original source.

III. COMPILATIONS BY THE SPIRITUALS IN THE BEGINNING OF THE XIVTH CENTURY

1. SPECULUM PERFECTIONIS *status Fratris Minoris scilicet Beati Francisci* (completed 1318) ed. Sabatier, *collection de documents pour l'histoire religieuse et littéraire du Moyen-âge,* Paris, Fischbacher, 1898. The editor wrongly entitles this work: "Sancti Francisci Legenda antiquissima auctore fratre Leone." In reality the *Speculum* was composed by a Friar of Portiuncula who inclined to the Spirituals and who utilized mainly the "Rotuli" or "Cedulæ Fratris Leonis" and also the *Vita Secunda* of Thomas de Celano. We quote: *Spec. Perf.* with the running number. An English translation of the text only was made by De la Warr, London, Burns and Oates, 1902.

2. ACTUS BEATI FRANCISCI ET SOCIORUM EIUS (1322-1328) ed. Sabatier, Paris, Fischbacher, 1902, published in Italian under the name of *Fioretti di San Francesco* in countless editions and translated into numerous languages. English translation: *The Little Flowers of St. Francis,* London, Cath. Truth Society, 1912. The original of the *Actus-Fioretti* was composed probably in whole or in part by Fr. Hugolinus of Monte Georgio.

3. FR. UBERTINUS DE CASALI, *Arbor vitæ crucifixæ Jesu* (1305) impressus Venetiis per Andream de Bonettis de Papia, 1485 (an unpaged incunabulum—for this reason only book and chapter can be quoted). To the *Arbor vitæ* must be added the official writings which Ubertinus composed against the Community in the dispute regarding the observance: (1) The *Responsio,* an answer to the four contested points between the Spirituals and the Community (1310); (2) the *Rotulus,* or article of accusation against the Community (1311); finally (3) the *Declaratio,* or the reply of Ubertinus (August, 1311). These writings were published by Fr. Franz Ehrle, S.J. *(Zur Vorgeschichte des Konzils von Vienne,* in: *Archiv für Litteratur-und Kirchengeschichte des Mittelalters* III, Berlin 1887, 1-195).

4. FR. ANGELUS CLARENUS, *Expositio Regulæ Fratrum Minorum* (1318-1326) ed. P. Livarius Oliger, O. F. M., Ad Claras Aquas 1912, and *Historia septem tribulationum Ordinis Minorum* (1313-

1324), ed. Döllinger, *Beiträge zur Sektengeschichte des Mittelalters*, 2 Teil, München, Beck, 1890. We still depend on Döllinger's edition, although it is very defective. Fr. Ehrle has published only fragments of the *Historia* (in *Archiv für Lit.—und Kircheng.* II und III Band). Fr. Tocco has published as yet only the first two "Tribulations" *(le due prime tribolazioni dell' Ordine francescano,* Roma, 1908).

These compilations by the Spirituals are of great moment insofar as they were intended to embody the earliest Franciscan traditions and in part really succeed in this task. The writings or memoirs of the first disciples of Francis form the basis for the *Speculum perfectionis* and also to a great extent for the compilations of Ubertinus and Angelus. The *Actus-Fioretti* likewise contain many historically correct data. Taken as a whole, however, they are the poetical expression of the "psyche" of St. Francis and his first companions; the spirit which the *Fioretti* breathes, is without doubt the spirit of the Poverello and his first disciples.

IV. BIOGRAPHIES OF DISCIPLES OF FRANCIS

1. VITA S. ANTONII auctore anonymo, ed. Léon de Kerval, *S. Antonii de Padua vitæ duæ, quarum altera hucusque inedita,* Paris, Fischbacher, 1904. The first only of these two Lives is important, the so-called Legenda Prima or antiquissima, which was written shortly after the canonization of the Saint (1232). Concerning the earlier editions of this *Vita,* cf. *Bibliotheca hagiographica latina,* 587 sqq.

2. VITA S. CLARÆ auctore Fr. Thomæ de Celano, ed. *Acta Sanctorum,* Augusti t. II, p. 754-757. It was composed following the canonization of St. Clare (1255), and is a rich mine of material for the student of early Franciscan history. Of importance are also the *Regula Sororum Pauperum,* ed. Sbaralea, *Bullarium franciscanum* I, 671-678, and the *Letters of St. Clare,* four to Blessed Agnes of Prague *(Acta SS.,* Martii t. I, p. 505-507), and one to Sister Ermentrude in Flanders (Wadding, *Annales Minorum,* Supplementum ad a. 1257, n. 20). Cf. Fr. Paschal Robinson, O. F. M. *Life of St. Clare,* Philadelphia, Dolphin Press, 1910, for the English translation of these sources.

3. VITA B. ÆGIDII, auctore Fr. Leone, ed. *Analecta Franciscana* III, Ad Claras Aquas 1897, 74-115. Concerning this edition of the *Vita* (taken from the *Chronica XXIV. Generalium)* and also two others undertaken by Fr. Lemmens and the Bollandists, cf. Fr. Gisbert Menge, O. F. M., *Der selige Ægidius von Assisi,* Paderborn 1906, VII-XV. The *Vita* was composed shortly after the death of Brother Giles (1261). Appended to the *Vita* are the

Dicta B. Ægidii, a collection of truly golden sayings of Brother Giles, gathered by companions of the Blessed and rendered available by Fr. Gisbert Menge in a critical Latin edition *(Dicta B. Ægidii Assis. secundum codd. mss. emendata et denuo edita a PP. Collegii S. Bonav.,* Ad Claras Aquas, 1905) and in a good German translation *(Der selige Ægidius,* Paderborn, 1906, 63-94). Fr. Paschal Robinson has given us an excellent English translation, *The Golden Sayings of Brother Giles,* Philadelphia, Dolphin Press, 1907.

V. THE EARLIEST FRANCISCAN CHRONICLES

1. CHRONICA FR. IORDANI DE JANO, ed. Böhmer, Paris, Fischbacher, 1908. The earlier editions by G. Voigt *(Abhandlungen der kgl. sächsischen Gesellschaft der Wissenschaften zu Leipzig* t. VI, 1870), and by the Collegium S. Bonaventuræ *(Analecta franc.* t. I), are lacking in completeness and accuracy. Although written as late as 1262, the Chronicle of Fr. Jordan is of great value, since its author became a Franciscan as early as 1217 or 1218, and consequently is an eye-witness to most events which he chronicles.

2. TRACTATUS FR. THOMÆ DE ECCLESTON *de Adventu Fratrum Minorum in Angliam,* ed. A. G. Little, Paris, Fischbacher, 1909. Earlier editions by Brewer *(Monumenta franciscana* I, London, 1858), Howlett *(Monum. franc.* II, London, 1882) and Collegium S. Bonaventuræ *(Analecta franciscana* I). Fr. Thomas of Eccleston joined the Friars about 1232 and completed his chronicle 1258-1259. He was for the main part an eye-witness of the chronicled events. English translation by Fr. Cuthbert, O. M. Cap., *The Chronicle of Thomas of Eccleston,* London, 1909.

3. CHRONICA FR. SALIMBENE DE ADAM, ed. Holder-Egger, *Monumenta Germaniæ historica, Scriptores* t. XXXII, Hannoveræ et Lipsiæ, 1905-1913. Before this edition, only the greatly abridged text of Bertani, *Chronica Fr. Salimbene Parmensis,* O. M., Parmæ 1857, was available. Fr. Salimbene was born 1221, joined the Friars in 1238, and completed his chronicle about 1288.

VI. RECORDS AND REPORTS NOT OF FRANCISCAN ORIGIN

1. PAPAL DOCUMENTS relating to the origin of the Franciscan Order, ed. Sbaralea, *Bullarium franciscanum* t. I and II, Romæ, 1759 and 1761.

2. IACOBI VITRIACENSIS de B. Francisci eiusque societate testimonia, ed. Böhmer, *Analekten zur Geschichte des Franziskus von*

Assisi, p. 94-106: two letters of Cardinal Jacques de Vitry written in 1216 and 1220 respectively, likewise a chapter of his *Historia orientalis,* written 1223-1226. To these are added: *Iacobi Vitria-censis sermones ad Fratres Minores duo,* ed. Fr. Hilarin Felder, Romæ, 1903, composed between 1228 and 1240.

3. TESTIMONIA MINORA SÆCULI XIII de S. P. Francisco, ed. Fr. Leonard Lemmens, O. F. M., *Archivum franc. historic.* I, 68-84; an excellent compilation and evaluation of the Franciscan texts of THOMAS OF SPALATO (died 1222), BURCHARD OF URSPERG (died 1230), ROGER OF WENDOVER (died 1236), WALTER OF GISBURNE and others. To these must be added several passages relating to Francis in STEPHANUS DE BORBONE, O.P., *Tractatus de diversis rebus prædicabilibus* (composed before 1260), ed. Lecoy de la Marche, *Anecdotes historiques, légendes et apologues tirés de recueil inédit d'Etienne de Bourbon, Dominicain de XIIIe siècle,* Paris, Renouard, 1877.

NOTES

CHAPTER I

1. Thus Thom. Cel. I, n. 21; II, n. 2; S. Clara, Regula sororum pauperum c. 6, Sbaralea, *Bullar. Francisc.* I, 674; Iordanus a Iano, *Chron.* n. 1.

2. Cf. *The Rule of St. Benedict* c. 58, also the copious references in Ducange-Carpenterius, *Glossarium mediæ et infimæ latinitatis, s. v.* "Conversio." St. Clare of Assisi likewise (*loc. cit.* c. 1) designates her embracing of religious life as a conversion.

3. Thom. Cel. I, n. 3–22; II, n. 3–14; *Tres Soc.* n. 3–25.

4. *Testamentum, Opusc.* ed. Böhmer 36, Lemmens 77.

5. Thom. Cel. I, n. 1–3; *Tres Soc.* n. 1–2.

6. *Tres Soc.* n. 3. Cf. Thom. Cel. II, n. 3.

7. H. Tilemann, *Studien zur Individualität des Franziskus von Assisi* Leipzig-Berlin, 1914, 201.

8. Thom. Cel. I, n. 2. 9. *Tres Soc.* n. 2.

10. Thom. Cel. II, n. 4; *Tres Soc.* n. 4. For the date of the captivity, cf. Pennacchi, *L'anno della prigionia di S. Francesco in Perugia,* Perugia 1915.

11. See Chapter II. 12. Thom. Cel. I, n. 3–4. 13. Thom. Cel. I, n. 5; *Tres Soc.* n. 5. 14. *Tres Soc. ibid.* 15. *Tres Soc.* n. 6. Cf. p. 21. 16. *Tres Soc.* n. 7. 17. *Tres Soc.* n. 8; Thom. Cel. I, n. 6. 18. Thom. Cel. I, n. 6. 19. Cf. Thom. Cel. I, n. 2 with n. 6–7. 20. Thom. Cel. I, n. 7. 21. *Loc. cit.* n. 7. 22. Cf. Thom. Cel. I, n. 21.

23. Thom. Cel. I, n. 8–21; *Tres Soc.* n. 8–25.

24. *Testament., Opusc.* ed. Böhmer 36 sq., Lemmens 77 sq.

25. Concerning the greatly uncertain chronology of St. Francis cf. Fr. Leone Patrem, *Cronologia di S. Francesco,* in: *Miscellanea franciscana* Vol. IX (1902), fasc. 3; Böhmer, *Analekten,* Tübingen 1904, 123 ff.; Fr. Paschal Robinson, *Quo anno Ordo fratrum Minorum inceperit,* in: *Archivum franciscanum historicum* II (1909), 181–196; Enrico Pessina, *Cronologia francescana, esposizione storico-cronologica della Vita di S. Francesco d'Assisi,* Napoli 1918; P. Dominic Mandic, *De protoregula Fratrum Minorum,* Mostar 1923.

26. Thom. Cel. I, n. 22; *Tres Soc.* n. 25; S. Bonav. c. 3, n. 1.

27. *Tres Soc.* n. 28 sq.; Thom. Cel. I, n. 24; II, n. 15; *Vita fr. Ægidii, Anal. franc.* III, 75; S. Bonav. c. 3, n. 3–4.

28. *Tres Soc.* n. 29.

29. Thom. Cel. I, n. 32 sq.; II, n. 16 sq.; *Tres Soc.* n. 46–51.

30. *Testamentum, Opusc.* ed. Böhmer 37, Lemmens 79.

31. Thom. Cel. I, n. 32; *Tres. Soc.* n. 51. 32. S. Bonav. c. 3, n. 8. 33. Thom. Cel. I, n. 22.

34. Thom. Cel. *loc. cit.*; *Tres Soc.* n. 29. The attempts made to reconstruct the primitive rule have so far led to no satisfactory results. The reconstruction proposed by Vlastimil Kybal (*Die Ordensregeln des hl. Franz von Assisi,* Leipzig 1915, 1–16) approaches perhaps quite closely to the original text, while that of Karl Müller (*Die Anfänge des Minoritenordens,* Freiburg, 1885, 4 f. 185–188), of Böhmer (*Analekten zur Geschichte des Franziskus von Assisi,* Tübingen, 1904, LV. 88 f.), and of Fr. Cuthbert, O. M. Cap. ("The Primitive Rule of St. Francis."

in: *Life of St. Francis of Assisi*, London, 1913, Append. I, p. 393-403) are somewhat too elaborate.   Cf. P. Dom. Mandic *loc. cit.* 46 sqq.

35. "In Pentecoste conveniebant omnes fratres apud S. Mariam et tractabant, qualiter melius possent regulam observare . . . Sanctus autem Franciscus
faciebat admonitiones, reprehensiones et præcepta, sicut ei iuxta consilium
Domini videbatur . . . , ut s. evangelium et regulam, quam promiserant,
firmiter observarent . . ." *Tres Soc.* n. 57. *Anonymus Perusinus* says expressly: "In quo capitulo tractabatur, qualiter aliam meliorem regulam possent
observare."

36. Proofs by Kybal *loc. cit.* 26-42.

37. *Epistula data Ianuæ* Octobr. 1216, Böhmer, *Analekten* 94.

38. While it was formerly thought that the rule of 1221 originated by simply
adding new chapters to the primitive rule of 1210 (Sabatier, *Speculum perfectionis* XXXVI sq.; P. van Ortroy, in: *Analecta Bolland.* XXIV, 413; Lemmens,
Opuscula S. Francisci 160; Felder, *Geschichte der wissenschaftlichen Studien im
Franziskanerorden* 102 *et al.*), Kybal has now, in my opinion, brought proof that
the rule of 1221 is a comprehensive new edition (Kybal *loc. cit.* 16-26), or as
Fr. Cuthbert has already stated (*loc. cit.* 263), a uniform revision.   This is not,
however, as Kybal thinks, to be regarded as an independent rule, unrelated to
the one of 1210, which in fact evolved by steps from the primitive rule in the
first decades of the Order.   That the opinion of Kybal is untenable is made
clear from the fact that the rule of 1221 is always designated in the MSS. as
"the first rule, approved by Innocent III (died 1216) without a·Bull" (Böhmer
1, Lemmens 24).   If Kybal asserts (*loc. cit.* 17 ff.) that this annotation on the
MS. is based on deception, reducible to a "pia fraus," one can only marvel at
such an arbitrary opinion.

39. Iordan. a Iano n. 15.   Caesar's fitness for this task is specially emphasized
by Fr. Jordan n. 9 in the words: "This Caesar was even as a secular cleric a
follower of evangelical perfection."

40. "Hæc est vita evangelii Iesu Christi, quam frater Franciscus petiit a
domino papa Innocentio concedi sibi et confirmari, et dominus papa concessit
et confirmavit eam sibi et suis fratribus habitis et futuris." *Regula* I, *Opusc.* ed.
Böhmer 1, Lemmens 24.

41. "Regula et vita istorum fratrum hæc est, scilicet vivere in obedientia, in
castitate et sine proprio, et Domini nostri Iesu Christi doctrinam et vestigia
sequi." *Regula* I, c. 1, *Opusc.* ed. Böhmer 1, Lemmens 25.

42. "Teneamus ergo verba, vitam et doctrinam et sanctum eius evangelium,
qui dignatus est rogare Patrem suum et nomen eius nobis manifestare." *Reg.*
I, c. 22, *Opusc.* ed. Böhmer 22, Lemmens 56.

43. *Spec. perf.* c. 1 and 11; Ubertino di Casale, *Arbor vitæ* lib. 5, c. 3, Sabatier,
Spec. perf. CXLIII.

44. *Spec. perf.* p. 256.   45. S. Bonav. c. 4, n. 11.

46. Thus Fr. Leo in the *Spec. perf.* c. 53 (according to the edition of 1509,
Sabatier p. 90): "B. Franciscus, dum fecit regulam, de omni capitulo separatim
consulebat Dominum, si esset secundum voluntatem suam."

47. "Ut sciant [ministri] omnes fratres teneri ad observandam perfectionem
sancti evangelii, volo quod in principio et in fine regulæ sit scriptum, quod
fratres teneantur sanctum evangelium Domini nostri Iesu Christi firmiter observare." *Spec. perf.* c. 3.

48. *Regula* II, *Opusc.* ed. Böhmer 29. 35, Lemmens 63. 74.

49. Thus the tradition of the Spirituals as given in the *Spec. perf.* c. 1-3.   It
is evidently a legendary fabrication insofar as the tradition relates that Francis
made erasures in the Rule in consequence of the energetic remonstrances of the
Ministers.   That the Vicar of the Order, Brother Elias, and his partisans desired
a mitigation of the rule, is clear from the narrative of St. Bonaventure, that
Elias had allowed the draft of the rule entrusted to him by Francis to disappear
through carelessness, and thus forced the Saint to make a second transcript,
which was, however, identical with the first: S. Bonav. c. 4, n. 11.

50. "Tempore, quo de regula confirmanda fiebat inter fratres collatio, Sancto

de huiusmodi negotio vehementer sollicito talia monstrantur in somniis."
Thom. Cel. II, n. 209.

51. Thom. Cel. II, n. 209; S. Bonav. c. 4, n. 11. 52. Thom. Cel. II, n. 208.
53. Kybal, 10 f. 54. Matth. xix, 21. 55. Matth. xvi, 24. 56. Luke xiv, 26.
57. Matth. xix, 29.

58. Böhmer 1, Lemmens 24 sq. The latter omits the words "Evangelii Iesu
Christi." They are, in fact, not to be found in the MSS. of the so-called Portiuncula Book, but are contained in the *Expositio Regulæ* of Fr. Angelus Clarenus
(1317, resp. 1321–1323), ed. P. Livarius Oliger, O.F.M., Ad Claras Aquas, 1912,
12.

59. Böhmer 29, Lemmens 63.

60. These regulations which Francis culled from the Gospel and placed in
his rule, are always designated by St. Bonaventure (e.g. *Expositio super regulam
Fratrum Minorum* c. 2, n. 17, *Opera* VIII, 400. 402; *Epistula de sandaliis apostolorum* n. 15, *Opera* VIII, 390) as the Rule of the Apostles (Regula Apostolorum).

61. *Tres Soc.* n. 51.

62. Thom. Cel. I, n. 18–20; II, n. 116; *Tres Soc.* n. 60. Cf. Lempp, *Die Anfänge des Klarissenordens*, in: *Zeitschrift für Kirchengeschichte* XIII (1892), 181–
245; Lemmens, *Die Anfänge des Klarissenordens*, in: *Römische Quartalschrift* XVI
(1902), 93–124; Wauer, *Entstehung und Ausbreitung des Klarissenordens besonders
in den deutschen Minoritenprovinzen*, Leipzig, 1906; Liv. Oliger, *De origine regularum ordinis S. Claræ*, in: *Archiv. franc. histor.* V, (1912), 181–209. 413–447;
René de Nantes, *Les origines de l'Ordre de Sainte Claire*, Paris 1912; Fr. Cuthbert, *St. Francis of Assisi*, p. 131–149.

63. "Ipsis [i.e. St. Clare and her companions] beatus Franciscus, quibus tamquam modo genitis non cibum solidum, sed qui videbatur competere, potum
lactis formulam vitæ tradidit." Letter of Gregory IX, dated May 11, 1238, to
Bl. Agnes of Prague, in: Sbaralea, *Bullar. franc.* I, Rome, 1759, 243.

64. *Opusc.* ed. Böhmer 35, Lemmens 75.

65. Thus e.g. in his Testament (Böhmer 36. 38, Lemmens 77. 80): "Dominus
dedit mihi fratri Francisco incipere facere pœnitentiam. . . . Ubicumque non
fuerint recepti, fugiant in aliam terram ad faciendam pœnitentiam." The
first disciples of Francis styled themselves "viri pœnitentiales" (*Tres Soc.* n.
37). The evangelical life of the Poor Ladies is likewise designated simply as
"Penance" by *Tres Soc.* n. 60 and by St. Clare herself: "Altissimus dignatus
est cor meum illustrare, ut exemplo et doctrina beatissimi Patris nostri Francisci pœnitentiam facerem" (*Regula et vita sororum pauperum* c. 6, Sbaralea,
Bullar franc. I, 674). It is plain that Francis calls the life after the manner of
the Gospel "penance" or "penitential life," for the same reason that St. John
the Baptist, Christ and the apostles call it thus: Matth. iii, 2; iv, 17; Luke v,
32; xiii, 5; Acts ii, 38; xi, 18; xvii, 30; Cf. *Life of St. Clare* by P. Robinson,
p. 110.

66. "Similiter et viri uxorati et mulieres maritatæ a lege matrimonii discedere
non valentes, de fratrum salubri consilio se in domibus propriis arctiori pœnitentiæ committebant." *Tres Soc.* n. 60. "Nam prædicationis ipsius [*sc.* Fran-
cisci] fervore quam plurimi secundum formam a Dei viro acceptam novis se
pœnitentiæ legibus vinciebant, quorum vivendi modum idem Christi famulus
Ordinem fratrum de pœnitentia nominari decrevit." S. Bonav. c. 4, n. 6. The
secretary of Bonaventure, Fr. Bernard of Bessa (*Liber de laudibus b. Francisci*,
c. 7, ed. P. Hilarin a Lucerna, 75 sq., *Analecta franc.* III, 686 sq.), gives interesting information regarding the Third Order. Regarding its origin and its
first rule cf. W. Götz, *Die Regel des Tertiarierordens*, in: *Zeitschrift für Kirchengeschichte* XXIII (1902) 97–107; P. Mandonnet, O. P., *Les Règles et le Gouverne-
ment de l'Ordo de Pœnitentia au XIIIe siècle*, Paris, 1902, in: *Opuscules de critique
historique* I (1903) 143–250; K. Müller, *zur Geschichte des Bussbrüderordens*, in:
Zeitschrift für Kirchengeschichte XXIII (1902), 496–524; Sabatier, *Regula antiqua
fratrum et sororum de Pœnitentia seu Tertii Ordinis sancti Francisci*, in: *Opusc.
de critique hist.* I, (1903), 1–30; H. Böhmer, *Analekten* XXXI–XXXV; P. Anas-
tasius van den Wyngaert O. F. M., *De Tertio Ordine s. Francisci iuxta Marianum*

Florentinum, in: *Archiv. franc. histor.* XIII (1920), 3–77; Cuthbert, *Life of St. Francis*, p. 271–290.

67. The opinion maintained by Rénan, Voigt, K. Müller, Sabatier and P. Mandonnet, that Francis did not originally intend to establish a Religious Order, but merely a fraternity which was to be open to all, (cf. Felder, *Geschichte der wissensch. Studien im Franziskanerorden*, Freiburg, 1904, p. 13, note 1), has to-day been entirely abandoned. This opinion, however, was based on a very correct conception insofar as Francis did not wish his ideals to be restricted to a monastic Order, but to permeate all classes of society and to "evangelize" them. The Church has at all times up to the present day (cf. Encycl. Bened. XV "Sacra propediem" of January 6, 1921, *Acta Ap. Sedis* XIII, 1921, 33–41) emphasized this world-embracing purpose of the Franciscan Order.

68. Basil., *Epist.* 295; Cassian, *Collat.* 21, 5; 21, 33; August. c. *Faust.* 5, 9; *Ep.* 220, 12; *In Ps. 132*, 9; *Sermo* 356, 1; Chrysost., *Act. Apost. homil.* 11, 3.

69. Ruperti Tuitiensis, *De vita vere apostolica*, especially lib. 4, Migne *Patrol. lat.* 170, 643, sq.; S. Bernard. *Sermones de diversis* 22, 2; 27, 3; 37, 7, Migne 183, 595. 613. 642.

70. Although monasteries and monastic institutions were numerous in that period, there existed in fact but two rules and two religious families. The monks strictly so-called (Benedictines, Cistercians or Bernardines, Carthusians and others), observed the rule of St. Benedict since the seventh century; the congregations of Hermits and Clerics Regular adopted the rule taken from the writings of the great Bishop of Hippo during the twelfth century, and for that reason were known as Augustinian Hermits and Augustinian Clerics Regular.

71. *Spec. perf.* c. 68. Cf. Thom. Cel. I, n. 32–33.

72. Thom. Cel. II, n. 150; Bern. a Bessa, *Lib. de laud.* c. 5; *Spec. perf.* c. 43. Similarly the tradition of the Preachers, Gerard of Fracheto, *Vitæ fratrum*, ed. Reichert, Lovanii 1896, 10 sq.

73. From first to last he was firmly convinced that Jesus Christ Himself had revealed the rule to him: *Testam. S. Franc.*; Thom. Cel. II, n. 15; *Anon. Perus.* c. 10; *Tres Soc.* n. 29; S. Bonav. c. 4, n. 11; *Spec. perf.* c. 68; Angelus de Clareno, *Expos. Reg., Verba S. Franc.* c. 5.

74. "De patientia et paupertate servanda sermonem protraxit, ceteris institutis sanctum evangelium anteponens." Thom. Cel. II, n. 216. 75. Thom. Cel. I, n. 7. 84.

76. *Tres Soc.* n. 17. Similarly Bernard a Bessa, c. 1, 5: "Relictis denique omnibus Christi vestigia devote secutus, veterem Apostolorum vitam redivivis actibus innovavit, suæque religionis domum non super arenam temporalium, sed super petram Christi in paupertatis evangelicæ perfectione fundavit."

77. Walteri Gisburnensis, *Chronica de gestis regum Angliæ*, ed. *Monumenta Germaniæ historica SS.* t. XXVIII, 631.

78. *Iacobi Vitriacensis de b. Francisco eiusque societate testimonia*, Böhmer 98. 101 sq. 105. These testimonials are found in two letters of Jacques de Vitry dated 1216 and 1220 respectively, also in his *Historia orientalis* lib. II, c. 32.

79. Humbertus de Romanis, *De eruditione prædicatorum* lib. 2, c. 36, *Maxima Bibliotheca Patrum*, t. XXV, p. 468.

80. Luke vi, 30. 81. *Tres Soc.* n. 44; Thom. Cel. I, n. 17. 82. Matth. v, 40.

83. *Tres Soc.* c. 10, ed. Amoni, Romæ 1880, p. 62. This passage is not found in the edition of Faloci-Pulignani. 84. Luke x, 8.

85. *Reg.* II, c. 3, *Opusc.* ed. Böhmer 31, Lemmens 67. 86. Matth. x, 12. 87. *Reg.* II, *loc. cit.*

88. Thom. Cel. I, n. 23; S. Bonav. c. 3, n. 2. 89. *Testam. Opusc.* ed. Böhmer 38, Lemmens 80.

90. Bro. Leo testifies in a note written by himself and found in a breviary he had received from Francis and which is still preserved in the Basilica of St. Clare at Assisi, that to his dying day the Saint had the gospel of the day read to himself whenever he was unable to attend Mass: Sabatier, *Spec. perf.* 175, note 2. Shortly before his death he asked the Gospel book to be brought and the

sublime passage to be read in which the Saviour takes leave of His disciples before the passion (John xiii, f.): Thom. Cel. I, n. 110.

91. "Non enim fuerat evangelii surdus auditor, sed laudabili memoriæ, quod audierat cuncta commendans, ad litteram diligenter implere curabat." Thom. Cel. I, n. 22.

CHAPTER II

1. 2 Tim. ii, 3. 2. *Ep.* 22, 30; Migne 22, 416. 3. *De opere monachorum* c. 28; Migne 40, 575.

4. "Ad te ergo nunc mihi sermo dirigitur, quisquis abrenuntians propriis voluntatibus Domino Christo, vero regi, militaturus obedientiæ fortissima atque præclara arma sumis." *S. Benedicti Regula*, Prolog.

5. Cf. Ducange-Carpenterius, *Glossarium mediæ et infimæ latinitatis, s. v.* The word is also used in this sense in the Franciscan sources and is thus applied to Francis himself. Thus, the Three Companions relate that Francis was not numbered among the common soldiers during his captivity at Perugia, but among the "milites," on account of his "nobility of manner." *Tres Soc.* n. 4. Similarly *Tres Soc.* n. 5; Thom. Cel. I, n. 4; II, n. 77; *Tract. de mirac.* n. 41. The following passage from Celano regarding St. Clare is also significant: "Pater eius miles, et tota ex utroque parente progenies militaris." (*Vita S. Claræ* c. 1, ed. *Acta SS.*, Augusti t. II, 755. Cf. P. Robinson, *Life of St. Clare*, p. 6, note 89).

6. *Rolandslied des Pfaffen Konrad*, 5159 f. 5169. The same motif underlies the original form of the Normanic Chanson de Roland, as also the Carlovingian Epics and the Legend of the Grail (Parsifal). Cf. Fr. Weiss, O. P., *Die Entwicklung des christlichen Rittertums, Studien über die Rolandssage*, in *Histor. Jahrbuch der Gorresgesellschaft* I, (1880), 107–140. 7. *Rolandslied*, 5820 ff.

8. This rule was composed with the co-operation of St. Bernard at the Synod of Troyes in 1128. Cf. G. Schnürer, *Die ursprüngliche Templerregel*, Freiburg i. B. 1903, 95–128.

9. "Præfatio Regulæ Commilitonum Christi . . . Hortamur itaque vos, qui usque nunc miliciam sæcularem, in qua Christus non fuit causa, sed solo humano favore amplexi estis. . . Ante omnia autem, quicumque vis, o Christi miles. . . inter militares, qui pro Christo animas suas dederunt, sortem obtinere mereberis." Schnürer, *loc. cit.* 130; Holstenius, *Codex Regularum* II, 431.

10. Cf. Schnürer, *Franz von Assisi* (München, 1907), 14 sq.; Jörgensen, *Der hl. Franz von Assisi*, 136. 11. *Tres Soc.* n. 5.

12. "Tentat proinde Franciscus adhuc divinam fugere manum, et paternæ correctionis paulisper oblitus, arridentibus sibi prosperis, cogitat quæ sunt mundi, ac ignorans consilium Dei, de gloria sæculi et vanitate facturum adhuc maxima se promittit." Thom. Cel. I, n. 4. 13. *Anon. Perus.* n. 5.

14. "Franciscus, quia levis animo erat et non modicum audax, ad eundum conspirat cum illo, generis nobilitate impar, sed magnanimitate superior, pauperior divitiis, sed profusior largitate." Thom. Cel. I, n. 4.

15. Thom. Cel. I, n. 4–5; *Tres Soc.* n. 5. 16. Thom. Cel. II, n. 6; *Tres Soc.* n. 6. 17. Thom. Cel. *ibid.*

18. Kluber, *Das Ritterwesen des Mittelalters nach seiner politischen und militarischen Verfassung*, Nürnberg 1786, p. 417. 19. Thom. Cel. I, n. 10 sq.; *Tres Soc.* n. 17.

20. "At ipse, quia novus Christi athleta erat, cum audiret persequentium minas ac eorum præsentiret adventum, dare locum ire volens, in quandam occultam caveam, quam ad hoc ipsemet paraverat, se mergebat." Thom. Cel. I. n. 10. 21. *Ibid.* n. 11.

22. "Christi miles fortissimus minas diaboli vilipendens orabat, ut Deus dirigeret viam suam." *Tres Soc.* n. 12. 23. Thom. Cel. II, n. 127.

24. *Testam.*, ed. Böhmer 36, Lemmens 77. 25. *Ibid.* 26. S. Bonav. *Leg.* c. 1, n. 5. 27. *Ibid.* Also Thom. Cel. I, n. 7; *Tres Soc.* c. 11. 28. Thom. Cel. I, n. 21; *Tres Soc.* n. 21–24. 29. S. Bonav. c. 2, n. 1. 8. 30. Thom. Cel. I, n.

55. 31. Thom. Cel. I, n. 55; II, n. 32. S. Bonav. c. 14, n. 1; Thom. Cel. I, n. 103. 33. *Vita Fr. Ægidii* p. 75.

34. Wadding, *Annales*, ad an. 1210, n. 3. Wadding borrowed this anecdote from: *Actus b. Francisci in valle Reatina.* Cf. *Act. SS.* Oct. t. II, p. 589. A separate edition of the *Actus* was published by F. Pennacchi (Foligno, 1911). 35. *Spec. perf.* c. 4.

36. *Ibid.* c. 72. We call attention to the historically interesting phenomenon that Francis was so completely charmed by the two decidedly Christian hero legends which dominated the Middle Ages from the twelfth century on. The first is the Legend of Charlemagne, in which the heroes are Charles and his twelve Paladins, principally Roland and Olivier. It found its fullest expression in the *Rolandslied* (between 1127 and 1139), and previously in the Normanic *Chanson de Roland* (about 1066). The second is the Legend of the Holy Grail, the most splendid form of which is found in the French *Parceval* (about 1175), and in the German *Parzival* by Wolfram von Eschenbach (beginning of the thirteenth century). Francis clearly refers to the *Chanson de Roland* and to *Parceval.* These romantic tales of chivalry were already sung throughout Italy in the twelfth century by the provençal "jongleurs." Cf. Gasparri, *Italien. Literat.* I, (1885), 112 ff.

37. Wolfram von Eschenbach, *Parzival* IX, 888–890. Cf. *Tristan* V, 5027–5028; *Rolandslied*, 1975–1977.

38. *Chanson de Roland*, 1820 ff., 3338 ff., 3831 f., 3964 ff.; *Rolandslied*, 6114 ff. 9009 ff. 39. *Rolandslied*, 2378 ff.; 2398 f. 40. Matth. x, 34. 38. 41. 1. Pet. ii, 21. 42. John viii, 12. 43. John xiii, 15. 44. Rom. viii, 29. 45. Gal. ii, 20.

46. *Regulæ antiquissimæ fragmenta*, Böhmer, *Analekten* 88; Kybal, *Die Ordensregeln des hl. Franz von Assisi*, 11.

47. *Regula* I, c. 22, 23. *Opusc.* ed. Böhmer 22 sq., Lemmens 56, 60.

48. *Epist. ad Capit. Generale, Opusc.* ed. Böhmer 57 sq., Lemmens 100.

49. *Verba admonitionis*, c. 6 *Opusc.* ed. Böhmer 44, Lemmens 9. sq.

50. Ultima voluntas, quam scripsit sororibus S. Claræ, *Opusc.* ed. Böhmer 35. 51. Thom. Cel. I, n. 84. 52. J. Görres, *Der hl. Franziskus von Assisi, ein Troubadour,* in: *Katholik* XX, (1826); Separatausgabe: Strassburg, Le Roux 1828, 50.

53. "Existimo autem beatum Franciscum speculum quoddam sanctissimum dominicæ sanctitatis et imaginem perfectionis ipsius." Thom. Cel. II, n. 26. 54. S. Bonav. c. 13, n. 2. 55. *Tres Soc.* n. 68. 56. *Epist. ad Capit. Gener., Opusc.* ed. Böhmer 57. 57. Thom. Cel. I, n. 115.

58. Böhmer, 71, places this Oratio "Absorbeat," the authenticity of which rests on the authority of Ubertino di Cassale (1305), among the "Dubia."

59. Thom. Cel. I, n. 84. 60. Thom. Cel. II, n. 199. 61. *Ibid.* 62. *Spec. perf.* c. 114; Thom. Cel. II, n. 200. 63. Thom. Cel. *ibid.* 64. *Spec. perf. ibid.* 65. Thom. Cel. I, n. 84. sq. 66. *Ibid.* n. 86.

67. "Totum viri Dei studium, tam publicum quam privatum, circa crucem Domini versabatur; et a principio temporis, quo Crucifixo cœperat militare, diversa circa eum crucis mysteria præfulserunt." *Tract de. mirac.* n. 2. Cf. S. Bonav. *Leg., de mirac.* 1, n. 2. 68. S. Bonav. c. 1, n. 5.

69. Thom. Cel. II, n. 10 sq. Cf. *idem, Tract. de mirac.* n. 2; *Tres Soc.* n. 14; S. Bon. *Leg.* c. 2, n. 1. 70. *Tres Soc.* n. 14; *Spec. perf.* c. 92. Cf. Thom. Cel. II, n. 11. 71. Thom. Cel., *Tract. de mirac.* n. 2.

72. "Familiare sibi signum tau, præ ceteris signis, quo solo et missivas cartulas consignabat et cellarum parietes ubilibet depingebat." *Ibid.* n. 3. "Hoc signo sanctus Franciscus suas consignabat litteras, quoties caritatis causa scriptum aliquod dirigebat." S. Bonav., *Leg., de mirac.* 10, n. 7.

73. "Nonne mos erat et primis filiis pia sanctione statutum, ut ubicumque crucis similitudinem cernerent, honorem ei debitæ reverentiæ consecrarent?" Thom. Cel. *ibid.* 74. Thom. Cel. *ibid.* 75. *Ibid.* 76. *Ibid.* Cf. *Actus* c. 1, n. 42. 77. *Actus* c. 38, n. 5. 78. *Actus* c. 4, n. 1. 79. Thom. Cel. I, n. 77.

80. Francis thus imitated the provençal troubadours, with whose songs and customs he was well acquainted. Cf. Görres, *loc. cit.*

81. Thom. Cel. II, n. 127.   Cf. *Spec. perf.* c. 93.   82. *Fioretti*, 3a Considerazione delle Sante Istimmate.

83. Thom. Cel. I, n. 93–96; *Tract. de mirac.* n. 4; *Tres Soc.* n. 17; S. Bonav. c. 13, n. 3; *Actus* c. 9; *Fioretti, ibid.*   These records describing the details of the stigmatization, evidently rest on the testimony of the one witness of the wondrous event, Brother Leo.   The narrative as given by the Three Companions, of whom Leo was one, comes from the latter himself.   Celano and Bonaventure received their information from the living companions of St. Francis, in this case also from Brother Leo.   The latter took great pleasure in relating the episode to the younger generation of Brothers, during whose times the *Fioretti* originated, as Eccleston expressly states.   Cf. Eccleston, ed. Brewer, *Monumenta franc.* I, 51; *Analecta franc.* I, 245; Little· 93; Cuthbert, *Chronicle of Eccleston* 205.   For Brother Leo's autographic note on the Stigmata of St. Francis see Böhmer 69, and P. Michael Bihl, *De Stigmatibus S. Franc. Assis., Archiv. franc. histor.* III, 406 sq.   How the comprehensive report of Brother Leo reached Brother Hugolinus, the author of the *Actus b. Francisci*, the latter relates himself: "Hanc historiam (of the stigmatization as given in the *Actus-Fioretti*) habuit frater Iacobus de Massa ab ore fratris Leonis et frater Hugolinus de Monte S. Mariæ ab ore dicti fratris Iacobi, et ego, qui scripsi, ab ore fratris Hugolini viri per omnia fide digni.   Ad laudem Dei." *Actus* c. 9, n. 71, ed. Sabatier 39.   As the reader is aware, we are interested only in the circumstances of the stigmatization.   Regarding the fact itself, Cf. our treatment of the subject in the new edition of P. Bernard Christen, *Leben des hl. Franziskus von Assisi*, Innsbruck, 1922, 380–390, and the article: *Trois témoignages inconnus sur les stigmates de S. François*, in: *Études franc.* t. XXXIV (1922), 121–125. Cf. also F. Pennacchi, *Saggio del processo per la canonizzazione di San Francesco*, in: *Miscell. francescana*, vol. XV (1914), 129–137.   In this study, which has not as yet received the attention it deserves, Professor Pennacchi publishes a notarial document dated 1226, in which a number of persons—not members of the Order—testify to having seen the Stigmata during the life and after the death of the Saint.   An exact description of the Stigmata according to these witnesses is appended, completely coinciding with that of Celano I, n. 95.

84. Thom. Cel., *Tract. de mirac.* n. 2.   85. Thom. Cel. I, n. 112.   86. Thom. Cel. I, n. 97.

87. Thom. Cel. I, n. 98. 99. 102. 105. 108; II, n. 44. 64. 126. 166; *Tract. de mirac.* n. 14.   88. Thom. Cel. I, n. 105. 107.   89. S. Bonav. c. 14, n. 2.   90. *ibid.* n. 107.

91. "O martyr et martyr, qui ridens et gaudens libentissime tolerabat, quod erat omnibus acerbissimum et gravissimum intueri!   Revera nullum in eo remanserat membrum absque nimio passionis dolore, et calore naturali sensim amisso, ad extrema quotidie properabat.   Stupebant medici, mirabantur fratres, quomodo spiritus vivere posset in carne sic mortua, cum, consumptis carnibus, sola cutis ossibus adhæreret." *Ibid.*   92. *Tres Soc.* n. 15.

93. "Voluit certe per omnia Christo crucifixo esse conformis, qui pauper et dolens et nudus in cruce pependit. . . . O vere Christianissimum virum, qui et vivens Christo viventi et moriens morienti et mortuus mortuo perfecta esse studuit imitatione conformis et expressa promeruit similitudine decorari." S. Bonav. c. 14, n. 4.   94. Thom. Cel. I, 95; II, 135–137.   95. *Ibid.* I, n. 112. 123.

CHAPTER III

1. Sabatier, *Spec. perf.* p. 120.   2. *Spec. perf.* c. 119.

3. "Missam vel unicam non audire cotidie, si vacaret. . ."   In the Friary he could hear but one Mass according to his regulation: "Moneo præterea et exhortor in Domino, ut in locis, in quibus fratres morantur, una tantum Missa celebretur in die secundum formam sanctæ ecclesiæ.   Si vero plures fuerint in loco sacerdotes, sit per amorem caritatis alter contentus audita celebratione

alterius sacerdotis." (*Epist. ad Capitulum Gener.*, *Opusc.* ed. Böhmer 60, Lemmens 104.) Francis made this regulation in consideration of human unworthiness, and for fear lest the Friars gradually lose their reverence for the Most Blessed Sacrament as a result of daily communion or celebration. In those and later years there were many learned and pious men who had the same opinion as Francis in this regard (Cf. Wadding-De la Haye, *S. Francisci Opuscula*, I, Augustæ, Veith 1739, p. 8; *Acta SS.* t. II, Oct. p. 998 sq.), until the Church declared that the daily and worthy celebration of the eucharistic sacrifice was more in accord with the wish of the Saviour, than the humble omission of it. (Benedict XIV, "De sacrificio Missæ," sectio 2, n. 9 sqq.). It is known that even St. Bonaventure, the spiritual heir of the Seraphic Patriarch, remained away from the altar for days, because "he deemed himself unworthy to receive holy communion" (*Catalogus Sanctorum Fratrum Minorum*, edited by Fr. L. Lemmens, O. F. M., Romæ 1902, 27). On the other hand, the same St. Bonaventure reprimands the priests "who not from respect, but through negligence omit the celebration, because he thereby, as far as is in him, deprives the Most Holy Trinity of honor, the angels of joy, the sinners of pardon, the just of grace, the poor souls of comfort, the Church of aid, himself of the remedy against his weakness and daily faults" (*De præparatione ad Missam* c. 1, n. 9, *Opera* VIII, 102).

4. "Erat enim frater ille [Benedictus de Pirato] sacerdos sanctus et discretus, qui beato Francisco celebrabat aliquando, ubi iacebat infirmus, quia semper quum poterat volebat habere vel audire missam quantumcumque esset infirmus." *Spec. perf.* c. 87. 5. Sabatier, *Spec. perf.* p. 175, note 2.

6. Thom. Cel. II, n. 201. 7. *Leg.* c. 9, n. 2. 8. Thom. Cel. II, n. 201. 9. At the Pentecost Chapter of 1217. 10. *Spec. perf.* c. 65. 11. Thom. Cel. II, n. 201. 12. *Tres Soc.* n. 8; Thom. Cel. II, n. 8. 13. *Tres. Soc.* c. 3; Thom. Cel. II, n. 8.

14. Thom. Cel. II, n. 201; *Spec. perf.* c. 65. One of these baking irons is still preserved in the monastery at Greccio. Cf. J. Jörgensen, *Das Pilgerbuch aus dem franziskanischen Italien*, Kempten, 1905, 94 f. 100. 15. *Spec. perf.* c. 56. 57. 16. *Tres Soc.* n. 21–24; Thom. Cel. I, n. 18. 17. S. Bonav. c. 2, n. 7. 18. Thom. Cel. I, n. 21; S. Bonav. c. 2, n. 8. 19. Wadding, *Annal.* ad a. 1213 n. 17.

20. The proofs in: Lud. Lipsin, *Compendiosa historia vitæ S. P. Francisci*, Assisii 1756, also Faloci-Pulignani, in: *Miscellanea francescana* Vol. II, 33–37.

21. *Anecdotes historiques d'Etienne de Bourbon*, éd. Lecoy de la Marche, Paris 1877, n. 316, p. 264 s.; n. 347, p. 304 s. 22. *Tres Soc.* n. 59. 23. *Tres Soc.* n. 57; Thom. Cel. II, n. 201.

24. *Verba admonitionis* c. 26, *Opusc.* ed. Böhmer 48 sq., Lemmens 18.

25. *Testamentum*, *Opusc.* ed. Böhmer 36 sq., Lemmens 78 sq.

26. Barth. de Pisa, *Conform.* 1. I, fructus XII, pars 2, ed. *Anal. franc.* IV, p. 595–598. 27. Böhmer XXIX.

28. Epistola quam misit omnibus fidelibus; Epist. ad Capit. generale; Epist. ad omnes clericos; Epist. ad universos custodes; Epist. ad populorum rectores.

29. John xiv, 6–9. 30. 1 Tim. vi, 16. 31. John iv, 24. 32. John i, 18. 33. John vi, 64. 34. Mark xiv, 22. 35. John vi, 55. 36. 1 Cor. xi, 29. 37. Ps. iv, 3. 38. John ix, 35. 39. Wisd. xviii, 15. 40. Matth. xxviii, 20.

41. *Verba admonitionis* c. 1, *Opusc.* ed. Böhmer 40 sq., Lemmens 3–5. 42. Hebr. xiii, 8. 43. Ps. cxviii, 21. 44. Ezech. xxxiii, 13.

45. *Epist. ad populorum rectores*, *Opusc.* ed. Böhmer 70 sq., Lemmens 111 sq. Text according to Gonzaga, *De origine seraphicæ religionis*, Venetiis 1603, 806 sq. 46. *Spec. perf.* c. 56. 47. 1 Cor. ii, 14.

48. *De reverentia corporis Domini et de munditia altaris*, *Opusc.* ed. Böhmer 62 sq., Lemmens 22 sq. 49. *Tres Soc.* n. 57. 50. John vi, 55. 51. Luke xxii, 19. 52. *Regula prima* c. 20, *Opusc.* ed. Böhmer 18, Lemmens 50.

53. Wadding ad a. 1216, n. 11; ad a. 1219, n. 38–80. 54. Col. i, 20. 55. Col. iii, 22. 56. Luke xxii, 19. 57. 1 Cor. xi, 27. 58. Hebr. x, 28. 59. Hebr. x, 29. 60. 1 Cor. xi, 29. 61. Jer. xlviii, 10. 62. Mal. ii, 2. 63. 1 Pet. i, 12. 64. Lev. xi, 44. 65. Ps. lxi, 9. 66. 1 Pet. v, 6.

67. *Epist. ad Capitulum Generale, Opusc.* ed. Böhmer 59 sq., Lemmens 100–103. Ubertino di Casale, *Arbor Vitæ* lib. 5, c. 7, remarks that Francis wrote this letter toward the end of his life, after he had withdrawn from the direction of the Order.

68. *Epist. ad universos custodes, Opusc.* ed. Böhmer 63 sq., Lemmens 113–115.

69. *Spec. perf.* c. 65.

70. Regarding these abuses cf. Anonymus of Passau: *De occasione errorum hæreticorum*, in: Preger, *Beiträge zur Geschichte der Waldensier im Mittelalter, in den Abhandlungen der Kgl. Bayrischen Akademie der Wissenschaften* 3, Kl., 13. Bd., 1. Abt., München 1875, 64 (242) ff. This excellent priest and inquisitor severely rebukes those who do not renew consecrated hosts in time, so that they swarm with worms; who frequently let the body and blood of the Lord fall to the ground; who preserve the Most Blessed Sacrament in their room or in a tree of the garden; who, while visiting the sick, hang the Holy Eucharist up in a room and go to the tavern; who administer the Sacrament to public sinners and refuse it to the worthy; who celebrate Mass while living in notorious sin; who use adulterated wine for the Sacrifice, pour more water than wine into the chalice, and celebrate again after consuming the ablution; who read several Masses on one day without reason; who protract the Mass unduly by excessively long and confused singing; who establish taverns in the churches and render unseemly plays therein. In these words the Anonymus of Passau sums up the abuses, which were constantly censured by the Popes and the Councils.

71. *S. Claræ Vita* c. 4, n. 28, ed. *Act. SS.*, Augusti t. II, p. 760.

72. *Catalogus Gen. Ministr.*, ed. P. Hilarinus 95; Bernard of Bessa adds dolefully: "Nowadays [about 1277] they suspend the Eucharist above the altar so that frequently, when the faithful are assembled, it cannot be reached, because the cord by which it is fastened, becomes obstructed or damaged and breaks, so that the body of Christ falls to the ground."

73. Cf. P. Hilaire de Paris, *St. Antoine de Padoue. La Légende primitive et autres pièces historiques*, Montreuil-sur-mer 1890, 107 f.

74. It is significant how frequently Berthold of Regensburg treats of the Eucharist in his sermons, and how he has appropriated the very conception of the Sacrament of the Altar which we have found in St. Francis. Cf. Franz Göbel, *Die Missionspredigten des Franziskaners Berthold von Regensburg*, 3. Aufl., Regensburg 1873, 181 f. 329–332. 493–500. Likewise in the Latin sermons, e.g. in Sermo VI of Rusticanus de tempore: "De honorificentia Christi sive Corporis Christi, et quomodo gravatur Christus contra illos, qui eum non honorant."

75. Cf. the beautiful sections on the Most Holy Sacrament in Alexander Alensis, *Summa* IV pars, q. 11 sq., *Venetiis apud Franciscum Franciscium*, Vol. IV, p. 122b–228c; S. Bonaventura, *Comment. in lib. IV Sent.* dist. 8–13, *Opera* t. IV, p. 177–313; *De præparatione ad Missam*, *Opera* t. VIII, 98–106; Duns Scotus, *Quæst. in lib. IV Sent.*, *Opera*, Parisiis, 1894, t. XVIII and XXIV.

76. Declared as such by Leo XIII, Bull "Providentissimus Deus," Nov. 28, 1897.

77. *Analecta Ord. Min. Cap.* t. XIII, Romæ 1897, 178–184; *Bullarium O. M. Cap.*, ed. a P. Michaele a Tugio, t. I, Romæ 1740, 54. 63. 98. 109. 134 sq.

CHAPTER IV

1. *Tres Soc.* n. 8; Thom. Cel. II, n. 8. 2. Thom. Cel. I, n. 8 sq. 18.

3. ". . . usque ad inferiorem gradum omnibus debitum honorem impendens. Nam apostolicam sumpturus legationem, fideque catholica integer totus, erga ministros et ministeria Dei reverentia plenus ab initio fuit." Thom. Cel. II, n. 8.

4. "Venerabatur sacerdotes, et omnem ecclesiasticum ordinem nimio amplexabatur affectu." Thom. Cel. I, n. 62.

5. Iulian. a Spira, *Vita S. Fr.* n. 28. 6. *Anon. Perus.* n. 37; *Tres Soc.* n. 57. 7. *Spec. perf.* c. 87. 8. Iulian. a Spira n. 27. 9. *Tres Soc.* n. 59.

10. "Fratres quoque, tunc sacerdotes Ordinis non habentes, confitebantur sæcularibus sacerdotibus, indifferenter bonis et malis, nec peccatum in aliquo considerantes." Iulian. a Spira n. 27.

11. Bern. a Bessa c. 2; Thom. Cel. I, n. 46.

12. Thom. Cel. I, n. 46; Leo, *Vita Fr. Ægidii* p. 79; Bern. a Bessa c. 2.

13. Thom. Cel. II, n. 146; Bern. a Bessa c. 5; *Spec. perf.* c. 53.

14. *Tres Soc.* n. 19 sq.; Thom. Cel. I, n. 14 sq.; II, n. 12.   15. Thom. Cel. I, n. 32.   16. Thom. Cel. II, n. 100.   17. Thom. Cel. I, n. 108; II, n. 50.   18. Thom. Cel. II, n. 220.   19. *Ibid.* I, n. 75.

20. *Regula bullata* c. 9, *Opusc.* ed. Böhmer 33, Lemmens 71.

21. Thom. Cel. II, n. 147.   22. *Spec. perf.* c. 50.   23. Cf. e. g. Iord. a Iano n. 22. 24.

24. Bull "Cum dilecti," issued by Honorius III, dated June 11, 1219, in: Sbaralea, *Bullar. franc.* I, p. 2, n. 2.

25. *Testam., Opusc.* ed. Böhmer 38, Lemmens 80.   26. *Testam., ibid.*   27. *Spec. perf.* c. 10.   28. *Ibid.*

29. "Frater Franciscus promittit obedientiam et reverentiam domino Innocentio papæ et eius successoribus" (Müller, *Versuch einer Rekonstruktion der ältesten Regel von 1209,* in: *Die Anfänge des Minoritenordens.* Freiburg i. Br. 1885, 185). In the final rule of 1223 Francis repeats this vow to "the Lord Pope Honorius and his canonically elected successors and to the Roman Church." *Regula bull.* c. 1, *Opusc.* ed. Böhmer 29, Lemmens 63.   30. *Tres Soc.* n. 46.

31. *Tres Soc.* n. 46–51; Thom. Cel. I, 32 sq.; II, 16, sq.; S. Bonav. c. 3 n. 8 sqq.; *Anon. Perus.* n. 31–36.

32. *Anon. Perus.* n. 36; *Tres Soc.* n. 52; Thom. Cel. II, n. 17.

33. "Paucis vero diebus morantes cum ipso, ita eum ædificaverunt sanctis sermonibus et exemplis, quod videns in opere fulgere quod de ipsis audierat, recommendavit se eorum orationibus humiliter et devote, et petivit etiam de gratia speciali, quod volebat ex tunc sicut unus de fratribus reputari." *Tres Soc.* n. 48.

34. "Venerabilis autem Pater Iohannes de Sancto Paulo cardinalis, qui b. Francisco consilium et protectionem frequenter impendebat, vitam et actus b. Francisci et omnium fratrum eius omnibus aliis cardinalibus commendabat. His auditis commota sunt viscera eorum ad diligendos fratres et unusquisque desiderabat ex fratribus in sua curia habere, non pro servitio aliquo recipiendo ab eis, sed propter devotionem et amorem, quem habebant plurimum erga fratres." *Anonym. Perus.* n. 42; *Tres Soc.* n. 61.

35. ". . . . . . .ut b. Franciscum et eius fratres intime diligeret, protegeret et foveret; qui revera ferventissime se habuit circa eos, ac si esset omnium pater. Immo plus quam patris carnalis dilectio ad carnales filios se extendat, amor huiusmodi spiritualiter efferbuit ad Virum Dei cum suis fratribus diligendum in Domino et fovendum." *Tres Soc.* n. 61; *Anonym. Perus.* n. 43.

36. Thom. Cel. I, n. 74. For the date cf. Sabatier, *Spec. perf.* p. 122, note 2.

37. *Tres Soc.* n. 61.   38. Thom. Cel. II, n. 23 sq.; *Tres Soc.* n. 63.   39. Iord. a Iano n. 11–14.   40. Iord. a Iano n. 14.   Cf. *Tres Soc.* n. 64 sq.   41. Thom. Cel. I, n. 74.

42. Bull "Mira circa nos," dated July 19, 1228, Sbaralea, *Bullar. franc.* I, p. 42, n. 25.

43. Bull "Quo elongati," dated Sept. 28, 1230, *ibid.* p. 68, n. 56.

44. 346 documents in all are found issued by Gregory IX from 1227-1240 in the interests of the Order, in Sbaralea, *ibid.*

45. Iord. a Iano n. 63.   46. Regula II, c. 12, *Opusc.* ed. Böhmer 35, Lemmens 74.   47. Thom. Cel. I, n. 62.   48. *Opusc.* ed. Böhmer 63, Lemmens 23.

49. "Admonebat sollicite fratres, ut sanctum evangelium et regulam promiserant, firmiter observarent, et ut maxime circa divina officia et ecclesiasticas ordinationes essent devoti et reverentes." *Tres Soc.* n. 57.

50. *Opusc.* ed. Böhmer 1-26, Lemmens 24-62.

51. "Postea non licebit ei ad aliam religionem accedere neque extra obedien-

tiam evagari iuxta mandatum domini papæ." Regula I, c. 2. This decree of the Pope was issued Sept. 22, 1220, cf. Bull "Cum secundum consilium," Sbaralea, *Bullar. franc.* I, p. 6.

52. "Nullus recipiatur contra formam et institutionem sanctæ ecclesiæ." Regula I, *ibid.*

53. *Ibid.* c. 3. While the first rule was still in use, probably about 1215, Innocent III arranged a special Office, called "Breviarium" on account of its brevity, for use at the Roman church, that is, for the chapel at the Roman Curia. Deference for the Church as well as practical reasons led Francis to adopt this Office in the final Rule (*Regula bull.* c. 3), and it soon came into general use. Cf. Hilarin Felder, *Die liturgischen Reimoffizien auf die hhl. Franziskus und Antonius gedichtet und komponiert durch Fr. Julian von Speier*, Freiburg i. d. Schw. 1901, 15–21.

54. Schnürer, *Die ursprüngliche Templerregel*, Freiburg i. Br. 1903, 135.

55. "Nullus fratrum prædicet contra formam et institutionem sanctæ romanæ ecclesiæ." *Regula* I, c. 17. 56. *Ibid.* c. 19. 57. *Ibid.* c. 20. 58. *Ibid.* c. 23.

59. "According to the final rule, the institution of Francis appears welded together as firmly as possible with the Roman Church, and the expressions used therein to enjoin the complete submission of the Brothers Minor, simply cannot be surpassed." H. Tilemann, *Studien zur Individ. des Franziskus von Assisi*, Leipzig-Berlin, 1914, 167. 60. *Opusc.* ed. Böhmer, 36. 39, Lemmens 78. 81. 82.

61. It is well known that Rénan (*François d'Assise*, in: *Nouvelles études d'historie religieuse*, Paris 1884, 243 sq.), Karl von Hase (*Franz von Assisi*, Leipzig, 1892, 4), H. Thode (*Franz von Assisi und die Anfänge der Kunst der Renaissance in Italien*, Berlin, 1885, 522, 525 ff.), Paul Sabatier (*Vie de S. François* IX f., XXV ff. 116. 288 f., 320 ff., 385 ff., also in his edition of the *Spec. perf. var. loc.*), and Vlastimil Kybal (*Die Ordensregeln des hl. Franz von Assisi*, Leipzig 1915, 88–92. 104–106. 153 f.; *Über das Testament des hl. Franz von Assisi*, in: *Mitteilungen des Instituts für österreichische Geschichtsforschung* XXXVI, 312–340) have attempted to represent Francis as the enemy of the Church, and the Church as the enemy of the Franciscan Ideal. They claim that originally and by nature Francis was an individualist and had the vocation of becoming in reality a forerunner of Luther; that he for a time bravely struggled against the fetters placed on him by the Roman Church, but that, worn out by the hopeless struggle, he was finally overcome by the powerful diplomacy of the Church and forced to abandon his original ideal. Against these fanciful assertions we simply place objective facts as we find them in the relation of Francis to the Church. A polemic dispute with the above-mentioned writers can be dispensed with all the more easily since they have been completely refuted by the non-Catholic historians Walter Götz (*Die ursprünglichen Ideale des hl. Franziskus von Assisi*, *Historische Vierteljahrsschrift* VI, 19–50; *Die Quellen zur Geschichte des hl. Franz von Assisi*, Gotha 1904), and H. Tilemann (*Studien zur Individualität des Franziskus von Assisi*, Leipzig 1914, 141–167. 202–210). By means of authentic sources, Götz and Tilemann reach the conclusion that Francis was at all times filled with deep devotion and loyalty toward the Church; that the Church on her part has never and in no wise done violence to his ideals or turned him from them; moreover, that his original ideals have in fact never changed, but remained the same until the very end of his life. Minor deflections from his original purpose must be charged to the process of harmonizing theory and practise.

62. "Minores fratres . . . apostolicæ sedi in omnibus obedientes." *Burchardi Urspergensis Chronicon*, ed. Abel-Weiland, *Monumenta Germ. histor. Scriptores* t. XXIII, 376.

63. Hil. Felder, *Die liturg. Reimoffizien auf die hhl. Franz. und Antonius*, 107.

64. Döllinger, *Beiträge zur Sektengeschichte des Mittelalters*, 1. Teil, München 1890, 98–241.

65. *S. Hildegardis Epistolæ*, Coloniæ 1556, 138.

66. *Cæsarii Heisterbacensis Dialogus miraculorum* 5, 19.

67. Dr. F. Imle, *Ein heiliger Lebenskünstler*, Paderborn 1914, 204. 68. *Vita fr. Ægidii*, 106.

CHAPTER V

1. "Inerat namque iuvenis Francisci præcordiis divinitus indita quædam ad pauperes miseratio liberalis, quæ secum ab infantia crescens, tanta cor ipsius benignitate repleverat, ut, iam evangelii non surdus auditor, omni proponeret se petenti tribuere (Lc. 6, 30), maxime si divinum allegaret amorem." S. Bonav. c. 1, n. 1.   2. *Tres Soc.* n. 3.   3. *Tres Soc.* n. 3.   4. S. Bonav. c. 1, n. 1.   5. *Tres Soc.* n. 7.   6. *Tres Soc.* n. 10.   7. Thom. Cel. I, n. 7; *Tres Soc.* n. 13.

8. ". . . . Cupiebat enim possidere sapientiam, quæ auro melior, et prudentiam acquirere, quæ pretiosior est argento." Thom. Cel. I, n. 8 sq.; cf. *Tres Soc.* n. 16.   9. *Tres Soc.* n. 20; Thom. Cel. I, n. 10–15.

10. Dante, *Divina Commedia*, Paradise, Canto XI. Transl. by Henry F. Cary.
11. Matth. x, 8–10.   12. Thom. Cel. I, n. 16. 21–22; *Tres Soc.* n. 25; Iord. a Iano n. 1–2; S. Bonav. c. 3.

13. Regarding Peter Catanii cf. Sabatier, *Spec. perf.* p. 70, note 2.
14. The full narrative in *Tres Soc.* n. 27–29; condensed Thom. Cel. I, n. 24.
15. *Tres Soc.* n. 33. 40.   16. *Tres Soc.* n. 46; Thom. Cel. I, n. 32.
17. *Testam., Opusc.* ed. Böhmer 37, Lemmens 79.   18. Thom. Cel. I, n. 32.
19. Thom. Cel. I, n. 32–34; *Tres Soc.* n. 46–53.

20. ". . . .ut in omnibus regulis suis commendaret potissime paupertatem, et omnes fratres sollicite redderet de pecunia evitanda; plures enim regulas fecit et eas expertus est, priusquam faceret illam, quam ultimo reliquit fratribus." *Tres Soc.* n. 35.

21. "Sæpe vero de paupertate sermonem faciens, ingerebat fratribus evangelicum illud: Vulpes foveas. . ." S. Bonav. c. 7, n. 2.   22. Thom. Cel. II, n. 70.   23. "Domina sancta Paupertas,Dominus te salvet!" *Opusc.* ed. Böhmer 64, Lemmens 20.   24. Thom. Cel. II, n. 82.

25. H. J. Schmitz, *Der Bettler von Assisi und das Rittertum, die Poesie und die Kunst seiner Zeit* (Frankfurter Broschüren, N. F. Band 5, Heft 2) p. 10.

26. Thom. Cel. II, n. 55.   27. *Opusc.* ed. Böhmer 37 sq., Lemmens 79 sq.

28. "Gaudet sanctus et iubilat præ laetitia cordis, quoniam fidem tenuisse Dominæ Paupertati usque in finem se videt." Thom. Cel. II, n. 215.

29. "De patientia et paupertate servanda sermonem protraxit, cæteris institutis sanctum evangelium anteponens." *Ibid.* n. 216. "Semper diligant et observent Dominam Paupertatem." *Spec. perf.* c. 87.   30. Thom. Cel. II, n. 214–216.

31. Dante, *Divina Commedia*, Paradise, Canto XI.

32. It was written but a few months after St. Francis had died (July, 1227), by one of the two Ministers General, either John Parenti, or, more probably, John of Parma.   Fr. Edouard d'Alençon has published the Latin original, with an Italian translation (*Sacrum Commercium B. Francisci cum Domina Paupertate*, Romæ 1900).   Another Italian translation made in the 14th century was published by Salv. Minocchi (*Le mistiche nozze di San Francesco e Madonna Povertà*, Firenze 1901).   Fr. Ubald d'Alençon has made a French version (*Les Noces mystiques du bienheureux François avec Madame la Pauvreté*, Paris, 1913), E. von Némethy, a German, (*Die mystische Hochzeit des hl. Franziskus mit der Frau Armut*, Jena 1913), and Montgomery Carmichael an English version (*The Lady Poverty*, London, Murray, 1902).

33. *Testamentum, Opusc.* ed Böhmer 37, Lemmens, 79; *Tres Soc.* n. 29.

34. Thus the Knights Templar were designated in the original rule: *Lucæ Holstenii Codex Regularum* t. II, Augustæ Vindelicorum 1759, 431; Schnürer, *Die ursprüngliche Templerregel*, Freiburg i. Br. 1903, 130.

35. *Regula Militum Hospitalis S. Ioannis Hierosolymitani* c. 7 sq., Holstenius *ibid.* p. 446.

36. *S. Bernardi Sermones de diversis* 22, 2; 27, 3; 37, 7; Migne, *Patr. lat.* 183, 596. 613. 642.

37. *De vita vere apostolica* lib. I, c. 3. 8; Migne, *Patr. lat.* 170, 615–616.

38. Matth. xix, 21.   39. *Tres Soc.* n. 51.   40. *Spec. perf.* c. 107.

41. "Inveni virum perfectissimum, qui vult secundum formam sancti evangelii vivere et evangelicam perfectionem in omnibus observare." *Tres Soc.* n. 48.

42. "Domina Clara prima plantula sororum pauperum Sancti Damiani de Assisio, æmulatrix præcipua Sancti Francisci in conservanda perfectione evangelica." *Spec. perf.* c. 108.

43. ". . . .eligendo vivere secundum perfectionem sancti evangelii. . ." Ex Regula sororum sanctæ Claræ, *Opusc.* ed. Böhmer 35, Lemmens 75.

44. Ultima voluntas, quam scripsit sororibus sanctæ Claræ, *Opusc.* ed. Böhmer 35, Lemmens 75.

45. "Vixerunt secundum formam sancti evangelii a Domino illis ostensum." *Tres Soc.* n. 29.

46. "Ipse Altissimus revelavit mihi, quod deberem vivere secundum formam sancti evangelii. . ." *Testament.*, *Opusc.* ed. Böhmer 37, Lemmens 79.

47. "Si enim Deus peccatoribus donat bona temporalia propter nutriendorum filiorum amorem, multo magis viris evangelicis, quibus hæc debentur ex merito, largietur." *Tres Soc.* n. 51.

48. "De patientia et paupertate servanda sermonem protraxit, cæteris institutis sanctum evangelium anteponens." Thom. Cel. II, n. 216.

49. *Opusc.*, ed. Lemmens 18. 20 sq., Böhmer: *Admonitiones* c. 27; *Laudes de virt.* 50. S. Bonav. c. 7, n. 1. Cf. Thom. Cel. II, n. 200. 51. Thom. Cel. II, n. 82.

52. Francesco Tresatti, *Le poesie spirituali del B. Iacopone da Todi*, bro. III, Oda 24, Str. 41, 51, 52, Venetia 1617, 351-353. 53. Thom. Cel. II, n. 93.

54. S. Bonav. c. 7, n. 6. The theological proof that poverty excels among the three evangelical counsels, and hence is the basic principle of evangelical perfection, is adduced by St. Bonaventure, *De perfectione evangelica* q. 2, a. 1, *Opera* t. V, 127 sqq. 55. Matth. x, 8-10. 56. Cf. p. 7.

57. Cf. the decrees of the councils of this period, Mansi, *Amplissima Collectio Conciliorum* t. XXII, 224, 792. 819.

58. "Omnes enim, a maximo usque ad minimum, avaritiæ student, diligunt munera, retributiones sequuntur, iustificantes impium pro muneribus et iusti iustitiam auferentes." *Innocentii III Regestorum* lib. 3, 24; Migne, *Patr. lat.* 214, 904. 59. Cf. Michael, *Geschichte des deutschen Volkes* II, 2, 295, 297.

60. Cf. the decrees of the third and fourth Lateran Councils, and of the Provincial Councils of this period, Mansi t. XXII.

61. "Quamvis ad abolendum simoniacam pravitatem a prædecessoribus nostris varia emanaverint instituta, usque adeo tamen. . . . morbus ille irrepsit, ut adhuc, peccatis exigentibus, nec levi potuerit medicamine nec igni curari." *Ibid.* lib. 1, 261; Migne, *Patr. lat.* 214, 220.

62. Cf. Karl Müller, *Die Waldenser und ihre einzelne Gruppen*, Gotha 1886, 108-116; J. B. Pierron, *Die katholischen Armen*, Freiburg i, Br. 1911, 129 ff. 63. Cf. p. 56-73.

64. The ideal love of womanhood as conceived by the Christian knight is expressed typically in the Song of Roland and in Parsifal; its erotic form, typifying a worldly and dissolute knighthood, in the *Artussage* and in *Tristan*.

65. This connubial union of Christ and poverty is described in exquisitely poetic form in the allegory "Sacrum Commercium," ed. Fr. Eduardus Alenç., p. 10-12; von Némethy, 12-16. Cf. *Actus b. Francisci* c. 13, 23-27. 66. Dante, *Div. Commedia*, Paradise, Canto XI.

67. "Hanc Filio Dei familiarem attendens, iam iamque toto orbe repulsam studet charitate perpetua desponsare. Amator ergo factus formæ illius, ut uxori fortius inhæreret. . ." Thom. Cel. II, n. 55.

68. Ultima voluntas quam scripsit S. Franciscus S. Claræ, *Opusc.* ed Böhmer 35, Lemmens 76. 69. Cf. e. g. *Tres Soc.* n. 8.

70. "Sic filium pauperis Dominæ legebat in pauperibus cunctis." Thom. Cel. II. n. 83.

71. "Christi Iesu paupertatem et Matris frequenter cum lacrymis revocabat ad mentem." S. Bonav. c. 7, n. 1.

72. ". . . inde hanc virtutem regiam esse dicebat, quæ in rege et regina tam præstanter effulsit." Thom. Cel. II, n. 199; *Tres Soc.* n. 15; S. Bonav. *ibid.*

73. "Hanc dignitatem regalem, quam pro nobis Dominus Iesus egenus factus assumpsit, ut sua nos ditaret inopia ac vere pauperes spiritu regni cœlorum reges institueret et heredes, nolo relinquere pro feudo divitiarum falsarum vobis ad horam concesso." S. Bonav. c. 7, n. 7. 74. *Tres Soc.* n. 28.
75. *Regula* I, c. 9, *Opusc.* ed. Böhmer 9 sq.; Lemmens 36 sq.
76. *Regula* II, c. 6, ed. Böhmer 32, Lemmens 68 sq.

CHAPTER VI

1. St. Dominic indeed resolved from the very beginning to avoid all luxury in his appearance as preacher, in order to combat the Albigenses more effectively, as his contemporaneous confrères Fr. Jordan (*Legend. B. Dominici* ed. Quétif-Echard, *Scriptores Ord. Præd.* 1, 5), and Fr. Etienne de Bourbon (*Anecdotes historiques* publiés par Lecoy de la Marche, Paris 1877, 79, n. 83; 213, n. 251) record. However, the true ideal of poverty was still strange to Dominic at that time. In 1212 and 1213, while he was harboring the project of founding a new Order and had already found associates for it, he accepted extensive foundations from Count de Montfort: "Necdum enim illa postmodum edita constitutio servabatur, ut nec recipere possessiones nec receptas iam retinere liceret." (Fr. Jordan *ibid.* I, 10, n. 21). In 1215 Bishop Fulco of Toulouse donated the sixth part of the revenues of the diocese to him (*Ibid.* I, 12, n. 23). Shortly after (1216), when Dominic met Francis in Rome, the former resolved to follow the Franciscan ideal and renounce the right of possession; this, however, became a law only in 1220: "Quapropter ne prædicationis, cui summopere debebant impendere, impediretur officium, proposuerat ex tunc (1216) terrenas possessiones et reditus prorsus abiicere, quod postmodum in primo capitulo generali Bononiæ anno Domini MCCXX celebrato affectu pariter et effectu per constitutionem perpetuæ fuit executioni mandatum." (Fr. Constantine of Orvieto, *Leg. B. Dominici* ed. Quétif-Echard, *ibid.* I, 28 f., n. 18; cf. Jordan *ibid.* I, 20, n. 38). In any case it is beyond doubt that the incentive to this resolution came from Francis. Dominic had just applied for the approbation of his Order. He was, however, not only forbidden to write a new rule, but a decree was issued forbidding the introduction of new rules in general (Fr. Constantine *ibid.* I, 28 f., n. 17 ff.). But since on the one hand the old rules did not answer his purpose, and on the other Francis had counseled against uniting the institution of St. Dominic with his own (Thom. Cel. II, n. 150), the latter wished to appropriate at least the original elements of the Franciscan Order, especially poverty as Fr. Angelus of Clareno remarks: "Sanctus vero Dominicus. . . . servatione evangelicæ paupertatis, quam vidit et audivit a S. Francisco et eius sociis, animatus superaddidit regulæ S. Augustini paupertatis evangelicæ altissimam perfectionem: non habere in communi." (Ehrle, *Die Briefsammlung des F. Angelus de Clareno*, in: *Archiv für Litteratur- und Kirchengeschichte* I, 559). Dominic di·l not, moreover, regard the repudiation of property as a means of sanctification as Francis did, but solely as a help to a more effective exercise of the apostolate. Cf. Denifle, *Die Konstitutionen des Predigerordens vom Jahre 1228*, in: *Archiv, loc. cit.* I, 182 f. Also: Berthold Altauer, *Die Armutsidee des hl. Dominikus*, in: *Theologie und Glaube* XI (1919), 405–417; *Die Beziehungen des hl. Dominikus zum hl. Franziskus*, in: *Franziskanische Studien* IX (1922), 1–28. According to Altauer, Dominic met Francis after 1218; consequently he would not have been influenced directly and personally by Francis in the question of poverty, but only indirectly by the Franciscan movement.

2. "Viri probatissimi et sapientissimi in religionibus . . . sic sua reliquerunt, quod communia possederunt." *De paupertate evangelica* q. 2, a. 2, *Opera* V, 136. A complete compilation of the respective precepts regarding poverty in the older rules was made in the ninth century by St. Benedict of Aniane in his *Concordia Regularum* c. 42; Migne, *Patrol. lat.* 103, 1057 sqq.

3. Cf. the Rule of the Templars written by St. Bernard at the Council of

Troyes in 1128 (Schnürer, *Die ursprüngliche Templerregel*, Freiburg i. Br. 1903, 135 ff.).

4. Cf. Fr. Eberhard Hoffmann, S. Ord. Cist., *Das Konverseninstitut des Zisterzienserordens*, Freiburg i. Schw., 1905; on page 27, the 15th chapter of the "Exordium parvum," composed by Abbot St. Stephen in 1120, can be found.

5. Cf. Karl Müller, *Die Waldenser und ihre einzelne Gruppen*, Gotha 1886, 7. f.

6. The Waldenses who returned to the Church, that is the "Catholic Poor Men" in France (since 1208), and the "re-united" Lombards of Italy (since 1210), retained the principle of absolute poverty after their conversion (cf. J. B. Pierron, *Die katholischen Armen*, Freiburg i. Br. 1911, 173. 176), but had little influence and disappeared after a few years.

7. *Tres Soc.* n. 35. Bishop Guido himself had several lawsuits of this kind with the Crucigeri as well as with the Benedictines of Monte Subasio. Cf. *Opera Honorii III.* ed. Horoy, *Medii ævi bibliotheca patristica*, Series prima, Paris 1879, I, 163. 200; Potthast, *Regesta Roman. Pontificum*, Berol. 1874, n. 7728. 7746.

8. Thom. Cel. I, n. 33. 9. *Tres Soc.* n. 51; cf. Thom. Cel. I, n. 32 sq.

10. "At sanctus Franciscus suasionem eius (Cardinalis Ioannis a S. Paulo) humiliter prout poterat, recusabat, non persuasa despiciendo, sed alia pie affectando altiori desiderio ferebatur." Thom. Cel. I, n. 33.

11. Matth. viii, 20; Luke ix, 58. 12. Matth. xix, 21; Mark x, 21; Luke xviii, 22. 13. Luke xiv, 33. 14. Matth. x, 8-10. 15. Luke xii, 33.

16. Although most Catholic as well as non-Catholic writers emphasize the harmony of the Franciscan ideal of poverty with that of the Gospel, Ad. Ott asserts (*Thomas von Aquin und das Mendikantentum*, Freiburg i. Br. 1908, 6 f.), that the Franciscan ideal, which demands absolute poverty of the individual as well as of the Order as such, must even be regarded as "Biblically recorded." This opinion is very ably refuted by Fr. Th. Soiron, O. F. M., *Das Armutsideal des hl. Franz von Assisi und die Lehre Jesu über die Armut*, in: *Franziskanische Studien* IV (1917), 1-17. Cf. Fr. Ubald d'Alençon, O. M. Cap., *L'âme franciscaine* 2me éd., Paris 1913, and the various articles by Fr. Antoine de Sérent dealing with this work (*L'âme franciscaine*, in: *Archiv. franc. histor.* VIII, 448-466), and also by Fr. Leone Bracalone, O. F. M. (*A proposito di una pubblicazione "L'Anima francescana,"* in: *Archiv. franc. histor.* VIII, 467-481).

17. Thom. Cel. II, n. 12; *Tres Soc.* n. 20. 18. Cf. p. 78 f. 19. Thom. Cel. II, n. 55. 20. *Tres Soc.* n. 28 sq.; Thom. Cel. I, n. 24. 21. *Opusc.* ed. Böhmer 37, Lemmens 79. 22. S. Bonav. c. 7, n. 3; Thom. Cel. II, n. 80. 23. Thom. Cel. II, n. 81. 24. *Ibid.* 25. *Spec. perf.* c. 57. 26. *Regula* I, c. 2, *Opusc.* ed. Böhmer 2, Lemmens 26.

27. "Sæpe etiam, si fratres egerent, potius ad alios recurrere quam ad intrantes ordinem docuit, primo quidem propter exemplum, deinde ad vitandam omnem turpis commodi speciem." Thom. Cel. II, n. 81. 28. Thom. Cel. II, n. 67; S. Bonav. c. 7, n. 4.

29. The Chaparon, which distinguished the garb of the novice from that of the professed Religious, consisted of a piece of cloth which covered head and shoulders. Later on the superiors made use of the authority granted by the rule and ordained that novices also could wear the cowl, but with a strip of cloth in front, and, in some Provinces, also in back.

30. *Regula* II, c. 2, *Opusc.* ed. Böhmer 30, Lemmens 64.

31. *Regula* I, c. 7, *Opusc.* ed. Böhmer 8, Lemmens 34.

32. *Regula* II, c. 6, *Opusc.* ed. Böhmer 32, Lemmens 68.

33. *Testam.*, *Opusc.* ed. Böhmer 38, Lemmens 80.

34. ". . . Et quum ex longa familiaritate, quam idem confessor [B. Franciscus] Nobiscum habuit, plenius noverimus intentionem ipsius; et in condendo prædictam regulam, obtinendo confirmationem ipsius per Sedem Apostolicam sibi astiterimus . . . declarari postulastis dubia et obscura Regulæ prædictæ, nec non super quibusdam difficilibus responderi . . . præsertim quum iam dixerint aliqui proprietatem mobilium pertinere ad totum Ordinem in communi. . ." Gregorii IX Bulla "Quo elongati," *Bullar. franc.* I, 68.

35. "Dicimus itaque, quod nec in communi nec in speciali debeant proprie-

tatem habere: sed utensilium ac librorum, et eorum mobilium, quæ licet habere, eorum usum habeant: et fratres secundum quod Generalis Minister vel Provinciales dixerint, iis utantur, salvo locorum et domorum dominio illis, ad quos noscitur pertinere." *Ibid.* 69.

36. *Salutatio virtutum, Opusc.* ed. Böhmer 65, Lemmens 21.

37. *Actus B. Francisci* c. 13, n. 22 sq.   38. Thom. Cel. II, n. 216.

39. A reference to Ps. lxx, 15: "Quoniam non cognovi litteraturam, introibo in potentias Domini."   40. S. Bonav. c. 7, n. 2; cf. Thom. Cel. II, n. 194.

41. *Testamentum, Opusc.* ed. Böhmer 37, Lemmens 79.   42. Thom. Cel. I, n. 39.

43. They soon after relinquished it in favor of St. Francis and his associates. Francis accepted it gratefully, but on the condition that the abbey retain the title to it, and that he be allowed to send the monks a basket of fish annually as tribute.

44. "Et fecerunt ibi unam domunculam, in qua aliquando pariter morarentur." *Tres Soc.* c. 9.   ". . . aliquam parvam et pauperculam domunculam ex luto et viminibus constructam, ubi fratres possint quiescere et operari. . ." *Spec. perf.* c. 55.

45. Formerly every village, and also many farms, had a bake-oven, separated from the other buildings. Whenever the oven had been fired during the day, the oven itself, or the building in which it stood, retained enough warmth to serve as welcome night-quarters for journeymen, soldiers and other homeless wayfarers.

46. "Nam, cum sæpe in maximis frigoribus necessario carerent hospitio, clibanus recolligebat eos, vel certe in cryptis seu speluncis humiliter noctibus latitabant." Thom. Cel. I, n. 39.   47. *Tres Soc.* n. 34, 38 sqq.

48. "Nihil insuper sibi proprium vindicabant, sed libris et aliis collatis, eisdem utebantur communiter secundum regulam ab apostolis traditam et conservatam." *Tres Soc.* n. 43.

49. "Cœperunt cum sancta paupertate ibidem habere commercium. . ."   50. Thom. Cel. I, n. 34. sq.

51. ". . . Nam, ut ait sanctus, citius de tugurio quam de palatio in cælum ascenditur. . ."

52. Thom. Cel. I, n. 42–44; *Tres Soc.* n. 55.

53. In some of the Provinces the brothers did not set foot before 1219; cf. Iord. a Iano, n. 3.

54. Francis himself undertook a journey to Syria in 1212 to convert the Saracens, and to Morocco in 1213 (according to Celano I, n. 55 sq.).   In 1219 he again journeyed to the Orient, as we shall presently see.

55. Iacobi Vitriacensis *Epistola data Ianuæ* a. 1216, Böhmer, *Analekten* 94; Iord. a Iano n. 16; *Tres Soc.* n. 57.   56. *Tres Soc.* n. 59 sq.

57. Iacobi Vitriacensis *Historia orientalis* lib. 2, c. 32, Böhmer *ibid.* 102–104.

58. *Vita B. Ægidii* c. 3, *Act. SS.*, Aprilis t. III, 227, 15.

59. "Fratres Minores ex parte sunt iuvenes et pueri.   Unde si iuxta ætatum suarum flexibilitatem sunt mutabiles et proclives, non est contra rerum naturam. Ipsi autem iam ad extremam dementiam pervenerunt, quia per civitates et oppida et loca solitaria sine discretione vagantur, horribilia et inhumana martiria tolerando." Buoncompagno, Rhetorica antiqua, Schönbach, *Beiträge zur Erklärung altdeutscher Dichtwerke*, II. Stück, S. 68, in: *Sitzungsberichte der Wiener Akademie, philos.-hist. Klasse*, Bd. 145 (1902), Wien 1903.

60. "Hæc tamen religio valde periculosa nobis videtur, eo quod non solum perfecti, sed etiam iuvenes et imperfecti, qui sub conventuali disciplina aliquo tempore artari et probari debuissent, per universum mundum bini et bini dividuntur." *Iacobi Vitriac. Epistola* a. 1220 Mart., Damiatæ, Böhmer, *Analekten* 101.   61. Iord. a Iano n. 3–11.   62. *Ibid.* n. 11–13.   63. *Ibid.* n. 14–15.

64. Regarding these changes cf. Karl Müller, *Die Anfänge des Minoritenordens und der Bussbruderschaften*, Freiburg i. Br. 1885, 68 ff.

65. Thom. Cel. II, n. 56.   66. *Spec. perf.* c. 10.

67. "Docebat suos habitacula paupercula facere, ligneas non lapideas, easque

vili schemate casellas erigere." Thom. Cel. II, n. 56; *Spec. perf.* c. 5. 10.   68. *Spec. perf.* c. 11.   69. *Determinationes quæst.* pars. s, q. 6, *Opera* VIII, 341.

70. "Volebat, ut fratres non in magna quantitate in locis collocarentur, quia sibi difficile videbatur in magna multitudine paupertatem observari." *Spec. perf.* c. 10.   71. *Spec. perf.* c. 7.   72. Iord. a Iano n. 16.   73. Eccleston coll. 6, p. 40.

74. Eccleston *ibid.;* Thom. Cel. II, n. 57; *Spec. perf.* c. 7.   75. *Spec. perf.* c. 10.   76. *Liber de laudibus b. Fr.* c. 4, 31.   77. *Determinationes quæst. ibid.*   78. *Ibid. quæst.* 15, p. 367.

79. Thom. Cel. II, n. 58; S. Bonav. c. 7, n. 2; *Spec. perf.* c. 6.

80. Thom. Cell. II, n. 59; *Spec. perf.* c. 9.

81. "Nolebat locellum aliquem fratres inhabitare, nisi certus ad quem proprietas pertineret, constaret patronus.   Leges enim peregrinorum in filiis suis semper quæsivit, sub alieno videlicet colligi tecto, pacifice pertransire, sitire ad patriam." Thom. Cel. II, n. 59.   82. Cf. p. 101 f.

83. "Docebat fratres, ut pauperum more pauperculas casa erigerent, quas non inhabitarent ut proprias, sed sicut peregrini et advenæ alienas." S. Bonav. c. 7, n. 2.

84. Regarding the first-named Orders no proof is necessary; regarding the Clerics Regular (from whom also the Dominicans originated), Fr. Denifle adduces numerous proofs in: *Archiv für Literatur-und Kirchengeschichte* I, 178 f.

85. The Benedictine Matthew of Paris, who was unfavorable to the Mendicants, criticizes just this in the Mendicants.   The geniune monastic life is represented, according to him, only by the Benedictines and Cistercians: "Non enim vagabantur per civitates et pagos, non erat eis pro claustrali maceria oceanus, sed infra muros suos clausi et stabiles conversantes." Matth. Paris., *Chronica maiora* ed. *Monum. Germ. hist. Script.* XXVIII, 355, lin. 9 sqq.

86. "Cantabiles mihi erant iustificationes tuæ in loco peregrinationis meae." Ps. cxviii, 54.   87. Iord. a Iano n. 43.   88. Cf. p. 129 ff.

89. "Dico ergo, quod fratribus horum concessus est usus, sed vetatur appropriatio.   Nam non dicit regula, quod fratres nihil habeant nec aliqua re utantur, quod esset insanum; sed, quod nihil sibi approprient." *De tribus quæstionibus* ed. *Opera* t. VIII, 333.

90. "Iniungo omnibus fratribus meis tam clericis quam laicis euntibus per mundum vel morantibus in locis, quod nullo modo apud se vel apud alium nec aliquo modo bestiam aliquam habeant.   Nec eis liceat equitare, nisi infirmitate vel magna necessitate cogantur." *Regula* I, c. 15, *Opusc.* ed. Böhmer 14, Lemmens 43.   In the second rule there is no precept prohibiting the keeping of beasts, but there is one forbidding to ride on horseback: *Reg.* II, c. 3, Böhmer 31, Lemmens 67.

91. On this score, riding was also forbidden in the rule of the Dominicans. Albert the Great traveled as Provincial and as Bishop always on foot.   Brothers who failed against this precept were punished with the discipline and fasting on bread and water.   (Sighart, *Albertus Magnus. Sein Leben und seine Wissenschaft*, Regensburg 1857, 86).   92. *Spec. perf.* c. 10.

93. "In libris testimonium Dei quærere non pretium, ædificationem non pulchritudinem edocebat." Thom. Cel. II, n. 62.

94. "In stratis et lectis ita abundabat copiosa paupertas, ut qui super paleam haberet panniculos semisanos pro matalaciis reputaret." *Spec. perf.* c. 6.

95. "Non solum domorum arrogantiam odiebat homo iste, verum domorum utensilia multa vel exquisita plurimum perhorrebat.   Nihil in mensis, nihil in vasis quo mundi recordaretur amabat, ut omnia peregrinationem, omnia cantaret exsilium." Thom. Cel. II, n. 60.

96. "Omni studio, omni sollicitudine custodiebat sanctam et divinam paupertatem, non patiens, ne quando ad superflua perveniret, nec vasculum in domo aliquod residere, cum sine ipso utcumque posset extremæ necessitatis evadere servitutem.   Impossibile namque fore, aiebat, satisfacere necessitati et voluptati non obedire." Thom. Cel. I, n. 51.

97. Thom. Cel. II, n. 61.   98. Matth. x, 9 sq.   99. *Testamentum*, ed. Böhmer 37, Lemmens 79.

100. Mark vi, 8 sq. Cf. P. Soiron, O. F. M., *Das Armutsideal des hl. Franz von Assisi*, in: *Franziskan. Studien* VII (1917) 10 f.

101. "Et dixit eis: Quando misi vos sine sacculo et pera et calceamentis, numquid aliquid defuit vobis? At illi dixerunt: Nihil. Dixit ergo eis: Sed nunc qui habet sacculum, tollat similiter et peram, et qui non habet, vendat tunicam suam et emat gladium." Luke xxii, 35 sq.

102. "Tunicas superiores. . . tunicas inferiores . . . et bracas . . ." Iord. a Iano n. 6; cf. *ibid.* n. 20, for the year 1221.   103. *Regula* I, c. 2, *Opusc.* ed. Böhmer 3, Lemmens 27.

104. This was intended by Francis from the beginning: "Parat sibi ex tunc tunicam crucis imaginem præferentem." Thom. Cel. I, n. 22.   Later writings assert the same.   105. *Regula* I, *ibid., Opusc.* ed. Böhmer 2, Lemmens 26.   106. *Ibid.* c. 14.   107. *Spec. perf.* c. 3.

108. The precept forbidding money was retained in a different connection, as we shall see.

109. Sandals also were worn by the brothers in the first years.   Francis himself put aside his shoes at the time of his final calling.   (Thom. Cel. I, n. 22; *Tres Soc.* n. 25).   That in the following years the brothers did not wear sandals is evident from the comparison which Abbot Burchard of Ursperg (died 1226) draws between the Poor Men of Lyons and the Minorites: "Pauperes de Lugduno . . . calceos desuper pedem precidebant et *quasi nudis pedibus* ambulabant. . . Pauperes Minores *precise nudis pedibus* tam æstate quam hieme ambulabant" (*Burchardi Urspergensis Chronicon* ed. Abel-Weiland, *Monum. Germ. hist. Script.* XXIII, 376).   As we have shown, Francis was acquainted only with the words of the Mission according to Matth. x, 10, and Luke x, 4, in which shoes are forbidden to the disciples, and not with those of Mark vi, 8 sq., in which sandals are allowed.   From various writings of St. Bonaventure we learn that in the meantime the use of sandals had become general in the Order and that this custom was rightly based on the words and example of Christ and the Apostles.   (*Apologia pauperum* c. 6, n. 6 sqq.; *Epistola de sandaliis Apostolorum; Expositio in Regulam Fratrum Minorum* c. 2, n. 17 sqq., *Opera* VIII, 268. 386-390. 402).   St. Bonaventure answers his opponent, who had asserted that it was contrary to the Gospel and improper for the Brothers to go without covering for the feet, with the striking retort: "Tu igitur, qui Evangelii doctor es et sectator, si huius evangelicæ perfectionis apicem non attingis usu, attingas saltem affectu pio, affatu veridico et catholico intellectu, et noli . . . contra evangelicorum pedum nuditatem pelles mortuas defensare." (*Ep. de sandaliis apostolorum* n. 16, *Opera* VIII, 390).

110. "Habeant unam tunicam cum caputio et aliam sine caputio, qui voluerint habere.   Et qui necessitate coguntur, possint portare calceamenta." *Reg.* II, c. 2, *Opusc.* ed. Böhmer 30, Lemmens 65.   In order to estimate this precept more correctly, we place the parallel ordinance of the oldest constitutions of the Dominican Order (1228) by its side: "Et non plures tunicas (defferant fratres) quam tres cum pellicio in yeme vel quatuor sine pellicio, quod semper tunica copertum deferatur.   Pellibus silvestribus et coopertoriis quarumcumque pellium fratres nostri non utantur.   Tunicæ circa cavillam pedis sufficit ut descendant, quibus cappa brevior sit et etiam pellicium.   Scapularia nostra circa cooperturam genuum sufficit ut descendant.   Caligas et soccos habebimus ut necesse fuerit et facultas permiserit.   Ocreas non habebimus nec chirothecas." (*Constitutiones antiquæ ord. fratrum prædicatorum* ed. P. Denifle in: *Archiv für Lit.- und Kirchengesch. des Mittelalters* I, 104).   Three coats therefore with fur, or four without fur; over that, scapular and mantle; shoes and stockings according to necessity, but no boots or gloves.

111. *Regula* II, c. 2.   112. Thom. Cell II, n. 65.

113. ". . . . secundum loca [individual houses] et tempora et frigidas regiones." *Regula* II, c. 4, *Opusc.* ed. Böhmer 32, Lemmens 67.

114. The luxury in clothing indulged in by many monks can best be judged

from the reformatory statutes of the Cistercians (S. *Stephani Abbatis Cist. Exordium parvum* c. 15, Migne, *Patrol. lat.* 166, 1507) and Cluniacensians (*Petri Venerab. Statuta Congregat. Cluniac.* c. 18, Migne, *Patrol. lat.* 189, 1030 sq.) and likewise from the contemporary decrees of Councils, e.g. of the Council of Paris, 1212: "Inhibemus districte illis [religiosis] auctoritate apostolica, ne chirothecis albis de corio, quibus uti solent sæculares, et quæ sunt quasi signum lasciviæ, utantur; vel calceamentis sæcularibus, puta hosellis, vel calceis nimis strictis et peracutis [pointed shoes], vel pileis, quae vulgo dicuntur de coton, vel opertoriis pretiosis, puta variis vel griseis, vel de ciragrallis, vel de cuniculis, vel de venetis. Pannis etiam non utantur nisi nigris vel albis, et non sumptuosis, aut satellis pictis vel discoloribus, suis vel alienis." Harduin, *Acta Conciliorum* VII, 2007, X.

115. *Regula* II, c. 2, ed. Böhmer 31, Lemmens 65.
116. *Regula* I, c. 2, ed. Böhmer 3, Lemmens 27.
117. "Tantum adhuc laxabitur rigor, dominabitur tepor, quod filii pauperis patris etiam scarlaticos portare, colore solum mutato, minime verebuntur." Thom. Cel. II, n. 69. Petrus Venerab. *loc. cit.* testifies that some monks were led by the "vestium damnata curiositas" to parade in scarlet clothing. 118. *Ibid.*
119. "Revera ipse a principio religionis usque ad mortem tunica sola, corda et femoralibus dives, nihil aliud habuit. Indicabat eius habitus pauper ubi suas divitias aggregaret." Thom. Cel. II, n. 55.
120. "Ut tales suo exemplo confunderet, super tunicam propriam rudem consuit saccum; in morte etiam exsequialem tunicam vili sacco petiit operiri." *Ibid.* n. 69. 121. Thom. Cel. II, n. 214 sq.
122. Ad. Harnack remarks rightly: "It is a well-known fact that poverty was the dominant theme in the history of the thirteenth and fourteenth centuries, that they argued as stubbornly and as hotly about it as about the natures of Christ from the fourth to the sixth century." *Dogmengeschichte* III, Freiburg i, Br. 1897, 388. Cf. Balthasar, *Geschichte des Armutsstreites im Franziskanerorden bis zum Konzil von Vienne*, Münster 1911.

CHAPTER VII

1. Cf. H. v. Scheel, *Der Begriff des Geldes in seiner historisch-ökonomischen Entwicklung*, in: *Jahrbücher für Nationalökonomie und Statistik* 6 (1866), 12–29; Walther Lotz, *Die Lehre vom Ursprung des Geldes, ibid.* 62 (1894), 337–359; Emil Michael, *Geschichte des deutschen Volkes seit dem dreizehnten Jahrhundert bis zum Ausgang des Mittelalters* I, Freiburg i. Br. 1897, 136–144.
2. See p. 78. 3. See p. 7.
4. "Verum summopere amicus Dei cuncta, quæ sunt mundi, despiciens, super omnia tamen exsecrabatur pecuniam. Inde illam a principio suæ conversionis præcipue vilipendit, et tamquam ipsum diabolum se sequentibus semper innuit fugiendam. Hæc ab ipso data erat solertia suis: ut stercus et pecuniam uno amoris pretio ponderarent." Thom. Cel. II, n. 65.
5. *Tres Soc.* n. 29.
6. "Cum autem Dominus Bernardus bona sua pauperibus largiretur aderat beatus Franciscus intuens virtuosam operationem Domini, et ipsum Dominum in corde suo glorificans et collaudans." *Ibid.* n. 30. 7. *Ibid.* n. 30–31.
8. "Noluit ergo vir, quod daretur eis aliquod tegumentum, licet esset tunc magnum frigus: quia putabat eos esse ribaldos et fures. . . Calefacti solo calore divino et cooperti tegumento Dominæ Paupertatis. . . ." *Tres Soc.* n. 39. 9. *Ibid.* n. 39 sq.
10. "Ipsi autem Christi pauperes neque sacculum in via portant . . . neque æs sive pecuniam aliquam in zonis suis, non possidentes aurum neque argentum. . ." (*Iacobi Vitriac. Historia orientalis* lib. 2, c. 32, Böhmer, *Analekten*

103). "Pauperes minores . . . neque pecuniam nec quidquam aliud præter victum accipiebant et si quando necessariam quisquam eis sponte conferebat. . ." (*Burchardi Ursperg. Chronicon* ed. Abel-Weiland, *Monum. Germ. hist. Script.* XXIII, 376). 11. *Tres Soc.* n. 41. 12. *Ibid.* n. 45. 13. Thom. Cel. II, n. 65.

14. Thom. Cel. II, n. 68. A similar occurrence is related by Thom. Cel. II, n. 66.

15. "Pecuniam contempsit in tantum, ut in omnibus regulis suis commendaret potissime paupertatem et omnes fratres sollicitos redderet de pecunia evitanda." *Tres Soc.* n. 35.

16. *Regula* I, c. 2, *Opusc.* ed. Böhmer 2, Lemmens 26.

17. *Regula* I, c. 7, *Opusc.* ed. Böhmer 7, Lemmens 33.

18. *Regula* I, c. 8, *Opusc.* ed. Böhmer 8 sq., Lemmens 35 sq.

19. *Regula* II, c. 4, *Opusc.* ed. Böhmer 31 sq., Lemmens 67.

20. The principal passage of this important decree is as follows: "Duximus respondendum, quod si rem necessariam velint fratres emere, vel solutionem facere pro iam empta, possint vel nuntium eius, a quo res emitur, vel aliquem alium volentibus sibi eleemosynam facere, præsentare, qui taliter præsentatus non est eorum nuntius, licet præsentetur ab ipsis, sed illius potius, cuius mandato solutionem fecit seu recipientis eandem. . . Si vero pro aliis imminentibus necessitatibus præsentetur, eleemosynam sibi commissam potest, sicut et dominus, apud spiritualem amicum fratrem deponere, per ipsum loco et tempore pro ipsorum huiusmodi necessitatibus, sicut expedire viderit, dispensandam. Ad quem etiam fratres pro huiusmodi necessitatibus poterunt habere recursum maxime si negligens fuerit, vel necessitates ignoraverit eorundem." Bull "Quo elongati," *Bullar. franc.* I, 69. 21. Luke xxii, 35–36. 22. Matth. xvii, 23 sqq. 23. John xii, 6.

24. St. Bonaventure remarks hereto: "Christus habuit loculos tribus de causis: pro pauperibus aliis, condescendo infirmis, in articulo necessitatis, utpote quando transibat per Samaritanos. In quo etiam articulo discipulis loculos habere permisit secundum illud: 'Quando misi vos sine sacculo et pera etc.' . . . . Modus habendi loculos in Domino in nullo minuit paupertatem. Sic enim Dominus condescendit infirmitati et necessitati, ut tamen salva esset forma paupertatis et exemplum, quod præcipue monstrare venerat hominibus." *De perfectione evangelica* q. IV, a. 1, *Opera* V, 131.

25. "Nautas quosdam Anconam tendentes, ut eum secum transveherent, exoravit. Verum hoc agere pertinacius recusantibus propter defectum expensarum, sanctus Dei, confidens plurimum de Domini bonitate, navem latenter cum socio introivit." Thom. Cel., *Tractatus de miraculis* n. 33. 26. Bull "Ex parte," March 17, 1226, *Bullar. franc.* I, 26, n. 25.

27. St. Benedict stresses this point in Rule c. 48: "Tunc fratres vere monachi sunt, si labore manuum suarum vivunt, sicut et Patres nostri et Apostoli."

28. "In bene moderatis monasteriis constitutum est, aliquid manibus operari, et cæteras horas habere ad legendum et orandum." *De opere monachorum* c. 29, Migne, *Patrol. lat.* 40, 576.

29. "Otiositas inimica est animæ; et ideo certis temporibus occupari debent fratres in labore manuum, certis iterum horis in lectione divina." *S. Benedicti Regula* c. 48.

30. "Si quis ita negligens et desidiosus fuerit, ut non velit aut non possit meditari aut legere, iniungatur ei opus, quod faciat, ut non vacet." *Ibid.*

31. *S. Bernardi Epistol.* I, n. 4; Migne, *Patrol. lat.* 182, 73.

32. *Dialogus inter Cluniacensem et Cisterciensem monachum*, in: Martène et Durand, *Thesaurus novus anecdotorum*, Lut. Paris. 1717, t. V, 1623, n. 52.

33. The "litteratura" of the monks from the 11th to the 13th century must of course not be rated too high. In many cases it consisted merely in memorizing the Psalter. A large number of monks were in fact illiterates. Cf. P. Eberhard Hoffmann, *Das Konverseninstitut des Zisterzienserordens*, Freiburg (Schweiz) 1905, 40. During the 13th century, however, the older monasteries again resumed literary labors. (Cf. Felder, *Geschichte der wissenschaftl. Studien*

im Franziskanerorden 118–120). 34. *Testamentum, Opusc.* ed. Böhmer 37,
Lemmens 79.

35. St. Thomas of Aquinas thus elucidates the relation between poverty and
labor: "Mercenarii [wage-earners] pauperes sunt, de laboribus suis victum
quærentes quotidianum; et ideo lex provide ordinavit, ut statim eis merces
solveretur, ne victus eis deficeret" (*Summa* I, 2, q. 105, a. 2 ad 6). Servants
and artisans were also classed as "mercenarii," receiving their livelihood in
return for their labors. Cf. Anton von Kostanecki, *Arbeit und Armut*, Freiburg
i. Br. 1909, 25–42. 36. *Testam., Opusc.* ed. Böhmer 36, Lemmens 77. Cf.
Thom. Cel. I, n. 17. 37. Thom. Cel. I, n. 16. 38. *Tres Soc.* n. 21 sqq. 39.
Thom. Cel. II, n. 120.

40. "Fecerat quadam quadragesima vasculum quoddam, circa quod minutia
temporis, ne penitus exciderent, applicaverat." *Ibid.* n. 97.

41. "Proponebat, Christo duce, ingentia se facturum. . . Flagrabat proinde
desiderio magno ad humilitatis reverti primordia, et præ amoris immensitate
spe gaudens, corpus suum, licet ad tantam iam devenisset extremitatem, revo-
care cogitavit ad pristinam servitutem. . . Volebat ad serviendum leprosis
redire denuo. . ." Thom. Cel. II, n. 103.

42. "Solliciti erant quotidie orare et laborare manibus suis, ut omnem otiosi-
tatem, animæ inimicam, a se penitus effugarent." *Tres Soc.* n. 41.

43. "Macerabant autem carnem suam multis ieiuniis, frigore et nuditate et
labore manuum suarum. Multoties enim, ut non starent otiosi, iuvabant pauperes homines in agris eorum, et postea ipsi dabant eisdem de pane amore Dei."
Spec. perf. c. 56.

44. "Conversabantur in eodem loco cum b. patre filii et fratres omnes in
labore multo et inopia universarum rerum." Thom. Cel. I, n. 42.

45. Two chapels of this leprosorium are still extant, San Rufino d'Arce and
Santa Maria Maddalena. For the illustrations see Schnürer, *Franz von Assisi*,
1907, 52.

46. Epist. I. data Ianuae a. 1216, Böhmer, *Analekten*, 98. Regarding the
Poor Clares, Jacques de Vitry also says: "Mulieres vero iuxta civitates in
diversis hospitiis commorantur, nihil accipiunt, sed de labore manuum vivunt."
Ibid. loc. cit. 47. Thom. Cel. I, n. 39 sq.

48. "Raro autem alicui pro tota die se obligabat, ut posset opportuno tempore orationi vacare. Si quando autem pro tota die se obligabat, semper reser-
vabat sibi, ut posset dicere horas suas." *Vita fr. Ægidii, Analecta franc.* III, 82.

49. "Omnia autem laboriosa, quae operabatur, voluntarie semper et alacriter
faciebat." *Ibid.* 84.

50. "Nullum laboritium quantumlibet vile verecundabatur facere, dummodo
illud honeste facere posset." *Ibid.* 82. 51. *Ibid.* 79. 52. *Ibid.* 77. 53. *Ibid.*
81 sq. 54. *Ibid.* 83 sq. 55. Ps. cxxvii, 2. 56. 2 Thess. iii, 10; 1 Cor. vii, 24.

57. *S. Hieronymus, Epist.* 125, n. 11; Migne, *Patrol. lat.* 22, 1078.

58. *S. Anselmus Cant., Epist.* lib. 3, 49; Migne, *Patrol. lat.* 159, 81.

59. *Regula* I, c. 7, ed. Böhmer 7 sq., Lemmens 33 sq.

60. *Regula* II, c. 5, *Opusc.* ed. Böhmer 32, Lemmens 68.

61. *Testamentum, Opusc.* ed. Böhmer 37 sq., Lemmens 79.

62. See Chapter XVII, "Franciscan Science."

63. Bull "Cum secundum," Sept. 22, 1220, *Bullar. francisc.* I, 6.

64. Cf. Felder, *Geschichte der wissenschaftl. Studien im Franziskanerorden*, 67 f.
65. *Ibid.* 71.

66. St. Bonaventure remarks regarding the chapter dealing with labor in the
rule of 1223, that Francis did not expect any monetary returns accruing from
the manual labor of the brothers, just as he himself did not earn as much as
twelve deniers during his whole life: "Ipse autem de labore manuum parvam
vim faciebat nisi propter otium declinandum, quia, cum ipse fuerit regulæ
observator perfectissimus, non credo, quod unquam lucratus fuerit de labore
manuum duodecim denariis vel eorum valorem; sed potissime fratres ad orationem monebat, nec volebat quod illam exstinguerent propter lucrum." *Epist.
de tribus quæst.* n. 9; *Opera* VIII, 334.

67. Larger vegetable gardens were laid out (since 1240) by the Minister General Fr. Haymo, who declared that it was evidently better that the brothers raise their own vegetables, than that they should beg for them. (Fr. Thomæ de Eccleston, *Tractatus de Adventu Fratrum Minorum in Angliam*, coll. 10, ed. Little, Paris 1909, 55 sq.). St. Bonaventure defended the laying out of spacious monastery gardens, declaring that they were necessary "for the raising of vegetables as well as for the sake of air, so that the sick may recuperate, the healthy relax, and those exhausted by mental labor may regain strength." (*Determinationes quæst.* pars 2, q. 6, *Opera* VIII, 341).

68. The legislators of the ancient monasteries, whose inmates were almost exclusively lay-brothers, excoriated idleness as did Francis. St. Augustine rebukes certain lazy monks with fine sarcasm, and continues: "It is not proper that the workmen do not work in that religious state in which senators become laborers, and that the servants indulge themselves, while the lords renounce all luxury" (*De opere monachorum* c. 25, n. 33; Migne, *Patrol. lat.* 40, 575). Benedict of Nursia inveighs severely against idleness, and directs that even delicate and sick brothers occupy themselves as much as their condition permits (*Regula S. Benedicti* c. 48). When later on some Benedictines, in particular those of Cluny, did away with manual labor, Peter the Venerable was forced to introduce it again (1146), giving as reason: "Otiositas . . . in tantum magnam partem nostrorum, maxime eorum qui conversi dicuntur, occupaverat, ut in claustris vel extra claustra, præter paucos legentes et raros scribentes, aut adhærentes claustri parietibus domitarent, aut ab ipso, ut ita dicam, ortu solis usque ad eius occasum, imo fere mediam noctem, quibus impune licebat, totam pene diem vanis, otiosis et (quod peius est) etiam detractoriis verbis consumerent" (*Statuta Congreg. Cluniac.* n. 39; Migne *Patrol. lat.* 189, 1037). 69. Thom. Cel. II, n. 161. 70. *Ibid.* n. 162.

71. Fr. Salimbene. *Liber de prælato*, Parmæ 1857, 404.

72. "Labori sunt astricti validi et fortes, et qui vitam in sæculo de labore corporis transigebant, et tales . . . plures erant in exordio religionis minorum fratrum; et ideo ad labores erant arctandi; nunc autem comparatione aliorum *paucissimi* sunt tales." *De perfectione evangelica* q. 2, a. 2, *Opera* V, 154.

73. St. Bonaventure says *loc. cit.* that the lay-brothers be "solicitous for the needs of the brothers—circa necessaria fratrum intenti."

74. The enemies of the Mendicant Orders, in particular William of St. Amour, asserted that Francis had obliged also the educated brothers to perform manual labor. This assertion was refuted by St. Bonaventure in various writings (*De perfectione evangelica* q. 2, *Opera* V, 144–165; *Epistola de tribus quæstionibus* n. 9, *Opera* VIII, 334; *Expositio super Regulam FF. Minorum* c. 5, *Opera* VIII, 419 sq.; *Apologia pauperum* c. 12, *Opera* VIII, 320 sq.) and condemned by Alexander IV in 1256 (Bull "Non sine," *Bullar. franc.* II, 165).

75. "Cum labore sudandum sit, ut veritas cognoscatur, ut cognita diligatur, et cognita et dilecta aliis proponatur." S. Bonav., *De perfect. evangel.* q. 2, a. 2, n. 9; *Opera* V, 145.

76. "Quanto enim spiritus melior est corpore, tanto spiritualis quam corporalis exercitatio fructuosior." *Ibid.* 165. "Labor sapientiæ simpliciter melior est corporeo labore." (S. Bonav., *Expositio Regulæ* c. 5, n. 4; *Opera* VIII, 420).

77. "Si enim corporalia faciendo meretur quis sustentamentum, multo fortius spiritualia opera impendendo, quæ corporalibus operibus merito præferuntur." S. Bonav., *De perf. evangel. ibid.* 145.

78. "Modus autem laudabilissimus corpori necessaria acquirendi est in prædicationis et doctrinæ laboribus exerceri. Labor enim mechanicus condigne certo pretio compensatur, non autem est compensatio receptio corporalium spiritualia seminanti." S. Bonav., *Expositio Regulæ* c. 5, n. 2, *ibid.* 420.

79. See Felder, *Geschichte der wissenschaftl. Studien* 348 ff. 80. See Felder *ibid.* 349 ff.

81. Guigo, *Statua Ordinis Carthusiensis* c. 28, ed. Holstenius, *Codex regularum* II, 322. 82. Matth. x, 10; Luke x, 7. 83. Luke x, 7. 84. Luke viii, 1–3; 22, 35.

85. 1 Cor. ix, 4, 7. 11. 14. The Apostle indeed gained his livelihood by manual labor, but he declares that he did so of his own choice and for the sake of example: 1 Cor. ix, 12. 15; 1 Thess. ii, 7–9; 2 Thess. iii, 8 sq.

86. "Si enim Deus peccatoribus donat bona temporalia propter nutriendorum filiorum amorem, multo magis viris evangelicis, quibus hæc debentur ex merito, largietur." *Tres Soc.* n. 51.

87. "Ministros verbi Dei tales volebat, qui studiis spiritualibus intendentes nullis aliis præpedirentur officiis." Thom. Cel. II, n. 163.

88. Regula II, c. 5. Not even the office of teaching or studies were to injure the spirit of prayer, as Francis wrote to St. Anthony: "Placet mihi, quod sacram theologiam fratribus legas, dummodo propter huius studium sanctæ orationis spiritum non exstinguant." Böhmer 71. 89. See p. 152 f. 90. *De perf. evangel.* q. 2, a. 2; *Opera* V, 134.

91. "Cum omnia bona ecclesiarum et monasteriorum non sint nisi eleemosynæ pauperum, ut Sancti dicunt et manifestum est." *Ibid.* q. 2, a. 3, n. 17, p. 160.

92. "Omnes quotquot validi et clerici et monachi, qui vivunt de huiusmodi bonis sine labore manuali . . de grossis et magnis eleemosynis. . ." *Ibid.*

93. The objection raised by William of St. Amour, by secular priests and monks, that it was improper for the Franciscans and Dominicans to live on alms and begging, is answered pointedly by St. Bonaventure: "Si enim illicitum est per eleemosynarum acceptionem pauperibus Christi accipere vitæ sustentamentum, multo fortius illicitum est accipere amplitudinem et multitudinem possessionum et redituum. Quis enim ita absurdus est, qui dicat, licere alicui accipere talentum auri et non frustum panis? Quod si hoc verum est; cum universarum ecclesiarum possessiones tam in religiosis proprietatem habentibus quam in clericis sæcularibus, habeantur per acceptionem eleemosynarum voluntarie et gratis datarum: videbitur ex hoc subverti status universarum ecclesiarum, si eleemosynas accipere vel de eleemosynis vivere, seu in parva quantitate seu in magna, illicitum iudicetur; nisi forte quis dicat, quod licitum est *accipere,* sed non est licitum *petere.* Sed mirum videtur, quod aliquis possit in illud quod maius est, et non in illud quod minus est; et quod aliquod monasterium possit recipere centum millia marcarum in reditibus ab aliquo principe, et unus pauperculus non possit suae indigentiæ relevationem suppliciter implorare . . . ; et quod aliquis possit petere aliqua expedientia ad alicuius divitis monasterii securitatem et abundantiam, et pauper voluntarius non possit petere vitæ sustentamentum." *Ibid.* q. 2, a. 2; *Opera* V, 142.

94. Matth. x, 9–10. 95. Luke viii, 2–3; John xii, 6.

96. Cf. S. Bonav., *De perf. evangel.* q. 2, a. 2; *Opera* V. 140.

97. "Pater sanctus utebatur eleemosynis ostiatim quæsitis multo libentius quam oblatis." Thom. Cel. II, n. 71.

98. "Contemptus sui est perfectionis, et maior contemptus maioris perfectionis; sed qui pro Christo mendicat maxime seipsum contemnit et abiicit; ergo talis perfectissime agit." S. Bonav. *ibid.* 139, n. 29.

99. "Omnino pauperis, secundum quod pauper, actus est egere et mendicare; ergo si esse pauperem bonum est, mendicare pro Christo laudabile est et perfectum." S. Bonav. *ibid.* n. 26.

100. The sources emphasize continually that Francis always chose this motive and this formula when begging. The *Spec. perf.* c. 23 gives the instruction of Francis more fully: "Quum frater vadit pro eleemosyna, prius debet dicere: Laudatus et benedictus sit Dominus Deus! Postea debet dicere: Facite nobis eleemosynam amore Domini Dei."

101. *Tres Soc.* n. 10. 102. *Tres Soc.* n. 22. 103. *Ibid.* n. 23. 104. *Ibid.* n. 24; Thom. Cel. II, n. 13.

105. "Ne vel semel sanctam illam sponsam offenderet, hoc facere solitus erat servus Dei excelsi. Si quando invitatus a dominis, mensis esset profusioribus honorandus, prius per propinquas vicinorum domos panum fragmenta quærebat, ac deinde sic ditatus inopia festinabat accumbere." Thom. Cel. II, n. 72.

106. Thom. Cel. II, n. 73. Cf. *Spec. perf.* c. 23 and S. Bonav. c. 7, n. 7. 107. S. Bonav. c. 7, n. 8.

108. "Nonnunquam seipsum exercitans et fratrum verecundiæ parcens, ipse solus in principio pro eleemosynis discurrebat." Thom. Cel. II, n. 74. 109. *Spec. perf.* c. 18.

110. "Verecundiam mendicandi inimicam saluti dicebat, verecundiam in mendicando eam, quæ pedem non retrahit, sanctam esse confirmans. Nasci ruborem in tenera fronte laudabat, pudore confundi non ita." Thom. Cel. II, n. 71. 111. Isaias l, 7. 112. *Regula* I, c. 9, *Opusc.* ed. Böhmer, 10 Lemmens 37. 113. Thom. Cel. II, n. 71; S. Bonav. c. 7, n. 8. 114. Thom. Cel. II, n. 74; cf. *Spec. perf.* c. 18. 115. *Tres Soc.* n. 35. 116. Iord. a Iano n. 27. 117. *Spec. perf.* c. 18. 118. Thom. Cel. II, n. 76; *Spec. perf.* c. 50.

119. "Dicebat sæpe beatus Franciscus, quod verus frater Minor non multum stare deberet, quin pro eleemosynis iret. Et quando nobilior, ait, filius meus est, tanto sit promptior ad eundum, quoniam taliter ei merita cumulantur. Thom. Cel. II, n. 75. 120. Thom. Cel. *ibid; Spec. perf.* c. 24. 121. Matth. vi, 34. 122. *Spec. perf.* c. 19.

123. "Prohibuit fratri, qui faciebat coquinam fratribus, ne poneret legumina de sero in aqua calida quando debebat ea dare fratribus ad manducandum die sequenti, sicut consuetum est: ut observarent illud verbum sancti evangelii: Nolite solliciti esse de crastino." *Ibid.*

124. "Si quis eis aliquid misercorditer contulerit, non reservant in posterum." Iacobi Vitriac. *Historia orientalis* lib. 2, c. 32, Böhmer, *Analekten* 103. "Nullum genus alimenti penes eos usque in crastinum reservatur, ut paupertas spiritus, quæ viget in mente, actu sicut habitu omnibus innotescat." Rogeri de Wendover, *Flores historiarum* ed. *Monum. Germ. hist. Script.* XXVIII, 41.

125. *Spec. perf.* c. 19. 126. *Chronica* n. 16. 127. Ps. lxxii, 78. 128. *Determinationes quæstionum*, pars I, q. 7, *Opera* VIII, 342.

129. "Dicebat b. Franciscus ista verba fratribus frequenter: 'Non fui latro de eleemosynis acquirendo eas vel utendo eis ultra necessitatem. Semper minus accepi quam me contingeret, ne alii pauperes defraudarentur portione, quia contrarium facere furtum esset." *Spec. perf.* c. 12.

130. "In eleemosynarum datione animarum lucrum potius quam carnis subsidium requirebat, et non minus in dando quam in accipiendo se ipsum ponebat cæteris in exemplum." Thom. Cel. II, n. 78.

131. *Vita fr. Ægidii* ed. *Anal. franc.* III, 77. 83.

132. *Regula* I, c. 9, *Opusc.* ed. Böhmer 10, Lemmens 37.

133. The opinion of Sabatier (*Spec. perf.* p. 64, note 1) that the Friars were originally allowed to beg only for the lepers, will appear evidently erroneous after reading our treatment of this subject. Sabatier quotes in defense of his opinion the following passage from the rule of 1221: "Et nullo modo fratres recipiant nec recipi faciant, nec quærant, nec quæri faciant pecuniam *vel* eleemosynam." But this quotation is false. The passage in question does not, read "pecuniam *vel* eleemosynam" but "pecuniam *pro* eleemosyna," in other words: the brothers are forbidden to accept money as alms.

134. *Regula* II, c. 6, *Opusc.* ed. Böhmer 32, Lemmens 68.

135. *Testamentum*, ed. Böhmer 37 sq., Lemmens 79.

136. S. *Paulini Poema* 24, v. 329-332; Migne, *Patrol. lat.* 61, 621.

137. S. August., *De opere monachorum*, c. 28 n. 36; Migne, *Patrol. lat.* 40, 575.

138. See Pierron, *Die katholischen Armen*, Freiburg, Herder 1911, 60 ff.

139. Copious proofs for this are brought forward by Fr. H. Denifle, O. P., *Die Konstitutionen des Predigerordens vom J. 1228*, in: *Archiv. für Literatur- und Kirchengesch.* I, (1885) 182 f.

140. "Cum dilecti filii Frater Franciscus et Socii eius de vita religione Minorum Fratrum abiectis vanitatibus huius mundi . . . serendo semina verbi Dei apostolorum exemplo diversas circumeant mansiones. . ." *Bullar. franc.* I, 2.

141. "Quia vero debemus religiosas fovere partes et maxime dicti Ordinis Fratres, qui relictis omnibus Christum sequuntur, pro eo pauperes et in paupertate vivere continua eligentes. . ." *Bullar. franc.* I, 23.

142. *De perfectione evangel.* q. 2, a. 2, conclusio; *Opera* V, 140 sq.

143. "Pro Christo, inquam, imitando, quantum ad contemptum sui, affectum

proximi et cultum Dei. Nam in his tribus potissime debemus Christum imitari. Quod quidem facit, qui voluntarie mendicat pro nomine Christi, ut seipsum vilificet et humiliet, ut proximum suum ædificet et provocet ad pietatem, et ut vacet Deo libera mente, deposita omni sæculi sollicitudine." *Ibid.* 140. 144. *Ibid.* 141.

145. "Quantum fratres declinabunt a paupertate, tantum mundus declinabit ab eis, et quærent et non invenient. Sed si Dominam meam Paupertatem complexi fuerint, mundus eos nutriet, quia mundo dati sunt ad salutem. Commercium est inter mundum et fratres: debent ipsi mundo bonum exemplum, debet eis mundus provisionem necessitatum." Thom. Cel. II, n. 70.

146. Luke xii, 6 f.; Matth. x, 29 f. 147. Matth. vi, 25 ff.; Luke xii, 24. 148. *Tres Soc.* n. 20.

149. Thom. Cel. I, n. 29. The biographer adds that Francis repeated these words: "Iacta cogitatum tuum in Domino, et ipse te enutriet," as often as he later on sent a brother anywhere in obedience.

150. *Actus B. Francisci et Sociorum eius* c. 13, ed. Paul Sabatier, Paris, 1902, 46 sq. 151. *Tres Soc.* n. 50. 152. *Ibid.* n. 51. 153. Deut. x, 18.

154. *Historia orientalis* lib. 2, c. 32, Böhmer, *Analekten* 104.

155. *Tres Soc.* n. 46. 156. Thom. Cel. *Tractatus de miraculis*, n. 33. 157. Thom. Cel. I, n. 34. 158. Thom. Cel. *Tractatus de miraculis* n. 33. 159. *Ibid.* 35. 160. *Ibid.* 161. S. Bonav. c. 7, n. 12. 162. Thom. Cel. *Tract. de mirac.* n. 36. 163. Thom. Cel. I, n. 77. 164. S. Bonav. c. 7, n. 13.

165. *De perf. evangel.* q. 2, a. 1; *Opera* V, 133 sq.

166. "Sic paternus ille oculus nequaquam despicit suos, quin potius maiori defectu mendicos maior providentia nutrit. Largiori mensa pauper pascitur quam tyrannus, quanto Deus homine profusior largitate." Thom. Cel. II, n. 44.

167. Jacopone, *Le poesie spirituali* lib. 3, oda 24, 16.

168. See Imle, *Ein heiliger Lebenskünstler*, Paderborn 1914, 163 f.

CHAPTER VIII

1. Harnack, *Lehrbuch der Dogmengeschichte* III, 3. Auflage, Freiburg i. Br. 1897, 380. 2. *Salutatio virtutum, Opusc.* ed. Böhmer 64 sq., Lemmens 20 sq. 3. *Spec. perf.* c. 86. 4. *Regula* II, c. 9; *Regula* II, c. 6 and 12, *Opusc.* ed. Böhmer 9. 32. 35, Lemmens 36. 68. 74.

5. "Beatus igitur pater Franciscus consolatione et gratia Spiritus sancti quotidie replebatur, omnique vigilantia et sollicitudine novos filios novis institutionibus informabat, sanctæ paupertatis beatæque simplicitatis viam gressu indeclinabili eos edocens ambulare." Thom. Cel. I, n. 26.

6. *Verba admonitionis* c. 5, *Opusc.* ed. Böhmer 43, Lemmens 8 sq. 7. Thom. Cel. II, n. 134.

8. *Verba admonitionis* c. 22, *Opusc.* ed. Böhmer 47, Lemmens 16. 9. Luke x, 20. 10. *Regula* I, c. 17, *Opusc.* ed. Böhmer 16 sq., Lemmens 46 sq.

11. *Verba admonitionis* c, 12. 17, *Opusc.* ed. Böhmer 45 sq., Lemmens 12. 14. 12. Is. liv, 1. 13. Thom. Cel. II, n. 164. 14. Thom. Cel. II, n. 194.

15. ". . . Cui et si concessum est litteraturæ præcellere, plus tamen in moribus piæ simplicitatis imaginem gerat teneatque virtutem." *Ibid.* 185.

16. "Et hæc fuit intentio beati Francisci et Regulæ, quod fratres primo studerent quantum ad id, quod est per se et principale intentum: fundare semetipsos in vera humilitate . ." Ubertino di Casale, *Rotilus, Archiv.* III, 127.

17. "Spiritus autem Domini . . . studet ad humilitatem et puram simplicitatem." *Regula* I, c. 17, *Opusc.* ed. Böhmer 16, Lemmens 47.

18. "Asserebat autem . . . ad scientiam Dei facile perventurum eum, qui Scripturæ intendens, humilis non præsumptuosus inquireret." Thom. Cel. I, n. 102. 19. Thom Cel. I, n. 104.

20. *Verba admonitionis* c. 4. 20. 24, *Opusc.* ed. Böhmer 43. 47. 48, Lemmens

8. 15. 17.   21. *Regula* II, c. 10, *Opusc.* ed. Böhmer 34, Lemmens 72.   22. *Verba admon.* c. 4; S. Bonav. c. 6, n. 5.

23. "Filius hominis non venit ministrari, sed ministrare." Matth. xx, 28. "Quicumque voluerit inter vos maior fieri, sit vester minister, et quicumque voluerit inter vos primus esse, erit vester servus." Matth. xx, 26. "Qui maior est in vobis, fiat sicut minor, et qui præcessor est, sicut ministrator." Luke xxii, 26.

24. Böhmer, *Analekten* 125, is in error, when he assumes that the fraternity did not receive the name "Minores" until 1216. In this very year Jaques de Vitry reports: "Fratres Minores vocabantur." Burchard of Ursperg also (*Chronicon, Monum. Germ. hist. Scriptores* t. XIII, 376) gives the impression that the Franciscans were always called thus: "Eo tempore mundo iam senescente exortæ sunt duæ religiones in ecclesia, cuius ut aquilæ iuventus renovatur . . . . videlicet *Minorum Fratrum* et Prædicatorum . . . maluerunt appellari *Minores Fratres* quam minores pauperes . . ." The decisive word, however, is spoken by Thomas of Celano, I, n. 38, when he writes regarding the origin of the fraternity and its appellation in the primitive rule: "Ordinem Fratrum Minorum primitus ipse [Franciscus] plantavit, et ea occasione hoc ei nomen imposuit: cum nempe sic in Regula scriberetur: *et sint minores:* ad huius sermonis prolationem ea quidem hora, volo, inquit, ut Ordo Fratrum Minorum fraternitas hæc vocetur." Likewise *Spec. perf.* c. 44. Aside from the Gospel, no doubt the one circumstance was also a factor in selecting this title; namely, that in the days of Francis the poorer classes in the cities were known as "Minores," while the wealthy classes, the merchants and nobles, were termed "Maiores." See Chapter XIV.

25. "Et nullus in vita ista vocetur prior, sed generaliter omnes vocentur Fratres Minores. Et alter alterius lavet pedes." *Regula* I, c. 6, *Opusc.* ed. Böhmer 7, Lemmens 32.

26. "Quamdiu fecistis uni ex his fratribus meis minimis, mihi fecistis . . . Quamdiu non fecistis uni de minoribus his, nec mihi fecistis." Matth. xxv, 40, 45.

27. "Hac igitur de causa humilitatis forma Franciscus fratres suos voluit vocari *Minores*, et prælatos sui Ordinis dici *ministros*, ut et verbis uteretur Evangelii, quod observare promiserat, et ex ipso nomine discerent discipuli eius, quod ad discendam humilitatem ad scholas humilis Christi venissent:" S. Bonav. c. 6, n. 5.

28. "Dicebat beatus Franciscus, quod ideo Deus voluit et revelavit ei, ut vocarentur Fratres Minores, quia iste est populus pauper et humilis, quem Filius Dei postulavit Patri suo, de quo populo ipsemet Filius Dei dicit in evangelio: 'Nolite timere pusillus grex, quia complacuit patri vestro dare vobis regnum.'" *Spec. perf.* c. 26.

29. *Epistola* I, *Opusc.* ed. Böhmer 53, Lemmens 93.   30. *Spec. perf.* c. 44.

31. ". . . nec præsint in domibus eorum, quibus serviunt . . ., sed sint minores et subditi omnibus, qui in eadem domo sunt." *Regula* I, c. 7, *Opusc.* ed. Böhmer 7, Lemmens 33.   32. Thom. Cel. II, n. 148.

33. "Videns autem quosdam prælationibus inhiare, quos præter alia vel sola reddebat indignos ambitio præsidendi, eos non esse fratres minores dicebat, sed vocationis, qua vocati erant, oblitos a gloria excidisse." Thom. Cel. II, n. 145.

34. "Humilis est homo per affectum inferioritatis sive minoritatis; esse humilem, hoc est esse omnium minorem; . . . esse humiles, hoc esse fratres Minores." S. Bonav. *De S. P. Nostro Francisco sermo* V. *Opera* IX, 594.

35. "Universis denique se subditum exhibebat." *Anonymus Perusinus*, n. 37. Cf. *Tres Soc.* n. 57.

36. "Et eramus idiotæ et subditi omnibus." *Testamentum, Opusc.* ed. Böhmer 37, Lemmens 79.

37. "Et omnes clericos et omnes religiosos habeamus pro dominis in his, quæ spectant ad salutem animæ." *Regula* I, c. 19, *Opusc.* ed. Böhmer 18, Lemmens 49.

38. "Et ipsos [pauperculos sacerdotes huius sæculi] et omnes alios volo

timere, amare et honorare sicut meos dominos." *Testamentum, Opusc.* ed. Böhmer 36, Lemmens 78. **39.** *Testamentum, Opusc.* ed. Böhmer 38, Lemmens 80. **40.** *Spec. perf.* c. 50.

41. B. Franciscus "omnia per humilitatem maluit vincere quam per iudicii potestatem." Iord. a Iano n. 13. **42.** *Tres Soc.* n. 57. **43.** Thom. Cel. II, n. 145. **44.** "Ad servandam sanctae humilitatis virtutem . . . Permansit exinde subditus usque ad mortem, humilius agens quam aliquis aliorum." Thom. Cel. II, n. 143.

45. "Nolo videri singularis hac praerogativa libertatis, ut habeam socium specialem, sed fratres me de loco ad locum associent, sicut Dominus inspiraverit eis . . . Vidi iam unum caecum, qui non habebat nisi unum catulum ducem sui itineris, et ego volo videri melior illo." *Spec. perf.* c. 40. **46.** S. Bonav. c. 6, n. 10.

47. "Quia erat humillimus, omnem mansuetudinem ostendebat ad omnes homines, omnium moribus se conformans, sanctior inter sanctos, inter peccatores quasi unus ex eis." Thom. Cel. I, n. 83. **48.** *Tres Soc.* n. 57. **49.** Thom. Cel. II, n. 31. **50.** *Actus b. Francisci* c. 8.

51. ". . . Videor mihi maximus peccatorum, quoniam si aliquem sceleratum tanta fuisset Deus misericordia prosecutus, decuplo me spiritualior esset." Thom. Cel. II, n. 123. Cf. S. Bonav. c. 6, n. 6; *Spec. perf.* c. 60. **52.** Thom. Cel. I, n. 34. **53.** Thom. Cel. II, n. 134; S. Bonav. c. 6, n. 3.

54. "Sciebat famae pretium conscientiae secretum minuere, longeque damnosius abuti quam carere virtutibus." Thom. Cel. II, n. 139. **55.** Iord. a Iano n. 8. **56.** Thom. Cel. I, n. 95 sq.; II, n. 135-138.

57. *Verba admon.* c. 28, *Opusc.* ed. Böhmer 49, Lemmens 19.

58. ". . . . Latroni tanta contulisset Altissimus, gratior te foret, Francisce." Thom. Cel. II, n. 133.

59. "Nam saepe, cum beatificaretur a pluribus, verba huiuscemodi respondebat: Filios et filias adhuc habere possum; nolite laudare securum. Nemo laudandus, cuius incertus est exitus." *Ibid.* n. 133. **60.** *Actus b. Francisci*, c. 10. **61.** *Ibid.* II, n. 130. **62.** *Ibid.* I, n. 53.

63. "In veritate, Domine Episcope, magnum honorem mihi fecisti, quoniam quae mea sunt auferentibus aliis, tu solus illaesa servasti. Separasti, inquam, pretiosum a vili, sicut discretus homo, Deo laudem, mihi vilitatem reddendo." Thom. Cel. II, n. 141. **64.** *Spec. perf.* 45.

65. "Quantum homo in oculis Dei est, tantum est et non plus." S. Bonav. c. 6, n. 1. **66.** Bötticher, *Das Hohelied vom Rittertum*, Berlin 1886, 47-50. 65.

67. "Dicebat, propter hoc Filium Dei de altitudine sinus paterni ad nostra despicabilia descendisse, ut tam exemplo quam verbo Dominus et Magister humilitatem doceret." S. Bonav. c. 6, n. 1.

68. "Taliter homo iste omnem gloriam, quae Christum non saperet, abiuraverat; taliter humanis favoribus aeternum irrogaverat anathema." Thom. Cel. II, n. 139.

69. Beatus Franciscus novus praeco Regis humilitatis et poenitentiae vias exemplo mirabili praeparans . . ." *Vita Fr. Aegidii*, ed. *Anal. franc.* III, 74.

70. "In hac [humilitate] studuit aedificare seipsum, ut fundamentum iaceret, quod a Christo didicerat . . . Humilis habitu, humilior sensu, humillimus reputatu. Non discernebatur Dei princeps, quod praelatus esset, nisi hac clarissima gemma, quia inter minores minimus erat." Thom. Cel. II, 140. **71.** *Ibid.* I, n. 34. **72.** *Ibid.* I, n. 38. 40. **73.** *Tres Soc.* n. 42. Likewise *Anonym. Perusin.* n. 26. **74.** *De laudibus B. Franc.* c. 7.

75. *Flores historiarum* ed. *Monum. Germ. hist. Script.* t. XXVIII, 41.

76. "Haec est vere religio pauperum Crucifixi et ordo praedicatorum, quos fratres Minores vocamus. Vere Minores et omnibus huius temporis regularibus in habitu et nuditate et mundi contemptu humiliores." *Historia orient.* lib. 2, c. 32, Böhmer, *Analekten* 102.

CHAPTER IX

1. *Regula* II, c. 1.   In substance also *Regula* I, c. 1.
2. "Non omnia pro Deo reliquisse dicebat eum, qui sensus proprii loculos retineret." Thom. Cel. II, n. 140.   3. See p. 61–73.   4. *Tres Soc.* n. 57.   5. *Actus b. franc.* c. 2 and 8.
6. "Dixit enim fratri Petro Catanii, cui pridem obedientiam sanctam promiserat: Rogo te propter Deum, ut vicem tuam de me uni de sociis meis committas, cui sicut tibi devotus obediam.   Scio, inquit, obedientiæ fructum, et quod nihil transeat temporis sine lucro, qui alterius iugo colla submiserit. Admissa igitur sua instantia, usque ad mortem subditus ubique permansit, guardiano proprio semper reverenter obtemperans." Thom. Cel. II, n. 151.   7. *Ibid.* n. 151.   8. *Testamentum*, ed. Böhmer 38, Lemmens 80.
9. "Guardianus eius, qui votum sancti divina verius inspiratione cognovit, . . . dixit ad patrem: Tunicam istam et femoralia cum cappellula, obedientiæ sanctæ mandato, a me tibi accomodatam cognoveris . . . Gaudet Sanctus et iubilat præ lætitia cordis." Thom. Cel. II, n. 215.   10. *Tres Soc.* n. 42.   11. Thom. Cel. I, n. 39. 45.   12. Iord. a Iano n. 18.   13. *Ibid.* n. 27.   14. *Ibid.* n. 47.
15. Eccleston, *De adventu FF. Min. in Angliam* coll. I, p. 6.
16. "Beatus autem Franciscus videns fratrem Ægidium gratia et virtute perfectum et paratum ac promptum ad omne opus bonum, intime diligebat eum et de ipso aliis fratribus dicebat: 'Iste est miles meus tabulæ rotundae.'" *Vita fr. Ægidii, Anal. franc.* III, p. 78.   17. *Ibid.*   18. *Ibid.* p. 80.
19. "Concessas post petitionem proprie licentias dixit, iniunctas vero nec postulatas sacras obedientias nominavit. Utramque bonam dicebat, sed aliam tutiorem." Thom. Cell. II, n. 152.   20. *Ibid.*
21. Regula I, c. 4. 5; II, c. 10, *Opusc.* ed. Böhmer 4. 34, Lemmens 29. 72.
22. Luke xiv, 33.   23. John xv, 13.   24. Luke ix, 62.   25. Proverbs xxvi, 11.   26. *Verba admon.* c. 3, *Opusc.* ed. Böhmer 42, Lemmens 6 sq.   27. Thom. Cel. II, n. 154.   28. *Vita b. Ægidii* 80; *Dicta b. Ægidii* 65–67.
29. *Regula* I, c. 5, *Opusc.* ed. Böhmer 6, Lemmens 32.   30. *Dicta b. Ægidii* 65. 66.
31. "Per caritatem spiritus voluntarie serviant et obediant invicem.   Et hæc est vera et sancta obedientia Domini nostri Iesu Christi." *Regula* I, c. 5, *Opusc.* ed. Böhmer 6, Lemmens 32.   32. *Opusc.* ed. Böhmer 37, Lemmens 79.   33. *Opusc.* ed. Böhmer 65, Lemmens 21.   34. Cf. p. 172 f.
35. "Et recordarentur ministri et servi, quod dicit Dominus (Matth. xx, 28): 'Non veni ministrari, sed ministrare'. . . Similiter omnes fratres non habeant aliquam potestatem vel dominationem maxime inter se. Sicut enim dicit Dominus in Evangelio (Matth. xx, 25): 'Principes gentium dominantur eorum et qui maiores sunt potestatem exercent in eos,' non sic erit inter fratres, sed 'quicumque voluerit inter eos maior fieri, sit eorum minister' (Matth. xxiii, 11) et servus, et 'qui maior est inter eos, fiat sicut minor' (Luke xxii, 26)." *Regula* I, c. 4. 5, *Opusc.* ed. Böhmer 5. 6, Lemmens 29 sq., 31.
36. Thus, *Regula* I, c. 4 twice, c. 5 three times, Regula II, c. 10 four times, etc.
37. "Et nullus vocetur prior . . ." *Regula* I, c. 6, *Opusc.* ed. Böhmer 7, Lemmens 32.   38. See Ducange-Carpent., *Glossarium ad Scriptores mediæ et infimæ latin. s. v.* "Custos" and "Guardianus."   39. Thom. Cel. II, n. 185.   40. *Ibid.* n. 187.   41. "Per obedientiam itaque raro præcipiendum censuit, nec primo fulminandum iaculum, quod esse deberet extremum.   Ad ensem, inquit, non cito manus mittenda est." *Ibid.* n. 153.
42. *Epist. ad fideles, Opusc.* ed. Böhmer 53, Lemmens 92.
43. *Regula* II, c. 10, *Opusc.* ed. Böhmer 34, Lemmens 71 sq.
44. "Honorari eum [ministrum] vice Christi vellem ab omnibus, et in necessariis omnibus ipsi cum benevolentia provideri." Thom. Cel. II, n. 186.   "Hos tamen [ministros] volebat omni honore præveniri et diligi, sicut qui pondus portarent sollicitudinum et laborum.   Summis eos præmiis apud Deum dignos

esse dicebat, qui tali forma talique lege creditas sibi animas gubernarent." *Ibid.* n. 187.

45. "Beatus servus, qui ita inventus fuerit inter subditos suos, sicuti quando esset inter dominos suos." Verba admon. c. 23, *Opusc.* ed. Böhmer 48, Lemmens 17.

46. "Et ego frater Franciscus, parvulus vester et servus." *Testamentum, Opusc.* ed. Böhmer 40, Lemmens 82. 47. Iord. a Iano n. 49.

48. "Simplicitas dicitur per oppositum duplicitati, qua scilicet aliquis aliud habet in corde et aliud ostendit exterius . . . qua homo unum prætendit et aliud intendit." S. Thomas Aq., *Summa theol.* 2, 2, q. 109, a. 2, ad 4. "Veritas idem videtur esse simplicitati, quia utrique opponitur simulatio." *Ibid.* 2, 2, q. 109, a. 2, 4. 49. Matth. xviii, 3. 50. Thom. Cel. II, n. 189. 51. Thom. Cel. II, n. 142.

52. "Erat enim gloriosus sanctus secum habitans, et deambulans in latitudine cordis sui in se dignum Deo habitaculum præparabat, et ideo aures eius non rapiebat clamor exterior, nec vox aliqua excutere poterat seu interrumpere ingens negotium, quod habebat in manibus . . . Dabat semper sanctæ simplicitati operam." *Ibid.* I, n. 43. 53. *Ibid.* II, n. 131. 54. *Ibid.* II, n. 52 sq. Cf. *Spec. perf.* c. 61. 55. *Ibid.* II, n. 130. 56. *Ibid.* 57. *Ibid.* II, n. 132. 58. *Actus b. Franc.* c. 2. 59. Thom. Cel. I, n. 54.

60. *Chronica Danorum et præcipue Silandiæ*, Lemmens, *Testimonia minora sæculi XIII. de S. P. Francisco, Archiv. franc. hist.* I, 77.

61. Walterus de Gysburne, *Chronica de gestis regum Angliæ*, Lemmens *ibid.* 78. 62. *Actus b. Franc.* c. 11. 32. 63. Thom. Cel. II, n. 39.

64. "Sic enim consueverant facere semper, cum veniebant ad eum, nec ab ipso cogitationem minimam vel primos etiam motus animi occultabant." Thom. Cel. I, n. 30.

65. "Sic enim eos repleverat sancta simplicitas, sic eos innocentia vitæ docebat, sic eos cordis puritas possidebat, ut duplicitatem animi penitus ignorarent." *Ibid.* n. 46. 66. Cf. Thomas de Eccleston coll. IV–VI. ed. Little 30–33.

67. *Vita fr. Iuniperi, Chron. XXIV Gen., Anal. franc.* III, 56. 68. *Spec. perf.* c. 58. 69. Thom. Cel. II, n. 190. 70. Matth. xi, 25; xviii, 18, 3; Luke x, 21.

71. "Fratres mei, fratres mei, Dominus vocavit me per viam simplicitatis et humilitatis, et hanc viam ostendit mihi in veritate pro me et pro illis, qui volunt mihi credere et imitari." *Spec. perf.* c. 68.

72. *Testamentum, Opusc.* ed. Böhmer 39, Lemmens 82.

73. "Hæc est [sancta simplicitas] quæ græcas glorias non optimas arbitrans, plus eligit facere quam discere vel docere. Hæc est, quæ in omnibus divinis legibus verbosas ambages, ornatus et faleras, ostentationes et curiositates perituris relinquens, quærit non corticem, sed medullam, non testam sed nucleum, non multa sed multum, summum et stabile bonum." Thom. Cel. II, n. 189.

74. Matth. vi, 2. 75. *Regula* I, c. 17, *Opusc.* ed. Böhmer 16, Lemmens 47. 76. *Epist. ad. fideles, Opusc.* ed. Böhmer 53, Lemmens 93.

77. "Ave regina sapientia! Deus te salvet cum tua sorore pura sancta simplicitate." *Salutatio virtutum, Opusc.* ed. Böhmer 64, Lemmens 20; Thom. Cel. II, n. 189.

78. "Volo, inquit, fratres meos discipulos evangelicos esse sicque in notitia veritatis proficere, quod in simplicitatis puritate concrescant, ut simplicitatem columbinam a prudentia serpentina non separent, quas Magister eximius ore suo benedicto coniunxit." S. Bonaventura c. 11, n. 1.

79. "Asserebat autem scientiatum ad scientiam Dei facile perventurum eum, qui Scripturæ intendens humilis, non præsumptuosus inquireret." Thom. Cel. II, n. 102.

80. "Homo cui etsi concessum est litteraturæ dono præcellere, plus tamen in moribus piæ simplicitatis imaginem gerat foveatque virtutem." *Ibid.* n. 185.

81. "Quando radebatur sanctus Franciscus, sæpe rasori dicebat: Cave, ne mihi magnam coronam facias. Volo enim, quod fratres mei simplices partem habeant in capite meo." *Ibid.* n. 193.

82. "Volebat denique religionem pauperibus et illitteratis, non solum diviti-

bus et sapientibus esse communem. Apud Deum, inquit, non est acceptio personarum, et generalis minister religionis, Spiritus Sanctus, æque super pauperem et simplicem requiescit. Hoc sane verbum voluit in Regula ponere, sed bullatio facta præclusit." *Ibid.* n. 193.

83. "Hanc [sanctam simplicitatem] in fratribus litteratis et laicis requirebat pater sanctissimus." *Ibid.* n. 189. 84. *Ibid.* n. 192.

CHAPTER X

1. "Inter alias virtutes, quas diligebat et desiderabat in fratribus post fundamentum sanctæ humilitatis, diligebat præcipue pulchritudinem et munditiam honestatis." *Spec. pref.* c. 86.

2. "Quæ mulier totius honestatis amica quoddam virtutis insigne præferebat in moribus, sanctæ illius Elisabeth, tam impositione nominis ad filium quam et spiritu prophetali, aliquo similitudinis privilegio gaudens." Thom. Cel. II, n. 3.

3. "Nam Francisci magnanimitatem et morum honestatem admirantibus convicinis, quasi divino instructa oraculo sic aiebat: Quid putatis iste filius meus erit? Meritorum gratia Dei filium ipsum noveritis affuturum." *Ibid.* 4. *Tres Soc.* n. 3.

5. "Rigidus in disciplina super custodiam suam stabat, curam permaximam gerens de utriusque hominis puritate servanda." S. Bonav. c. 5, n. 3.

6. "Si qua, ut assolet, carnis tentatio eum quandoque pulsaret, in quadam fovea glacie plena, cum hiems existeret, se mergebat, in ea tam diu persistens, quoadusque carnalis omnis recederet corruptela." Thom. Cel. I, n. 42.

7. "Tolerabilius viro spirituali fore incomparabiliter asserebat magnum sustinere frigus in carne, quam ardorem carnalis libidinis vel modicum sentire in mente." S. Bonav. *ibid.* 8. Bern. a Bessa c. 5.

9. *Vita fratris Leonis, Chron. XXIV Gen., Anal. franc.* III, 68; Bern. a Bessa *ibid.*

10. "O quam pulcher, quam gloriosus apparebat in vitæ innocentia, in puritate cordis, in aspectu angelico!" Thom. Cel. I, n. 83. 11. Thom. Cel. II, n. 112. 12. *Ibid.* n. 114. 13. *Ibid.* n. 112.

14. "Fateor veritatem, carissime, nullam me si aspicerem recogniturum in facie, nisi duas. Illius, inquit, et illius vultus cognitus est, alterius nescio." *Ibid.* 15. *Ibid.* n. 114.

16. ". . . Ex nimia securitate minus cavetur hostis. Diabolus si de suo capillum potest habere in homine, cito illum excrescere facit in trabem. Nec si per multos annos deiicere non potuit, quem tentavit, moram causatur, dummodo sibi cedat in fine. Hoc est enim opus suum, nec est ad alia die noctuque sollicitus." *Ibid.* n. 113. 17. Matth. v, 28.

18. *Regula* I, c. 12, *Opusc.* ed. Böhmer 13, Lemmens 41.

19. *Regula* II, c. 11, *Opusc.* ed. Böhmer 35, Lemmens 73.

20. "Nolo, quod aliquis ad visitandum eas spontaneum se offerat; sed invitos et plurimum renitentes iubeo ipsarum servitiis deputari, spirituales dumtaxat viros, digna et longæva conversatione probatos." Thom. Cel. II, 205. 21. *Ibid.* n. 206. 22. *Ibid.* n. 205. 207.

23. "Unum atque eundem spiritum, dicens, fratres et dominas illas pauperculas de hoc sæculo eduxisse." *Ibid.* n. 204. 24. *Ibid.* n. 205.

25. *Forma vivendi sororibus s. Claræ data, Opusc.* ed. Böhmer 35, Lemmens 75.

26. ". . . promisit eis et aliis paupertatem in simili conversatione profitentibus firmiter suum et fratrum suorum auxilium et consilium perpetuo exhibere. Hæc semper, dum vixit, diligenter exsolvit, et fieri semper, cum morti proximus esset, non negligenter mandavit." Thom. Cel. II, n. 204. Cf. Thom. Cel. II, n. 116 sq.; *Spec. perf.* c. 90.

27. "Iacoba de Septem Soliis, claritate et sanctitate pari in urbe romana, privilegium amoris præcipui meruerat apud sanctum." Thom. Cel., *Tract. de miraculis* n. 37.

28. "Domina Iacoba eum ardenter dilexerat exsulem." *Ibid.* 29. *Ibid.* n. 37-39. 30. See especially Mark vi, 12; Luke v, 32; Acts xxvi, 20.

31. Among the many proofs the following is particularly relevant: "Franciscus hortabatur omnes, ut amarent et timerent Deum atque pœnitentiam agerent de peccatis . . . Qui vero eos audiebant dicebant: Qui sunt isti, et quæ dicunt? Erat enim tunc amor et timor Dei quasi ubique exstinctus et via pœnitentiæ penitus nesciebatur, imo stultitia reputabatur. Nam in tam prævaluerat carnis illecebra, mundi cupiditas, superbia vitæ, quod totus mundus in his tribus malignitatibus positus videbatur." *Tres Socii,* n. 33 sq.

32. ". . . viri pœnitentiales de Assisio." *Ibid.* n. 58.

33. "Dominus ita dedit mihi fratri Francisco incipere facere pœnitentiam." *Testam., Opusc.* ed. Böhmer 36, Lemmens 77.

34. "Cernebant eum a pristinis moribus alteratum et carnis maceratione valde confectum, et ideo totum quod agebat exinanitioni et dementiæ imputabant." Thom. Cel. I, n. 11. 35. S. Bonav. c. 2, n. 4.

36. "Parat sibi ex tunc tunicam crucis imaginem præferentem, ut in ea propulset omnes dæmoniacas phantasias: parat asperrimam et incultam, et quæ a mundo nullatenus valeat concupisci." Thom. Cel. I, n. 22. 37. S. Bonav. c. 5, n. 2. 38. *Ibid.* 39. Eccleston, *De Adventu Fratrum Minorum in Angliam* coll. 13, p. 91.

40. "Accubitum vero suum, ubique receptus hospitio, nullis sinebat stramentis seu vestibus operiri, sed nuda humus, tunicula interposita, nuda suscipiebat membra; cum quandoque corpusculum suum somni beneficio recrearet, sæpius sedens, nec aliter se deponens, dormiebat, pro cervicali ligno vel lapide utens." Thom. Cel. I, n. 52. Cf. C. Bonav. *ibid.* "Vestitus etiam de nocte dormivit, mattam pro stratu cubiculi habuit, saccum capiti pro cervicali supposuit cuculla solummodo et cilicio, quibus in die vestitus incessit, pro nocturnalibus, operimentis contentus." Rogeri de Wendover, *Chronica maiora,* ap. Lemmens, *Testimonia minora sæculi XIII, Archiv. franc.* I, 81.

41. "Tanta disciplinæ rigiditate sensuales appetitus arcebat, ut vix necessaria sumeret sustentationi naturæ." S. Bonav. c. 5, n. 1.

42. "Impossibile namque fore, aiebat, satisfacere necessitati et voluptati non obedire." Thom. Cel. I, n. 51. 43. *Actus b. Francisci* c. 6. 44. Luke x, 7.

45. Thom. Cel. *ibid.*; Iulian. de Spira, *Leg.* n. 32; *Tres Soc.* n. 14 sq.

46. "Homo habens animal suum, quamvis multum laboret magna deferens onera et quamvis ipsum bene pasceret, tamen per viam non recte vadit sine virga correctionis; sic est de corpore pœnitentis." *Dicta b. Ægidii* 31.

47. "Exinde se tanta carnis maceratione afflixit, quod sanus et infirmus corpori suo nimis austerus existens, vix aut nunquam sibi voluit indulgere." *Tres Soc.* n. 14.

48. "Nunquam parcebat corpori Christi strenuus miles, exponens illud, tamquam alienum a se, omnibus tam operum quam verborum iniuriis." Thom. Cel. II, n. 21. 49. Thom. Cel. II, n. 116 sq.

50. "Tanta enim in eo carnis ad spiritum erat concordia, tanta obedientia, quod cum ille omnem niteretur apprehendere sanctitatem, ipsa nihilominus non solum non repugnabat, sed et præcurrere satagebat, iuxta quod scriptum est (Ps. lvii, 2): Sitivit in te anima mea, quam multipliciter tibi caro mea." Thom. Cel. I, n. 97. "Nam et calor spiritus ita iam levigaverat corpus, ut anima sitiente in Deum, sitiret et quam multipliciter caro illa sanctissima." *Ibid.* II, n. 129.

51. "Assiduitas vero subiectionis fecerat eam voluntariem, et ex cotidiana inclinatione sui situm apprehenderat tantæ virtutis, quoniam consuetudo saepe vertitur in naturam." *Ibid.* I, n. 97. 52. See p. 35 ff. 53. Thom. Cel. II, n. 210. 54. *Ibid.* n. 211.

55. "Die mortis eius instante confessus est, se multum peccasse in fratrem corpus." *Tres Soc.* n. 14.

56. *Verba admon.* c. 10, *Opusc.* ed. Böhmer 45, Lemmens 11.

57. "Sanctus Franciscus quotidianam, immo continuam sui et suorum inquisitionem diligentissime faciebat, et nil in eis residere patiens lubricum, ab ipsorum

cordibus omnem negligentiam abigebat . . . Docebat eos non solum mortíficare vitia et carnis incentiva reprimere, verum etiam et ipsos exteriores sensus, per quos mors intrat ad animam." Thom. Cel. I, n, 42 sq.

58. Thomas of Celano is no doubt in error when he states that Otto IV passed through Assisi on his way to Rome. (Thom. Cel. I, n. 43). The Emperor chose the Via Aemilia and Flaminia from Faenza in order to reach Rome (Böhmer-Ficker, *Reg. Imperat.* ad a, 1209, p. 96). On his return from Rome, however, he stopped at Foligno and Terni and thus had to touch Assisi. 59. Thom. Cel. I, n. 43.

60. "Et quidem tantæ mortificationis exemplum cæteri ferventissime sequebantur." *Ibid.* I, n. 42.

61. "Sic etiam et tota illa prima schola sua omnibus se subdebat incommodis ut nefas duceretur si quis in aliquo alio quam in consolatione spiritus respiraret." *Ibid.* II, n. 21.

62. "Fratres Minores vere possunt inter discipulos Domini computari, quia spernentes sæcularia desideria carnem suam macerant et tormentant et Christum nudis pedibus et cilicio induti sequuntur." *Rhetorica antiqua,* apud Schönbach, Wien 1903.

63. "Aut propter summam perfectionem Domino adhæserunt, aut certe insani sunt, quia desperata videtur eorum via, cum parco cibo utantur et nudis pedibus ambulent atque vilissimis vestibus sunt induti." *Tres Soc.* n. 34.

64. "Per viam crucis et semitas iustitiæ incedentes de arcta via pœnitentiæ et observationis evangelicæ offendicula removebant, ut posteris iter planum fieret." *Ibid.* n. 45.

65. Thom. Cel. I, n. 39–41. Cf. Thom. Cel. I, n. 20; II, n. 21; *Anonym. Perusin.* n. 23; Iordan. a Iano n. 21; Eccleston, *De adventu fratrum Min. in Angliam* ed. Little p. 8–10. 15. 28. 43 sq.; *Vita S. Claræ* c. 3, n. 17 sqq.; *Vita fr. Ægidii* p. 78 sq. 88.

66. "Nam cum circulis ferreis et loricis se cingerent et vestirent, vigiliis multis et ieiuniis maceratis continuis, multoties defecissent, nisi pii patris monitione assidua rigorem tantæ abstinentiæ relaxassent." Thom. Cel. II, n. 21.

67. "Hoc solo documento dissona fuit manus a lingua in patre sanctissimo. Corpus enim suum utique innocens flagellis et penuriis subigebat, multiplicans ei vulnera sine causa." Thom. Cel. II, n.129. 68. *Spec. perf.* c. 27.

69. "Arguebat præterea pius pater fratres suos, qui nimis erant sibi ipsis austeri, vigiliis et ieiuniis et corporalibus exercitiis nimium insudantes . . . Quos vir Dei prohibebat, admonens eos benigne et rationabiliter reprehendens atque ipsorum vulnera alligans salutarium vinculis præceptorum." *Tres Soc.* n. 59. The *Spec. perf.* c. 27 states that Francis on this occasion forbade girdles and other instruments of penance, and ordained that the Friars should wear nothing but the habit on the body. The *Fioretti* c. 18 locates this incident at the so-called Chapter of the Mats, and plainly exaggerates the narrative of the Three Companions and of the *Speculum perfectionis* thus: "St. Francis commanded under holy obedience as prudent father that everyone who wore a spiked shirt or iron rings should remove them and place them before him. This was done. Thus well-nigh five hundred spiked shirts and many more rings for arms and body were counted. A whole mountain of them was piled together, and St. Francis commanded them to let them lie."

70. Thom. Cel. II, n. 129. Cf. *Spec. perf.* c. 97.

71. Eccleston, *De adventu* coll. XIV, p. 106.

72. ". . . Sale conditum sacrificium Deo semper reddere iubet, et, ut vires proprias in Dei obsequio unusquisque consideret, monet attente. Peccatum simile asserit, indiscrete corpori subtrahere debitum, sicut imperante gula ei exhibere superfluum." *Ibid.* II, n. 22. Cf. *Spec. perf.* c. 27. In the same manner St. Clare admonishes her spiritual daughter Agnes of Prague (*Acta SS.*, Martii t. I, 507 B): "A nimio abstinentiæ rigore, quem te sectari cogñovi, abstinere te vehementer in Domino rogo: ut vivens et sperans in Domino, rationabile obsequium exhibeas et holocaustum tuum sale prudentiæ sit conditum."

73. "Docuit eos insuper discretionem sequi ut aurigam virtutum, non eam.

quam caro suadet, sed quam edocuit Christus, cuius sacratissimam vitam expressum constat esse perfectionis exemplar." S. Bonav. c. 5, n. 7.

74. Cf. *S. Columbani Regula cœnobialis* c. 10, Migne, *Patrol. lat.* t. 80, 216–224.

75. "Ideoque quoties pueri vel'adolescentiores ætate aut qui minus intelligere possunt, quanta pœna sit excommunicationis: hi tales dum delinquunt aut ieiuniis nimiis affligantur aut acribus verberibus coerceantur, ut sanentur." *S. P. Benedicti Regula* c. 30, Migne, *Patrol. lat.* t. 66, 533.

76. "Si autem [quis frater] improbus est, vindictæ corporali subdatur . . . . Si quis frater frequenter correptus pro qualibet culpa, si etiam excommunicatus, non emendaverit, acrior ei accedat correptio, id est, ut verberum vindicta in eum procedat." *Ibid.* c. 23. 28, Migne, t. 66, 501.519.

77. "Statutum est, ne staminiæ [woolen shirts], quæ ex more antiquo propter graviora quælibet fratribus acrius flagellandis scindi solebant et usque ad cingulum violenter detrahi, ulterius scinderentur, sed staminia integra manente, verberibus subiiciendus frater ea ex toto exueretur." *Petri Venerabilis Statuta Congregat. Cluniacensis* 53, Migne, *Patrol. lat.* t. 189, 1043.

78. ". . . Denudatus, ut dignam suis meritis accipiat sententiam, vapulet, quantum placuerit prælato . . . Et si placuerit ei [prælato], denuo vapulet ad pedes singulorum, primo prælati, deinde utriusque lateris sessorum." *Constitutiones antiquæ ordinis fratrum prædicatorum* I. dist. 23, ed. Denifle.

79. *Regula* I, c. 5, *Opusc.* ed. Böhmer 5, Lemmens 31. Similarly *Regula* II, c. 7, *Opus.* ed. Böhmer 33, Lemmens 69.

80. "Si quis fratrum diabolo instigante fornicaretur, habitu ordinis exuatur, quem ex sua turpi iniquitate amisit, et ex toto deponat et a nostra religione penitus expellatur. Et postea pœnitentiam faciat de peccatis suis." *Regula* I, c. 13, *Opusc.* ed. Böhmer 13, Lemmens 42.

81. In the third chapter of both rules Francis prescribes fasting from All Saints until Christmas, from Epiphany until Easter and on all Fridays of the year. For the Poor Clares he prescribed (according to a letter of St. Clare to Bl. Agnes of Prague, *Act. SS.*, Martii t. 507 A-B) continual fasting, except during the Paschal season, on Sundays, feast days, and the ordinary Thursdays (Gregory IX annulled even these exemptions, but Innocent IV amplified them considerably: *Bullar. francisc.* I, 265. 396. 478). This greater severity in regard to the Poor Clares may be perhaps explained from the fact that they were not destined for the arduous labors of the Apostolate. — The older statutes of the Dominican Order of 1228 (*ibid.* dist. I, 8, p. 198) prescribe fasting from Sept. 15 until Easter and on all Fridays. The Benedictine rule (c. 41) ordains fasting from Sept. 13 until Easter and on Wednesdays and Fridays from Pentecost until Sept. 13. St. Columba commands uninterrupted fasting: "Ergo quotidie ieiunandum est, sicut quotidie orandum est, quotidie laborandum, quotidieque est legendum." (*Reg. cœnobial.* c. 3, Migne, *Patrol. lat.* t. 80, 211.)

82. Outside the fasting season Francis, like all other Founders, allowed two meals, at noon and in the evening, according to the express declaration of St. Clare, *ibid.*

83. Meat was allowed only to the sick, e. g. according to the rule of St. Benedict, c. 39, also the *Constitutiones antiquæ fratrum prædicatorum* I, 11. Columba prescribes outright: "Cibus sit vilis et vespertinus monachorum, satietatem fugiens et potus ebrietatem; ut et sustineat et non noceat. Olera, legumina, farina aquis mixta, cum parvo panis paximatio, ne venter oneretur et mens suffocetur."

84. "Secundum primam regulam fratres omni carnali feria carnes comedebant." Iordan. a Iano n. 11.

85. Luke x, 8. 86. *Opusc.* ed. Böhmer 4.31, Lemmens 29.67.

87. "Isti vicarii [frater Matthæus de Narnio et frater Gregorius de Neapoli] cum quibusdam fratribus senioribus Italiæ unum capitulum celebrarunt, in quo statuerunt, ut fratres diebus carnalibus procuratis non uterentur, sed tantum sponte a fidelibus oblatas manducarent." Iordan. a Iano n. 11.

88. "Constitutionibus perlectis cum beatus Franciscus esset in mensa et carnes appositas ad manducandum coram se haberet, dixit fratri Petro: 'Domine

Petre, quid faciemus?' Et ille respondit: 'Ha, Domine Francisce, quod vobis placet, quia potestatem habetis vos.' . . . Et sic tandem beatus Franciscus intulit: 'Comedamus ergo secundum evangelium quæ nobis apponuntur.' " Iordan. a Iano n. 12.

CHAPTER XI

1. "Naturaliter erat hilaris et iocundus." *Tres Soc.* n. 4.

2. "Hic postquam fuit adultus et subtilis ingenii factus, artem patris, id est negotiationem exercuit. Sed dissimiliter valde, quoniam ipse hilarior et liberalior, deditus iocis et cantibus . . . iuvenis iocundus." *Tres Soc.* 2. 3.

3. "In eodem indumento pannum valde carum panno vilissimo consui faciebat." *Tres Soc.* n. 2. 4. Thom. Cel. I, n. 1–3; II, n. 7; *Tres Soc.* n. 1–2.

5. "Admirationi omnibus erat, et in pompa vanæ gloriæ præire cæteros nitebatur, in iocis, in curiosis, in scurrilibus et inanibus verbis, in cantilenis." Thom. Cel., I, n. 2.   6. *Das Ritterwesen des Mittelalters*, Klüber, Nürnberg 1786, I. Bd. 417.   7. "Car d'armes est li mestier tiex. Bruit es chans et joie à l'ostel." *Ibid.*

8. "Non videbatur tristari, sed quodammodo iucundare . . . lætabatur in carcere constitutus." *Tres Soc.* n. 4.   9. "Tantoque deinceps repletus est gaudio, quod non se capiens præ lætititia, etiam nolens ad aures hominum aliquid eructabat." Thom. Cel. I, n. 7.

10. "In his, quæ prius horrebas, hauries magnam dulcedinem et suavitatem immensam. Gavisus ergo in his et in Domino confortatus . . ." *Tres Soc.* n. 11.

11. *Tres Soc.* n. 13. 12. Thom. Cel. I, n. 16. 13. Thom. Cel. I, n. 93; II, n. 125.

14. "In hoc autem summum et præcipuum studium habuit beatus Franciscus, ut extra orationem haberet continue interius et exterius lætitiam spiritualem." *Spec. perf.* c. 95.

15. "Cum magno fervore spiritus et gaudio mentis cœpit omnibus pœnitentiam prædicare." Thom. Cel. I, n. 23. 16. *Ibid.* n. 36 sq. 17. *Legenda minor*, ed. a PP. Collegii S. Bonaventuræ, Ad Claras Aquas 1898, 236.

18. "Dulcissima melodia spiritus intra ipsum ebulliens exterius gallicum dabat sonum, et vena divini susurrii, quam auris eius suscipiebat furtive, gallicum erumpebat in iubilum." Thom. Cel. II, n. 127. 19. *Ibid.* 20. *Tres Soc.* n. 22.

21. "O martyr et martyr, qui ridens et gaudens libentissime tolerabat, quod erat omnibus acerbissimum et gravissimum intueri." Thom. Cel. I, n. 107.

22. *Ibid.* n. 213. 23. *Paul Wilhelm von Keppler*, Mehr Freude, Freiburg i. Br. 1909, 122. 24. Thom. Cel. I, n. 109. *Spec. perf.* c. 121. 25. *Spec. perf. ibid.*

26. Thom. Cel. I, n. 109. 27. "Tutissimum remedium contra mille inimici insidias vel astutias lætitiam spiritualem sanctus iste affirmabat." Thom. Cel. II, n. 125. 28. *Ibid.*

29. "Non decet servum Dei tristem vel turbulentum se monstrare hominibus, sed semper honestum. Offensas tuas in tuo cubiculo discute, et coram Deo tuo lacrimare et ingemisce. Cum redis ad fratres, mœrore deposito, cæteris conformare." *Ibid.* n. 128. Cf. *Spec. perf.* c. 96.

30. "Multum invident mihi æmuli salutis humanæ, et semper conantur quem in me non possunt, in sociis conturbare." *Ibid.*

31. Matth. vi, 16. By "hypocrites" Christ means the Pharisees.

32. "Et caveant fratres, quod non se ostendant tristes extrinsecus et nubilosos hypocritas; sed ostendant se gaudentes in Domino et hilares et convenienter gratiosos." *Regula* I, c. 7, *Opusc.* ed. Böhmer 8, Lemmens 34. Kybal regards this passage as a part of the primitive Franciscan rule.

33. "Tantum autem diligebat virum spirituali lætitia plenum, quod pro generali commonitione in quodam capitulo scribi fecit hæc verba: Caveant fratres, ne se ostendant extrinsecus nubilosos . . ." Thom. Cel. II, n. 128.

34. "Quanta autem tunc temporis [at the Chapter of the Mats in 1221] inter fratres fuerit caritas, patientia, humilitas et obedientia et fraterna iocunditas, quis valet explicare?" Iord. a Iano n. 16.

35. "Homines autem illius religionis semel in anno cum multiplici lucro ad locum determinatum conveniunt, ut simul in Domino gaudeant et epulentur, et consilio bonorum virorum suas faciunt et promulgant institutiones sanctas et a domino papa confirmatas." *Epistula data Ianuæ* a. 1216, Octob., Böhmer, *Analekten* 98.

36 ". . . ut irent per mundum prædicando et cantando Laudes Domini. Dicebat enim, quod volebat, ut ille, qui sciret, prædicaret populo, et post prædicationem omnes cantarent simul Laudes Domini tamquam ioculatores Domini." *Spec. perf.* c. 100.

37. "Quid enim sunt servi Dei, nisi quidam ioculatores eius [Domini] qui corda hominum erigere debent et movere ad lætitiam spiritualem?" *Ibid.*

38. "Verum spiritualem amplectens lætitiam, ineptam studiose vitabat, sciens ferventer diligendum, quod perficit, nec minus vigilanter, quod inficit, fugiendum." Thom. Cel. II, n. 130. 39. *Ibid.* n. 130 sqq.

40. "Non quod intelligendum sit vel credendum, quod pater noster omnis maturitatis et honestatis amator voluerit hanc lætitiam ostendi per risum vel etiam per minimum verbum vanum, quum per hoc non lætitia spiritualis sed vanitas et fatuitas potius ostendatur, imo et in servo Dei risum et verbum otiosum singulariter abhorrebat." *Spec. perf.* c. 189.

41. "Beatus ille religiosus, qui non habet iucunditatem et lætitiam nisi in sanctissimis eloquiis et operibus Domini et cum his perducit homines ad amorem Dei in gaudio et lætitia. Et væ illi religioso, qui delectat se in verbis otiosis et inanibus et cum his perducit homines ad risum." *Verba admon. Opusc.* ed. Böhmer 47, n. 20, Lemmens 15, n. 21. 42. See Chapter X, p. 221 ff.

43. "Frater Petrus de Teukesbury, minister Alemanniæ . . . dixit fratri prædicatori: 'Tria sunt necessaria ad salutem temporalem, cibus, somnus et iocus.' Item iniunxit fratri melancholico, ut biberet calicem plenum optimo vino pro pœnitentia, et cum ebibisset, licet invitissime, dixit ei: 'Frater carissime, si haberes frequenter talem pœnitentiam, haberes utique meliorem conscientiam.'" Thom. de Eccleston, coll. XV, p. 115. 44. Thom. Cel. II, n. 126.

45. Cf. Felder, *Geschichte der wissenschaftlichen Studien im Franziskanerordern*, Freiburg, Herder 1904, 426–447.

46. "Vocavit unum de sociis, qui fuerat in sæculo citharista, dicens: Frater, filii sæculi huius divina non intelligunt sacramenta. Instrumenta quippe musica, divinis quondam laudibus deputata, in aurium voluptatem libido humana convertit." Thom. Cel. II. n. 126. 47. Cf. p. 233.

48. "Frater Iuniperus egregius Domini ioculator, quia calida sæpe verba de Domino eructabat." Thom. Cel., *Vita S. Claræ* c. 6, n. 51.

49. *Vita fr. Ægidii, Anal. franc.* III, 105 sq.

50. "Morbum accidiæ pessimum summa cura vitabat, ita cum vel parum menti illapsum sentiret, ad orationem, citissime curreret." Thom. Cel. II, n. 125.

51. "Servus Dei pro aliquo, ut assolet, conturbatus illico surgere ad orationem debet, et tamdiu coram summo Patre persistere, donec reddat ei sui salutaris lætitiam. Si enim in mœstitia fecerit moram, adolescet babilonicum illud, quod tandem nisi per lacrimas expurgetur, mansuram generabit in corde rubiginem." Thom. Cel. II, n. 125. 52. *Tres Soc.* n. 32. 53. *Ibid.* n. 33. 54. *Ibid.* n. 39. 55. *Ibid.* n. 41. 56. *Ibid.* n. 45. 57. Thom. Cel. I, n. 35. 58. Keppler *loc. cit.*

59. "Cum magna penuria de duabus buccellis panis et septem rapis malum famis misere et sitim gaudio cordis temperabant, immo potius provocabant. Et collatione habita inter se, quomodo ventrem vacuum implere possent . . . , decreverunt, ut de aqua puri fluentis prætereuntis biberent, ne venter vacuus murmuraret." Iord. a. Iano n. 21. 60. Eccleston coll. I, p. 8 sq.

61. "Fuerunt tamen fratres omni tempore inter se ita iocundi et læti, ut vix in aspectu mutuo se temperarent a risu." *Ibid.* p. 32. 62. Thom. Cel. II, n. 76.

63. Thom. Cel. I, n. 34; *Spec. perf.* c. 90. 64. *Verba admon.* n. 27, *Opusc.* ed. Böhmer 49, Lemmens 18. 65. See p. 230 f. 66. *Tres Soc.* n. 22.

67. *Tres Soc.* c. 10, ed. Amoni p. 62. This passage is not in the edition of Faloci-Pulignani.

68. *Actus b. Francisci* c. 7. This poetic narrative of the *Actus-Fioretti* no

doubt has its source in the older historical version discovered lately by P. Bughetti,
O. F. M., in a MS. of the Biblioteca Nazionale at Florence: see Facchinetti,
S. Francesco d'Assisi, Milano 1921, 177 sq.

CHAPTER XII

1. Matth. xxiii, 8.   2. Cf. *S. Columbani Regula cœnobialis* c. 10; *S. Benedicti Regula* c. 21 sqq.
3. The word "Frater" is found in the first rule of St. Francis at least one
hundred and four times, in the much shorter second rule forty-seven times, in the
Testament twelve times; similarly in other writings of the Saint.   The rule of
the Order is called "regula et vita Minorum Fratrum" (e.g. in the beginning of
the second rule).   The Order itself is called by Francis with preference "Fraternitas" (in the first rule three times, in the second four times, in the Testament
twice, etc.); however, we also read in Thom. Cel. I, n. 38: "Ordinem Fratrum
Minorum primitus ipse plantavit et ea scilicet occasione hoc ei nomen imposuit . . . Volo, inquit, ut Ordo Fratrum Minorum fraternitas hæc vocetur."
4. "Et nullus vocetur Prior, sed generaliter omnes vocentur Fratres Minores."
Regula I, c. 6.
5. The passage (Matth. xxiii, 8–10) is quoted literally in the first rule, ch. 22,
thus: "Omnes autem vos fratres estis; et patrem nolite vocare vobis super
terram, unus est enim Pater vester, qui in cœlis est.   Nec vocemini magistri;
unus est enim Magister vester, qui in cœlis est, Christus."
6. Thom. Cel. II, n. 180. 191.
7. "Domina sancta caritas, Dominus te salvet . . . Sancta caritas confundit
omnes diabolicas et carnales tentationes et omnes carnales timores." *Salutatio
virtutum*, *Opusc.* ed. Böhmer 64 sq., Lemmens 20 sq.   8. John xv, 12.   9. 1
John iii, 18.
10. *Regula* I, c. 5. 7. 11; II, c. 6, *Opusc.* ed.   Böhmer 6, 8. 12. 21, Lemmens
32. 34. 40. 69.
11. *Regula* I, c. 6; II, c. 7; *De religiosa habitatione in eremo, Opusc.* ed. Böhmer 7. 33. 67, Lemmens 32. 70. 83; Thom. Cel. I, n. 98; II, n. 177. 184 sq.   12.
Luke xvii, 10.   13. Luke v, 22.   14. Cf. Matth. vii, 3 and Luke vi, 41.
15. *Regula* I, c. 5. 11, *Opusc.* ed. Böhmer 6. 12, Lemmens 32. 40 sq.
16. *Verba admon.* n. 8, *Opusc.* ed. Böhmer 44, Lemmens 10.
17. "Demum cum animus caritate repletus Deo odibiles odiat, vigebat
istud in sancto Francisco.   Detrectatores quippe super aliud vitiosorum genus
horribiliter exsecrans, venenum in lingua ferre eos dicebat aliosque veneno
inficere."   Thom. Cel. II, n. 182.
18. "Ideoque rumigerulos pulicesque mordaces, si quando loquerentur,
vitabat avertebatque prout vidimus aures, ne tali polluerentur auditu."   *Ibid.*
19. *Ibid.*   20. *Ibid.*   21. *Ibid.* n. 183.
22. "Revera super constantiæ fundamentum caritatis nobilis structura surrexit, in qua vivi lapides, ex omnibus mundi partibus coacervati, ædificati sunt
in habitaculum Spiritus Sancti.   O quanto caritatis ardore flagrabant novi
Christi discipuli!   Quantus in eis piæ societatis vigebat amor!   Cum enim alicubi pariter convenirent, vel in via, ut moris est, sibi invicem obviarent, ibi
spiculum spiritalis resultabat amoris, super omnem amorem veræ dilectionis
seminarium spargens.   Quid illud?   Casti amplexus, suaves affectus, osculum
sanctum, dulce colloquium, risus modestus, aspectus iucundus, oculus simplex,
animus supplex, lingua placabilis, responsio mollis, idem propositum, promptum
obsequium et indefessa manus . . . Desiderabiliter conveniebant, delectabilius
simul erant; sed gravis erat utrinque separatio socialis, amarum divortium,
acerba disiunctio."   Thom. Cel. I, n. 38 sq.   "Hoc solummodo suavissimum
cordis eorum contristare videbatur affectum, quod ab invicem separari oportebat.   Unde frequenter usque ad partes remotas fratres recedentes conduce-
bant, et effusis abunde in recessu lacrymis affectionis fidem mutuo demonstra-

bant." Thom. de Eccleston coll. V, p. 33. "Quando autem se invicem revidebant, tanta iucunditate replebantur et gaudio, ac si nihil recordarentur eorum, quæ passi fuerant ab iniquis . . . Amore intime se diligebant, et serviebant unus alteri, ac nutriebant eum, sicut mater filium unicum et dilectum." *Tres Soc.* n. 41.

23. "Et quidem cum cuncta terrena despicerent et se ipsos nunquam amore privato diligerent, totius affectum in communi refundentes, se ipsos dare in pretium satagebant, ut fraternæ necessitati subvenirent." Thom. Cel. I, n. 39. "Tantum caritatis ardebat in eis, quod facile eis videbatur tradere corpora sua morti non solum pro Christi amore, sed etiam pro salute animæ vel corporum suorum fratrum." *Tres Soc.* n. 41. 24. *Ibid.* n. 42.

25. Thom. Cel. II, n. 155; *Spec. perf.* c. 51.

26. *Tres Soc.* n. 43; Thom. Cel. *ibid.* The Three Companions state expressly: "ut pedem fratris turbati faceret poni super os suum," while Thom. Cel. (and *Spec. perf.*) writes: "ut læsi pedem vel inviti beatis osculis demulceret."

27. Iord. a Iano n. 55. 28. Thom. de Eccleston coll. VII, p. 44. 29. *Ibid.* coll. II, p. 10. 30. Thom. Cel., *Vita S. Claræ* c. 5, n. 38, p. 762.

31. "Præcipua namque ante omnia in eis viget virtus mutuæ ac continuæ caritatis, quae ita ipsarum in unam copulat voluntates, ut cum vel quadraginta vel quinquaginta pariter alicubi commorentur, idem velle et idem nolle unum in eis spiritus faciat de diversis." Thom. Cel. I, n. 19.

32. "Sanctus Franciscus vero de tanti viri adventu et conversione gavisus est valde . . . Beatus igitur Franciscus consolatione et gratia Spiritus Sancti quotidie replebatur, omnique vigilantia et sollicitudine novos filios novis institutionibus informabat." Thom. Cel. I, n. 25. 26.

33. "At illi, cum gaudio et lætitia multa suscipientes obedientiæ sanctæ mandatum, coram sancto Francisco supplices se prosternebant in terram; ipse vero amplexans eos dulciter et devote dicebat singulis: Iacta cogitatum tuum in Domino, et ipse te enutriet. Hoc verbum dicebat, quoties ad obedientiam fratres aliquos transmittebat." *Ibid.* n. 29. 34. *Ibid.* n. 30 sq.

35. "Curialissimus erat." *Ibid.* n. 17. "O quam pulcher, quam splendidus, quam gloriosus apparebat . . . in simplicitate verborum . . . in charitate fraterna . . . in concordi obsequio, in aspectu angelico! Dulcis in moribus, natura placidus, affabilis in sermone, commodissimus in exhortatione, fidelissimus in commisso, providus in consilio, . . . gratiosus in omnibus. Mente serenus, animo dulcis . . . rigidus in se, pius in aliis . . . omnium moribus utiliter se conformans." *Ibid.* n. 83. "Adeo amabilis est, ut ab omnibus hominibus veneretur." Iacobus Vitriacensis, *Epist. VI.* scripta a. 1220, Böhmer, *Analekten* 101. Cf. p. 177 f., 225 f.

36. Thom. Cel. II, n. 22; *Spec. perf.* c. 27. Cf. p. 222 f.

37. Thom. Cel. II, n. 181. 38. *Ibid.* II, n. 174.

39. Thom. Cel. I, n. 108; II, n. 216; *Spec. perf.* c. 88.

40. Thom. Cel. II, n. 217; *Spec. perf.* c. 88. 41. John xiii, 1.

42. "Multa sibi ad infirmos compassio, multa pro illorum necessitatibus sollicitudo." Thom. Cel. II, n. 175. 43. *Ibid.*

44. Thom. Cel. II, n. 176; *Spec. perf.* c. 28.

45. "Omnium languentium in se transformabat affectus, verba præbens compassionis, ubi subventionis non poterat." Thom. Cel. II, n. 175.

46. "Si quis fratrum in infirmitatem ceciderit, ubicumque fuerit, alii fratres non dimittant eum, nisi constituatur unus de fratribus vel plures, si necesse fuerit, qui serviant ei, sicut vellent sibi serviri; sed in maxima necessitate possunt ipsum dimittere alicui personæ, quæ debeat suæ satisfacere infirmitati." *Regula* I, c. 10, *Opusc.* ed. Böhmer 11, Lemmens 39.

47. *Regula* II, c. 6, *Opusc.* ed. Böhmer 32, Lemmens 69.

48. "Et specialiter monuit eas [Pauperes Dominas] ut de eleemosynis, quas Dominus daret eis, cum hilaritate et gratiarum actione discrete suis corporibus providerent." *Spec. perf.* c. 90.

49. According to a letter written by St. Clare to Bl. Agnes of Prague, Francis ordained: "Præter debiles et infirmas [quibus quoscumque cibos cum omni sollicitudine dari admonuit ac imperavit] nemini liceat ex nobis, quæ corpore

sana ac fortis est, aliis cibis, quam quadragesimalibus uti, tum feriato tum festo die." *Act. S.*, Martii t. I, 507, A–B.

50. ". . . maxime, ut sanæ in laboribus, quos sustinebant pro sororibus suis infirmis, et ipsæ infirmæ in suis infirmitatibus exsisterent patientes." *Spec. perf.* c. 90.   51. *Regula* II, c. 10, *Opusc.* ed. Böhmer 34, Lemmens 72.   52. Acts xiii, 48.   53. Apoc. iii, 19.

54. Regula I, c. 10, *Opusc.* ed. Böhmer 11, Lemmens 39.   An almost identical version was contained according to Thom. Cel. II, n. 175 in a still older, but no longer extant, compilation of the rule.

55. Thom. Cel. I, n. 101; *Spec. perf.* c. 91.   56. Cf. p. 230 f.   57. *Spec. Perf.* c. 89.   58. Thom. Cel. II, n. 9. 115–123.   59. Thom. Cel. II, n. 118.

60. "Si qui autem de fratribus . . . aliquam tentationem vel tribulationem habebant, audiendo beatum Franciscum loquentem ita dulciter et ferventer . . . liberabantur a tentationibus, et tribulationibus sublevabantur mirifice.   Compatiens namque loquebatur eis non ut iudex, sed ut pater misericors filiis, et medicus bonus infirmis, sciens cum infirmantibus infirmari, et cum tribulatis affligi." *Tres Soc*, n. 59.   61. Thom. Cel. II, n. 110.   62. Thom. Cel. I, n. 49 sq.   63. Thom. Cel. II, n. 49.   64. *Ibid.* n. 42.   65. Thom. Cel. II, n. 50.

66. *Spec. perf.* c. 90.   Cf. the Testament of St. Clare (*Act. S.*, Augusti t. II, p. 747), also her rule c. 6 (Sbaralea, *Bullar. francisc.* I, p. 675).

67. Thom. Cel. II, n. 155. 178. 188.

68. "Corripiebat nihilominus omnes delinquentes, atque contumaces et rebelles animadversione debita coercebat." *Tres Soc.* n. 59.   69. Thom. Cel. II, n. 156 sq.

70. "Illos autem infirmos suaviori fovebat clementia, patientia supportabat, quos velut fluctuantes parvulos tentationibus agitatos et spiritu deficientes sciebat." Thom. Cel. II, n. 177.

71. *Regula* I, c. 5, *Opusc.* ed.   Böhmer 5, Lemmens 31.

72. *Regula* II, c. 7, *Opusc.* ed.   Böhmer 33, Lemmens 69.

73. *Epist. ad quendam ministrum*, *Opusc.* ed.   Böhmer 28, Lemmens 109.

74. Thom. Cel. II, n. 185.   75. *Ibid.* n. 143.

76. "Condescendebat humiliter eius animus omnes fovens, omnibus deferens." Bern. a Bessa, *Liber de laudibus* c. 3.

77. Thus *Regula* I, c. 11. 14. 16; *Regula* II, c. 3, *Opusc.* ed. Böhmer 12. 13. 15. 31, Lemmens 40. 42. 45. 67.   78. *Tres Soc.* n. 58.   79. Thom. Cel. I, n. 29.

80. Matth. v, 39.   81. Luke vi, 29, 30.   82. Mark viii, 35; Luke ix, 24.   83. Matth. v, 10.   84. John xv, 20.   85. Matth. x, 23.   86. Matth. v, 11 f; Luke vi, 22 f.

87. *Regula* I, a. 14. 16. 22. *Opusc.* ed.   Böhmer 13. 15. 19, Lemmens 42. 45. 51.   Cf. *Regula* II, c. 10; *Admonitiones* n. 15.   The primitive history of the French province relates various incidents from which it is manifest that the Friars followed these injunctions literally.   Cf. e. g. *Tres Soc.* n. 38–41; Iord. a Iano n. 6; *Vita fr. Ægidii* 77. 83; *Dicta b. Ægidii* 18 sq.

88. "Et quicumque ad eos venerit amicus vel adversarius, fur vel latro, benigne recipiatur." *Regula* I, c. 7, *Opusc.* ed. Böhmer 8, Lemmens 34.   89. *Spec. perf.* c. 66.

CHAPTER XIII

1. 1 John iii, 18.   2. S. Kurth, *La Lèpre avant les Croisades en Occident*, Paris 1907.

3. The leper hospitals frequently had their own chapels and chaplains.   The Third Lateran Council (1179) at least decreed that the larger leper hospitals have their own chaplains, because the inmates were forbidden to enter the public churches: Harduin, *Acta Conciliorum* t. VI, pars II, n. XXIII.

4. Cf. Lütolf, *Die Leprosen*, in: *Schweizerischer Geschichtsfreund* XVI, 187–248.

5. "Ipse enim Christus in carne apparens multas curialitates leprosis exhibuit,

tangendo eos propria manu et sanando multos et dulciter eos alloquendo, sicut patet ex evangelio." Humbertus de Romanis, O. P., *De eruditione prædicatorum* lib. 2, c. 41, ed. *Maxima Bibliotheca Veterum Patrum* t. 25, Lugduni 1677, 477.

6. Is. 53, 4. One frequently meets with this reference to the prophecy of Isaias in medieval writers, e. g. S. Bonav. c. 1, n. 6 and Humbertus de Romanis *Ibid.*

7. According to the testament of Louis VIII (1226): "Donamus et legamus duobus millibus domorum leprosorum decem millia librarum, videlicet cuilibet earum centum solidos." Martin-Doisy, *Dictionnaire de l'économie chrétienne* II, 415. 8. Martin-Doisy *loc. cit.* IV, 126.

9. *Historia occidentalis* c. 29, ed Franc. Moschi, Duaci 1597, 338 sq.

10. Cf. the historically interesting sermon sketch of Humbert de Romanis *ibid.* "Ad Fratres et Sorores in domibus leprosorum."

11. "Consueverat multum horrere leprosos . . . In tantum enim, ut dixit, sibi amara fuerat visio leprosorum, ut non solum eos nollet videre, sed nec eorum habitaculis propinquare. Et si aliquando contingebat ipsum iuxta domos eorum transire aut eos videre, licet pietate moveretur ad faciendum eis eleemosynam, per interpositam personam, vultum tamen semper avertens, nares suas propriis manibus obturabat." *Tres Soc.* n. 11. "In tantum namque, ut dicebat, aliquando amara ei leprosorum visio exsistebat, ut, cum tempore vanitatis suæ per duo fere milliaria eminus ipsorum domos respiceret, nares suas propriis manibus obturaret." Thom. Cel. I, 17. "Inter omnia infelicia monstra mundi Franciscus naturaliter leprosos abhorrens . . ." Thom. Cel. II, n. 9. 12. S. Bonav. c. 1, n. 4.

13. "Francisce, inquit illi Deus in spiritu, pro carnaliter et vane dilectis iam spiritualia commutato, et amara pro dulcibus sumens contemne te ipsum, me si velis agnoscere; nam et ordine verso sapient tibi quæ dico." Thom. Cel. II, n. 9. 14. Thom. Cel. II, n. 9; *Tres Soc.* n. 11; S. Bonav. c. 1, n. 5.

15. Thom. Cel. II, n. 9; *Tres Soc.* n. 11.

16. *Testament., Opusc.* ed. Böhmer 36, Lemmens 77. 17. S. Bonav. c. 1, n. 6.

18. Thom. Cel. I, n. 17; *Tres Soc.* n. 11; S. Bonav. c. 2, n. 6.

19. "Diebus vero manibus propriis qui poterant laborabant, exsistentes in domibus leprosorum vel in aliis locis honestis, servientes omnibus humiliter et devote." Thom. Cel. I, n. 39. 20. *Spec. perf.* c. 44.

21. "Fratres tamen in manifesta necessitate leprosorum possint pro eis quærere eleemosynam." *Regula* I, c. 8, *Opusc.* ed. Böhmer 9, Lemmens 36.

22. In order to gain a proper conception of the immense difficulties connected with the care of the lepers, and of the heroism with which Francis and his brothers served them, one should read the 28th chapter of the *Actus* (the 25th of the *Fioretti*): "How St. Francis cured a leper in body and soul." This legend is probably based on fact, even as regards the miraculous cure related therein. The historians testify that Francis during his life (S. Bonav. c. 2, n. 6) and after his death (Thom. Cel. I, n. 146; II, n. 146 sq.) performed miraculous cures of lepers. 23. *Spec. perf.* c. 58.

24. We have seen that for the same reasons the Friars no longer labored in the houses of strangers. In the *Vita B. Christophori de Romandiola*, ed. *Analecta franc.* III, 161, it is stated expressly that the Friars had devoted themselves so extensively to the care of the lepers in the beginning, because they had no houses of their own.

25. Don Pietro Pirri, San Lazzaro del Valloncello. *Memorie di un grande leprosario francescano nell' Umbria*, Perugia 1915.

26. The same Albert of Pisa related later as Provincial of England how he at one time lived and labored with St. Francis in a leper hospital: Eccleston coll. XIV, p. 106. 27. Iord, a Iano n. 32. 39.

28. Eccleston, *De adventu FF. Min. in Angliam* coll. I and II, ed. Little p. 8. 13.

29. "Volebat ad serviendum leprosis redire denuo et haberi contemptui sicut aliquando habebatur." Thom. Cel. I, n. 103.

30. "Cum aliquem fratrum vel sororum contigerit infirmari, ministri per se

vel per alios, si infirmus eis fecerit nuntiari, semel in hebdomada visitent infirmantem et ad pœnitentiam commoveant et, sicut viderint expedire, necessaria corporis, quibus indiget, de communi administrent." *Regula antiquissima fratrum et sororum pœnitentium* c. 8, *Opusc.* ed. Böhmer 78.
31. *Vita auctore Gaufredo de Bello-loco Regis confessario* c. 3, *Act SS.*, Augusti t. V, p. 548, n. 29 sq. 32. Appendix *Vitæ* I, c. 4, n. 23, *ibid.* p. 564.
33. Le Comte de Montalembert, *Historie de Ste Elisabeth de Hongrie*, Paris 1903, 111–114. 117–119.
34. Concerning the love of Francis for the poor while in the world cf. p. 76 f.
35. Joh. Bapt. v. Weiss, *Weltgeschichte* IV, 3. Aufl., Graz und Leipzig 1891, 623. 36. "Pauperes quoque intime diligebat, eis viscerose compatiens, omnibusque se subditum exhibebat." *Tres Soc.* n. 57. 37. Thom. Cel. II, n. 83. 38. Thom. Cel. II, n. 84. 39. *Tres Soc.* n. 57.
40. "Et debent gaudere, quando conversantur inter viles et despectas personas, inter pauperes et debiles, infirmos et leprosos et iuxta viam mendicantes." *Regula* I, c. 9, *Opusc.* ed. Böhmer 10, Lemmens 37.
41. "Molestissimum erat ei, cum alicui pauperi cerneret exprobrari, vel in aliquam creaturarum maledictionis verbum audiret ab aliquo intorqueri." Thom. Cel. I, n. 76.
42. "Qui pauperi maledicit, Christo iniuriam facit, cuius portat nobile signum, qui se pro nobis fecit pauperem in hoc mundo." Thom. Cel. I, n. 76.
43. "Cum pauperem vides, o frater, speculum tibi proponitur Domini et pauperis Matris eius. In infirmis similiter, infirmitates, quas pro nobis assumpsit, considera." Thom. Cel. II, n. 85.
44. "Eia semper mirrhæ fasciculus commorabatur Francisco, semper respicit in faciem Christi sui, semper virum dolorum et scientem infirmitates attrectat." *Ibid.* 45. *Ibid.* II, n. 89.
46. "In eleemosynarum datione animarum lucrum potius quam carnis subsidium requirebat, et non minus in dando quam in accipiendo se ipsum ponebat cæteris in exemplum." *Ibid.* II, n. 78.
47. ". . . Da matri nostræ Novum Testamentum, ut vendat illud pro sua necessitate, quia per ipsum monemur subvenire pauperibus. Credo equidem, quod magis inde placebit donum quam lectio. Datur ergo mulieri liber, et primum Testamentum, quod in Ordine fuit, sacra hac pietate distrahitur." *Ibid.* n. 91.
48. "Sed iam pauperum amator exstitit præcipuus, iam id quod perfecte futurus erat sacra spirabant initia. Frequenter proinde exuens semetipsum pauperes induit, quibus se similem fieri nondum operis executione sed toto iam corde contendit . . ." *Ibid.* II, n. 8.
49. ". . . Audis, inquit, frater, quid hæc paupercula dicit? Amore Dei toleremus algorem, et da pauperculæ pannum, ut tunicam compleat. Dederat ipse, donat et socius, et uterque nudus remanet, ut vetula vestiatur." *Ibid.* II, n. 86. 50. *Ibid.* I, n. 76. 51. *Ibid.* II, n. 88.
52. ". . . Oportet, frater, ut reddamus mantellum paupercolo, cuius est. Mutuo accepimus ipsum donec pauperiorem invenire contigerit . . . Ego fur esse nolo; pro furto nobis imputaretur, si non daremus magis indigenti . . ." *Ibid.* n. 87. 53. *Ibid.* n. 92; cf. n. 196.
54. "Licet tunica vili satis et hispida foret contentus, illam multoties cum aliquo paupere dividere cupiebat." *Ibid.* I, n. 76.
55. "Semel aliquando, cum a paupere peteretur, nihilque haberet in manibus, gaidam propriæ tunicæ dissuit et pauperi erogavit. Nonnumquam etiam ob simile opus femoralia traxit." *Ibid.* II, n. 90.
56. "Frequenter proinde inveniens pauperes lignis vel aliis sarcinis oneratos, ad adiuvandum illos proprios humeros, licet nimium debiles, supponebat." *Ibid.* I, n. 76. 57. "Talibus erga pauperes affluebat pietatis visceribus, talibusque vestigia pauperis Christi prosequebatur affectibus." *Ibid.* II, n. 90. 58. See p. 97 ff. 59. *Tres Soc.* n. 43 sq. 60. *Vita fr. Ægidii* 76. 61. *Ibid.* 76. 62. *Ibid.* 77.
63. "Ille esset bonus activus, qui si possibile esset, omnes huius mundi pau-

peres pasceret, omnes vestiret, omnia eis necessaria tribueret abundanter . . ."
Dicta b. Ægidii 51.

64. *B. Luchesii Vita antiquior* n. 2 sq., *Act. SS.*, Aprilis t. III, p. 602 sq.

65. De Montalembert, *Historie de Ste Elisabeth* II, 115 ss. 133 ss.

66. ". . . Dicebat eisdem, quod cum oporteret quandoque in expensis exce-dere, potius eligebat, quod excessus fieret in eleemosynis propter Dominum, quam in sæcularibus et mundanis: ut excessus, qui fiebat in spiritualibus, excusaret atque redimeret excessum, quem frequenter oportebat fieri in mundanis." *S. Ludovici Vita Auctore Gaufredo de Bello-loco Regis confessario*, c. 3, *Act. SS.*, Augusti t. V, p. 548 sq., n. 27-31.

67. Thom. Cel. I, n. 76.

CHAPTER XIV

1. Thom. Cel. II, n. 111.   2. *Ibid.* n. 35 sq. Cf. *Actus* c. 23.   3. *Ibid.* II, n. 4.
4. Matth. x, 12. See p. 7 f.
5. "Salutationem hanc revelavit mihi Dominus, ut diceremus: Dominus det tibi pacem." *Testam., Opusc.* ed. Böhmer 38, Lemmens 80.
6. *Regula* I, c. 14, *Opusc.* ed. Böhmer 13, Lemmens 42.   7. *Spec. perf.* c. 26.
8. "In omni prædicatione sua, priusquam convenientibus proponeret verbum Dei, pacem imprecabatur dicens: Dominus det vobis pacem.   Hanc viris et mulieribus, hanc obviis et obviantibus semper devotissime nuntiabat.   Propterea multi, qui pacem oderant pariter et salutem, Domino cooperante, pacem amplexati sunt toto corde, facti et ipsi filii pacis et æmuli salutis æternæ." Thom. Cel. I, n. 23. Cf. *Tres Soc.* n. 26; Julian. a Spira, *Leg.* n. 16. I refer also to the interesting testimony of Bl. Angela of Foligno, *Vita* c. 9, n. 131, *Act. SS.*, Ianuarii t. I, 207: "Apparuit mihi B. Franciscus totus gloriosus salutationem consuetam offerens, quæ est ista: 'Pax Altissimi tecum sit!' Salutat autem semper voce piissima, humillima, gratiosa et affectuosa."
9. This follows from a statement of the Archdeacon Thomas of Spalato, of which we shall presently speak. See p. 291 f. 10. *Tres Soc.* n. 29. 11. *Spec. perf.* c. 101.
12. Humbertus de Romanis, O. P. (*De eruditione prædicatorum* lib. 2, c. 26, *Max. Bibl. PP.* t. XXV, 468) stresses this: "Fratres Minores declinent occupationes turbativas, ut pacem (quam optare eos Beatus Franciscus voluit docendo eos dicere 'Dominus det vobis pacem') habere possint."
13. "In his omnibus pacem et mansuetudinem cum omnibus sequebantur." Thom. Cel. I, n. 41.
14. "Sicut pacem annuntiatis ore, sic in cordibus vestris et amplius habeatis. Nullus per vos provocetur ad iram vel scandala, sed omnes per mansuetudinem vestram ad pacem, benignitatem et misericordiam provocentur. Nam ad hoc vocati sumus, ut vulneratos curemus, alligemus contractos et erroneos revocamus." *Tres Soc.* n. 58. This text is mutilated in Faloci-Pulignani, while Amoni, *Leg. trium Soc.* p. 84, offers the correct reading.
15. "Ambidexter et fortis existe, ut audias verbum angelicum, quod scriptum est in libro iudicum (6, 12): 'Pax tibi, virorum fortissime'. . . Propter favorem popularem milites sæculares ventum seminant inturbidum, metunt et laborare vel pugnare non cessant; quanto magis Christi militibus pugnandum est strenue pro salute sua, non pro gloria populari, sed pro gloria beatitudinis sempiternæ. Sicut autem de lege bellorum hoc legimus institutum, ut ex donativo, quod milites consequuntur, pars quædam, de qua sustentari possent, eisdem erat pro necessariis conferenda, pars autem alia, ne consumerentur inaniter custodita et tempore suo reddenda; ita si legitime certaveris, pax tibi reddetur pectoris, et tandem pax æternitatis, hæc pax super pacem." Guilberti Tornacensis Tractatus de pace animique tranquillitate c. 19, ed. *Max. Bibl. PP.* t. 25, 391, G-H. Regarding the author cf. Wadding-Sbaralea, *Scriptores Ordinis Minorum*, Romæ 1806, 100. 308 sq.

16. The use of the terms "minores" and "maiores" in the quoted sense was quite general. Cf. Ducange-Carpentarius, *Glossarium*, s. v., as also the very significant text in Petrus de Vineis (died 1249), *Epistolæ* lib. 5, c. 12, Basileæ 1566, 590: "Eidem ut reformetur pax inter *minores* et *maiores*. Pati nolentes, ut *minores a maioribus* opprimantur, discretioni tuæ præcipiendo mandamus, quatenus inter *milites et populares* civitatis procures pacem et concordiam reformare."

17. Regarding this entire description cf. Francesco Pennacchi, *L'anno della prigionia di S. Francesco in Perugia*, Perugia 1915 (*Estratto dall' Archivio per la Storia ecclesiastica dell' Umbria*, vol. II, Foligno 1915). This treatise of Pennacchi will call for a revision of the chronology of the youth of Francis, which is very uncertain as it is. Heretofore it was commonly assumed that the war between Assisi and Perugia and the following captivity of the Saint took place in the years 1201-02. If we assume instead the years 1204-5 and it appears that nothing can be said against this chronology of Pennacchi—then the statement of *Tres Soc.* n. 5, according to which several years passed between the liberation of Francis and his journey to Apulia, can no longer be upheld.

18. Cristofani, *Delle storie di Assisi* libri sei, terza ediz., Assisi 1902, 79.

19. See Pennacchi *ibid.* 5. sq.   20. See p. 172.   21. Bonav. c. 4, n. 4.

22. Since Cristofani discovered and published the Pact of 1210, historians have constantly stressed the part which Francis took in the reconciliation of the Maiores and Minores of Assisi. Cf. Pennacchi, *Il patto d'Assisi e San Francesco*, Assisi 1911.   23. Thom. Cel. II, n. 108; S. Bonav. c. 6, n. 9.   24. Harduin, *Acta Concil.* VI, 2, 1724.

25. "... Deveniens ergo Perusium populo congregato incipit prædicare; cumque milites in equis, ut assolet, currerent et in ludis militaribus arma tenentes verbum Dei præpedirent ... sæviunt in milites populares, et verso gladio nobiles in plebeios; ultimo tanta immanitate certatum est, quod etiam vicini, quos offenderant, condolebant." Thom. Cel. II, n. 37.

26. "... Tota verborum eius discurrebat materies ad extinguendas inimicitias et ad pacis federa reformanda ... Sed tantam Deus verbis illius contulit efficaciam, ut multi trinus nobilium, inter quas antiquarum inimicitiarum furor immanis multa sanguinis effusione fuerat debachatus, ad pacis consilium reducerentur..." Thomæ, Archidiaconi Spalatensis *Historia Pontificum Salonitanorum* ed. Heinemann, *Monum. Germ. hist. Script.* XXIX, Hannoveræ 1892, 580. The passage is found likewise in Sigonius, *De episcopis Bononsiensibus* libri quinque ed. *Opera omnia* III, Mediol. 1732-1737, col. 432, also in Böhmer, *Analekten* 106.   27. In the earliest Papal documents they are always, later on commonly, called "Penitents."

28. "Arma mortalia contra quempiam non recipiant vel secum ferant. Omnes a iuramentis solemnibus abstineant nisi necessitate cogente in casibus a summo pontifice exceptis in sua indulgentia videlicet pro pace, fide, calumnia et testimonio ... Si contra ius vel privilegia fratres vel sorores a potestatibus vel rectoribus locorum in quibus habitant vexentur, ministri loci, quod videbitur expedire, cum consilio domini episcopi faciant." *Regula et vita fratrum vel sororum de pænitentia* c. 6, n. 3-4; c. 10, n. 3, *Opusc.* ed. Böhmer 76. 79. In the above form these regulations no doubt originated after 1221, since they appear to presuppose the Papal decrees of 1221, 1227 and 1228. But just these decrees, whereby the exemption of the Tertiaries from the obligation of oaths and from military duty is protected, show that the regulations in question were contained in *substance* in the Regula pænitentium from the beginning.

29. "Significatum est nobis, quod Faventiæ et in quibusdam aliis civitatibus et locis vicinis quidam sunt, quibus illum Dominus inspiravit affectum, ut mundi iam gloriam non quærentes, sed ex humilitate abiicientes in sæculo semet ipsos ad pænitentiam se converterint et ad hoc totum deputaverint tempus suum signum humilitatis et pænitentiæ in habitu exhibentes. Quia vero tales super iuramento de armis sumendis et sequendis locorum potestatibus exhibendo multoties molestantur ex eo, quod nunquam defecit, qui bonis actibus invideret,

fraternitati tuæ per apostolica scripta mandamus, quatenus, cum a talibus fueris requisitus, molestatores suos super huius modi iuramento præmissa monitione sublata appelationis impedimento auctoritate nostra compescas." Sbaralea, *Bullar. francisc.* I, p. 8, n. 8.

30. We give the entire passage, which is not easily accessible: "Nam fratres Prædicatores et Minores, qui post suarum religionum exordia, contra nos odio et rancore concepto vitam et conversationem nostram reprobam prædicando multifariam depravarunt, nos et iura nostra minoraverunt in tantum, quod simus iam ad nihilum redacti et qui olim ratione officii dominabamur regibus, principes ligabamus, increpationes faciebamus in populis, nunc simus in opprobrium et derisum: et celeberrima laus nostra versa est in fabulam omni carni. Tacemus autem qualiter prædicti fratres, in alienam messem paulatim manum immittentes, clerum singulis dignitatibus supplantarunt: et sibi pænitentias et baptismata, infirmantium unctiones et cœmeteria usurpantes, in se omnem vim et authoritatem clericalis ministerii astrinxerunt. Nunc autem, ut iura nostra potentius enervarent, et a nobis devotionem præciderent singulorum, duas novas fraternitates creaverunt: ad quas sic generaliter mares et feminas receperunt, quod vix unus et una remansit, cuius nomen in altera non sit scriptum." Petrus de Vineis, *Epistolæ* lib. I, c. 37, Basileæ 1566, p. 234. Cf. Huillard-Bréholles, *Vie et correspondance de Pierre de la vigne, ministre de l'empereur Frédéric II*, Paris 1865, 148–153. The document is found among the letters of Peter de Vineis, but was not written by him, but addressed to him. See P. Frédégand, O. M. Cap., *Examen critique d'une phrase attribue à Pierre de la Vigne*, in: *Études franciscaines* t. XXXIV (1922) 538–560.

31. Georg Schanz, *Zur Geschichte der deutschen Gesellenverbände im Mittelalter*, Leipzig 1876, 70, Anmerk. 1.

32. "Multi magni genere tam viri quam mulieres, maxime in Italiæ partibus, huiusmodi statum vivendi assumpserunt." *De eruditione prædicatorum* lib. 2, c. 39, *Max. Bibl. PP.* t. XXV, 475.

33. Bernard a Bessa, *Liber de laudibus* c. 7, p. 75, says expressly: "In regulis seu vivendi formis istorum [fratrum et sororum de pænitentia] dictandis sacræ memoriæ dominus papa Gregorius, in minori adhuc officio constitutus, beato Francisco intima familiaritate coniunctus, devote supplebat, quod viro sancto in dictandi scientia deerat." 34. Sbaralea assigns June 25, 1227.

35. Breve "Nimis patenter," Sbaralea I, 30, n. 7; Potthast, *Regesta Pontif. Rom.* n. 7919. 36. Breve "Detestanda humani generis," Sbaralea I, 39, n. 20; Potthast n. 8159.

37. Breve "Cum dilecti" dated June 4, (Sbaralea gives June 7,) 1230, Sbaralea I, 65, n. 53, Potthast 8565; Breve "Nimis patenter," April 5, 1231, Sbaralea I, 71, n. 59, Potthast 8697 b; Breve "Ut cum maiori libertate," Nov. 21, 1234, Sbaralea I, 142, n. 149, Potthast 9768.

38. Cf. the exhaustive work of Leo L. Dubois, *Saint Francis, Social Reformer*, New York 1905.

39. "The Beggar of Assisi is the representative of the great lower mass of the people, the third estate, striving for a self-reliant and independent position, but at the same time also the representative of each individual of this mass, as he becomes conscious of his rights toward the world." Henry Thode, *Franz von Assisi und die Anfänge der Kunst der Renaissance in Italien*, Berlin 1885, 521.

40. "Nella regola di San Francesco era stata la consecrazione e in qualche modo il primo inizio della italiana democrazia." Gino Capponi, *Storia della Republica di Firenze I*, Firenze 1875, 180. Likewise Cristofani *loc cit.* I, 70, also A. Cantono, *San Francesco d'Assisi e la democrazia cristiana*, in: *Fede e scienza* Roma 1903.

41. *Regula* II, c. 2; *Tres Soc.* n. 57 sq. 42. Thom. Cel. II, n. 89. See p. 294. 43. See p. 288.

44. *Monum. Germ. hist. Leg.* sect. IV, t. I (1893) 603, Anmerk. L.; cf. Kluck, hohn, *Geschichte des Gottesfriedens*, Leipzig 1857, 56–73. 45. Matth. v. 9.

CHAPTER XV

1. "Apostolicus vir Franciscus." *Tres Soc.* n. 68.
2. The oldest liturgical Office in honor of St. Francis begins with the words: "Franciscus vir catholicus et totus apostolicus . . ." Hil. Felder, O. M. Cap., *Die Reimoffizien auf die hl. Franziskus und Antonius gedichtet und komponiert durch Fr. Julian von Speier* (died *c.* 1250), Freiburg, 1901, p. 107.   3. See p. 13.
4. *Vita Columbani Abbatis discipulorumque eius* lib. I, c. 4, ed. Krusch, *Monum. Germ. hist. Script. Rer. Meroving.* t. IV, Hannoveræ et Lipsiæ 1902, 70 sq.
5. Cf. *S. Columbani Regula cœnobialis* ed. Migne, *Patr. lat.* t. 80, col. 209–230.
6. "Si quis de ordine sacerdotum in monasteriis se suscipi rogaverit, non quidem citius ei assentiatur; tamen si omnino perstiterit in hac supplicatione, sciat se omnem regulæ disciplinam servaturum; nec aliquid ei relaxabitur . . . Concedatur ei tamen post abbatem stare et benedicere aut missas tenere . . . Clericorum autem si quis eodem desiderio monasterio sociari voluerit, loco mediocri collocentur et ipsi . . . Si quis abbas sibi presbyterum vel diaconum ordinari petierit de suis eligat qui dignus sit sacerdotio fungi.   Ordinatus autem caveat elationem aut superbiam nec quidquam præsumat, nisi quod ei ab abbate præcipitur . . . Locum vero illum semper attendat quo ingressus est in monasterium, præter officium altaris . . ." *S. Benedicti Regula* c. 60. 62.
7. Ruperti Abbatis Tuitiensis, *De vita vere apostolica* lib. 2, c. 16. 17; lib. 3, c. 7. 8; lib. 4, c. 11; Migne, *Patr. lat.* t. 170, col. 631–634. 637. 648.
8. On certain feasts an address was to be made to the monks assembled at Chapter.   On certain days likewise the Abbot or his representative was to preach to the people who were present in the monastery church. Cf. Martène, *De antiquis monachorum ritibus*, Lugduni 1690, 266. 334. 342. 602.
9. Cf. Lecoy de la Marche, *La chaire française au moyen-âge, spécialement au 13ième siècle*, Paris 1886, 26 s.
10. Several decrees of this kind are found in *Decretum Gratiani*, secunda pars, causa 16, q. 1, ed. *Christ. Freisleben* t. I, Coloniæ Munatianæ 1757, 661 sqq.
11. S. Hieronym., *Contra. Vigilantium* n. 15, Migne. *Patr. lat.* 23, 351.
12. "Monachis quamvis religiosis, ad normam sancti Benedicti intra claustrum morari præcipimus, vicos, castella, civitates peragrare prohibemus, et a populorum prædicatione omnino cessare censuimus." *Decret. Grat. ibid.* p. 663, can. 11.   13. Serm. 28 de tempore: "De quatuor vitiis."
14. For the proofs see P. Denifle, O. P., *Die Konstitutionen des Predigerordens vom Jahre 1228*, in: *Archiv. für Literatur-und Kirchengeschichte* I, 175.
15. In the liturgical Office of St. Dominic the first antiphon of the second nocturn reads: "Sub Augustini regula mente profecit sedula; tandem virum canonicum auget in apostolicum."   The author of this Office is one of the immediate successors of St. Dominic, either Jordan of Saxony or Constantin of Orvieto.
16. "Ipsi supra regulam addiderunt . . . prædicationem."   Humbert. de Romanis, *De eruditione prædicatorum* lib. 2, c. 10, ed. *Max. Bibl. PP.* t. XXV, 461.
17. "Utraque religio, scilicet monachorum et canonicorum regularium ordinatur ad opera vitæ contemplativæ: inter quæ præcipua sunt ea, quæ aguntur in divinis mysteriis." *Summa theol.* 2, 2, q. 189, a. 8, ad 2.   Cf. S. Bonav., *Quæstiones disputatæ de perfectione evangelica* q. 2, a. 3, n. 12, *Opera* V, 164 sq.; *Determinationes quæstionum circa regulam FF. Minorum* q. 2, *Opera* VIII, 338 sq.
18. See p. 1–18.
19. Cf. regarding these and other itinerant preachers of the beginning of the 12th century, J. Walter, *Die ersten Wanderprediger Frankreichs*, zwei Teile, Leipzig 1903 und 1906.
20. See p. 70. K. Müller, *Die Waldenser und ihre einzelnen Gruppen bis zum Anfang des 14. Jahrhunderts*, Gotha 1886; Haupt, *Waldensertum und Inquisition*, Freiburg 1890.
21. Tiraboschi, *Vetera Humiliatorum Monumenta* II, Mediolani 1767, 133 sq.
22. *Innocentii III Epistolæ* lib. 11, 196; Migne, *Patr. lat.* 215, col. 1513.   Cf. Pierron, *Die katholischen Armen*, Freiburg 1911.   23. Cf. p. 19–37.

24. Froissard, in Löber, *Über Ritterschaft und Adel im späteren Mittelalter,* Abhandlung der Münchener Akademie, 1861, I, 412. 25. See p. 264 ff.
26. "Præco sum magni Regis, quid ad vos?" Thom. Cel. I, n. 16.
27. Joh. Bapt. von Weiss, *Weltgeschichte* IV, 3. Aufl. Graz und Leipzig 1891, 625–633. 28. Cf. Ducange-Carpentarius s. v. "præco, præconare." 29. *Tres Soc.* n. 11–13. 30. Thom. Cel. I, n. 16; II, n. 10 sq.; *Tres Soc.* n. 13. 31. Thom. Cel. II, n. 11. 32. See p. 7 f. 76.
33. Thom. Cel. I, n. 22; *Tres Soc.* n. 25; S. Bonav. c. 3, n. 1.
34. ". . . imitator evangelicæ paupertatis effectus et sedulus evangelii prædicator." Iord. a. Iano n. 2. 35. Iord. a. Iano n. 2.
36. "Exinde cum magno fervore spiritus et gaudio mentis cepit omnibus pœnitentiam prædicare, verbo simplici, sed corde magnifico ædificans audientes. Erat verbum eius velut ignis ardens, penetrans intima cordis, et omnium mentes admiratione replebat." Thom. Cel. I, n. 23. 37. *Ibid.*
38. *Tres Soc.* n. 28 sq.; Thom. Cel. I, n. 24; II, n. 15; *Vita fr. Ægidii* 75; S. Bonav. c. 3, n. 3–4. 39. *Tres Soc.* n. 33.
40. Thom. Cel. I, n. 25. 29; *Tres Soc.* n. 35. 41. *Tres Soc.* n. 36. Cf. ed. Amoni p. 56. The text recension in Faloci-Pulignani as well as in Amoni is faulty.
42. "Ite, charissimi, bini et bini per diversas partes orbis, annuntiantes hominibus pacem et pœnitentiam in remissionem peccatorum; et estote patientes in tribulatione, securi quia propositum et promissum suum Dominus adimplebit. Interrogantibus humiliter respondete, persequentibus benedicite, vobis iniuriantibus et calumniam inferentibus gratias agite, quia pro his regnum nobis præparatur eternum." Thom. Cel. I, n. 29.
43. Thom. Cel. I, n. 29 sq.; S. Bonav. c. 4, n. 33. 44. *Tres Soc.* n. 37. 45. *Tres Soc.* n. 37–45. 46. Matth. x, 5–14; Mark vi, 7–13; Luke ix, 1–6; x, 1–11.
47. "Video, fratres, quod congregationem nostram vult Dominus misericorditer augmentare. Euntes ergo ad matrem nostram sanctam romanam ecclesiam notificemus summo Pontifici, quod Dominus per nos facere cœpit, ut de voluntate et præcepto ipsius, quod cœpimus prosequamur." *Tres Soc.* n. 46.
48. "Inveni virum perfectissimum, qui vult secundum formam sancti Evangelii vivere et evangelicam perfectionem observare; per quem credo, quod velit Dominus per universum mundum totam suam Ecclesiam renovare." *Anonym. Perus.* n. 33; cf. *Tres Soc.* n. 46.
49. "Vere hic est ille, qui opere et doctrina Christi sustentabit Ecclesiam." Thom. Cel. II, n. 17; *Tres Soc.* n. 51.
50. "Ite cum Domino, fratres, et sicut ipse Dominus inspirare dignabitur, omnibus pœnitentiam prædicate. Cum autem omnipotens Deus vos multiplicaverit numero maiori et gratia, referetis nobis, et nos plura his concedemus ac maiora vobis securius committemus." *Tres Soc.* n. 49; cf. Thom. Cel. *ibid.*
51. "Dedit etiam sibi [Francisco] licentiam prædicandi ubique pœnitentiam ac fratribus suis, ita tamen, ut qui prædicaturi erant, a beato Francisco licentiam obtinerent, et hoc idem postea in Concistorio approbavit." *Tres Soc.* n. 51. 52. *Ibid.* n. 52.
53. Cf. Lecoy de la Marche, *La chaire française au moyen-âge,* 2. ed., Paris 1886, 23 s. 26. Also *Odonis, episcopi Parisiensis, Constitutiones synodicæ of* 1198, in: Harduin, *Acta Concil.* t. VI, pars 2, p. 1945 n. 41, and *Richardi Poore Constitutiones* of 1217, in: Harduin *ibid.* VII, p. 103, n. 50.
54. *Tres Soc.* n. 33. 37. and Brother Leo in : *Vita fr. Ægidii* ed. *Analecta franc.* III, 76. See p. 326.
55. "Exinde beatus Franciscus circumiens civitates et castra, cœpit ubique amplius et perfectius prædicare . . . Erat enim vericidus prædicator, ex auctoritate apostolica roboratus . . ." *Tres Soc.* n. 54. 56. *Ibid.* 57 Thom. Cel. I, n. 36–37.
58. Harnack says rightly, *Lehrbuch der Dogmengeschichte* III, 3. Aufl., Leipzig 1897, 383: "While into the ideal of poverty and the ascetical renunciation the new moment of the *apostolic* life was received, this ideal took on an immanent

484   THE IDEALS OF ST. FRANCIS

gigantic power of *propaganda*, such as monasticism had never possessed, and such as—neither formerly nor now—belongs to its real nature."

59. "In pentecoste conveniebant omnes fratres apud Sanctam Mariam, et tractabant, qualiter melius possent regulam observare, atque constituebant fratres per diversas provincias, qui populo prædicarent." *Tres Soc.* n. 57.

60. ". . . Fervente desiderio et vehemente studio singulis diebus laborant, ut animas, quæ pereunt, a sæculi vanitatibus retrahant et eas secum ducant. Et iam per gratiam Dei magnum fructum fecerunt et multos lucrati sunt . . . Per totum annum disperguntur per Lombardiam et Thusciam et Apuliam et Siciliam . . . Dominus per huiusmodi simplices et pauperes homines multas animas ante finem mundi vult salvare." Iacobi Vitriac. *Epistula data Ianuae* a. 1216. Oct. in: Böhmer, *Analekten* 98 sq.

61. Thom. Cel. I, n. 74 sq.; *Spec. perf.* c. 65. Regarding the date see Potthast, *Regesta* n. 5487 sq.; Guido Levi, *Società di storia patria* XII, p. 241 sqq.; Sabatier, *Spec. perf.* p. 122, note 2.

62. S. Bonav. c. 4, n. 9; *Spec. perf.* c. 65; *Chron. XXIV General.* ed. *Anal. francisc.* III, p. 10. 63. Iord. a Iano n. 4.

64. Sbaralea, *Bullar. francisc.* I, p. 2, n. 2; Potthast, *Regesta* n. 6081. 65. Iord. a Iano n. 3–8. 66. *Ibid.* n. 5. 67. *Ibid.* n. 17. 68. *Ibid.* 69. *Ibid.* n. 18 sq.

70. Thomas de Eccleston, *Tractatus de adventu FF. Minorum in Angliam, passim.* 71. See p. 306. 72. Thom. Cel. I. n. 89. 120. 73. Thom. Cel. I, n. 55; S. Bonav. c. 9, n. 5.

74. Cf. P. Albert M. Weiss, *Die Entwicklung des christlichen Rittertums*, in: *Histor. Jahrbuch der Görresgesellschaft* I, (1880) 118 f. 129 f. 133–136. 138–140.

75. Verses 77–82. 76. Verses 227–232. 77. See p. 24. 78. Thom. Cel. I, n. 55; *Tract. de mirac.* n. 33. 79. Thom. Cel. *ibid.*; S. Bonav. c. 9, n. 5.

80. Thom. Cel. I, n. 56. Cf. S. Bonav. c. 9, n. 6. 81. Iord. a Iano n. 10. 82. S. Bonav. c. 9, n. 7.

83. Regarding the sojourn of Francis in the Christian and the Saracen camp we have two reports of the eye-witness Jacques de Vitry, in: Böhmer, *Analekten* 101 f. 104 f. Cf. Thom. Cel. I, n. 57; II, n. 30; S. Bonav. c. 5, n. 7–9; Iord. a Iano n. 10.

84. *Opusc.* ed. Böhmer 14–17, Lemmens 43–48.

85. *Opusc.* ed. Böhmer 33 sq. 35, Lemmens 71. 73 sq.

86. The parallel passage in the 16th chapter of the older rule reads: "Wherefore, whoever of the brothers may wish, by divine inspiration, to go among the Saracens and other infidels, let them go with the permission of their minister and servant. But let the minister give them leave and not refuse them, if he sees they are fit to be sent; he will be held to render an account to the Lord if in this or in other things he acts indiscreetly."

87. "Summam vero [obedientiam] et in qua nihil haberet caro et sanguis illam esse credebat, qua divina inspiratione inter fideles itur, sive ob proximorum lucrum, sive ob martyrii desiderium. Hanc vero petere multum Deo iudicabat acceptum." Thom. Cel. II, n. 152. Higher than the obedience to go among the infidels, Francis esteemed only the one to go among the Germans. The first expedition to Germany (1219) was treated so cruelly because of the suspected heresy of the Friars, that the Saint would oblige no brother to journey thither. Two years later he therefore promised the Friars who volunteered for Germany a more abundant blessing than to the missionaries among the Saracens: "Qui zelo Dei et animarum inspirati ire vellent [in Theutoniam], eandem eis obedientiam immo ampliorem dare vult [Franciscus], quam daret euntibus ultra mare." Iord. a Iano n. 17.

88. *Vita fr. Ægidii* ed. *Anal. francisc.* III, 78. 89. Iord. a Iano n. 7.

90. Iac. Vitriac. *Historia orientalis* lib. II, c. 32, Böhmer *Analekten* 105.

91. A Legend of these first martyrs of the Order is mentioned by Iord. a Iano n. 8, with the remark that it had been submitted to St. Francis. The report of an eye-witness was published by Karl Müller, *Die Anfänge des Minoriten-*

ordens, Freiburg i. Br. 1885, 204–210. A somewhat later description of the martyrdom was published in the *Analecta francisc.* III, 579–596.

92. Wadding, *Annales Minorum* ad a. 1220, n. 38.

93. *Vita primitiva S. Antonii* c. 5–6 ed. L. de Kerval p. 29–34.

94. *Act. SS.*, Octobr. t. VI, 378–392. 95. Iac. Vitriac., *Historia orientalis* lib. II, c. 32, Böhmer, *Analekten* 104. 105.

96. Cf. the respective Bulls of Gregory IX of 1233: *Bullar. francisc.* I, p. 100–107, n. 97–103. 106. From these Papal documents it becomes evident that the Friars were still active in the Saracen missions.

97. Most noted are the two Tartar missionaries and geographers, John de Plano Carpinis (Pian di Carpine) and William Rubruck. The former, at the behest of Innocent IV, passed along the coast of the Caspian Sea and Lake Aral through Mongolia to the camp of the Great Khan at Karakorum southeast of the Sea of Baikal; the latter journeyed first to Armenia, then to Sarai and thence to Karakorum. On the entire journey they preached the Gospel and collected valuable information regarding the country and people of interior Asia, which was heretofore unknown to the West. See D'Avezac, *Relation des Mongoles ou Tartares par le frère Jean du Plan de Carpin*, première édition complète, Paris 1838; P. Viator, O. M. Cap., *Le premier apôtre franciscain de la Tartarie (1182–1252): Fr. Jean de Plan-Carpin*, in: *Études francisc.* V. (1901) 505–520. 600–618; W. Rockhill, *The Journey of William of Rubruck to the Eastern Parts of the World*, London 1905; H. Matrod, *Le voyage de Fr. Guillaume de Rubrouck (1253–1255)*, in: *Études francisc.* XIX (1908) 5–24. 132–152. 349–367. 625–639; XX (1908) 142–156. 243–255. 498–508. 682–692; A. Batton, *Wilhelm von Rubruck, Ein Weltreisender aus dem Franziskanerorden*, München 1921.

98. According to the testimony of Pope Clement V: "In terris Saracenorum-Paganorum, Græcorum, Bulgarorum, Cumanorum, Yberorum, Alanorum, Gazarorum, Gothorum, Sichorum, Rutenorum, Iacobinorum, Nubianorum, Nestorianorum, Georgianorum, Armenorum, Indorum, Meclitorum aliarumque non credentium nationum Orientis et Aquilonis." Wadding, *Annales Minorum* VI, 97.

99. "Mare magnum iam aggredior, tractatum de gloriosis et tantis fratrum Minorum per orbem universum laboribus, agonibus et necibus in obsequium Christi et eius Ecclesiæ pro fidei catholicæ defensione atque propagatione toleratis." *Dominicus de Gubernatis a Sospitello, Orbis seraphicus* t. V (*de missionibus* t. primus), Romæ 1689. 100. Mark xvi, 15. 101. Thom. Cel. II, n. 172.

102. "Conferebant pariter veri cultores iustitiæ, utrum inter homines conversari deberent, an ad loca solitaria se conferre. Sed sanctus Franciscus, qui non de industria propria confidebat, sed sancta oratione omnia præveniebat negotia, elegit non sibi vivere soli, sed ei, qui pro omnibus mortuus est, sciens se ad hoc missum, ut Deo animas lucraretur, quas diabolus conabatur auferre." *Ibid.* I, n. 35.

103. The entire episode, which is related by S. Bonav. c. 12, n. 1–2 (and in substance also by *Actus B. Francisci* c. 16), is hardly identical with the one just described from Thom. Cel. I, n. 35. The latter episode happened on the return of the twelve Friars from Rome (1209); the former must be dated a few years later, because the Poor Clares (dating from 1212) are mentioned in it. Other incidents also of the two reports do not agree. 104. *Ibid.* I, n. 97.

105. "Tantum quoque animarum diligebat salutem et proximorum sitiebat lucra, ut cum per se ambulare non posset, asello vectus circuiret terras." *Ibid.* n. 98; S. Bonav. c. 14, n. 1.

106. S. Bonav. *ibid.*; Thom. Cel. I, n. 103.

107. "Animarum zelo, quo perfecte repletus erat, volebat sibi filios vera similitudine respondere." Thom. Cel. II, n. 155.

108. ". . . proximorum lucra sitiebant ardenter, quos desiderabant ut salvi essent." *Ibid.* I, n. 27.

CHAPTER XVI

1. Among the first twelve, Fr. Sylvester (Thom. Cel. II, n. 109) alone seems to have been a priest.   2. See p. 306.

3. "Nos plura concedemus ac maiora vobis securius committemus." *Tres Soc.* n. 49.

4. "Omnis utriusque sexus fidelis, postquam ad annos discretionis pervenerit, omnia sua solus peccata saltem semel in anno fideliter confiteatur proprio sacerdoti . . . Si quis autem alieno sacerdoti voluerit iusta de causa sua confiteri peccata, licentiam prius postulet et obtineat a proprio sacerdote, cum aliter ille ipsum non possit absolvere vel ligare." Denzinger-Bannwart, *Enchiridion symbolorum* ed. 12, n. 437.

5. "Quod vero pœnitentiam dare prohibentur [monachi], inde est, quia nulli sacerdotum licet alterius parochianum ligare vel solvere." *Decret. Gratian.* pars II, causa 16, q. 1, c. 19 ed. H. Freiesleben, Coloniæ Munatianæ 1757, 665.

6. *Regula* I, c. 20; II, c. 7. *Opusc.* ed. Böhmer 20. 33, Lemmens 49 sq. 69 sq.

7. Proof in: Felder, *Geschichte der wissenschaftl. Studien im Franziskanerorden,* 68.

8. Cf. S. Bonav., *Sentent.* lib. IV, dist. 17, pars 3, a. 1, q. 2, conclusio, *Opera* IV, 453 sq.; *Determinat. quæst.,* pars 1, q. 2, *Opera* VIII, 338 sq.; *Quare Fratres Minores prædicent et confessiones audiant* n. 13 sqq., *Opera* VIII, 378 sqq.

9. Eccleston coll. VI, ed. Little 34 sq. For the date see *ibid.* p. 35, nota b.

10. ". . . propter infatigabilem animarum zelum prædicando, docendo, confessiones audiendo usque ad solis occasum quam sæpe ieiunus manebat." *Vita s. Antonii* c. 11, n. 7 ed. L. de Kerval.   11. *Ibid.* c. 13, n. 7.

12. Antonius "tantam utriusque sexus multitudinem ad confitenda peccata mittebat, ut nec fratres nec alii sacerdotes, quorum non parva sequebatur eum frequentia, audiendis confessionibus sufficerent." *Ibid.* c. 13, n. 13.

13. "Fuerunt quoque et fratres plurimi, qui licet prædicationis vel lectionis officium non haberent, de gratissimo favore prælatorum, per obœdientiam et ordinationem ministri provincialis in diversis locis confessiones tam religiosorum quam sæcularium audiebant." Eccleston coll. XII, p. 75.   14. *Ibid.* p. 75-78.

15. Sbaralea, *Bullar. francisc.* I, p. 74-77, n. 63-66. Gregory IX writes: "Non desunt *plerique* tam ecclesiarum prælati, quam alii qui cæca cupiditate traducti propriæ aviditate substrahi reputantes, quidquid prædictis Fratribus fidelium pietas elargitur, quietem ipsorum multipliciter inquietant . . . Volunt namque, *etsi non omnes,* ipsis invitis, eorum confessiones audire ac eis iniungere pœnitentias et eucharistiam exhibere: nec volunt ut Corpus Christi in eorum oratoriis reservetur; et Fratres ipsorum defunctos ad ecclesias suas sepelire compellunt . . . Volunt etiam in domibus eorundem certum numerum Fratrum sacerdotum, clericorum et laicorum, necnon cereorum, lampadarum et ornamentorum pro sua voluntate taxare; . . . Nec permittunt, ut novi sacerdotes eorum alibi quam in ecclesiis suis celebrent primas missas; eos nihilominus compellentes, ut in quotidianis missis, quas in suis locis et altaribus celebrant, oblationes ad opus eorum recipiant et reservent. Quidquid etam eis, dum celebrant missarum solemnia intra domorum suarum ambitum, pia fidelium devotione donatur, ab ipsis extorquere oblationis nomine contendentes; quod eisdem tam in ornamentis altaris quam in libris ecclesiasticis absolute confertur, vendicant perperam iuri suo . . ." *Ibid.* p. 75 sq., n. 66.   16. *Ibid.* p. 214 sq., n. 224.

17. Bulls of June 12, 1234, *ibid* p. 128, n. 131, and of June 24, 1235, *ibid.* p. 167, n. 173. to be compared with the Bull of Innocent III, June 11, 1219, *ibid.* p. 2, n. 2.

18. Bull of Febr. 1, 1230, *ibid.* p. 58, n. 46.

19. Bulls of April 3, and May 17, 1233, *ibid.* p. 101, n. 97; p. 103, n. 101.

20. ". . . dilectos Fratres Ordinis memorati [Minorum] pro reverentia divina et nostra ad officium prædicandi, ad quod sunt ex professione sui Ordinis deputati, benigne recipere procuretis; ac populos vobis commissos, ut ex ore ipsorum verbi Dei semen devote suscipiant, admonentes, ut in suis necessitatibus eis

libenter assistatis; nec impediatis, quominus illi, qui ad eorum prædicationem accesserint, cum eorum sacerdotibus valeant confiteri . . . et dicti Fratres per cooperationem vestram suscepti ministerii sui fructum felicius consequantur." *Ibid.* p. 215, n. 224.

21. The negligence of some preachers in hearing confessions is reprimanded by Fr. Humbertus de Romanis, *De eruditione prædicatorum* lib. 1, c. 43, p. 455, with the following words: "Circa audientiam confessionum a prædicatoribus est notandum, quod multi in prædicatione commoti solent interdum libenter venire ad confitendum prædicatori: sed sunt aliqui prædicatores, qui omnino refugiunt confessiones audire, quamvis ad hoc habeant competentem suffici-entiam. Isti sunt similes agricolæ, qui libenter seminat et nihil vult metere. Per prædicationem enim seminatur, per confessionem vero colligitur fructus . . . Ad prædicatorem, si sit sufficienter idoneus ad confessiones audiendas, pertinet quod eas libenter audiat."

22. Cf. the utterance, given in the following note, of Innocent IV, in the Bull "Esti animarum," also the letter mentioned on p. 293, addressed to Peter de Vineis, the chancellor of Frederick II, and especially the notorious writings of William of St. Amour: *Tractatus de periculis novissimorum temporum, Opera omnia*, Constantiæ 1632, 17–72.

23. On March 27, 1248, he wrote to the Bishop of Pampeluna: ". . . intel-leximus quod tu Fratribus Minoribus, ne in tua civitate ac diœcesi officium prædicationis exerceant et confessiones fidelium audiant pro tuæ interdicis arbi-trio voluntatis . . . mandamus, quatenus prædictos Fratres verbum Dei pro-ponere ac fidelium confessiones in præfatis civitate ac diœcesi libere audire per-mittas" (*Bullar. francisc.* I, p. 510, n. 269). He wrote in a similar strain on Jan. 11, 1249 (*ibid.* p. 528, n. 298), to the Archbishop of Cologne.

24. In this Bull "Etsi animarum" of Nov. 21, 1254, (Denifle-Chatelain, Chartul. Universit. Paris. t. I, p. 267–272, n. 240), which was addressed to all Religious, but in fact was meant only for the Dominicans and Minorites—the other monks were not active in the apostolate—(cf. Eccleston coll. XV, p. 118), we read the following: "Sane gravis et clamosa querela nostris assidue auribus inculcatur, quod nonnulli vestrum suis iuribus et finibus non contenti paro-chianos alienos . . . in foro pœnitentiali periculose absolvunt . . . nec ipsos sine sui sacerdotis licentia ad pœnitentiam ullatenus admittatis, cum si quis alieno sacerdoti iusta de causa sua voluerit confiteri peccata, secundum statuta Concilii [Lateran. IV] licentiam prius postulare ac obtinere debeat a proprio sacerdote, vel saltem prius sibi confiteri et recipere absolutionis beneficium ab eodem."

25. Bull "Nec insolitum" of Dec. 22, 1254, *Bullar. francisc.* II. p. 3, n. 2. Alexander IV wrote it on the day following his coronation, after he had already revoked orally the Bull "Esti animarum" of his predecessor on the day of his election, Dec. 12, 1254 (Eccleston coll. XV, p. 119 sq.; *Chron. XXIV Ministr. General.* ed. *Anal. francisc.* III, 278).

26. Bull "Patris æterni" of April 9, 1255, *Bullar. francisc.* II, p. 29 sq., n. 39.

27. Their respective writings were published together by (Soldati), *SS. Thomæ et Bonaventuræ opuscula adversus Guillelmum de S. Amore*, Romæ 1773.

28. See the comprehensive article of Bäumker, Wilhelm von St. Amour, in: *Kirchenlexicon* XII, 2 Aufl., 1901, 1580–1586.

29. Especially in the two treatises: *Determinationes quæstionum* pars 1, q. 2, and *Quare Fratres Minores prædicent et confessiones audiant, Opera* VIII, 337–381. 30. *Ibid.* 338–380. 31. *Ibid.* 338 sq. 380, n. 19. 32. *Ibid.* 339. 377, n. 11. 33. *Ibid.* 339. 377, n. 9. 34. *Ibid.* 372–374. 35. *Ibid.* 338, n. 12.

36. Opera IV, 452–455; VIII, 356. 378. 380 This was done, as Bonaventure declares in these passages again and again, with reference to the decree of the Fourth Lateran Council, according to which everyone was obliged to confess at least once a year to his pastor.

37. "Missi sunt Fratres a Sede apostolica per mundum, muniti eius testimonio, qui prædictos defectus clericorum, ubi necesse fuerit, suppleant et indigentiæ fidelium subveniant, et non tantum laicos, sed et ipsos clericos et religiosos

prædicationibus instruant, exhortationibus a malo retrahant et in bono confortent, et in confessionibus pœnitentes absolvant et ad vitam gratiæ trahant, insuper exemplis ædificent, et orationibus gratiam eis et veniam impetrent apud Deum." *Opera* VIII, 380, n. 17.

38. Humbertus de Romanis (*De eruditione prædicatorum* lib. I, c. 20, *Max. Bibl. PP.* t. 25, 442) furnishes the telling as well as spirited proof, that the office of preaching is to be esteemed higher than all works of penance and mercy, indeed, even higher than the administration of the Sacraments. Even the hearing of confessions is not to be preferred to preaching, inasmuch as through confession only one, but by preaching many, are helped to salvation. 39. See p. 306. 40. Thom. Cel. I, n. 23.

41. "Licet autem vir Dei nondum plene populo prædicaret, quando tamen per civitates et castella transibat, hortabatur omnes, ut amarent et timerent Deum, atque pœnitentiam agerent de peccatis. Frater autem Ægidius admonebat audientes, ut ei crederent, quia eis optime consulebat." *Tres Soc.* n. 33. Exactly so Brother Leo in the *Vita fr. Ægidii* ed. *Anal franc.* III, 76; cf. *Vita B. Ægidii* in the *Scripta fr. Leonia* ed. Lemmens p. 41, n. 3.

42. *Act SS.*, April t. III, p. 229 sqq.; Menge, *Dicta B. Ægidii*, Ad Claras Aquas 1905. 43. See p. 134.

44. "Vadens autem sic per mundum hortabatur homines et mulieres, ut Deum diligerent et timerent et pœnitentiam facerent pro peccatis." *Vita fr. Ægidii* 77.

45. "Quocumque vero intrabant civitatem vel castellum aut villam vel domum, annuntiabant pacem, confortantes omnes, ut timerent et amarent creatorem cæli et terræ, eiusque mandata servarent." *Tres Soc.* n. 37.

46. "Hii autem . . . fervente desiderio et vehemente studio singulis diebus laborant, ut animas quæ pereunt, a sæculi vanitatibus retrahant et eas secum ducant. Et iam per gratiam Dei magnum fructum fecerunt et multos lucrati sunt . . . De die intrant in civitates et villas, ut aliquos lucri faciant operam dantes actioni, nocte vero revertuntur ad eremum vel loca solitaria vacantes contemplationi." Iacobi Vitriac. *Epist. data Iannæ* Oct. 1216, Böhmer, *Analekten* 98, n. 8. 9. 47. Matth. iii, 2 and Luke iii, 8. 48. Luke vi, 37 f. 49. Mark xi, 26. 50. *Regula* I, c. 21, *Opusc.* ed. Böhmer 18 sq., Lemmens 50 sq.

51. That not only the simple exhortatory address but also the formal discourse was in use in the first decade of the Order, I have proved extensively against Karl Müller and Paul Sabatier in my: *Geschichte der wissenschaftl. Studien*, 33–48. The fact has since been admitted quite generally. 52. See p. 306 f. 53. See p. 306 ff.

54. "Contrahentibus autem Fratribus moram in loco præfato, vir sanctus die quadam sabbati civitatem intravit Assisii, prædicaturus mane diei dominicæ, ut moris erat, in ecclesia cathedrali. Cumque in quodam tugurio sito in horto canonicorum vir Deo devotus in oratione Dei more solito pernoctaret . . ." S. Bonav. c. 4, n. 4. In his Testament, in which Francis points to his earliest activity, he declares: "Si invenirem pauperculos sacerdotes huius sæculi, in ecclesiis, in quibus morantur, nolo prædicare ultra voluntatem ipsorum" (*Opusc.* ed. Böhmer 36, Lemmens 78). Roger of Wendover, *Flores historiarum*, ed. *Monum. Germ. hist. Script.* XXVIII, 41, relates of the first Franciscan preachers: "Diebus autem dominicis et festivis de suis habitaculis exeuntes prædicaverunt in ecclesiis parochialibus evangelium verbi, edentes et bibentes quæ apud illos erant, quibus officium prædicationis impendebant." That Francis and his brothers were heard also outside of the churches, in the market-places, etc., can easily be seen from the oldest sources, and is self-evident considering the custom of the time. Preaching was done, no doubt, mostly in sacred places (cf. Lecoy de la Marche, *La chaire française au moyen-âge* 226 ss.), yet the itinerant preachers regarded any place as their pulpit where the people congregated, (cf. *idem. Anecdotes historiques d'Etienne de Bourbon* 73–75. 161 s. 229. 292), speaking on all possible occasions, such as at solemn investitures of knights, at tournaments, at parliament meetings, fairs, etc. (cf. Humbertus de Romanis, *De eruditione prædicatorum* lib. 2, *Max. Bibl. PP.* XXV, 506–568).

55 "In Pentecoste conveniebant omnes fratres apud sanctam Mariam et tractabant, qualiter melius possent regulam observare, atque constituebant fratres per diversas provincias, qui populo prædicarent." *Tres Soc.* n. 57.

56. "Quicumque ex ipsis habebat spiritum Dei et eloquentiam idoneam ad prædicandum, sive clericus sive laicus esset, dabat ei licentiam prædicandi." *Ibid.* n. 59. 57. *Regula* I, c. 17, *Opusc.* ed. Böhmer 15 sq., Lemmens 46.

58. *Regula* II, c. 9, *Opusc.* ed. Böhmer 33, Lemmens 71. Kybal (*Die Ordens-regeln* 151) is in error when he states that according to the final rule only learned brothers were permitted to preach, while in the rule of 1221 the brothers were selected without reference to their education. In the rule of 1223 the ability of the Friars in regard to the office of preaching is simply emphasized more than in the one of 1221. Kybal furthermore misunderstands the 17th chapter of the rule of 1221. Its meaning is that the Minister is to take the education of the candidates into consideration; once a preacher has been approved (approved does not mean "learned"), he retains the office as long as the superiors see fit; if they command that the preacher or the Minister lay down his office, the one as well as the other is to obey willingly.

59. "Generalis Minister dictam examinationem, approbationem et missionem . . . nulli potest absenti committere, sed qui examinatione indigere creduntur, mittantur ad ipsum, ut, cum Ministris provincialibus conveniat super hoc in capitulo generali. Si qui vero examinari non egent pro eo, quod in theologica facultate et prædicationis officio sunt instructi, si ætatis maturitas et alia, quæ requiruntur in talibus, conveniant in eisdem, possunt, nisi quibus Minister generalis contradixerit, eo modo, quo dictum est, populo prædicare." Bull "Quo elongati," Sept. 28, 1230, *Bullar. franc.* I, p. 69, n. 56.

60. "Nos devotionis vestræ precibus inclinati, ut singuli vestrum in suis Provinciis cum Diffinitoribus in provincialibus capitulis congregatis fratres in sacra pagina eruditos examinare ac approbare et eisdem officium prædicationis, Deum habendo præ oculis, committere valeant, vobis auctoritate præsentium concedimus facultatem." Bull "Prohibente Regula," Dec. 12, 1240, *Bullar. francisc.* I, p. 287, n. 325.

61. Thom. Cel. I, n. 22; *Tres Soc.* n. 25. 62. Thom. Cel. I, n. 23. 63. *Ibid.* n. 29.

64. "Ite cum Domino, fratres, et prout Dominus vobis inspirare dignabitur, omnibus pœnitentiam prædicate. Cum enim omnipotens Dominus vos numero multiplicabit et gratia, ad me cum gaudio referetis, et ego vobis his plura concedam et securius maiora committam." Thom. Cel. I, n. 33. Likewise *ibid.* II, n. 17, and *Tres Soc.* n. 49–51.

65. "Dominus ita dedit mihi fratri Francisco facere pœnitentiam . . . ubicumque [fratres] non fuerint recepti, fugiant ad aliam terram ad faciendam pœnitentiam cum benedictione Dei." *Testament., Opusc.* ed Böhmer 36, Lemmens 77.

66. "Cœperunt . . . viri quidam ipsius exemplo ad pœnitentiam animari." *Tres Soc.* n. 27.

67. ". . . confitebantur, quod erant viri pœnitentiales de civitate Assisii oriundi." *Ibid.* n. 37.

68. "Fratres minores monendi sunt . . . ut exemplum pœnitentiæ, quod mundo ostendunt, non maculent aliqua nota in eis reprehensibili, ut sic immaculatum servitium eorum sit aptius exemplar." Fr. Humberti de Romanis *De eruditione prædicatorum* lib. II, tract. 2, c. 26, *Max. Bibl. PP.* 25, 468.

69. Iacobi Vitriac., *Epist. data* 16 Oct. 1216, Böhmer 98, n. 8.

70. Thom. Cel. I, n. 37; *Tres Soc.* n. 54.

71. The proofs that the Second as well as the Third Order were designated as Orders of Penance, are found on p. 12f. Officially of course this title was reserved for the Tertiaries. Moreover, religious life as such, whether the eremitical or the monastic, was called "life of penance" and "state of penance." Jordan of Giano, for instance, says (n. 1): "Franciscus vir negotiator . . . in habitu heremitico modum pœnitentiæ est aggressus." Rupert of Deutz (*De vita vere apostolica* lib. I, c. 8, Migne. *Patr. lat.* 170, 616), in speaking of the essence of monastic life, remarks: "Monachi . . . vitam noscuntur pœniten-

tium agere." He then explains (*ibid.* 633), that "not only all monks, but also the patriarchs, prophets, apostles and all saints have led a life of penance."
72. Cf. the first Chapter.
73. "Nec tamen Sanctus his contentus ordinibus, satagebat omnium hominum generi salutis et pœnitentiæ viam dare." *Liber de laudibus b. Francisci* c. 7. Similarly Thom. Cel. I, n. 37. 74. *Tres Soc.* n. 33. 75. *Ibid.* n. 37. 76. *Ibid.* n. 36.
77. ". . . eos [viros sæculares] provocans ad emendatioris vitæ viam et pœnitentiam peccatorum." Thom. Cel. I, n. 31. 78. *Ibid.* n. 36 sq.
79. Opusculum commonitorium et exhortatorium sive epistolam quam misit omnibus fidelibus, *Opusc.* ed. Böhmer 49–57, Lemmens 87–98.
80. Thom. Cel. II, n. 35. 81. Iord. a Iano n. 16. 82. See p. 291. 83. Thom. Cel. II, n. 191. 84. See p. 327 f. 85. *Regula* II, c. 9, *Opusc.* ed. Böhmer 34, Lemmens 71.
86. "Vocati ab archiepiscopo lugdunensi . . . prohibuit eis, ne intromitterent se de Scripturis exponendis vel prædicandis." Etienne de Bourbon, *Anecdotes historiques* éd. Lecoy de la Marche 291 s.
87. ". . . Licentia diœcesani episcopi verbum exhortationis proponent his, qui convenerint ad audiendum verbum Dei, monentes et inducentes eos ad mores honestos et opera pietatis, ita quod de articulis fidei et sacramentis Ecclesiæ non loquantur." Tiraboschi, *Vetera Humiliatorum monumenta* II, Mediolani 1767, 134.
88. That under "the articles of faith and the Sacraments of the Church" the dogmatic, under the "good morals and pious works" the moral truths are to be understood, is plain. This distinction was quite universal since the twelfth century. Alexander III himself, who was the first to grant the Waldenses permission to preach (Anonymus Laudanensis, *Recueil des Hist. des Gaules* XIII, 682; *Monum. Germ. hist. Script.* XXVI, 449), divides the whole of theology into: "fides, sacramenta, caritas" (mores honesti et opera pietatis).
89. "Cum autem ex magna parte clerici simus et pene omnes litterati, lectioni, exhortationi et disputationi contra omnes errorum sectas decrevimus desudare." *Innocentii III Epist.* lib. 11, c. 196, Migne, *Patr. lat.* 215, 1513. Cf. Pierron, *Die katholischen Armen*, 1911, where p. 172 ff. the entire rule of this fraternity is printed.
90. See the rules of the re-united Lombards of 1210 and 1212 in Pierron, *loc. cit.* 176–182.
91. "Et eramus idiotæ." *Testam., Opusc.* ed. Böhmer 37, Lemmens 81. 92. See p. 331 f.
93. ". . . ad prædicandam fidem christianam et pœnitentiam Sarazenis et ceteris infidelibus." Thom. Cel. I, n. 55. Cf. p. 312 f.
94. *Regula* I, c. 16, *Opusc.* ed. Böhmer 14, Lemmens 44.
95. *Odonis episcopi Parisiens. Synod. constitutiones* (1198), v. 32, in: Harduin, *Acta Concil.* VI, pars 2, 1944.
96. Synod of Trier (1227), in: Mansi, *Concil. Collectio* XXII, 31, n. VIII.
97. Synod of Gran (1114), Mansi XXI, 100, c. 2.
98. *Richardi Poore constitut.* (1217), c. 3, n. 4, Harduin VII, 90.
99. Synod of Gran *ibid.* 100. Synod of Trier *ibid.* 101. *Richardi Poore constitut. ibid.* 102. See the following decree of the Fourth Lateran Council.
103. "Unde cum contingat, quod episcopi propter occupationes multiplices, vel invaletudines corporales, aut hostiles incursus, seu occupationes alias: (ne dicamus defectum scientiæ, quod in eis est reprobandum omnino, nec de cetero tolerandum): per seipsos non sufficiunt ministrare populo verbum Dei, maxime per amplas diœceses et diffusas: generali constitutione sancimus, ut episcopi viros idoneos ad sanctæ prædicationis officium salubriter exsequendum assumant, potentes in opere et sermone, qui plebes sibi commissas, vice ipsorum, cum per se idem nequiverint, sollicite visitantes, eas verbo ædificent et exemplo . . . Unde præcipimus tam in cathedralibus quam in aliis conventualibus ecclesiis viros idoneos ordinari, quos episcopi possint coadiutores et cooperatores habere, non solum in prædicationis officio, verum etiam in audiendis confessionibus et pœni-

tentiis iniungendis ac ceteris, quæ ad salutem pertinent animarum . . ." *Concil. Later. IV*, c. 10, Harduin VII, 27.

104. ". . . serendo semina verbi Dei apostolorum exemplo diversas circumeunt mansiones." Bull "Cum dilecti," June 11, 1219, *Bullar. francisc.* I, p. 2, n. 2.

105. ". . . in tantum prædicationis opus explere studuit, ut nomen evangelistæ gestorum strenuitate compensaret . . . quum multos hæretica cerneret pravitate delusos, . . . versuta hæreticorum dogmata sole lucidius confutavit. Ita demum verbum virtutis eius et doctrina salutaris in cordibus audientium radices fixit, ut eliminata erroris spurcitia non parva credentium turba Domino fideliter adhæreret. In quibus hæresiarcham unum, Bonillum nomine, ab annis triginta errore infidelitatis abductum." *Vita S. Antonii* c. 9, n. 3–6.

106. "Ita quod vulgato ubique vocabulo hæreticorum indefessus malleus dicebatur." Legenda "Benignitas" (*ca.* 1300) ed. L. de Kerval p. 220. The part which the refutation of heresies played in dogmatic sermons, may be conjectured from the fact that in Lombardy alone there existed seventeen different non-Catholoc creeds. Cf. Felice Tocco, *L'eresia nel Medioevo*, Firenze 1884, 146, nota. 107. See p. 335.

108. The most important of these instructions on the exercise of the office of preaching are from the pen of the Cistercian Alanus de Insulis (died 1202), *Summa de arte prædicatoria* (Migne, *Patr. lat.* 210. 111–198), and of the Dominican General Humbertus de Romanis (*ca.* 1250), *De eruditione prædicatorum* (*Max. Bibl. PP.* XXV, 420–567). Both restrict themselves to moral themes, i. e. to sermon sketches on vices and virtues, for special occasions and set instructions. Somewhat later the "Ars concionandi" originated, which was ascribed to St. Bonaventure, but is no doubt not genuine. In this work also moral themes are proposed almost exclusively (cf. S. Bonav. *Opera* IX, 8 sqq.). It closes with the remark: ". . . non est conandum indifferenter causas rerum omnium et effectus sustinere, sed maxime rerum moralium, quas volumus commendare vel reprobare, scilicet virtutum, vel vitiorum, vel eorum, quæ faciunt ad meritum . . . Unde verissime theologia habet cognoscere vitia et virtutes." *Ibid.* n. 51, p. 20 sq. 109. Bull "Quoniam abundavit," April 6, 1237, *Bullar. francisc.* I, p. 214, n. 224. 110. Bull "Patris æterni," April 9, 1255, *Bullar. francisc.* II, p. 29 sq., n. 39.

111. They are far more numerous than one might surmise. Lecoy de la Marche, *La chaire française au moyen-âge*, Paris, 1886, 495–531, enumerates about fifty Minorite preachers of the thirteenth century, of whom manuscript sermons are preserved in the Bibliothèque Nationale at Paris. Cf. the sermons of St. Bonaventure, *Opera* VIII, 23–731. The sermons which were published under the name of St. Anthony of Padua, must be examined as to their authenticity before an opinion may be ventured. The various editions of these are mentioned by Léon de Kerval, *S. Antonii Vitæ duæ*, Paris 1904.

112. We base this opinion not so much on the German sermons which have been published under the name of Berthold of Regensburg, but on the much more numerous Latin sermons, of which he is undoubtedly the author.

113. Cf. of the excellent article of Anton Schönbach, *Das Wirken Bertholds gegen die Ketzer*, in: *Sitzungsberichte der K. Akademie der Wissenschaften in Wien.* 147 Band, Wien 1904.

114. He deplores the fact that so many preachers only moralize: "Scio plurimos minus curare aliqua de fide in sermonibus proponere, sed pro communi utilitate nihil utilius iudico in prædicatione, quam quasi semper aliqua de fide inserere, maxime in tanta, ut ardentius cordibus imprimatur. Nimis enim heu hæretici nunc latenter multiplicantur et fervor fidei etiam in cordibus fidelium nimis debilitatur." Thus Berthold in a sermon on faith (de fide), Schönbach, *loc. cit.* 12; cf. 29.

115. *Rogeri Baconis Compendium studii philosophiæ* c. 5. ed, Brewer, London 1859, 427.

116. See Anselm. Cantuar. *De concordia præscientiæ Dei cum libero arbitrio* q. 3, c. 6 ed. Migne, *Patr. lat.* 158, 528.

117. See Felder, *Geschichte der wissenschaftl. Studien* 490–496.

118. "Principalis intentio ecclesiæ et ultimus finis est opus prædicationis, ut infideles ad fidem convertantur et fideles in fide et moribus conserventur. Sed quia utrumque vulgus prædicantium ignorat, ideo convertit se ad summam et infinitam curiositatem, scilicet per divisiones porphyrianas, et per consonantias ineptas verborum et clausularum, et per consonantias vocales, in quibus est sola vanitas verbosa, omni carens ornatu rhetorico et virtute persuadendi. Quoddam enim phantasma est pueriliter effusum et a pueris inventum, vacuis ab omni sapientia et eloquendi potestate . . . Et tamen est ibi maxima temporis consumptio. Nam propter curiositatis superfluitatem plus in decuplo laborant circa huiusmodi telam araneæ construendam, quam circa sententiam sermonis." *Rogeri Baconis Opus tertium* c. 75 ed. Brewer 304. "Quæ fiunt in textu principaliter legendo et prædicando sunt tria principaliter: scilicet divisiones per membra varia . . . concordantiæ violentes . . . et consonantiæ rhythmicæ." *Ibid.*, *Opus minus* 323. 119. See p. 44-55. 120. See p. 303. 307.

121. *Epistola ad omnes fideles, Opusc.* ed. Böhmer 55 sq., Lemmens 95–97. 122. Ps. cxliii, 1.

123. "In hoc capitulo beatus Franciscus assumpto themate: 'Benedictus Dominus Deus meus, qui docet manus meas ad prelium' fratribus prædicavit et docens virtutes et monens ad patientiam et ad exempla mundo demonstranda. Similiter fiebat sermo ad populum, et fiebat edificatio in populo et in clero." Iord. a. Iano n. 16.

124. "Procedit sapiens sacco vestitus et cinere adspersus caput, et mirantibus cunctis, facto plus prædicans, abbreviat verba: 'Magna, inquit, promisimus, maiora promissa sunt, servemus hæc, suspiremus ad illa. Voluptas brevis, pœna perpetua, modica passio, gloria infinita. Multorum vocatio, omnium retributio.' Erumpunt in lacrimas auditorum corda compuncta, vereque sapientem venerantur ut sanctum. 'Hæccine, ait simplex in corde suo, totum mihi præripuit sapiens quidquid facere vel dicere statui. Sed novi quid faciam. Scio quosdam versus de psalmis; geram ergo sapientis morem, postquam ille simplicis morem gessit.' Advenit crastina sessio, surgit simplex, psalmum proponit in themate. Divino igitur afflatus spiritu tam ferventer, subtiliter, dulciter ex inspirato Dei dono perorat, ut omnes repleti stupore dicant: 'Cum simplicibus sermocinatio eius.'" Thom. Cel. II, n. 192.

125. "Eodem anno in die assumptionis Dei genetricis, cum essem Bononie in studio, vidi sanctum Franciscum predicantem in platea ante palacium publicum, ubi tota pene civitas convenerat. Fuit autem exordium sermonis eius: 'Angeli, homines, demones.' De his tribus spiritibus racionalibus ita bene et diserte proposuit, ut multis literatis, qui aderant, fieret admiracioni non modice sermo hominis ydiote. Nec tamen ipse modum predicantis tenuit, sed quasi concionantis. Tota verborum eius discurrebat materies ad extinguendas inimicicias et ad pacis fœdera reformanda.'" Thomæ, Archidiaconi Spalatensis *Historia Pontificum Salonitanorum et Spalatinorum* ed. Heinemann, *Monum. Germ. hist. Script.* XXIX, Hannoveræ 1892, 580.

126. "Non distinctionum clavibus utebatur, quia quos ipse non inveniebat non ordinabat sermones." Thom. Cel. II, n. 107. 127. See above, note 118.

128. Lecoy de la Marche, who is very competent, says (*La chaire française au moyen-âge* 140): "Les Frères Mineurs ont suivi, au XIIIième siècle, la même voie que les Frères Prêcheurs. On peut dire, cependant, que leur prédication a toujours conservé une allure plus populaire . . . Alors même qu'ils subissent l'empire de la scolastique, leur langage garde plus de simplicité; il exerce d'action sur les masses. C'est ce qu'indiquent, du moins, la nature de leur succès et les récits de contemporains."

129. "Sed licet vulgus prædicantium sic utatur [the learned dialectic sermon is meant], tamen aliqui modum alium habentes, infinitam faciunt utilitatem, ut est frater Bertholdus Alemannus, qui solus plus facit de utilitate magnifica in prædicatione, quam fere omnes alii fratres ordinis utriusque." *Rogeri Baconis Opus tertium* c, 75, p. 310.

130. ". . . alta et clara voce laudes gallice cantans benedicebat et glorificabat Altissimi bonitatem." *Tres Soc.* n. 33. 131. Thom. Cel. I, n. 72.

132. Very many preachers were wont, as was the custom for centuries (cf. Conc. Remens. II, can, 15. in Harduin IV, 1019; Conc. Moguntinum I, c. 2, *ibid.* V, 8; Hincmari archiep. Remens. Capitula 8, *ibid.* V, 392), to memorize a number of homilies from the Fathers or other model sermons of noted homiletes, and to recite them uniformly for years (cf. Lecoy de la Marche, 322). 133. Ps. xliii, 16.

134. Thom. Cel. I, n. 73; S. Bonav. c. 12, n. 7; Stephanus de Borbone, O. P. *Tractatus de septem donis Spiritus Sancti* pars 4, titulus 5, in: Lecoy de la Marche, *Anecdotes historiques d'Etienne de Bourbon* 215, s., n. 254; 407, n. 473.

135. "Revera constantissimus erat valde, et in nullo, nisi quod erat Domini, attendebat. Nam cum inter multa millia hominum verbum Dei sæpissime prædicaret, ita securus erat, ac si cum familiari socio loqueretur. Populorum maximam multitudinem quasi virum unum cernebat, et uni quasi multitudini diligentissime prædicabat." Thom. Cel. I, n. 72. "Eadem mentis constantia magnis loquebatur et parvis, eademque spiritus iucunditate paucis loquebatur et multis." S. Bonav. c. 12, n. 8.

136. "Facundissimus homo, facie hilaris, vultu benignus . . . lingua placabilis, ignea et acuta; vox vehemens, dulcis, clara et sonora . . . Dabat voci suæ vocem virtutis vera virtus et sapientia Christus." Thom. Cel. I, n. 83; II, n. 107.

137. "Erant autem verba eius non inania, nec risu digna, sed virtute Spiritus Sancti plena, cordis medullas penetrantia, ita ut in stuporem vehementer converterent audientes." *Tres Soc.* n. 26. "Erat enim verbum eius velut ignis ardens (Eccli. xlviii, 1), penetrans intima cordis, omniumque mentes admiratione replebat, cum non humanæ inventionis ornatum prætenderet, sed divinæ revelationis afflatum redoleret." S. Bonav. c. 12, n. 7.

138. "Nec tamen ipse modum predicantis tenuit, sed quasi concionantis." Ex Thomæ *Historia pontificum Salonitanorum et Spalatensium,* Böhmer 106.

139. "Omnis ætas omnisque sexus properabat virum novum mundo cælitus datum et cernere et audiere." S. Bonav. c. 12, n. 8.

140. ". . . de toto corpore fecerat linguam." Thom. Cel. I, n. 97.

141. Böhmer, *Analekten* L, where the references are also given for the above.

142. "Qui [Franciscus] coram tantis principibus assistens, licentia et benedictione suscepta, intrepidus loqui cœpit. Et quidem cum tanto fervore spiritus loquebatur, quod non se capiens præ lætitia, cum ex ore verbum proferret, pedes quasi saliendo movebat, non ut lasciviens, sed ut igne divini amoris ardens, non ad risum movens, sed planctum doloris extorquens. Multi enim ipsorum compuncti sunt, divinam gratiam et tantam viri constantiam admirantes. Verum venerabilis Dominus episcopus Hostiensis timore suspensus erat, totis visceribus orans ad Dominum, ne beati viri contemneretur simplicitas, quoniam in eum sancti gloria resultabat et dedecus, eo quod erat pater super eius familiam constitutus." Thom. Cel. I, n. 73. This record evidently is traceable to Cardinal Hugolino himself, who had commissioned Thomas of Celano to write the life of Francis. 143. *Spec. perf.* c. 100, p. 197 sq.

144. "Quoniam sibi primo suaserat opere, quod verbis aliis suadebat, et non timens reprehensorem, veritatem fidentissime loquebatur." Thom. Cel. I, n. 36. Likewise *Tres Soc.* n. 54.

145. "Nam cum doctrina evangelica, etsi non particulariter sed generaliter defecisset, missus est hic a Deo, ut universaliter per totum mundum, apostolorum exemplo, perhiberet testimonium veritati. Sicque factum est, ut doctrina sua omnem mundi sapientiam ostenderet evidentissime fore stultam, et brevi spatio temporis ad veram sapientiam Dei, per stultitiam prædicationis, inclinaverit, Christo duce." Thom. Cel. I, n. 89.

146. "Sicque in præparatione Evangelii discalceatus in ecclesiis parochialibus et aliis fidelium conventiculis prædicationis officium implevit [Franciscus]; quod tanto efficacius cordibus audientium imprimere potuit quanto a carnalibus desideriis et gastrimargiæ crapulis exstitit alienus." Rogerus de Wendover,

Chronica, Archiv. francisc. hist. I, 81. "Non solum autem prædicatione, sed exemplo vitæ sanctæ et conversationis perfectæ multos non solum inferiores ordinis homines, sed generosos et nobiles ad mundi contemptum invitant, qui relictis oppidis et casalibus et amplis possessionibus temporales divitias in spirituales felici commercio commutantes habitum fratrum Minorum . . . assumpserunt." Iacobi Vitriac. *Hist. orientalis* c. 32, Böhmer 103 sq.

147. "Saluti namque animarum præstare nihil dicebat . . . Hinc sibi in oratione luctamen, in prædicatione discursus, in exemplis dandis excessus." Thom. Cel. II, n. 172.

148. "Affirmabat Minores fratres novissimo tempore idcirco a Deo missos ut peccatorum obvolutis caligine lucis exempla monstrarent." *Ibid.* n. 155.

149. "Eamus per mundum exhortando omnes plus exemplo quam verbo ad agendam pœnitentiam de peccatis suis et habendam memoriam mandatorum Dei." *Tres Soc.* n. 36.

150. "Commercium est inter mundum et fratres; debent ipsi mundo bonum exemplum, debet mundus eis provisionem necessariam. Quando ipsi retraxerint bonum exemplum fide mentita, retrahit mundus manum iusta censura." Thom. Cel. II, n. 70.

151. "Omnes tamen fratres operibus prædicent." *Regula* I, c. 17, *Opusc.* ed. Böhmer 16, Lemmens 46. 152. Ezech. iii, 18.

153. "Dixit ad eum b. Franciscus: Si verbum universaliter debet intelligi, taliter ego accipio, quod servus Dei sic debet vita et sanctitate in se ardere, ut luce exempli et lingua conversationis omnes impios reprehendant. Sic, inquam, splendor vitæ eius et odor famæ ipsius omnibus annuntiabit iniquitatem eorum." Thom. Cel. II, n. 103. 154. *Spec. perf.* c. 87, p. 177. 155. Thom. Cel. II, n. 156. 156. *Ibid.* n. 155.

157. "Non se poterat præ gaudio capere sanctus Franciscus tali respersus filiorum odore. Subito surrexit in laudem, et quasi hæc sola sibi gloria foret, audire bona de fratribus, plenis eructavit visceribus: Gratias tibi ago, Domine, pauperum sanctificator et rector, qui me de fratribus meis tali lætificasti auditu. Benedic, precor, illos fratres benedictione largissima, et omnes, qui per bona exempla redolere faciunt professionem suam, speciali dono sanctifica." *Ibid.* n. 178.

CHAPTER XVII

1. Twenty years ago I treated this subject in my book: *Geschichte der wissenschaftlichen Studien im Franziskanerorden bis um die Mitte des 13. Jahrhunderts,* Freiburg i, Br. 1904. This book dispelled the erroneous impressions of many students who claimed that Francis and his primitive institute were opposed to the study of sciences; doubts, however, were expressed that "perhaps the author in defending St. Francis from the patently unjust accusation of being averse to science and of underestimating its value, has somewhat overshot the mark." (P. Eubel, *Lit. Rundschau,* 1905, 332). Franz X. Seppelt reviewed my arguments in a treatise (*Wissenschaft und Franziskanerorden, ihr Verhältniss im ersten Jahrzehnt des letzteren,* in: *Kirchengeschichtliche Abhandlungen herausgeg. von Sdralek,* 4, Bd., Breslau 1906, 151–179), insofar as they had reference to the time preceding 1221. My arguments, he says in conclusion, "appear at times to confound conditions of a later period with those of the first decade of the Order, and are not free from a tendency to see all later developments in embryonic state in the first happenings of the Order" (*loc. cit.* 178). However, despite the difference of opinions as regards particulars, the sum total of the conclusions reached on both sides amounts to almost the same thing. I expressed my opinion in the words: "It would be a false deduction were one, basing his conclusions on the apostolate of the Friars prior to 1219, to look for important, even if private, contributions to scientific research among the Friars of this period." (*Geschichte* 49). Seppelt (*loc. cit.* 169) expresses himself in

almost the same words: "If we do not wish to lose ourselves in idle speculations but adhere to solid facts, and not strip the term 'science' of its meaning as then understood, we can hardly speak of science as existing in the Order." The present chapter aims at presenting the matter again in a comprehensive way with reference to our former treatment of the subject and taking into account all well-founded observations of our critics.

2. S. Bonaventura, *Determinationes quæstionum*, pars I, q. 3: "Cur fratres intendant studio litterarum?" *Opera* VIII, 339. With the Dominicans also studies had to be placed entirely in the service of the apostolate. "Cum Ordo noster specialiter ob prædicationem et animarum salutem ab initio noscatur institutus fuisse et studium nostrum ab hoc principaliter ardenterque summopere debet intendere, ut proximorum animabus possimus utiles esse," we read in the Prologue to the Constitutions of the Order of Preachers of 1228, published by P. Denifle, in: *Archiv für Lit.-und Kirchengeschichte, des Mittelalters* I, 194. If we find no traces of scientific activity in the contemporary Orders of monks, it is due to the fact that they were not engaged in the active ministry.

3. Rogerus de Wendover, *Chronica*, in: *Archiv, francisc.* I, 81; Matthæus Paris. *Historia maior* ed. Wats, London 1640, 222; cf. 339 sqq.

4. "Quamvis homo iste beatus nullis fuerit scientiæ studiis enutritus." Thomas Cel. II, n. 102. According to Fr. Stephen de Borbone, Francis was "simplex in litteratura," "homo valde parum litteratus" (Lecoy de la Marche, *Anecdotes d'Etienne de Bourbon* p. 215, n. 254; p. 407, n. 473). Likewise the *Spec. perf.* c. 45. According to Angelus Clarinus (*Historia septem tribulationum* ed Döllinger, *Beiträge zur Sektengeschichte* II, 441. 451) Francis was "illitteratus respectu multorum sapientium [Ordinis Min.] patrum."

5. ". . . cum beatus Franciscus idiotam se diceret." Thom. Cel. II, n. 103.

6. Cf. Ducange-Carpenterius, *Glossar. ad scriptores mediæ et infimæ latinitatis* s. v. "idiota."

7. "Et eramus idiotæ et omnibus subditi." *Testament., Opusc.* ed. Böhmer 37, Lemmens 79.

8. Thus Fr. Sylvester (Thom. Cel. II, n. 109), Fr. Petrus Catanei (Iord. a Iano n. 11 sq.). 9. Thom. Cel. I, n. 23; S. Bonav. c. 15, n. 5.

10. Thom. Cel. I, n. 16; II, n. 13. 127. Of course "at that time French and Italian were little more than dialects of one common mother-tongue, so that their use was customary even in the lower classes of the people." M. (argaret) L. (iscow), *Der heilige Franziskus, Preussische Jahrbücher*, Bd. 87 (1897) 288. 11. Thom. Cel. I, n. 22.

12. Cf. Emil Michael, *Geschichte des deutschen Volkes seit dem 13. Jahrhundert* I, 3. Aufl., Freiburg 1897, 229 f.

13. Referring to a still living eye-witness, St. Bonaventure declares (*Epistola de tribus quæstionibus ad Magistrum innominatum, Opera* VIII, 334, n. 10): ". . . Cum paucas litteras sciret, postmodum in litteris profecit in Ordine, non solum orando, sed etiam legendo."

14. "Infirmanti sibi et undique pervaso doloribus dixit aliquando socius eius: Pater, semper ad Scripturas confugium habuisti, semper illæ tibi dolorum præbuere remedia. Fac, oro, et nunc tibi de prophetis aliquid legi . . ." Thom. Cel. II, n. 105.

15. "Legebat quandoque in sacris libris, et quod animo semel iniecerat, indelebiliter scribebat in corde. Memoriam pro libris habebat, quia non frustra semel capiebat auditus, quod continua devotione ruminabat affectus. Hunc discendi legendique modum fructuosum dicebat, non per millenos evagari tractatus . . . Enodabat frequenter quædam dubia quæstionum, et imperitus verbis intellectum et virtutem luculenter promebat." *Ibid.* 102. 16. Seppelt *loc. cit.* 170. 17. Thom. Cel. II, n. 103.

18. "Fratres mei, theologia huius viri, puritate et contemplatione subnixa, est aquila volans; nostra vero scientia ventre graditur super terram." *Ibid.*

19. According to Angelus Clarinus, *Historia septem tribulationum*, tribul. 1, ed. Döllinger, *Beiträge zur Sektengeschichte* II, 442.

20. "Quamvis homo iste beatus nullis fuerit scientiæ studiis enutritus, tamen

quæ de sursum est a Deo sapientiam discens, et æternæ lucis irradiatus fulgoribus de scripturis [of theology] non infime sentiebat.   Penetrabat enim ab omni labe purum ingenium mysteriorum abscondita, et ubi magistralis scientia foris est, affectus introibat amantis."   Thom. Cel. II, n. 102.

21. "Hic vero, cum in via Dei et ipsius cognitione a primævo iuventutis flore, parum vel nihil esset instructus . . . gratia et virtute Altissimi super omnes tempore suo repertos divina sapientia est repletus."   Thom. Cel. I, n. 89.

22. Cf. Léon le Monnier, *Histoire de St. François* II, 4me éd., Paris 1891, 85.

23. Dante, *Divina Com.*, Paradiso, canto II.

24. "Hi sunt duo Cherubim, pleni scientia . . ," say the two Generals of the Mendicant Orders, Fr. Humbertus de Romanis and Fr. John of Parma, in their joint circular of 1255, in: Wadding, *Annal.* ad a. 1255, n. 12.   25. Dante *loc. cit.* verse 37–39.

26. "Circuibat proinde fortissimus miles Christi Franciscus civitates et castella, non in persuasibilibus humanae sapientiæ verbis, sed in doctrina et virtute Spiritus annuntians regnum Dei."   Thom. Cel. I, n. 36; Cf. n. 72. 89.   Exactly so *Tres Soc.* n. 54.

27. "Prædicat . . . eructans de pleno, quidquid Spiritus suggerit."   Thom. Cel. II, n. 25.

28. "Nolite timere, quia pusilli et despecti videamini et insipientes, sed secure annuntiate simpliciter pœnitentiam, confidentes in Domino, qui vicit mundum, quod spiritu suo loquitur per vos et in vobis ad exhortandum omnes, ut convertantur ad ipsum et eius mandata observent."   *Tres Soc.* n. 36.

29. "Quicumque ex ipsis spiritum Dei habebat et eloquentiam idoneam ad prædicandum, sive clericus sive laicus esset, dabat ei licentiam prædicandi." *Tres Soc.* n. 59.   30. Cf. p. 335 f.

31. "Ad prædicatores pertinet scientia, ut sint exercitati in utroque Testamento et sententiarum examine discreti."   Alanus ab Insulis, *Summa de arte prædicatoria* c. 38, Migne, *Patr. lat.* 210, 183.

32. *Odonis episc. Paris. Synodicæ constitut.* n. 41, Harduin VI, 1945.

33. Mansi, *Conciliorum collectio* XXII, 31–32.   34. See p. 337.   35. See p. 335 f.

36. Gualteri Mapes, *De nugis curialium*, Camden Society 1850, 64 f.   37. See p. 335 f.

38. Cf. Denifle, *Die Konstitutionen des Predigerordens vom Jahre 1228*, in: *Archiv. für Lit.-und Kirchengeschichte des Mittelalters* I, 184–192.   39. See p. 336 ff.   40. See p. 321 ff.   41. See p. 372 ff.

42. Cf. Felder, *Geschichte der wissenschaftl. Studien* 49 f.   43. Denifle *loc. cit.* 223, n. 31.   44. S. Bonav., *Epist. de tribus quæstionibus* n. 10, *Opera* VIII, 334.

45. "Bonum est Scripturæ testimonia legere, bonum est Dominum Deum nostrum in ipsis exquirere; mihi vero tantum iam ipse de Scripturis adlegi, quod meditanti et revolventi satissimum est."   Thom. Cel. II, n. 105.

46. "Ministros verbi Dei tales volebat, qui studiis spiritualibus intendentes nullis aliis præpedirentur officiis.   Hos enim a quodam magno rege dicebat electos ad edicta, quæ ex eius ore'perciperent, populis demandanda."   *Ibid.* n. 163.

47. Proved in: Felder, *Geschichte der wissenschaftl. Studien* 74–76.

48. As is well known, Dominic simply adopted the Augustinian rule, which has no place for studies.   Still, even during the lifetime of the Founder decisive norms of study were issued for the members of the Order (Fr. Humbertus de Romanis, *De eruditione prædicatorum, Max. bibl. PP.* XXV, 631 F, and especially Denifle *loc. cit.* 187), to which the relevant decisions of the oldest Constitutions of the Order dating from 1228 are attached (Denifle *loc. cit.* 194. 197. 222. 223.).   49. Regula II, c. 5, *Opusc.* ed Böhmer 32, Lemmens 68.

50. See p. 129 ff.   The fifth chapter of the rule is interpreted thus by the oldest constitutions of the Order, published in the lifetime of the last disciples of Francis: "Cum Regula dicat, quod fratres, quibus dedit Dominus gratiam laborandi, laborent fideliter et devote, ordinamus quod fratres tam clerici quam laici compellantur per suos superiores in scribendo, studendo et aliis laboribus sibi competentibus exerceri" (P. Ehrle, *Die ältesten Generalkonstitutionen des Franziskanerordens*, in: *Archiv. für Lit.-und Kirchengeschichte* IV, 104).   "Quia igitur

quidam Fratrum gratiam habent laborandi spiritualiter, quidam vero corporaliter, omnibus dans regulam generalem, dicit, ut unusquisque gratia sua utatur." S. Bonav., *Expositio Regulæ FF. Min.* c. 5, n. 4, *Opera* VIII, 420. Cf. *idem, De perf. evang.* q. 2, a. 3, n. 16, *Opera* V, 165.

51. "Et non curent nescientes litteras litteras discere." *Regula* II, c. 10, *Opusc.* ed. Böhmer 34, Lemmens 72.

52. "Fratri laico volenti habere psalterium, et ab eo licentiam postulanti, cinerem pro psalterio obtulit." Thom. Cel. II, n. 195. This anecdote is related more fully in *Spec. perf.* c. 4 and by Fr. Ubertinus de Casali, *Declaratio,* ed. Ehrle. *Archiv* III, 177.

53. "Dolebat si, virtute neglecta, scientia quæreretur, præsertim si non in ea vocatione quisque persisteret, in qua vocatus a principio fuerit." Thom. Cel. II, n. 195. The same regulations for the lay brothers are found in the constitutions of the Order of Preachers of 1228 (*loc. cit.* 127): "Conversis, qui nunc habent psalteria, tantum duobus annis liceat retinere ab inde, et ipsis aliis psalteria inhibemus . . . Item nullus conversus fiat canonicus, nec in libris causa studendi se audeat occupare."

54. S. Bonav. c. 11. n. 1. 55. 1 Cor. vii, 20.

56. S. Bonav., *Epistola de tribus quæst.* n. 10, *Opera* VIII, 334.

57. *Regula* II, c. 9, *Opusc.* ed. Böhmer 33, Lemmens 71.

58. ". . . quod in theologica facultate et prædicationis officio sunt instructi." Bulla "Quo elongati" of Sept. 28, 1230, *Bullar. francisc.* I, 69, n. 56.

59. ". . . Fratres in sacra Pagina eruditos examinare ac approbare et eis officium prædicationis, Deum habendo præ oculis, committere valeant . . ." Bulla "Prohibente Regula" of Dec. 12, 1240, *Bullar. francisc.* I, 287, n. 325.

60. *Regula* II, *ibid.* 61. See p. 340.

62. *Rogeri Baconis Compendium studii philosophiæ* c. 5, ed. Brewer 427.

63. See p. 337, 338. 64. Migne, *Patr. lat.* 205, 25.

65. *De adventu Min. in Angliam* ed. Little 60. 66. See Felder *loc. cit.* 263 ff.

67. Fr. Nicolai Triveti, O. P. *Annales sex regum Angliæ, qui a comitibus andegavensibus originem traxerunt* ed. Thomas Hog, Londiniæ 1845, 212. 68. *Ibid.* 230.

69. "Licet autem fratres summæ simplicitati et conscientiæ puritati summopere studerent in omnibus, in audienda tamen lege divina et scholasticis exercitiis ita fuerunt ferventes, ut scholas theologiæ, quantumcumque distarent adire quotidie nudis pedibus in frigoris asperitate et luti profunditate non pigritarentur." *Ibid.* 33. 70. Cf. Felder *loc. cit.* 380–546. 71. Proved in Felder *loc. cit.* 135–141.

72. According to *Chron. XXIV General.* ed. *Anal. francisc.* III, 132, it was done by means of the following letter: "Carissimo meo fratri Antonio frater Franciscus salutem in Domino. Placet mihi, quod sacram theologiam legas fratribus, dummodo propter huiusmodi studium sanctæ orationis et devotionis spiritum non extinguant, sicut in Regula continetur. Vale." According to Fr. Nicolaus Glassberger, *Chronica* ed. *Anal. francisc.* II, 34, the letter reads exactly as cited, while Petr. Rodulph. Tossinian., *Historiarum seraphicæ religionis libri tres.* lib. 1, Venetiis 1586, 78, and other writers since the fifteenth century give a somewhat varying text version. The wording of the letter is therefore not certain, but it is evident from Thom. Cel. (see note 76), that Francis in fact wrote to Anthony.

73. "Fratri Antonio episcopo meo." Thom. Cel. II, n. 163. 74. Iord. a. Iano n. 12.

75. "Quos [litteratos et nobiles], ut erat animo nobilissimus et discretus honorifice atque digne pertractans, quod suum erat unicuique piissime impendebat. Revera discretione præcipua præditus, considerabat prudenter in omnibus cunctorum graduum dignitatem." Thom. Cel. I, n. 57.

76. "Reverendum hoc dicebat officium [prædicationis], et qui illud administrarent, omnibus venerandos . . . Sacræ vero theologiæ doctores amplioribus dignos censebat honoribus." *Ibid.* II, n. 163.

77. "Et omnes theologos et qui ministrant sanctissima verba divina debemus

honorare et venerari sicut qui ministrant nobis spiritum et vitam." *Testam.,* *Opusc.* ed. Böhmer 37, Lemmens 79. S. Bonav., *Epist. de tribus quæst,* n. 10, *Opera* VIII, 335, remarks hereto: "In morte mandavit fratribus, quod doctores sacræ Scripturæ in summa veneratione haberent tamquam illos, a quibus perciperent verba vitæ."

78. "Cœperunt multi de populo, nobiles et ignobiles, clerici et laici, divina inspiratione compuncti, ad sanctum Franciscum accedere, cupientes sub eius disciplina et magisterio perpetuo militare." Thom. Cel. I, n. 37.

79. "Statim namque quamplures boni et idonei viri, clerici et laici . . . eum devote secuti sunt." *Ibid.* n. 56.

80. ". . . quidam litterati viri et quidam nobiles ei gratissime adhæserunt." *Ibid.* n. 57.

81. "Triginta viri clerici et laici tunc temporis ab ipso sanctæ Religionis habitum susceperunt." *Ibid.* n. 62.

82. Festinabant proinde multi homines, nobiles et ignobiles, clerici et laici divina inspiratione inflati beati Francisci vestigiis adhærere." *Tres Soc.* n. 54. Likewise Walteri de Gysburne *Chronica de gestis regum Angliæ* ed. *Monum. Germ. hist. Script.* XXVIII, 631, lin. 31–36.

83. Matthæi Paris. *Chron. maiora* ed. *Monum. Germ. hist. Script.* XXVIII, 248, lin. 1–6. 84. Iacobi Vitriac. *Epist.* scripta a. 1220, Mart., Böhmer 101 sq.

85. Proved in Felder, *loc. cit.* 113–120.

86. *Rogeri Baconis Compendium studii philosophiæ* c. 5, ed. Brewer 426 sq.

87. For these statements see Felder *loc. cit.* 113–120.

88. Bernard a Bessa (*Catalogus Gen. Ministr.* ed. P. Hilarin. 97, *Annal. francisc.* III, 695) says of him: "Vir adeo in sapientia etiam humana famosus, ut raros in ea pares Italia putaretur habere." Salimbene de Parma (*Chron.* 404) enumerates the many faults of Brother Elias and then adds: "Hoc solum habuit bonum frater Helyas, quia Ordinem fratrum Minorum ad studium theologiæ promovit." 89. See Felder *loc. cit.* 121, note 4.

90. For these and the following statements see Felder, *loc. cit.* 123–316.

91. ". . . Cum etiam propter litteratorum inopiam nec adhuc per sæculares potuerit observari statutum Lateranensis Concilii, ut in singulis ecclesiis essent aliqui, qui theologiam docerent; quod tamen per religiosos gratia Dei cernis multo latius impletum, quam etiam fuerit statutum." Contra impugnantes Dei cultum et religionem c. 4, n. 12, ed. (Soldati), *SS. Thomæ et Bonaventuræ Opuscula contra Guillelmum de S. Amore,* Romæ 1773, 76.

92. "Propter scholarium apud nos in theologia studentium raritatem, cum iam in civitatibus et aliis locis maioribus universis per fratres eosdem mendicantes et alios non sine grandi periculo dictæ litteræ doceantur." Denifle-Chatelain, *Chartular. Universit. Paris.* I, 254, n. 230.

93. "Nunquam fuit tanta apparentia sapientiæ, nec tantum exercitium studii in tot facultatibus, in tot regionibus, sicut iam a quadraginta annis. Ubique enim doctores sunt dispersi, et maxime in theologia in omni civitate, et in omni castro, et in omni burgo; præcipue per duos Ordines studentes, quod non accidit nisi a quadraginta annis, vel circiter." *Compendium studii phil.* c. 1, ed. Brewer 398.

94. The larger number of schools of the Mendicants were public, and open to all. Just as no one dreamed of closing the churches to the public, and of restricting the word of God to one class, just so little would a professor of theology have thought ordinarily of keeping his lecture room open only for the clerics of his house or monastery. Closed schools or houses of study in the stricter sense existed only where no thorough schooling was aimed at or where the attendance of scholars living elsewhere was not to be reckoned with. See the proofs in Felder *loc. cit.* 329–332.

95. "Propter quod accidit, ut sæculares a quadraginta annis nullum composuerint in theologia tractatum, nec reputant se aliquid posse scire, nisi per decem annos, vel amplius, audiant pueros duorum Ordinum. Nec aliter præsumunt legere sententias, nec incipere in theologia, nec unam lectionem, nec disputationem, nec prædicationem, nisi per quaternos puerorum in dictis Ordinibus;

sicut manifestum est omnibus in studio Parisiis et ubique." *Roger. Bacon. ibid* c. 5, p. 428 sq. "Pueri duorum Ordinum" are called by Bacon the Mendicant teachers as Albert the Great, Thomas of Aquinas, etc. *Ibid.* p. 426.

96. The famous doctor and preacher Petrus Cantor expresses the view of his time on the unity of studies and preaching in the words: "In tribus igitur consistit exercitium sacræ Scripturæ [i. e. of theology]: circa lectionem, disputationem et prædicationem . . . Lectio autem est quasi fundamentum et substratum sequentium; quia per eam ceteræ utilitates comparantur. Disputatio quasi paries est in hoc exercitio et ædificio, quia nihil plene intelligitur, fideliterve prædicatur, nisi prius dente disputationis frangatur. Prædicatio vero, cui subserviunt priora, quasi tectum est tegens fideles ab æstu et turbine vitiorum. Post lectionem igitur sacræ Scripturæ, et dubitabilium per disputationum inquisitionem, et non prius, prædicandum est." *Verbum abbreviatum* c. 1, Migne, *Patr. lat.* 205, 25. Substantially the same is said by Alanus ab Insulis (*Summa de arte prædicatoria, præfatio*, Migne 210, 111) and Peter d'Ailly (*Tractatus Universitatis* ed. D'Argentré,[*Collectio iudiciorum de novis erroribus* I, 2, Paris 1728, 77).

97. That Brother Leo is evidently to be regarded as the author of these reports, follows from the unassailed passage: ". . . Nos qui cum ipso Francisco fuimus, ad hoc respondemus sicut audivimus ab ore eius, quoniam ipse dixit fratribus hæc . . ." *Spec. perf.* c. 2, ed. Sabatier p. 6.

98. Angelus Clarenus, *Expositio Regulæ Fratrum Minorum* ed. Livarius Oliger 209; *Historia septem tribulationum* ed. Döllinger, *Beiträge zur Sektengeschichte*, 2. Teil, 445.

99. ". . . Beatus Franciscus expressit intentionem suam et de libris et de studio, sicut dictum est supra; sicut aperte patet in dictis fratris Leonis manu sua conscriptis, sicut ab ore sancti patris audivit, et ego ipse audivi a pluribus aliis sociis beati Francisci, quos vidi." *Responsio* ed. Ehrle 76, line 9–12. Likewise *ibid.* 168, 1. 24–30 and *Arbor vitæ* lib. 5, c. 3. 5.

100. "Nihil insuper sibi proprium vindicabant, sed libris et aliis collatis eisdem utebantur communiter." *Tres Soc.* n. 43; cf. *Spec. perf.* p. 14.

101. "In libris testimonium Dei quærere non pretium, ædificationem non pulchritudinem edocebat. Paucos tamen haberi volebat, eosdemque ad fratrum egentium necessitatem paratos." Thom. Cel. II, n. 62.

102. S. Bonav., *Epist. de tribus quæst.* n. 6, *Opera* VIII, 332 sq.

103. ". . . sicut dixit sanctus Leo ex ore ipsius [Francisci] volebat, quod in communi ad hoc [studium] haberentur libri sufficientes et pauperes, non superflui nec curiosi." Ubertinus, *Arbor vitæ* lib. 5, c. 5. 104. Ubertinus, *Responsio* 73, line 35.

105. "Et quum ex longa familiaritate, quam idem confessor Nobiscum habuit, plenius noverimus intentionem ipsius, et in condendo prædictam Regulam [of 1223], obtinendo confirmationem ipsius per Sedem Apostolicam sibi astiterimus. . . ." Bulla "Quo elongati" *Bullar. francisc.* I, 68. Cf. p. 102 f. 106. *Bullar. francisc.* III, 409.

107. "Voluit ergo dicere decretalis [Nic. III], quod secundum qualitatem locorum plures essent libri vel pautiores in locis, et secundum qualitatem personarum et offitiorum eis impositorum plures de libris communibus eis pro tunc concederentur ad usum; et finitis offitiis et cessantibus necessitatibus de usu predictorum librorum, ad armarium commune redirent, ut possent aliorum fratrum usibus applicari." Ubertinus, *Declaratio* 179 sq. 108. *Ibid.* 109. *Ibid.*

110. ". . . Cum quidam minister libros ambitiosos multumque valentes eius licentia retinendos expeteret, audivit ab ipso: Librum evangelii, quod promisi, pro tuis libris perdere nolo. Tu quidem quod volueris facies; mea non fiet licentia." *Ibid.*

111. *Spec. perf.* c. 2, ed. Sabatier p. 7 sq.; Fr. Ubertinus, *Arbor vitæ* lib. 5, c. 3 and *Responsio* 75, also *Declaratio* 177; Fr. Angelus, *Expositio* 32 sq. 65, and *Historia septem tribul.* 445 (Döllinger in this case as in many others gives a mutilated text, as I have convinced myself by an examination of the Cod. 7 Plut. 20, fol. 12b–13a of the Laurenziana at Florence, which he used).

112. *Spec. perf.* p. 6: "Nos qui cum ipso fuimus ad hoc respondemus, sicut

audivimus ab ore eius." Fr. Angelus, *Expositio* 65: "Et sicut frater Leo scribit et alii sotii eiusdem Sancti." Fr. Ubertinus, *Declaratio* 178, 1.9–12: "Hæc omnia scripta sunt per manum fratris Leonis in libro, qui est Assizii et in rotulis, quos habemus, ut superius est expressum. Ex quibus patet, quod intentio sancti Francisci omnem appropriationem librorum exsufflat." In the *Arbor vitæ* lib. 5, c. 3 Ubertinus says that the "rotuli fratris Leonis" are preserved in the convent of St. Clare at Assisi.

113. *Spec. perf.* p. 4 sqq.; Ubertinus, *Arbor vitæ, ibid.; Responsio* 75; *Declaratio* 177.

114. "Unde quotquot fratres veniebant ad eum pro habendo consilio eius super huiusmodi, hoc modo respondebat eis." *Spec. perf.* p. 12; likewise Ubertinus, *Declaratio* 177, appealing to the testimony of Br. Leo.

115. "Absit autem quod pater noster beatus Franciscus intenderet, quod quilibet frater sibi salmas librorum conquireret vel sic sibi appropriaret et quod quando frater mutatur de loco ad locum semper post se salmam deferret." Ubertinus, *Rotulus* 111, line 20–23; cf. *Declaratio* 179, line 29ff.; *Arbor vitæ* lib. 5, c. 5. It need hardly be said that such a "salma" or "sarcina" of writings easily represented the value of an important library according to present ideas.

116. "Expresse autem asseruit beatus Franciscus, quod qui vult esse verus frater minor, non debet habere nec libros nec aliud quid suo usui appropriatum exceptis necessariis vestimentis, unde nunquam voluit concedere, quod aliquis frater haberet librum aliquem ad suum proprium usum, quantumcumque a sibi carissimis instantissime fuerit requisitus, sed volebat, quod libri ad divinum cultum et sacrarum scripturarum studium essent in communi et in illis addiscerent illi, quibus Deus daret gratiam intellectus." Ubertinus, *Rotulus* 111 line 13 ff. "Et licet hec [the office of preaching] supponant scientiam, et scientia studium et studium usum librorum; tamen ex his que dicta sunt supra de verbis sancti fratris Leonis . . . non fuit intentio beati Francisci, quod fratres haberent tot salmas librorum ad usum proprium immo nec unicum librum." *Arbor vitæ* lib. 5, c. 5.

117. Ubertinus, *Declaratio* 179 sq. This view is shared in the passages cited above of Thom. Cel. II, n. 62 and of *Tres Soc.* n. 43.

118. *Spec. perf.* c. 2 p. 12; Ubertinus, *Declaratio* 178, line 1 ff.

119. *Regula* I, c. 3; II, c. 3, *Opusc.* ed. Böhmer 4. 31, Lemmens 28. 66. Cf. my treatise: *St. François d'Assise et le Bréviaire romain*, in: *Études franciscaines* V, Paris 1901, 490 ss. 120. *Spec. perf.* p. 3. 6. 26 sqq. 121. *Spec. perf. ibid.;* Ubertinus, *Declaratio* 177 sqq.

122. ". . . beatus Franciscus tempore suo non fecit ita Regulam et paupertatem [quoad libros] observari a fratribus . . . nec ita observandum mandavit . . . quia valde timebat scandalum et in se et in fratribus, nolebat contendere cum ipsis, sed condescendebat invitus voluntati eorum." *Spec. perf.* p. 6.

123. "Unde ipse ad litteram observavit totum sanctum evangelium [cf. Luke ix, 3 to which reference is made] a principio, ex quo cœpit habere fratres, usque ad diem mortis suæ." *Spec. perf.* p. 9; cf. 6 sq.

124. "Sufficere, inquit, debet huic pro se habitus et libellus, pro fratribus vero pennarium et sigillum. Non sit aggregator librorum." Thom. Cel. II, 185.

125. "Libros continue suos, videlicet bibliothecas in forulis a collo dependentes baiulantes." Matthæi Paris. *Historia Anglorum* ed. *Monum. Germ. hist. Script.* XXVIII, 397. One is indeed inclined to think here of the breviary which the Friars carried with them.

126. "Nullus frater libros scribat vel scribi faciat ad vendendum, nec minister provincialis audeat habere vel retinere aliquos libros absque licentia generalis ministri, nec aliqui fratres accipiant vel habeant absque licentia suorum provincialium ministorum. Et nulla biblia emenda precium 20 librarum turonensium excedat. Si contingat aliquem fratrem transferri de una provincia ad aliam ad morandum, libros ei concessos ad usum possit habere; post mortem vero suam libri scripti vel empti de elemosina ad illam provinciam revertantur, ad quam dicta elemosina pertinebat; et ad hoc fideliter faciendum ministri firmiter, in quorum provinciis decesserit, teneantur . . . Nullus libros aliquos

retineat sibi assignatos, nisi sint totaliter in ordinis potestate, quod libere per ministros dari valeant et aufferri." The oldest editions of the General Constitutions of the Franciscan Order ed. Ehrle, *Archiv. für Lit.-und Kirchengesch.* VI, 111. 127. See "Humility." 128. See p. 169 f. 204 f. 129. See p. 356. 130. See p. 497, note 72.

131. "Fuit ergo sua intencio, quod...fratres, quibus daret Deus aptitudinem intellectus, in illis [libris] legendo et alios instruendo proficerent, ita tamen quod magis esset principalis intencio et occupatio oracionis quam studii, et studium oracionem dirigeret, et oracio studium illustraret." Ubertinus, *Responsio 75;* *Declaratio 178.* In both places Ubertinus traces his statements to Fr. Leo.
132. Thom. Cel. II, n. 195. 133. *Ibid.*
134. "Et dicebat: Multi sunt, qui totum studium et sollicitudinem suam die noctuque ponunt in scientia, dimittentes vocationem suam, sanctam et devotam orationem suam." Fr. Leo, *S. Francisci intentio Regulæ* ed. Lemmens, *Documenta antiqua franciscana*, pars 1, Ad Claras Aquas 1901, 90.
135. Thom. Cel. II, n. 189 is alone when he says: "Hæc est [simplicitas], quae græcas glorias non optimas arbitrans, plus eligit facere quam discere vel docere." This possibly might be a reference to Greek philosophy; still it is a personal reflection of Thom. Cel., not a statement of Francis.
136. For the following account see my *Geschichte der wissenschaftl. Studien im Franziskanerorden*, especially p. 447-490, where the gradual introduction of philosophy into the schools of the thirteenth century, especially into those of the Mendicants, is explained at length.
137. The earlier translations by Boethius (died *ca.* 524) were lost in the disintegration of the ancient culture, with the exception of the two first books of the *Organon*, i. e. of the Aristotelian logics. See *loc. cit.* 200.
138. *Chartul. Univers. Paris.* ed. Denifle-Chatelain I, n. 11, p. 70; n. 59, p. 114-116; n. 79, p. 138; n. 87, p. 143.
139. *Die Konstitutionen des Predigerordens vom Jahre* 1228 ed. Denifle, *Archiv.* I, 222. 140. See Felder *loc. cit.* 457-459. 141. See *loc. cit.* 198 ff. 459 ff. 142. 1 Kings xiii, 19. 143. See Felder *loc. cit.* 461. 144. *Expositio 210.*
145. *Historia septem tribul.* ed. Ehrle, *Archiv.* II, 356-358 (Döllinger 466 f. this passage is again badly mutilated, although he could have copied it from Ehrle). Insofar as Angelus gives the impression that the study of philosophy was finally and universally introduced already under Crescentius, he is in error. Its introduction began at that time and was completed in the course of the next 30-40 years. This development found its conclusion in the General Constitutions of 1292, which ordained: "Iura vero et physica in scolis theologiæ ab eodem lectore et eodem tempore non legantur, sed alibi et ab aliis, ubi fuerit opportunum; seculares autem ad huiusmodi lectiones nullatenus admittantur. Nec ratione huiusmodi studii ab humilitatis obsequiis et divinis officiis eximantur, parcatur tamen iuvenibus a discursu." Ehrle, *Die ältesten Redaktionen der Generalkonstitutionen des Franziskanerordens*, in: *Archiv* VI, 108. Cf. Felder *loc. cit.* 462-466. 146. Felder *loc. cit.* 463.
147. "Cum ex duobus parietibus construatur ædificium Ordinis, scilicet moribus bonis et scientia, parietem scientiæ fecerunt ultra cælum et cælestia sublimem, in tantum ut quærerent, an Deus sit; parietem vero morum permiserunt ita bassum esse, ut pro laude magna dicatur de fratre: 'securus homo est'; unde non convenienter videbantur ædificare." Thom. de Eccleston, *De adventu Min. in Angliam* coll. XIII, p. 92.
148. Ehrle, *Petrus Johannes Olivi, sein Leben und seine Schriften*, in: *Archiv* III, 480 f. 503 f.
149. Angelus, *Expositio 214*; Ubertinus, *Rotulus 111.*
150. *Determinationes quæst.* pars 1, q. 3, *Opera VIII, 339.*
151. *Apologia pauperum* c. 12, n. 13, *Opera VIII, 320.*
152. *Collatio XVII in Hexaemeron*, n. 25, *Opera V, 413.*
153. *Collatio XIX in Hexaemeron*, n. 14, *Opera V, 422.*
154. *Epist. de tribus quæst.* n. 12 sq., *Opera VIII, 335 sq.*
155. *Collatio XXII in Hexaemeron* n. 21; *Opera V, 440.* That theology was

the only thing worth striving for in science, and that all other departments of learning were but ways and means to this ultimate goal of all earthly knowledge, was in general the principle of the entire Scholastic system of the Middle Ages. For the proof see Felder 380 ff.

156. *De reductione artium ad theol.* n. 7. 26, *Opera* V, 322. 326.

157. *Epist. de tribus quæst. ibid.*

158. *Breviloquium,* Prol. n. 3, *Opera* V, 205.

159. "Alii principaliter intendunt speculationi et postea unctioni; alii principaliter unctioni et postea speculationi. Et utinam iste amor vel unctio non recedat!" *Collatio XXII in Hexaemeron* n. 21, *Opera* V. 440.

160. "Hic sicut in luminibus scientiarum et maxime in Scripturis sacris videbatur miranda capacitate proficere, ita in devotionis gratia continuum sumebat augmentum. Siquidem omnem veritatem, quam percipiebat intellectu, ad formam orationis et laudationis divinæ reducens, continuo ruminabat affectu." *Catalogus Gener. Ministr.* ed. P. Hilarinus a Lucerna 112.

CHAPTER XVIII

1. *Dogmengeschichte* III, 3. Aufl., Freiburg i. Br. 1897, 380.

2. *Studein zur Individualität des Franziskus von Assisi,* Leipzig-Berlin 1914, 213.

3. "Otium sanctum, quo sapientiam cordis inscriberet, faciebat de tempore suo." Thom. Cel. II, n. 94.

4. "Nam eius tutissimus portus erat oratio, non unius existens momenti, vacuave aut præsumptuosa, sed longa tempore, plena devotione, humilitate placida; . . . ambulans, sedens, comedens et bibens orationi erat intentus." *Ibid.* I, n. 71. "Nam ambulans et sedens, intus et foris, laborans et vacans, orationi adeo erat intentus, ut illi videretur non solum quidquid erat in eo cordis et corporis, verum etiam operis et temporis dedicasse." S. Bonav. c. 10, n. 1.

5. Cant. ii, 14. 6. Thom. Cel. I, n. 71.

7. "Si quando visitationes sæcularium seu quævis alia negotia ingruebant, præcisis potius quam finitis ad intima recurrebat. Insipidus quidem erat mundus cælesti dulcedine pasto, et ad grossa hominum divinæ delitiæ facerant delicatum." *Ibid.* II, n. 94. 8. Ps. cviii, 11. 9. Thom. Cel. I, n. 96. 10. *Ibid.* II, n. 100. 11. *Ibid.* n. 99.

12. "Cum in publico subito afficeretur, visitatus a Domino, ne sine cella foret, de mantello cellulam faciebat. Nonnunquam mantello carens, ne manna absconditum proderet, manica vultum tegebat. Semper aliquid obiiciebat adstantibus, ne sponsi tactum cognoscerent, ita ut in arto navis plurimis insertus oraret invisus." *Ibid.* II, n. 94 sq. 13. *Ibid.* n. 98; S. Bonav. c. 10, n. 2.

14. "Sancta oratione omnia præveniebat negotia." *Ibid.* I, n. 35.

15. "Eos vero dicebat male dividere, qui prædicationi totum, devotioni nihil impendunt. Laudabat revera prædicatorem, sed eum, qui pro tempore sibi saperet sibique gustaret." *Ibid.* II, n. 164.

16. "Dicebat autem: Prius prædicator haurire secretis orationibus debet, quod postea sacris effundat sermonibus; prius intus calescere, quam foris frigida verba proferre." *Ibid.* n. 163.

17. "Hii autem circa temporalia nullatenus occupantur, sed fervente desiderio et vehemente studio singulis diebus laborant, ut animas, quæ pereunt, a sæculi vanitatibus retrahant . . . De die intrant civitates et villas, ut aliquos lucri faciant operam dantes actioni, nocte vero revertuntur ad eremum vel loca solitaria vacantes contemplationi." *Epist. data Ianuæ* a. 1216. Böhmer, *Analekten* 98.

18. "Videbat eum tota nocte orantem, rarissime dormientem, laudantem Dominum et gloriosam Virginem matrem eius." Thom. Cel. I, n. 24.

19. "Si sero incipiebat, vix mane finiebat." *Ibid.* n. 71.

20. S. Bonav. c. 13, n. 1. Cf. Thom. Cel. I, n. 71: "Eligebat proinde frequen-

ter solitaria loca, ut ex toto animum in Deum posset dirigere, nec tamen pigritabatur, cum tempus esset opportunum, se negotiis ingerere ac saluti libens intendere proximorum."

21. Thom. Cel. I, n. 71. 91. sq. 104; II, n. 35. 45. 95.

22. "Mos erat sancto Francisco integrum diem solitaria in cella transigere, nec ad fratres reverti, nisi sumendi cibi necessitas perurgeret. Non tamen signatis horis cœnaturus exibat, quoniam edacior contemplationis fames totum sibi frequentius vindicabat." *Ibid.* II, n. 45.

23. "Suspendebatur multoties tanta contemplationis dulcedine, ut supra semetipsum raptus, quod ultra humanum sensum experiebatur, nemini revelaret." *Ibid.* n. 98. 24. *Ibid.* n. 99. 25. *Ibid.* 26. *Ibid.* n. 95; S. Bonav. c. 10, n. 4.

27. *De religiosa habitatione in eremo, Opusc.* ed. Böhmer 67, Lemmens 83 sq.

28. Thom. Cel. II, n. 178. 29. Bull "Quia populorum tumultus," *Bullar. francisc.* I, 20, n. 17. 30. Ubertinus, *Arbor vitæ* lib. 5, n. 3.

31. "Orationis gratiam viro religioso desiderandam super omnia firmiter asserebat, nullumque credens sine ipsa in Dei prosperari servitio, modis quibus poterat, fratres suos ad eius studium excitabat." S. Bonav. c. 10, n. 1.

32. Thom. Cel. I, n. 45. 33. *Ibid.* II, n. 160.

34. Thom. Cel. I, n. 20. 40; *Tres Soc.* n. 41; *Fr. Ægid. Assis. Vita* 76. 78. 79. 85. 86. 109. 110. 113; Dicta 10. 41–52. 70–74; *S. Claræ Assis. Vita* c. 3, n. 19 sq., p. 759; c. 5, n. 36, p. 762; *S. Antonii Pat. Legenda prima* c. 7, n. 6–10, p. 36 sq.; c. 15, n. 1–7, p. 50–52; Thom. de Ecclest. coll. IV, p. 28; coll. V. p. 30 sq.; coll. XIV, p. 97 etc.

35. ". . . semper adorare et videre Dominum Deum vivum et verum mundo corde et animo." *Admonitiones* n. 16, *Opusc.* ed. Böhmer 46, Lemmens 14.

36. *Opusc.* ed. Böhmer 17, Lemmens 47 sq.

37. Böhmer 19, Lemmens 50. 38. Böhmer 21, Lemmens 54 sq.

39. Cf. I Mos. 1, 26, and 2, 15. 40. Matth. xxv, 34. 41. Matth. xvii, 5. 42. *Regula* I, c. 23, *Opusc.* ed. Böhmer 23–26, Lemmens 57–62.

43. Paul Sabatier (*Vie de S. François d'Assise*, 21. éd., Paris 1899, 295 s.), writes the following beautiful and apposite words: "Ces naïves répétitions n'ont-elles pas un charme mystérieux qui s'insinue délicieusement jusqu'au fond du cœur? N'y a-t-il pas là une sorte de sacrement dont les paroles ne sont que le véhicule grossier? François se réfugie en Dieu, comme l'enfant va se jeter dans le sein de sa mère et dans l'incohérence de sa faiblesse et de sa joie, lui balbutie tous les mots qu'il sait, et par lesquels il ne veut que répéter l'éternel, je suis a toi, de l'amour et de la foi."

44. Cf. Felder, *Jesus Christus* I, 3. Aufl., Paderborn 1923, 331, 352 f.

45. Harnack, *Dogmengeschichte* III, 380.

46. "Tota in Christum unum anima sitiebat, totum illi non solum cordis sed corporis dedicabat." Thom. Cel. II, n. 94.

47. *Officium Passionis Domini, Opusc.* ed. Böhmer 107–122, Lemmens 126–148.

48. ". . . ad reverentiam et memoriam et laudem passionis Domini . . ." Böhmer 107, Lemmens 126. 49. Böhmer 121 sq., Lemmens 147 sq.

50. *Vita S. Claræ* c. 4, n. 30 sq., *Act. SS.*, Augusti t. II, p. 761.

51. *Act. SS.*, Martii t. I, p. 505–507. 52. *Vita S. Claræ* c. 6, n. 51, p. 764.

53. Franz Pfeiffer (*Deutsche Mystiker* I, 2. Aufl., Göttingen 1907. 309–386) has published a number of these old German texts. 54. *Loc. cit.* 375.

55. For a selection of apposite passages from Bonaventure see P. Ephrem Longpré, O. F. M., *La théologie mystique de S. Bonaventure*, in: *Archiv. franc.* XIV (1921) 68–71.

56. See the thorough investigation made by P. Symphorien, O. M. Cap., *L'influence spirituelle de saint Bonaventure et l'imitation de Jésus-Christ*, in: *Études franciscaines* XXXIII (1921) 36–96. 235–255. 344–359. 433–467; XXXIV (1922) 23–65. 158–194.

57. This has been already established by Mgr. Puyol, *L'auteur de l'imitation* 121–126.

58. "Summum nostrum studium sit: in vita Iesu Christi meditari . . . Cum Christum habueris, dives es et sufficit tibi." *Imitatio* lib. I, c. 1; lib. II, c. 1.

59. "Non pluribus indigeo, fili. Scio Christum pauperem crucifixum." Thom. Cel. II, n. 105.

60. Cf. P. Athanasius Bierbaum, O. F. M., *Der heilige Franziskus von Assisi und die Gottesmutter*, Paderborn 1904.

61. ". . . devotione fervebat erga totius bonitatis Matrem." Thom. Cel. I, n. 21. "Devotionem ferventem habebat ad Dominam mundi." S. Bonav. c. 2, n. 8.

62. "Matrem Iesu indicibili complectebatur amore, eo quod Dominum maiestatis fratrem nobis effecerit." Thom. Cel. II, n. 198.

63. "Beata Virgo Maria sic honoratur, ut dignum est, quia ipsum portavit in sanctissimo utero." *Epistl. ad Capitulum Generale, Opusc.* ed. Böhmer 59, Lemmens 102. 64. Thom. Cel. II, n. 200.

65. *Regula* I, c. 9, *Opusc.* ed Böhmer 10, Lemmens 37. 66. Thom. Cel. II, n. 83. 67. *Ibid.* n. 200. 68. Thom. Cel. *ibid.; Tres Soc.* n. 15. 69. *Opusc.* ed. Böhmer 35, Lemmens 76. 70. S. Bonav. c. 3, n. 1. 71. *Ibid.* c. 4, n. 5.

72. Hettinger, *Aus Welt und Kirche* I, 1902, p. 229.

73. Thom. Cel. I, n. 21. 106; II, n. 18 sq. 160. 74. *Ibid.* n. 108.

75. "Sed quod lætificat plurimum, Ordinis advocatam ipsam constituit, suisque alis quos relicturus erat filios usque in finem fovendos et protegendos submisit." *Ibid.* II, n. 198. The biographer adds the supplication: "Exercise, then, O Advocate of the poor, thy office in our behalf until the time ordained by the Father!"

76. *Opusc.* ed. Böhmer 66. 107, Lemmens 119. 126. The statute, however, prescribing a solemn Mass in honor of the Immaculate Virgin on Saturdays, and which has been ascribed to St. Francis (Wadding, *Annales* ad annum 1219, n. 30), in reality owes its origin to St. Bonaventure. The latter decreed at the General Chapter of 1269: "Ordinamus ob reverentiam gloriosæ Virginis, ut in quolibet Sabbato ad ipsius honorem dicatur sollemniter missa, quando fieri poterit bono modo. Ad cuius etiam honorem fratres prædicent populo, quod quando auditur campana completorii ipsa beata Virgo aliquotiens salutetur." Little, "Decrees of the General Chapters of the Friars Minor 1260 to 1282," in: *The English Historical Review* Vol. XIII (1898) 705.

77. "Peculiares illi persolvebat laudes, fundebat preces, offerebat affectus, quot et qualiter humana promere lingua non posset." Thom. Cel. II, n. 198.

78. S. Bonav. c. 9, n. 3. 79. *Opusc.* ed. Böhmer 61. 72, Lemmens 105. 121.

80. "Videbat [Bernardus] eum tota nocte orantem rarissime dormientem, laudantem Deum et gloriosam Virginem matrem eius." Thom. Cel. I, n. 24.

81. *Opusc.* ed. Böhmer 108, Lemmens 128. 82. *Opusc.* ed. Böhmer 70, Lemmens 123.

83. "Angelos, qui nobiscum in acie sunt, quive nobiscum ambulant in medio umbræ mortis, maximo venerabatur affectu. Tales ubique socios reverendos esse dicebat, tales nihilominus invocandos custodes." Thom. Cel. II, n. 197.

84. "Inoffensos eorum aspectus servare docebat, nec præsumere coram eis, quod non coram hominibus fieret. Pro eo, quod in conspectu angelorum psallebatur in choro, omnes qui possent in oratorium convenire volebat, et ibidem psallere sapienter." *Ibid.*

85. J. B. Weiss, *Weltgeschichte* IV, 3. Aufl., Graz 1891, 623.

86. Emil Michael, *Geschichte des deutschen Volkes* I, 3. Aufl., Freiburg 1897, 214 f.

87. "Beatum vero Michaëlem, eo quod animarum repræsentandarum haberet officium, sæpe dicebat excellentius honorandum." Thom. Cel. *ibid.;* cf. S. Bonav. c. 9, n. 3.

88. Thom. Cel. *ibid.*; S. Bonav. *ibid.* Before the feast of the Assumption he likewise fasted forty days in honor of the Mother of God: S. Bonav. *ibid.*

89. "Dicebat enim: Quilibet pro tanti honore principis aliquid laudis vel muneris specialis Deo deberet offerre." Thom. Cel. *ibid.*

90. S. Bonav. *ibid.* 91. Thom. Cel. II, n. 202.

NOTES

92. *Admonitiones* c. 6, *Opusc.* ed. Böhmer 44, Lemmens 9 sq. 93. *Spec. perf.* c. 4. 94. *Regula* I, c. 3, *Opusc.* ed. Böhmer 3 sq., Lemmens 28.

95. "Officium dicebamus clerici secundum alios clericos." *Opusc.* ed. Böhmer 37, Lemmens 79.

96. *Regula* II, c. 3, *Opusc.* ed. Böhmer 31, Lemmens 66. The Papal chapel made use of the so-called *Psalterium romanum*, which St. Jerome had corrected according to the Septuagint. This translation had never become popular, while the one made from the *Hexapla* of Origen (the so-called *Psalterium gallicanum*) was universally adopted. The popular tendency of St. Francis and the familiarity of his Friars with the ordinary *Psalterium* was the decisive factor in selecting the latter. And since he had brought the Breviary adopted by him and which had formerly been in use in the Capella papalis only, so prominently to the front that it was soon introduced throughout the world as the Breviary of the Friars Minor, the natural result was that the version of the Psalms in use in the Papel chapel or the Roman Church was discontinued, and the popular translation, thanks to the Seraph of Assisi, has been preserved to this day in the Breviary. The reasons which led St. Francis to adopt the Roman Breviary, and the influence which he and his Order exercised on the formation and the spread of this Breviary, have been treated extensively in my article in the *Études franciscaines* V (1901) 490–504: *St. François d'Assise et le Bréviaire romain.*

97. "Et quamvis sim simplex et infirmus, tamen semper volo habere clericum, qui mihi faciat officium, sicut in regula continetur. Et omnes alii fratres teneantur . . . facere officium secundum regulam. Et qui inventi essent, qui non facerent officium secundum regulam et vellent alio modo variare . . ., omnes fratres, ubicumque sunt, per obedientiam teneantur . . . ipsum fortiter custodire sicuti hominem in vinculis die noctuque," etc. *Testament., Opusc.* ed. Böhmer 38 sq., Lemmens 81. 98. See p. 399.

99. The proof herefor has been adduced in my: *Geschichte der wissenschaftl. Studien* 426–439. Cf. Fr. Antoine de Sérent, O. F. M., *L'âme franciscaine*, in: *Archiv. francisc.* VIII (1915) 452–458. 100. *Epist. ad Capitul. General., Opusc.* ed. Böhmer 61, Lemmens 106.

101. S. Bonav. c. 10, n. 6. 102. Thom. Cel. II, n. 96 sq.

103. "Deprecati sunt eum fratres tempore illo, ut doceret eos orare, quoniam in simplicitate spiritus ambulantes adhuc ecclesiasticum officium ignorabant. Quibus ipse ait: 'Cum orabitis, dicite: Pater noster, et Adoramus te, Christe, et ad omnes ecclesias tuas, quæ sunt in universo mundo, et benedicimus tibi, quia per sanctam crucem tuam redemisti mundum.'" *Ibid.* I, n. 45.

104. "Dum enim, igne Spiritus Sancti succensi, non solum constitutis horis, verum etiam qualibet hora, cum parum eos terrena sollicitudo vel molesta curarum anxietas occuparet, Pater noster in melodia spiritus voce supplici decantarent . . ." *Ibid.* n. 47.

105. *Regula* I, c. 3, *Opusc.* ed. Böhmer 4, Lemmens 28.

106. *Regula* II, c. 3, *Opusc.* ed. Böhmer 31, Lemmens 66.

107. Schnürer, *Die ursprüngliche Templerregel*, Freiburg 1903, 135.

108. P. Eberhard Hoffmann, *Das Konverseninstitut des Zisterzienserordens*, Freiburg 1905, 62.

109. See note 103, 110. See *Regula* I, c. 22, *Opusc.* ed. Böhmer 21, Lemmens 55. 111. Mark xi, 25; Matth. vi, 9; Luke xi, 2.

112. *Laudes, Opusc.* ed. Böhmer 71–73, Lemmens 119–121. Böhmer inserts the *Expositio super orationem dominicam* among the "Dubia," but his reasons are not well-founded (*Analekten* XXX). Lemmens regards the little opus as undoubtedly genuine, and for very good reasons (*Opuscula* 196 sq.).

113. Böhmer 71–73, Lemmens 119–121.

114. *Die sieben Vorregeln der Tugend*, in: Pfeiffer, *Deutsche Mystiker* 324 f. 115. See p. 388.

116. "Contemplatio et sapientia æternorum." Thom. Cel. II, n. 82. Under "contemplation" was meant mysticism in actu, under "wisdom" mysticism in habitu. See Zahn, *Einführung in die christliche Mystik*, Paderborn 1918, 38.

117. "Sanctus Franciscus Spiritu Dei plenus desiderio flagravit . . ., ut totus

posset adhærere Deo assiduæ contemplationis eius gustum." S. Bonav. *Determinat. quæst.* pars I, q. I, *Opera* VIII, 338.

118. See pp. 389–392.   119. See pp. 392–394.

120. "Desideravit dissolvi et esse cum Christo." Thom. Cel. I, n. 71.

121. See pp. 395–399.   122. See pp. 400–403.   123. See pp. 403–405.   124. See pp. 384–386.   125. Thom. Cel. I, n. 45; II, n. 105.

126. Thom. Cel. II, n. 200; *Tres Soc.* n. 15.   127. See pp. 381 ff.   128. See pp. 382f.–384f.

129. "Hominum conversationem fugere proponebat et ad loca remotissima se conferre, ut sic exutus omni cura, et aliorum sollicitudine deposita, solus carnis paries inter se et Deum interim separaret." Thom. Cel. I, n. 103. "Corpore peregrinus a Domino vir Dei Franciscus præsentem spiritum cælo contendebat inferre, et angelorum civem iam factum solus carnis paries disiungebat." *Ibid.* II, n. 94.

130. ". . . ut ipse liberius suam intentionem dirigere posset ad Deum, et beatarum mansionum in cælo positarum, frequenter mente excedens, circuire posset ac ingredi officinas, et in pinguedine gratiæ coram placidissimo et serenissimo universorum Domino se in cælestibus præsentare . . ." *Ibid.* I, n. 102.

131. Especially pp. 28–37.

132. "Alii pietate commoti movebantur ad lacrimas, videntes eum . . . ad tantam ebrietatem divini amoris tam cito venisse." *Tres Soc.* n. 21.

133. "Amore divino fervens semper ad fortia mittere manum, et dilatato corde viam mandatorum Dei ambulans, perfectionis summam attingere cupiebat." Thom. Cel. I, n. 55.   134. *Ibid.* I, n. 82.

135. "Caritatem ferventem, qua Sponsi amicus Franciscus ardebat, quis enarrare sufficiat! Totus namque quasi quidam carbo ignitus divini amoris flamma videbatur absorptus." S. Bonav. c. 9, n. 1.

136. "L'un fu tutto serafico in ardore." Dante, *Divina Com.*, Paradiso XI, 37.

137. Thom. Cel. I, n. 16.   138. *Tres Soc.* n. 21; Thom. Cel. II, n. 13.   139. *Tres Soc.* n. 33.   140. Thom. Cel. II, n. 127.   141. *Tres Soc.* n. 15.

142. "Talis deberet esse Fratrum conversatio inter gentes, ut quicumque audiret vel videret eos, glorificaret Patrem cælestem et devote laudaret." *Tres Soc.* n. 58.

143. "Per ipsum [fratrem Martinum de Bartona] scripsit beatus Franciscus propria manu litteram, sub divo in pluvia non madefactus, ministro et fratribus Franciæ, ut visis litteris iubilarent laudes Deo Trinitati dicentes: Benedicamus Patrem et Filium cum Sancto Spiritu." Eccleston coll. VI, p. 40.

144. *Epist. ad omnes custodes, Opusc.* ed. Böhmer 64, Lemmens 114.

145. *Epist. ad omnes fideles, Opusc.* ed. Böhmer 51. 54, Lemmens 90. 94 sq. 146. Cf. p. 388 ff.   147. *Opusc.* ed. Böhmer 66 sq., 107, Lemmens 119. 126.

148. Böhmer 67, Lemmens 121–123.   149. Böhmer 67, Lemmens 123.   150. Böhmer 109, Lemmens 128.   151. Schnürer, *Franz von Assisi* 113.

152. The Laudes Dei are written on a sheet which the Saint gave to Brother Leo. The latter added to it the annotation: "Blessed Francis two years before his death kept a Lent in the place of Mount La Verna in honor of the Blessed Virgin Mary, the Mother of the Lord, and of blessed Michael the Archangel, from the feast of the Assumption of the holy Virgin Mary until the September feast of St. Michael. And the hand of the Lord was laid upon him; after the vision and speech of the Seraph and the impression of the Stigmata of Christ on his body, he made and wrote with his own hand the "Praises" written on the other side of the sheet, giving thanks to the Lord for the benefits conferred on him." The precious sheet, which contains also the blessing of St. Francis to Brother Leo, is preserved to this day in a reliquary in the Sacro Convento at Assisi; the text, however, has suffered, because Brother Leo, according to the wish of the Saint, carried the sheet on his person during his life (he died in 1271). We give the "Praises" according to the reconstruction of Faloci-Pulignano, Gli autografi di S. Francesco, *Miscellanea francesc.* Vol. VI, 35 sgg. Cf. Lemmens, *Opusc.* p. 198.   Thom. Cel. II, n. 49. and P. Robinson, *The Writings of St. Francis*, p. 146 ff.

153. "Paucos dies, qui usque ad transitum eius restabant, expendit in laudem, socios suos valde dilectos secum Christum laudare instituens. Invitabat etiam omnes creaturas ad laudem Dei, et per verba quædam, quæ olim composuerat, ipse eas ad divinum hortabatur amorem." Thom. Cel. II, n. 217.

154. ". . . novam laudem de creaturis Domini." *Spec. perf.* c. 100, p. 197. See the conclusion of the following chapter.

CHAPTER XIX

1. Cf. Zöpf, *Das Heiligen-Leben im 10. Jahrhundert*, Leipzig u. Berlin 1908, 219–229.

2. Cf. Biese, *Die Entwicklung des Naturgefühls im Mittelalter*, Leipzig 1888.

3. "We may not hesitate a moment to declare his [Francis'] canticles and lyrics important documents of a newly-awakened love of nature." H. Tilemann *Studien zur Individualität des Franziskus von Assisi*, Leipzig 1914, 210.

4. Böhmer, *Analekten* XLIX–LII, proves conclusively that Francis was by nature and by disposition a thoroughly poetical personality.

5. "Absorptus totus in amore Dei beatus Franciscus non solum in anima sua iam omni virtutum perfectione ornata, sed in qualibet creatura bonitatem Dei perfecte cernebat, propter quod singulari et viscerosa dilectione afficiebatur ad creaturas." *Spec. perf.* c. 113, p. 223. Tilemann also *loc. cit.* 186 f. emphasizes this as the characteristic trait of his love of nature.

6. "Quis enarrare sufficeret dulcedinem, contemplans in creaturis sapientiam Creatoris, potentiam et bonitatem eius." Thom. Cel. I, n. 80.

7. "Revera, miro atque ineffabili gaudio ex hac consideratione sæpissime replebatur, cum respiciebat solem, cum lunam cernebat, cum stellas et firmamentum intuebatur." *Ibid.*

8. "Omnes denique creaturas fraterno nomine nuncupabat et modo præcellenti atque cæteris inexperto creaturam occulta cordis acie decernebat, utpote qui iam evaserat in libertatem filiorum Dei." *Ibid.* n. 81. "Consideratione quoque primæ originis omnium abundantiore pietate repletus, creaturas quantumlibet parvas fratris vel sororis appelabat nominibus pro eo, quod sciebat eas unum secum habere principium." S. Bonav. c. 8, n. 6.

9. "Affluebat spiritu charitatis, pietatis viscera gestans, non solum erga homines necessitatem patientes, verum etiam erga muta brutaque animalia, reptilia, volatilia et cæteras sensibiles et insensibiles creaturas." Thom. Cel. I, n. 77.

10. "Molestissimum erat ei, cum alicui pauperum cerneret exprobrari, vel in aliquam creaturarum maledictionis verbum audiret ab aliquo intorqueri." *Ibid.* n. 76. 11. *Ibid.* I, n. 59. 12. *Ibid.* II, n. 170. 13. *Ibid.* I, n. 60. 14. *Ibid.* I, n. 60 sq. 15. *Ibid.* II, n. 167.

16. The author of the *Legenda de passione sancti Verecundi militis et martiris* gives the following incident as related by two eye-witnesses: "Beatus Franciscus ex maxima carnis maceratione, nocturnis vigiliis, orationibus et ieiuniis consumptus ac debilitatus, cum ambulare non posset, et præcipue, postquam fuit insignitus vulneribus Salvatoris, pedester incedere non valens, portabatur asello; et cum quodam sero iam nocte transiret cum fratre socio per viam S. Verecundi [abbey near Gubbio] asello equitans et sacco rudi amictus humeros et circa scapulas, laboratores agrorum vocabant eum dicentes: 'Frater Francisce, mane hic nobiscum et noli ultra pergere, quia lupi ferales hic discurrunt, qui asellum tuum comedent et lædent vos.' Tunc beatus Franciscus dixit: 'Nihil nocui fratri lupo, ut fratrem nostrum asellum audeat devorare. Valete, filii, et Deum timete.' Et sic frater Franciscus pertransivit illæsus. Hæc nobis retulit agricola, qui præsens fuit." Faloci-Pulignani, *S. Francesco e il Monastero di S. Verecondo presso Gubbio*, in: *Miscellanea francesc.* t. X, p. 7; Lemmens, *Testimonia minora sæculi XIII de S. Francisco*, in: *Archiv. francisc.* I, 69 sq. 17. Thom. Cel. II, n. 35 sq.

18. "De lupo ferocissimo per sanctum Franciscum reducto ad magnam mansuetudinem." *Actus b. Francisci* c. 23; *Fioretti* c. 21.

19. Bernard. de Bessa, *Liber de laudibus b. Francisci* c. 6, p. 42.

20. Thom. Cel. I, n. 61.   21. Thom. Cel., *Tract de miraculis* n. 15.

22. "Credo ad innocentiam primam redierat, cui, cum volebat, mansuebantur immitia." Thom. Cel. II, n. 166.

23. "Et mirum certe, cum ipsæ irrationales creaturæ ipsius erga se affectum pietatis cognoscerent et amorem dulcissimum præsentirent." *Ibid.* I, n. 59.

24. "Nituntur proinde creaturæ omnes vicem amoris rependere Sancto et gratitudine sua pro meritis respondere; blandienti arrident, roganti annuunt, obediunt imperanti." *Ibid.* II, n. 166.

25. "Creatoris præcipuum amatorem non mirum si venerantur reliquæ creaturæ." *Ibid.* II, n. 168.

26. "Sic enim gloriosus pater Franciscus, in via obedientiæ ambulans et divinæ subiectionis perfecte iugum amplectens, in creaturarum obedientia magnam coram Deo adeptus est dignitatem." *Ibid.* I, n. 61.

27. "Quia enim ad tantam pervenerat puritatem, ut caro spiritui et spiritus Deo harmonia mirabili concordarent, divina ordinatione fiebat, ut creatura Factori suo deserviens voluntati et imperio eius mirabiliter subiaceret." S. Bonav. c. 5, n. 9.

28. Iulian. a Spira, *Officia rhythmica* 108.   29. Ps. viii, 1.   30. Rom. i, 20.

31. "Mundum quasi peregrinationis exsilium exire festinans, iuvabatur felix iste viator hiis quæ in mundo sunt non modicum quidem.   Nempe ad principes tenebrarum utebatur eo ut campo certaminis, ad Deum vero ut clarissimo speculo bonitatis.   In artificio quolibet commendat artificem." Thom. Cel. II, n. 165.

32. "Exsultat in cunctis operibus manuum Domini, et per iucunditatis spectacula vivificam intuetur rationem et causam.   Cognoscit in pulchris pulcherrimum; cuncta sibi bona, qui nos fecit est optimus, clamant.   Per impressa rebus vestigia insequitur ubique dilectum, facit sibi de omnibus scalam, qua perveniatur ad solium." *Ibid.*

33. "Sic et omnia illa, præcipue in quibus filii Dei posset, aliqua similitudo allegorica reperiri, amplexabatur carius et videbat libentius." *Ibid.* I, n. 77.

34. See pp. 19–37.   35. John viii, 12.   36. Luke xii, 49.

37. "Inter omnes creaturas inferiores et insensibiles singulariter afficiebatur ad ignem propter pulchritudinem et utilitatem eius, propter quod nunquam voluit illius officium impedire." *Spec. perf.* c. 11.

38. "Parcit lucernis, lampadibus et candelis, nolens sua manu deturbare fulgorem, qui nutus esset lucis æternæ." Thom. Cel. II, n. 165.   39. *Spec. perf. ibid.*

40. "Post ignem singulariter diligebat aquam, per quam figuratur sancta pœnitentia et tribulatio, quibus sordes animæ abluuntur, et quia prima ablutio animæ fit per aquam baptismi." *Spec. perf.* c. 118.   41. *Ibid.*   42. 1 Cor. x, 4.

43. Ps. lx, 3.

44. "Super petras ambulat reverenter, eius intuitu qui dicitur petra.   Cum opus esset versiculo: In petra exaltasti me; ut reverentius aliquid diceret, suptus pedes, inquit, exaltasti me." Thom. Cel. *ibid.*   45. Job. xiv, 7.

46. "Ligna cædentes fratres prohibet totam succidere arborem, ut spem habeat iterum pullandi." Thom. Cel. *ibid.*   ". . . ut talis arboris semper aliqua pars remaneret integra amore illius, qui salutem nostram in ligno crucis voluit operari." *Spec. perf.* c. 118.   47. Cant. ii, 1.   48. Is. xi, 1.

49. "Quantam putas eius menti exhilarationem florum speciositas importabat, cum eorum venustatis cerneret formam, et suavitatis olentiam præsentiret? Statim ad illius floris pulchritudinem considerationis oculum deflectebat, qui, lucidus in vernali tempore de radice Iesse progrediens ad odorem suum suscitavit innumera millia mortuorum." Thom. Cel. I, n. 81.

50. "Iubet hortulanum indefossos limites circa hortum dimittere, ut suis temporibus herbarum viror et florum venustas prædicent speciosum omnium rerum Pater.   Hortulum in horto herbis odoriferis et florificis præcipit designari, ut in

memoriam suavitatis æternæ avocent speculantes." Thom. Cel. *ibid.* "...
amore illius, qui dicitur flos campi et lilium convallium." *Spec. perf. ibid.* 51.
Ps. xxi, 7.

52. "Circa vermiculos etiam nimio flagrabat amore, quia legerat de Salvatore
dictum: Ego sum vermis et non homo. Et idcirco eos colligebat de via, in tuto
recondens loco, ne transeuntium vestigiis tererentur." Thom. Cel. I, n. 80; cf.
II, n. 165.

53. "Quid de aliis inferioribus creaturis dicam, cum et apibus in hieme, ne
frigoris algore deficerent, vel sive optimum vinum faceret exhiberi? Quarum
efficaciam operum et ingenii excellentiam ad Domini gloriam tanto præconio
extollebat, ut diem unam plerumque in earum cæterarumque creaturarum laudibus consummaret." *Ibid.* I, n. 80. 54. John i, 29.

55. "Sed in omni genere animalium speciali dilectione ac promptiori affectu
agniculos diligebat, eo quod Domini nostri Iesu Christi humilitas in sacra Scrip-
tura agno assimilatur frequentius et convenientius coaptatur." Thom. Cel.
ibid. n. 77. 56. *Ibid.* II, n. 111. 57. *Ibid.* I, n. 77 sq. 58. *Ibid.* n. 79.

59. Thom. Cel., *Legenda ad usum chori* ed. P. Eduardus Alenc. n. 7, p. 439.

60. "Contemplatio est tanto eminentior, ... quanto melius scit considerare
Deum in exterioribus creaturis." S. Bonav., *Sent.* lib. 2, dist. 23, a. 2, q. 3,
concl., *Opera* II, 545 a. Similarly S. Thom. Aq. 2, 2, q. 180, a. 4.

61. "Ad summum perfectionis apicem sanctus iste pertingens, columbina
simplicitate plenus omnes creaturas ad Creatoris hortatur amorem." Thom.
Cel. *ibid.*

62. "Sicut enim olim tres pueri in camino ignis ardentis positi ad laudandum
et glorificandum Creatorem universitatis elementa omnia invitabant, sic et iste
vir, spiritu Dei plenus in omnibus elementis et creaturis Creatorem omnium et
Gubernatorem glorificare, laudare et benedicere non cessabat." Thom. Cel.
I, n. 80.

63. "Inauditæ devotionis affectu complectitur omnia, alloquens ea de Domino
et in laudem eius adhortans." *Ibid.* II, n. 165.

64. "Cumque florum copiam inveniret, ita prædicabat eis et ad laudem eos
dominicam invitabat, ac si ratione vigerent. Sic et segetes et vineas, lapides
et sylvas, et omnia speciosa camporum, irrigua fontium, et hortorum virentia
quæque, terram et ignem, aërem et ventum sincerissima puritate ad divinum
monebat amorem et libens obsequium hortabatur." *Ibid.* I, n. 81.

65. S. Bonav. c. 8, n. 7 66. Thom. Cel. II, n. 168. 67. *Ibid.* II, n. 171. 68.
Ibid. I, n. 58. 69. Iulian. a Spira *ibid.* 122.

70 "Et propter multas consolationes, quas habuit et habebat in creaturis,
parum ante obitum suum composuit quasdam laudes Domini de creaturis suis
ad incitandum corda audientium eas ad laudem Dei et ut ipse Dominus in creaturis suis ab hominibus laudaretur." *Spec. perf.* c. 118. "Laudes de creaturis
tunc quasdam composuit, et eas utcumque ad Creatorem laudandum accendit."
Thom. Cel. II, n. 213. 71. Matth. xvii, 2. 72. Mal. iv, 2.

73. This translation is taken from Fr. Paschal Robinson: *The Writings of
Saint Francis of Assisi*, Dolphin Press 1906, p. 152. For the history of the
origin of the Canticle of the Sun cf. Christen-Felder, *Leben des heiligen Franziskus
von Assisi*, Innsbruck 1922, 397–406. 74. *Spec. perf.* c. 119. 75. *Ibid.* c. 100.

76. Thom. Cel. II, n. 117; *Spec. perf.* c. 121.

77. *Spec. perf.* c. 122. 123. 78. *Ibid.* c. 100.

79. Harnack, *Dogmengeschichte* III, 3. Aufl., 382.

INDEX

Names of persons and places which are irrelevant to subjects treated are omitted. Likewise authorities which recur frequently (e.g. Thomas of Celano).

A

Adam of Marsh, 374.
Agnes of Prague, 394.
Alanus ab Insulis, 354, 499 [96].
Albert of Pisa, 197, 222, 269.
Albert the Great, 455 [91].
Alexander II, 299.
Alexander III, 490 [88].
Alexander IV, 324, 338.
Alms, as source of Franciscan livelihood, 142-155;—and the ancient Orders, 143ff.;—and the Gospel, 143; esteemed by Francis, 144-147; quest of—loved and p r a c t i s e d by F r a n c i s, 143-147; recommended to the Friars, 147-150; manner of seeking, 149f.; when improper, 150-152;—and idleness, 152-154;—and the apostolate, 154f.
Angela of Foligno, 479 [8].
Angelus Clarinus, 366f., 376, 495 [4], 495 [19], 499 [111].
Angels, venerated by Francis, 399f.
Anonymus of Passau, on disrespect toward the Eucharist, 447 [70].
Anselm of Canterbury, 339.
Anthony of Padua, 55, 315, 322, 337, 360.
Apostles, Mission of, and Francis, 7, 79.
Apostolate, Franciscan, 297-349; among the faithful, 298-311; among the infidels, 311-

317; of the sacrament of Penance, 321-325; of preaching, 325-347: of example, 347-349;—and poverty, 87-89;—and prayer, 383ff.
Apostolic life, 13ff., 302, 350.
Apulia, journey of Francis to, 4, 20.
Aristotle, 340, 373f.
Arms, bearing of—forbidden to Tertiaries, 292f.
Augustine, St., 130, 153, 460 [68].
Augustinians, 14ff., 204, 299f.

B

Banditry and feudal system, 289f.
Bees and Francis, 421.
Begging, See Alms, Quest of alms, Mendicatio.
Benedict of Nursia, 14-16, 19, 224, 298f., 460 [68].
Benedictines, 130f., 204, 224, 298f., 460 [68].
Bernard of Clairvaux, 392.
Bernard of Quintavalle, 7, 79, 84, 97, 121, 202, 303, 304.
Berthold of Regensburg, 338f., 343, 447 [74].
Birds, sermon to the—425.
Bishops, reverence of Francis toward—58-60.
Blessed Sacrament, See Eucharist.
Bonaventure, St., on the daily celebration of the Mass, 445 [3]; love of Francis for the

511

T

Teaching, office of—in the Order, 141, 362–369.
Tertiaries, 12f., 270, 280–282, 292–295.
Theology, *See* Science.
Third Order, *See* Tertiaries.
Thomas of Aquinas, 299f.
Thomas of Spalato, 292, 492 [125].
Treuga Dei, Franciscan, 296.
Trinity, devotion of Francis to —388–392.
Troubadours and Francis, 1, 227, 242, 345–347, 428f.

U

Ubertinus of Casale, 369–371, 376, 388, 497 [52], 499 [112], 501 [131].
Urban II, 290.
Use of temporal things, 103–119.
Utensils of the Friars, 114f.

V

Vocation of Francis, 4–8, 20–23, 77ff.
Vows, 87f.

W

Waldenses, 71, 89, 154, 354.
Walter of Gisburne, 15, 498 [82].
Walter Mapes, 354f.
Wandering preachers, 299f., 337, 354f.
Water, loved by Francis, 420.
Wealth, despised by Francis, 2.
William of Esseby, 190.
William of St. Amour, 324, 356, 461 [98], 498 [91].
Wolf of Gubbio, 416f.
Womanhood and knighthood, 90.
Worms and Francis, 421.

Z

Zeal for souls of Francis, 317–320. *Cf.* Apostolate.

PRINTED BY BENZIGER BROTHERS, NEW YORK